Signature Interiors

BETA-PLUS

Introduction

"*Signature Interiors*" invites you on a captivating journey through the realms of design excellence, unveiling the visionary works of 25 upcoming and renowned architects and interior designers from diverse corners of the globe. This curated collection transcends geographical boundaries to showcase a kaleidoscope of design perspectives, each bearing the distinctive mark of its creator. From a Victorian building in London to an elegant home in Sydney and an apartment overlooking Madison Square Park in New York to a beautiful Haussmannian apartment with view of the Eiffel Tower in Paris to a vast townhouse in Warsaw, a villa near Antwerp, four residences in Spain (Madrid, Barcelona, Málaga, Mallorca), a characterful house in Toronto, a modern beach home in Amangansett and many other locations, these designers weave cultural influences into every thread of their creations.

Dive into a world where spaces become narratives and design transforms into an art form. "*Signature Interiors*" introduces you to the brilliant minds behind the scenes, highlighting their unique stories, inspirations, and the innovative approaches that set them apart. Whether it's minimalistic elegance, understated luxury or an eclectic fusion of different interior styles, this book celebrates the harmonious blend of creativity and functionality.

Beta-Plus Publishing takes you on a visual odyssey, where design is not merely an arrangement of elements but an eloquent expression of individuality. Discover the stories behind the designs, the inspirations that fuel the creativity, and the meticulous craftsmanship that transforms spaces into living art. "*Signature Interiors*" is a testament to the prowess of these designers, offering a glimpse into the future of interior aesthetics while paying homage to the timeless elegance of their craft. Each page is a celebration of innovation, a testament to the transformative power of design, and an ode to the 25 luminaries who have left an indelible mark on the world of interiors.

Wim Pauwels
Publisher

Contents

8-23	Oskar Firek Architects
24-41	Rhyme
42-63	Arjaan De Feyter
64-79	HUTCH Design
80-101	Smac Studio
102-115	William McIntosh Design
116-129	Maximale
130-143	Georgina Jeffries
144-157	Aleksandr Orlov and Elena Semenova
158-175	Pauline Vanthournout
176-189	Vanessa Schorreels
190-203	Carla Barton
204-217	Montana Burnett
218-231	Chused & Co
232-245	Véronique Cotrel
246-259	Angel Martin
260-275	Marie-Emilie Geerinckx
276-289	Studio Zung
290-301	Ann-Sophie Princen
302-321	Grain Designoffice
322-335	Meg Cassidy
336-347	Fabian Freytag
348-365	Paulien De Lange
366-379	Özge Öztürk & Alexandre Simeray (OZA Design)
380-391	Laura Sainderichin

Oskar Firek Architects

The portfolio of Oskar Firek Architects is a collection of private and commercial investment projects. Each project stands out for its attention to detail and emphasis on highlighting the unique character of interiors through continuous reliance on passion, perfectionism, and integrity in the creative process. The designs of apartments, houses, or apartments correspond to the personalities of the owners, and the functional spaces are a practical extension of the brand's concept.

The design studio was founded in 2012 by Oskar Firek, the son of artist-sculptors associated with the Krakow Academy of Fine Arts. From a young age, the architect observed the creative process and immersed himself in art, which sparked his fascination with painting, sculpture, and ceramics. Deeply rooted aesthetics have a clear influence on the projects created by OF A, where a commitment to natural materials, clean forms, and functional spaces serves as the foundation of their work.

Oskar Firek Architects primarily undertakes projects in Poland but also has experience working with international investments and their supervision. Due to their attention to detail and authenticity, their projects are aimed at the most demanding clients. Conscious of abandoning trends in favor of simplicity, harmony, and preserving personal character, they create timeless designs within interiors.

www.oskarfirek.com

Photography: ONI Studio

Located in Warsaw's Mokotów district (Poland), this vast townhouse designed by Oskar Firek Architects between 2021 and 2023 spans 230 square meters across four levels.

The ground floor is the heart of the home, featuring a welcoming living area that seamlessly connects to the garden.

On the second level, the master bedroom offers a private and comfortable retreat, while the children's bedrooms and a guest area occupy a separate floor.

The basement houses all the technical facilities, a garage, and a gym.

What truly sets this project apart is its considered use of materials and the harmonious blend of classic and modern furniture. The interior showcases a striking mix of styles and bold color choices, reflecting the owner's unique personality.

Throughout the space, you'll discover captivating artworks by renowned artists, including Malwina Konopacka, Edward Dwurnik, Marcin Zawicki, Adam Bakalarz, Nikodem Szpunar, and Jan Możdzyński.

Custom-designed furniture and unique objects contribute to the space's coherence and vibrancy.

This distinctive interior is the result of a collaborative effort between the designers and the homeowner, infusing the space with its own character.

Rhyme

Rhyme is an interior design and architecture studio that provides a well-thought-out service and individualized approach coupled with deliberate and exclusive aesthetics.

"Rhyme" also means rhythm, harmony, poetry. Their design process combines many elements: textures, colors, materials, light, etc., in order to create a specific rhythm and harmony of space. It's all about the individual characteristics, mood, nuances, and original perspective that the authors put into their works.

Rhyme Studio is open tot making projects all over the world. If their way of work, their taste and subtle sense of beauty are close to the client, then there are no boundaries for cooperation. Trust, engagement and dialogue, continuous search for aesthetics and perfectionism are those characteristics that Rhyme values in its team members. No wonder that it is manifested in all the aspects, both in the studio's internal activities and when communicating with the clients.

www.rhyme.team

Photography: Mikhail Loskutov

"Copper House" is a 78 square meter apartment in Moscow. The owner contacted Rhyme in an early stadium because "he did not want to live in this apartment". The apartment was already purchased with repairs from the developer, which neither qualitatively nor aesthetically met the requirements of Rhyme's client.

When Rhyme visited the flat for the first time, they understood that those repairs must be completely dismantled. Therefore Rhyme removed all the repairs to keep only the base. There was nothing but concrete after this intervention. Rhyme wanted to maximize the potential inherent to the architecture of this apartment. It has many advantages. The first is high ceilings. The second is panoramic windows, located quite densely - many windows for one room. Rhyme wanted to open the space as much as possible and let natural light into the apartment. The flat is quite small, but there is everything you need: a large kitchen-living room, a small hallway, two bathrooms and two bedrooms. Rhyme made the interior, thought out and worked out to the smallest details, but at the same times there is no feeling of "polishing" in it, in the bad meaning of the word "done". There is an element of randomness, lightness, and some carelessness in it.

Working on the palette of this apartment, Rhyme followed this logic: the most concentrated color part, the most contrasting, bright color part is concentrated in the living room area, and gradually, towards the bedrooms, the interior becomes calmer. Considering the fact that the presence of color in the interior was an important wish of the client, the sofa area is made in almost opposite contrasting colors. There is a red-mustard sofa, a turquoise carpet, that was made according to Rhyme's design specifically for this living room. It has a complex shape, a complex relief and a complex color. The burgundy armchair complements an unusual color combination. There is a chair with a pattern similar to a fir tree next to it, and a marble stand with burgundy veins. And all this culminates in a huge round mirror of Christophe Gagnon in electric blue color. There is no dining table in this apartment, because the customer didn't really need it. But there is a beautiful small island table where you can have a quick snack or breakfast. It was quite difficult to work with the kitchen, because quartzite is a capricious material and practically does not lend itself to repolishing or restoration. The use of such quartzite made this small kitchen really spectacular. The bedroom has more restrained colors. There are also interesting items that are made according to Rhyme's sketches in the bedroom: a carpet, a console table, a stand made of stone. And an important design feature of this room is that in order to keep two windows in one room, Rhyme did not make a separate dressing room and placed wardrobes along the wall in which they made a passage to the bathroom. A free-standing sink is installed in the master's bathroom, delicately hidden with the necessary part behind the mirrored facades and a long Agape mixer tap.

With the overal simplicity of the project, so restrained, Rhyme paid special attention to the details: handles, switches, carvings on doors. All these were developed according to proportions, dosage and materials. When working on any project, a very light feeling remained - the feeling of work in one breath, from the start to the end.

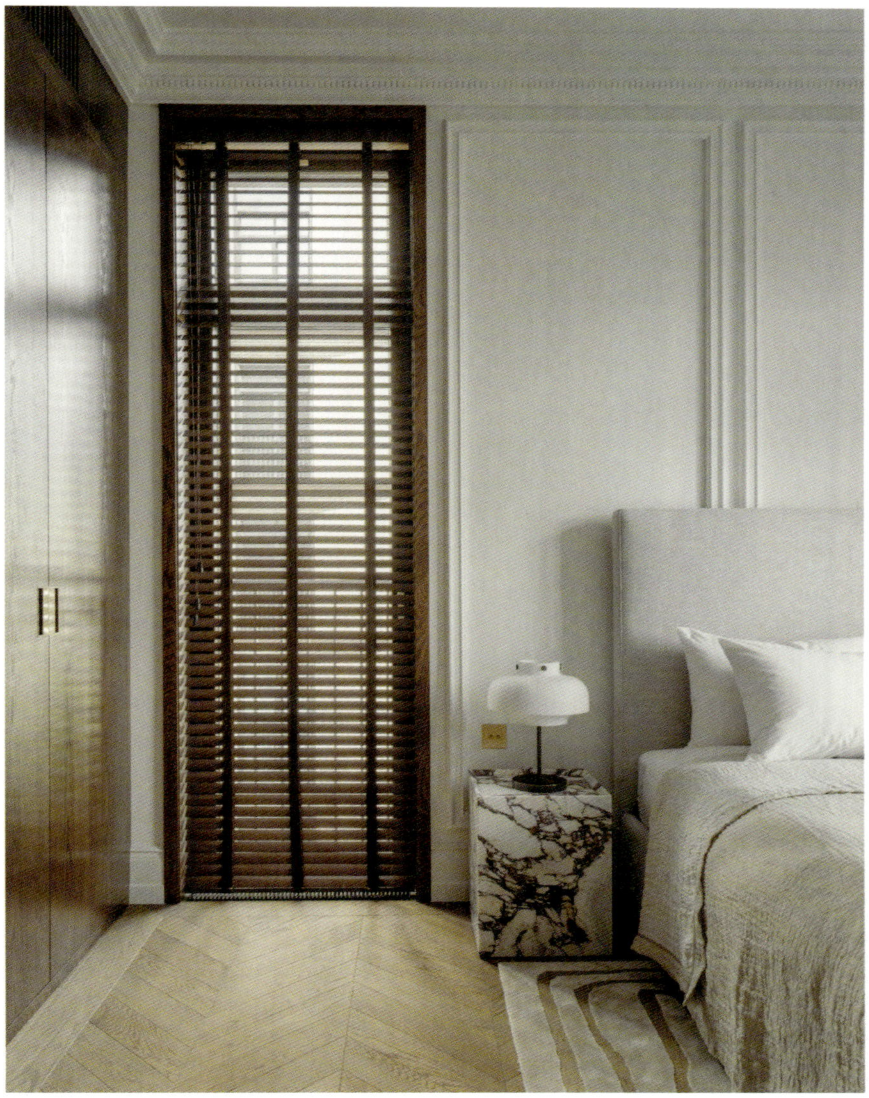

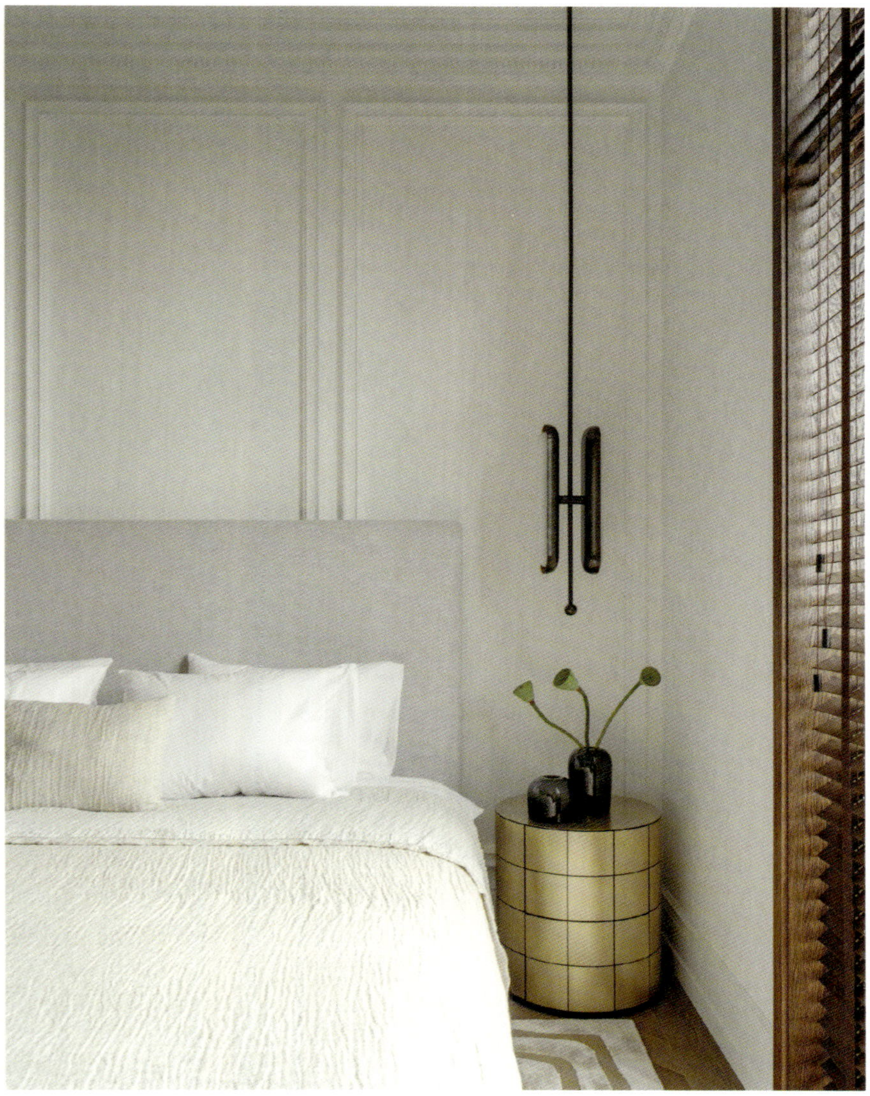

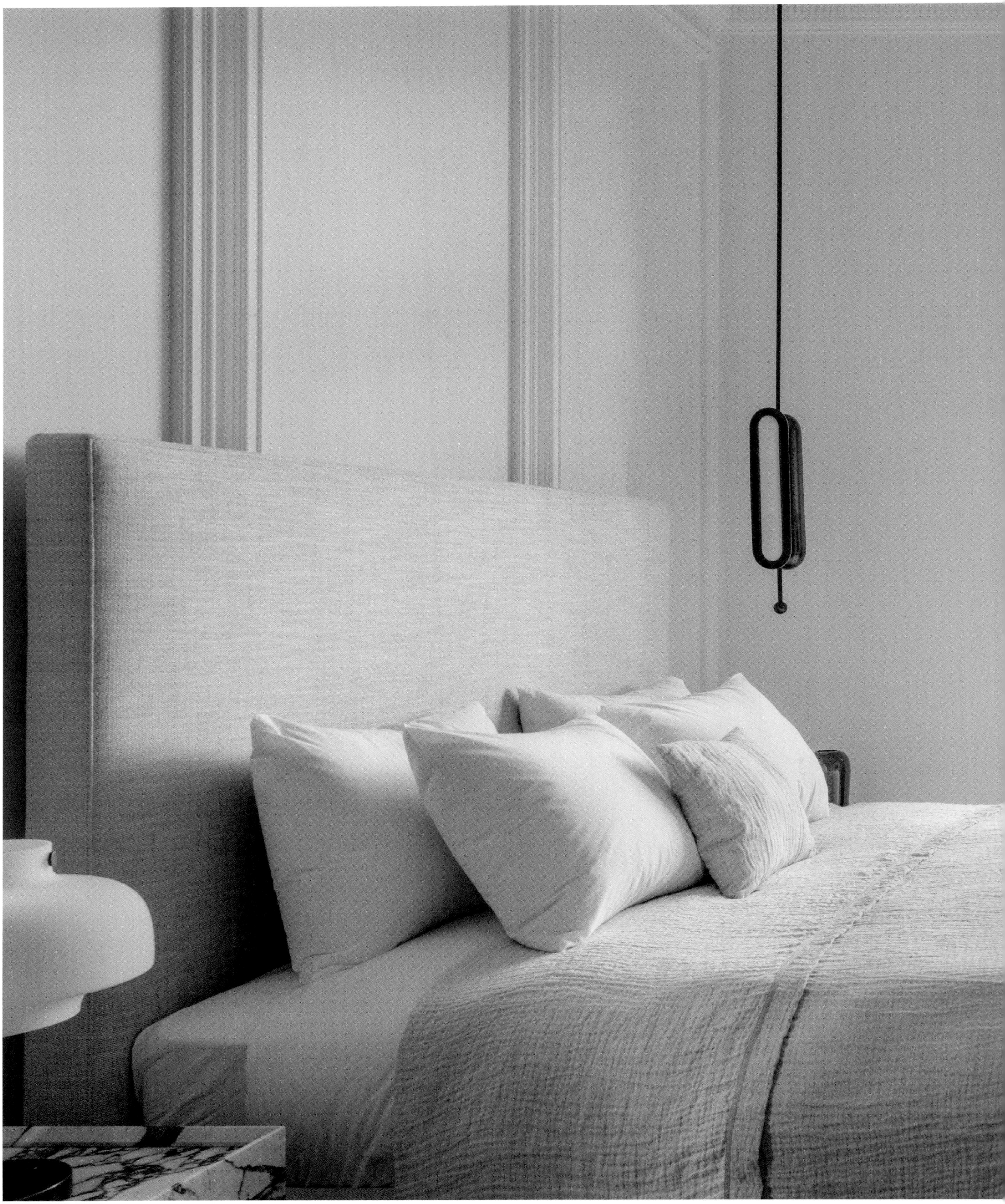

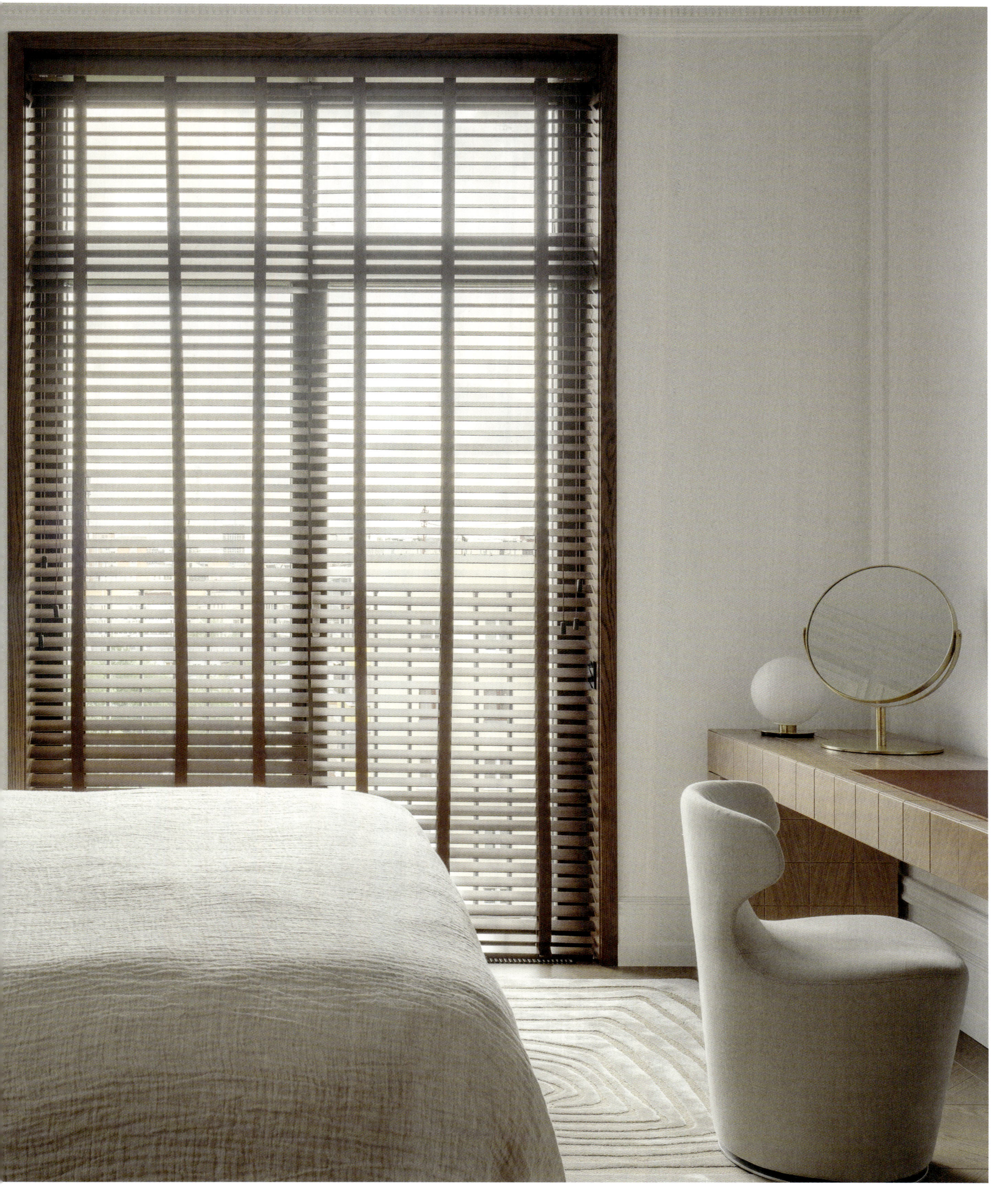

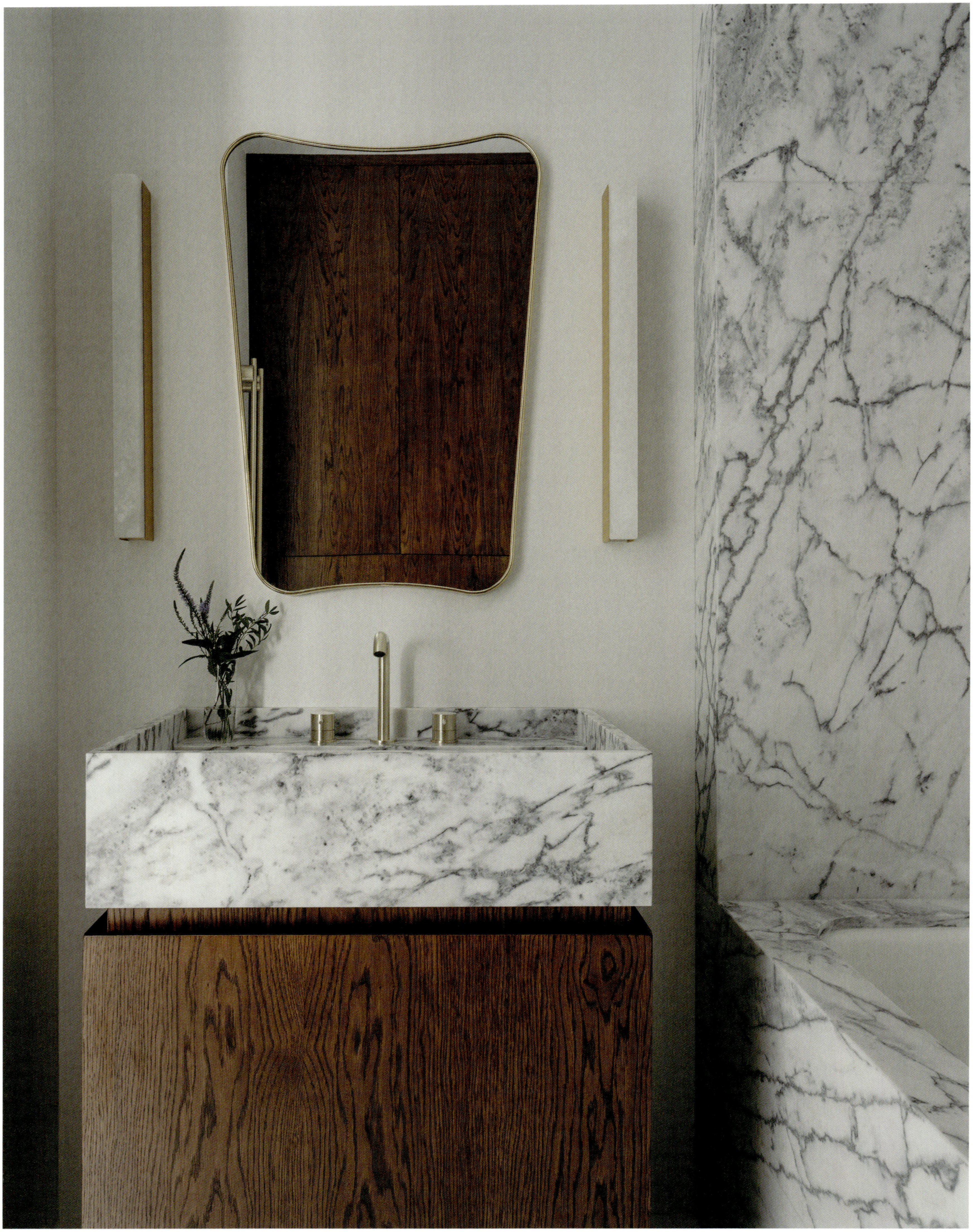

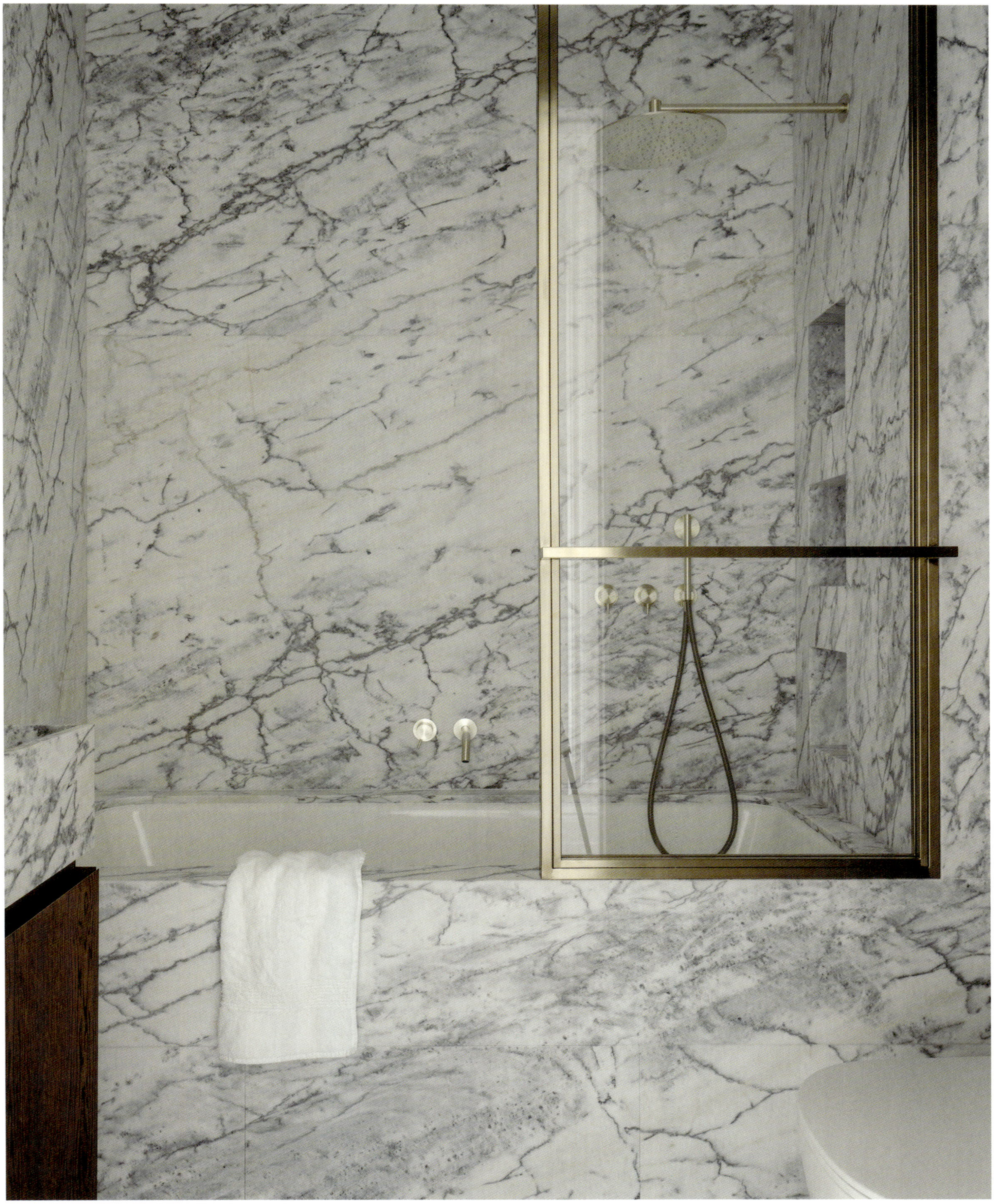

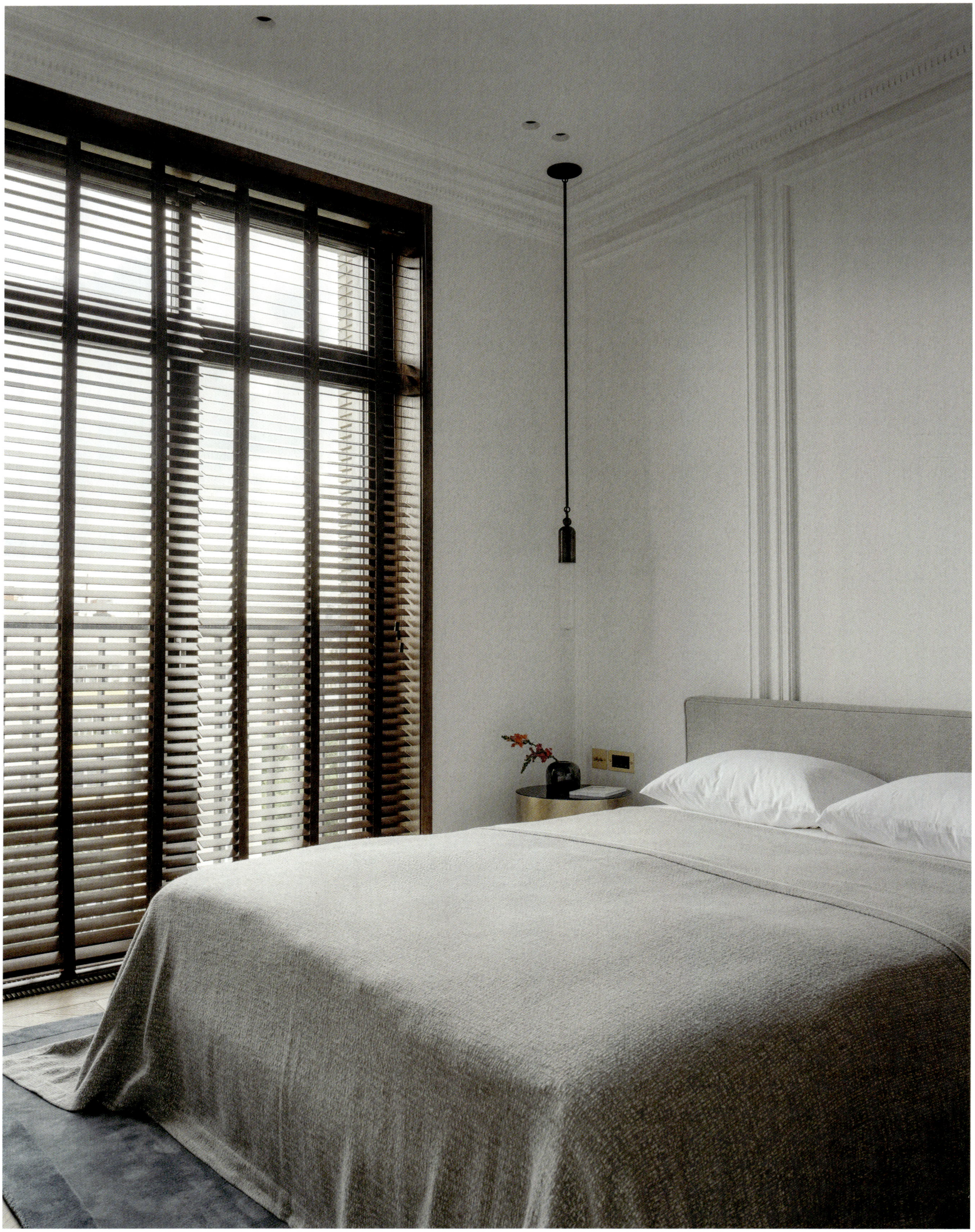

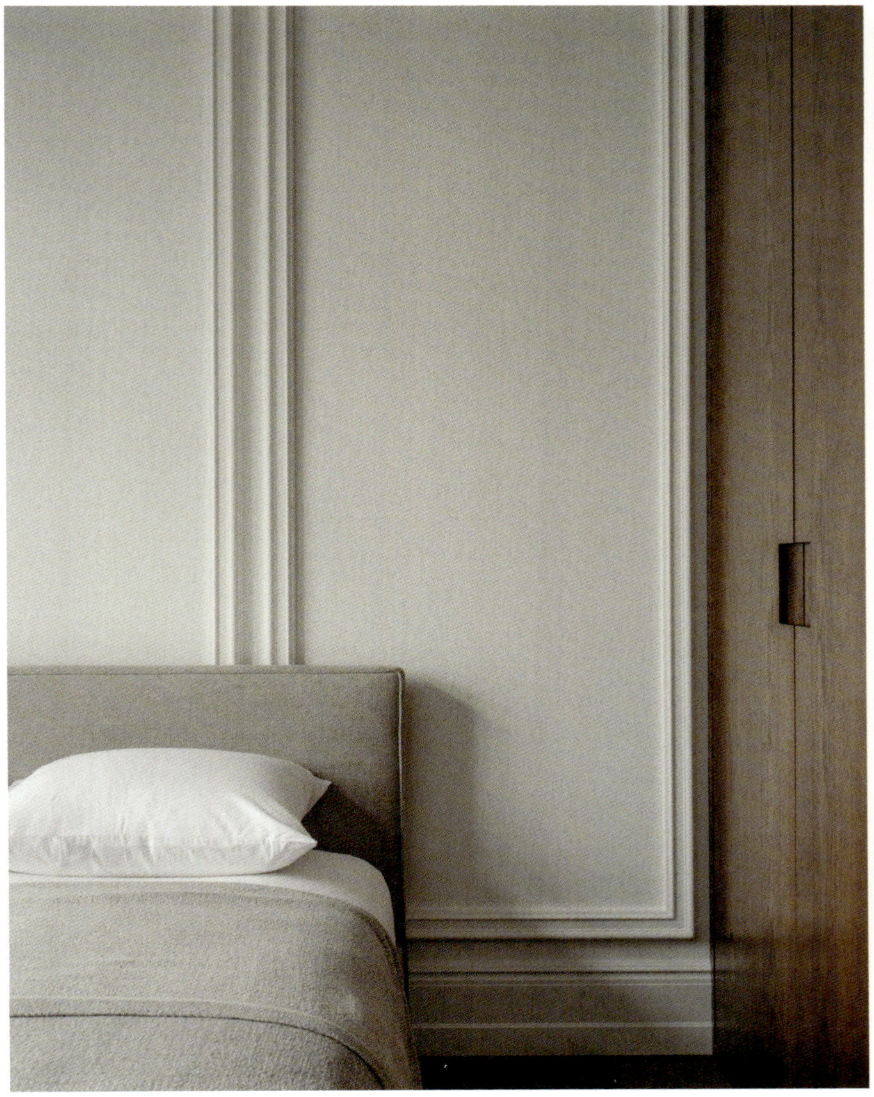

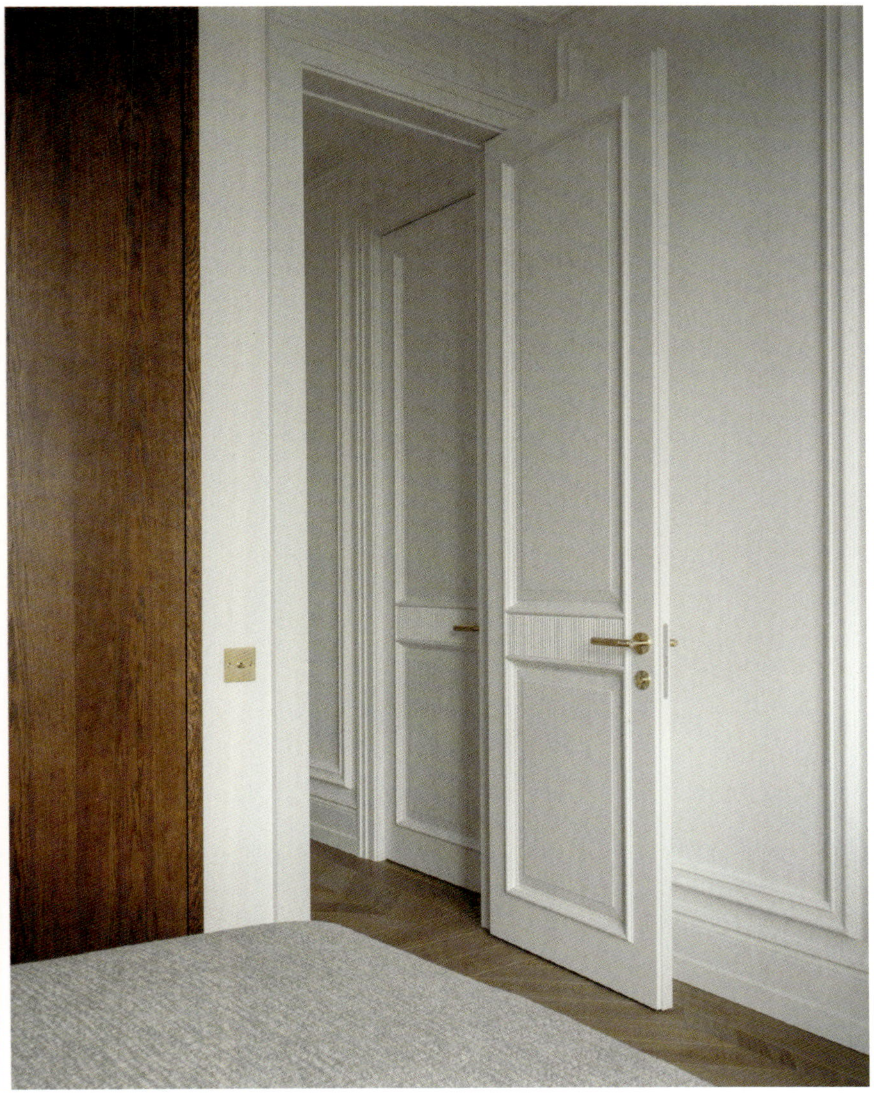

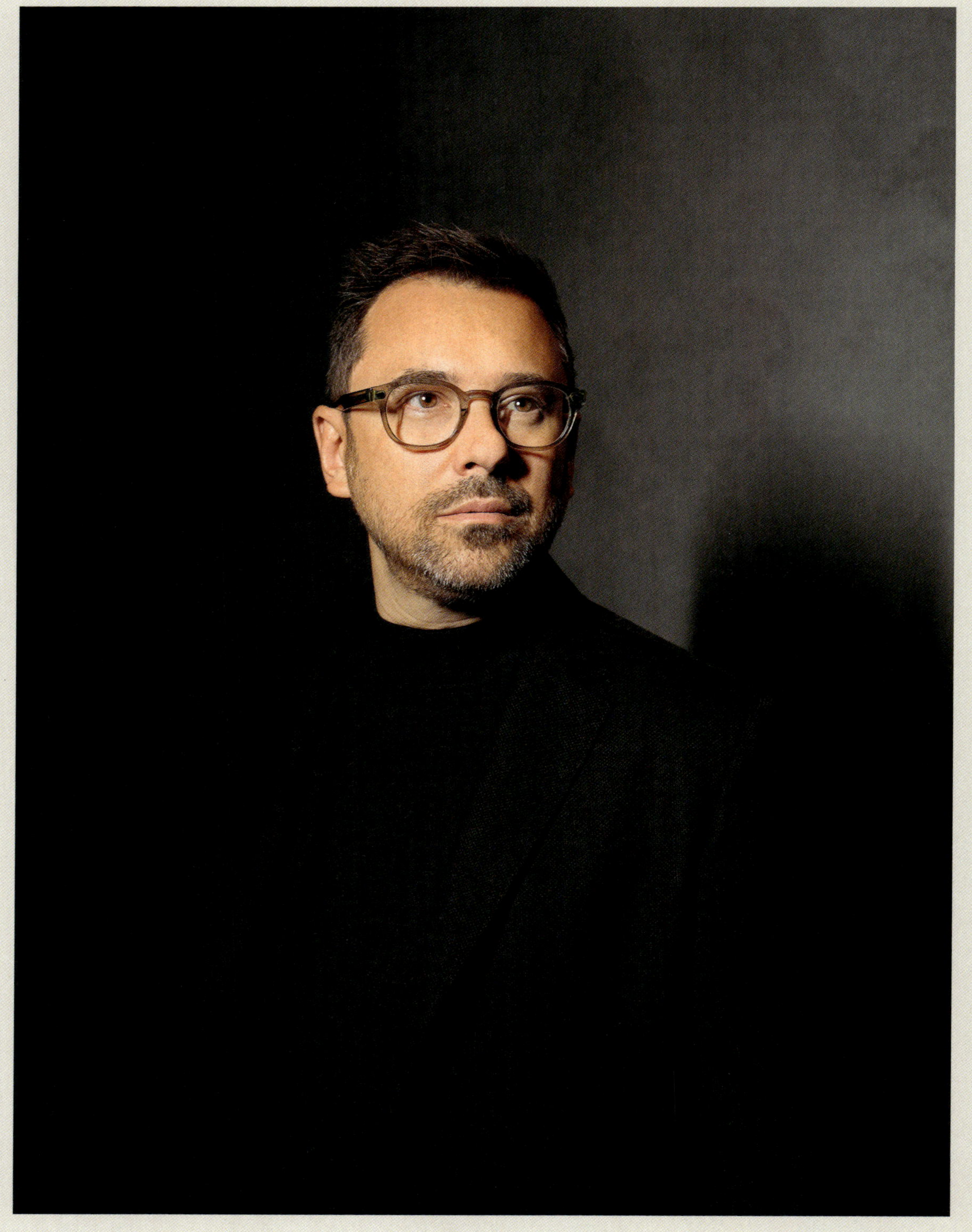

Arjaan De Feyter

Interior designer Arjaan De Feyter graduated from the Henry van de Velde Institute in Antwerp in 1999. Almost immediately after, he started his own design office. At the same time he was a freelance collaborator with a renowned Antwerp interior designer with an international clientele until 2005.

The eponymous Design Office concentrates mainly on total customized concepts for interiors. Often with a flawless symbiosis between several disciplines.

Questioning the assignment and the user, dealing critically with spatiality, livability and circulation are often central to his approach. Challenging traditional housing forms, creating multifunctional design solutions and/or interiors that can grow with the times in terms of material, sustainability and functionality are a matter of course.

The Design Office has many different types of references. Mainly active in the residential sector where the detail and high level of finishing prevails, this is also his dada and hence the focus on these types of projects. But also many other types of projects including offices, medical cabinets, installations, restoration projects from cultural heritage to new construction projects, etc. belong to the oeuvre.

Also in the certain large project development projects where the link with historical heritage is central, he has had the opportunity to set a new course on how interiors can be handled differently at that level. Intensive collaborations with notorious technical firms and top architects including David Chipperfield came about in this regard.

As an interior architect, he has received various recognitions including a mention in the Yearbook of Architecture, won the Steel Construction Prize, was invited to the KUL for the workshop "Working with the Masters" and has been able to participate in interesting exhibitions including the famous Venice Architecture Biennale 2020.

Since 2006, Arjaan De Feyter is also attached to the Faculty of Design Sciences at the University of Antwerp, where he teaches Interior Design as a practical lecturer.

www.arjaandefeyter.be

Photography: Jan Liégeois

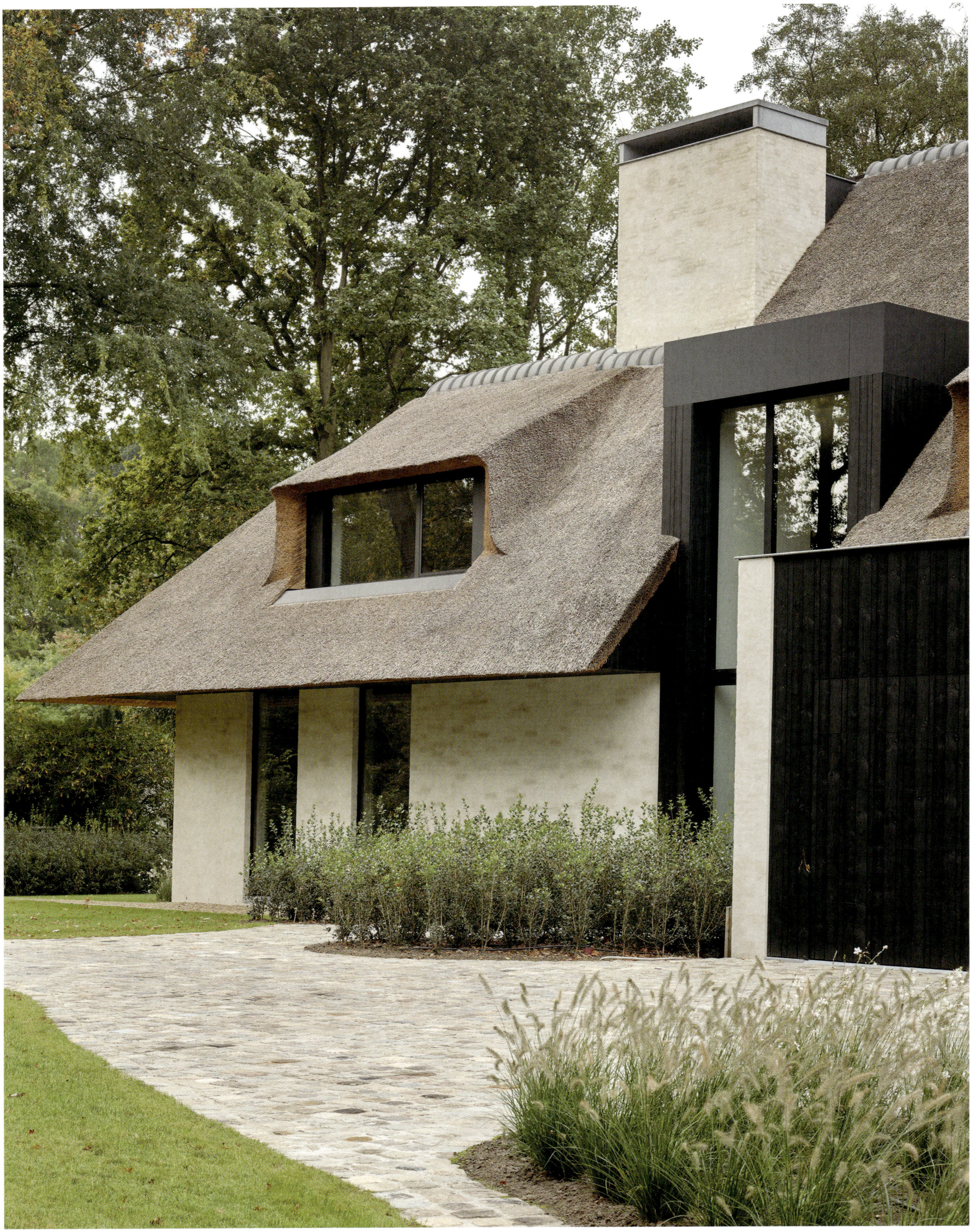

Located in the green outskirts of Antwerp, this beautiful new home designed by DCX Architects was carefully incorporated into the already existing forest environment with beautiful trees and natural pond.

Warm facade materials such as chipped brick, black sintered wood and thatch are combined with large expanses of glass and cut-out dormers to connect interior and exterior, classic and modern, warm and sleek. From an underground gym that receives natural light by creating a rolling landscape, to a guest room on the top floor with hotel suite allure and its own intimate terrace. This home forms a beautiful whole with terrace, outdoor pool and forest surroundings thanks to Kevin Mampay's landscape design, while all interior spaces are carefully coordinated to the design of interior designer Arjaan De Feyter.

Upon entering the home, the sculptural spiral staircase immediately catches the eye. A first imposing eye-catcher that makes the connection with the upper floors and, above all, strongly stimulates curiosity about what the rest of the house has to offer.

By centrally positioning the monumental gas fireplace, the immense living space is divided between the sitting area on the one hand and the dining area on the other. This serves as a room divider creating intimacy between the two functions, without losing the open character of the space. One can enjoy the open gas fireplace from all sides.

Furthermore, maximum contact with the green environment is created through the large window openings, also provided with overhanging canopies that serve as sun protection but also create cozy covered areas on the terrace.

The natural stone floor on the ground floor is entirely in Muschelkalk, a light gray hard German limestone. For the kitchen, a contrasting stone radiates enough personality and strength but also brings color in a natural way, and timelessly matches the rest of the color palette. Arjaan chose a Rouge Royal, a Belgian "marble" / limestone with a soft brown / red color and broad white-gray veins and fossils. A natural stone that is still barely quarried and has fallen into oblivion over the years. Yet it has been used in many iconic buildings such as the Antwerp City Hall and Central Station.

An admittedly classic touch in the contemporary setting, further combined with smoked oak custom furniture and bronze accents. A variation on this color palette was incidentally continued on the second floor where a full soft taupe-pink carpet is laid in the master suite. Children's bathrooms are each given their own personal preferred color.

Interior Architecture: Arjaan De Feyter. Architecture: DCX Architects. Landscape design: Kevin Mampay.

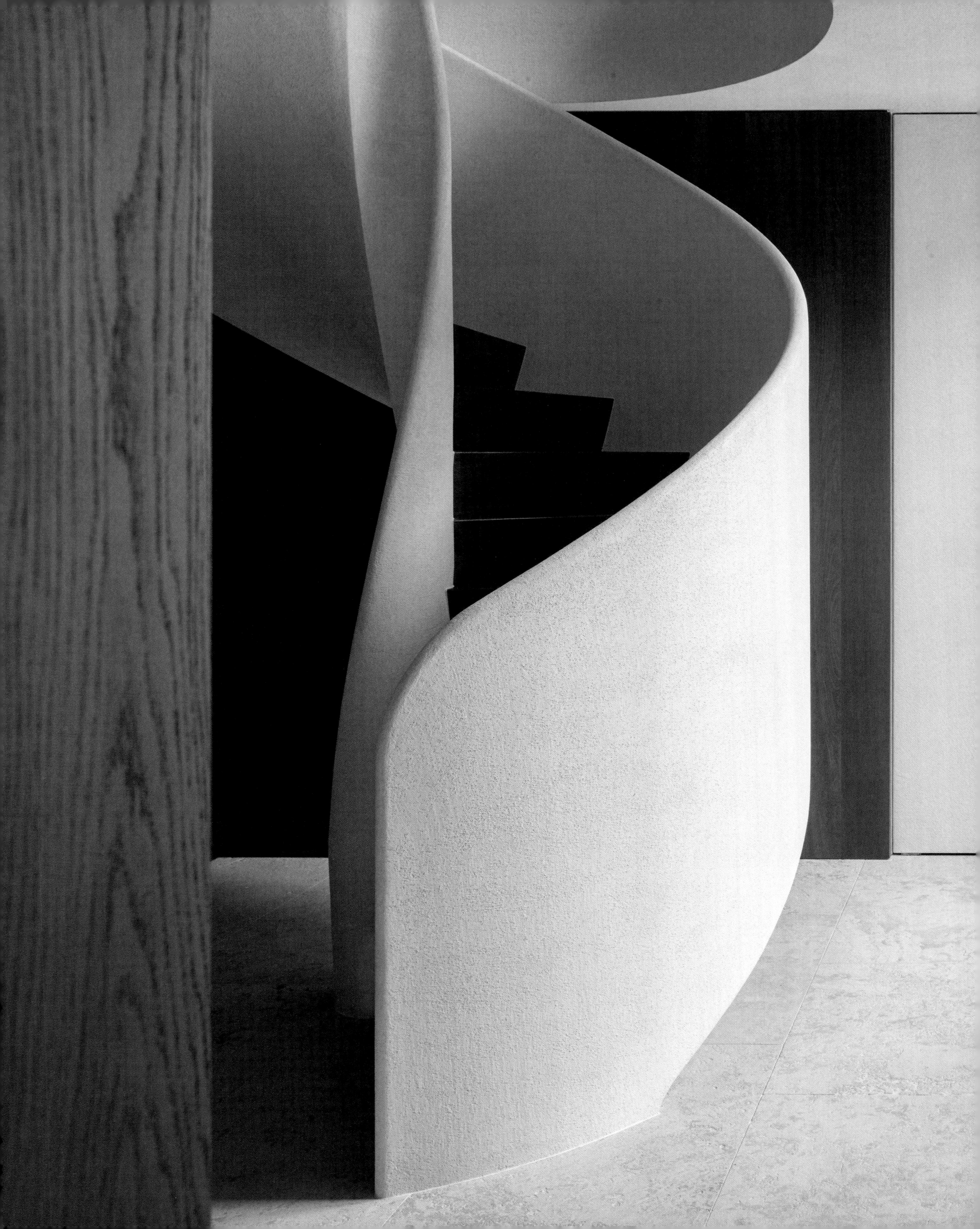

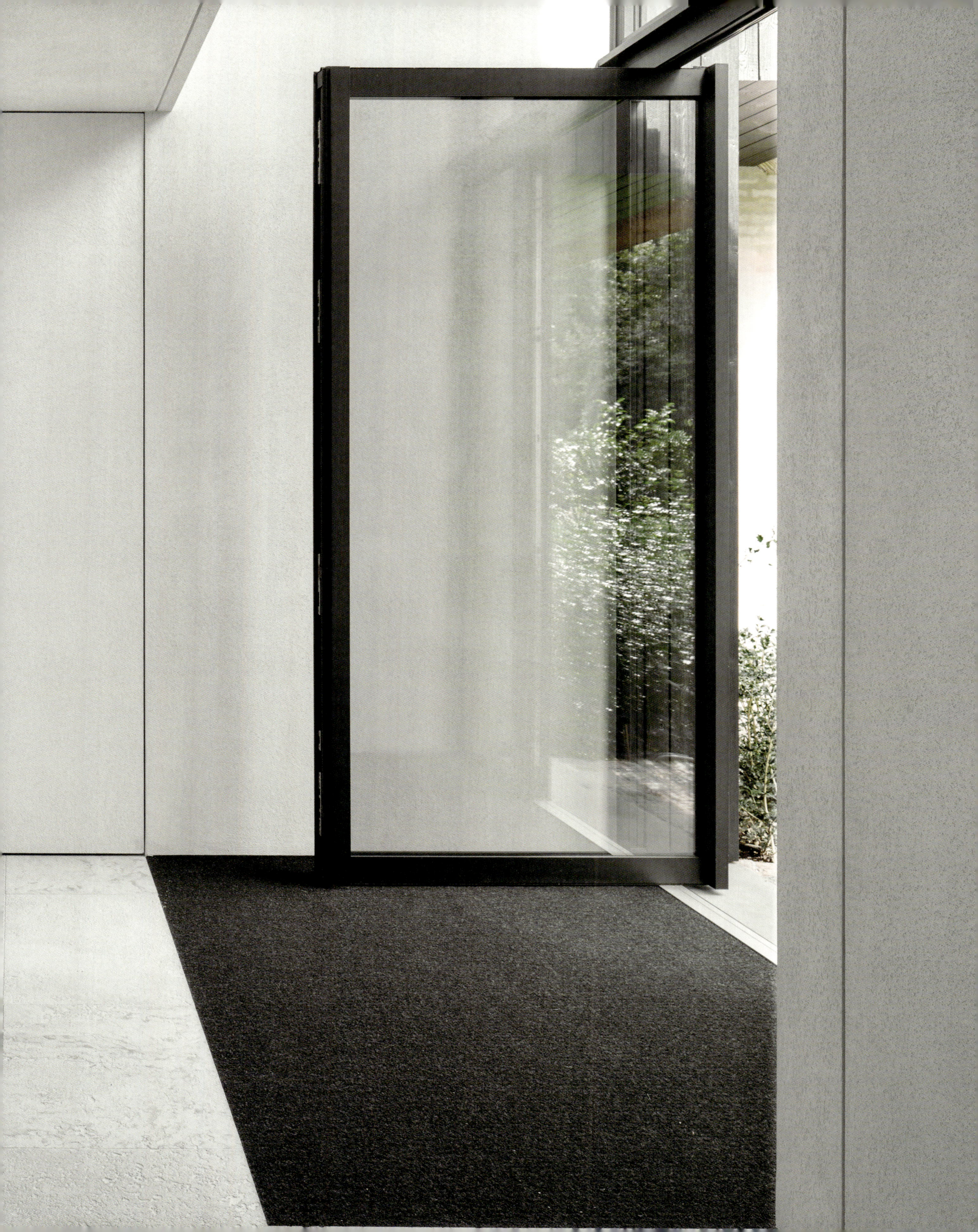

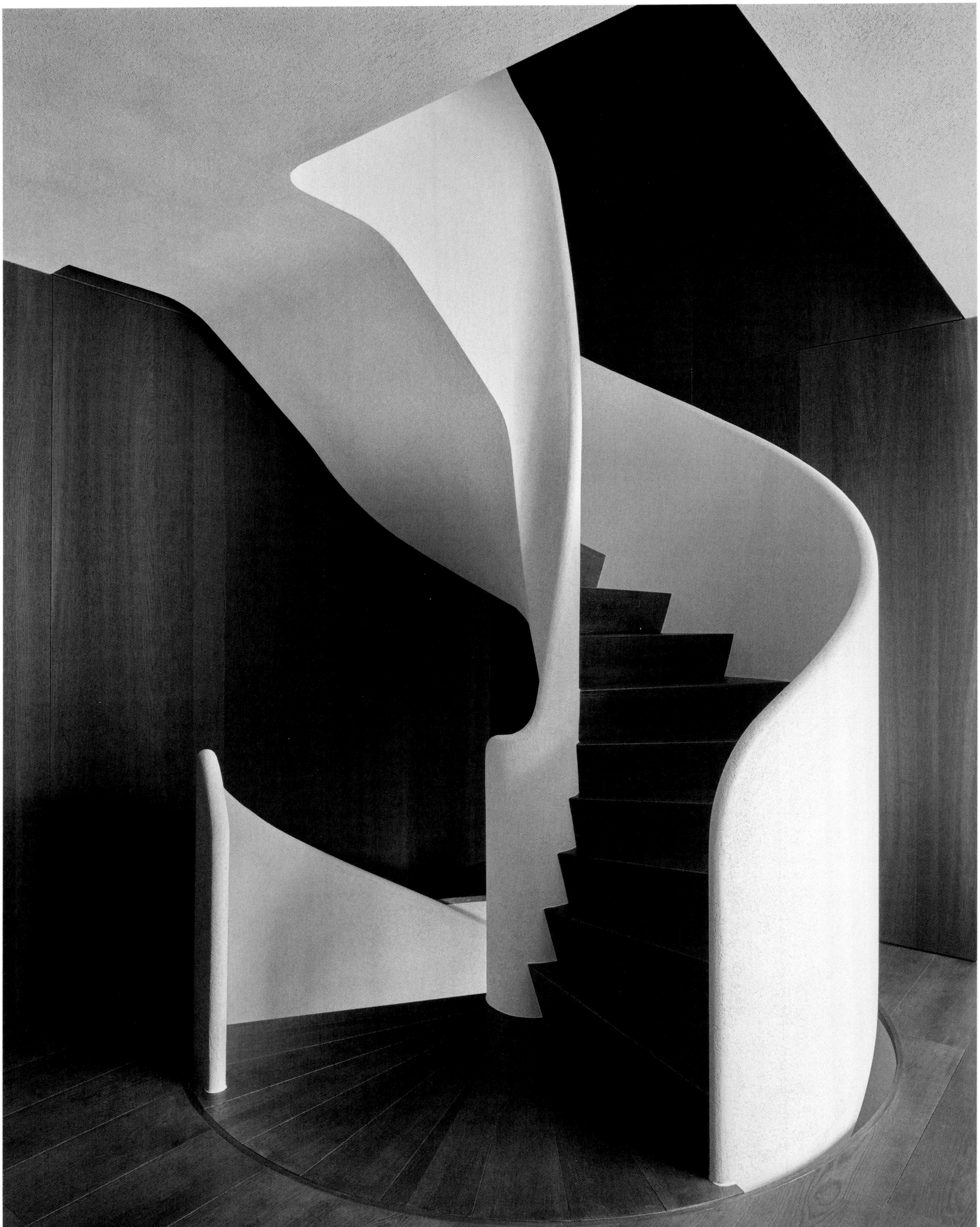

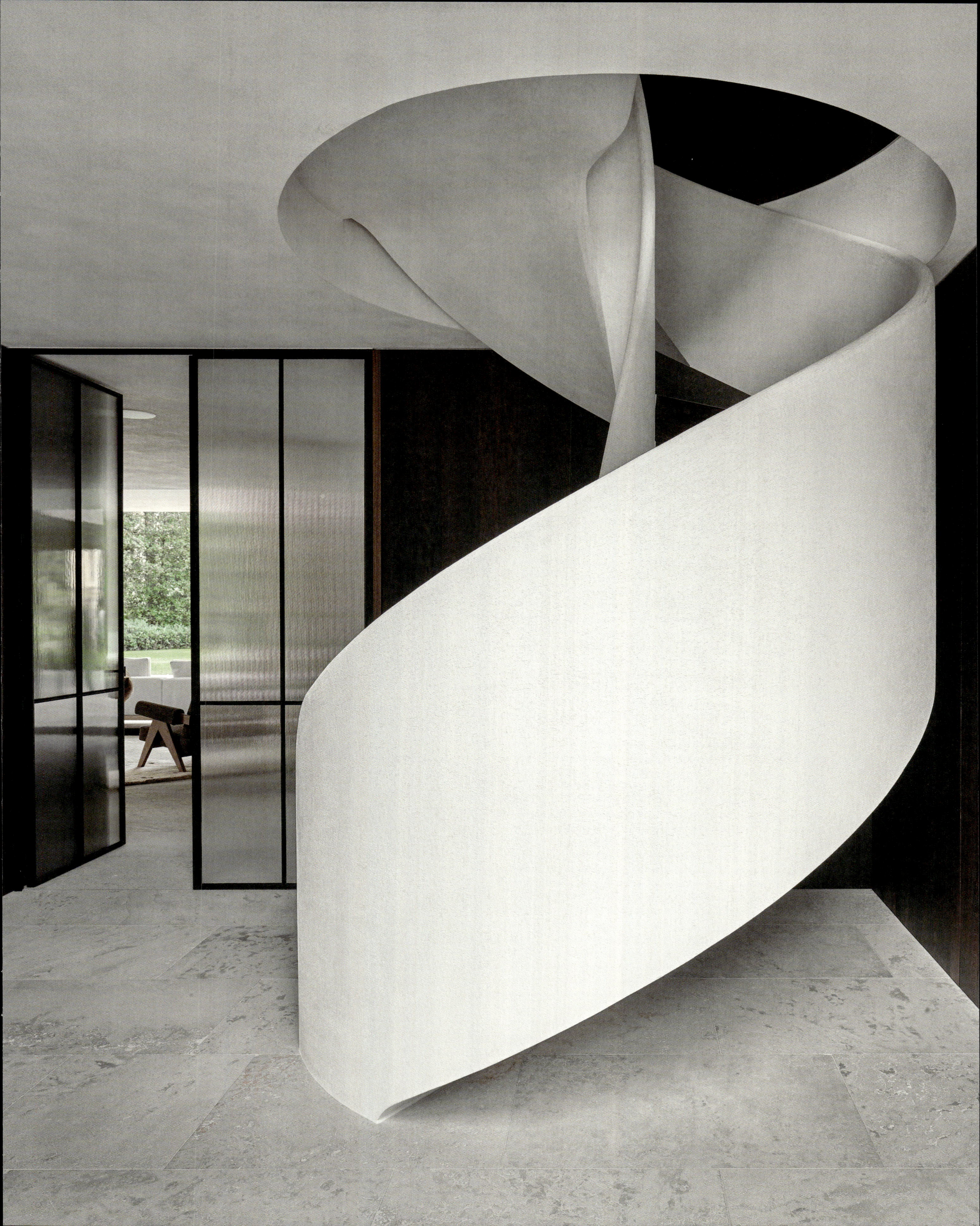

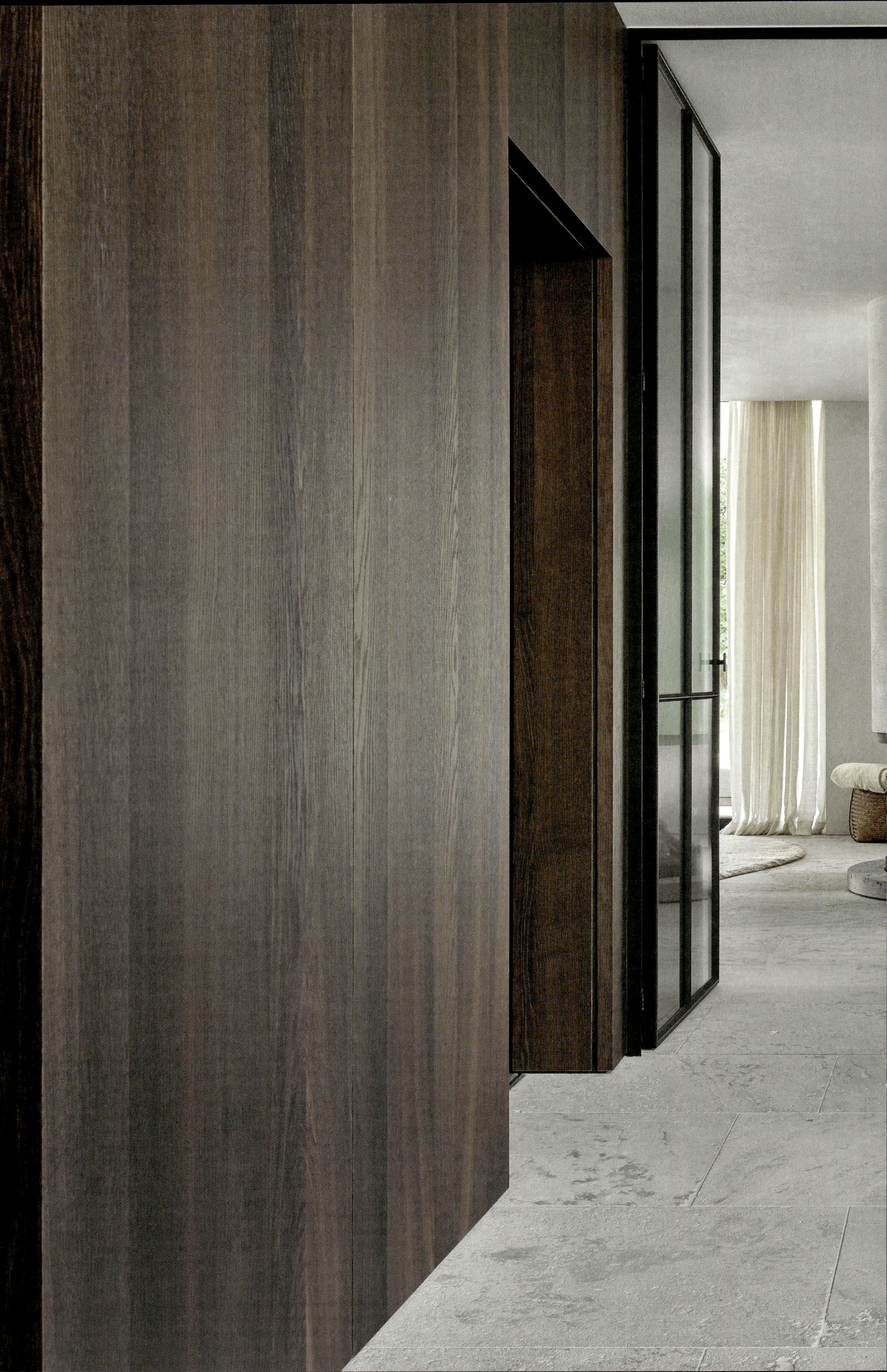

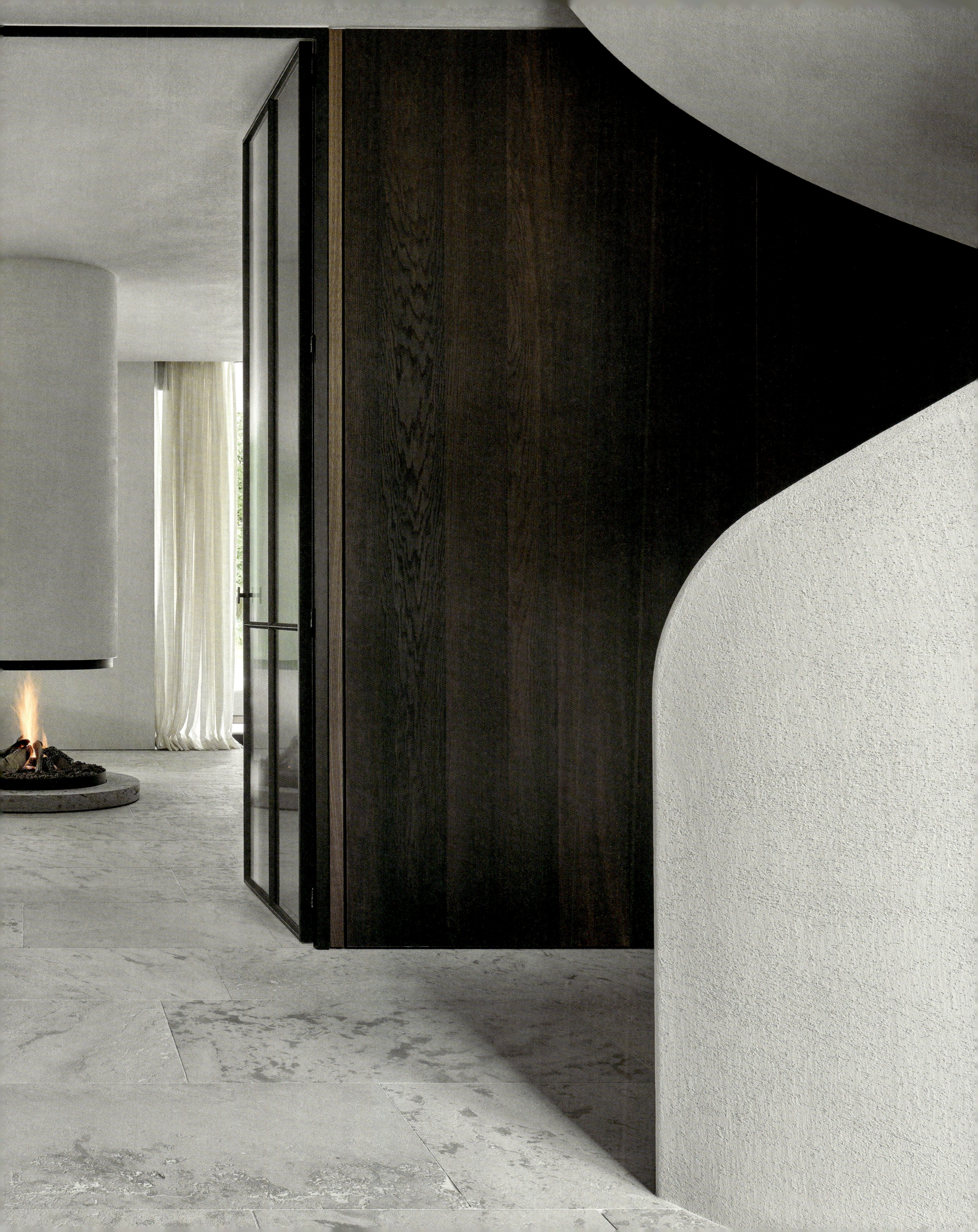

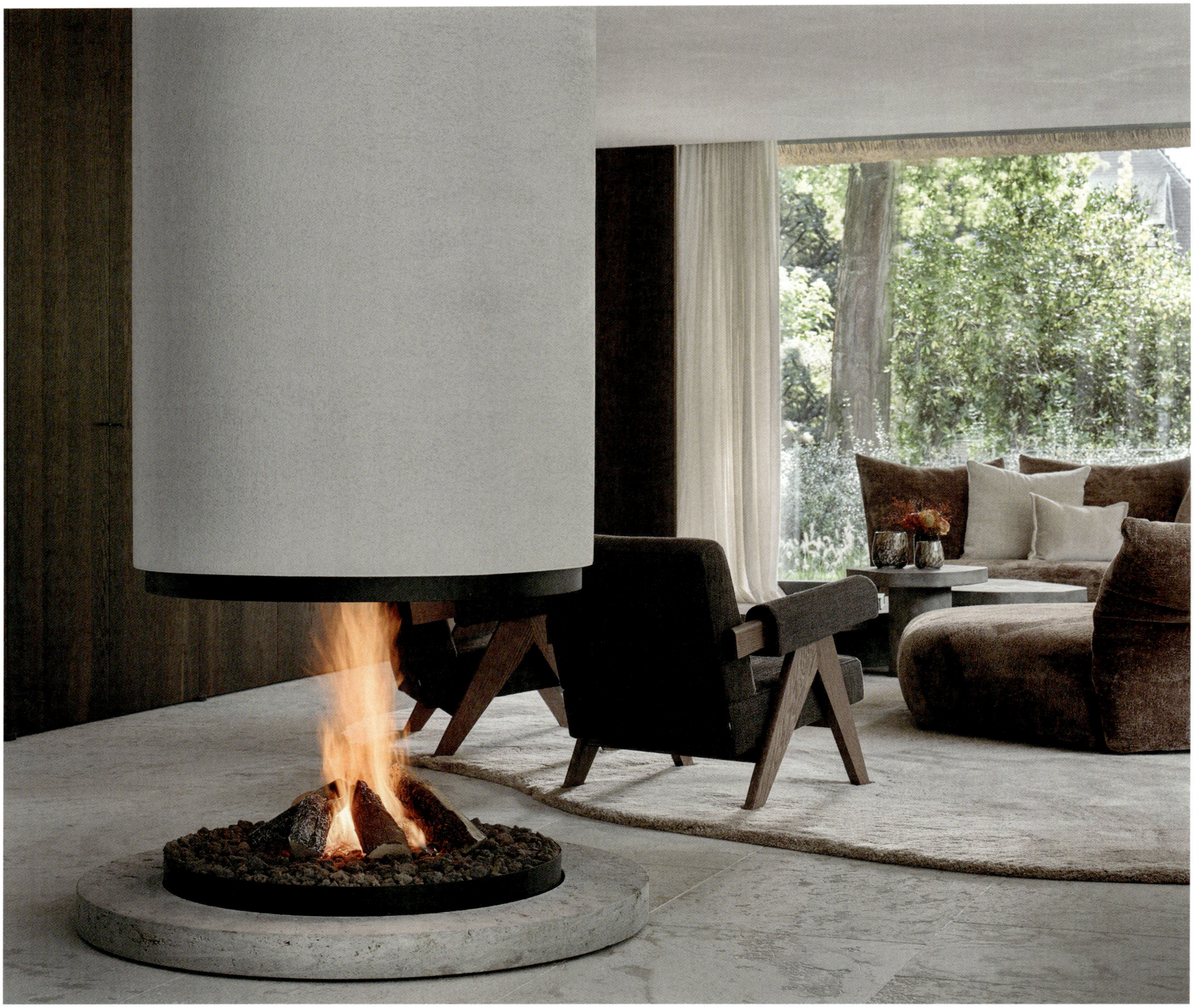

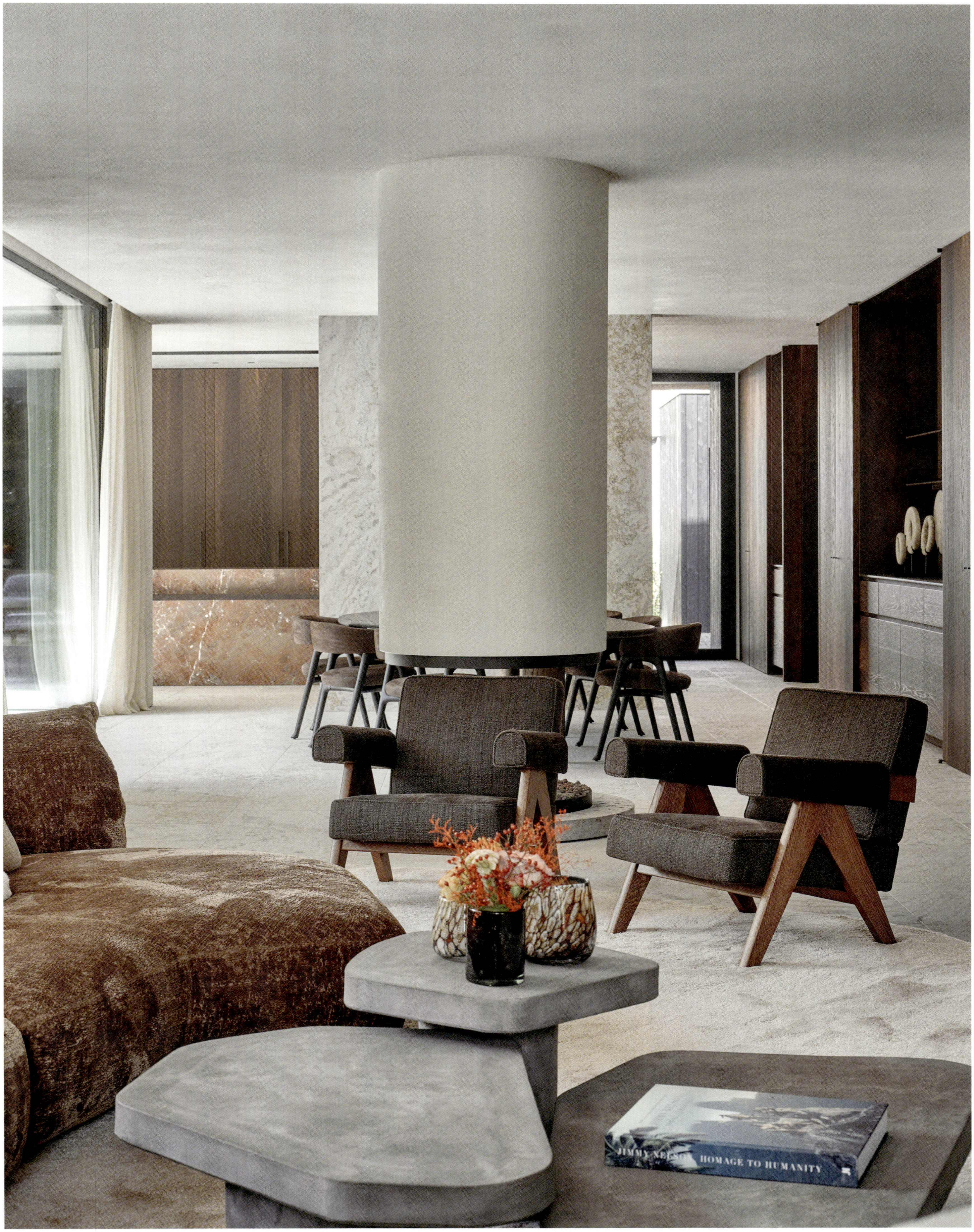
HOMAGE TO HUMANITY

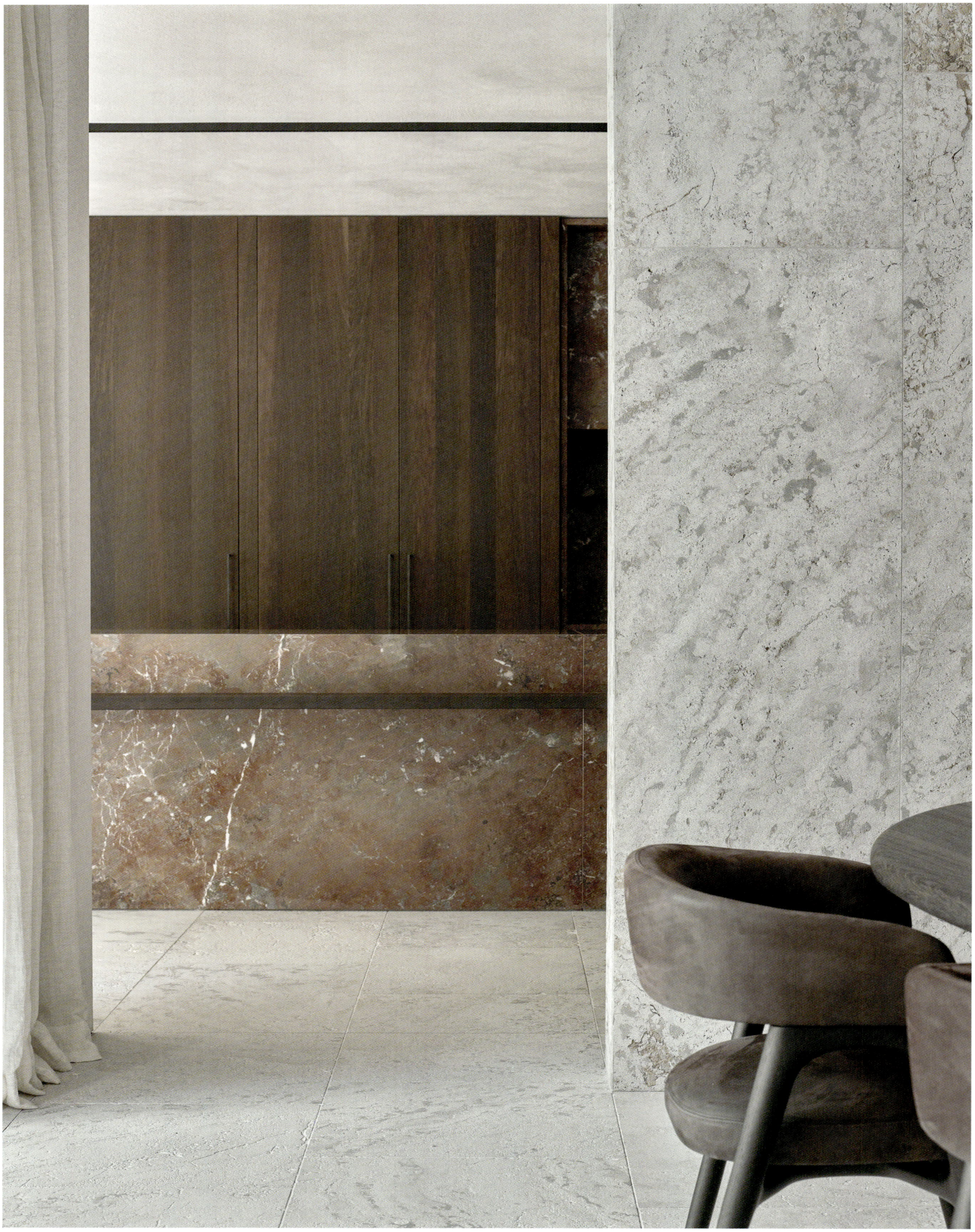

55

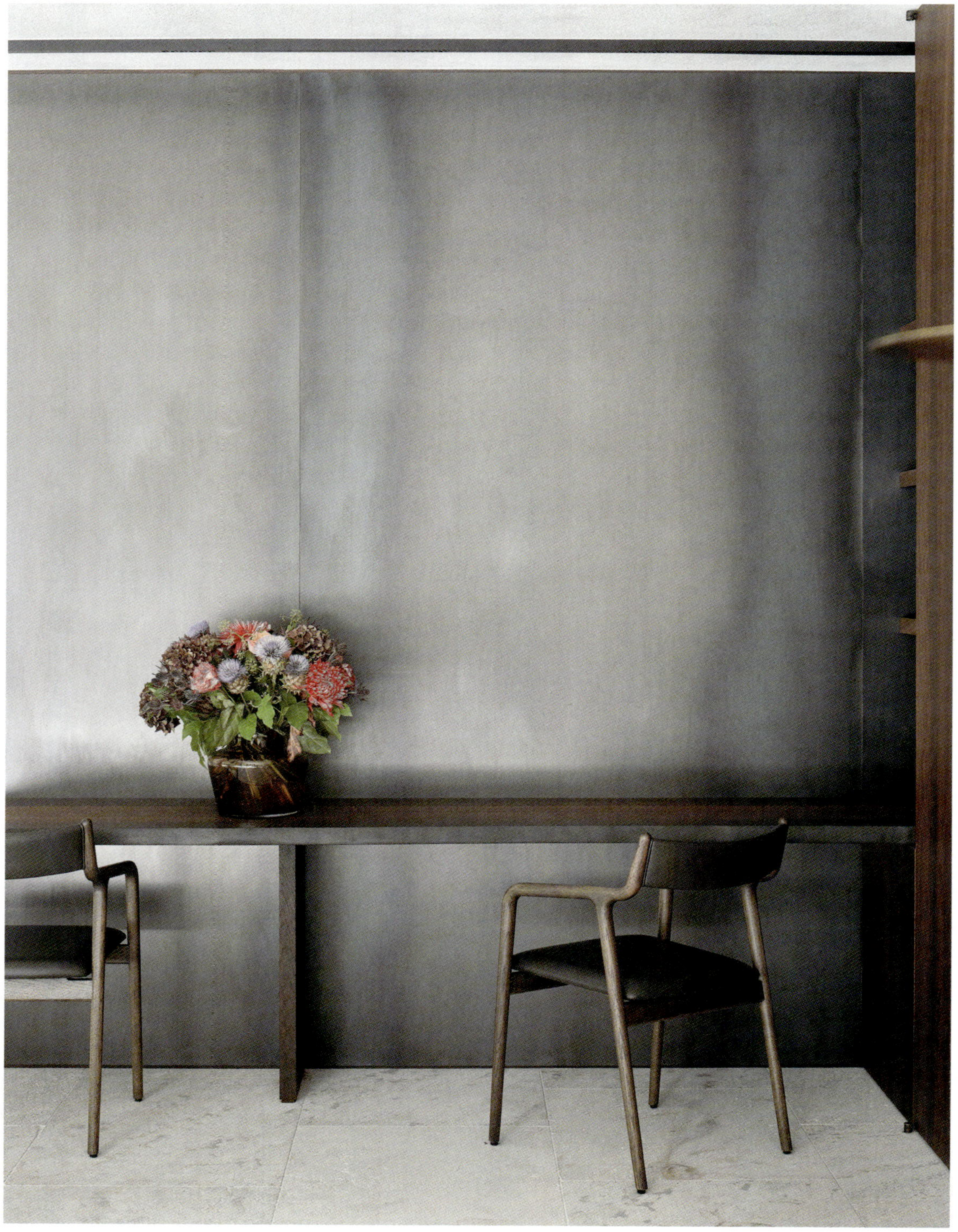

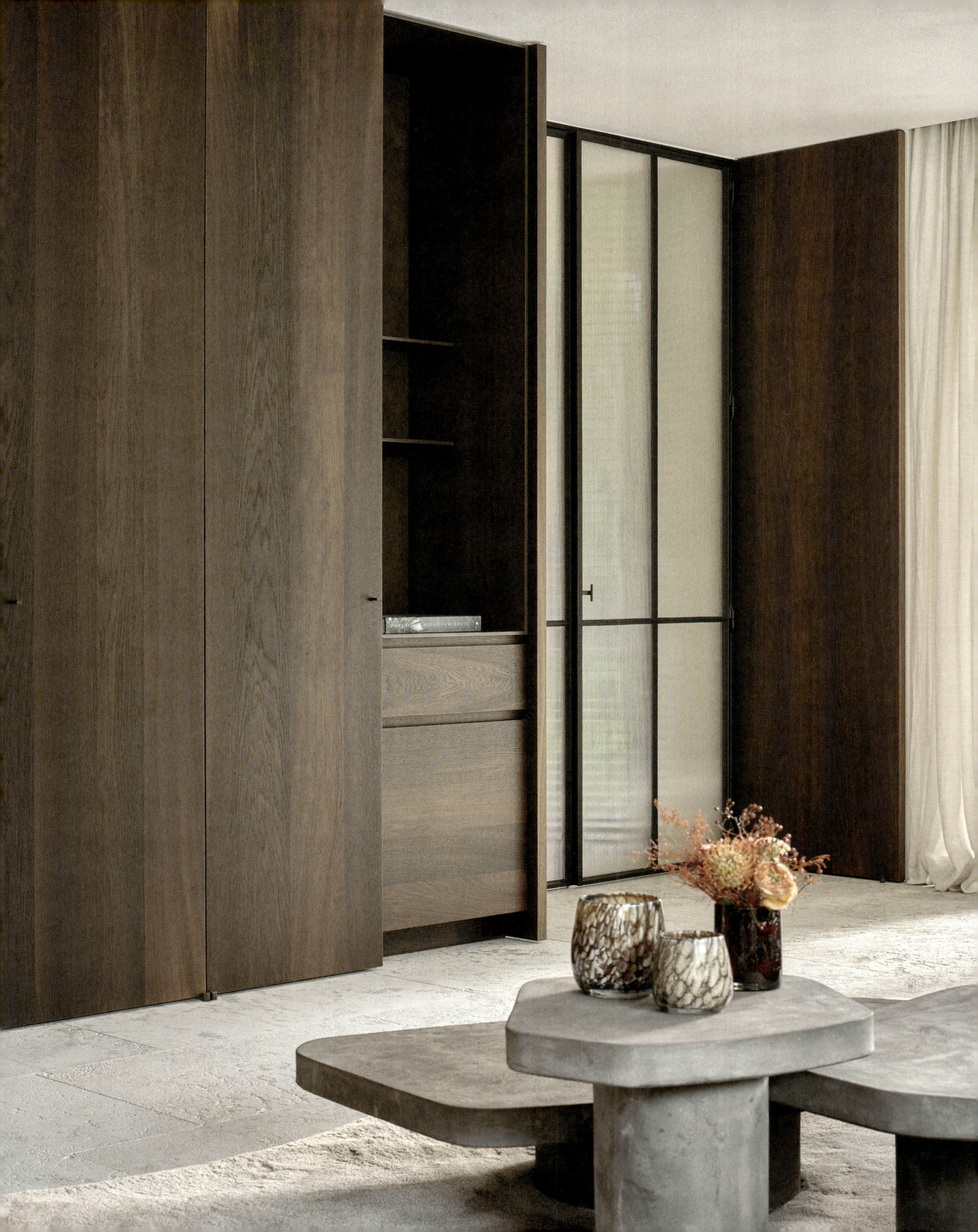

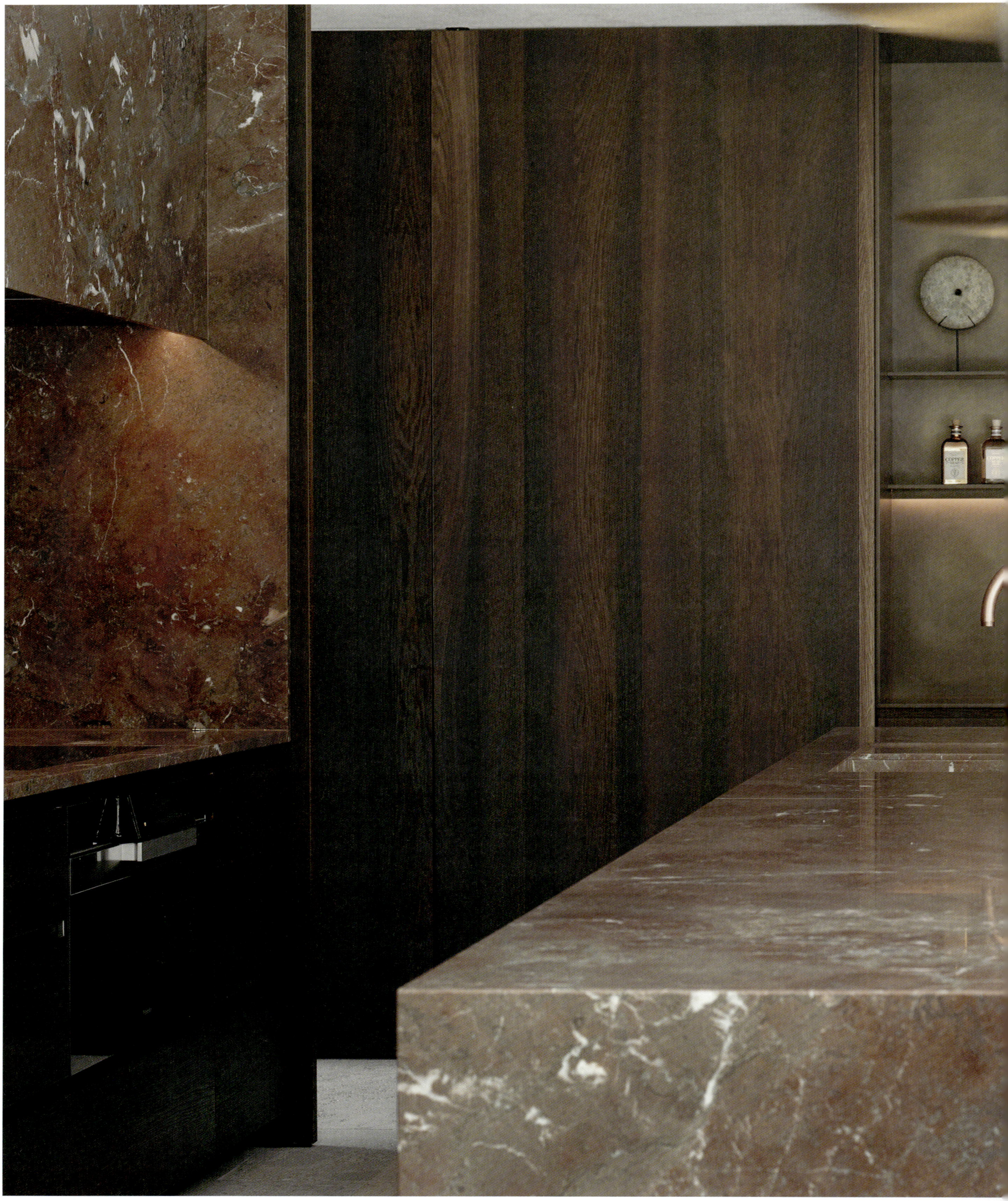

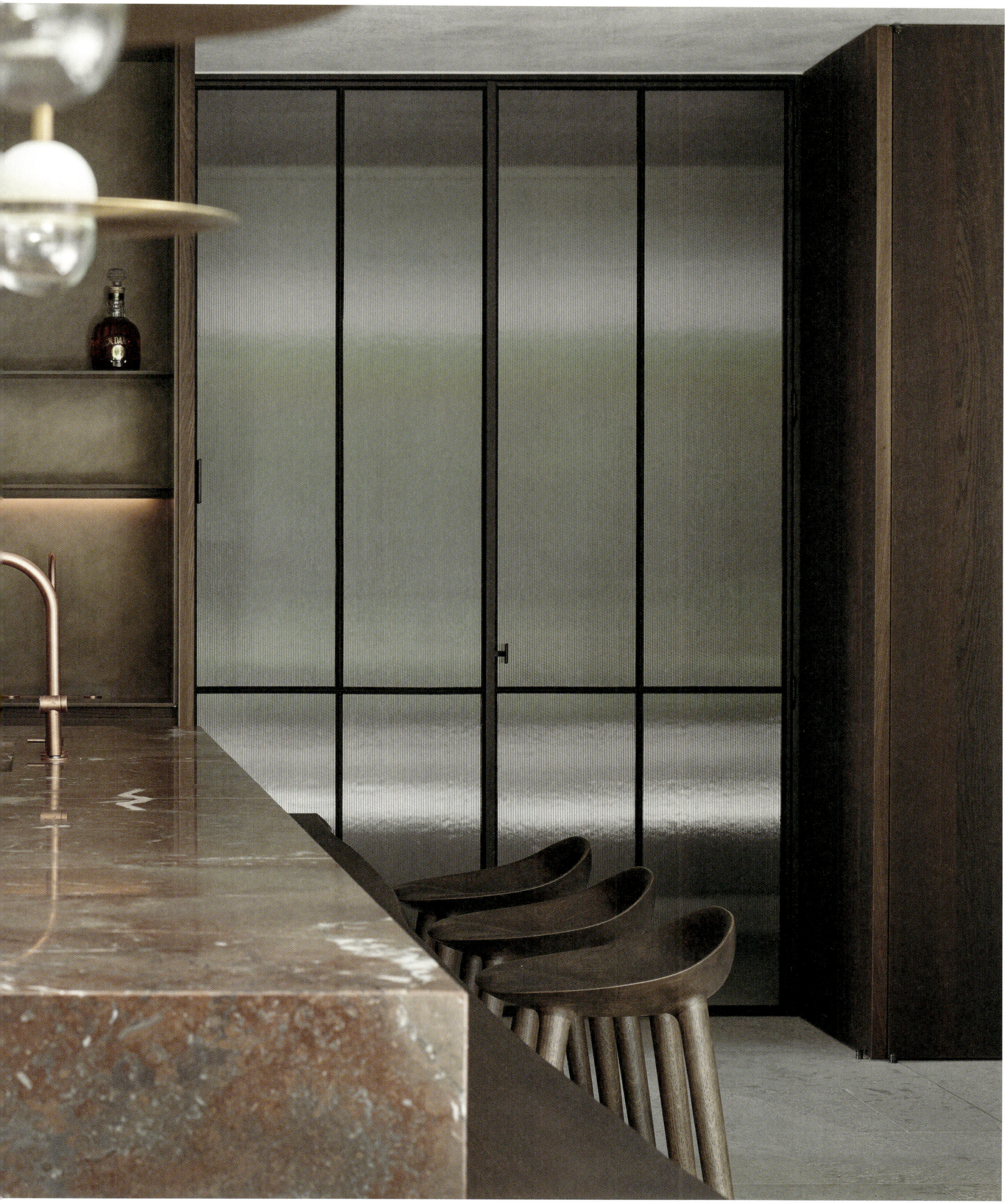

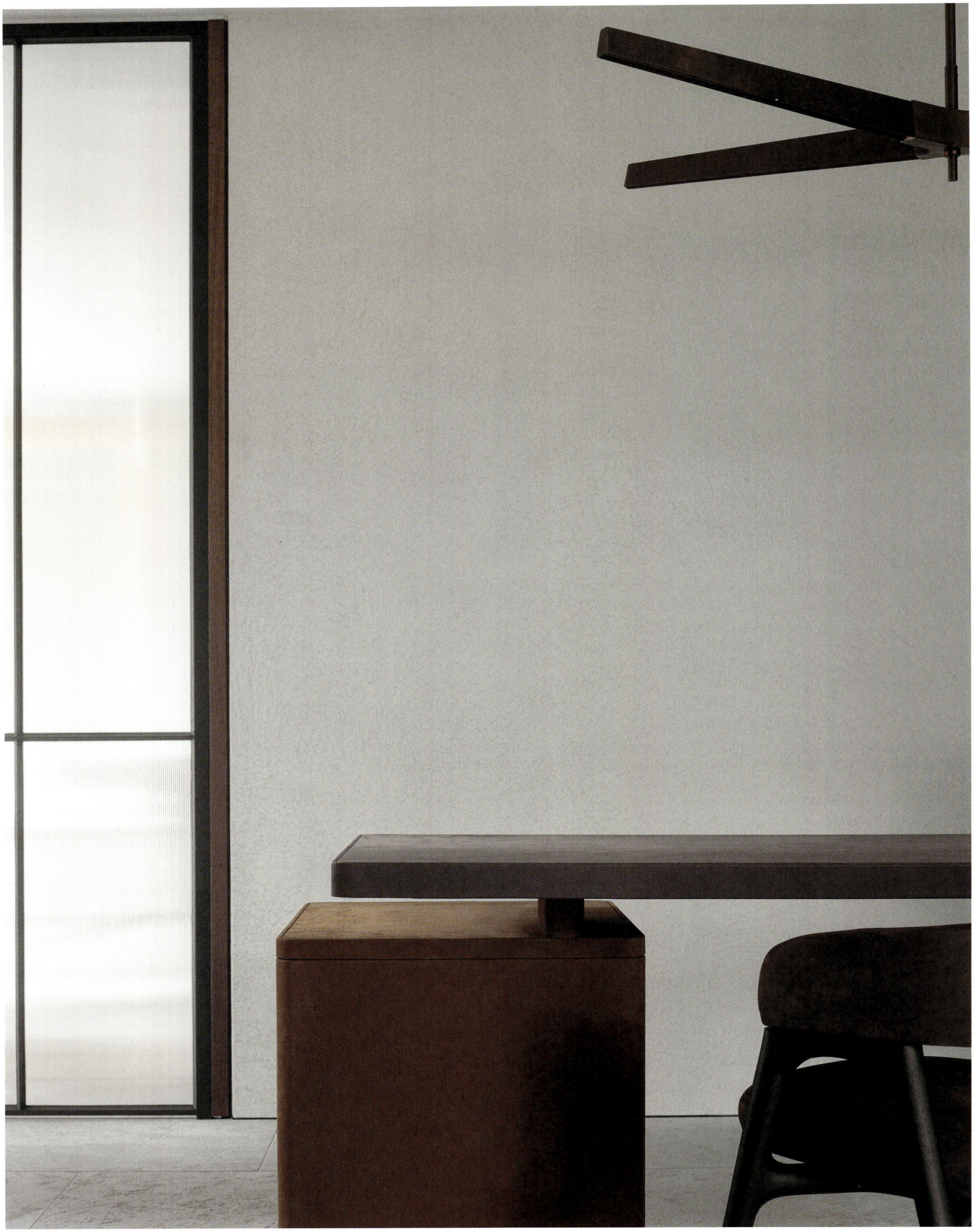

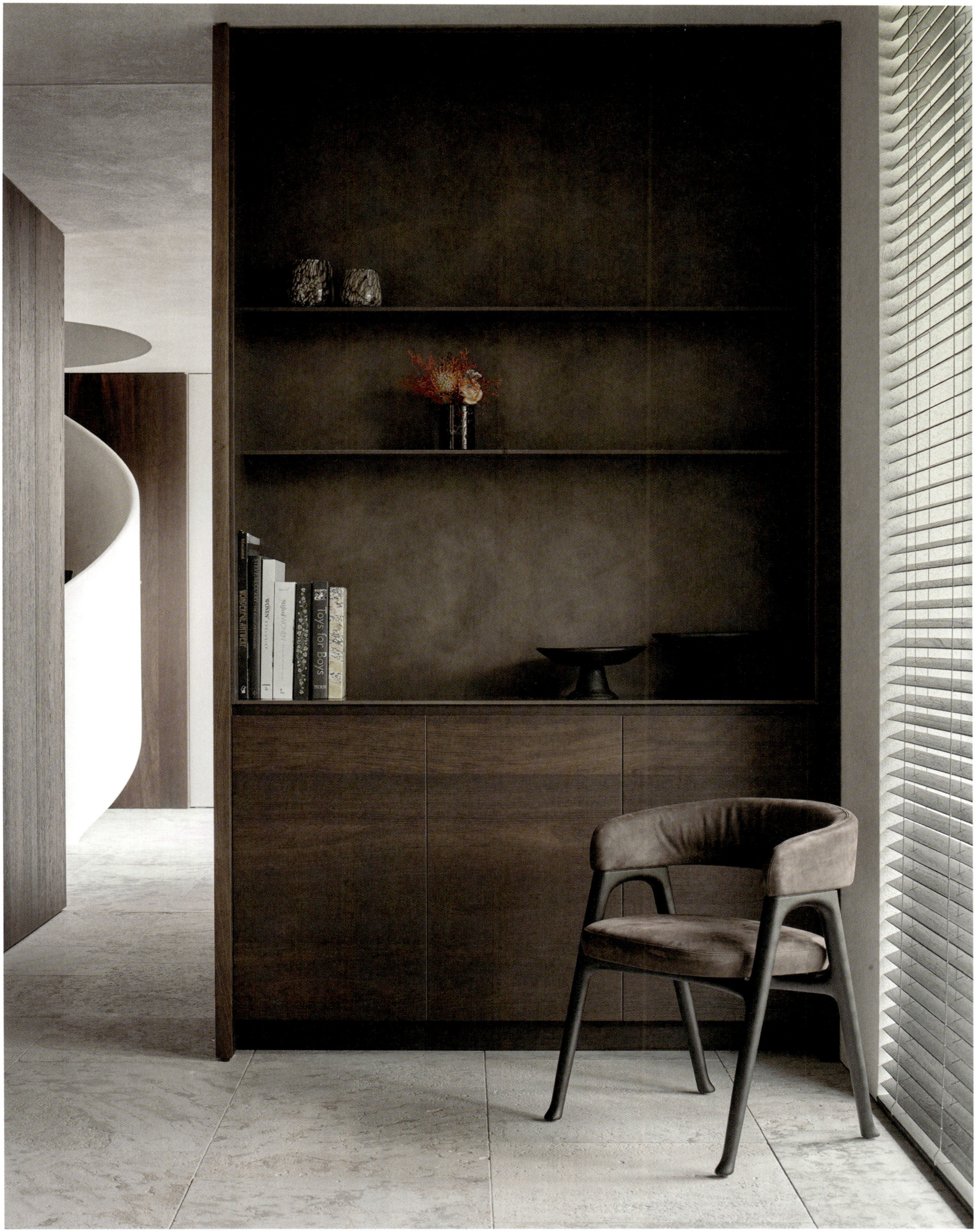
Toys for Boys

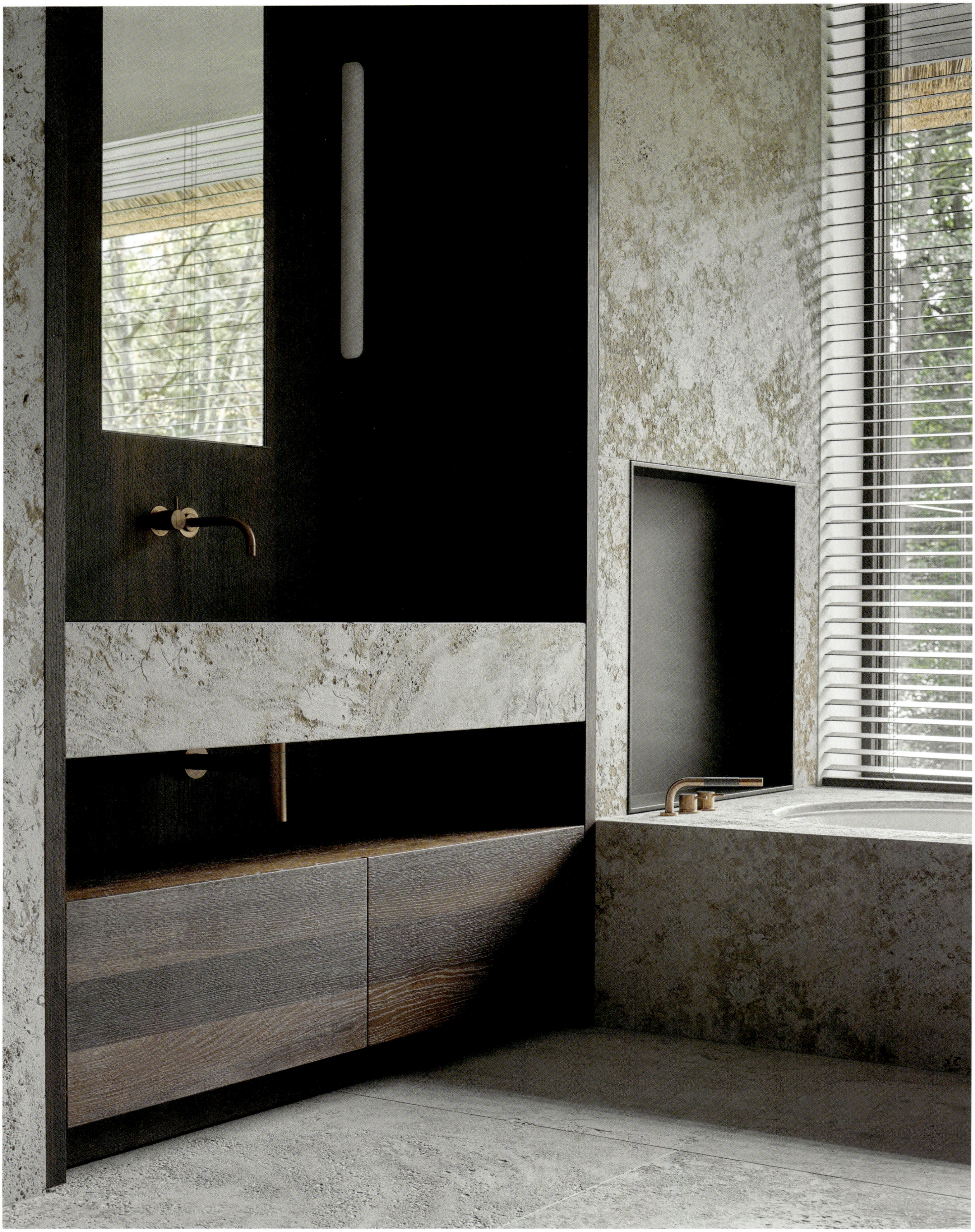

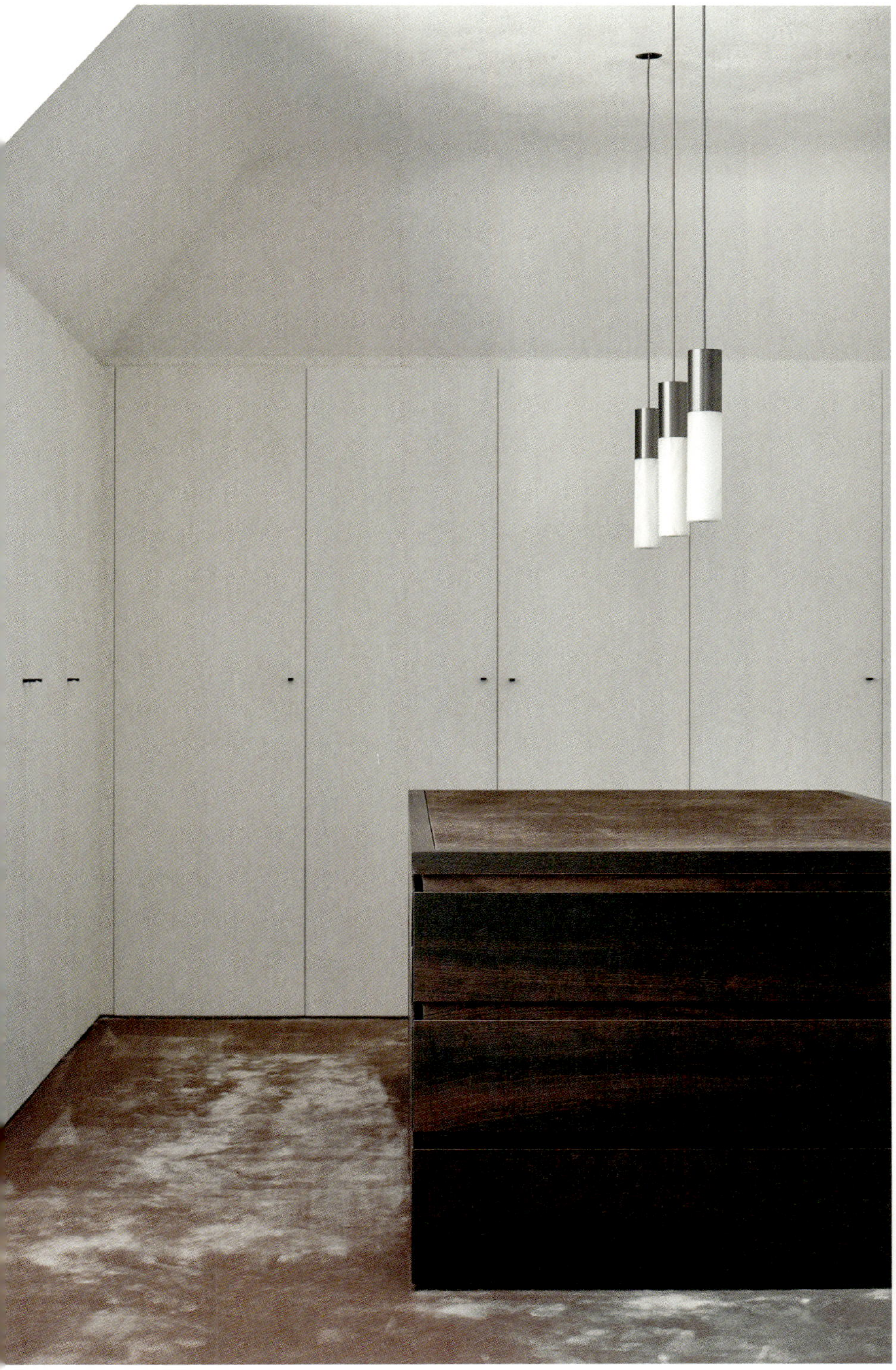

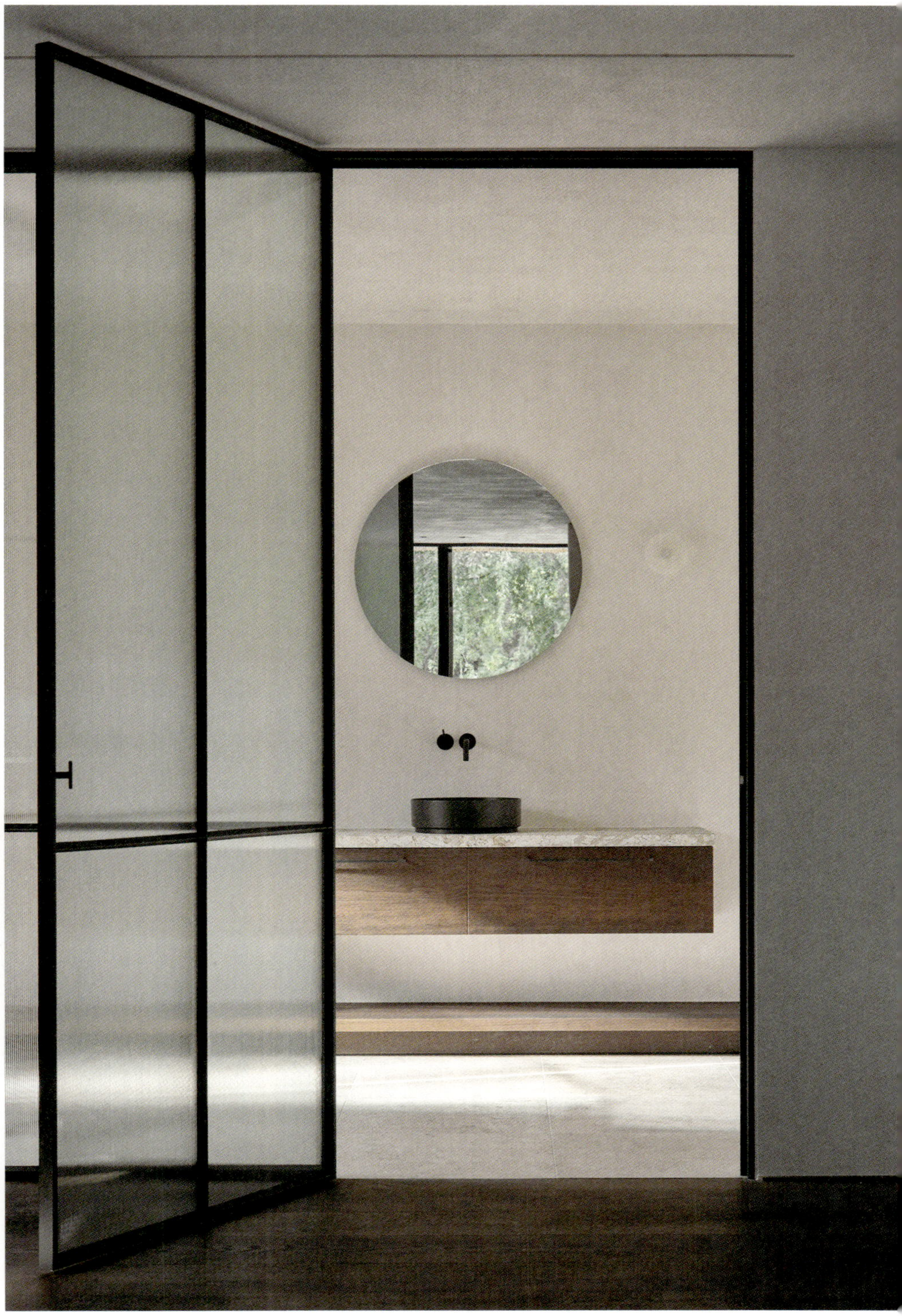

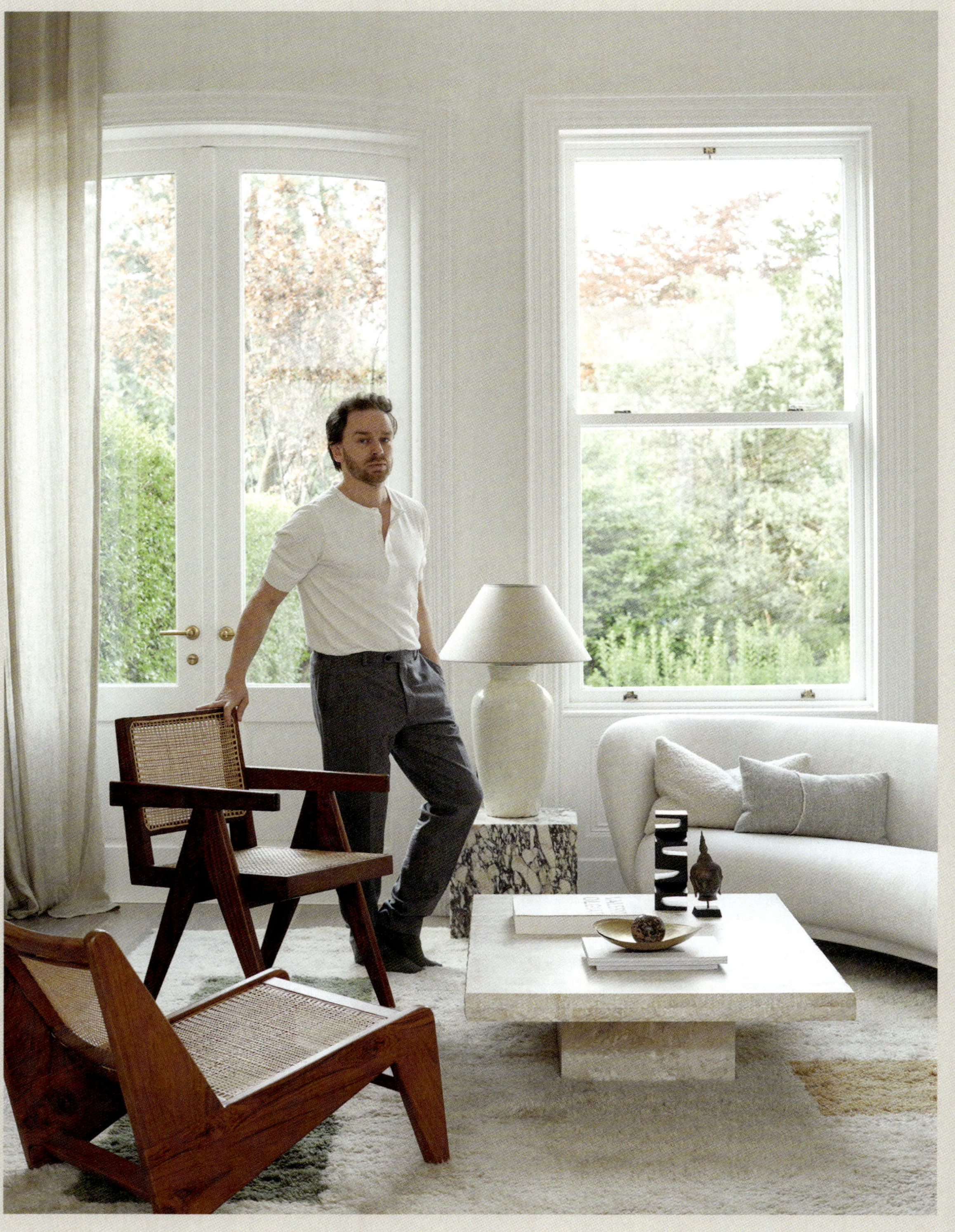

HUTCH Design

HUTCH design is a London-based studio founded in 2017 by architect and interior designer Craig Hutchinson.

For Craig, "modern living" means allowing people to live creatively and to have their home tailor-made to facilitate their lifestyle, whilst also enabling individuals to add their own unique personality to the space.

Integral to his approach is how the home responds to its surrounding site and context. The relationship between different spaces in the home, how light enters a space, the type of materials used are all at the very heart of his design philosophy.

Craig is interested in exploring and combining natural materials, and particularly in how the interplay between them accentuates their individual qualities and characteristics.

Home, for him, means a place to completely disconnect. A safe space to relax, and to separate one's self from the stressful nature of busy modern life. Almost like a retreat.

www.hutchdesign.co

Photography: Helen Cathcart - Stylism: Sarah Birks

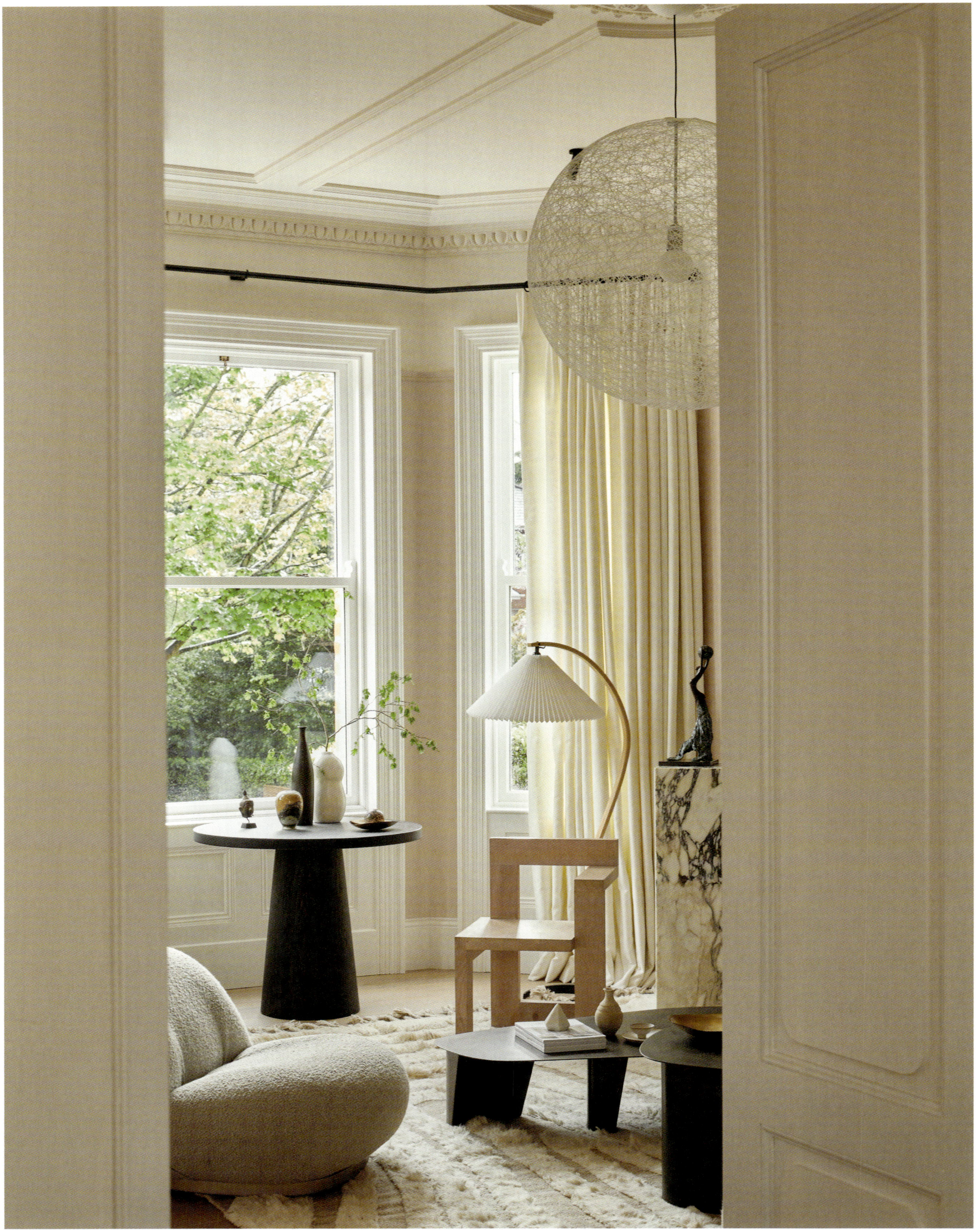

"No. 8" is a remarkable transformation by HUTCH Design of a 120-year-old derelict Victorian building into a contemporary home for a young family with three small children.

The exceptional three-storey residence in Belfast (Northern Ireland) now offers five bedrooms and three bathrooms. With a completely redesigned layout that includes impressive double-height volumes and an interconnected sequence of spaces – views flow seamlessly from the front to the back of the house.

HUTCH Design worked closely with the clients to create their dream home, creating open living spaces with ample storage alongside more private, quiet areas. Light airy spaces, soft, neutral tones, and natural materials create a warm, calming and informal home comfortable for family life. The designers positioned the kitchen as the focal point of the ground floor living-dining-kitchen area, perfect for family and entertaining.

Externally, the building was completely restored with a new roof, sash windows, repointed brickwork and lime-rendered facades – fitting for the surrounding historic Conservation Area.

No.8 exemplifies understated, calming luxury with luminous, inviting spaces. Combining comfort and contemporary design, it is a beautiful home to be lived in.

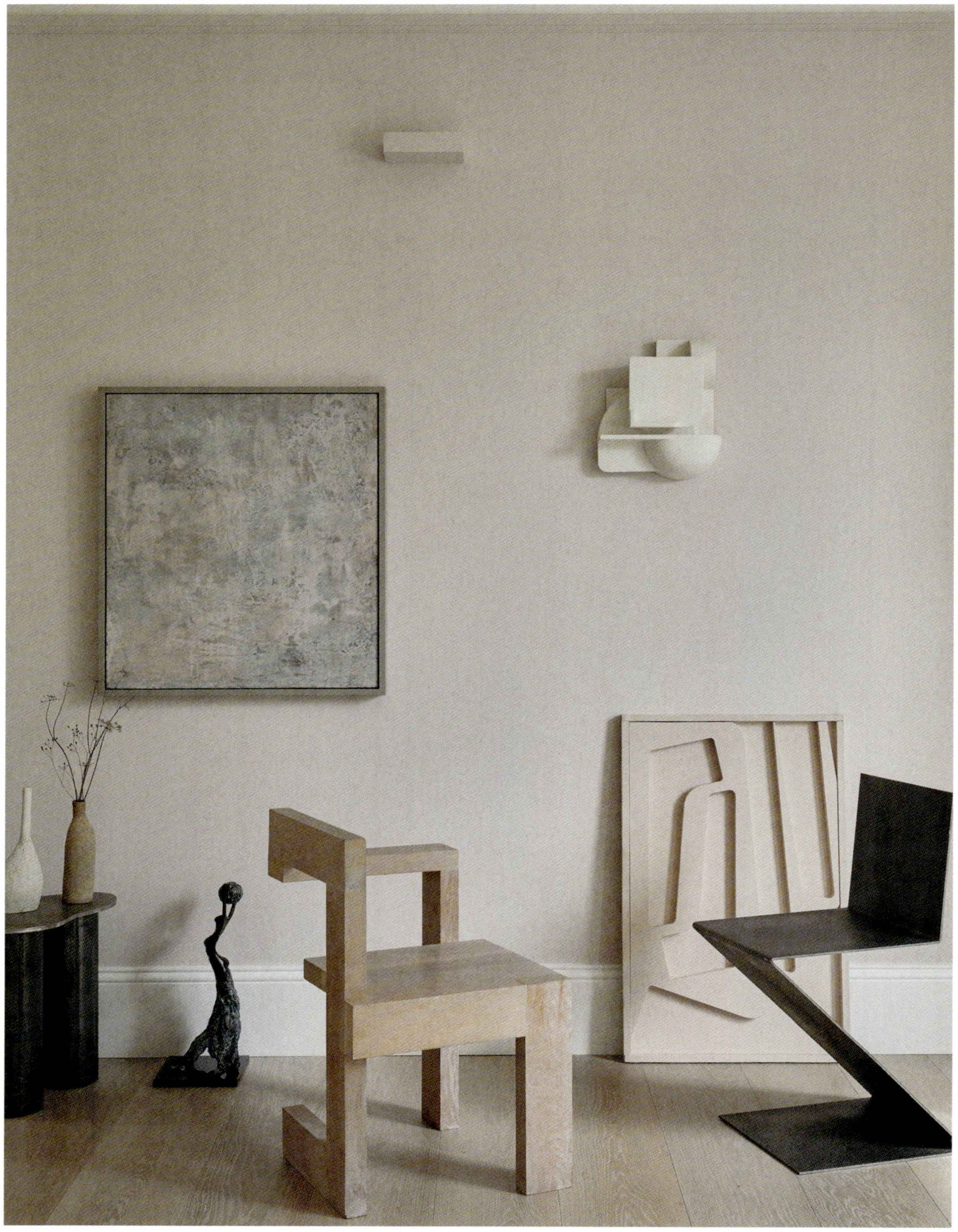

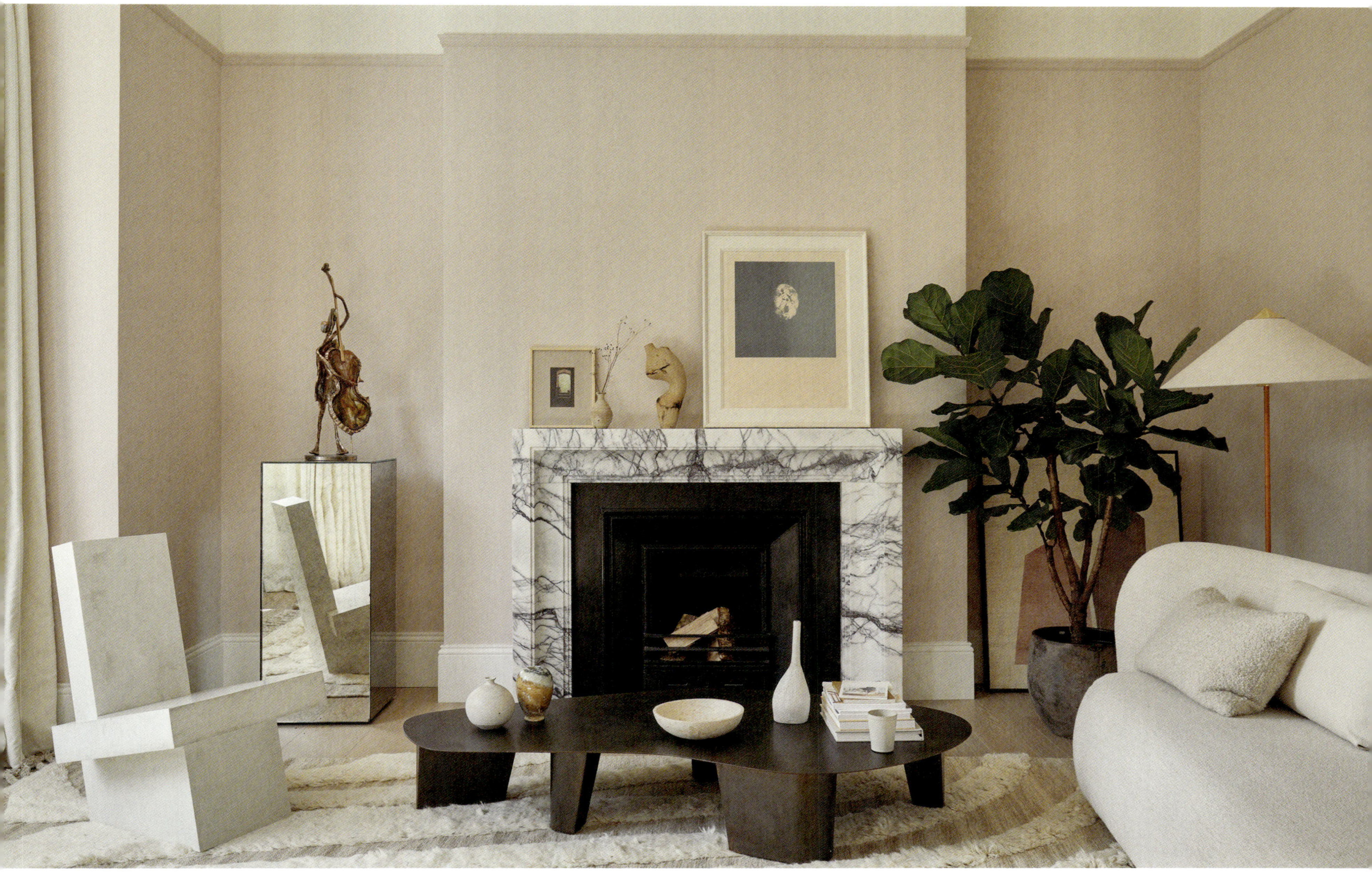

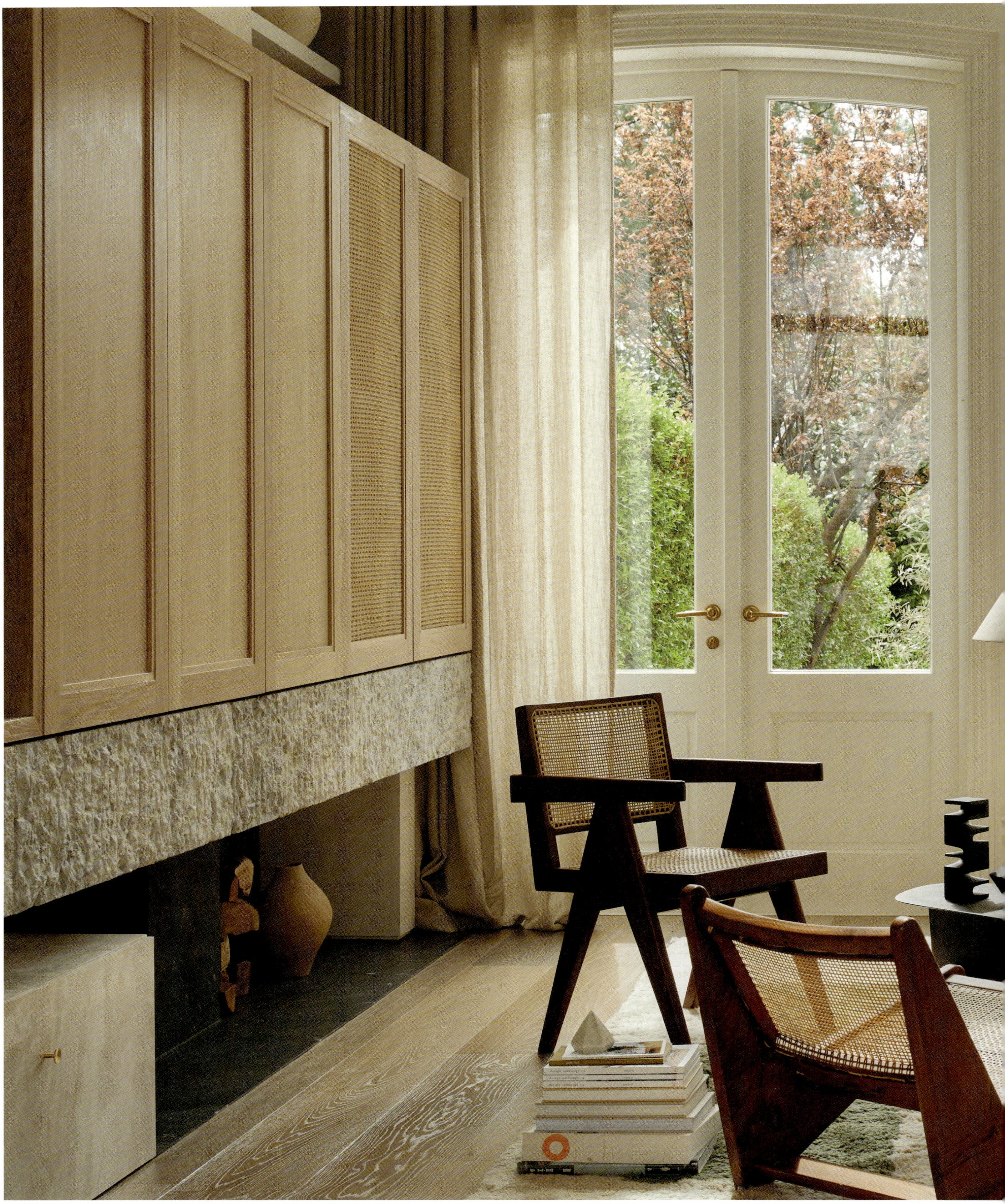

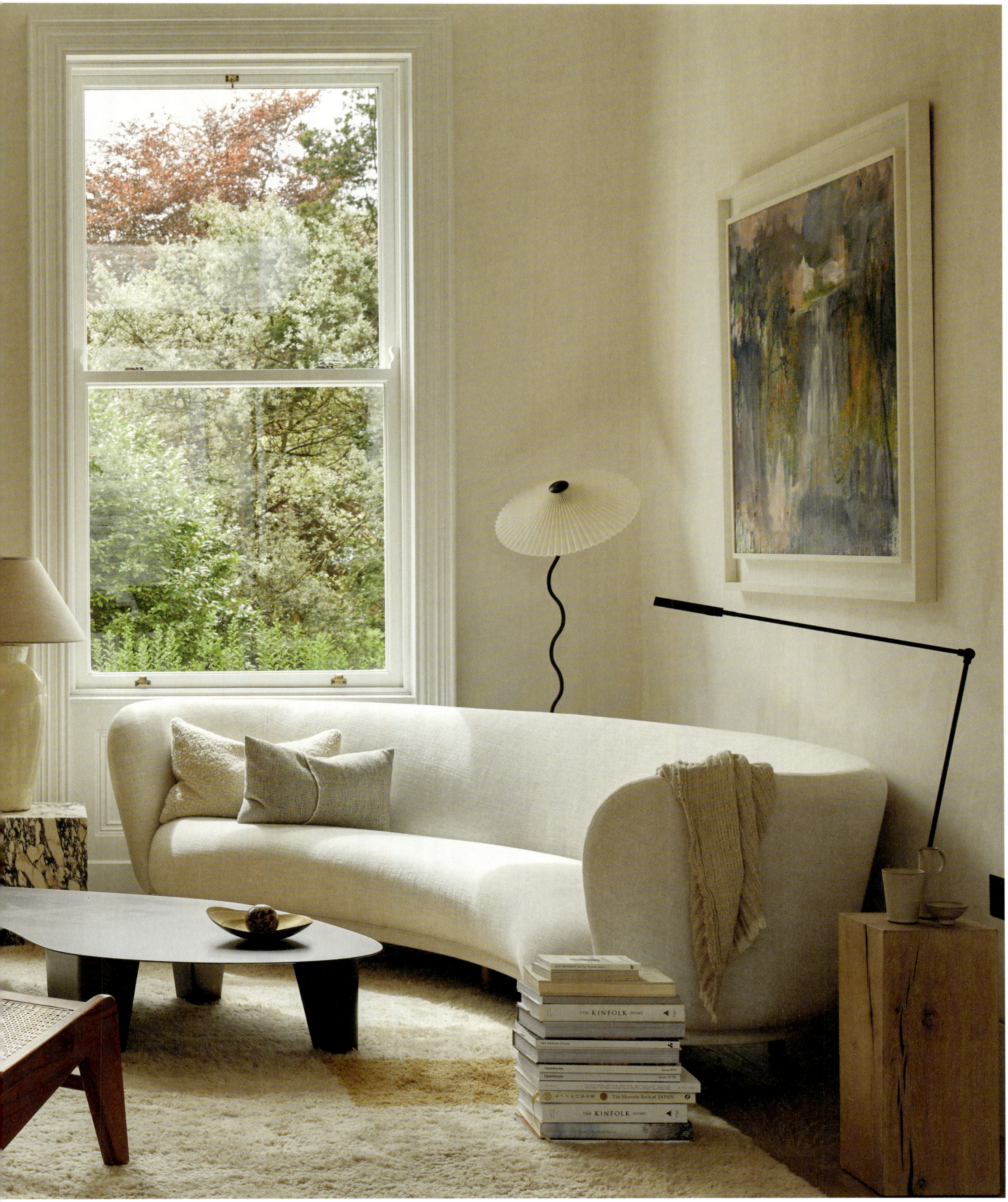

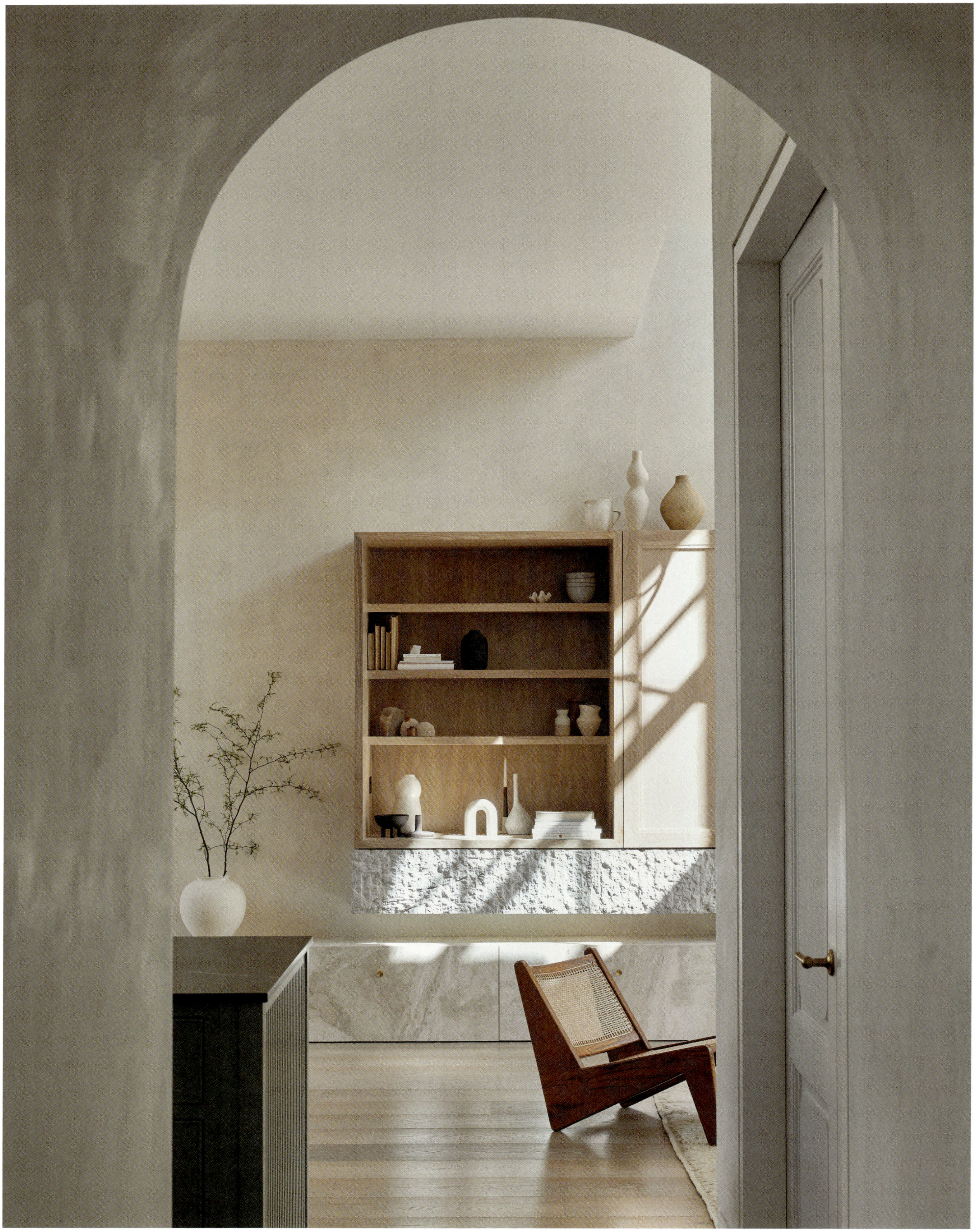

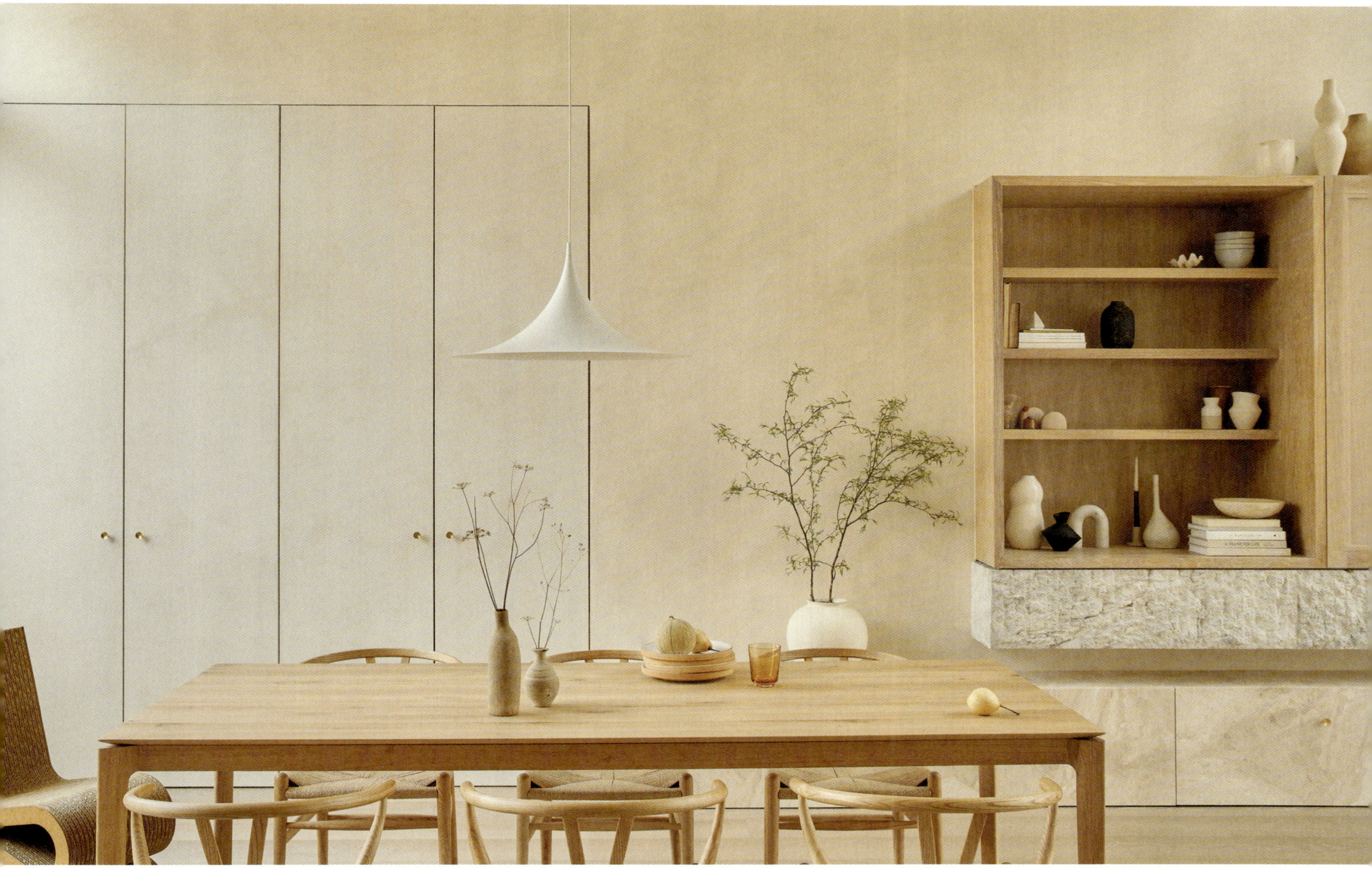

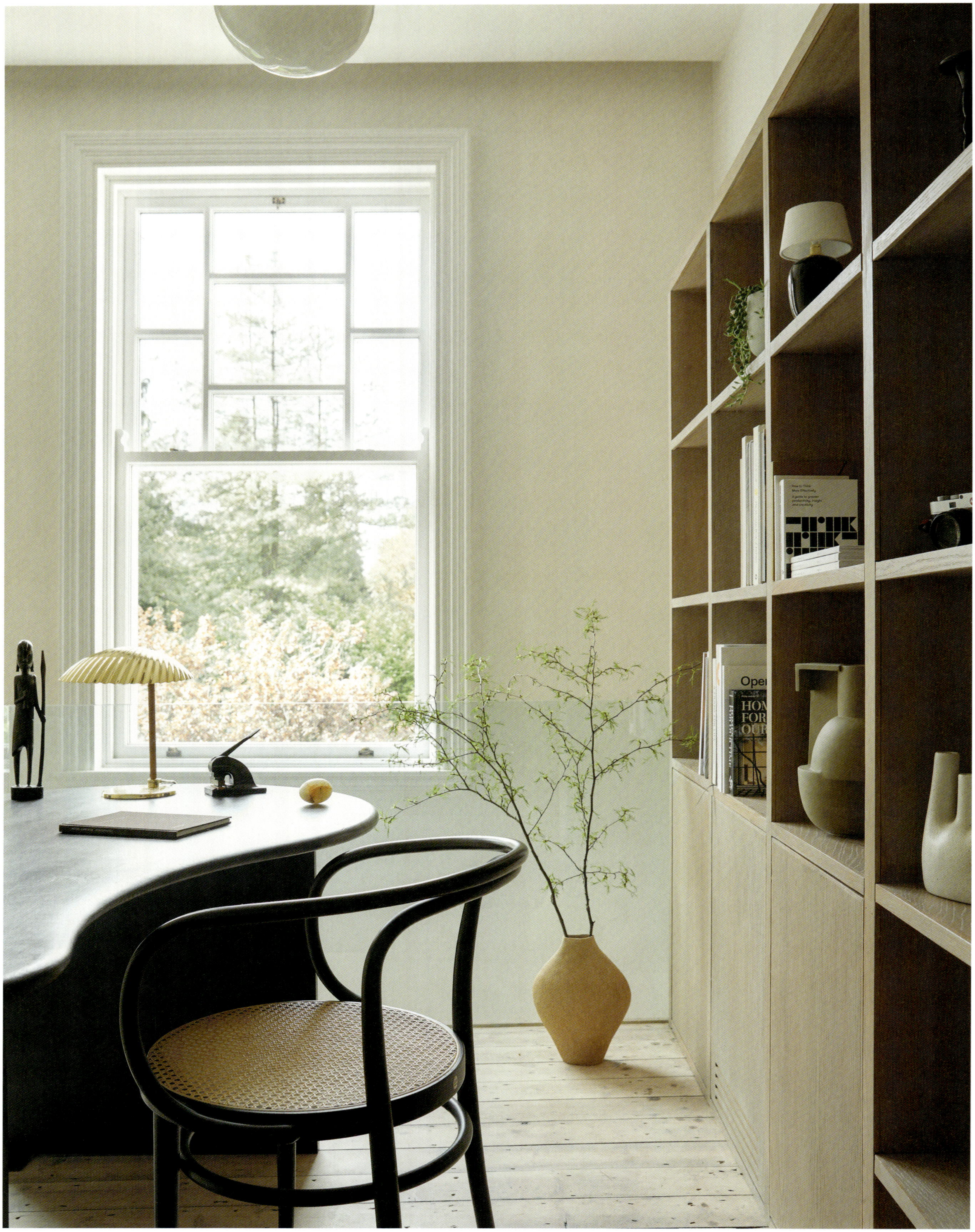

75

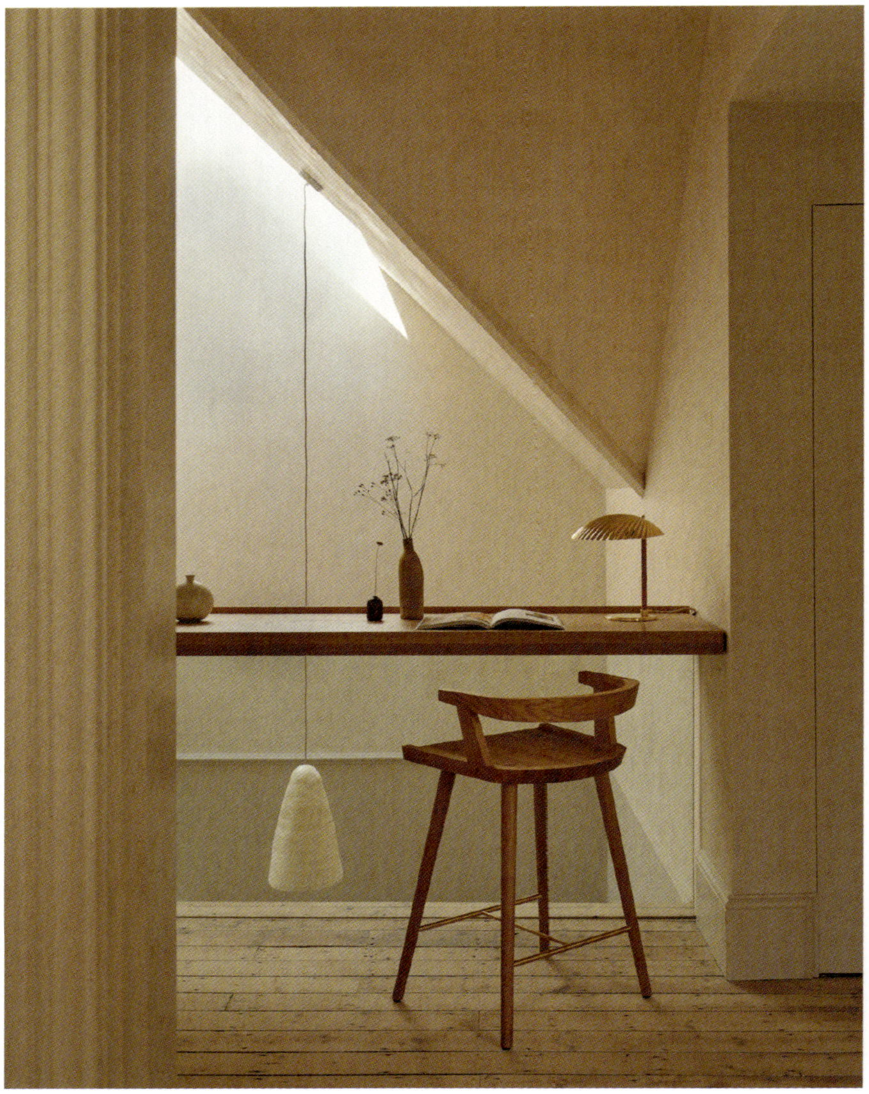
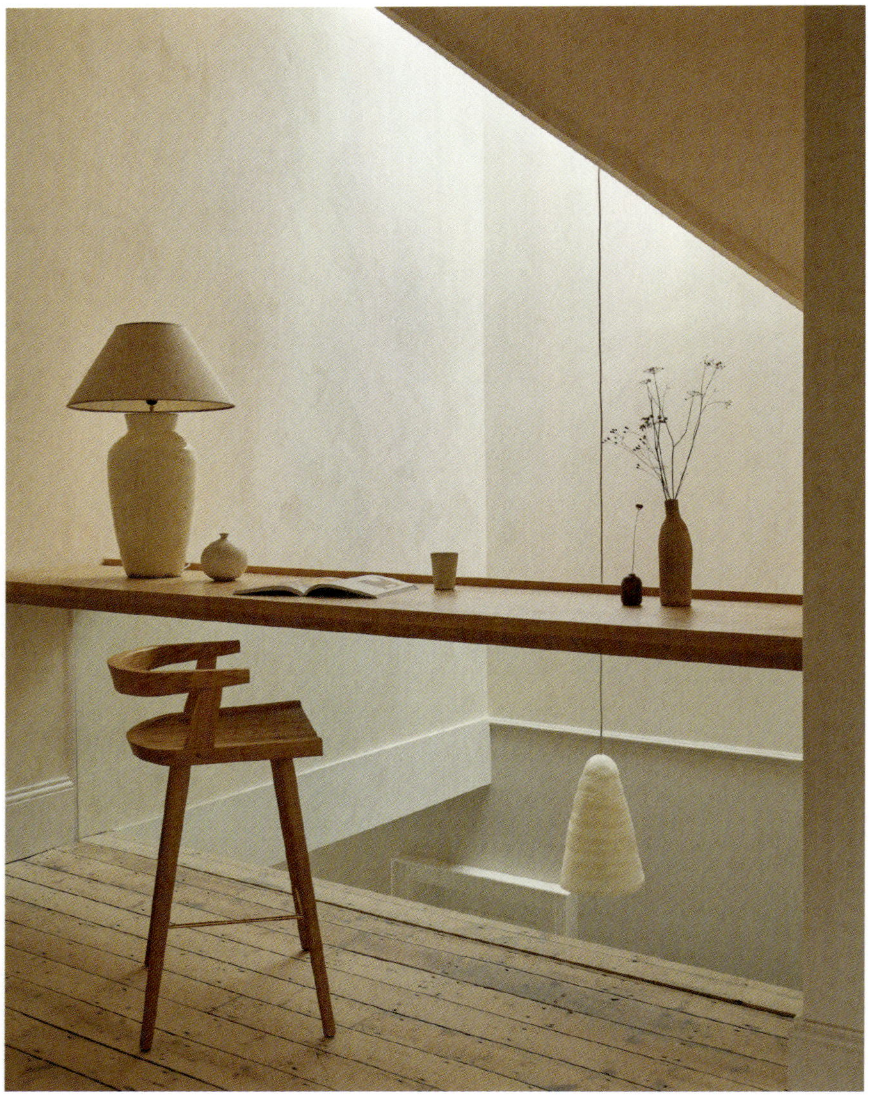

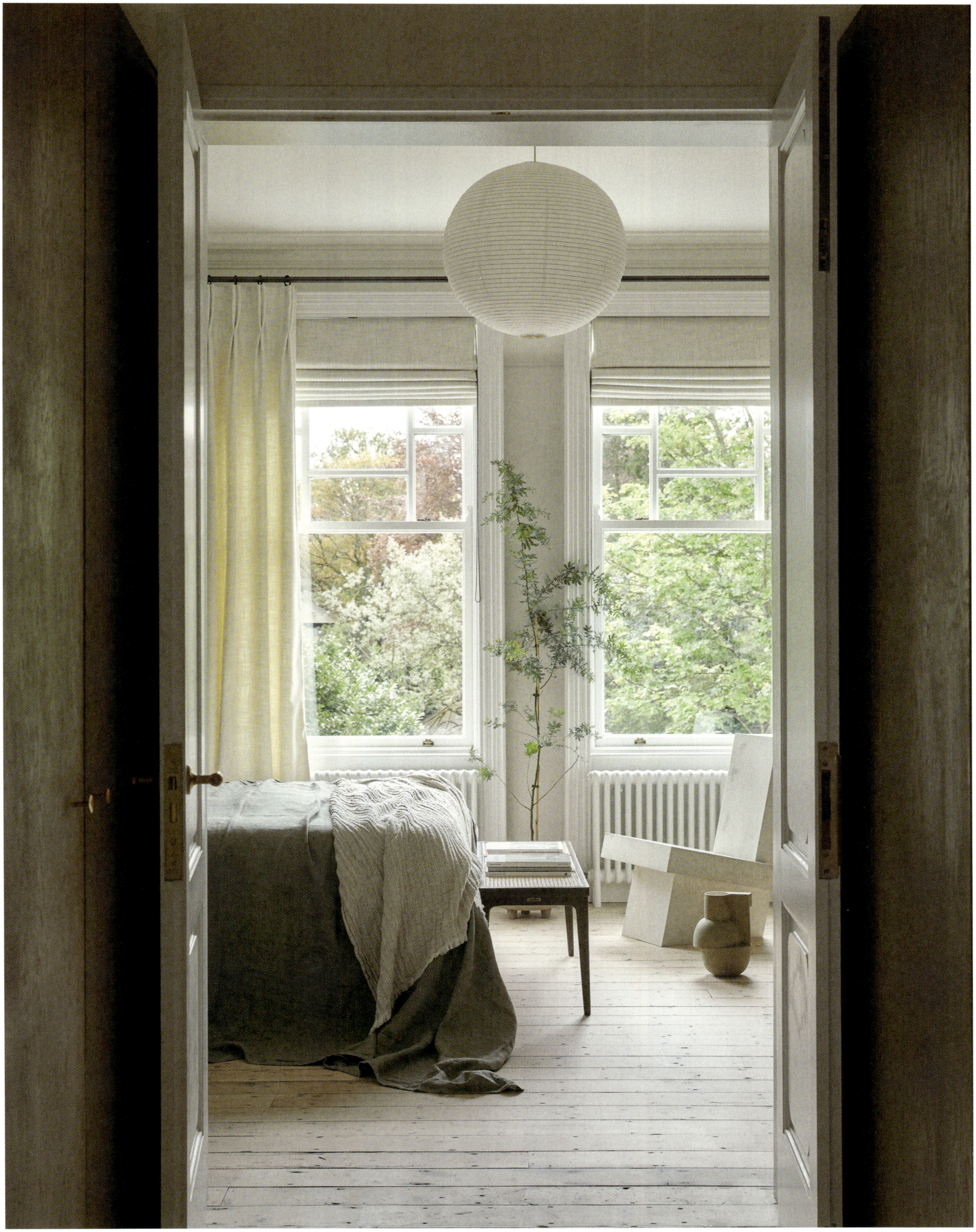

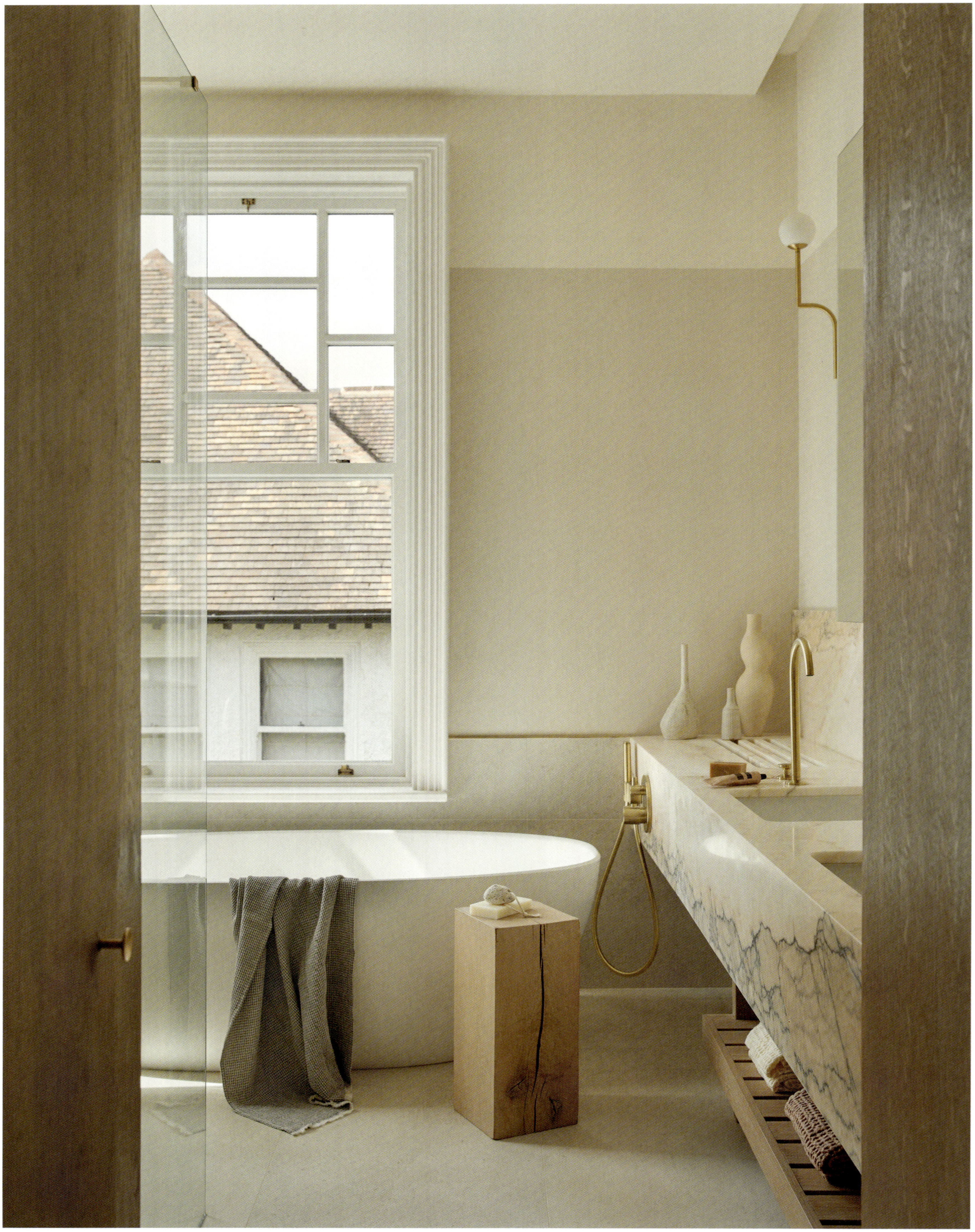

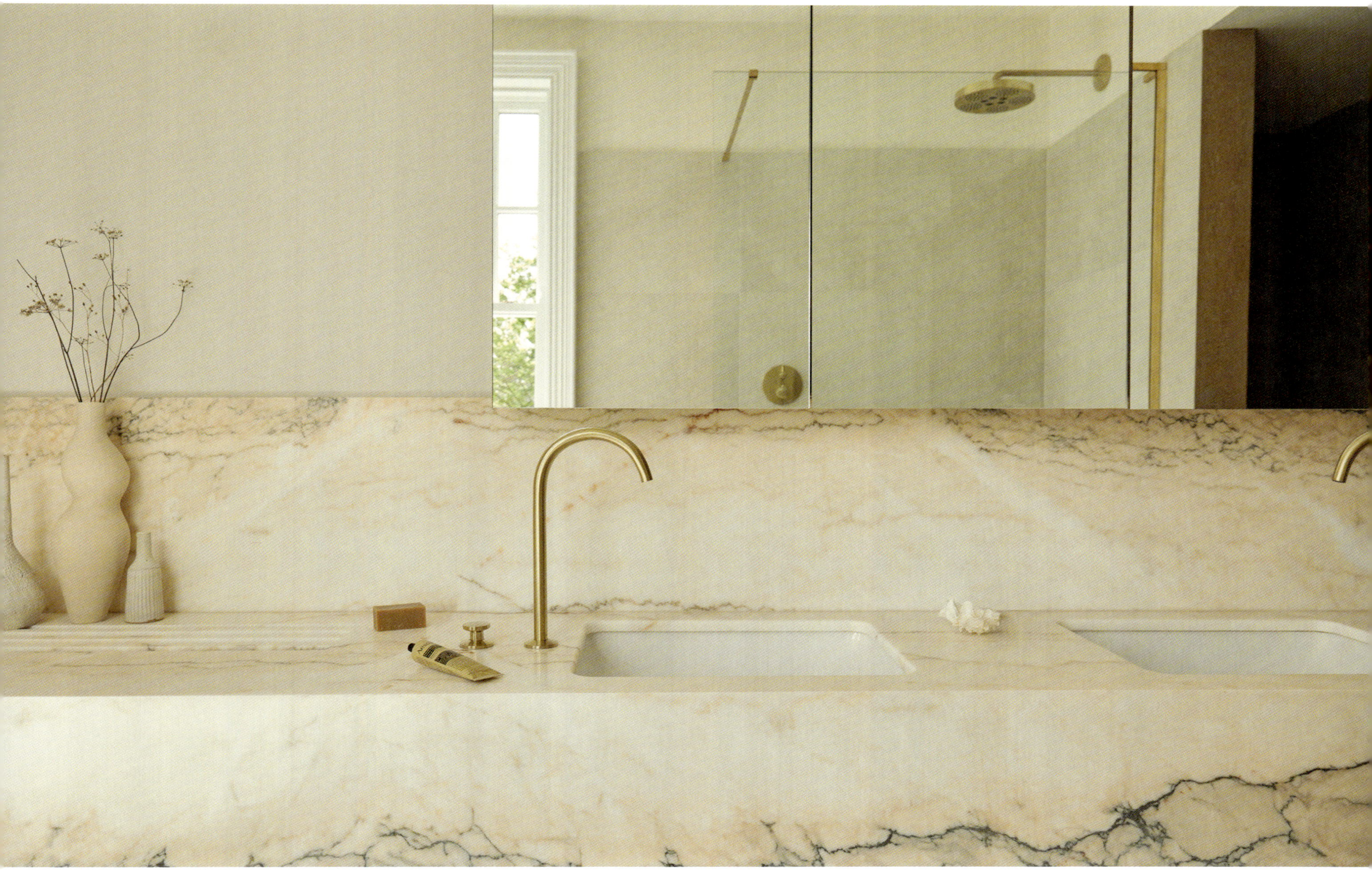

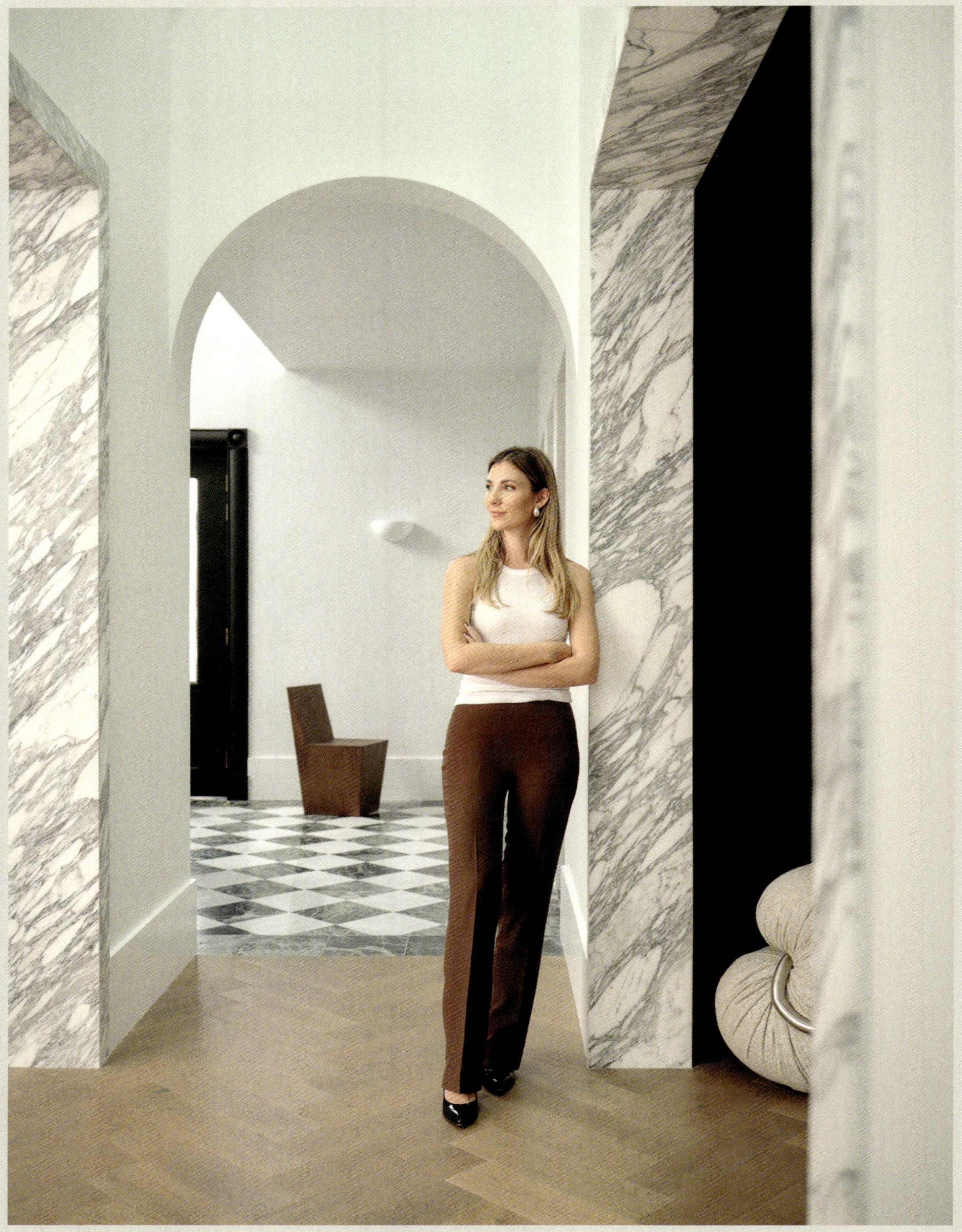

Smac Studio

Smac Studio is an award-winning firm that has been featured in local and international publications, including Vogue Living, Belle, Domino, Dwell, The Local Project and Est Living. The studio is based in Paddington, NSW, Australia.

With degrees in Architecture and Interior Architecture, the Smac Studio team has a knack for clever spatial planning. This is an interior design firm that does much more than choose furniture — registered as Class One and Class Two building practitioners, they move walls and reconfigure floor plans to create beautiful flow and function in your home.

With a Bachelor of Architecture from the University of Sydney, Principal Shona McElroy's creativity and unexpected design details have seen her nominated for an Australian Interior Design Award, a Dezeen House Interior Award and IDEA Emerging Designer of the Year.

Smac Studio's ideal way to work is from concept to completion. Shona and Ally like to come on board early (often before the Development Application) and work collaboratively with the clients. However, they can get in touch at any stage of your project. This is a fresh, approachable team who are easy to work with, have their clients at their core and never build the same thing twice.

www.smacstudio.com.au

Photography: Dave Wheeler - Styling: Claire Delmar

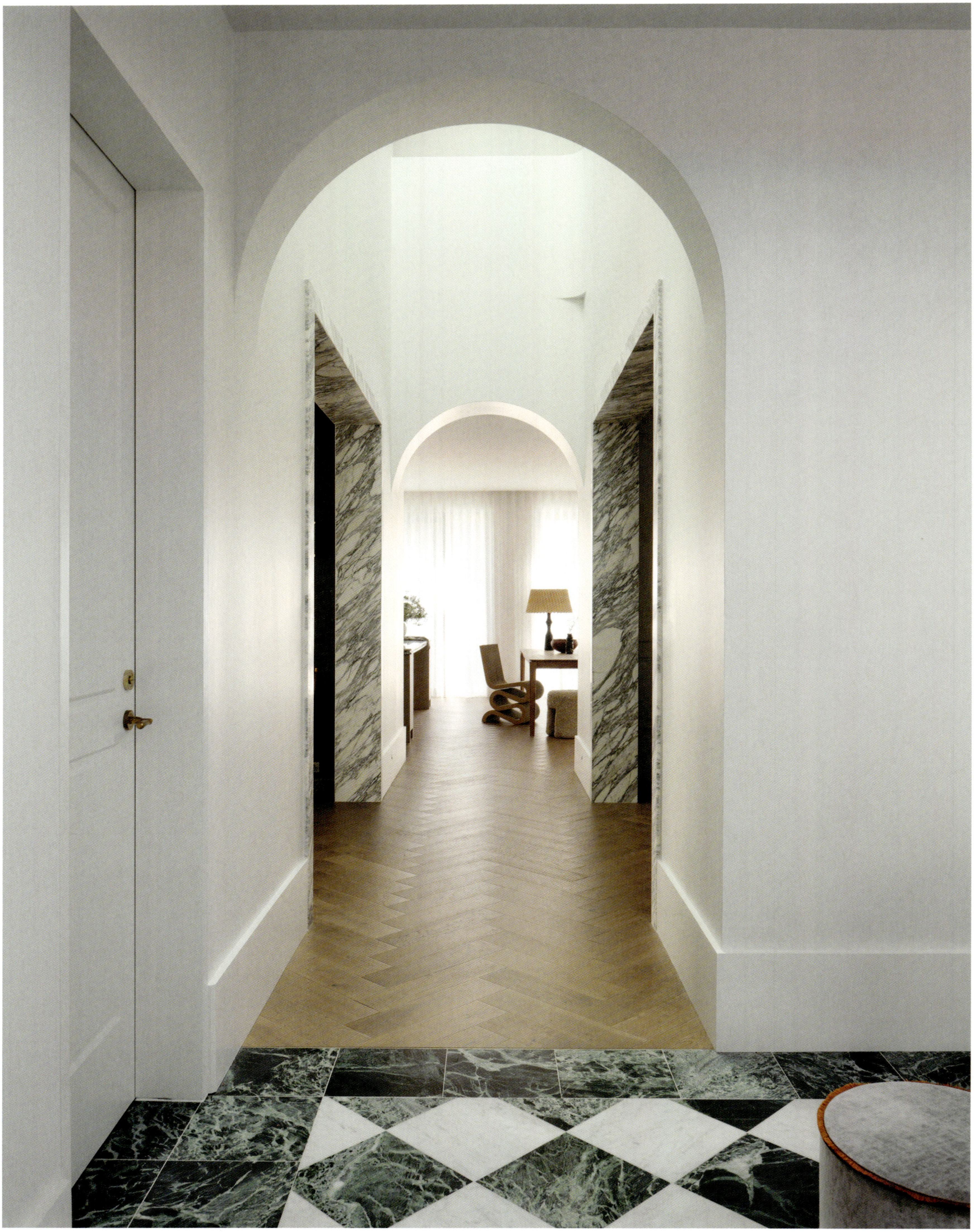

Smac Studio Interior Design has transformed a fragmented, terracotta-toned 1980s property into an elegant open plan home. Located in Vaucluse, Sydney, original arched windows look onto Australia's oldest lighthouse.

The new owners wanted large, melded spaces for entertaining and more natural light. The original architect took a trip to Tuscany in the 1980s — he returned full of inspiration and built this home for his family. It was very important for Shona McElroy, Principal of Smac Studio, to honor his vision, to preserve the Italian spirit of the house.

The extensive renovation saw three small rooms reconfigured into one expansive kitchen, living and dining area. The rear wall was moved out to create more internal space and lavish slabs of Arrabescato marble now grace the kitchen island, splashback and fireplace.

The entrance foyer also received a notable update. Previously the floor was dark green stone and walls were limewash orange. Black steel balustrades carved the staircase at sharp angles. Smac Studio smoothed the hard edges into inviting Venetian plaster curves and created a checkerboard floor from Carrara and Verdi Alpi marble. Verdi Alpi was the original stone slab on the floor, so this design decision is a tribute to that.

The biggest challenge with the renovation was time. Smac Studio only had three months to design and nine months to build. There were problems with lead times for certain items, so things were changing on the fly, but Shona still got all the elements she wanted in the beginning. Those elements were curvature, a journey from formal entrance to informal open plan living, a marble checkerboard floor and artful lighting. Even though the build time was short they didn't skimp on character. Shona loves all the different layers, materials and shifts of light as you move through this home.

She likes to think this house is like a little black dress with a pearl necklace — a timeless aesthetic.

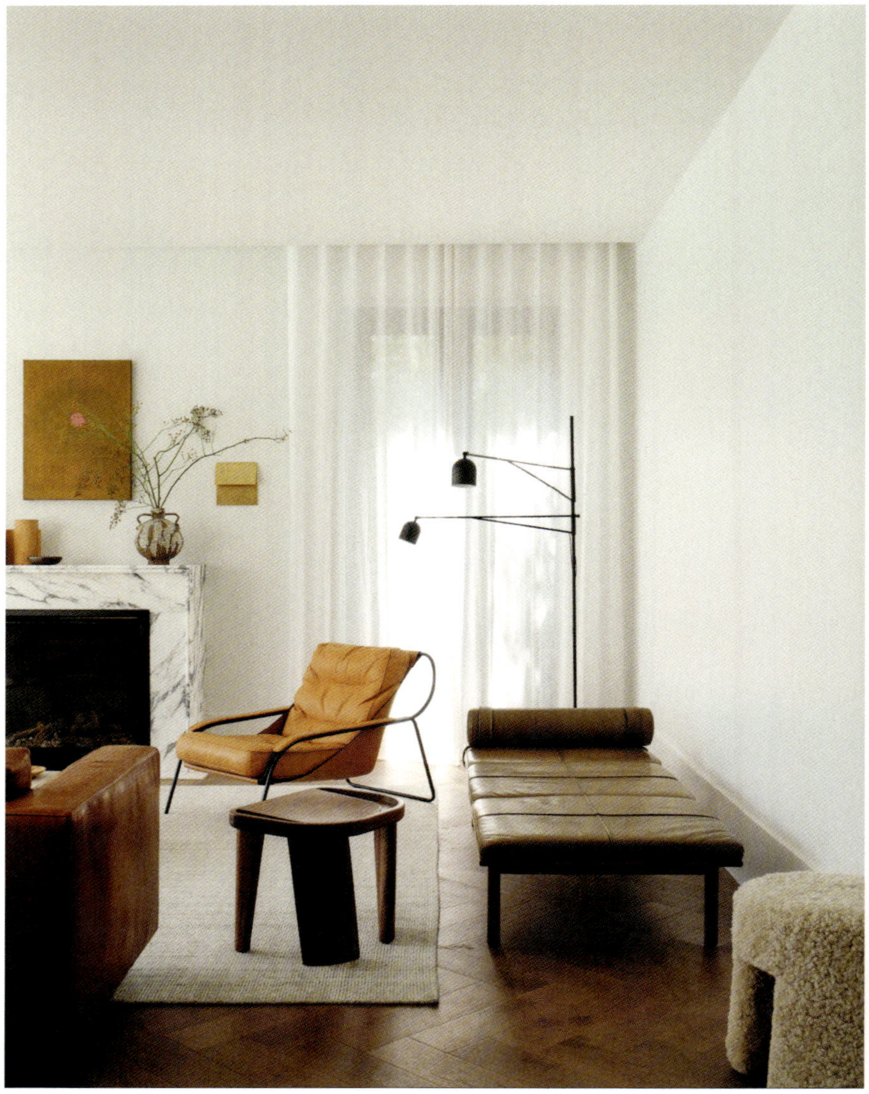

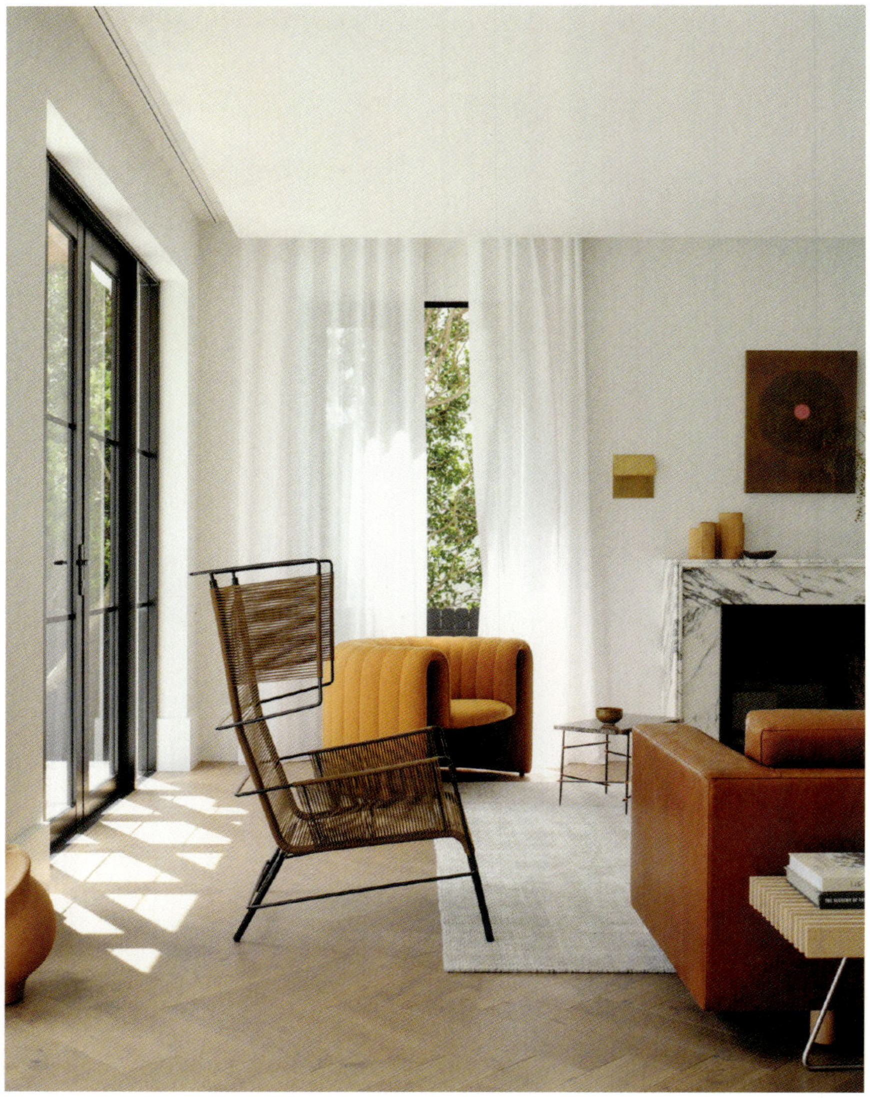

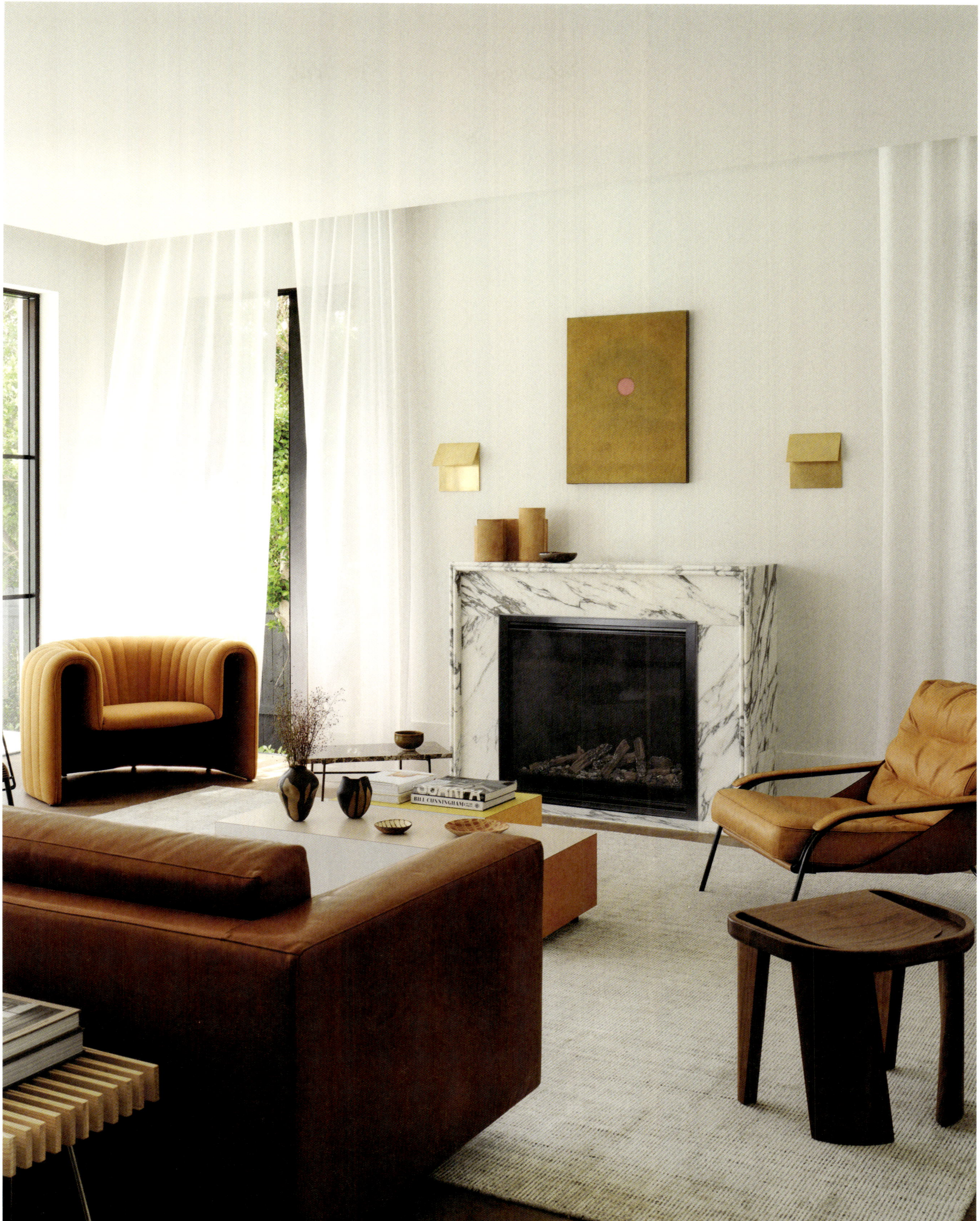
BILL CUNNINGHAM

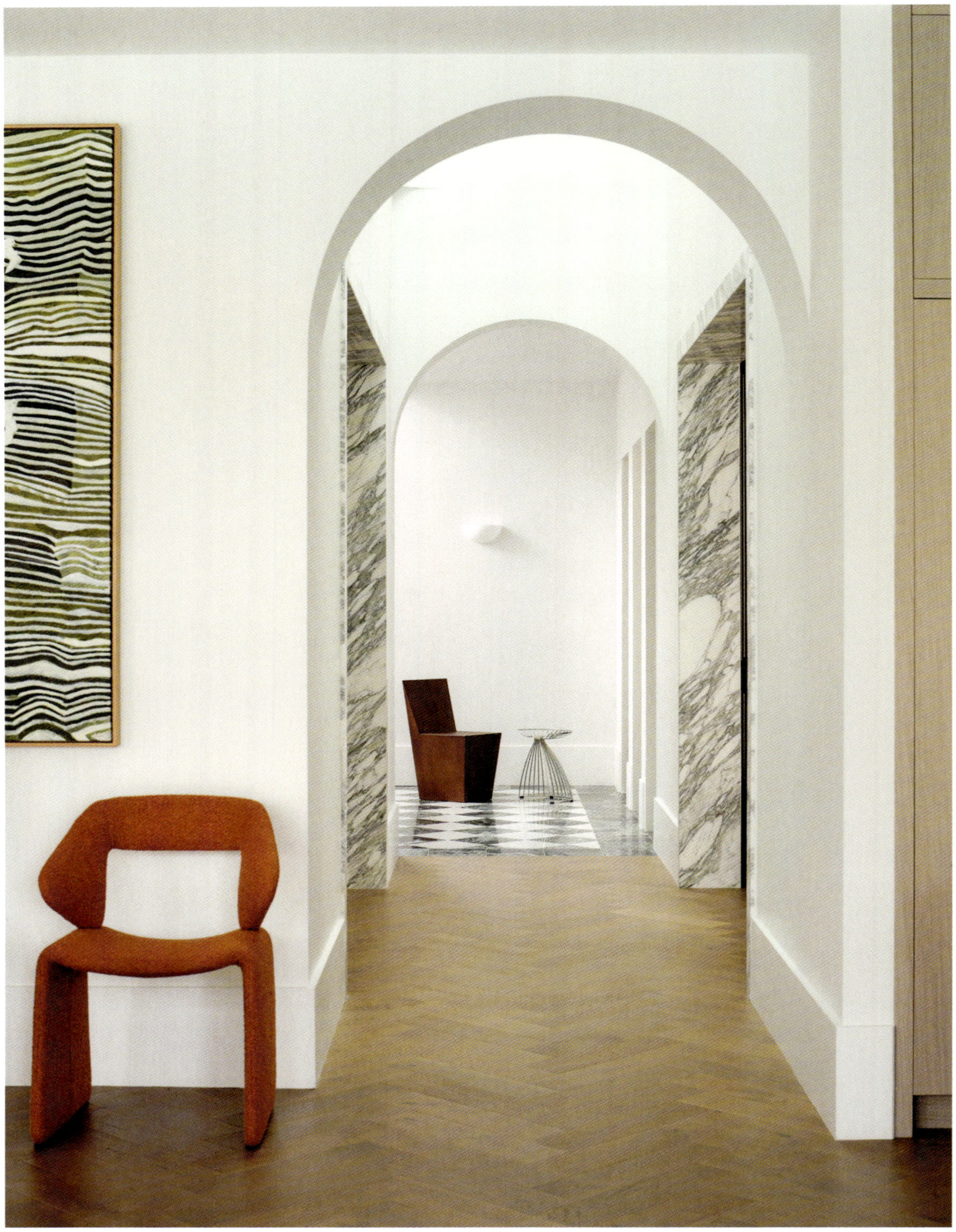

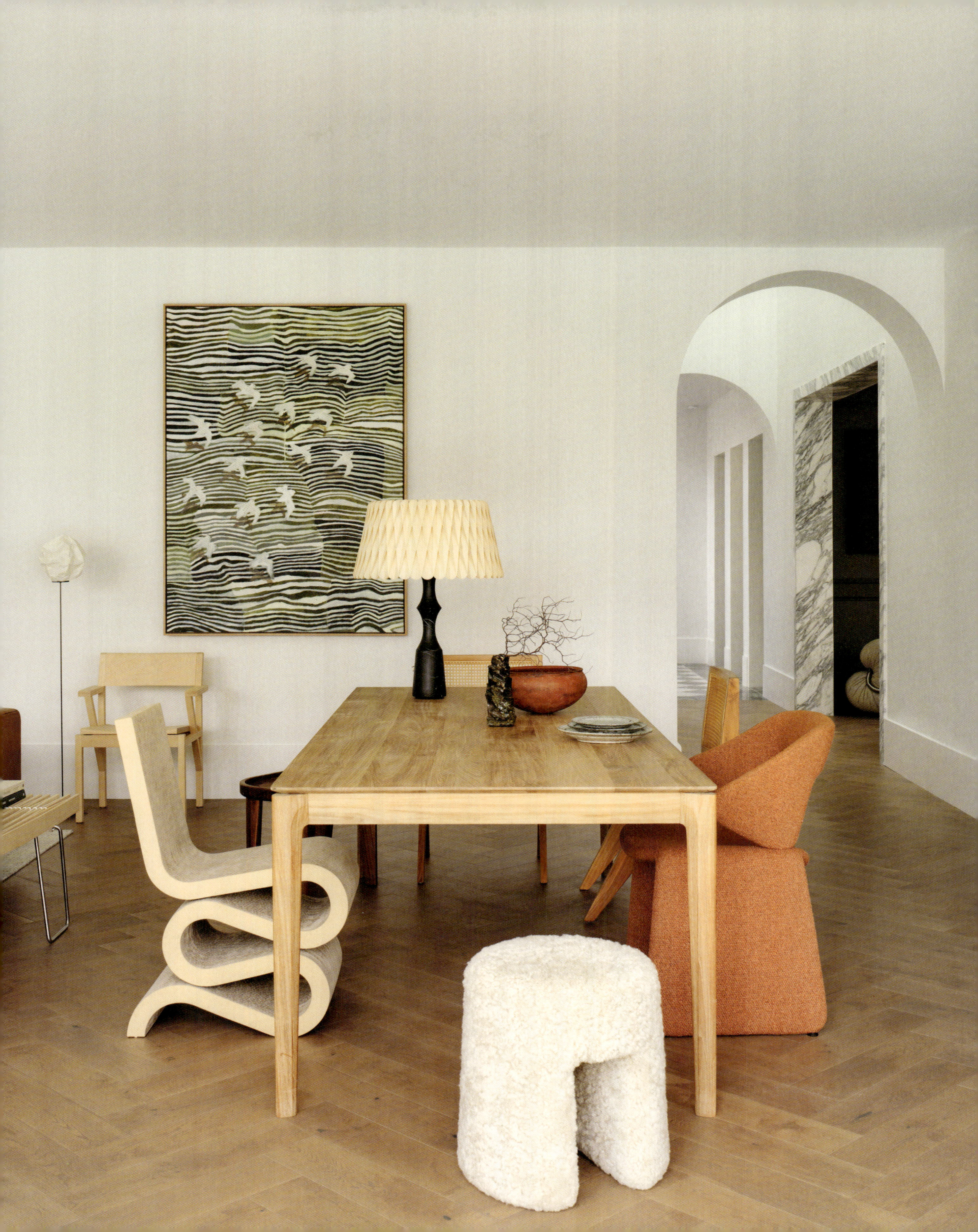

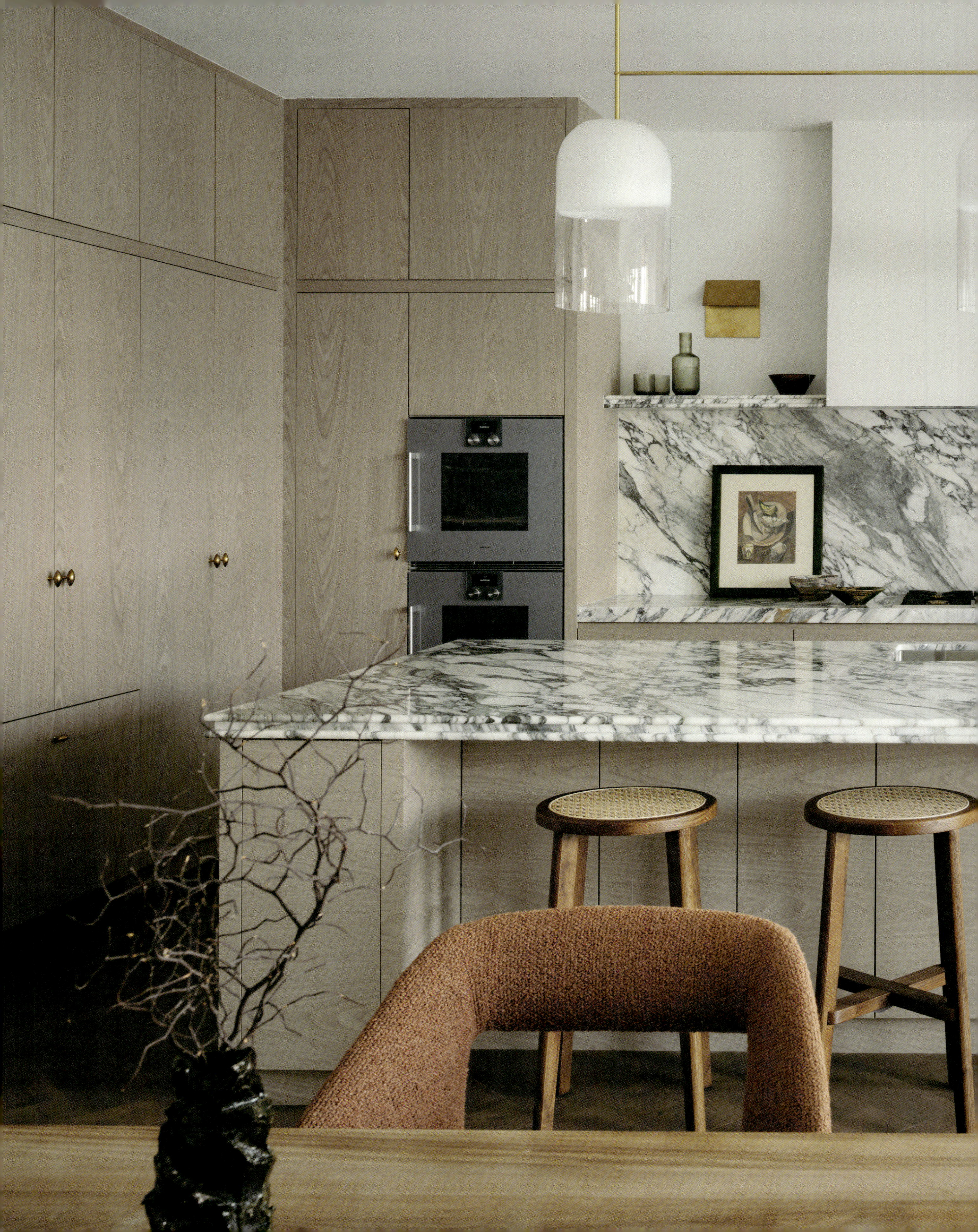

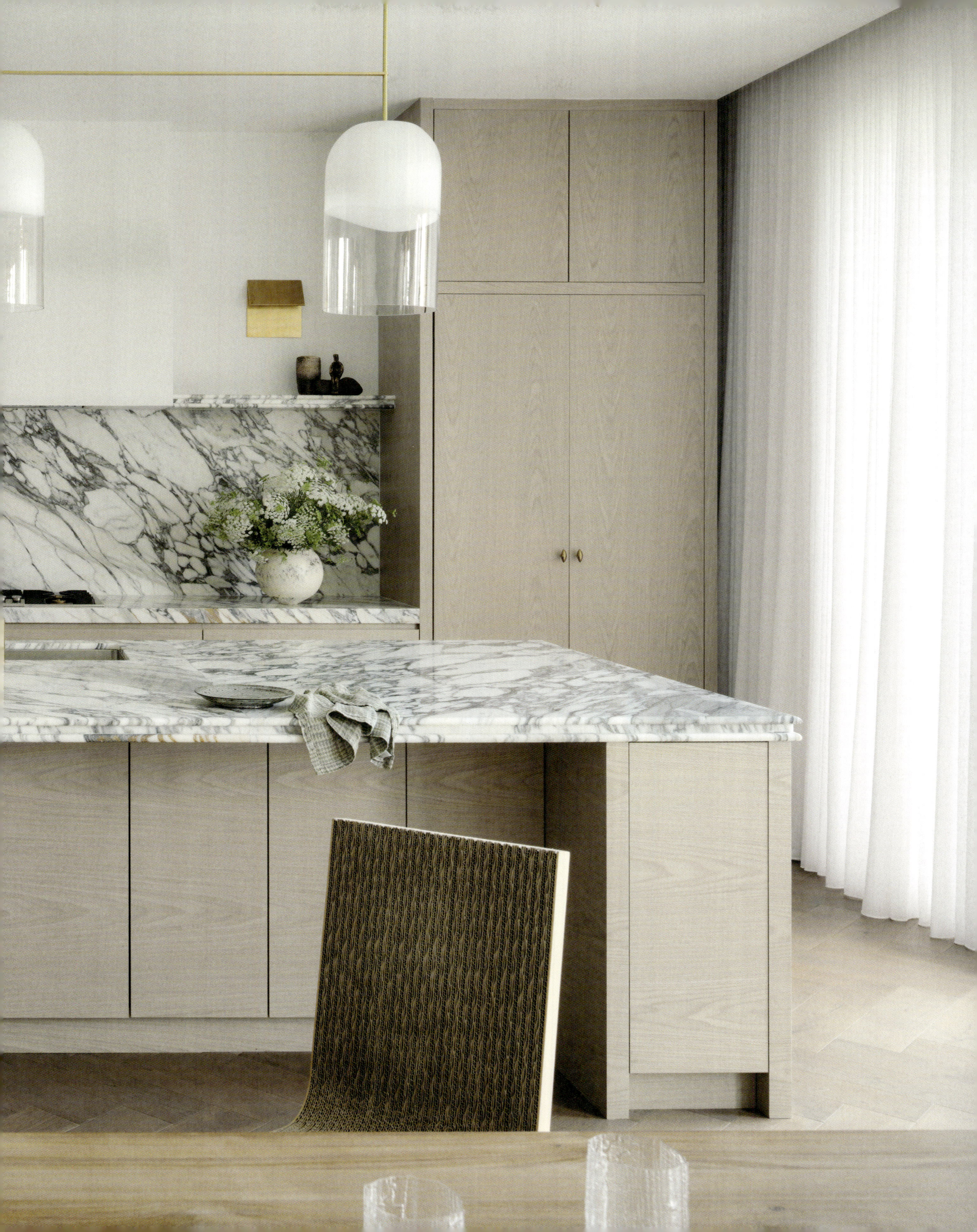

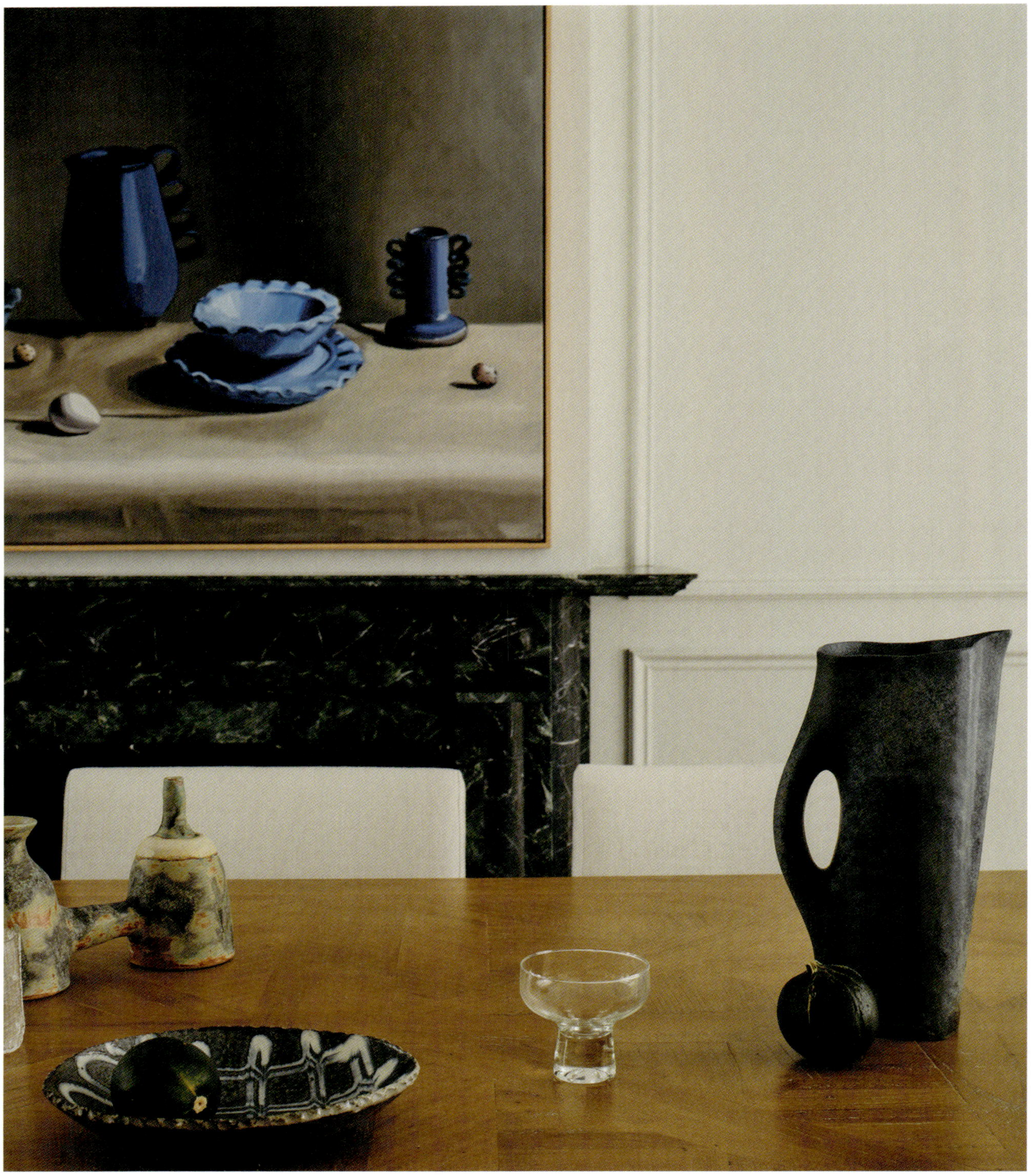

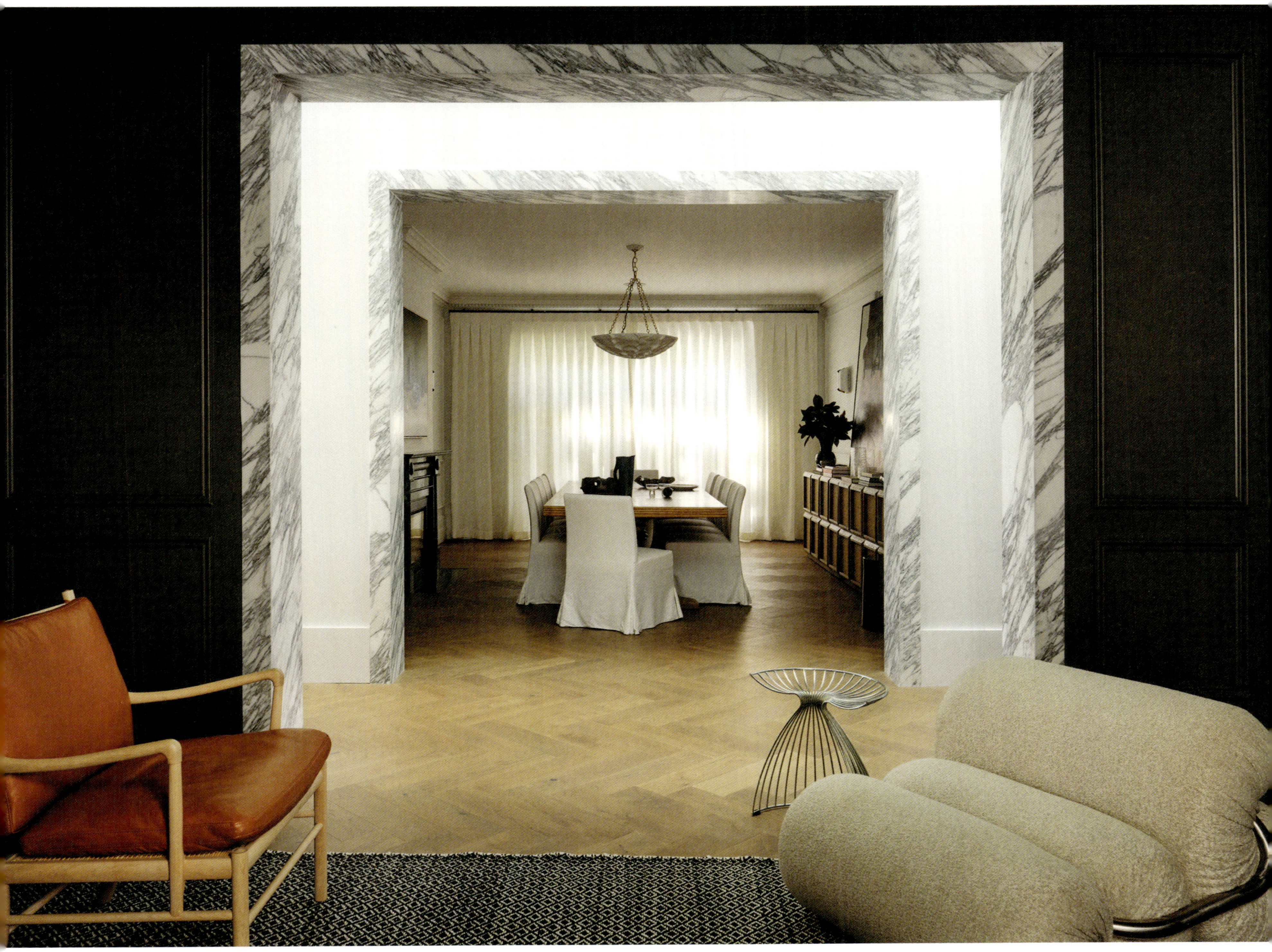

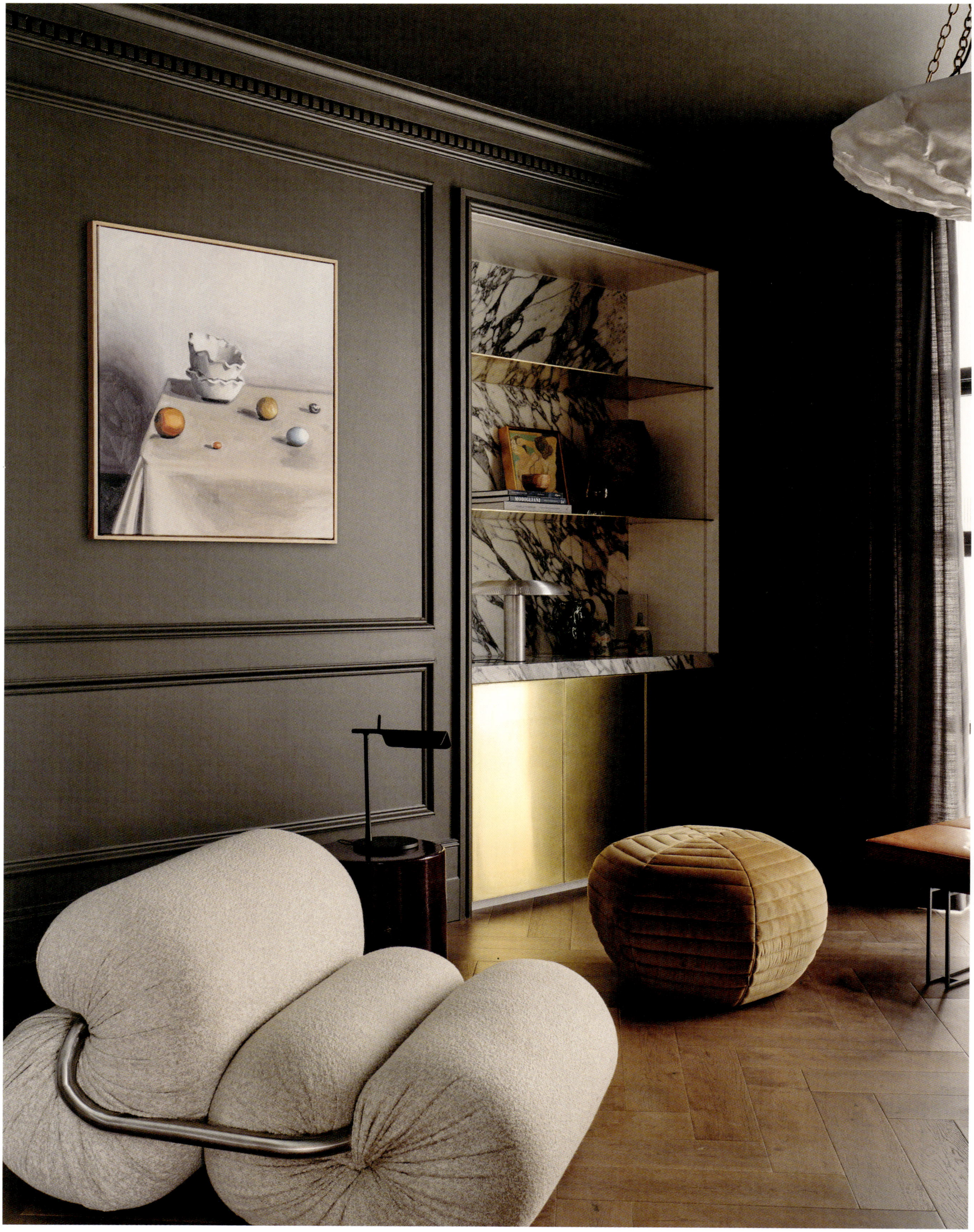
MODIGLIANI

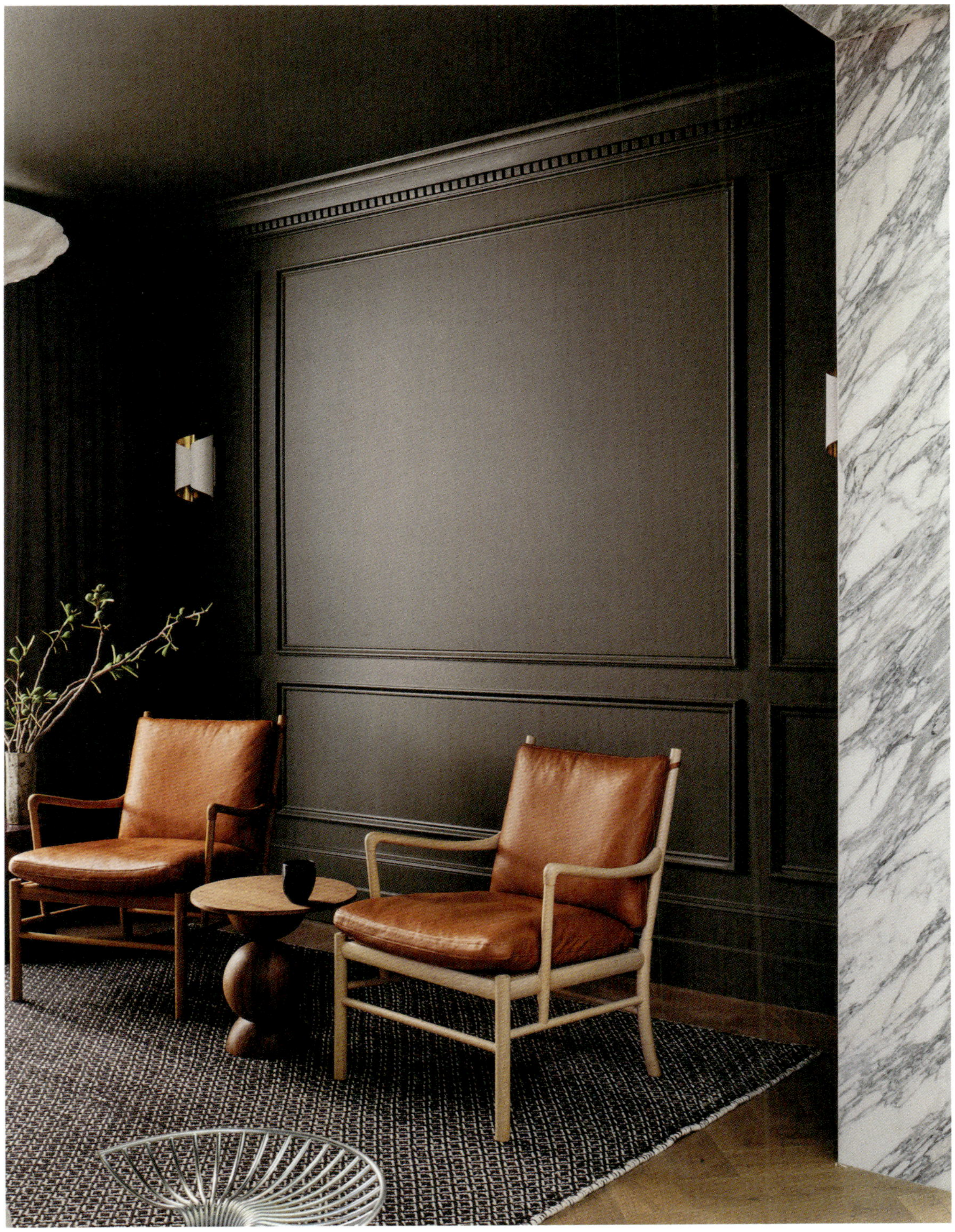

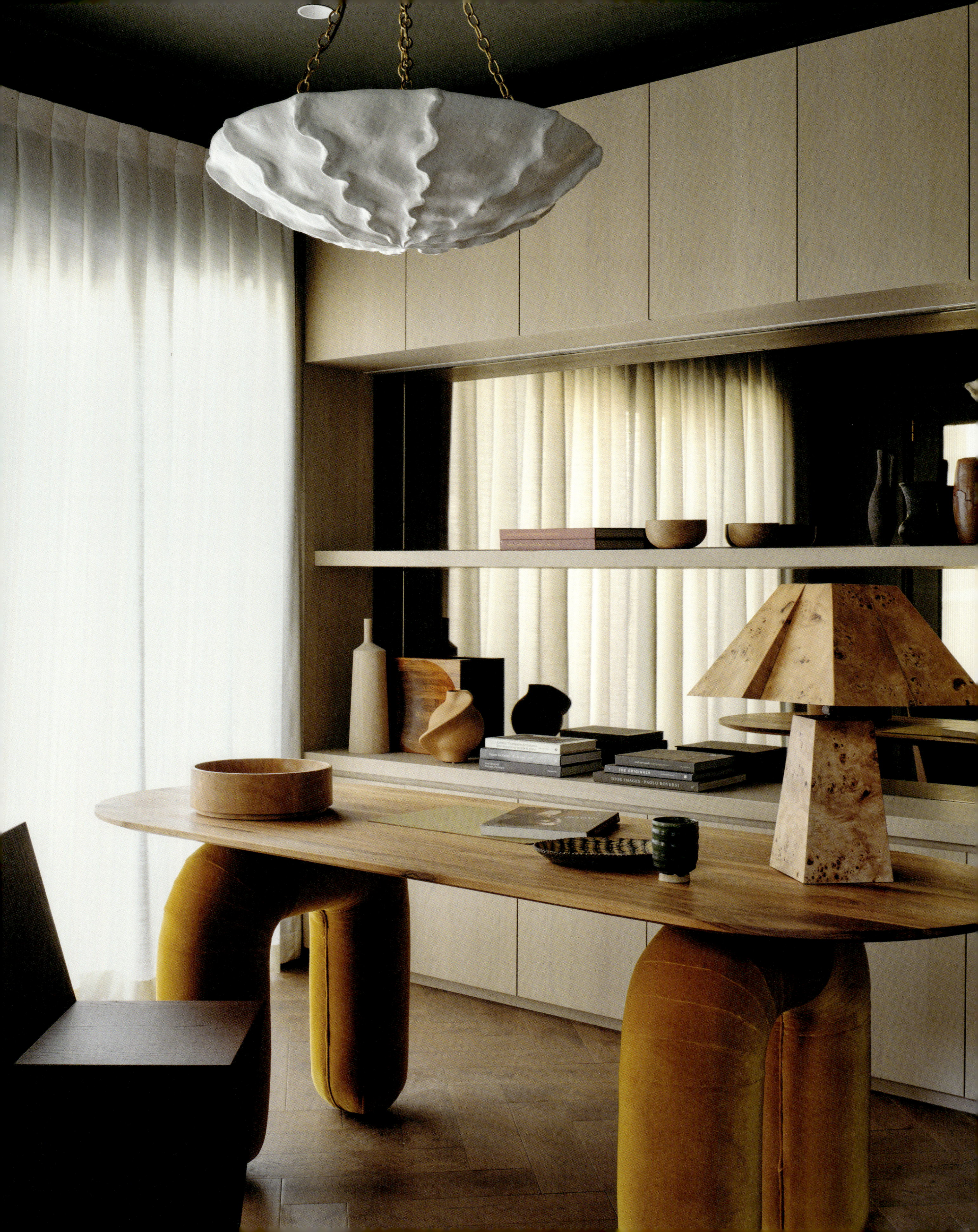
THE ORIGINALS
DIOR IMAGES · PAOLO ROVERSI

95

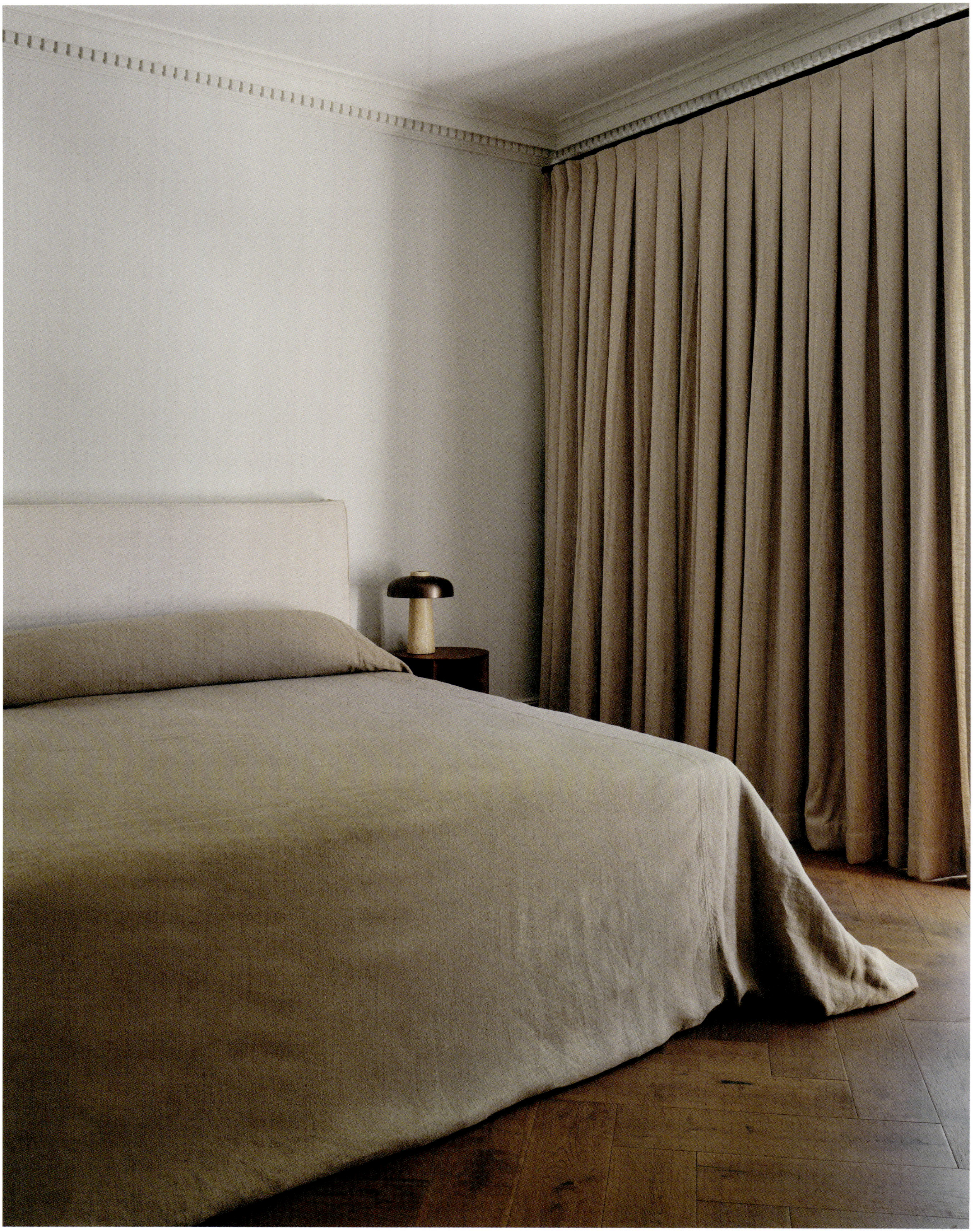

97

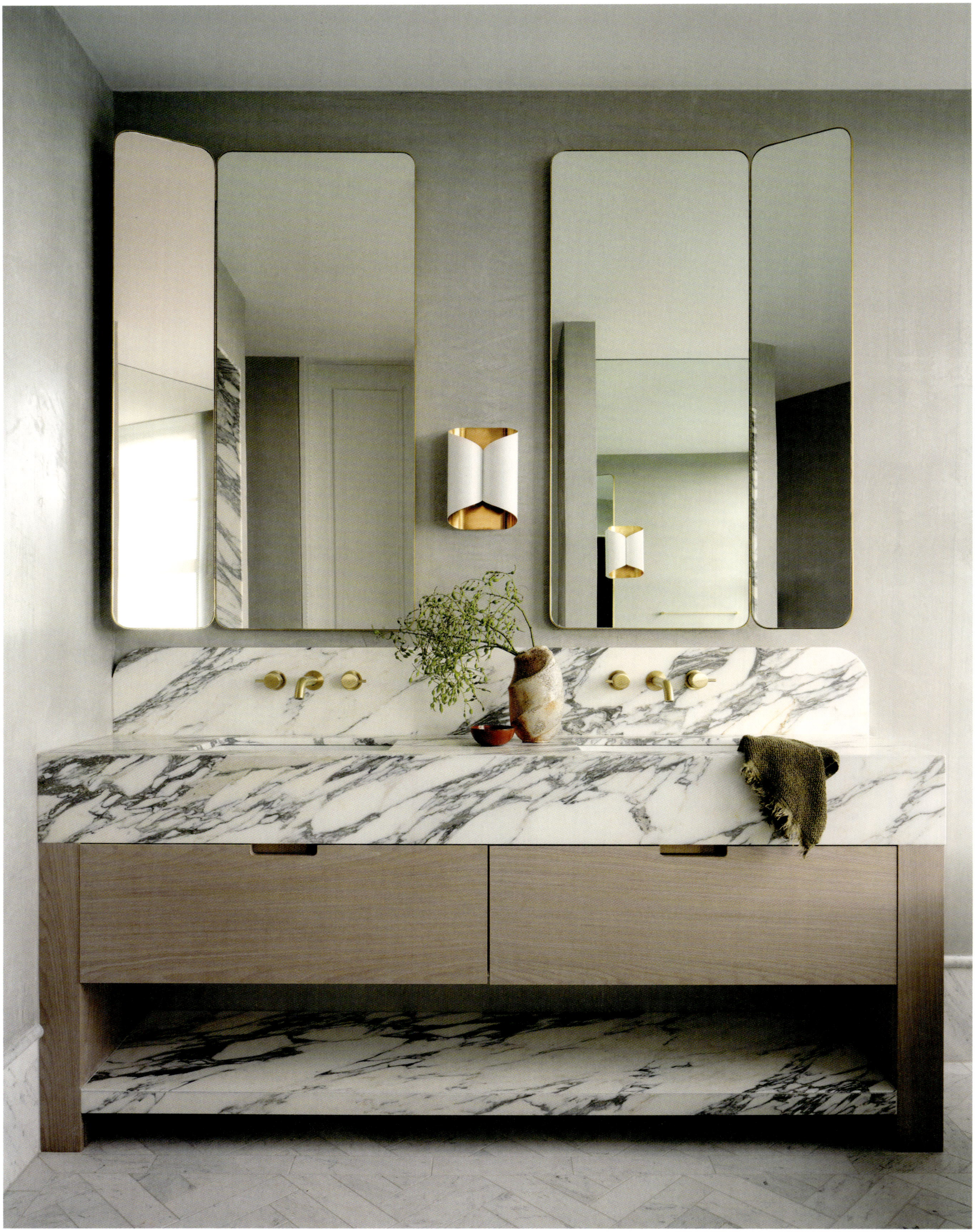

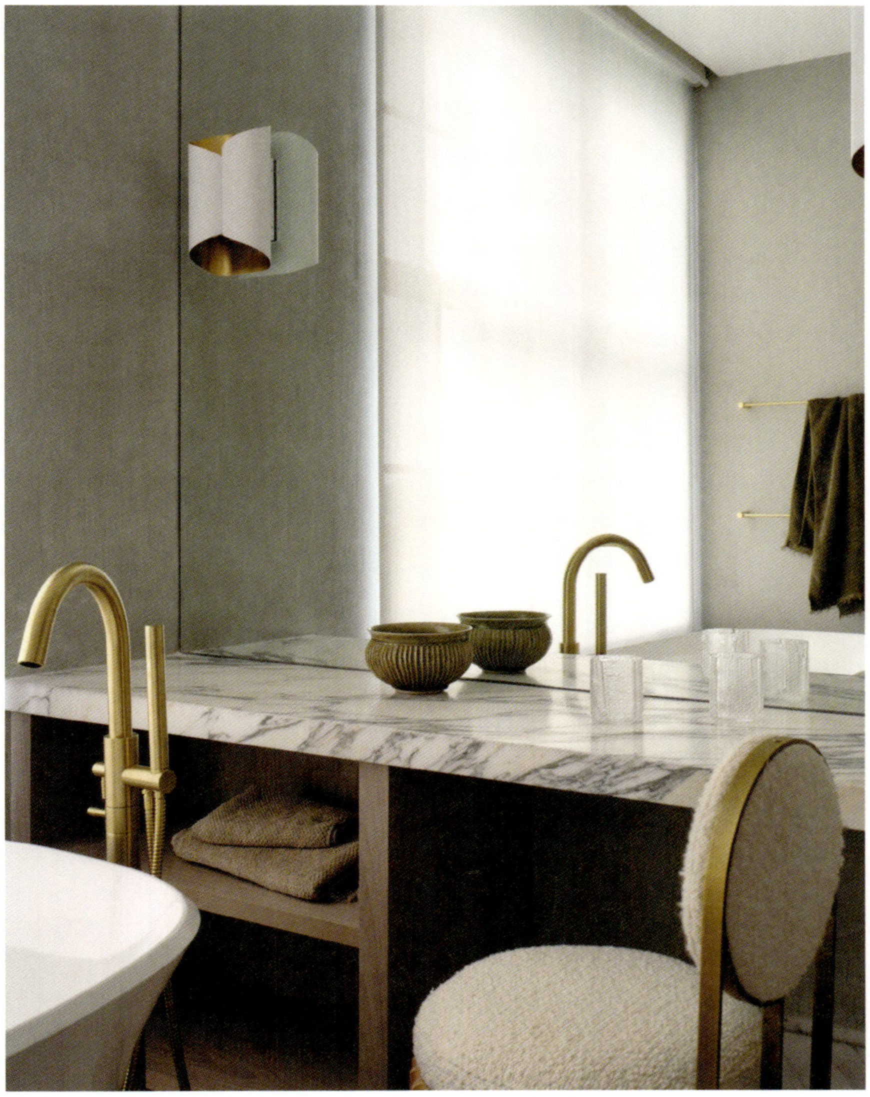
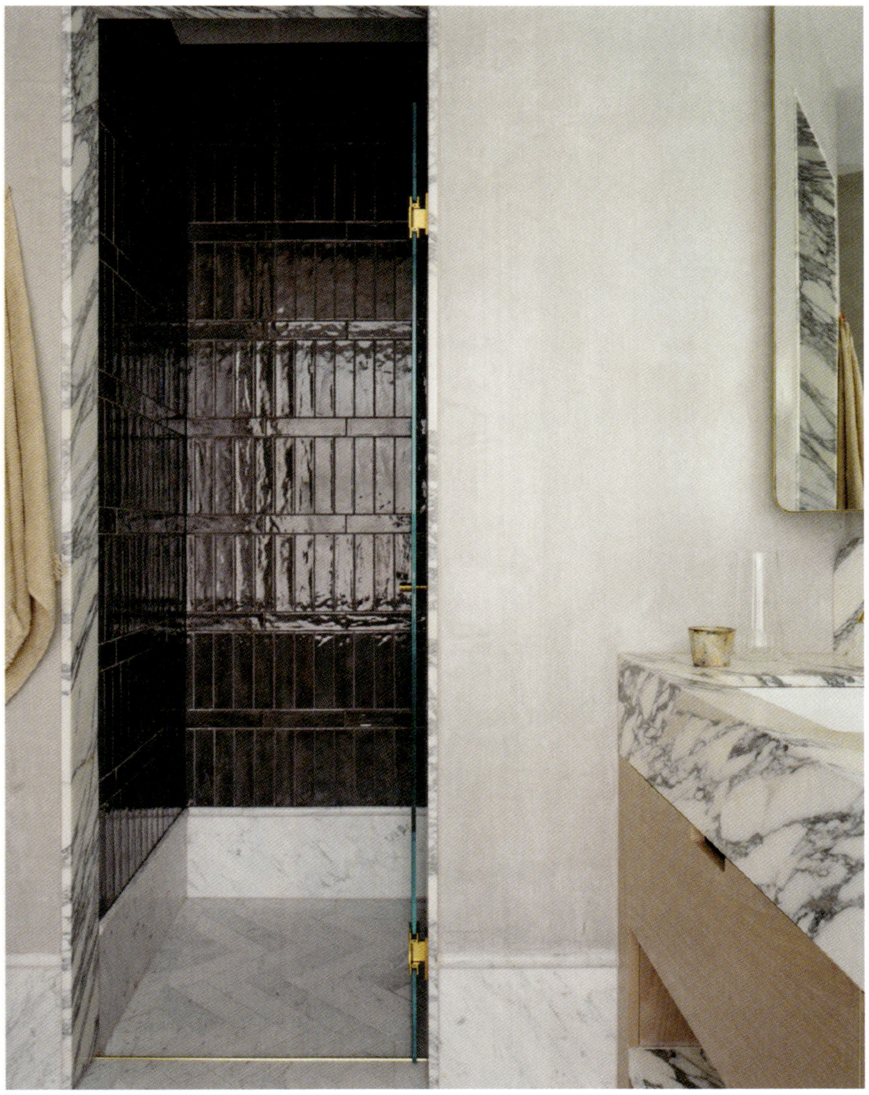

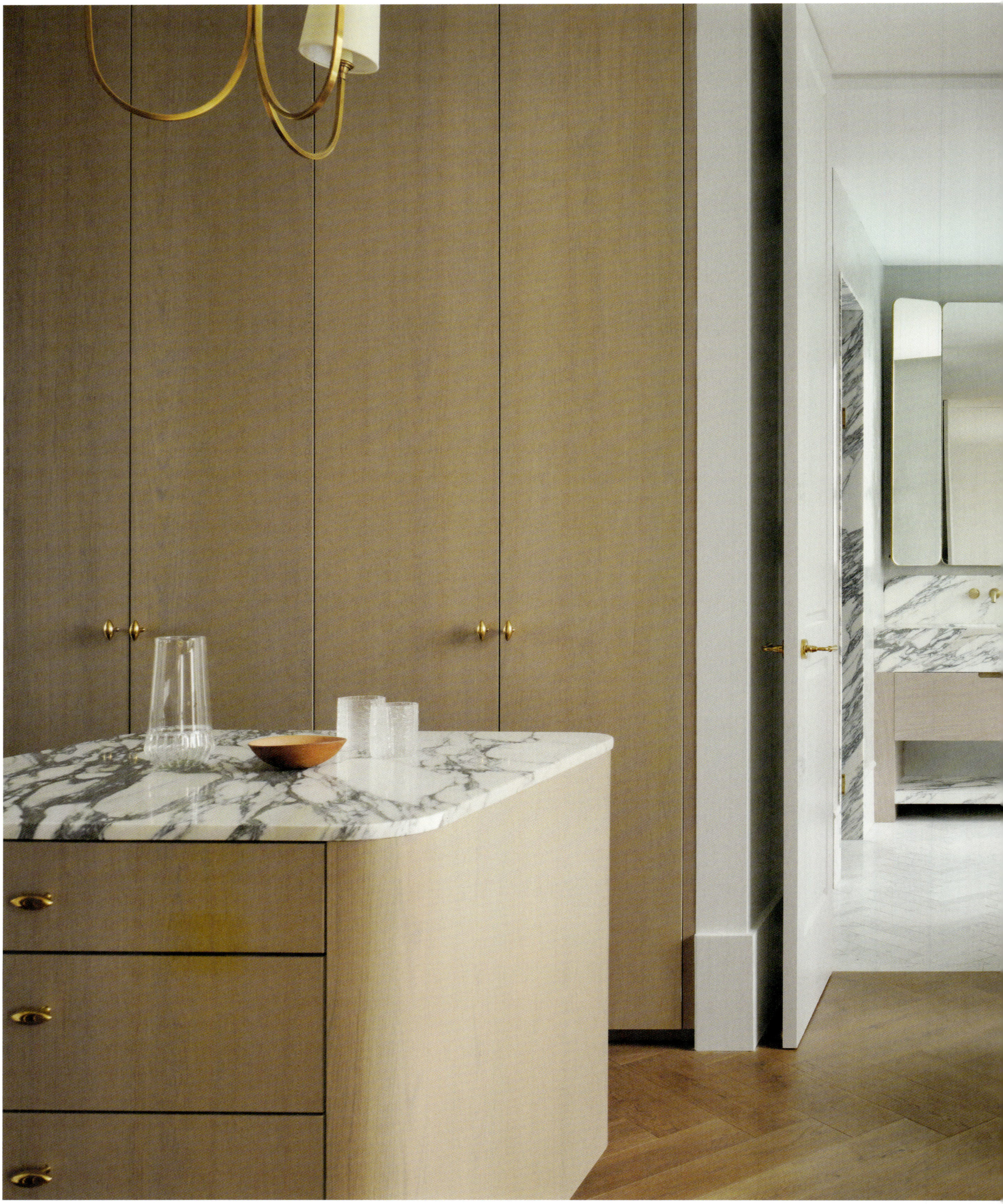

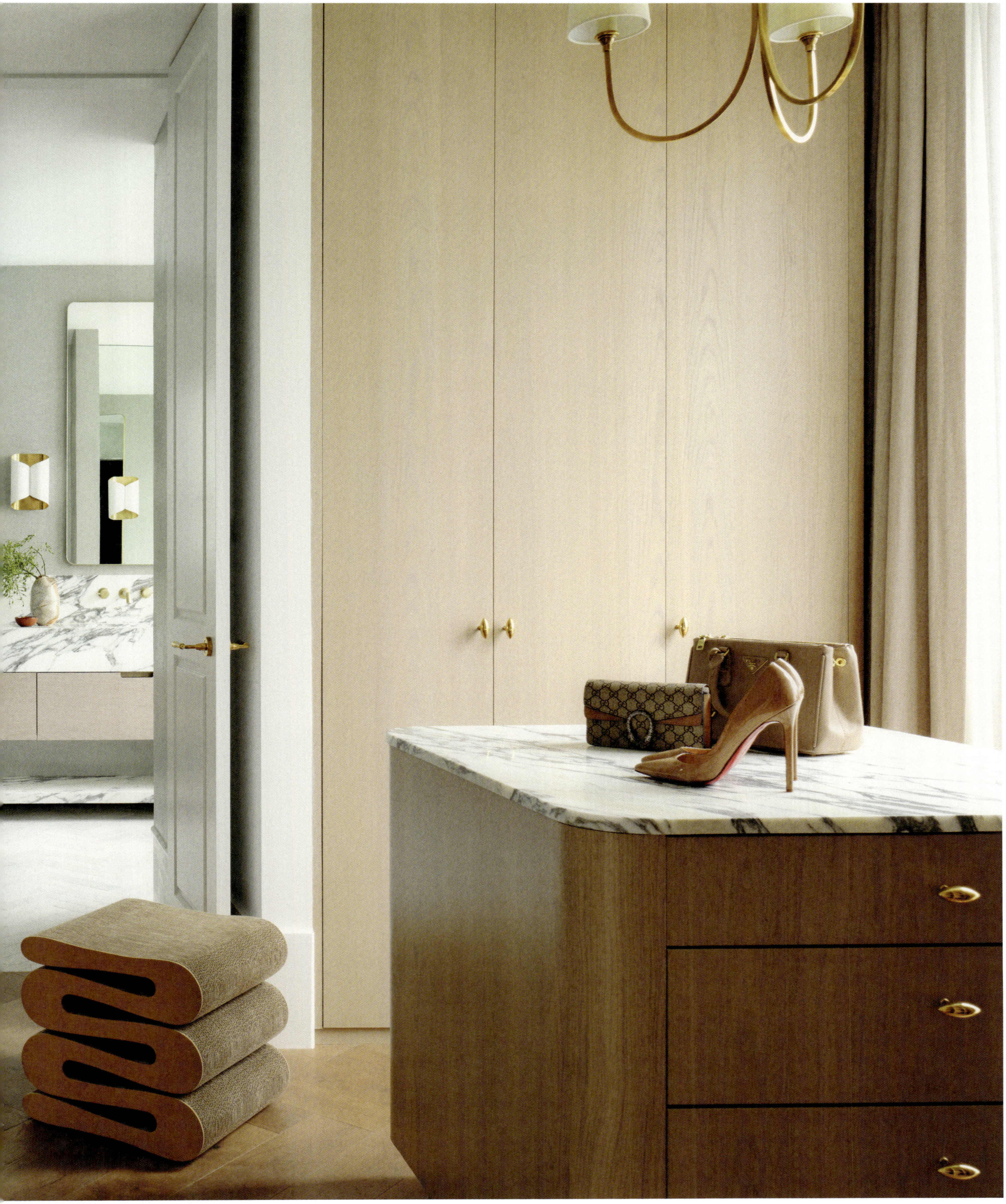

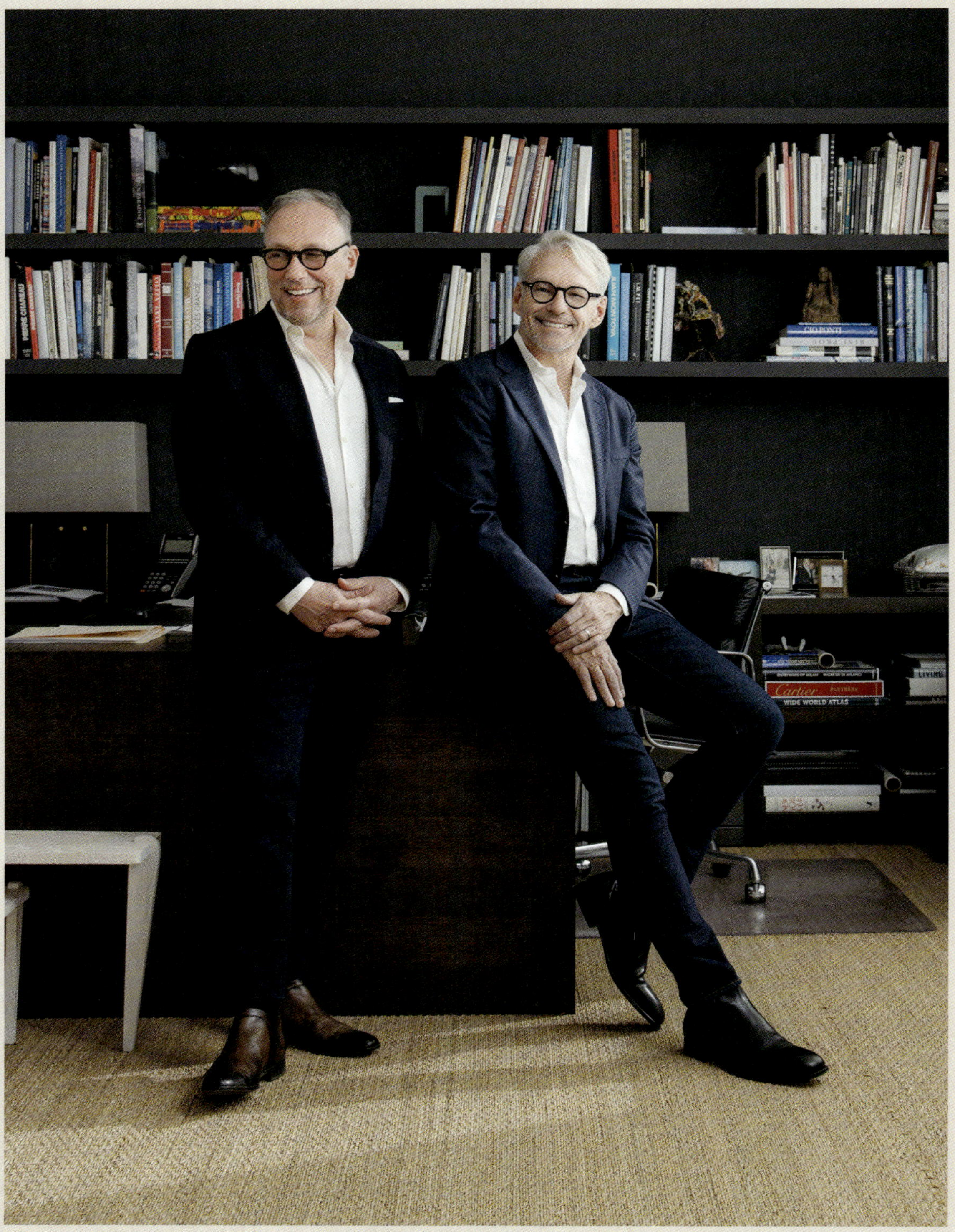

William McIntosh Design

William McIntosh Design, is a New York City based interior design and decoration firm led by award-winning designers William McIntosh and Martin Raffone. The partners create sophisticated interiors that are individually conceived, refined meticulously crafted. Luxury is the hallmark of the New York City based firm, whose work forges a perfect balance of traditional and modern sensibilities. The resulting environments are inviting, stylish, and above all, resolutely livable. The firm's work is at once familiar but also reveals surprises and new interpretations, embracing both the period and the modern.

McIntosh and Raffone have completed elegant, polished interiors in many of Manhattan's "it" buildings—including 432 Park Avenue, the Plaza, the Puck Building, and Herzog & de Meuron's 160 Leroy Street—as well as projects in Miami, Palm Beach, San Francisco, London, and lush retreats from St Barths to Morocco.

Individually and as a team, McIntosh and Raffone have been featured in many world-renowned publications including Architectural Digest, Departures Magazine, Elle Décor, Palm Beach Cottages and Gardens, and Traditional Home.

Principal William McIntosh studied Interior Design at Pratt Institute in New York. After his graduation he worked for the noted Interior Design firms of Timothy MacDonald Incorporated and Bray-Schaible Design. He established his namesake firm in 1990. With a team of dedicated professionals including Architects, Designers, Artists, and Craftsmen, McIntosh continues to produce the thoughtful, intelligent, and personal interiors that have established him among a loyal international clientele.

Partner and Creative Director Martin Raffone is a master in creating and curating distinct interior environments via the integrative use of architecture, furniture, lighting, and accessories. A graduate of Parsons School of Design and possessing more than twenty-five years' experience in the conception and decoration of private residences world-wide, he brings his sharp personal style and discerning eye to every project. Working in collaborative environments with both design clients, as well as vendors, fabricators, and contractors, is integral to his process and ultimately the successful outcome of the work.

www.williammcintoshdesign.com

Photography: Richard Powers - Styling: Anita Sarsidi

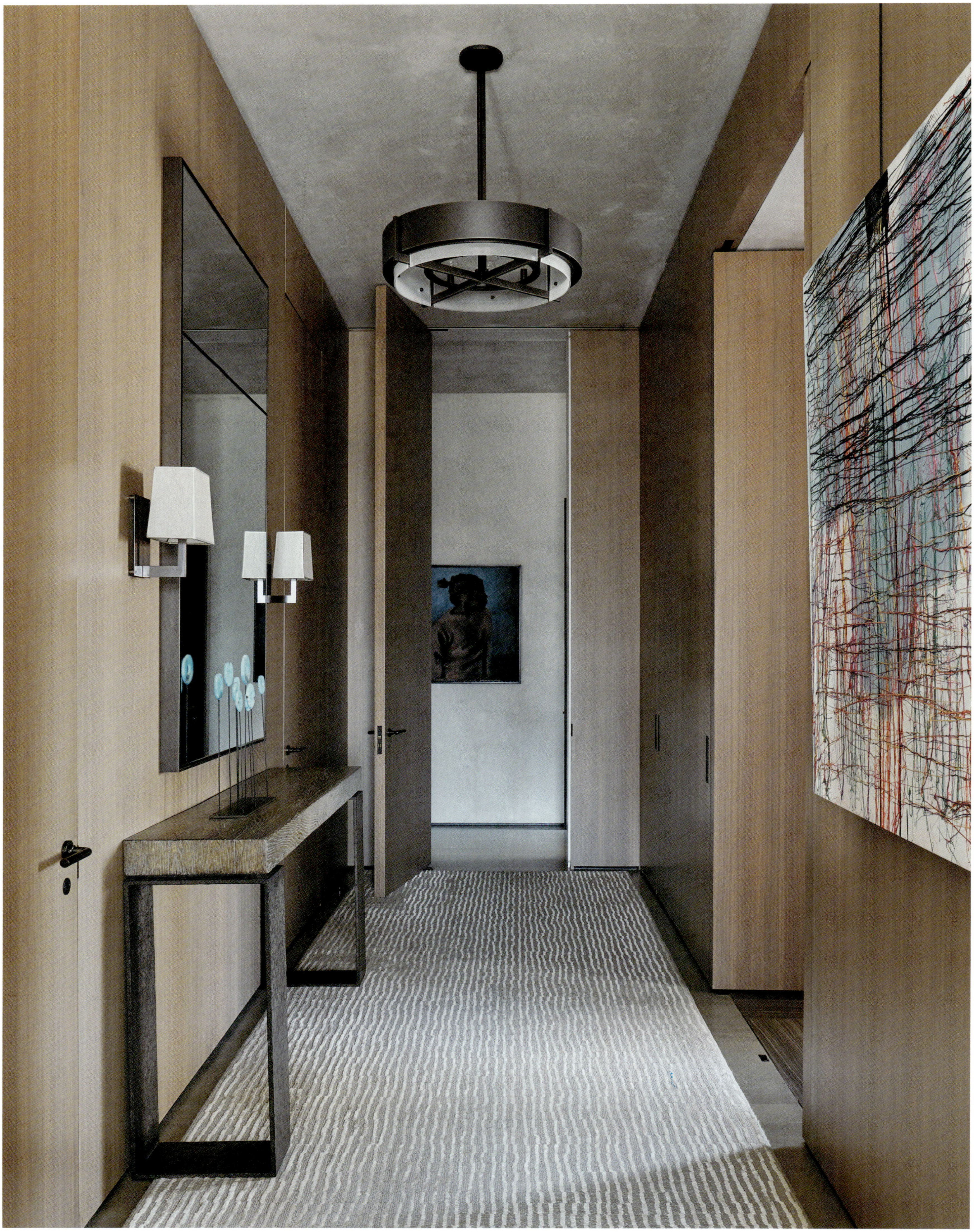

A powerful and daring combination of architecture and art come together in this 6,000 square foot family apartment overlooking Madison Square Park. A formal sequence of spaces provides a bracing background for a collection of museum quality art and furniture. Superbly curated by William McIntosh Design's Creative Director, Martin Raffone, the result is a home that is both exhilarating and comfortable .

No expense was spared in the conception and execution of the unique finish materials, custom components and furnishings. The result is powerfully impressive design that functions for both family, public and charitable events.

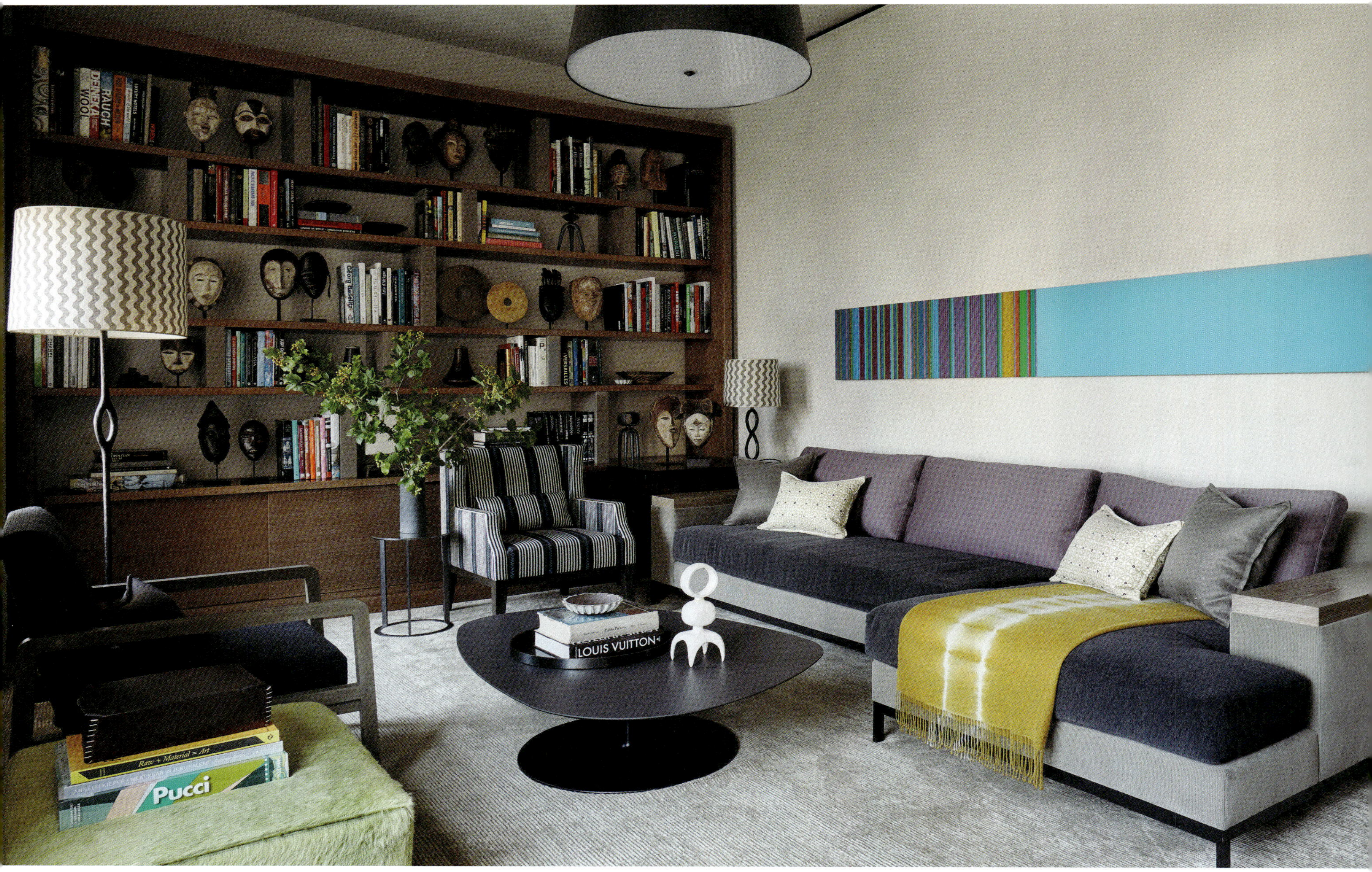
LOUIS VUITTON
Raw + Material = Art
Pucci

107

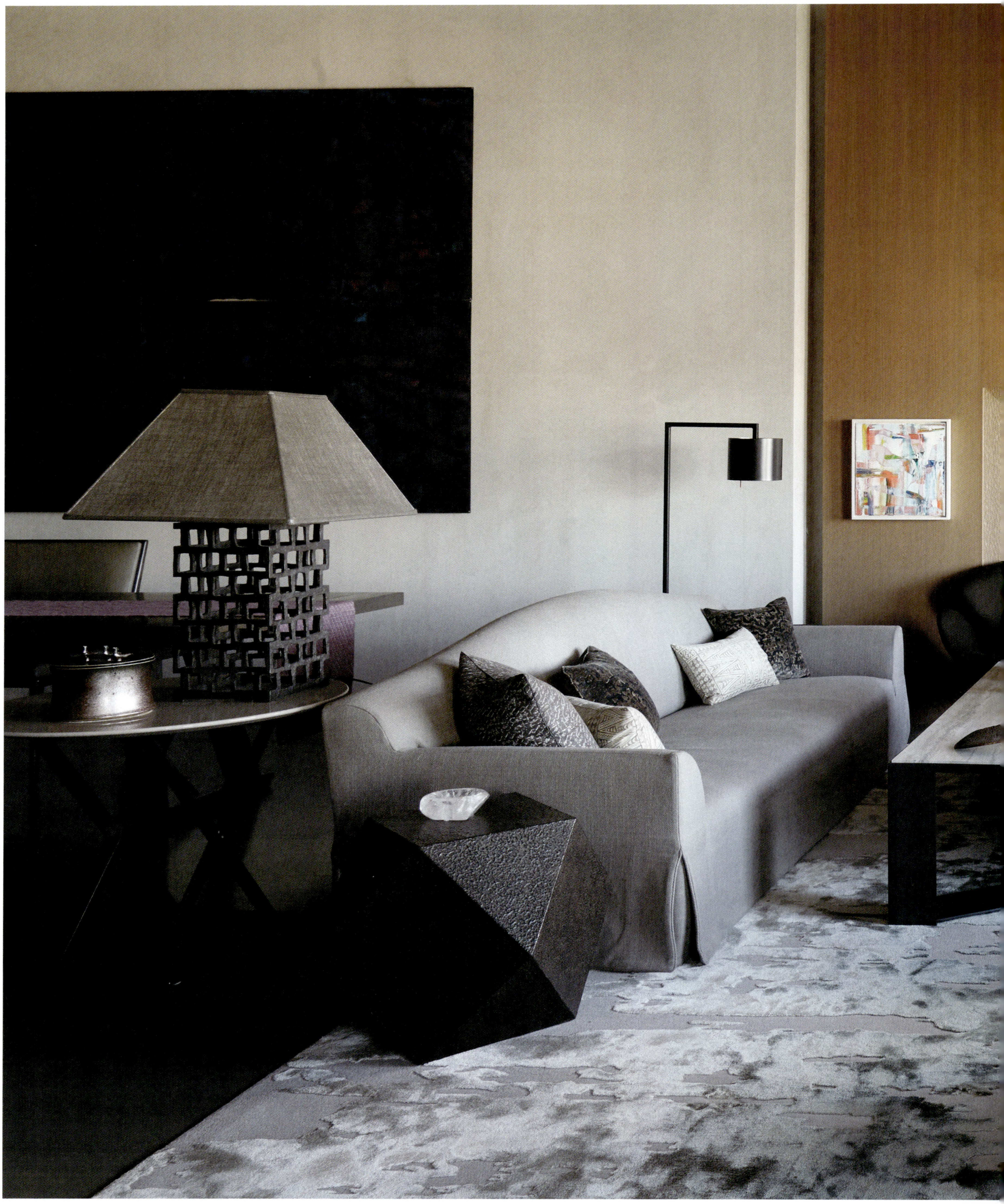

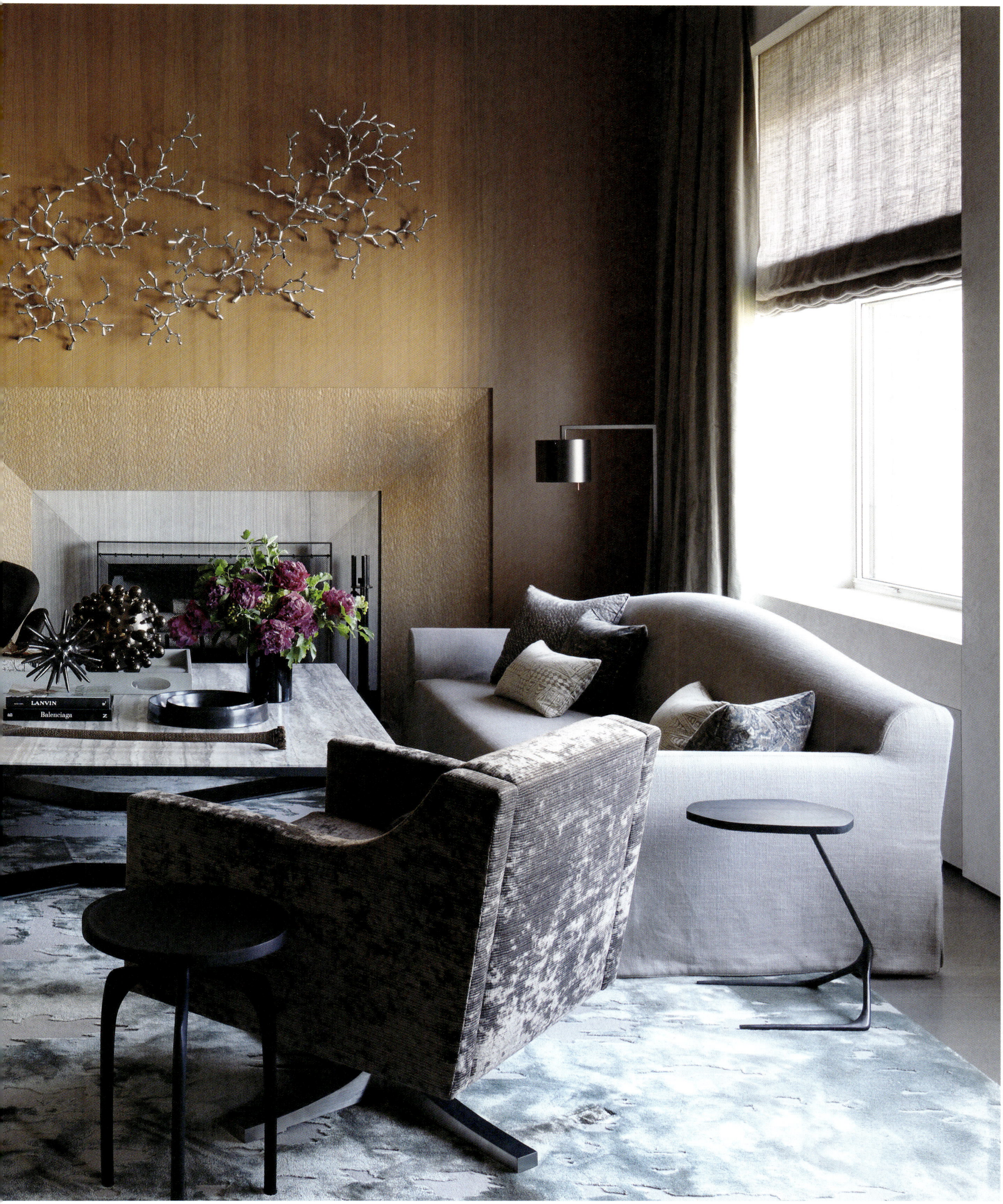
LANVIN
Balenciaga

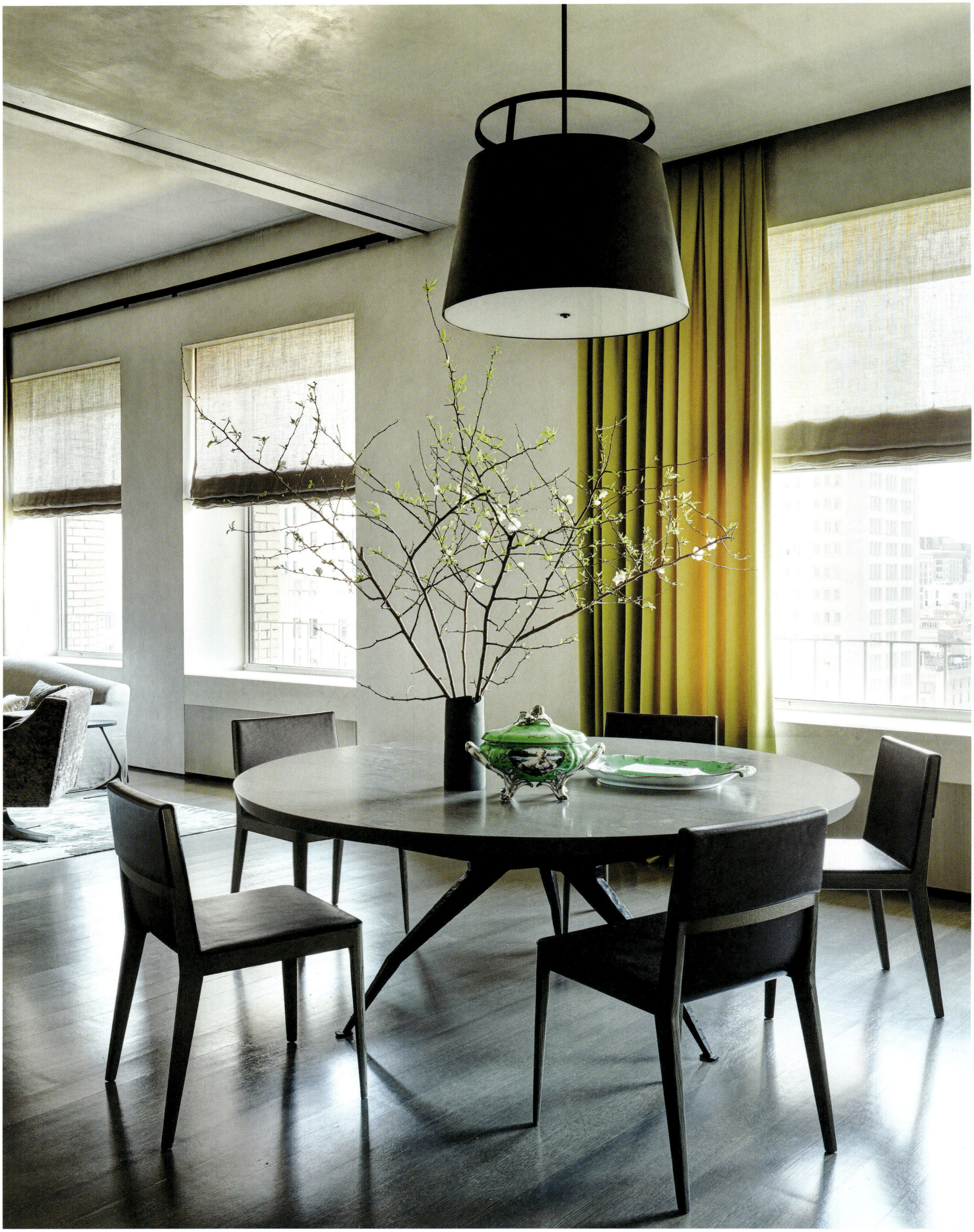

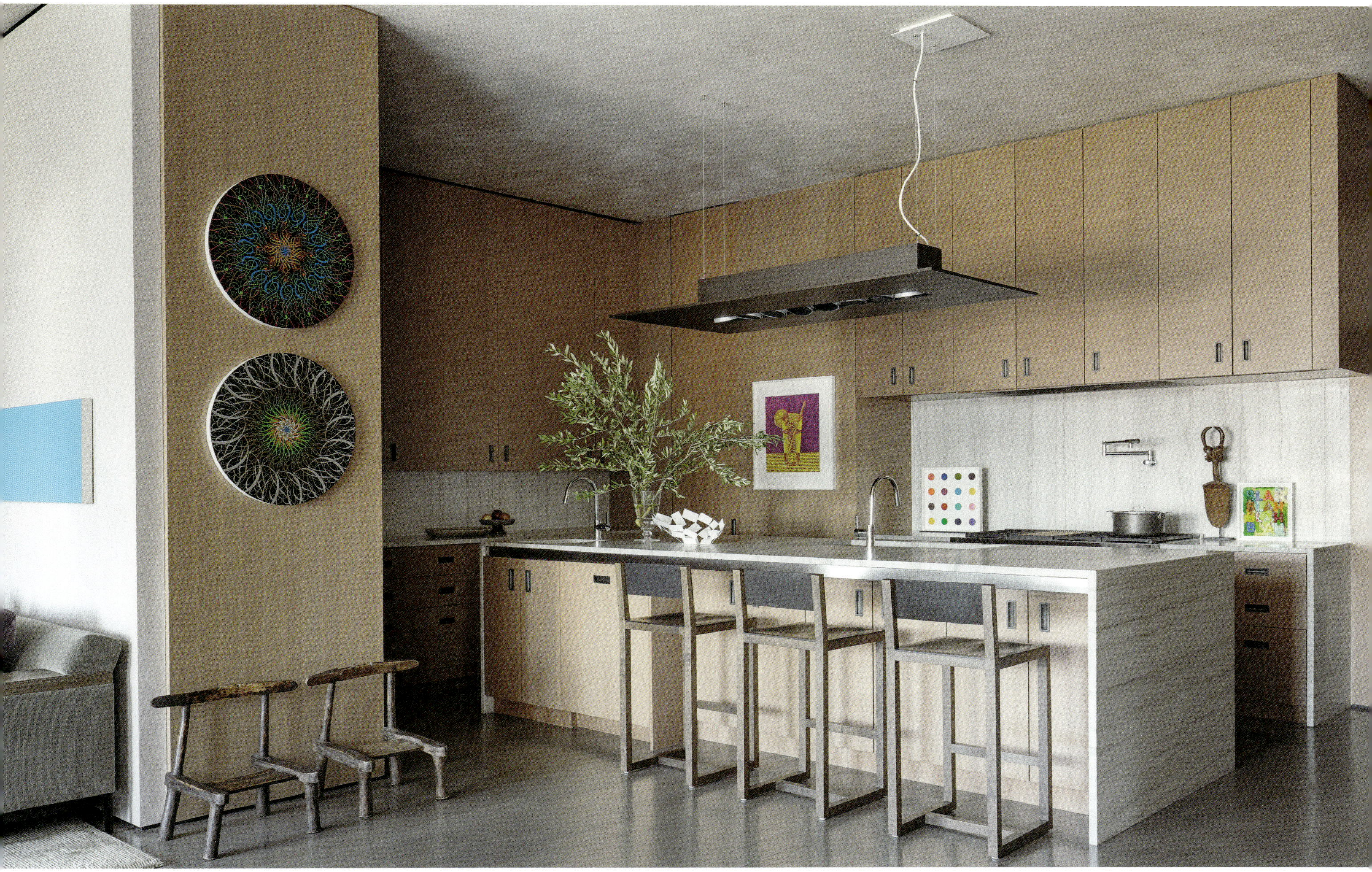

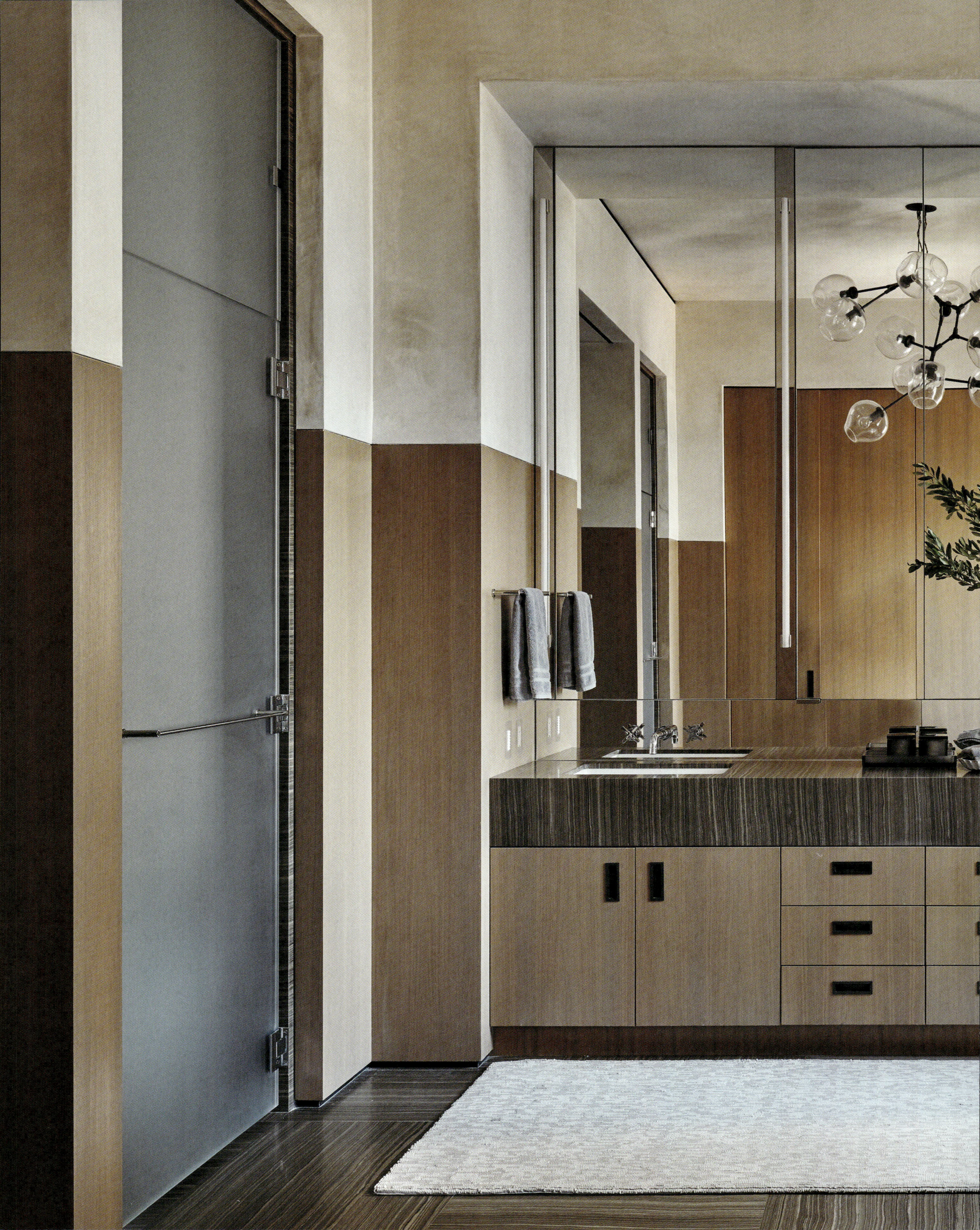

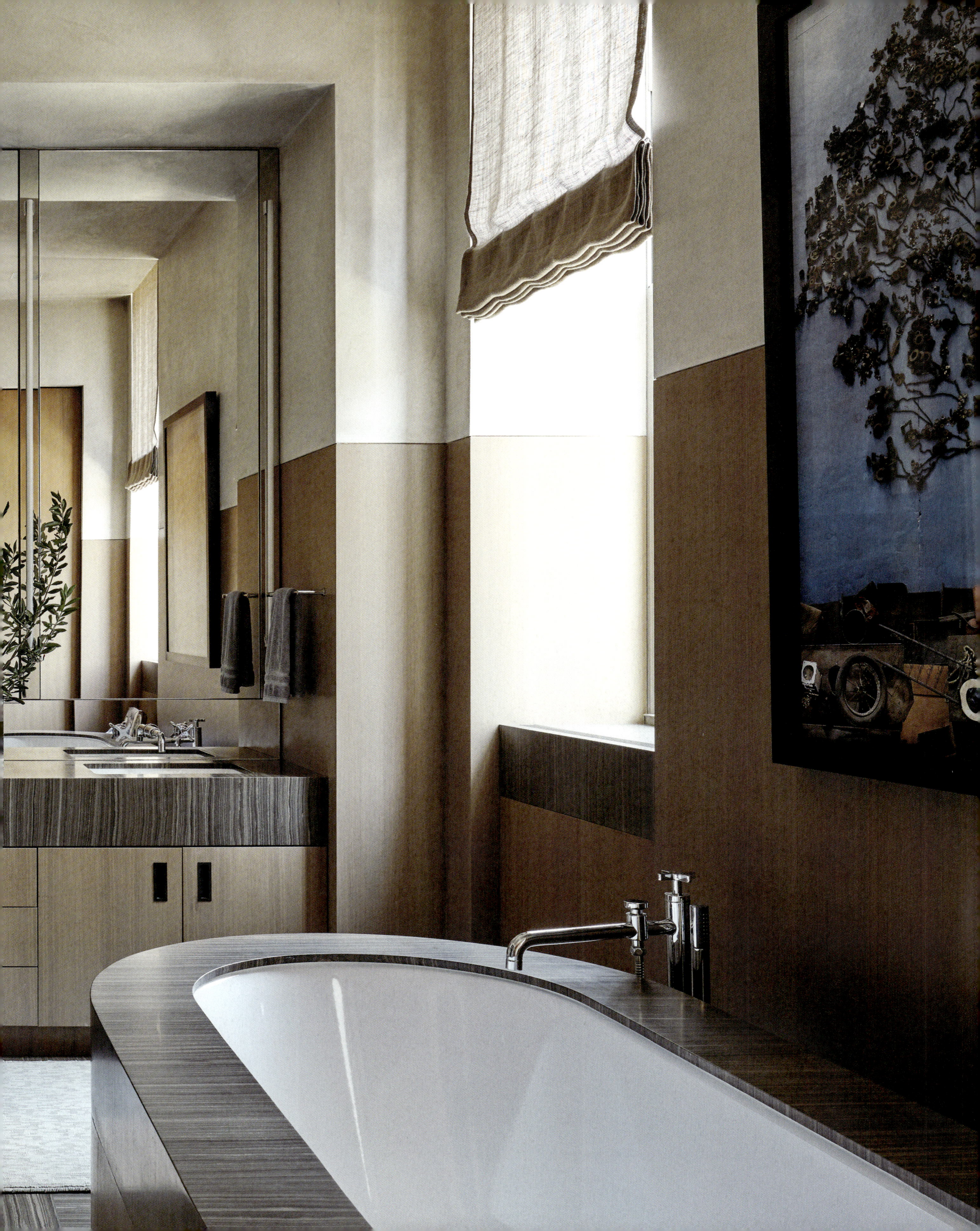

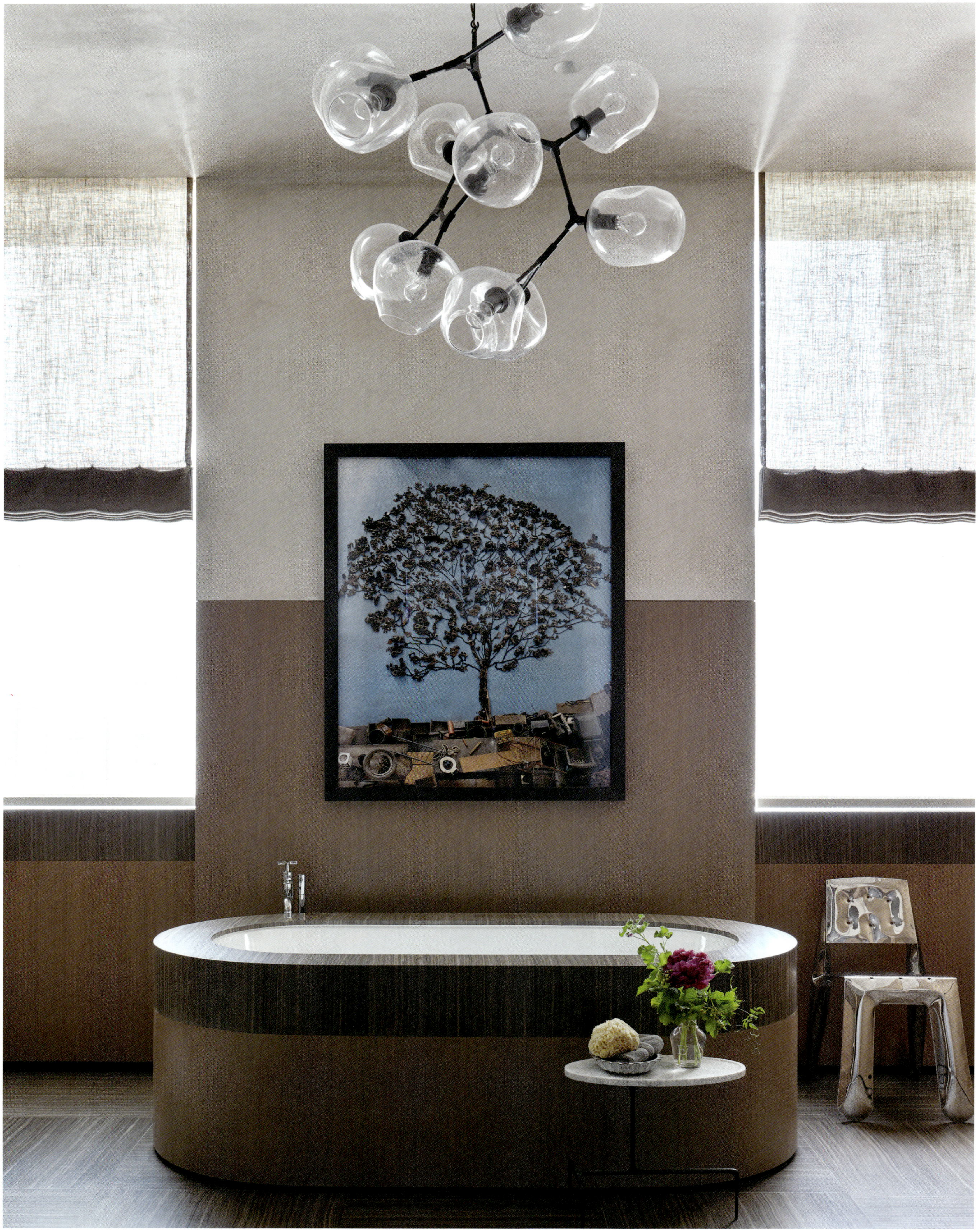

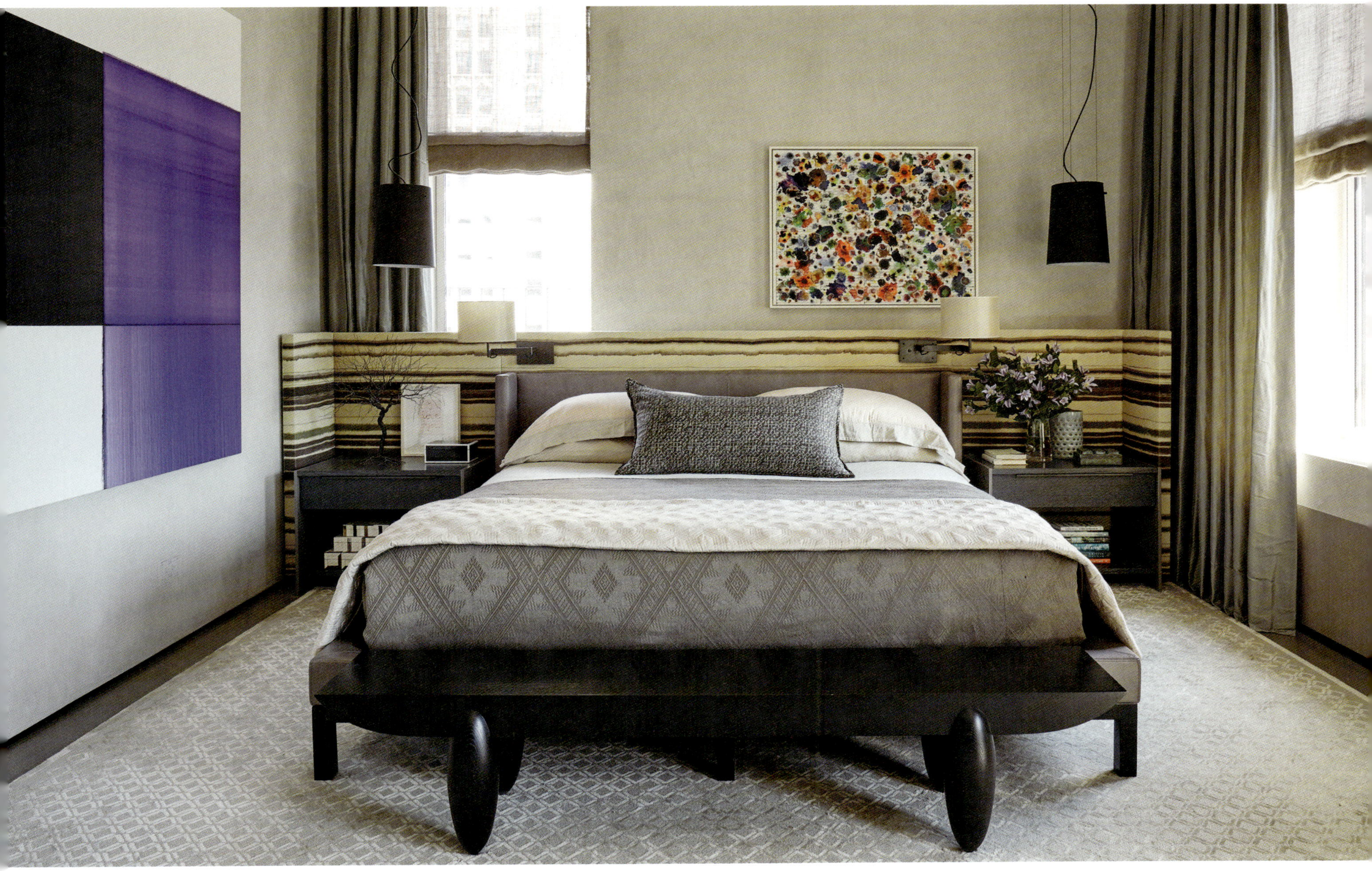

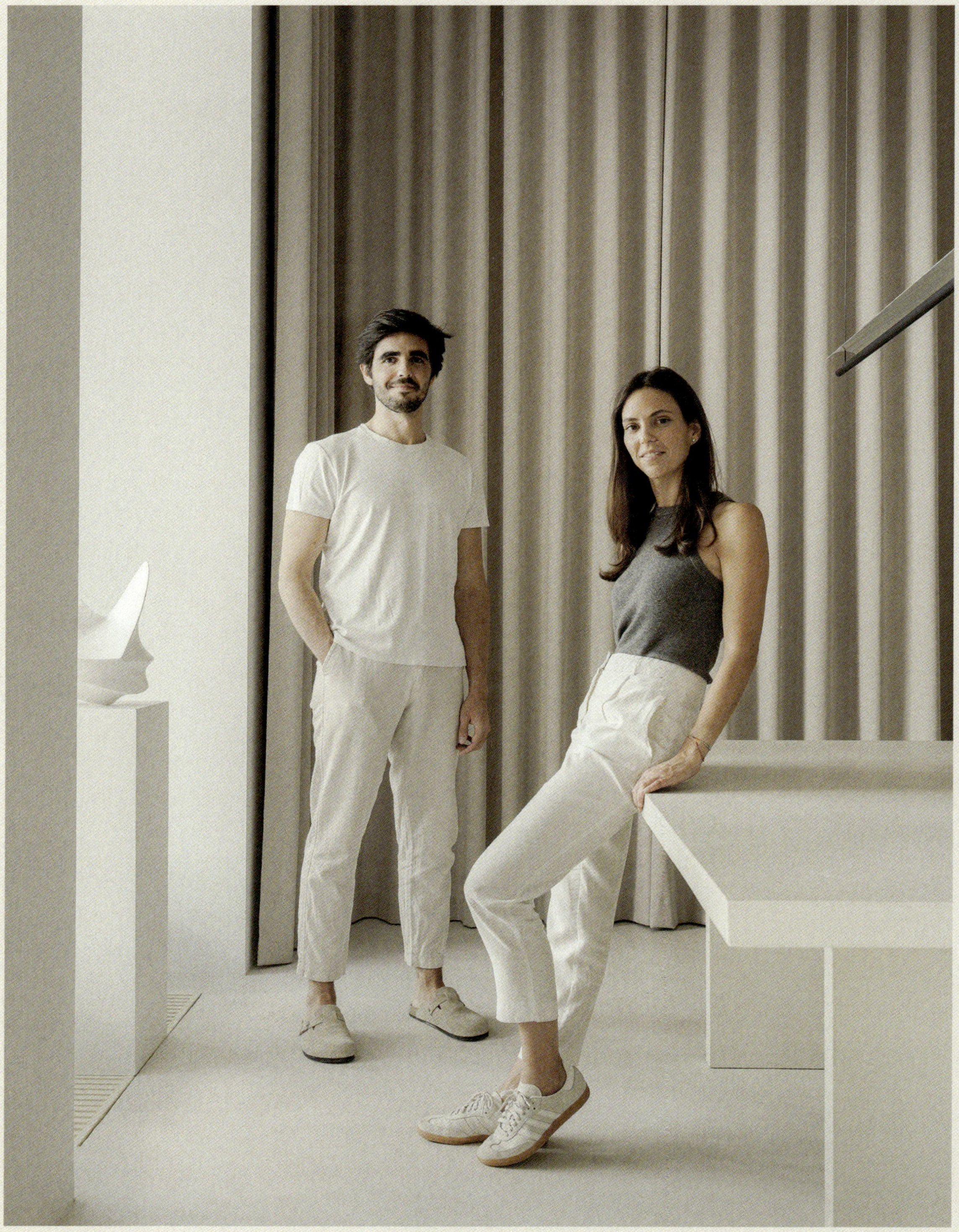

Maximale

Maximale is an architectural firm based in Madrid founded in 2022 by Pablo Delgado and Cristina Garau, architects from the University of Seville and Navarra respectively. Their work develops projects of various scales and typologies based on the search for concrete strategies to achieve technical and aesthetic solutions applied individually to each project.

Through an analytical and conceptual approach, Maximale Studio defines an architecture that uses light and geometry to achieve proportion, harmony and coherence. Their projects seek answers to social, cultural or environmental needs, promoting a constant dialogue between different disciplines such as art, design and research.

Maximale is the result of the training and professional experience of its founders in an international context. Their career began in Amsterdam, Paris and Venice and continued in London, where Pablo developed retail projects for brands such as Burberry and Tiffany and Cristina worked on large-scale projects in the architectural firms BIG and Adjaye Associates.

www.maximalestudio.com

Photography: David Zarzoso

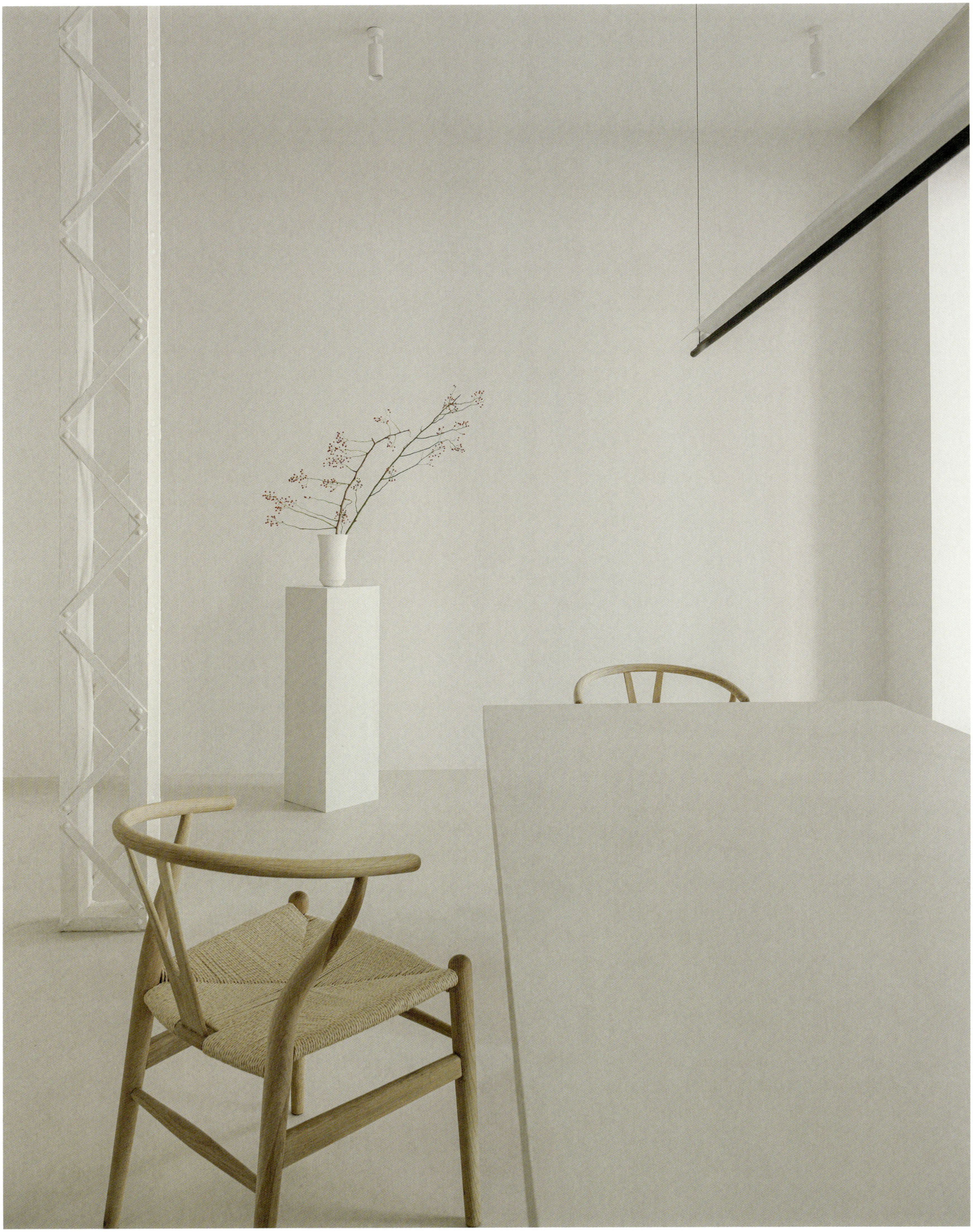

In this publication, Maximale presents three recent projects.

On page 118 their own Espacio Maximale in Madrid, a 70 square meter working and meeting place for the development of their architectural practice. It is conceived as a workshop where to produce, but also as a space that invites reflection and meeting. The project program defines the two essential areas in the operation of the studio. A first reception space at street level linked to the meeting that is succeeded by a second area related to work. Both spaces are differentiated by a small change in height around which the auxiliary uses and a small rest patio are articulated. The neutral and harmonious tones allow a slow and continuous reading of the space. Its location at street level in the Chamberí neighborhood invites to have a more direct contact with clients, collaborators, friends and professionals of the sector allowing to develop visits, talks, meetings and workshops.

On pages 120-123 a 250 square meter house in Sant Cugat, Barcelona, seeks to redefine the pre-existing spaces and routes through simplification and cohesion. In order to disarticulate the previous compartmentalization on the first floor, the proposal dilutes the formal limits and incorporates curved lines. The materiality in these spaces is homogeneous and continuous through muted tones and a stone pavement that spreads outward in the form of terraces. These gradually give way to nature in the form of a domestic garden, to end up merging with the Serra de Collserola Natural Park. The upper levels are given a greater warmth through the use of oak wood in the pavement. The existing roof, also made of wood, has a clear geometry that defines the floor plan distribution with its beams. In this way, the main room is presented as a space of seclusion bathed in light from the south and west.

On pages 124-129 Maximale shows a 450 square meter residence in Málaga. The project is based on the premise of respecting the past of a historic building in the center of Málaga, while seeking to respond to the specific requirements of temporary users and, therefore, with minimal housing needs. It comprises a set of 7 apartments together with their respective common areas, recovering artistic and architectural elements of great value. Inside, the apartments reflect on the current functionality and the absence of ornamentation while establishing a dialogue with the vibrant details of this unique building. All floors are resolved in two different typologies of pre-existing dwellings in which, as one ascends, the specific elements of the façade and roof bathe the space in light and warmth.

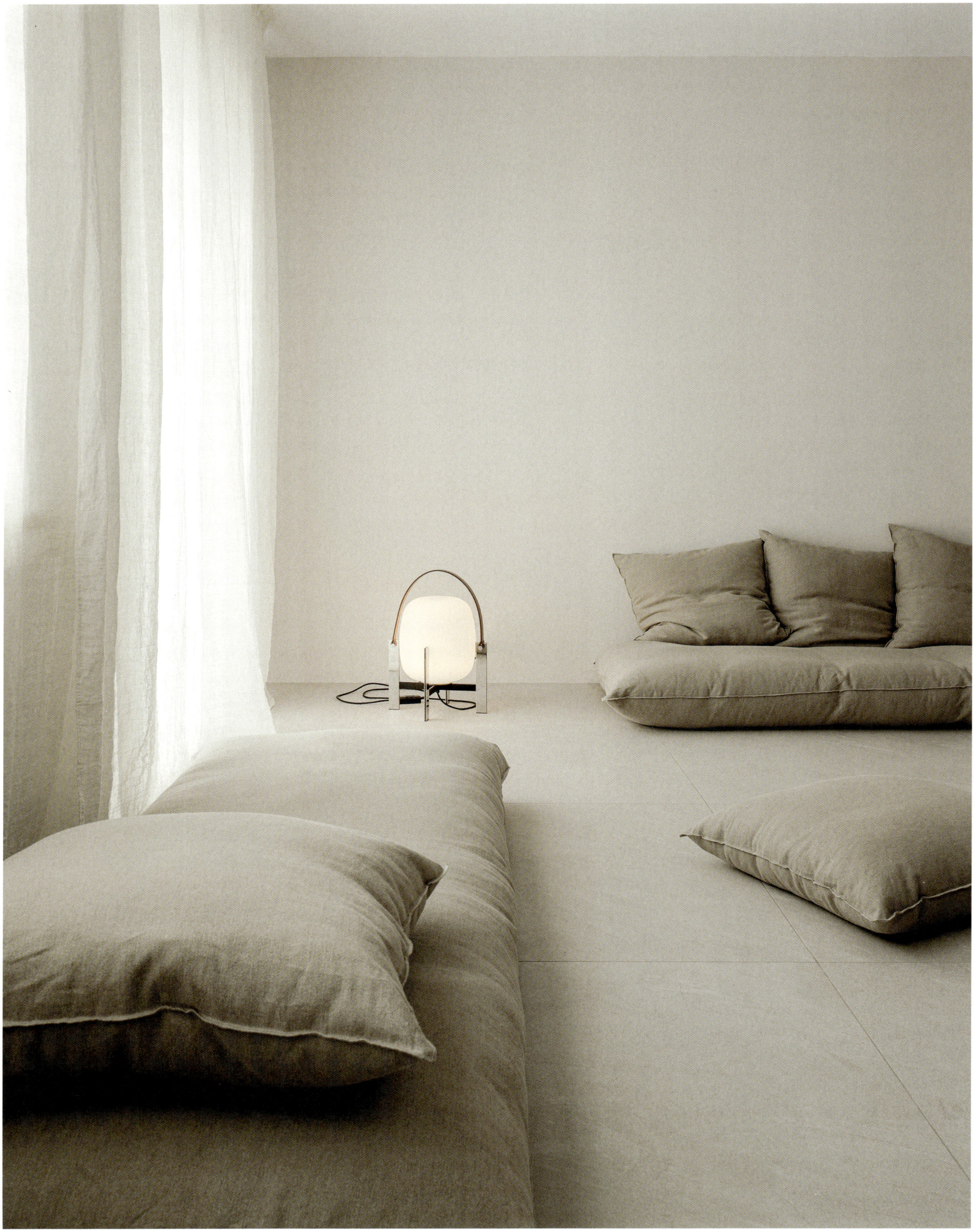

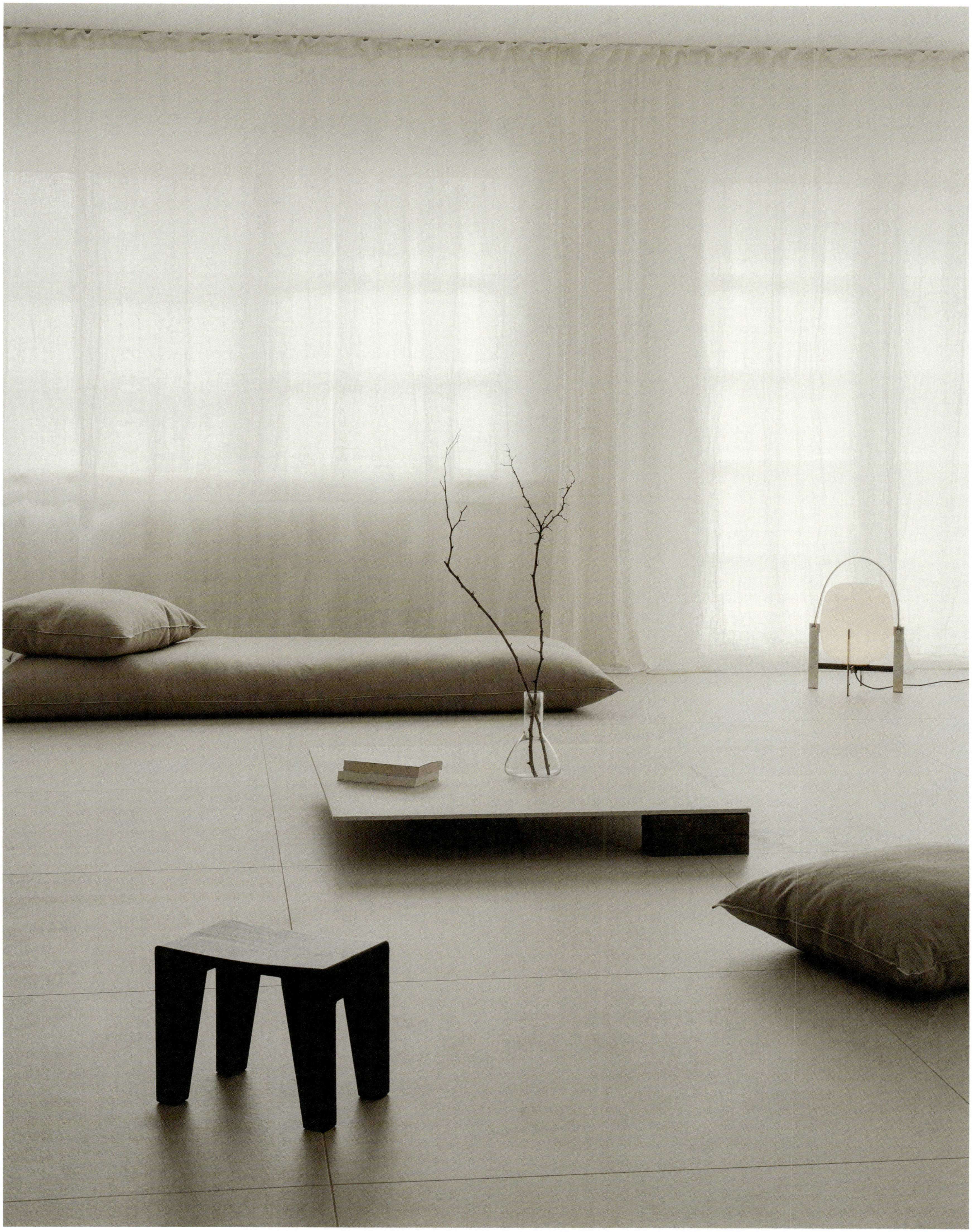

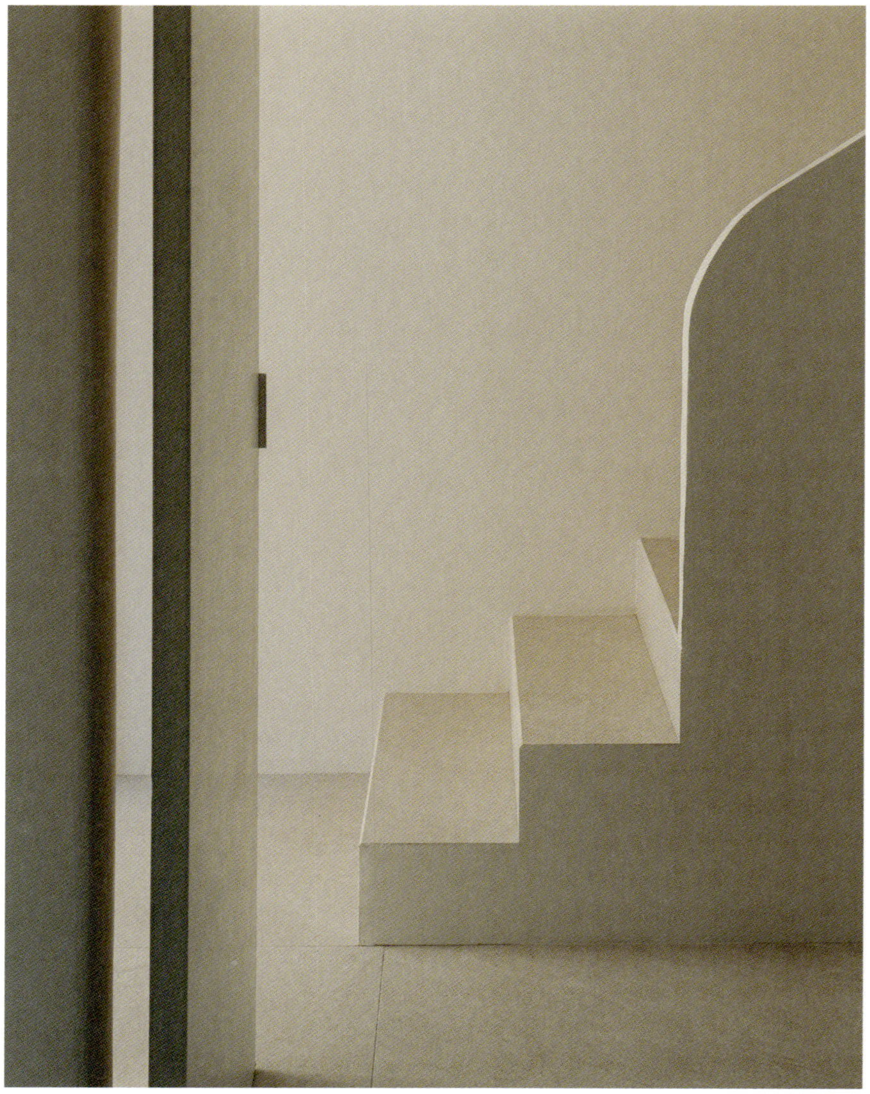

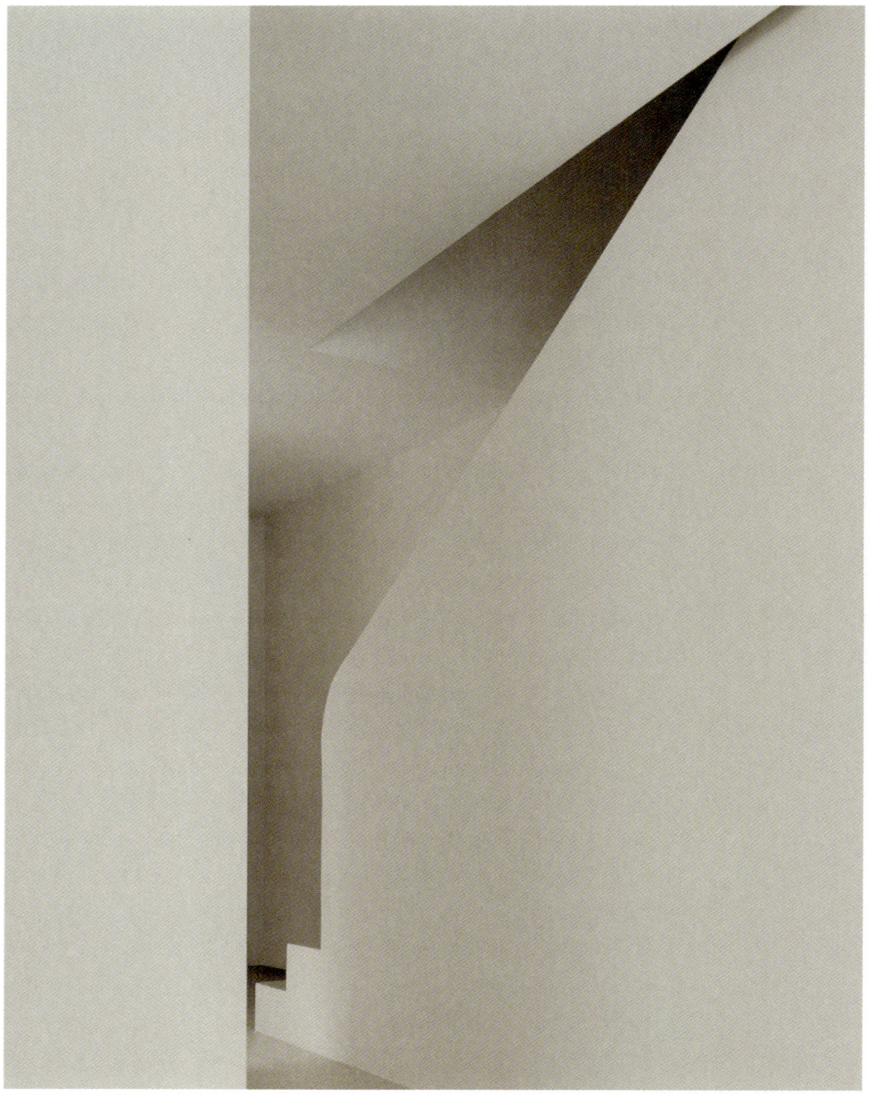

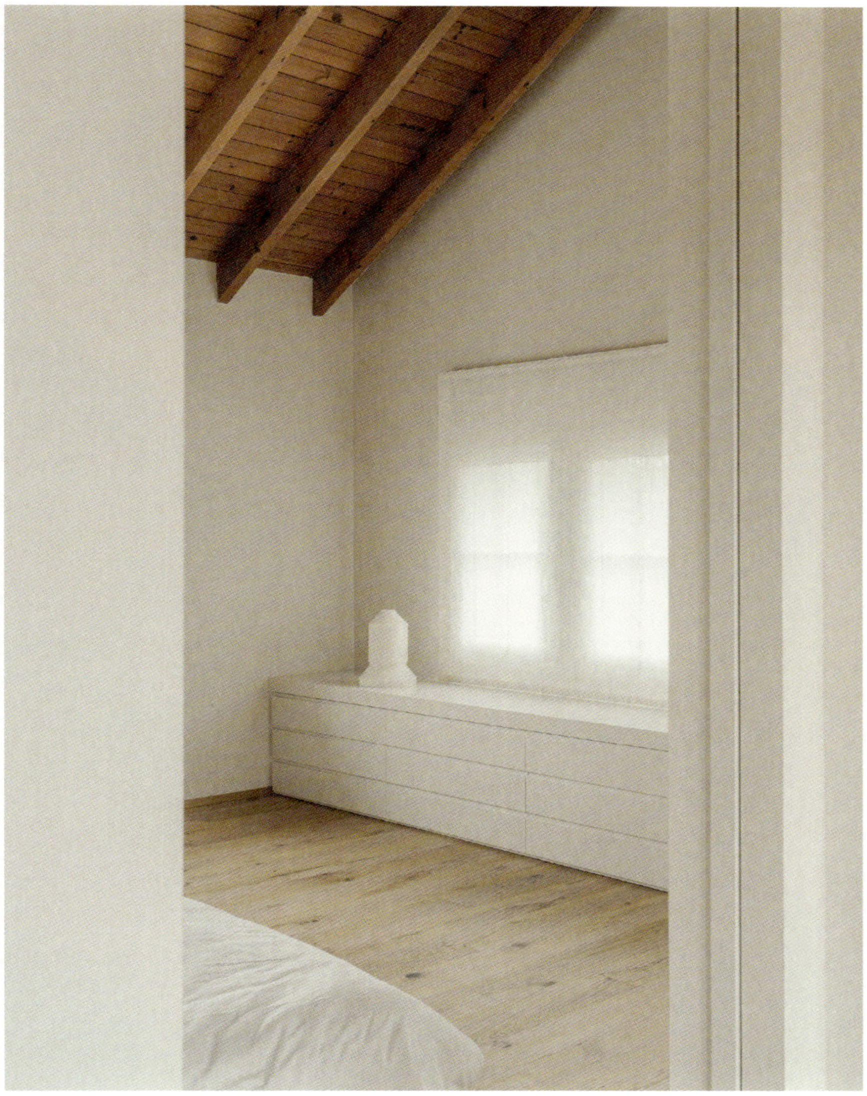

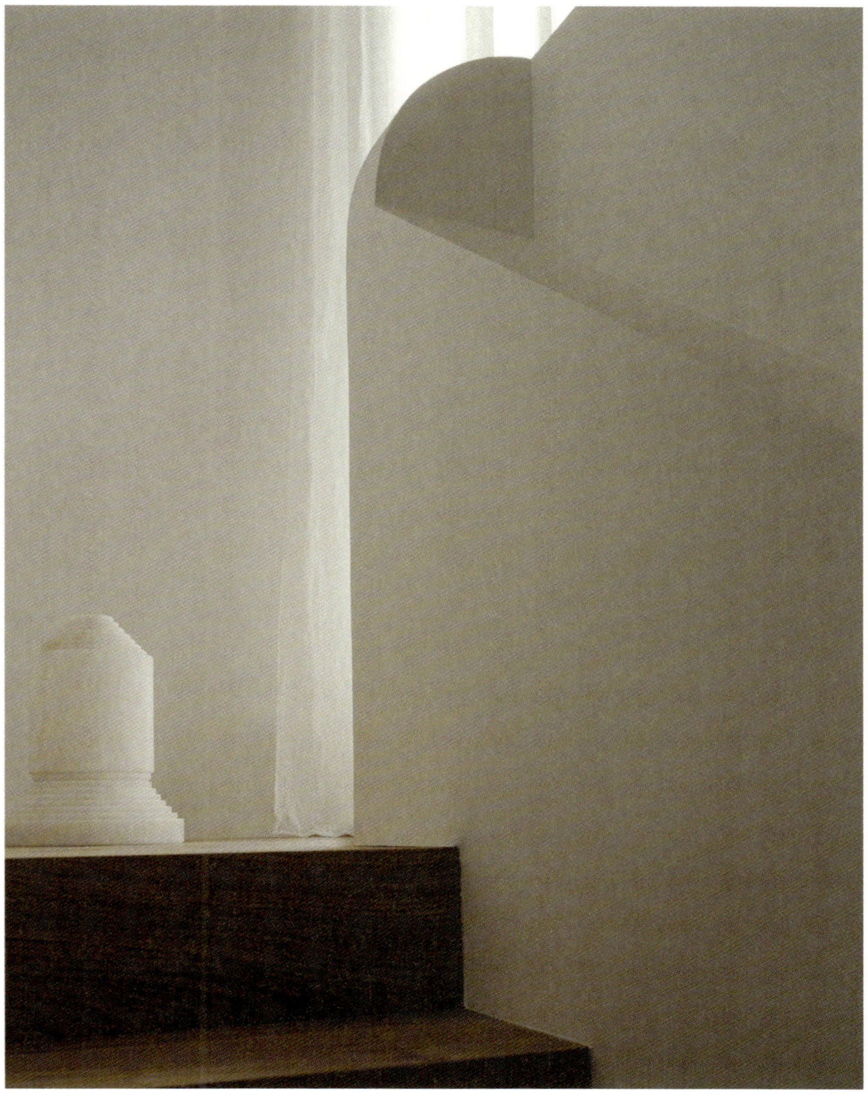

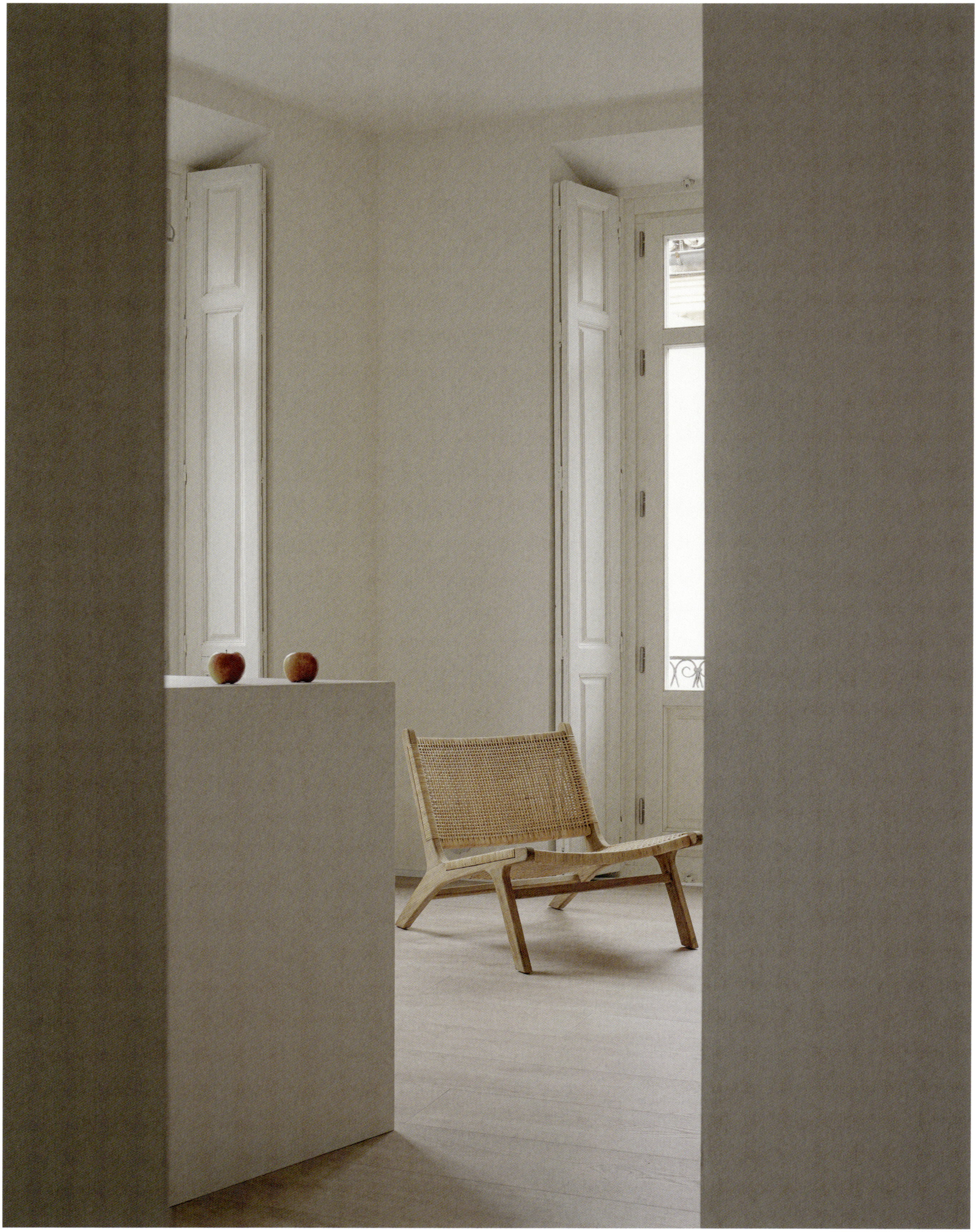

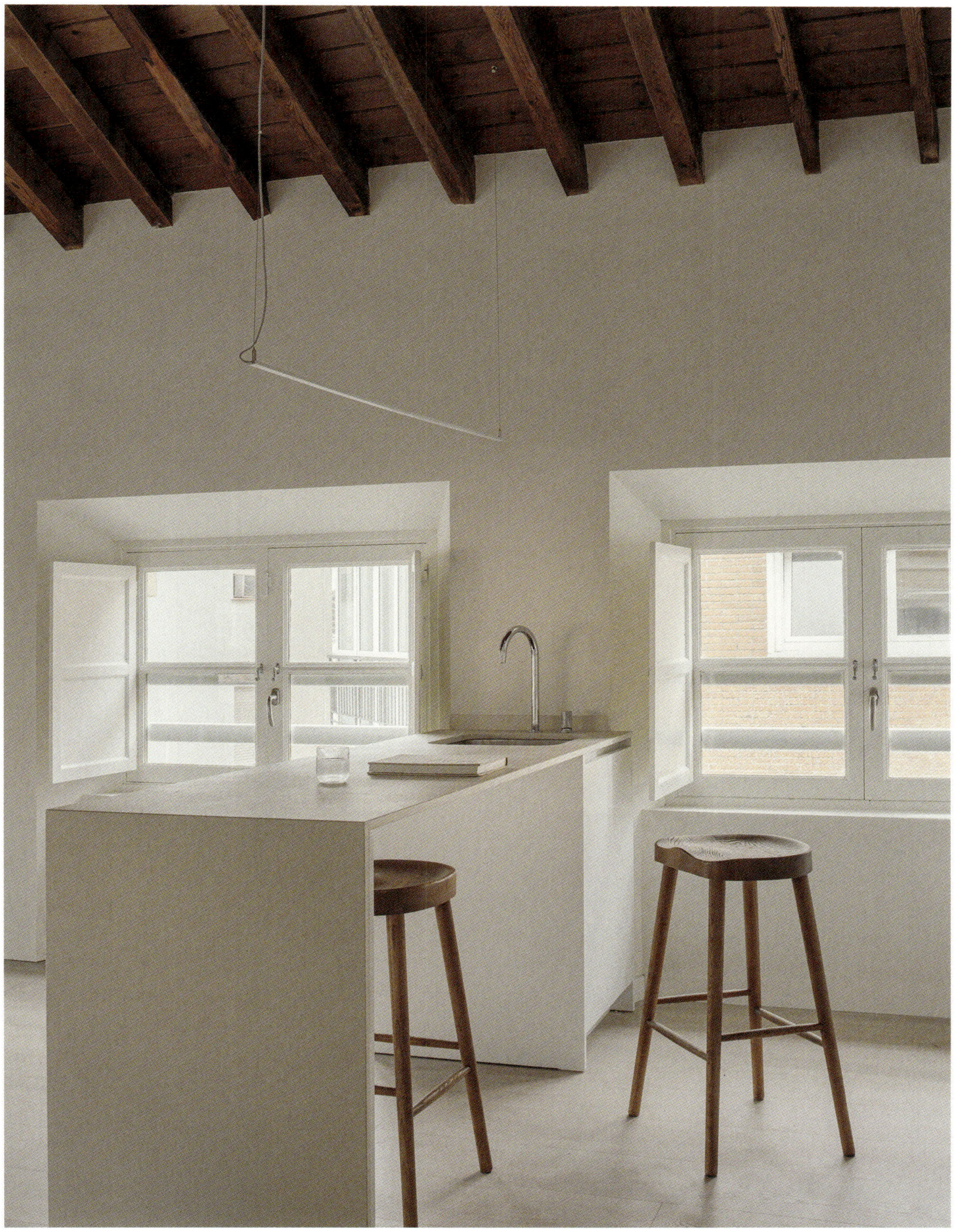

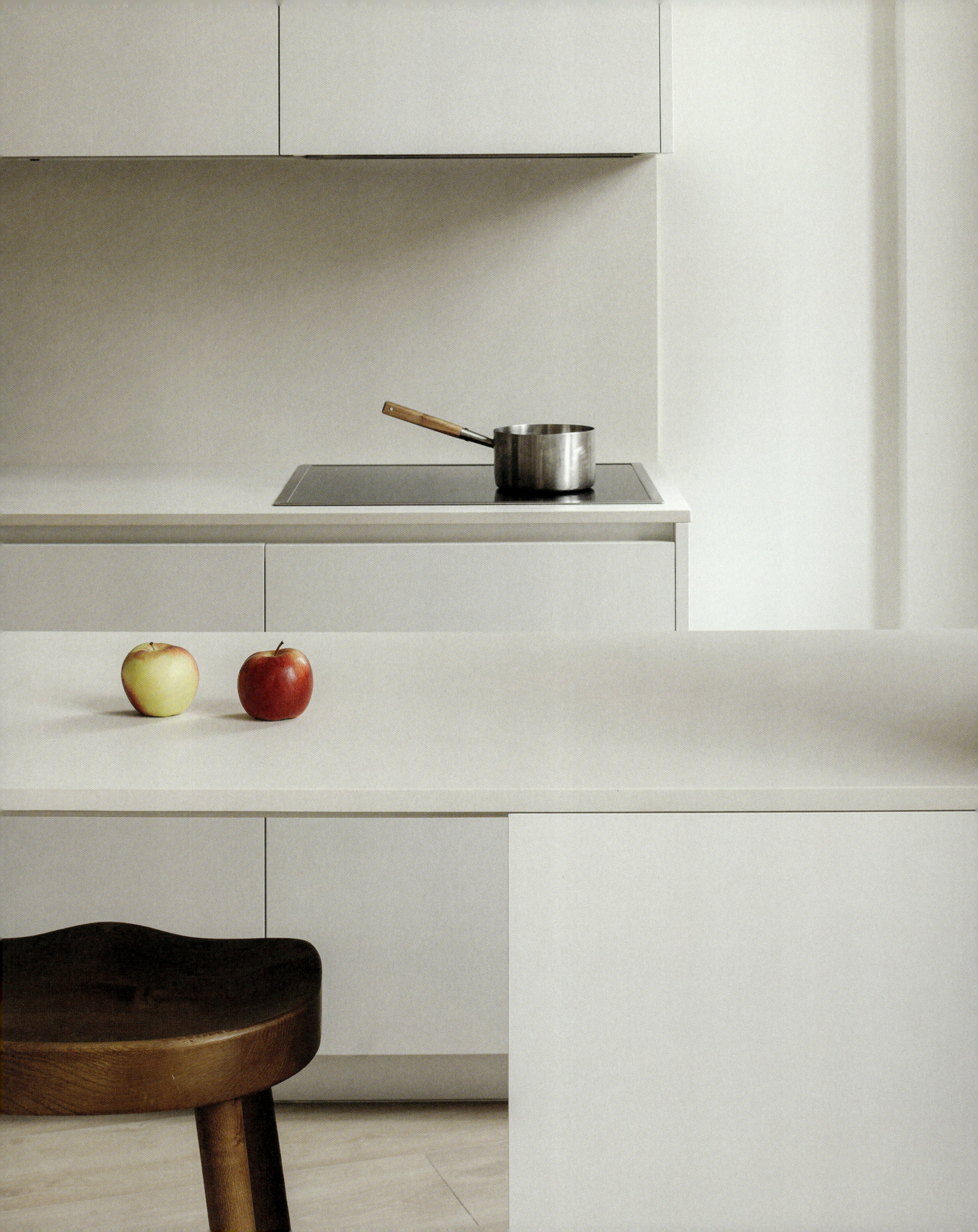

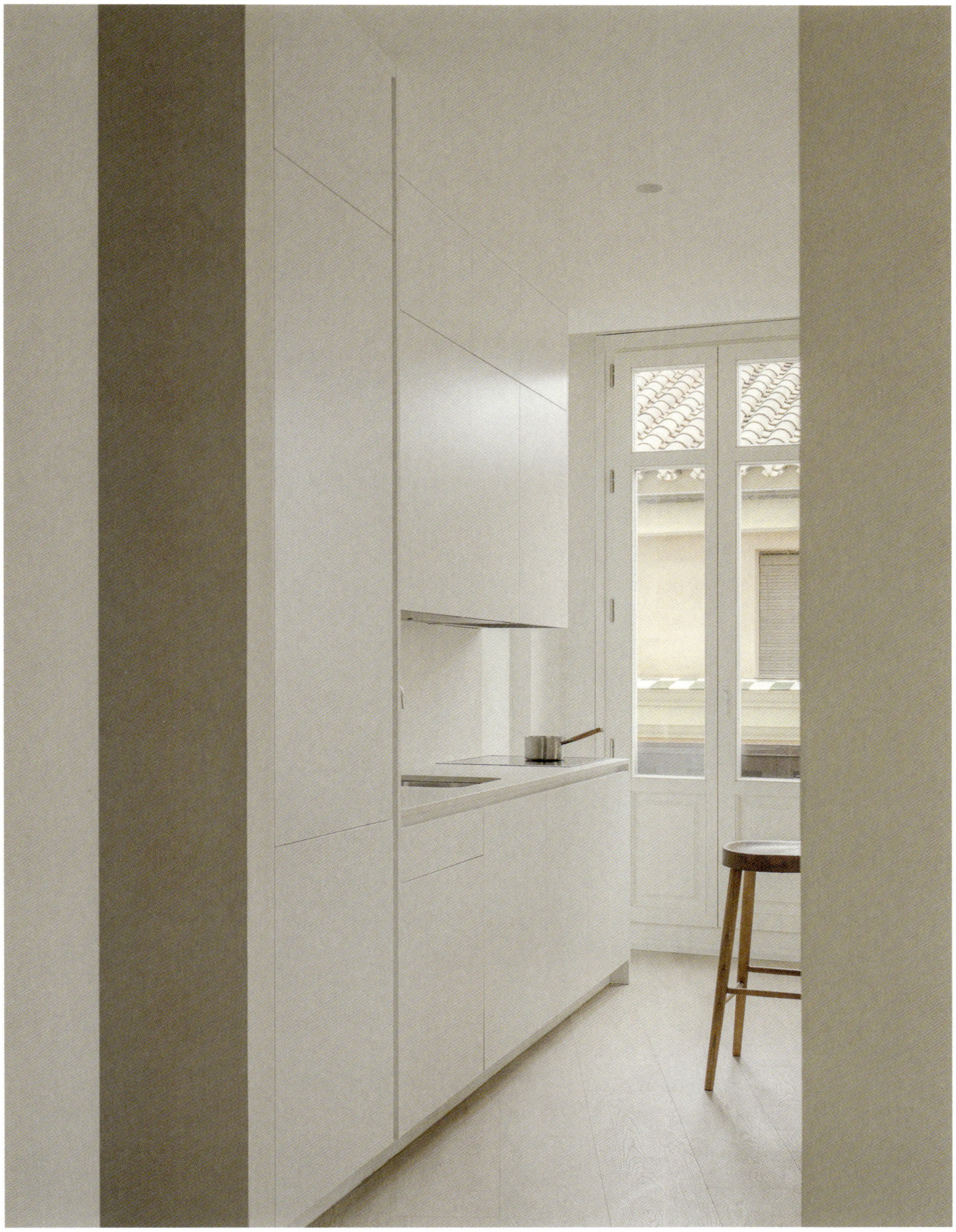

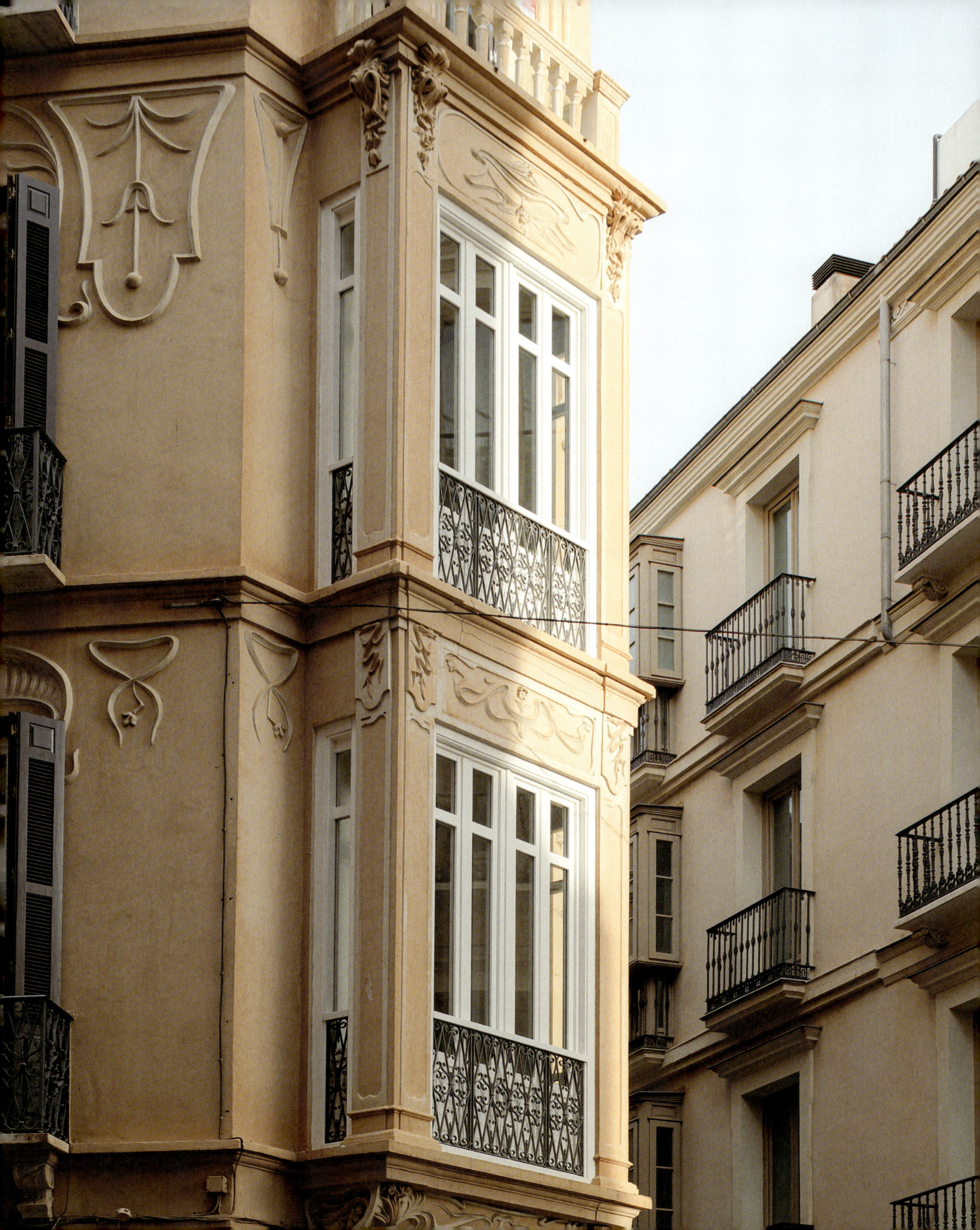

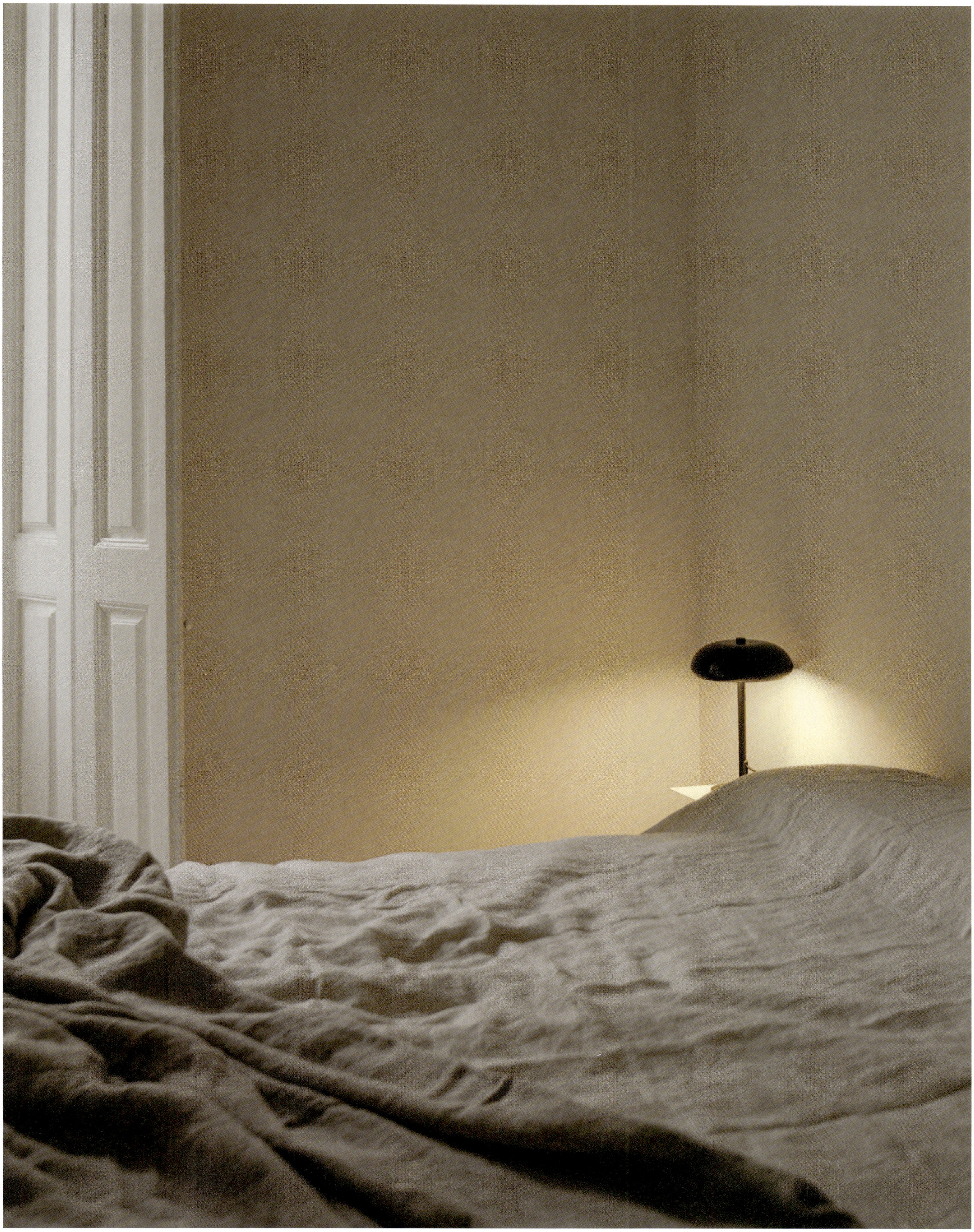

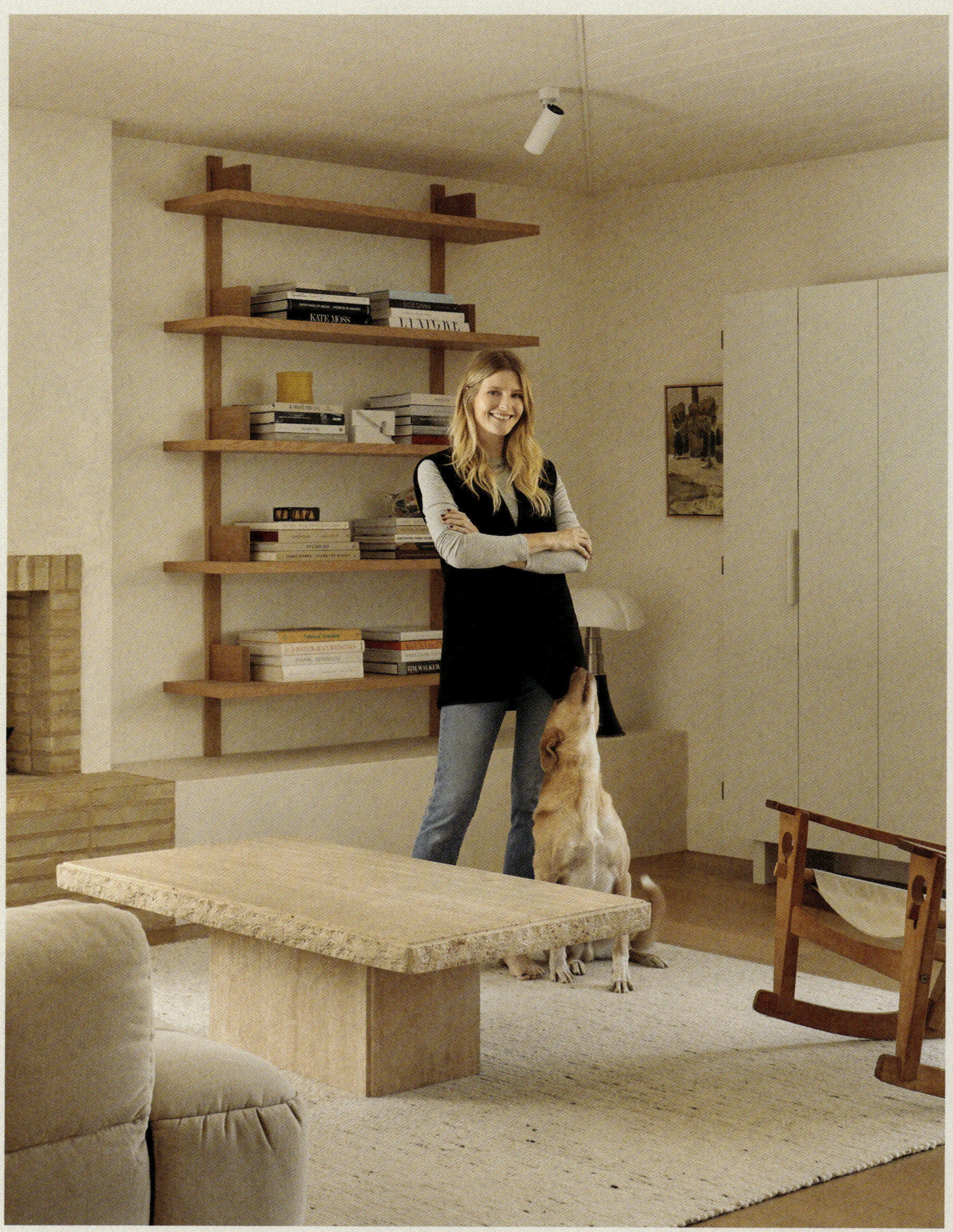
KATE MOSS

Georgina Jeffries

Georgina Jeffries is an interior design practice anchored by a belief in the emotional capacity of design to enhance liveability. This foundational philosophy underpins her wide portfolio of residential projects, which consistently explore proportion, light and balance to deliver honest and nurturing spaces that elevate daily life.

A harmony between nostalgia, refuge and occasion is a creative hallmark of the practice, driven by the natural ability of founder Georgina Jeffries to balance poetry and approachability. Embracing the unique narratives of coastal, country and city living, their work is unified by enduring materials, quality craftsmanship and a refined response to detail, crafting authentic, place-specific interiors with romantic inflections.

Based in Lorne and Prahran, Georgina Jeffries' small yet dexterous team of multi-disciplinary design professionals offer a tailored client experience across residential interior design and decoration. Their inclusive and collaborative spirit, led by director, Georgina Jeffries, honors the unique perspectives of each participant to enrich built outcomes.

Understanding that design excellence is the outcome of authentic working relationships, Georgina considers her collaborators as an extension of the team. Their reliable network of builders, joiners, sales representatives and consultants consistently support their design ambitions – a wonderful asset to their daily practice.

Georgina Jeffries and her team offer full scope interior design services in the residential market. They harness a customized approach to tailor spaces to our clients' individual needs, while skillfully translating the brief into highly considered and unexpected design outcomes. Embracing a collaborative and consultative attitude, they guide their clients through six project stages that capture the design intent and ensure seamless on-site delivery – from initial design to final styling.

Georgina Jeffries offer stand-alone design services to assist with the procurement and placement of furniture, art and décor. The design team develops a styling approach in response to the narrative of the client and home, informing a careful curation of custom, vintage and designed pieces that render the home usable, beautiful and complete.

www.georginajeffries.com

Photography: Lillie Thompson (p.132 & 134-139) / Cricket Saleh (p.140-143)

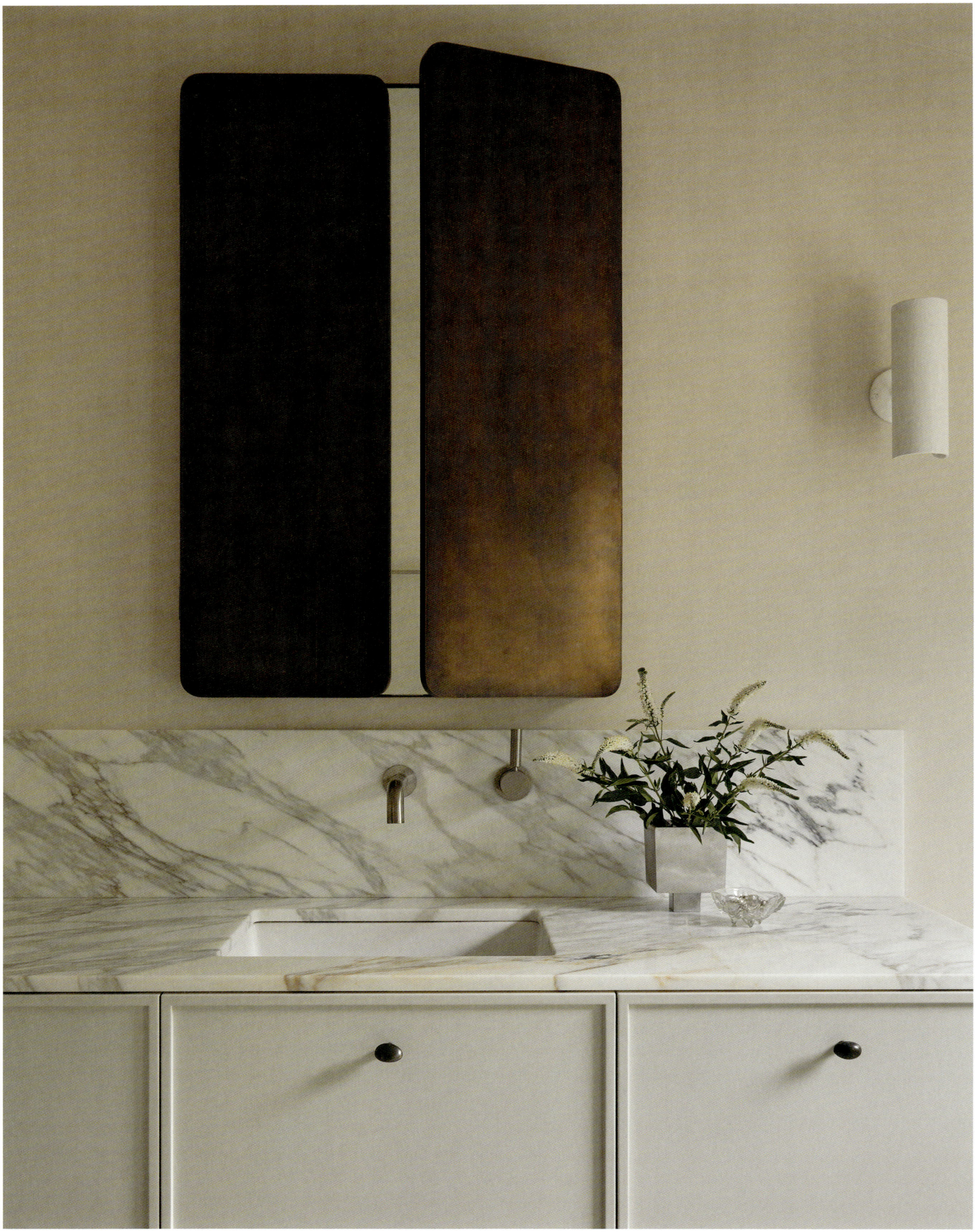

On pages 132 and pages 134 to 139: this 1916 weatherboard cottage along the Great Ocean Road in Lorne (Victoria, Australia) has been designed and transformed into a vibrant and animated residence by Georgina Jeffries and her team. The brief was centered around celebrating the home's history, supporting family life and establishing a connection to the garden. Inspired by the home's existing charm and character, merging shards of the past with a more modern approach became a labor of love for the owners. As her own retreat, Georgina brought together a custom style with her partner's landscape and construction background to handcraft this restful home. This unique renovation project captures the casual and relaxed simplicity of life by the sea while remaining connected to and grounded in its original and handcrafted origins. Through a careful and deliberate overlay of natural and subtle textural elements, the interior spaces are modest and layered with unexpected character. The existing volumes and sense of scale have been maintained and opened up to create a more fluid internal experience that also connects outward to the garden. By framing the views and creating a balance between the inside and outside, the warmth of the interior feels cocooning. The use of wood throughout the building softens the spaces and adds depth. This element, along with natural stone, also weaves a sense of permanence into the joinery, kitchen, bedrooms and bathrooms. While the house is visually connected through a conscious choice of materials, nature is also present throughout. As her own signature style, Georgina integrates artisanal gestures, adds personal expression and adds a handmade element. Working with artisans, skilled joiners and metalworkers, unique pieces and moments can be found throughout the home, leaving a distinct mark. Interior design: Georgina Jeffries. Builder: Howley Construction & Troy Fynmore. Landscape: Dirt Landscapes.

On pages 140 to 143: "Martini" is a calming beach retreat enveloped in a sophisticated palette and dynamic tactility. Natural materiality, organic lines and gentle hues imbue a refined sense of composure within the Portsea home. Architecture & Interiors: Inglis Architects. Interior furnishing, object & art: Georgina Jeffries. Landscape: Eckersleys with build by DMS Landscapes. Build: Made Build.

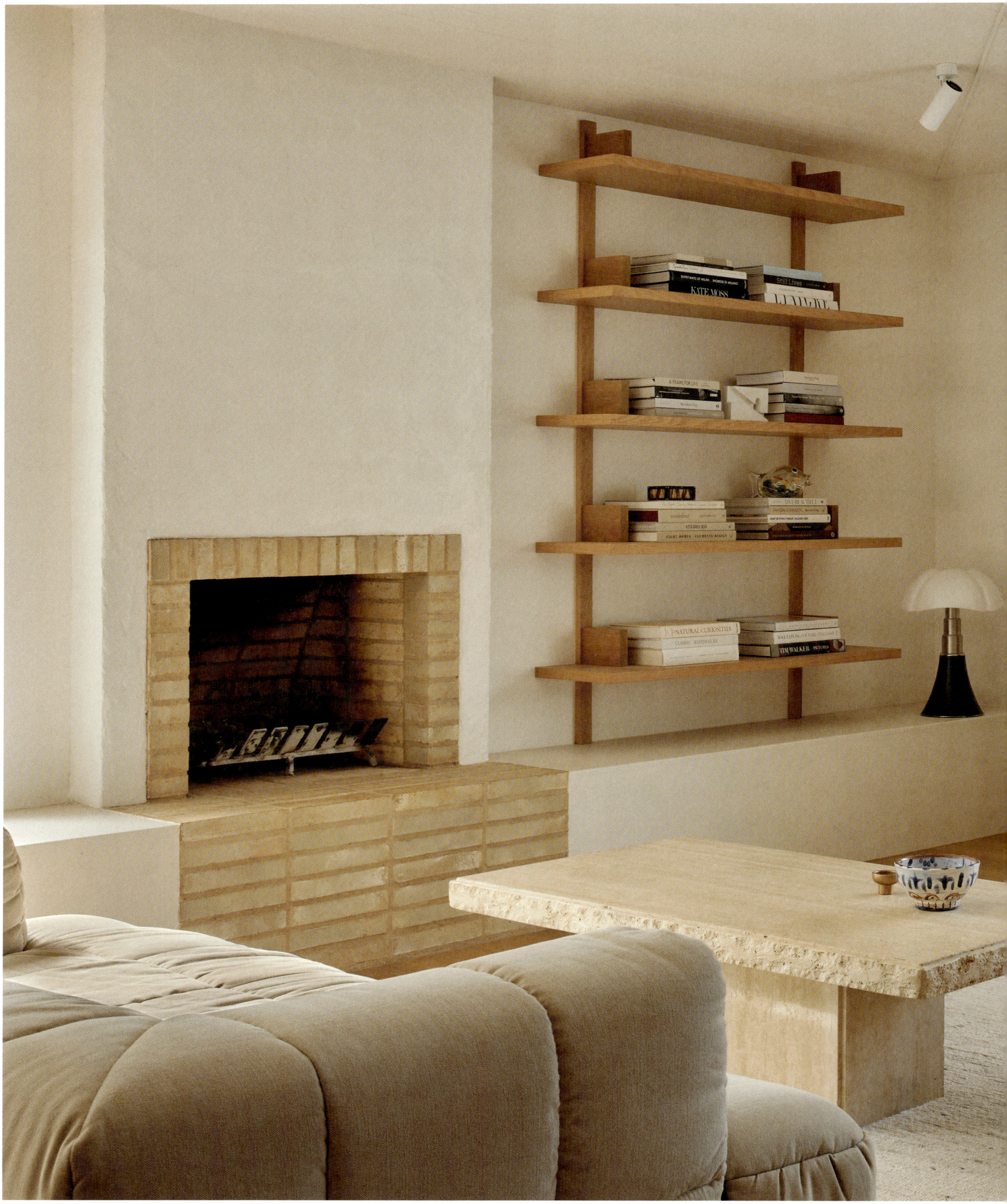

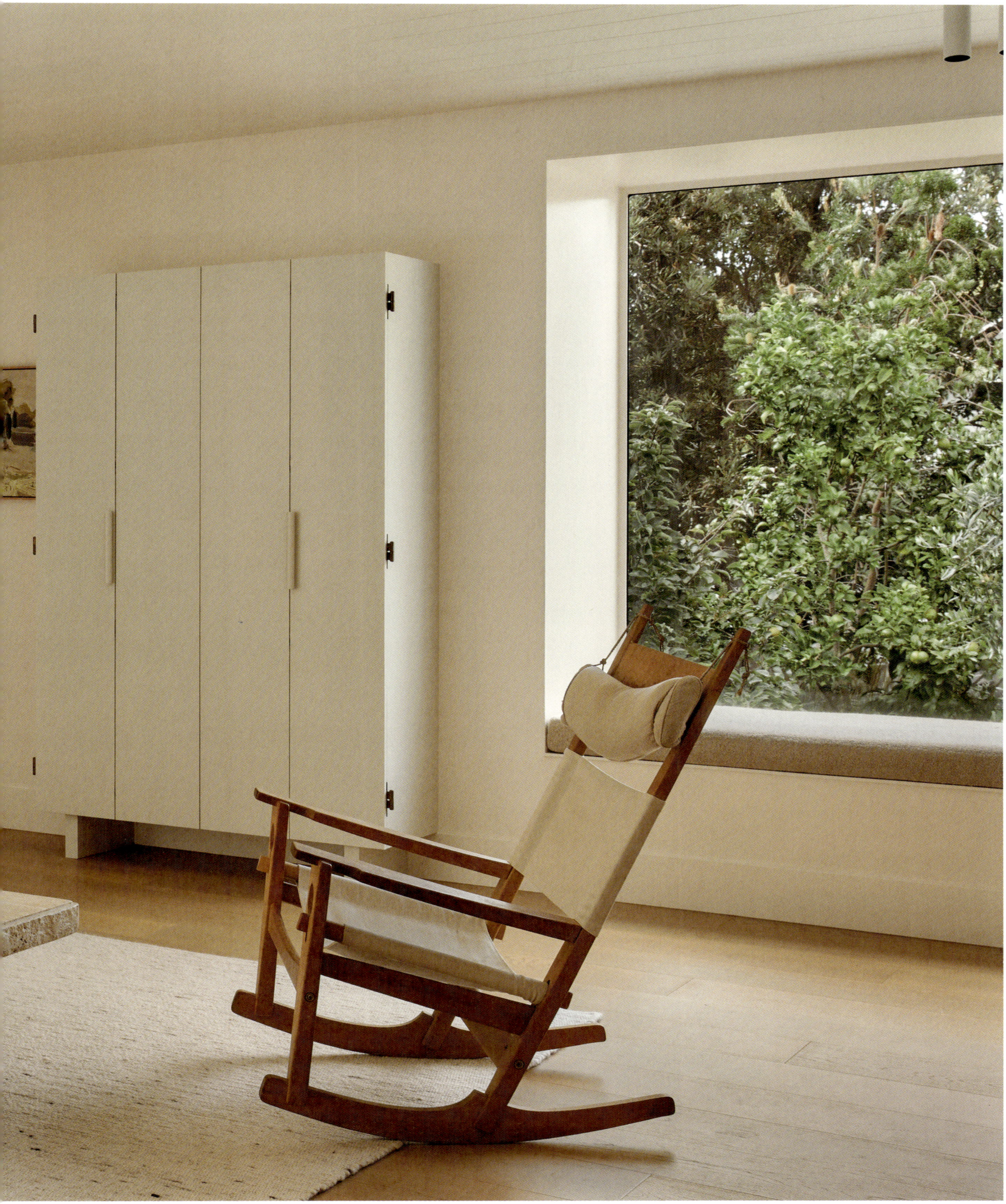

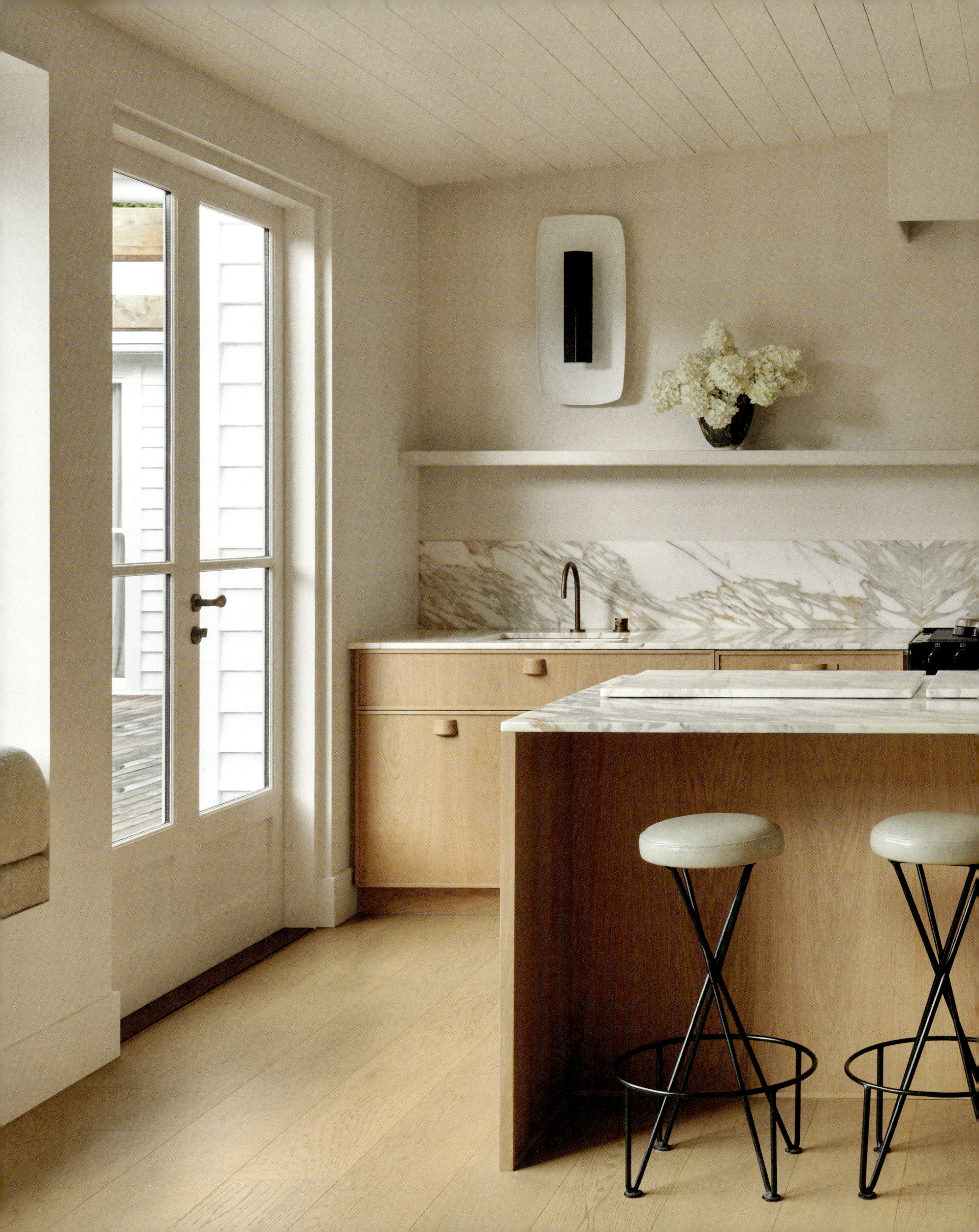

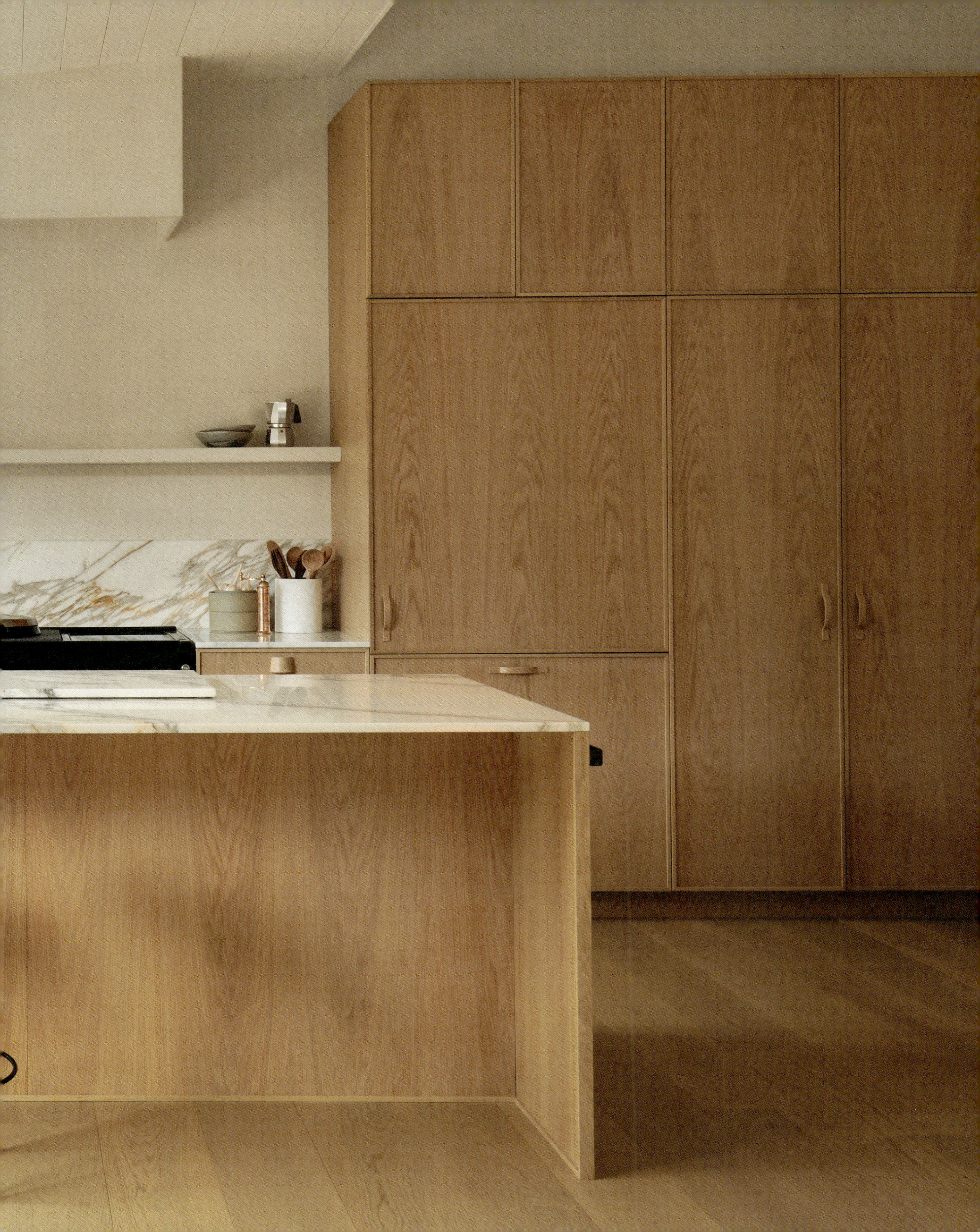

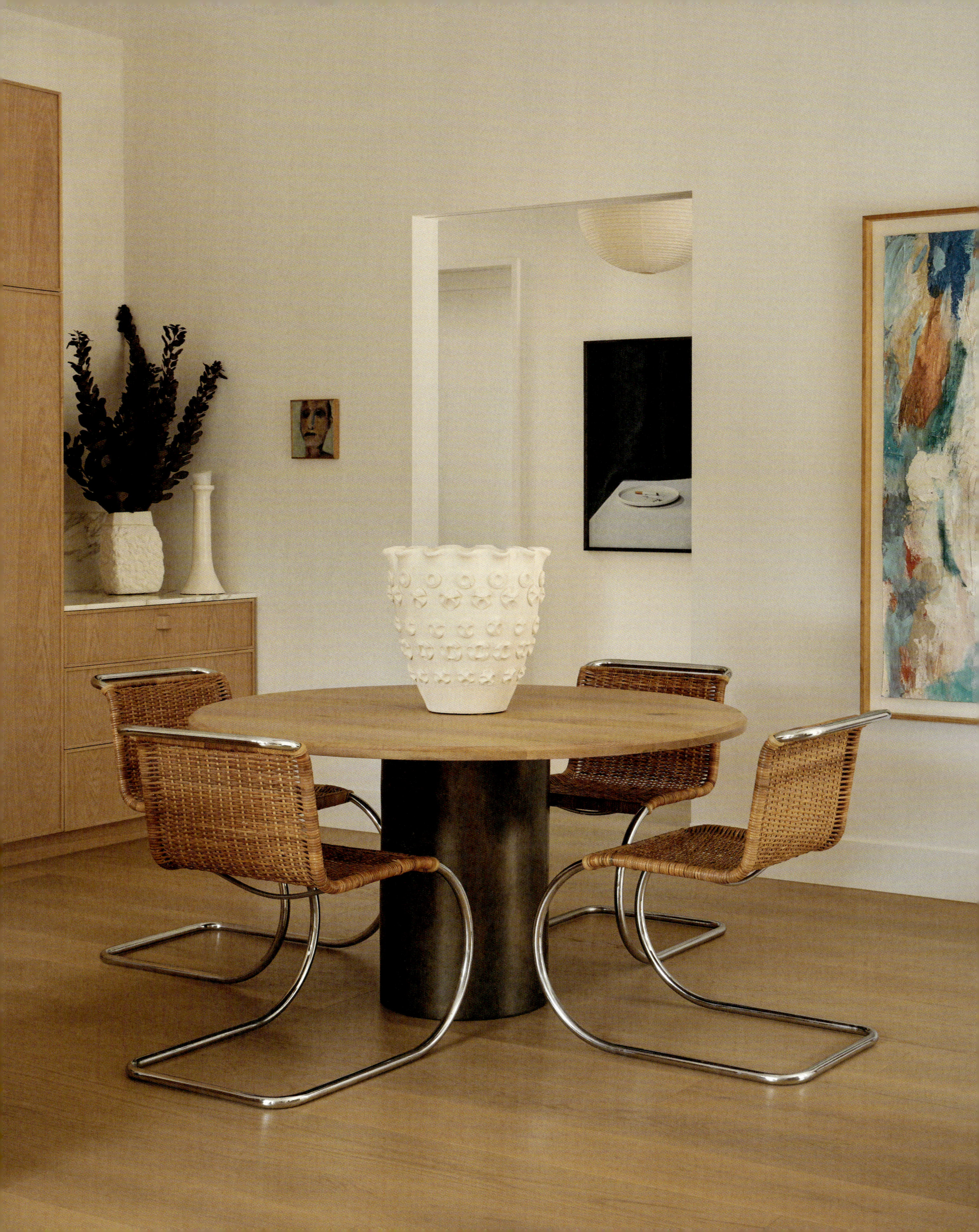

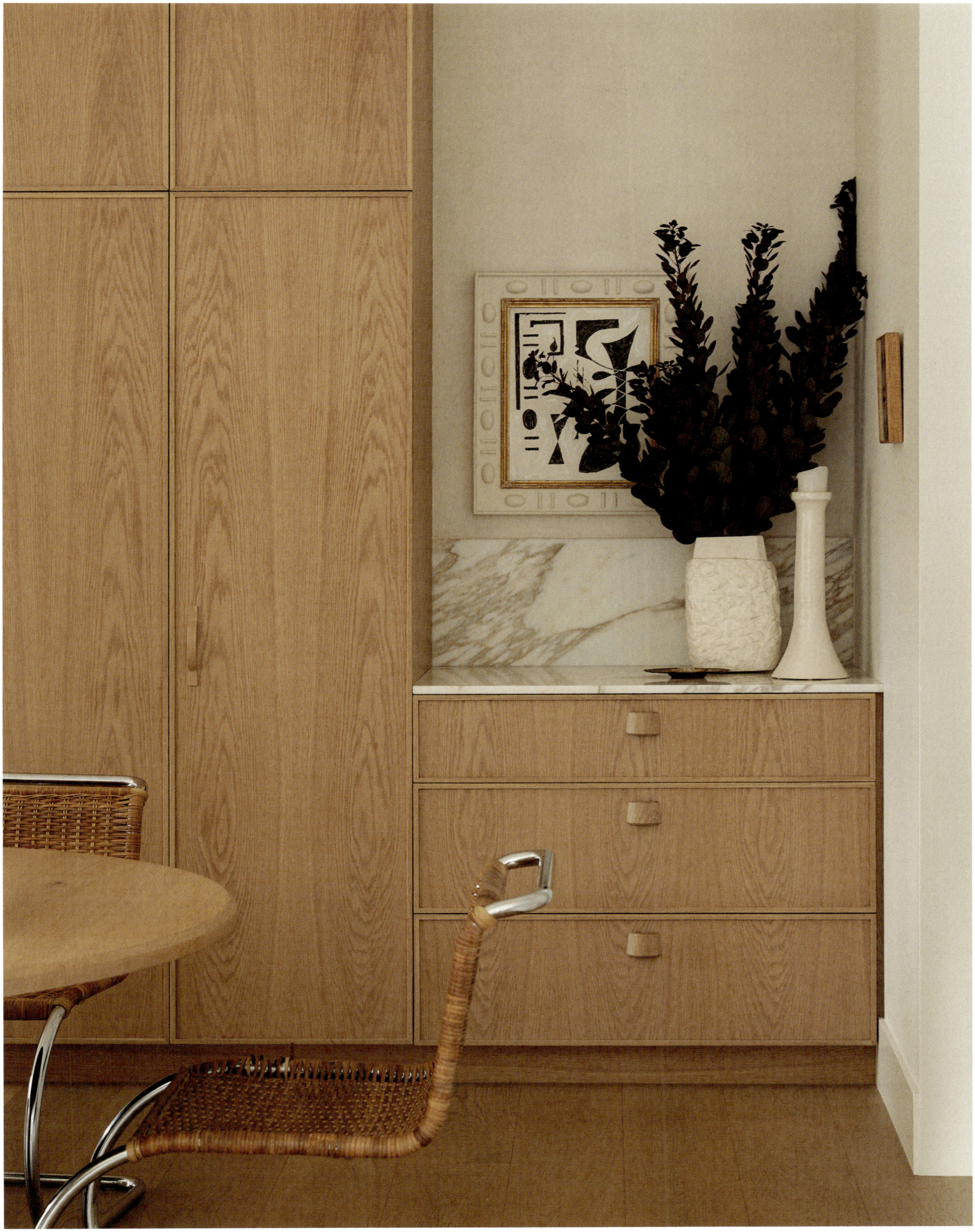

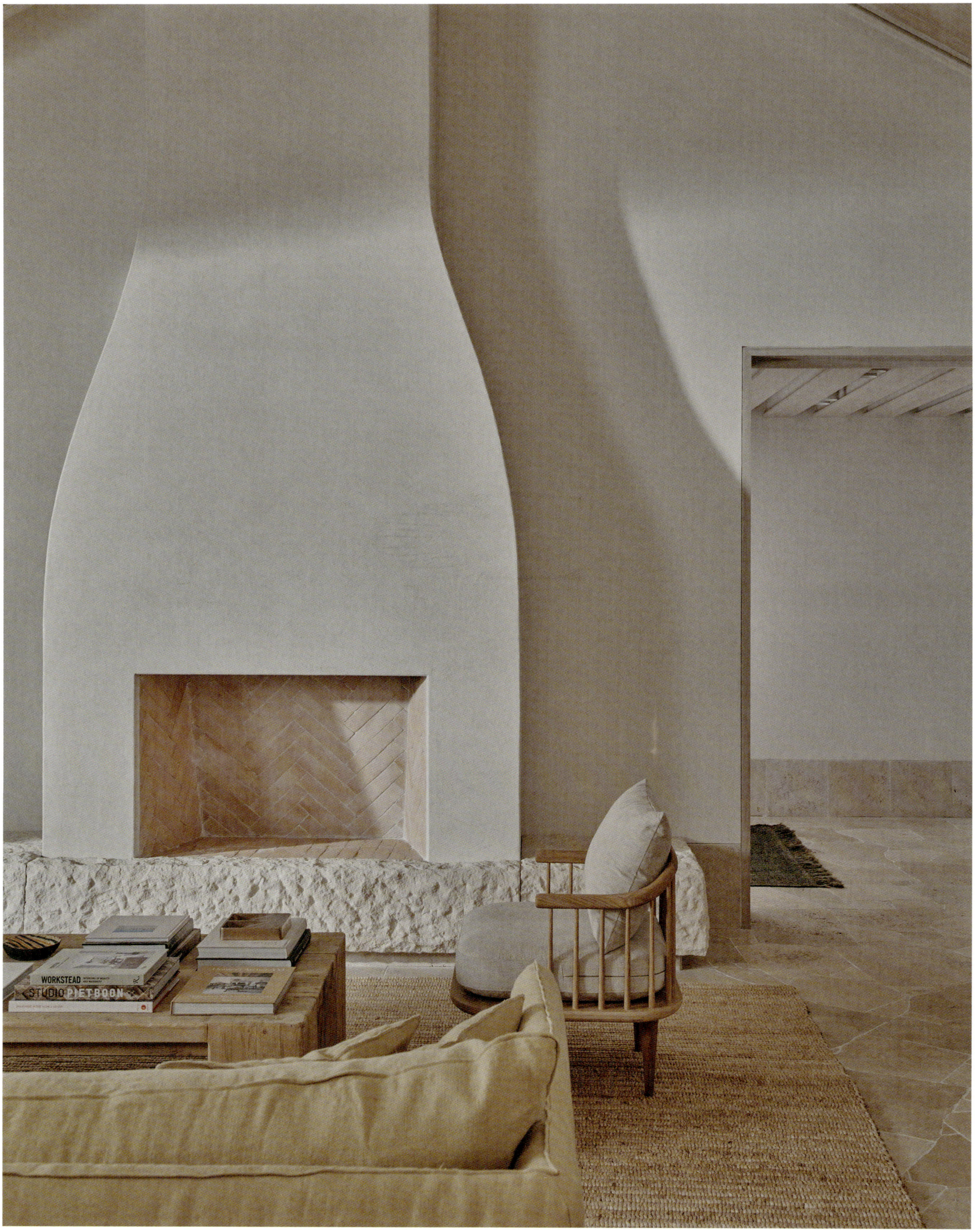
WORKSTEAD
STUDIO PIETBOON

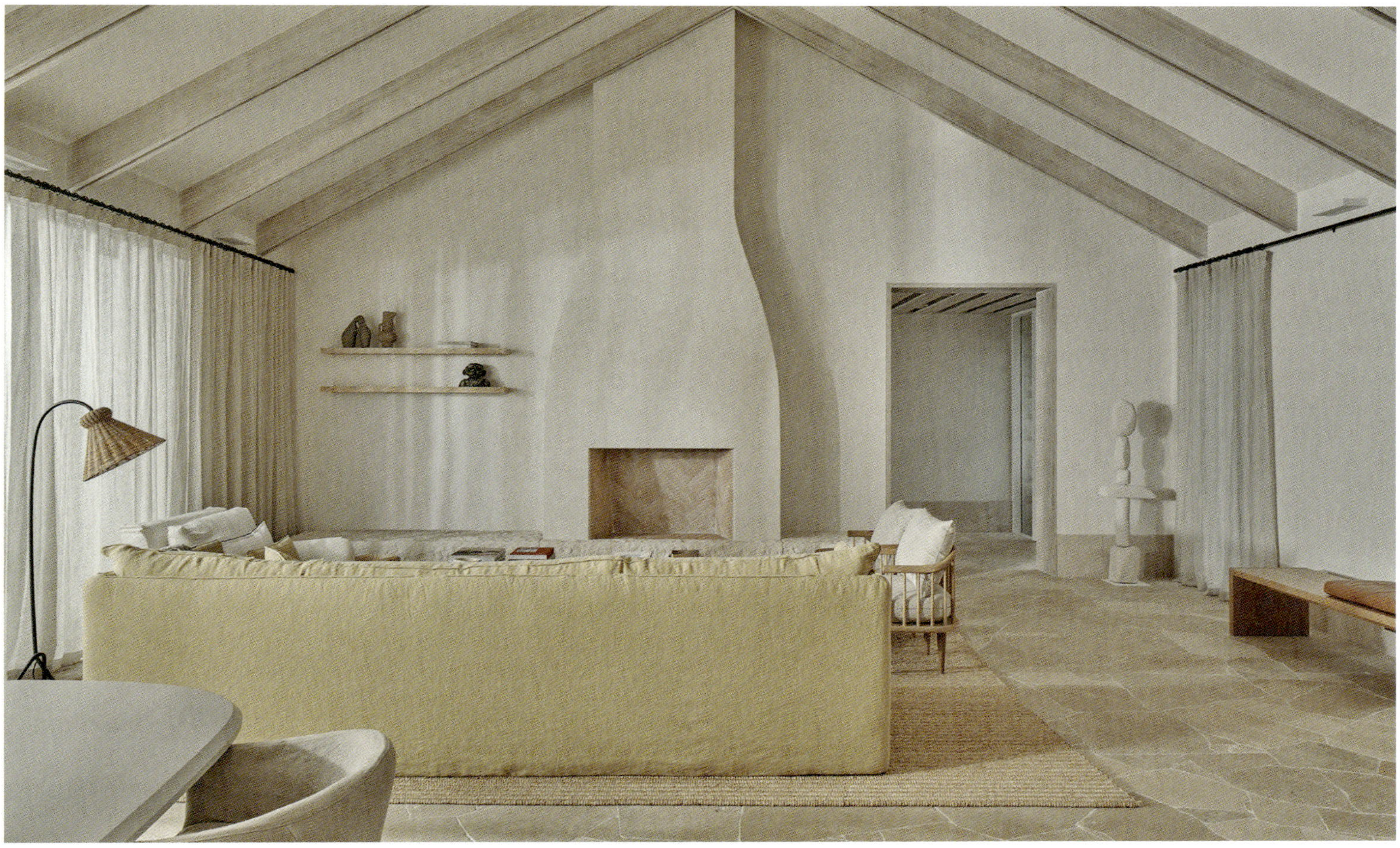

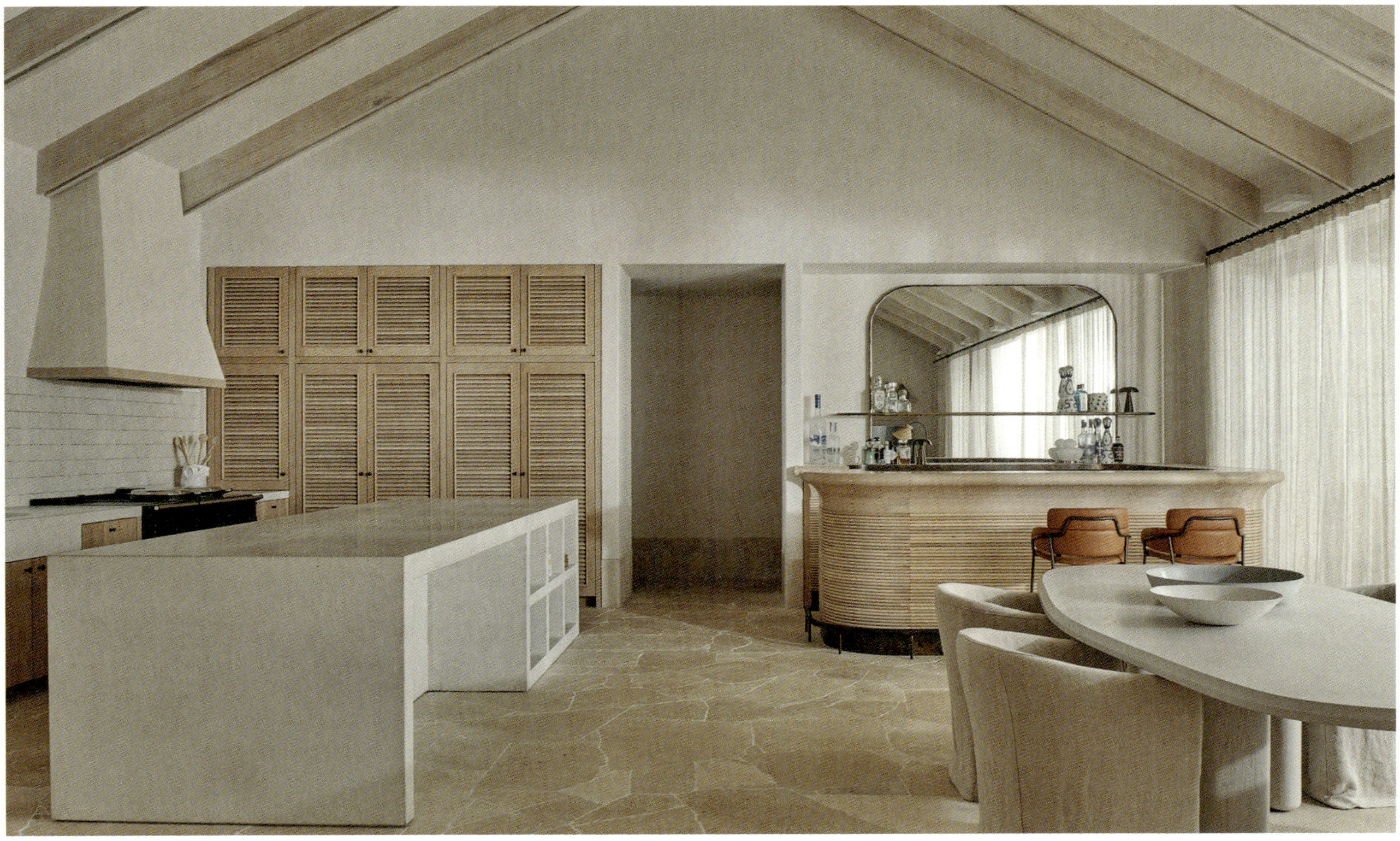

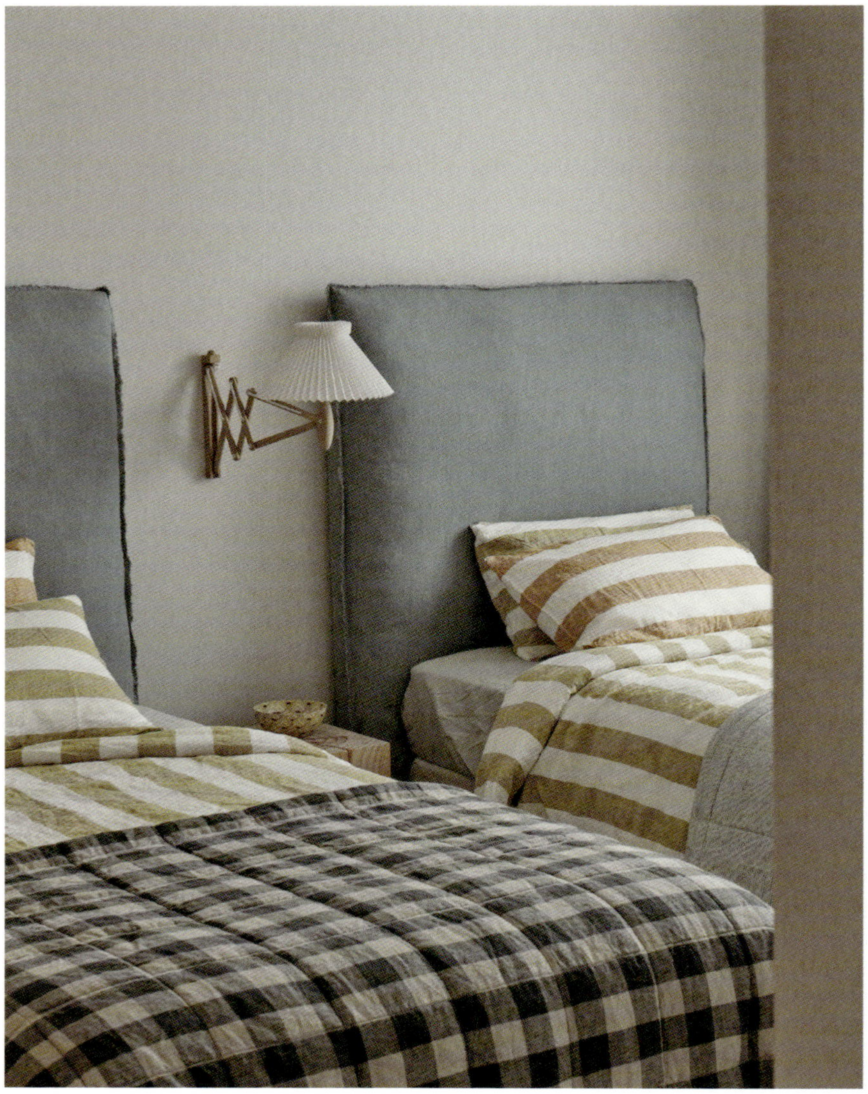

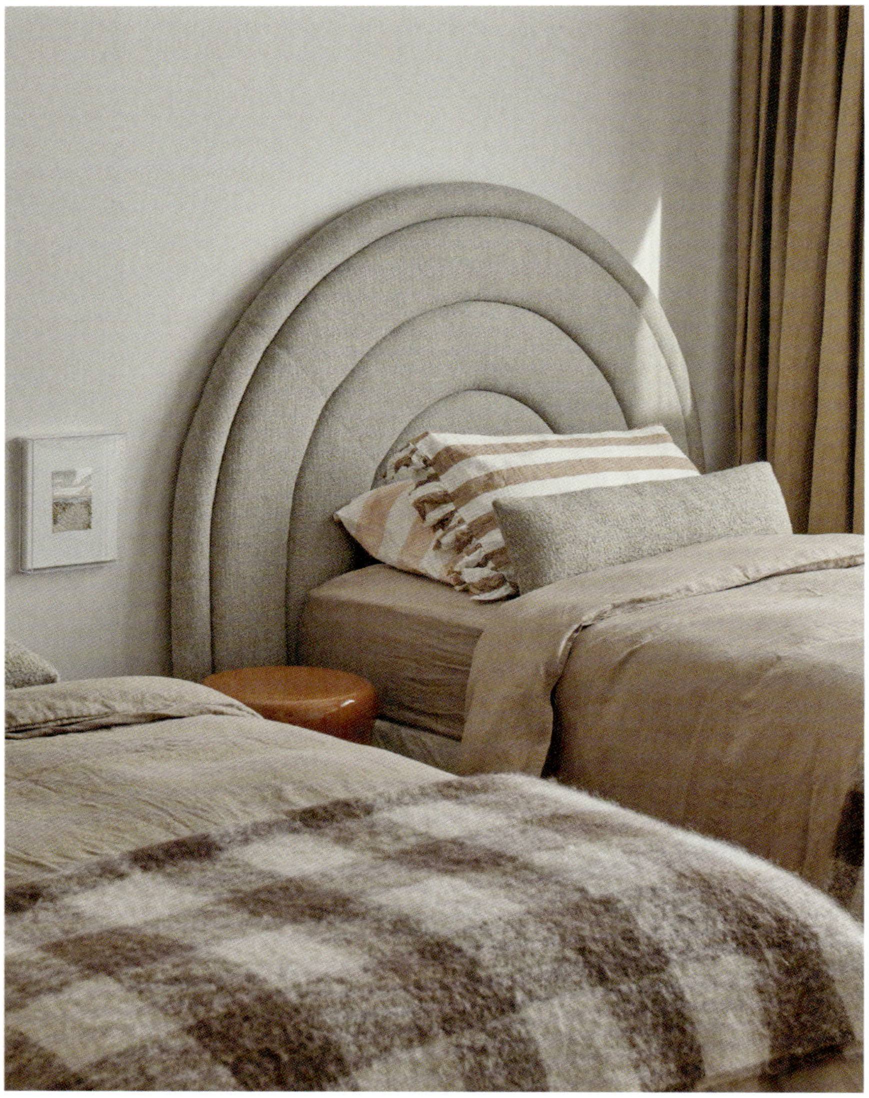

143

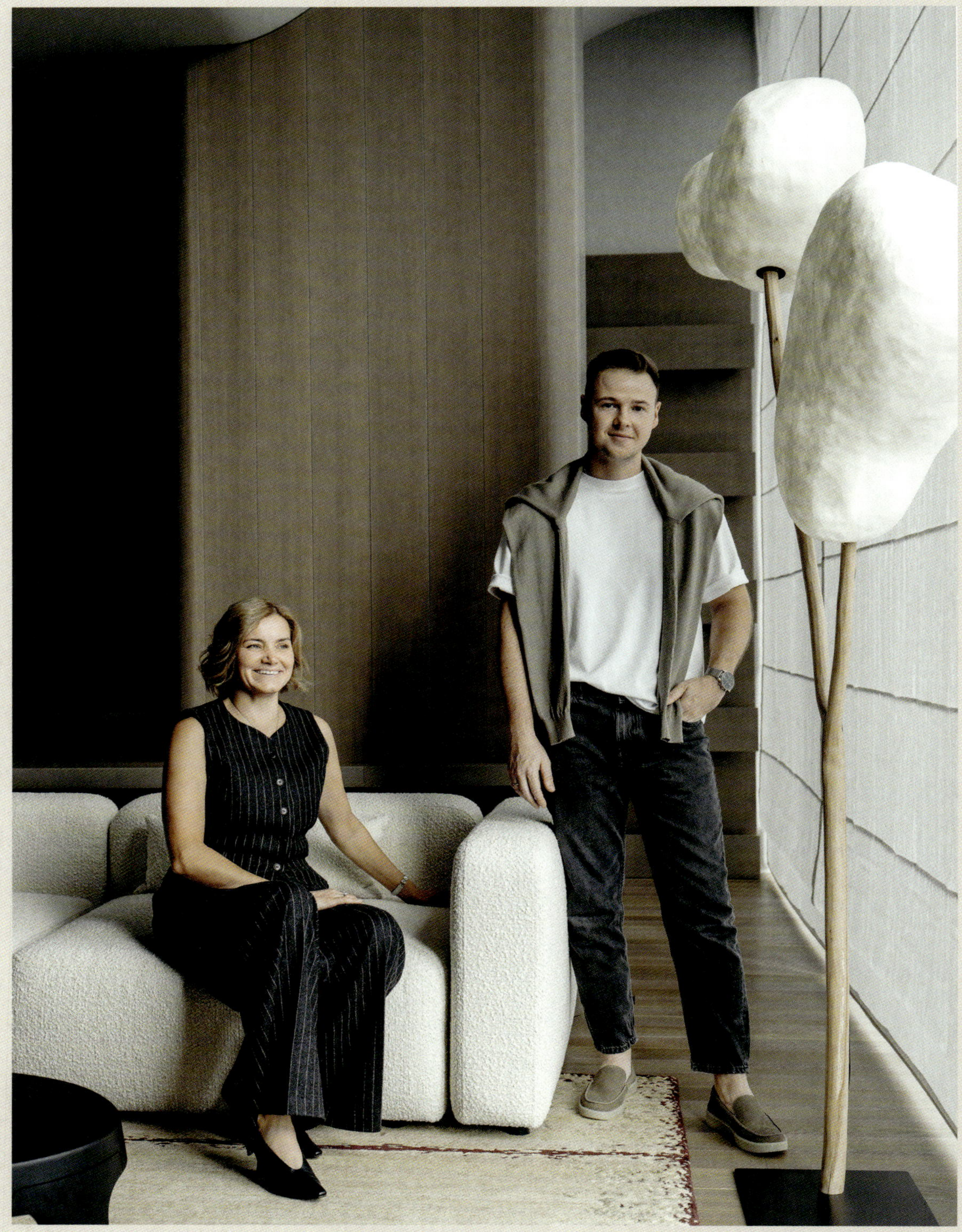

Aleksandr Orlov and Elena Semenova

The creative duo of Aleksandr Orlov and Elena Semenova was born during their studies at the Moscow "Details" School-Studio in 2018.

Elena is responsible for project implementation, international logistics and individual selection of art in galleries around the world.

Aleksandr develops the conceptual basis and main idea of the project, its graphic presentation and semantic content of objects, as well as the development of unique items.

Every project starts with a concept. To experience the complete narrative of the project, research is necessary: studying the culture of the place, history, and characteristic facts.

In the future, these features will help in the search for shapes, their colors, textures and the choice of materials.

www.orlovsemenova.com

Photography: Mikhail Loskutov

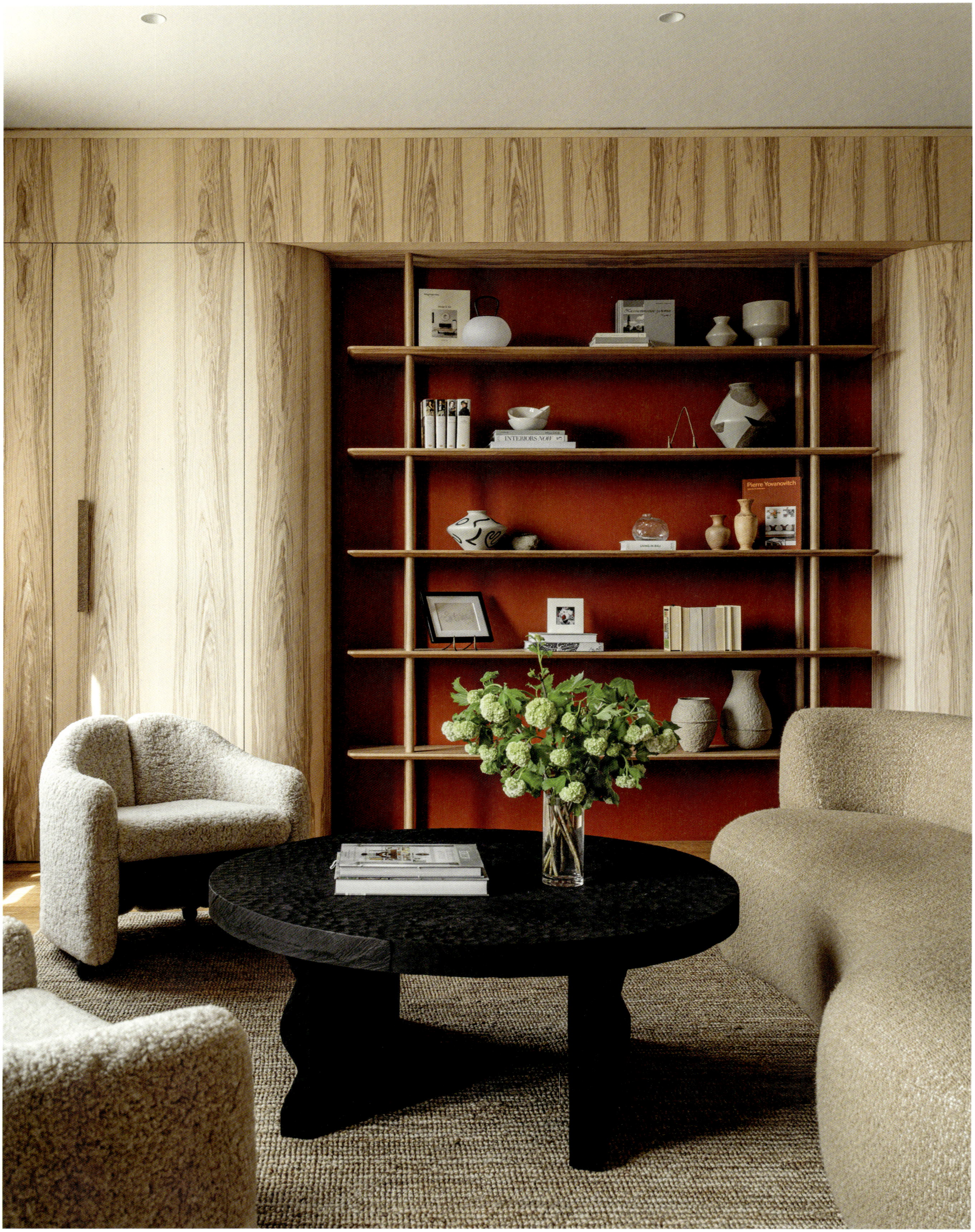
INTERIORS NOIR
Pierre Yovanovitch

The clients for this project present as a harmonious family unit composed of a married couple, their daughter, and an older son who lives independently but consistently congregates for family festivities.

Communication was primarily established with the clients themselves, ensuring that all directives were thoughtfully considered. These clients exemplify a pragmatic approach to life, devoid of excesses, with a keen comprehension that each element within their home should bear purpose and significance according to their unique perspectives. Additionally, they display vested interests in vigorous sports, regular travel, and curating a collection of icons housed within their country dwelling, which dramatically inspired the concept of this project. Their specific requests comprised a range of items from lesser-known or even indistinctive manufacturers.

They demonstrated a penchant for custom-made pieces based on the exclusive designs by Aleksandr and Elena. There was also a notable inclination towards the works by select French artisans, including Pierre Yovanovitch and Christophe Delcourt. Their prioritized desires entailed a capacious living room equipped with an ample table for engaging in board games, and unobstructed frameless windows to maintain an open vista of the exterior surroundings.

The residential location in question is nested in a contemporary building within the residential complex, "Heart of the Capital," favorably situated on the banks of the Moscow River. This apartment was specifically chosen due to its exceptional river views and enchanting sunsets. Moreover, the property boasts a corner layout, augmented ceilings, and substantial windows, thereby saturating the apartment with considerable light. Special value was placed on the picturesque sunrises and sunsets.

The unity of the two apartments was created via a concealed conduit traversing the facade of the kitchen on one side and the closet on the other. Nevertheless, the apartment displayed limitations, primarily the curved layout of the living room. To mitigate this challenge, the designers tactfully deployed a Christophe Delcourt sofa.

Due to the curvilinear and angled nature of the apartment, the layout resolution was not immediately apparent. The definitive strategy comprised positioning Delcourt's substantial sofa in alignment with the living room windows. The decor utilizes a bespoke method of accumulating distinctive items from a diverse palette of styles and epochs into a cohesive composition. The furniture for the project was sourced through Booroom Gallery, 1stdibs, coupled with designer pieces by Delcourt and Yovanovitch, carefully selected by Aleksandr Orlov and Elena Semenova. The aesthetic color palette drew inspiration from the Trinity icon by Andrei Rublev, resulting in an interior predominantly characterized by blue, red, and yellow hues.

The clients bestowed complete trust in Aleksandr and Elena, even bringing several vintage items in suitcases upon their request. Consequently, Aleksandr Orlov and Elena Semenova take immense pride in the curated selection of unique furniture pieces widely regarded as distinctive within the context of Russia.

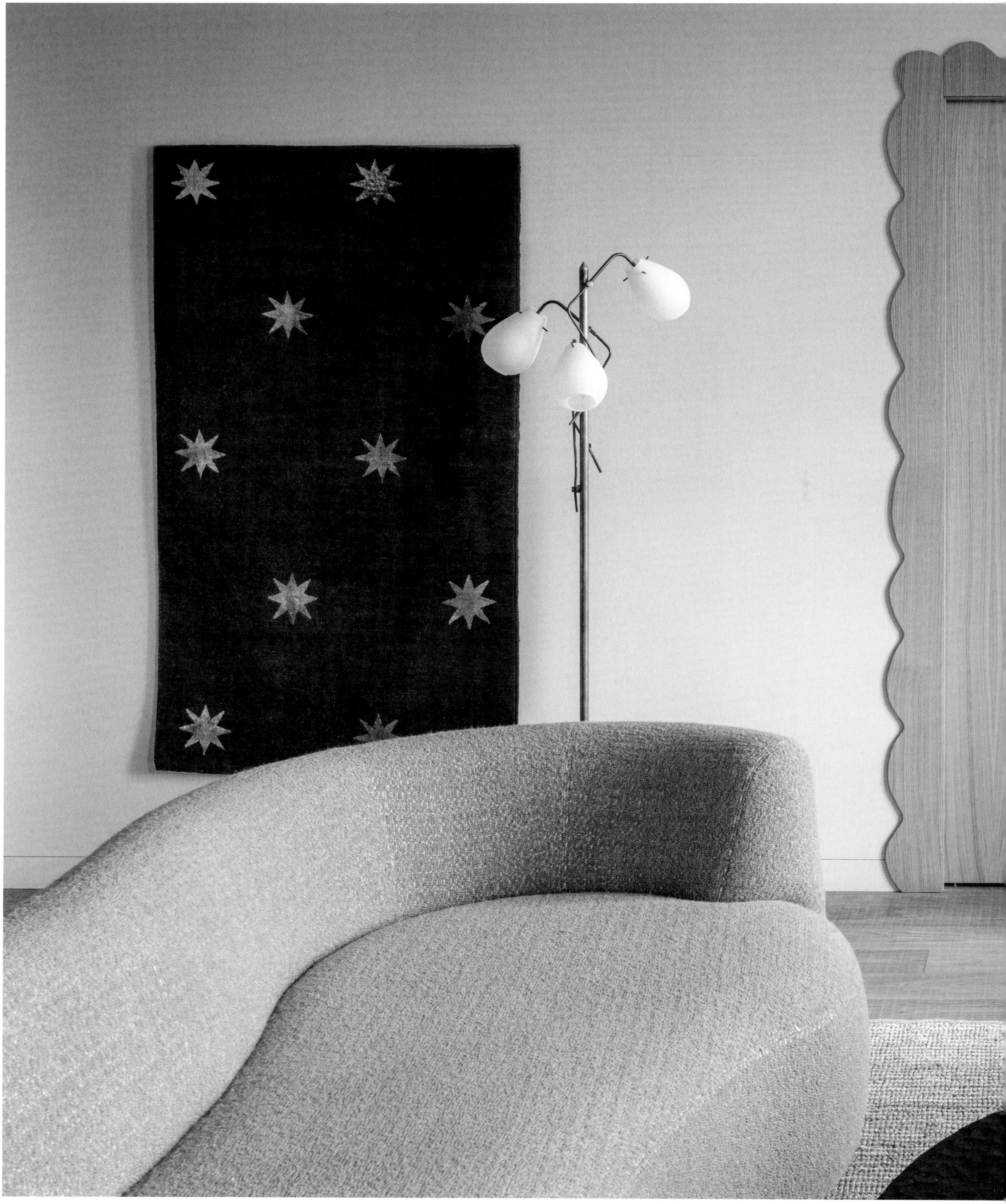

149

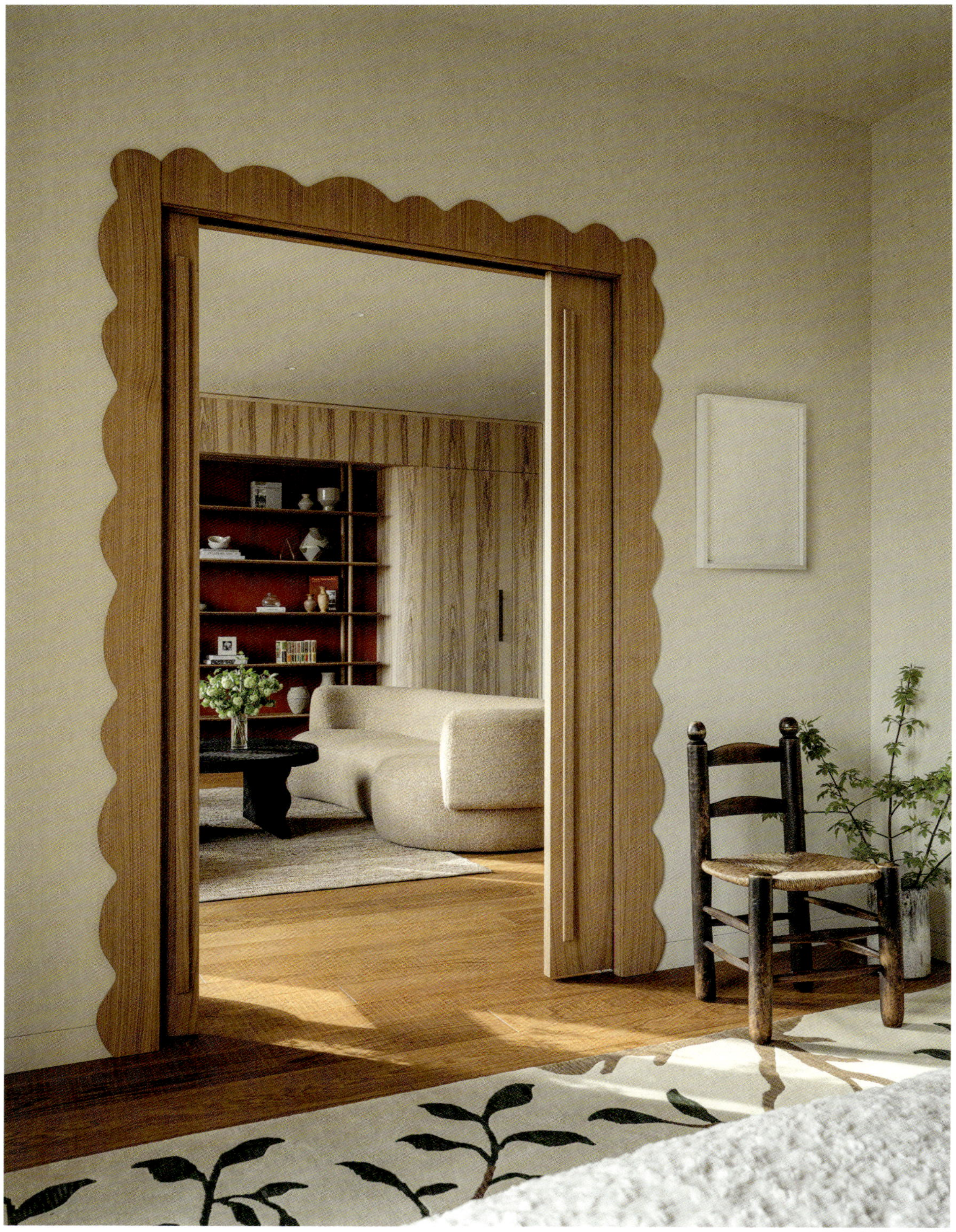

151

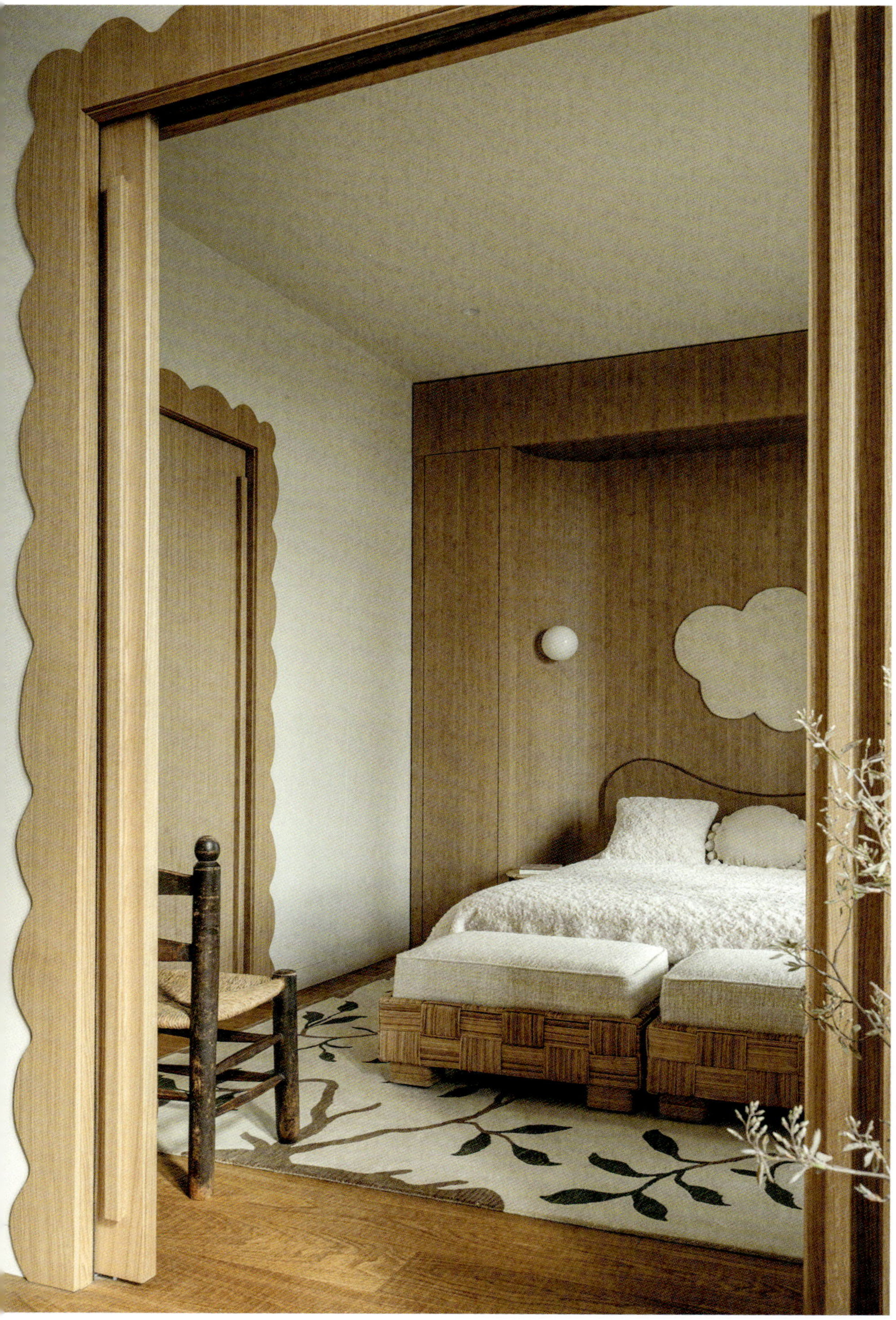
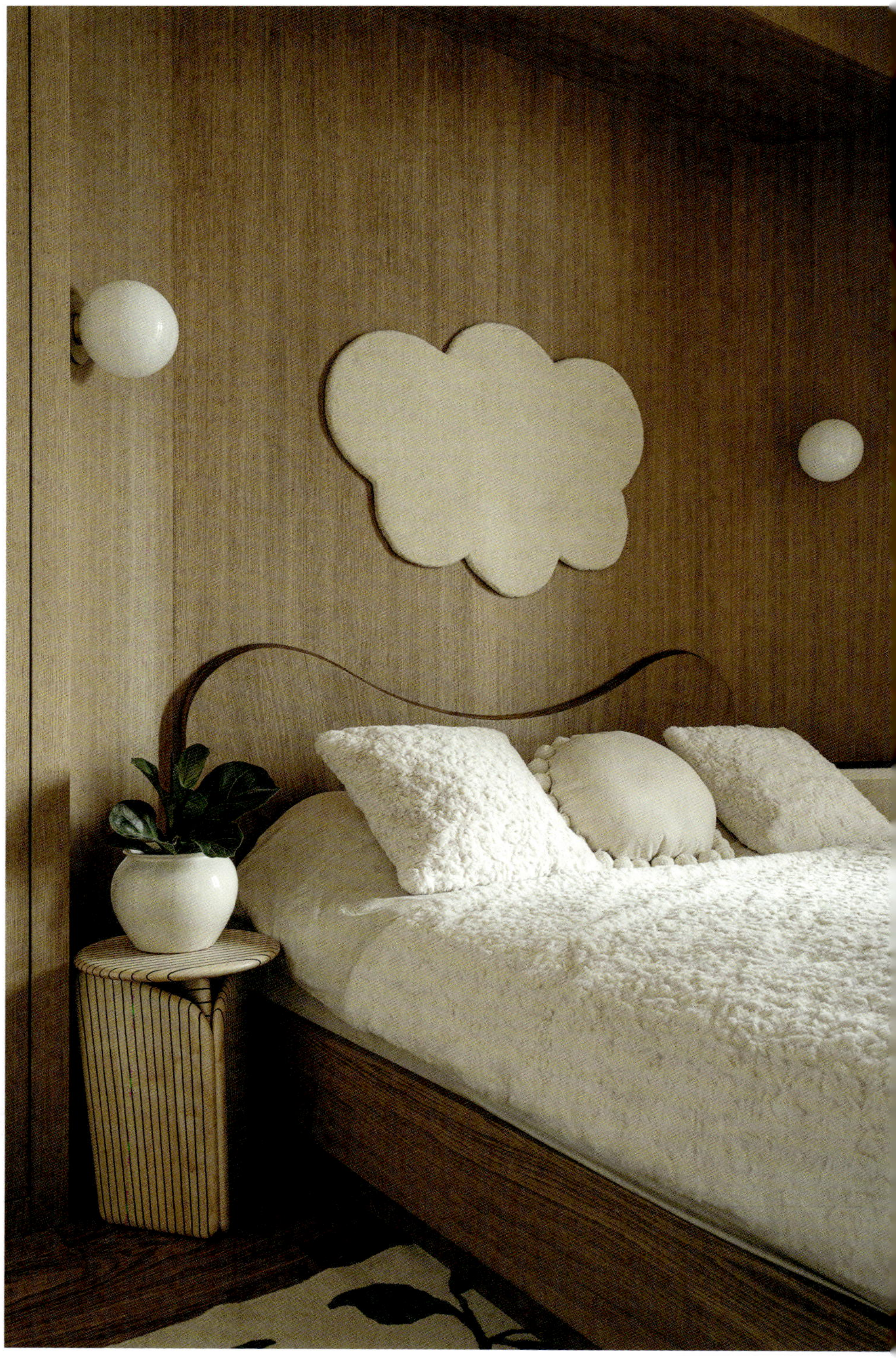

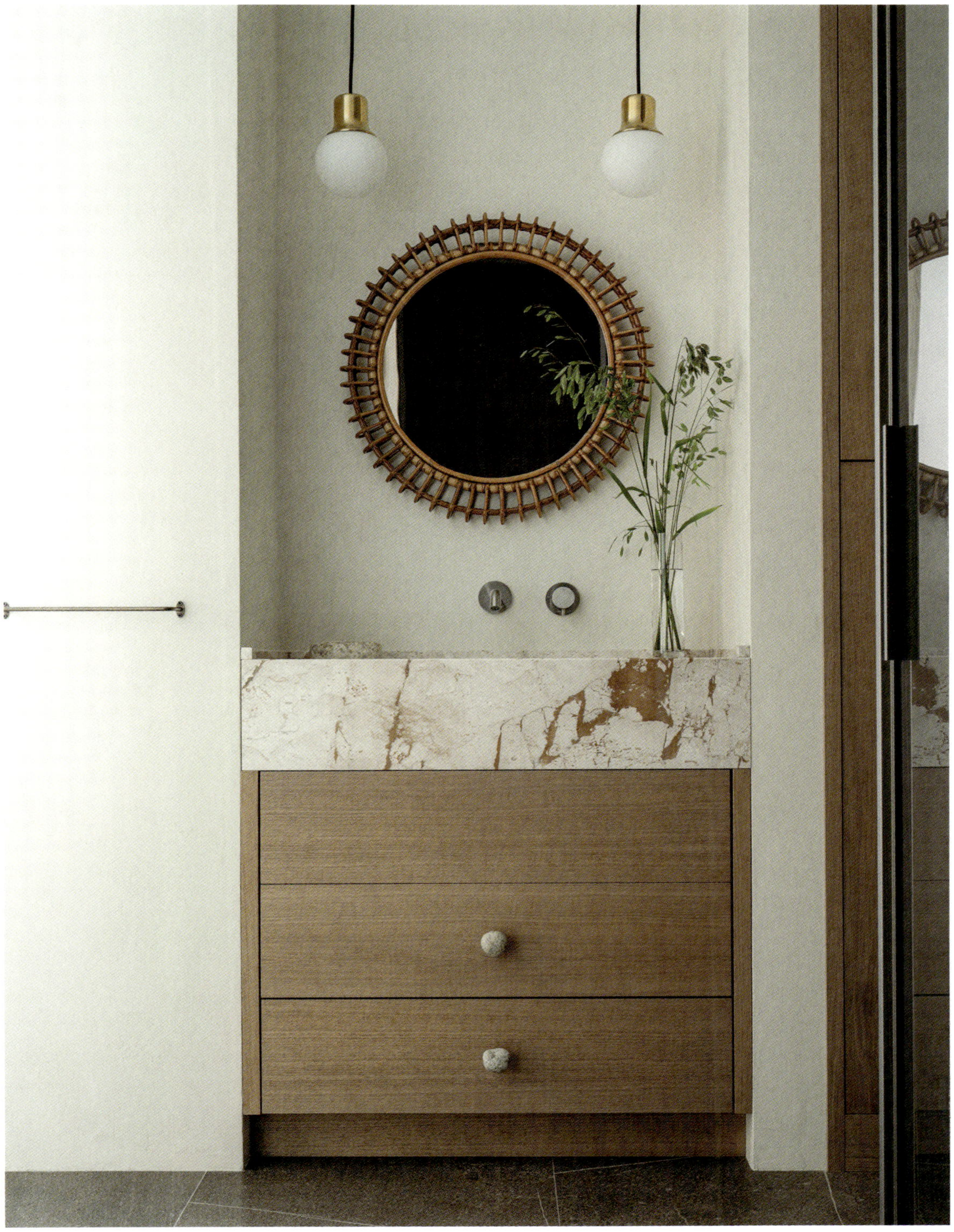

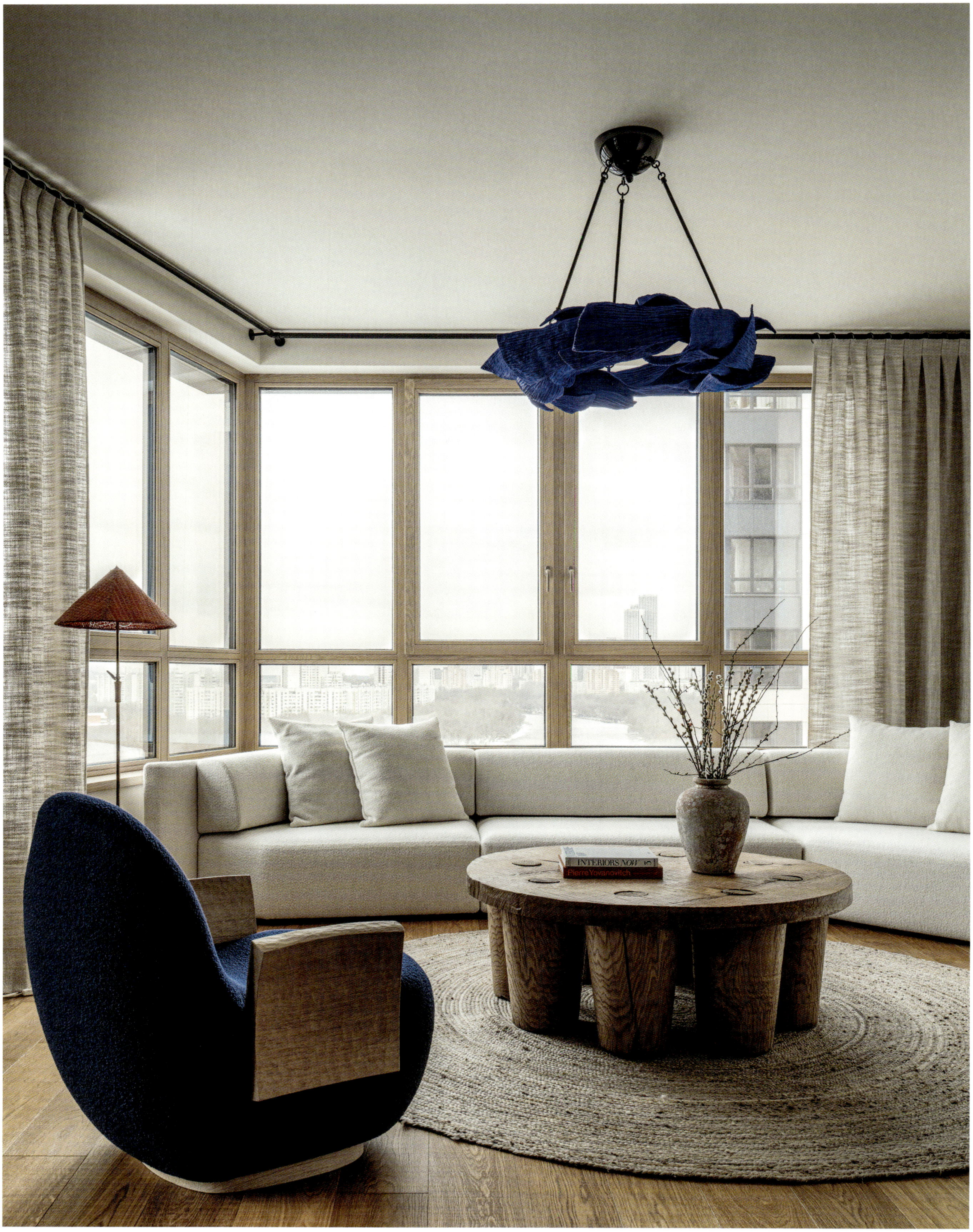
INTERIORS NOW
Pierre Yovanovitch

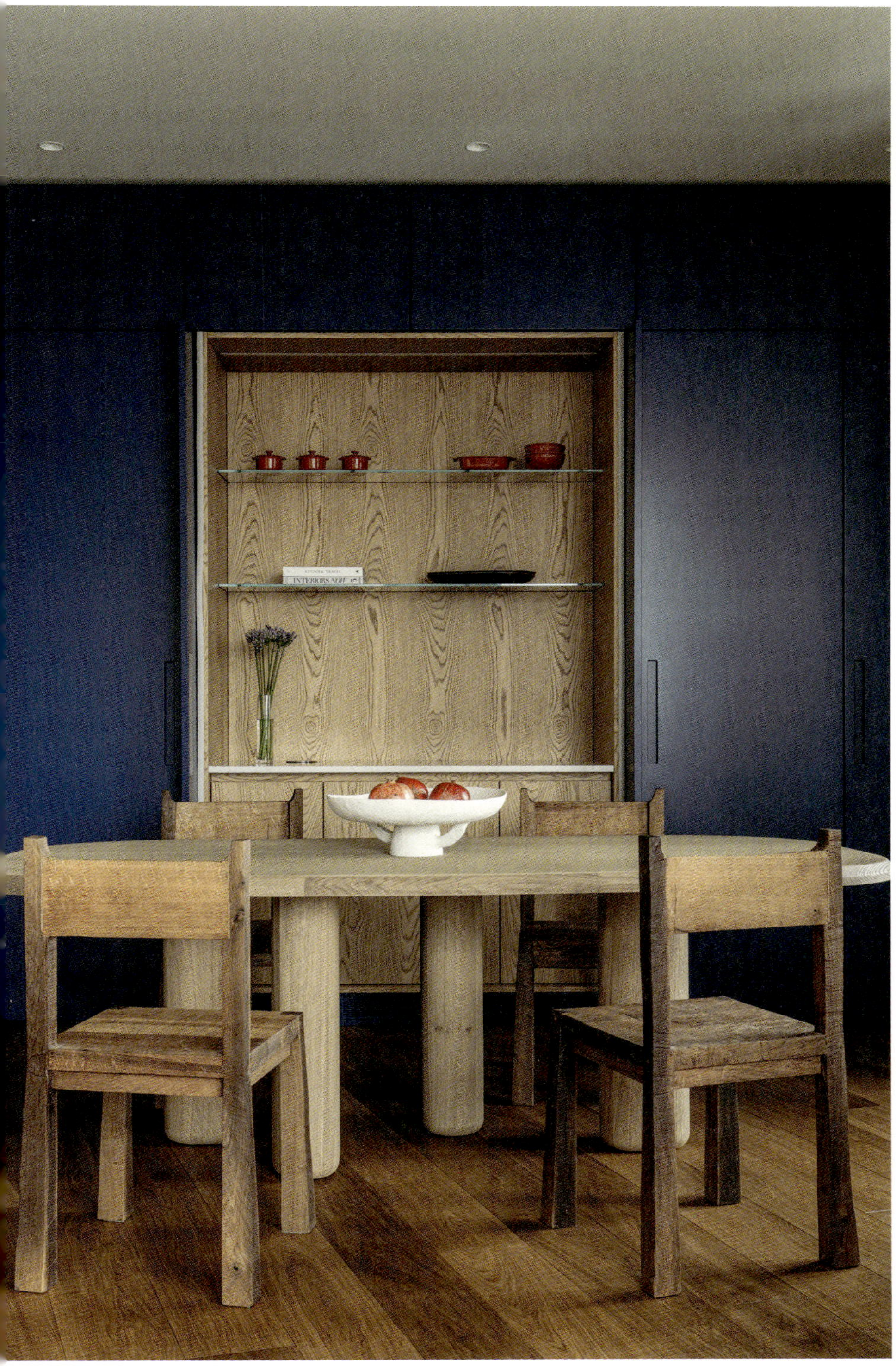

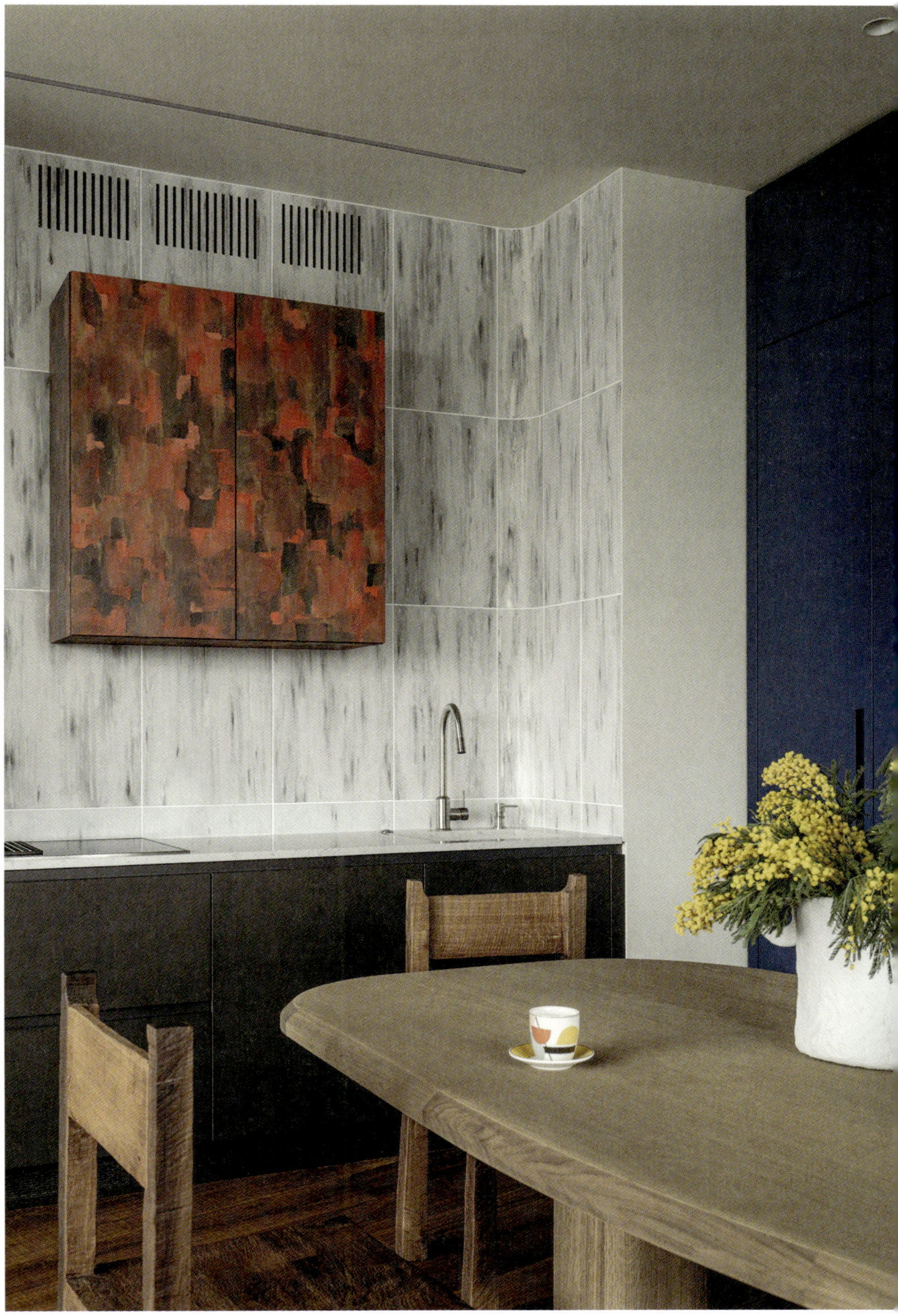

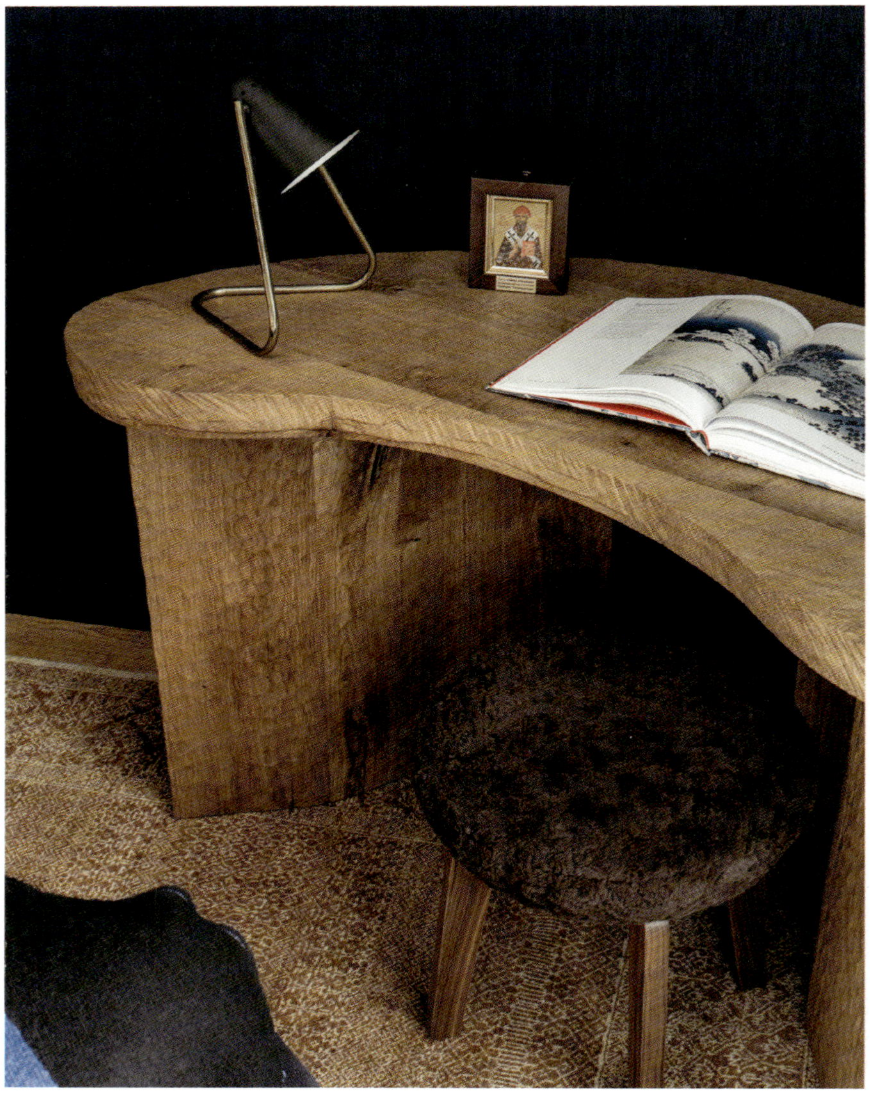

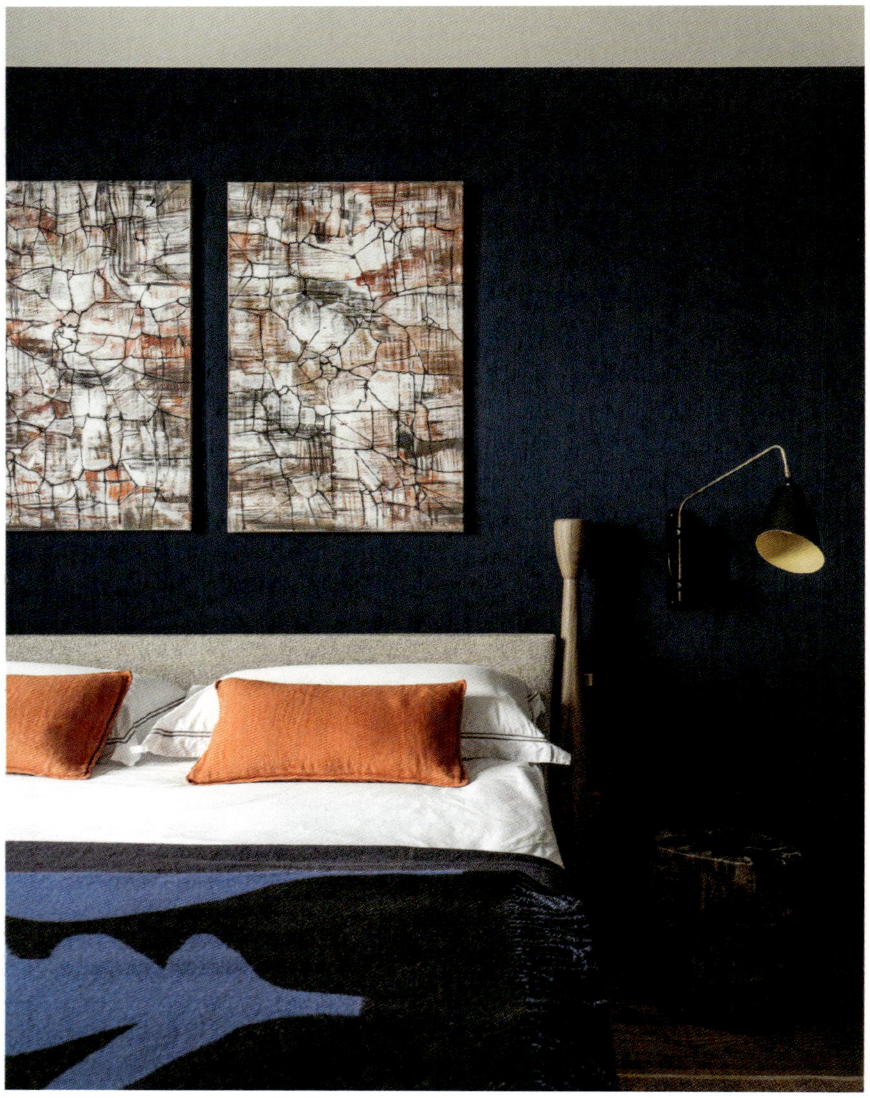

157

Portrait by Piet-Albert Goethals

Pauline Vanthournout

The love for art and architecture is in the DNA of the Vanthournout family and the passion for interior design continues to flow through her veins.

She is a spontaneous, colorful, energetic person full of crazy and innovative ideas. She defines a home as the reflection of the client's personality. By analyzing their wishes, she creates the projects whilst adding her own little twist. She is not afraid to use color, nor different materials. Her creations stand out and she always tries to look at things with a refreshing view, a different perspective … An innovative and contemporary style.

After her studies, Pauline ended up in Paris, where she worked at Chanel Image department. At Chanel she designed shops, pop-up stores and scenographies for traveling exhibitions.

After more than 10 amazing years working for Chanel and traveling around the world, Pauline decided to make a professional switch and she opened her own office in Belgium: PVIA Interior.

www.paulinevanthournout.com

Photography: Jan Verlinde

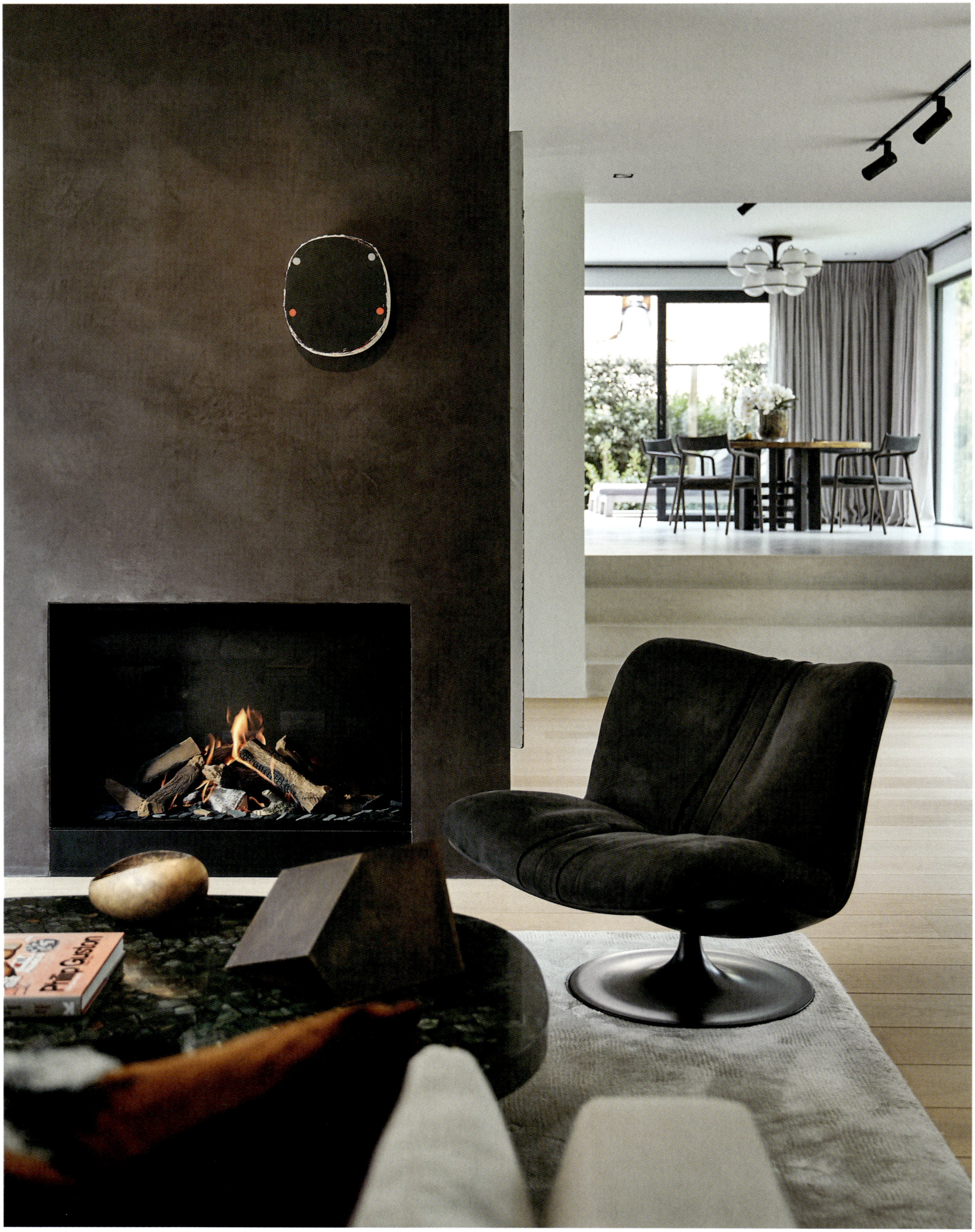
Philip Guston

In this publication, Pauline Vanthournout presents two of her most recent interior designs: villas in Knokke (pages 160 to 167) and Sint-Martens-Latem (pages 168 to 175).

On pages 160 to 167: for this villa in Le Zoute, Pauline worked closely with Maruani Mercier, gallery owners who represent major contemporary artists around the world. For Pauline Vanthournout, each project is unique and particularly interesting: you get to know so many different people, each with their own style. Pauline had the privilege of renovating and designing for this exceptional gallery owner. That of course means: a multitude of walls! So Pauline decided to close off some of the windows to provide additional space for art. Some of these walls have earthy tones, others remained white. Surprising furniture, incredible art, with a discreet yet striking design. Like, for example, the self-contained bench at the bookcase, a place for reflection on art, but also to give the space its finishing touch.

On pages 168 to 175: an amazing dynamic and very classic young family asked Pauline to create their everlasting home. She is always honored when clients entrust her with the design of their interiors, their own oasis of calm. This house has classic cottage architecture - a style that could not be neglected in its design. Pauline didn't feel like using the typical dark woods in an already classic home, so here she introduced the silver-gray vibe she really loves. Silver travertine, silver larch wood, libraries with silver leaf, stainless steel for all the details, silver rugs, gray silver lacquered upholstery… all the elements remain in the pantone range of those warm, unique shades of gray. The volumes in the house are just great, which has led to a very open interior, all spaces are somehow connected. A nice flow and fun way of living was the message of this project.

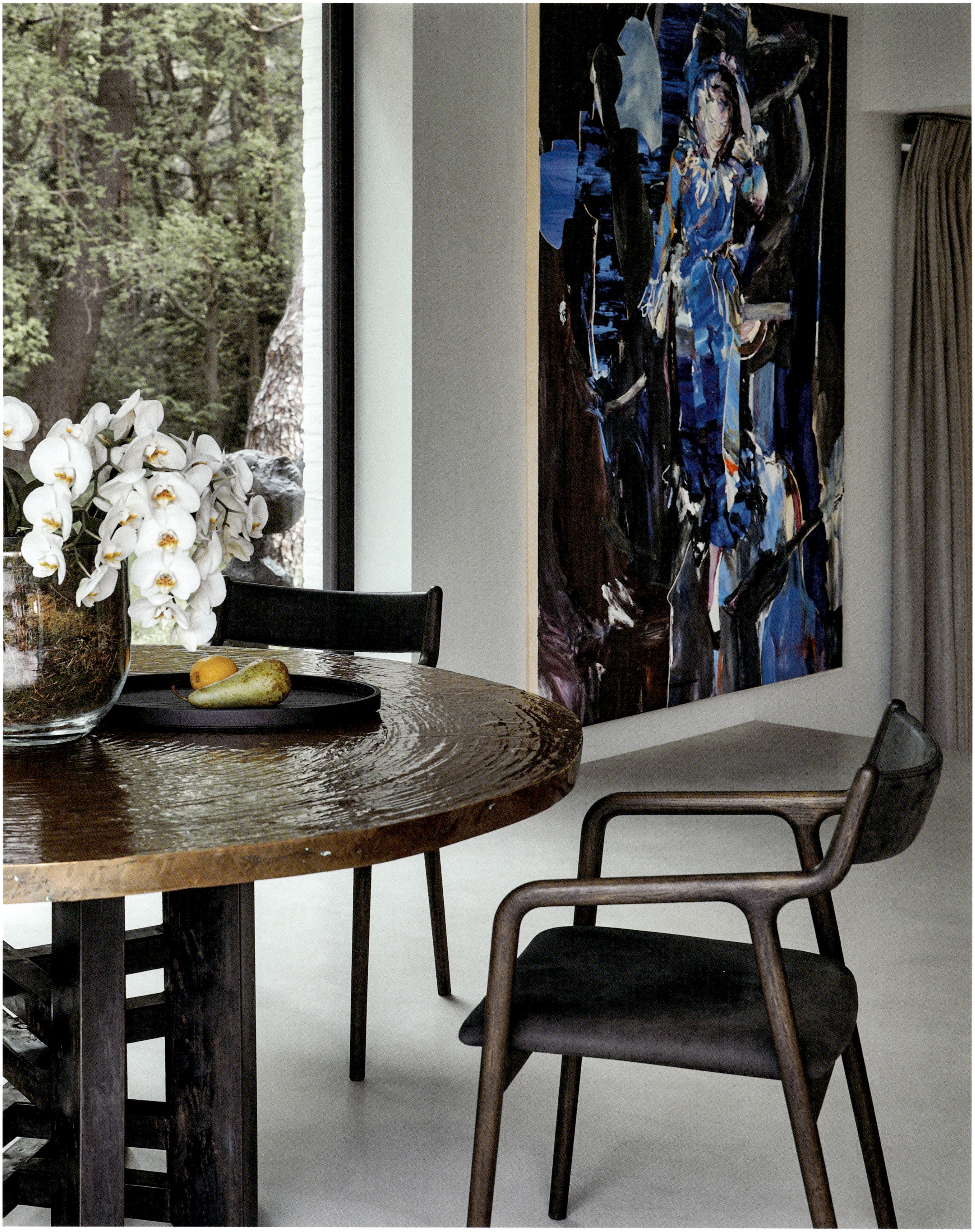

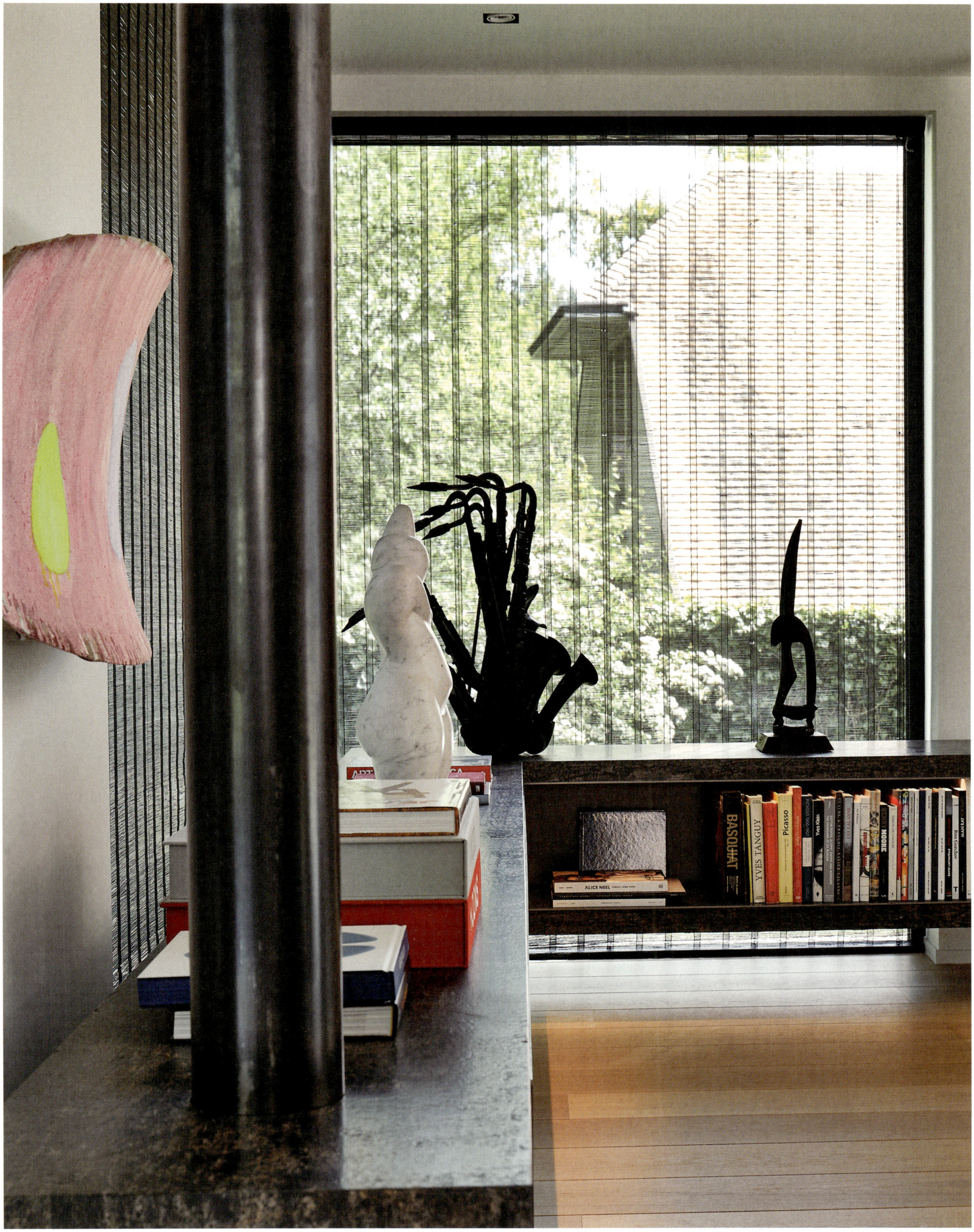
ALICE NEEL
BASQUIAT
YVES TANGUY
Picasso

WOOL
KOONS
Philip Guston
Philip Guston
A Life Spent Painting
Robert Storr

165

THE IMPOSSIBLE COLLECTION OF DESIGN
THE IMPOSSIBLE COLLECTION
JAMES TURRELL
PHOTOGRAPHS

167

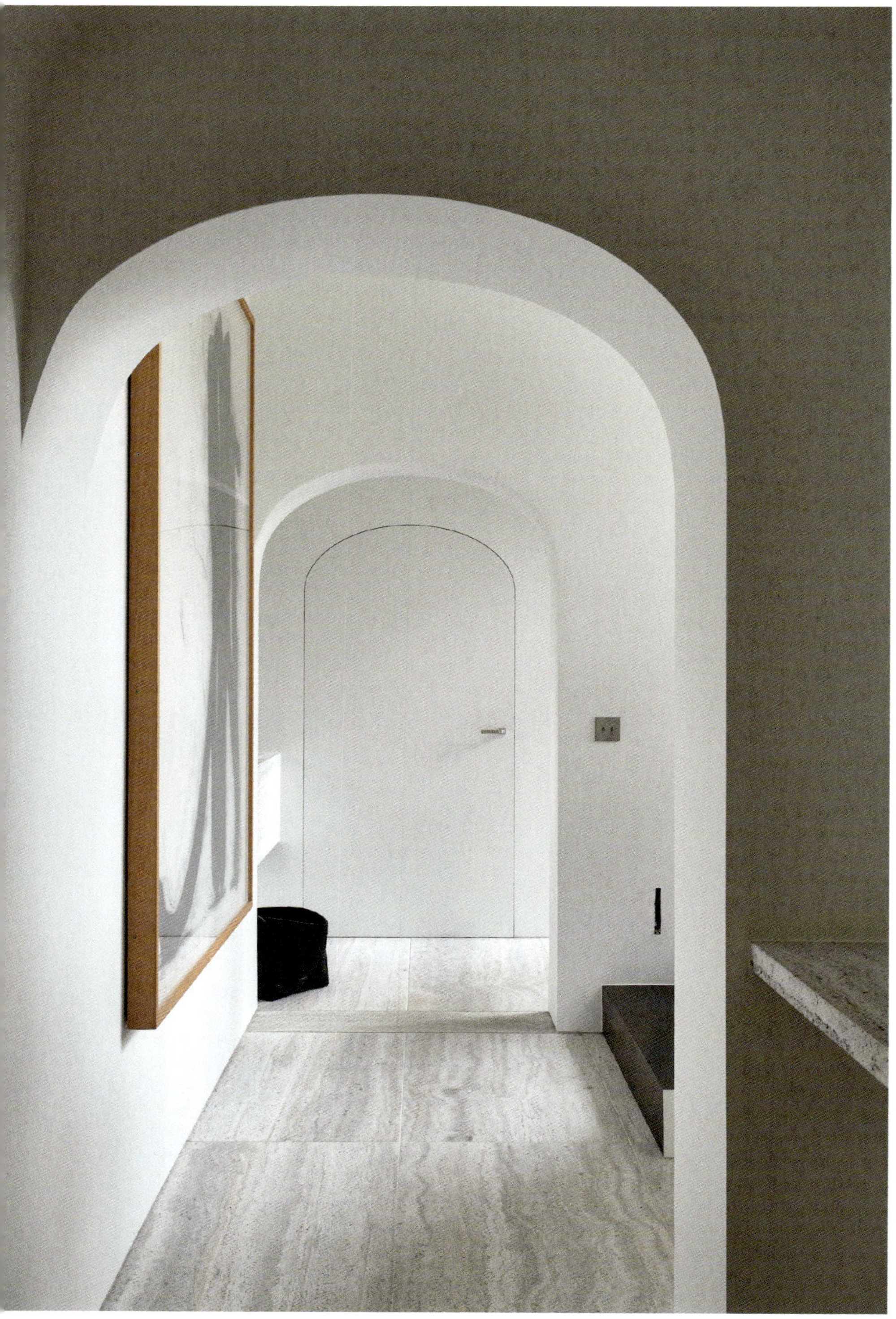

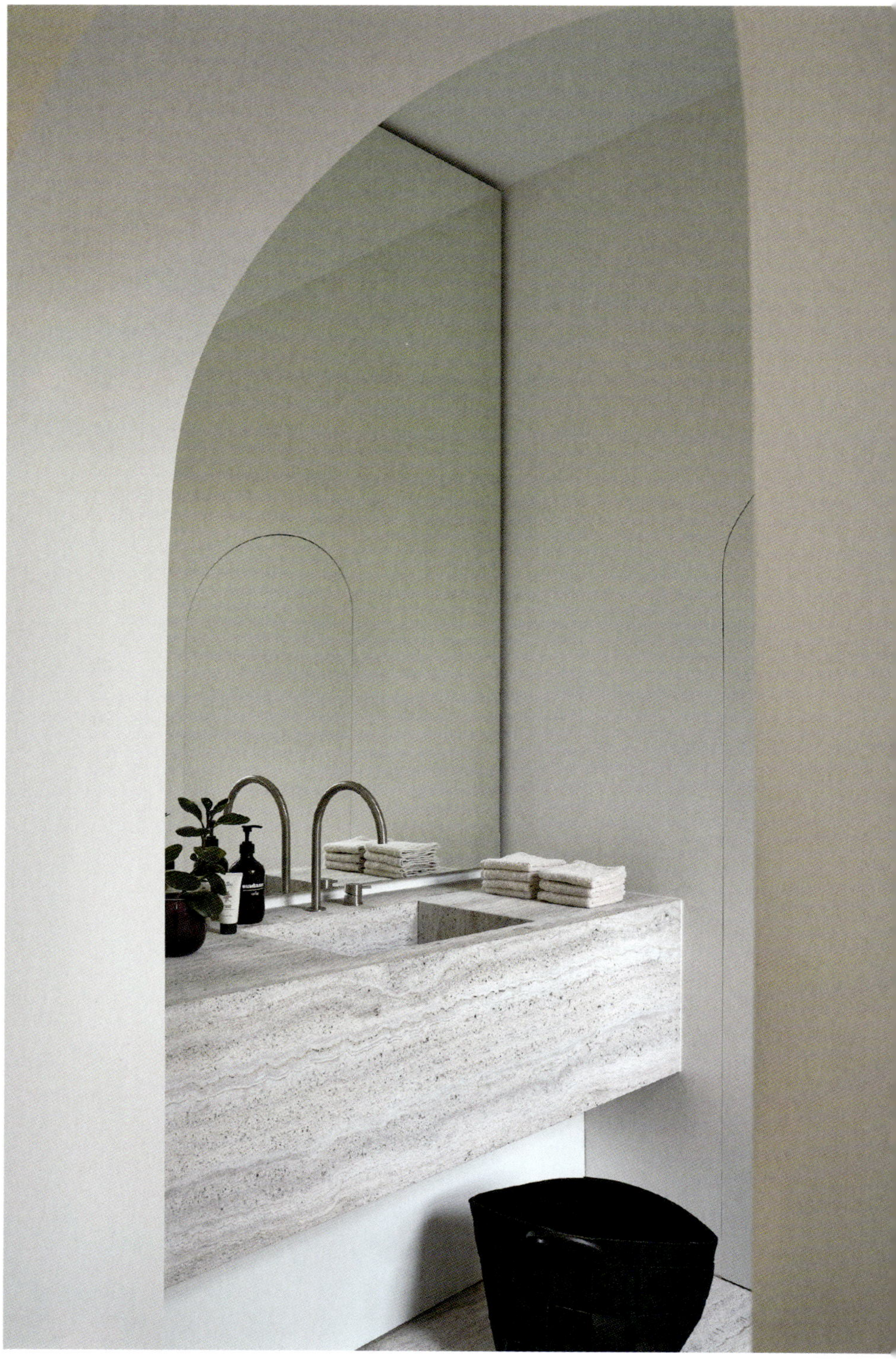

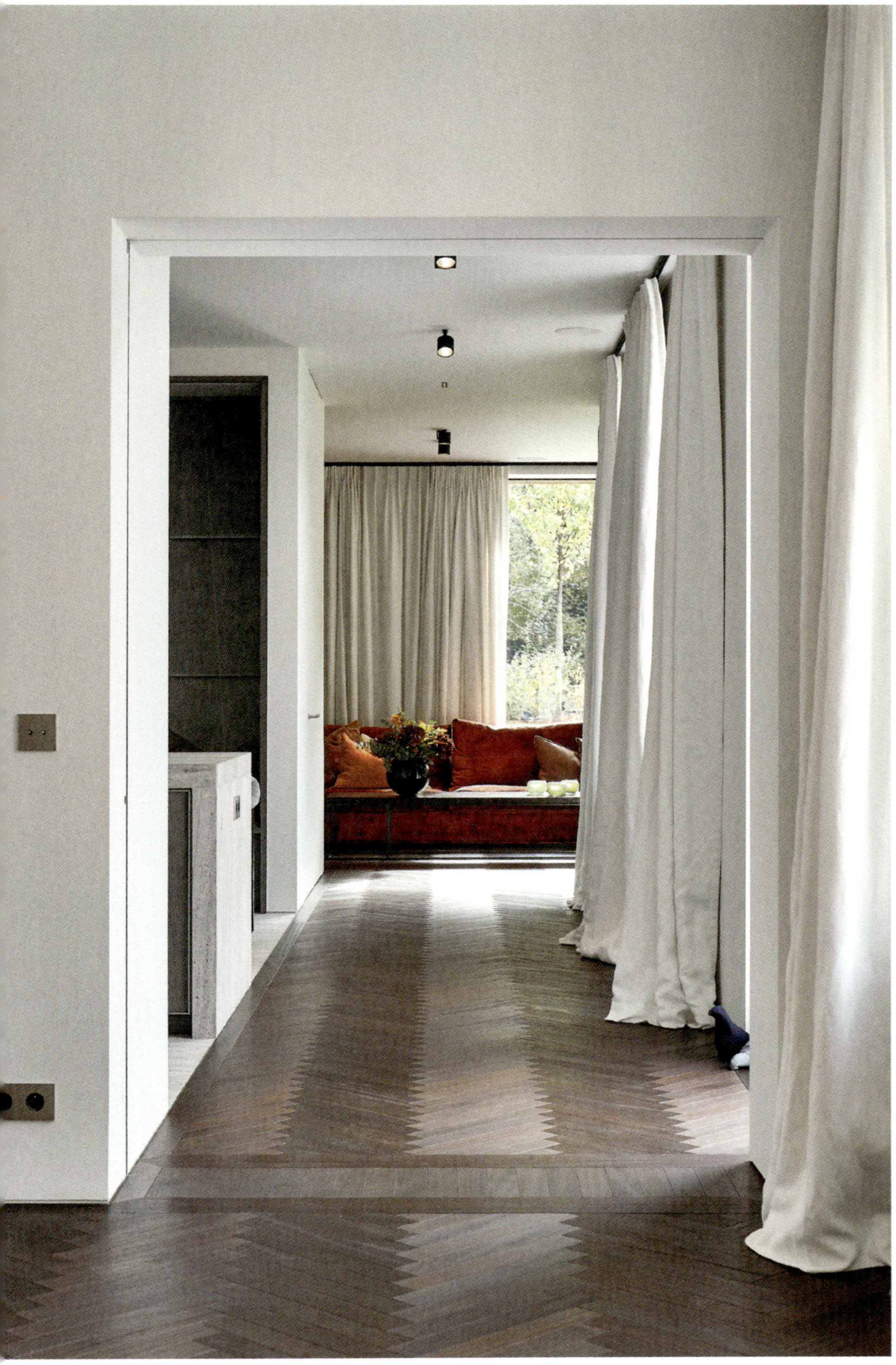

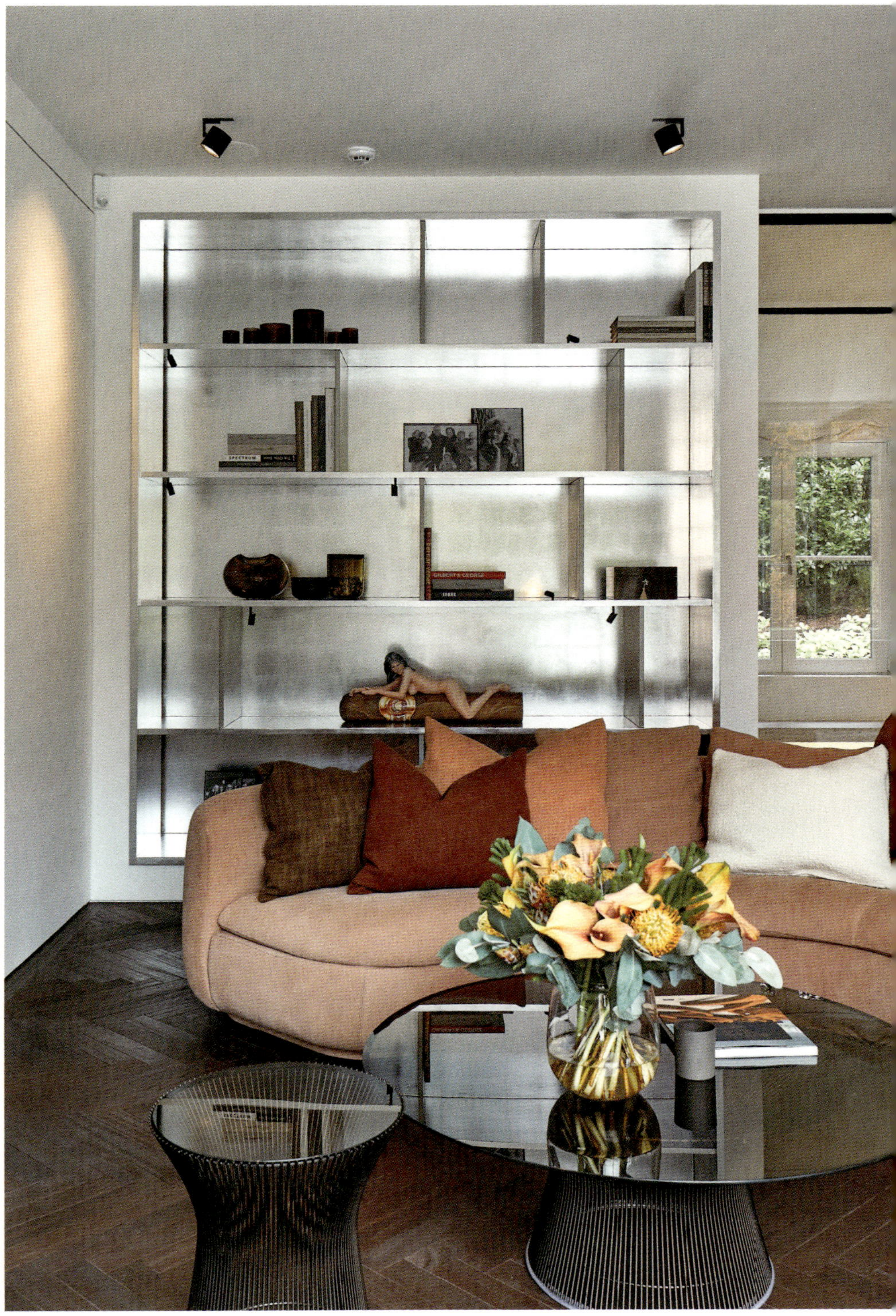

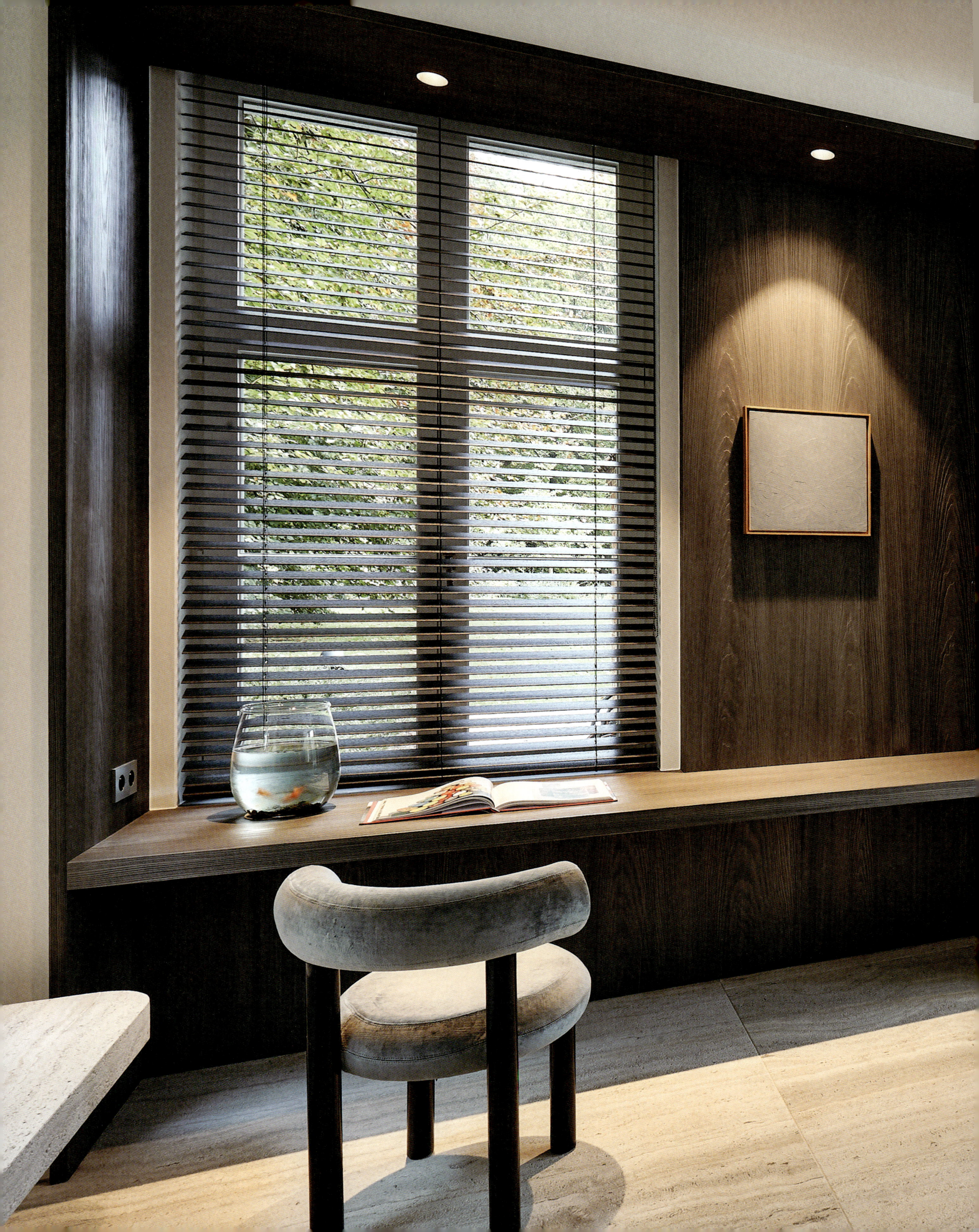

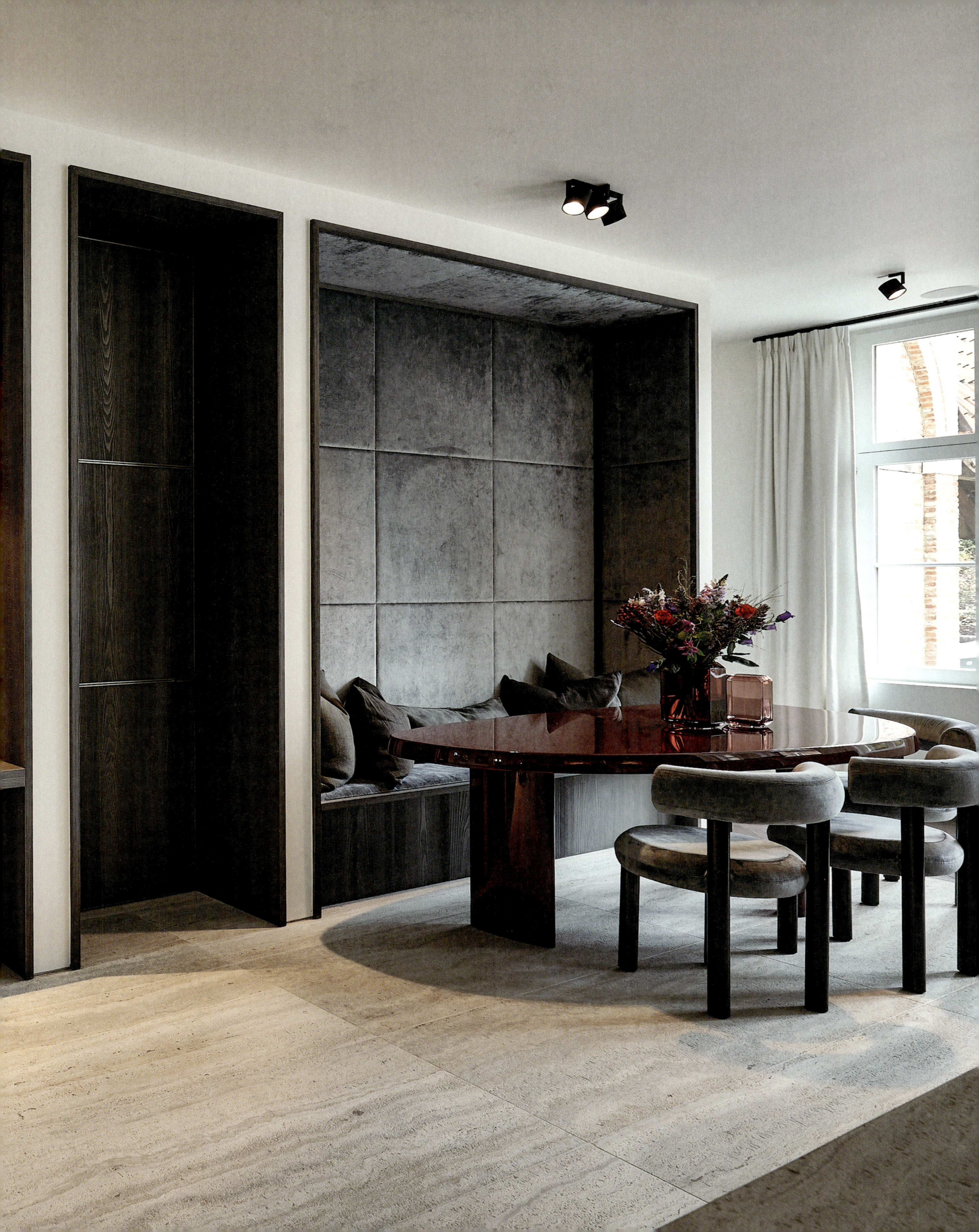

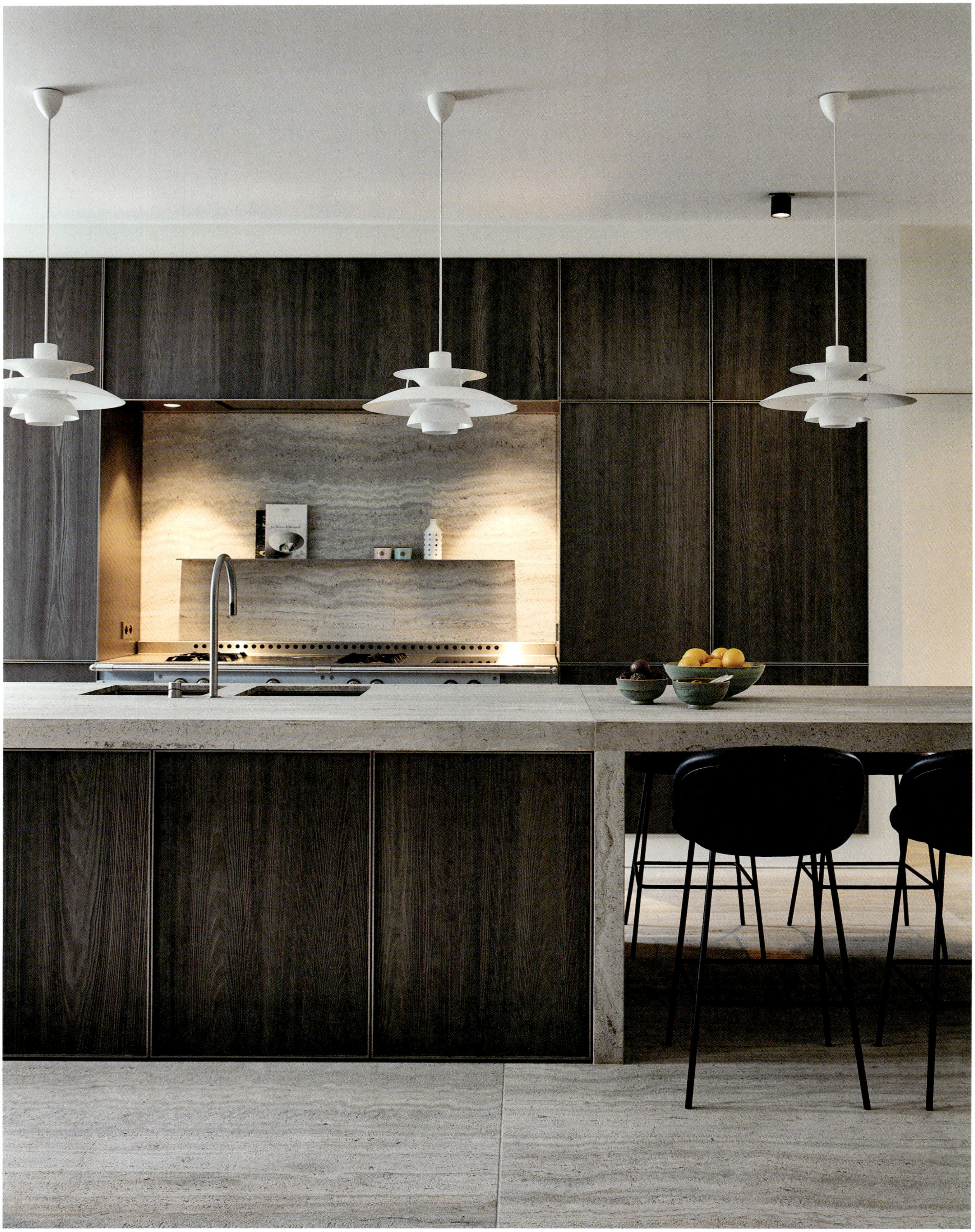

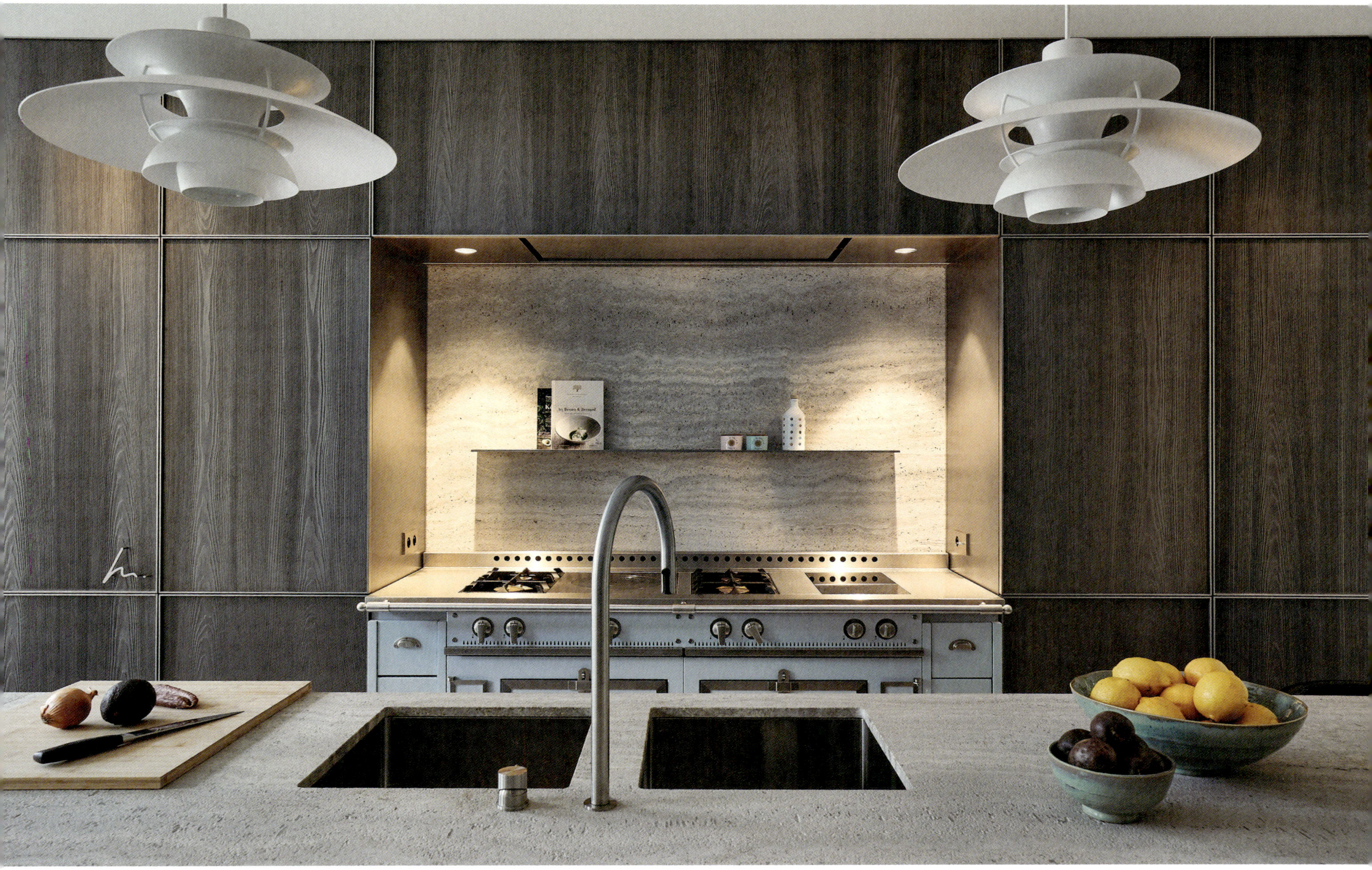

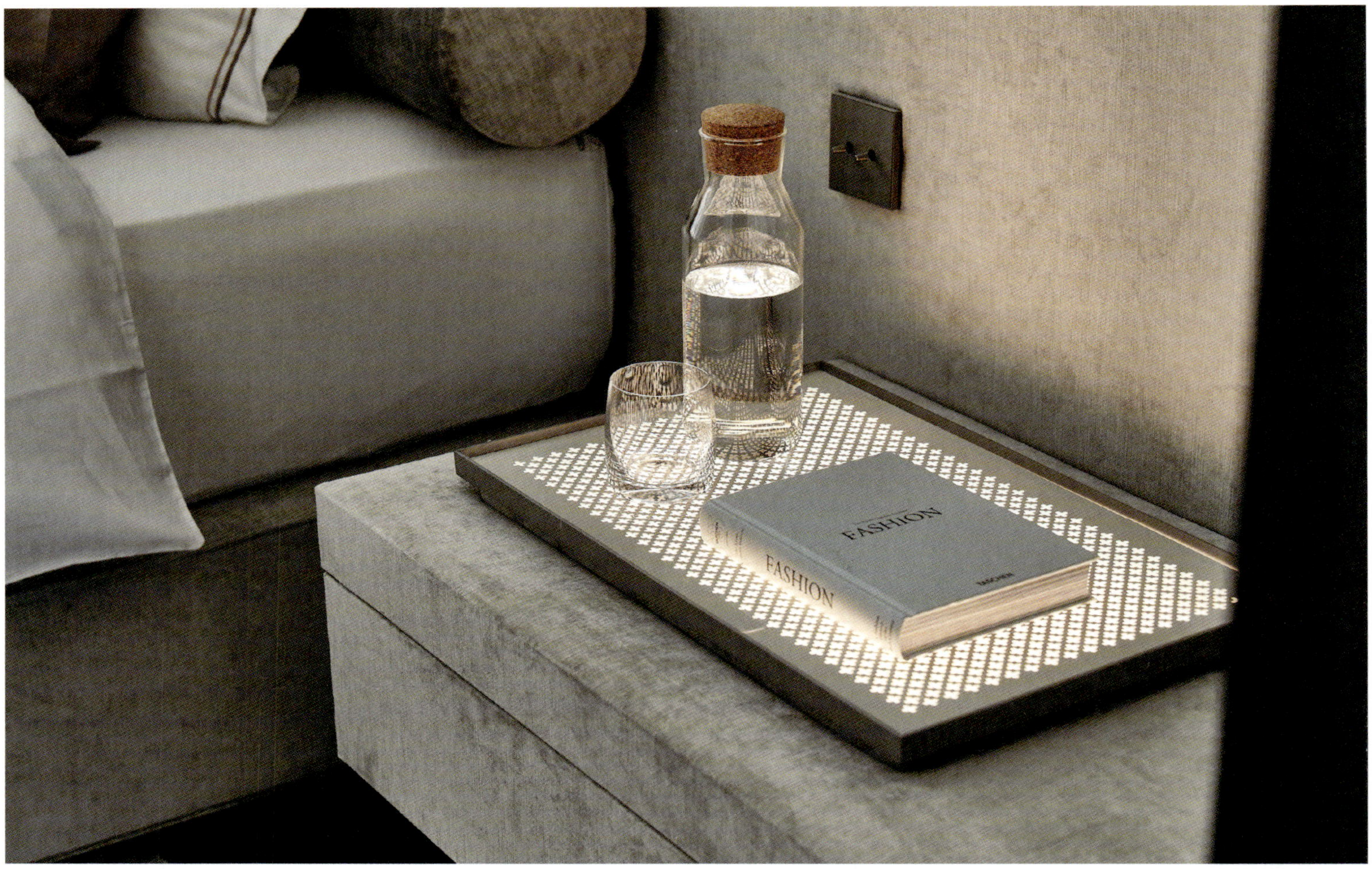
FASHION
TASCHEN
FASHION

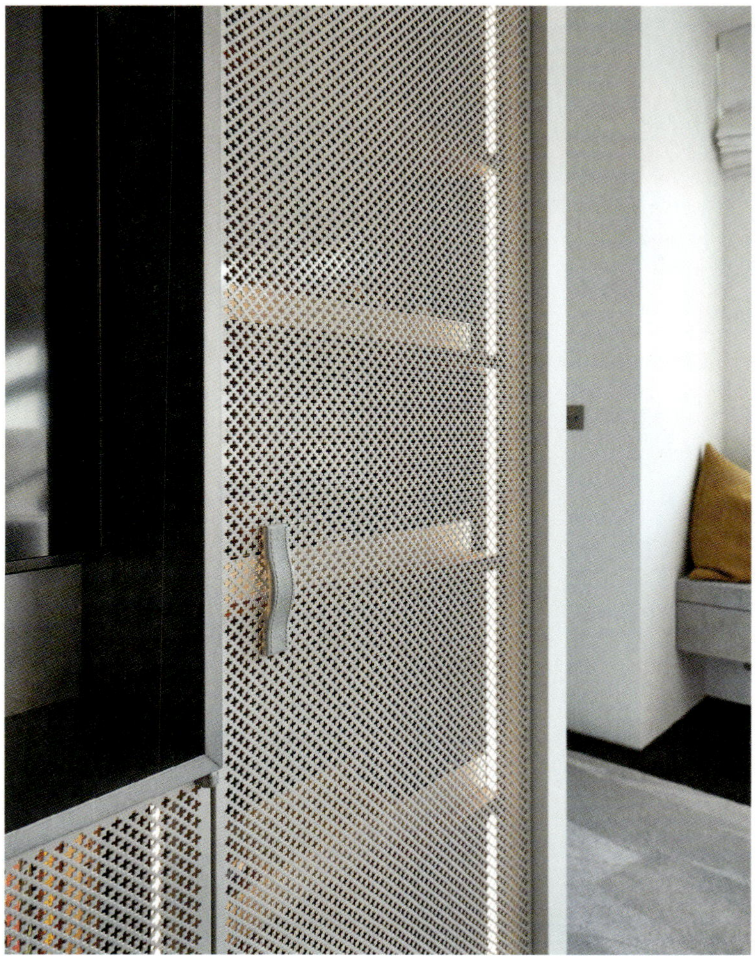

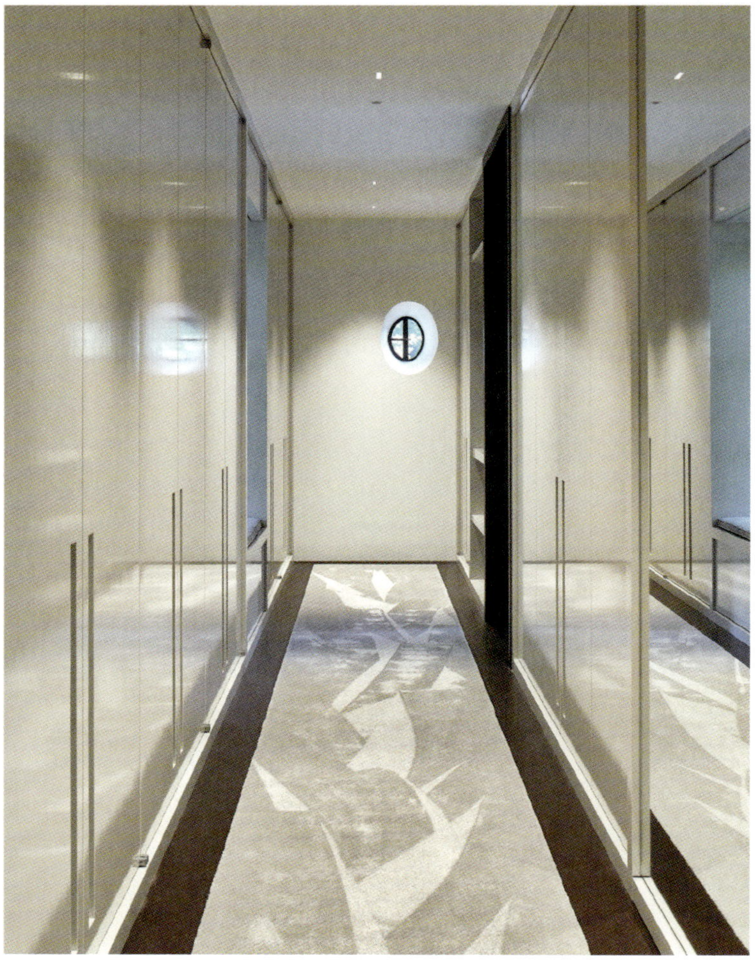

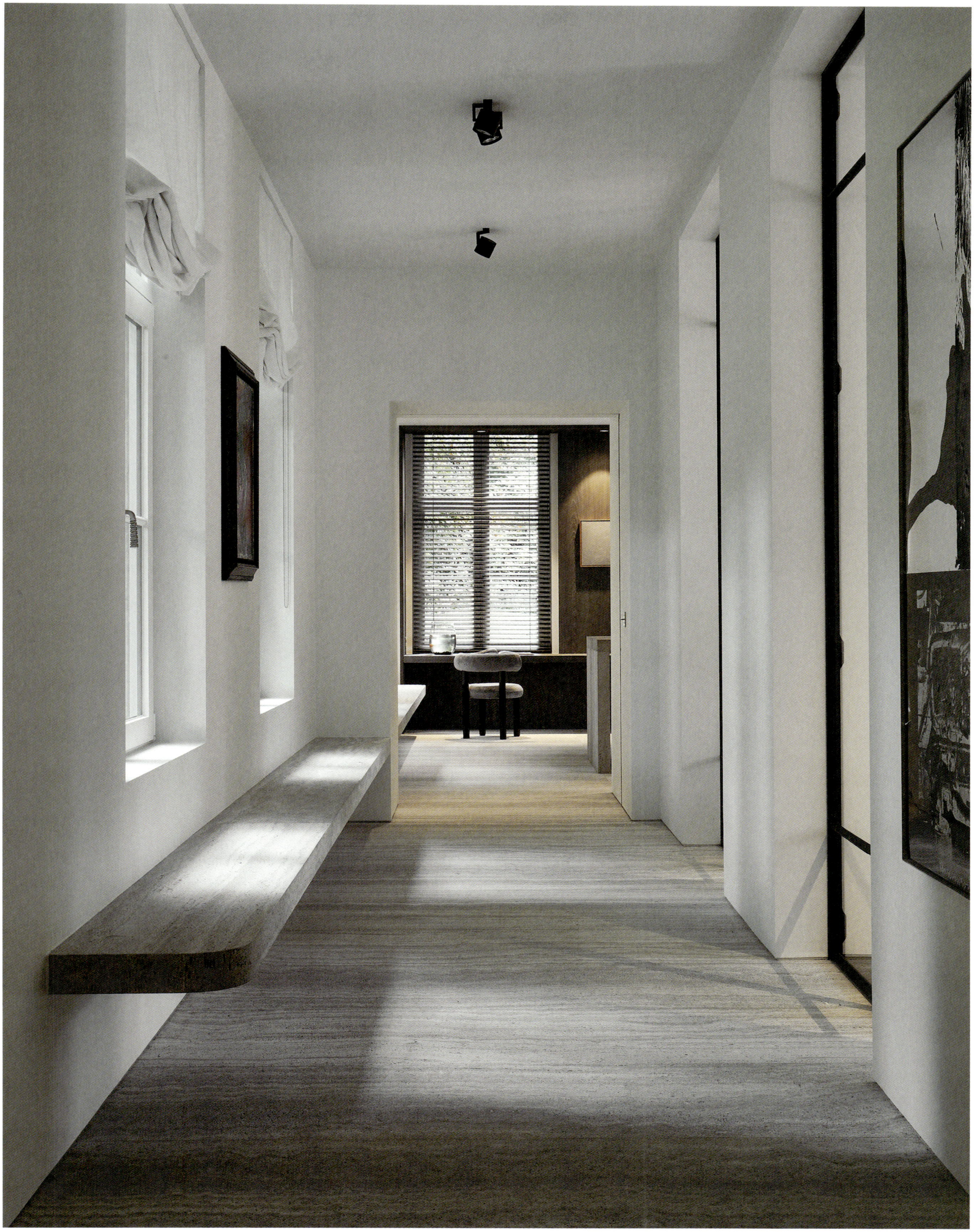

Portrait by An Van Daele

Vanessa Schorreels

Vanessa Schorreels' love for interior design took time to mature. Today her style has grown into a layered and grounded vision. Her gratitude for the beauty of nature is never far away in her designs. She is fascinated by the beautiful, little things in everyday's life. Vanessa has developed a finesse for influences and she demonstrates a similar attentiveness in the way she works. A sustained dialogue with her client is indispensable to her. A clear view of how people use her spaces and how she can make their experience as optimal as possible is equally important. She goes for a natural palette in a multitude of textures every time. Vanessa highly values innovation and derives great satisfaction from developing materials and details together with her craftsmen.

Contrasts and harmony are always balanced in Vanessa's portfolio thanks to her sensitivity to color palettes. Her passion for art forms part of her interior designs - favorite artists and sources of inspiration are Imi Knoebel, Donald Judd and Mark Rothko. From this flows a choice in materials. Smooth surfaces are challenged by a coarse counterpoint; hot and cold are practiced interacting. All these choices unite in a clear signature. She goes for purity in her designs, even when it seems challenging with the multitude of inspirations she brings together in her style.

www.vanessaschorreels.be

Photography: Cafeine (Thomas De Bruyne)

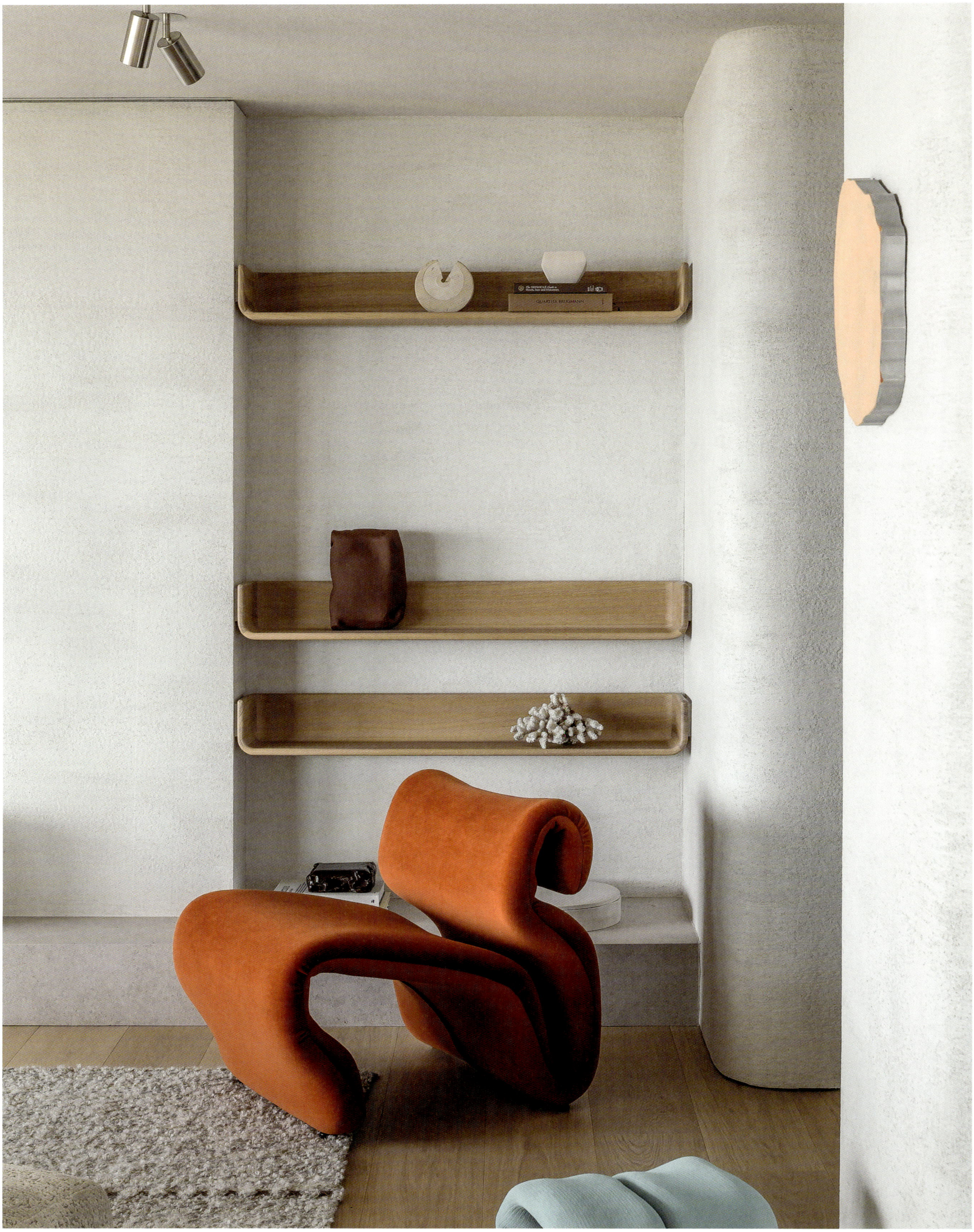

"Reness" is a minimalist home located on the Belgian coast designed by Vanessa Schorreels. The design concept draws its inspiration from the breathtaking sea views that dominate the apartment's vista. The design palette revolves around reflections, delicate textures, and an understated color scheme. It prioritizes the essentials, leaving ample room for personal interpretation and imagination. In this respect, the design pays homage to the influential designer Charlotte Perriand, who found inspiration in the organic forms of Normandy's beaches and the rugged beauty of nature. Reness exudes a sense of warm minimalism, creating a serene ambiance with subtle hints of brutalism through its monolithic forms and robust materials.

What sets this apartment apart is its meticulous attention to craftsmanship, extending from the kitchen to the restrooms and from the living spaces to the bedrooms. Handcrafted details and carefully curated artistic objects, as well as artworks that subtly reference the sea, imbue the space with an authentic character. The Noguchi vintage lamp, suspended like a work of art above the table and the vintage Perriand chairs are just two of the many visual delights. Reness is designed to foster gatherings and shared moments with friends and family around a central table and a central tailor-made couch. Every detail has been thoughtfully considered to enhance the overall experience.

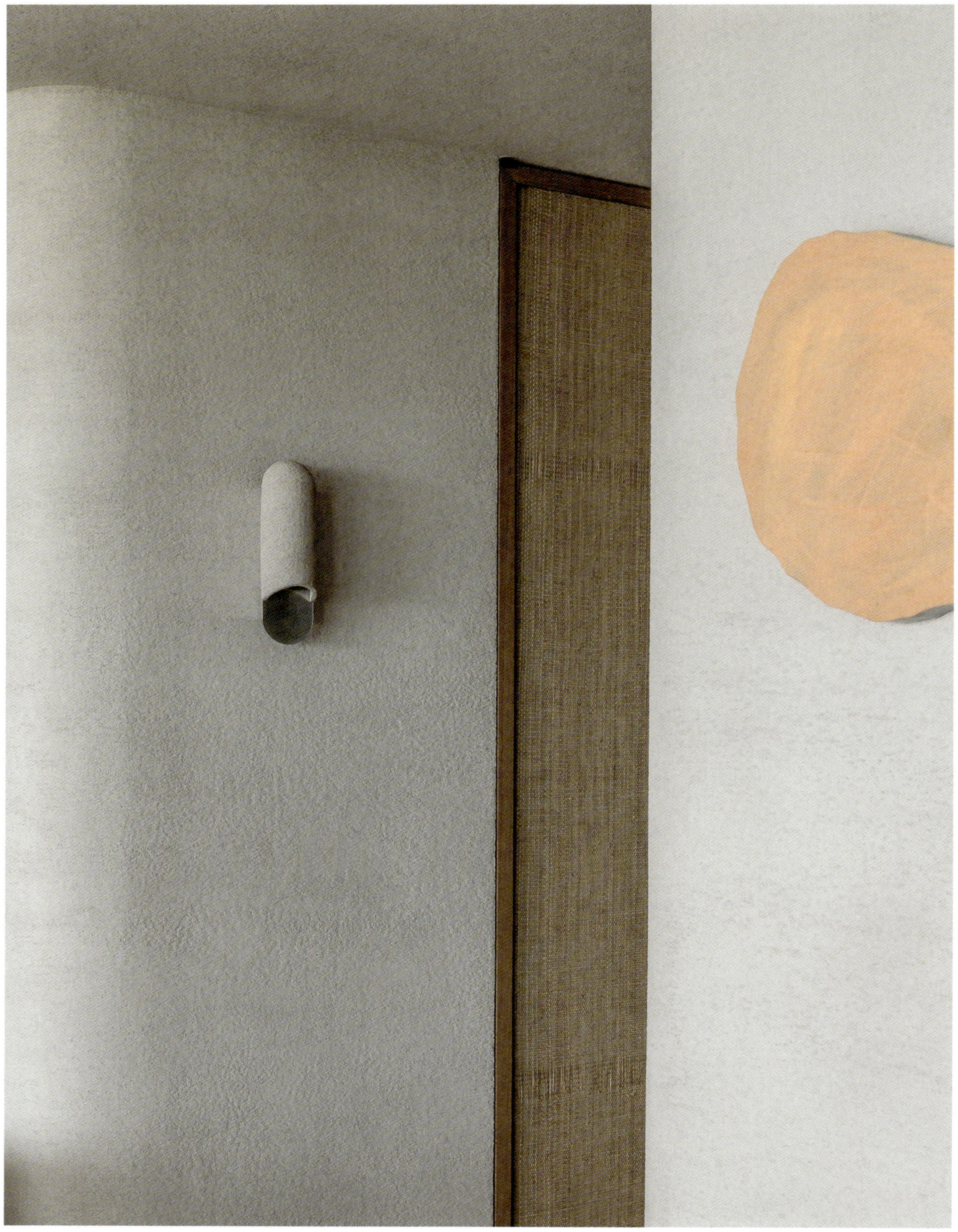

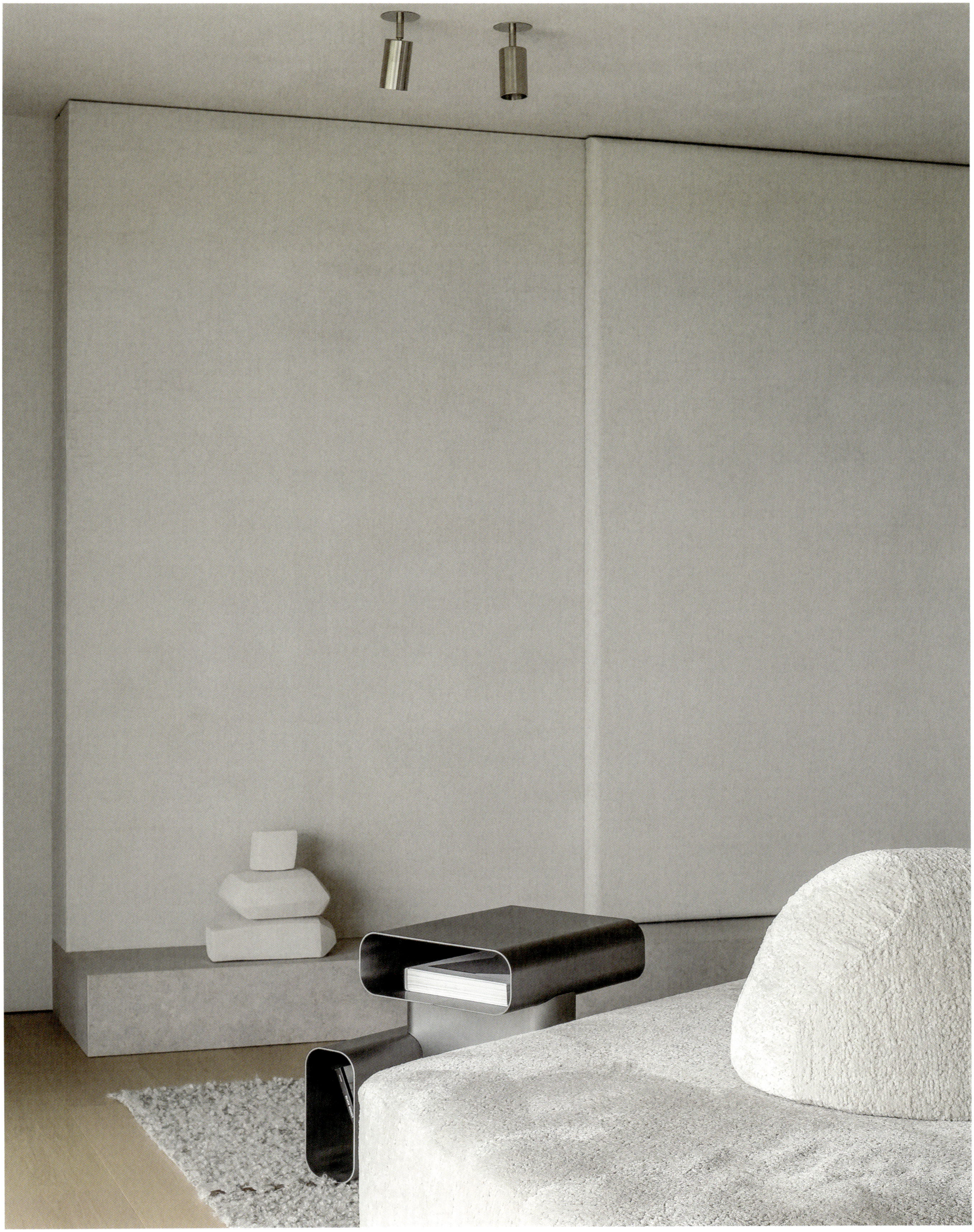

182

183

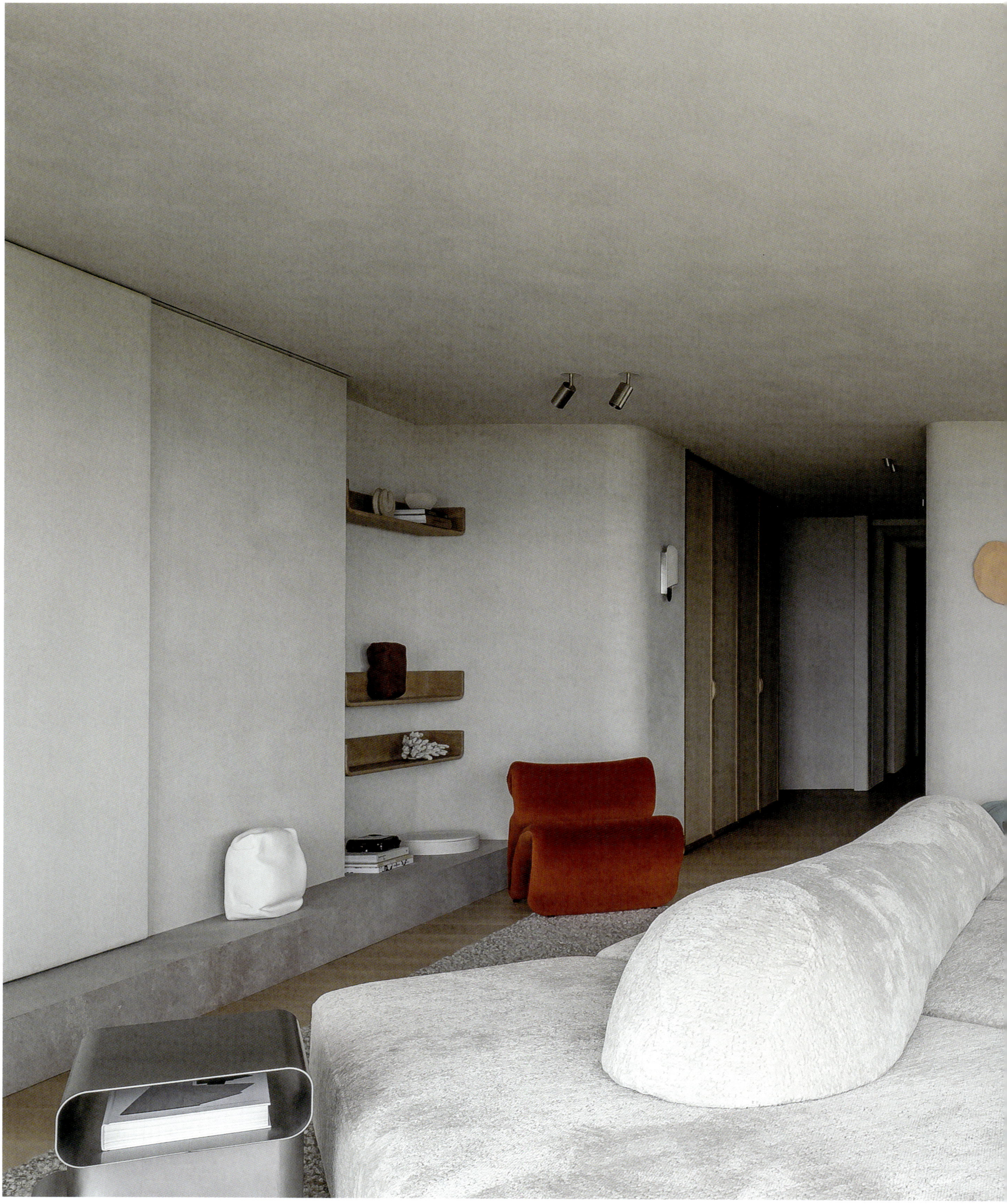

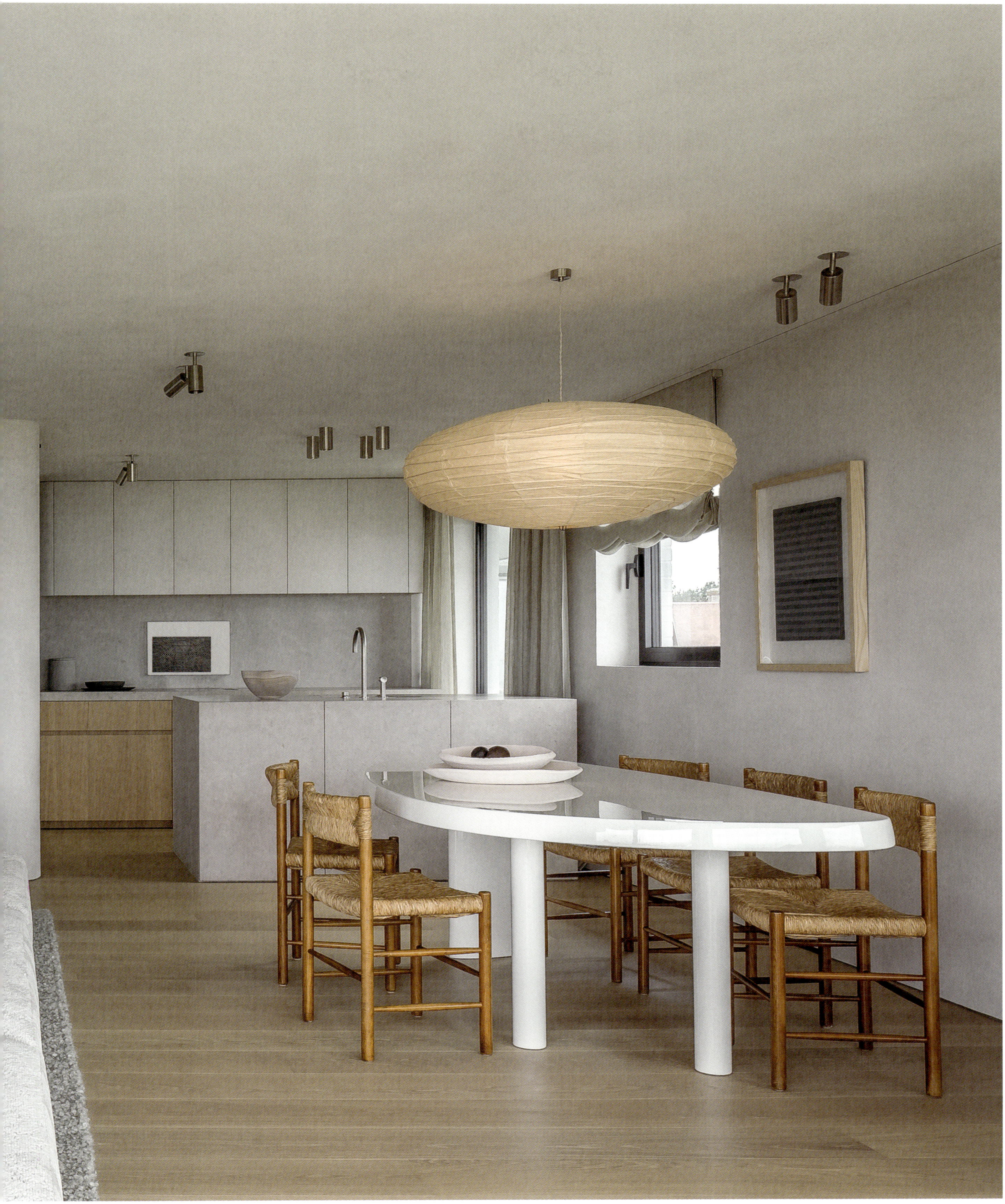

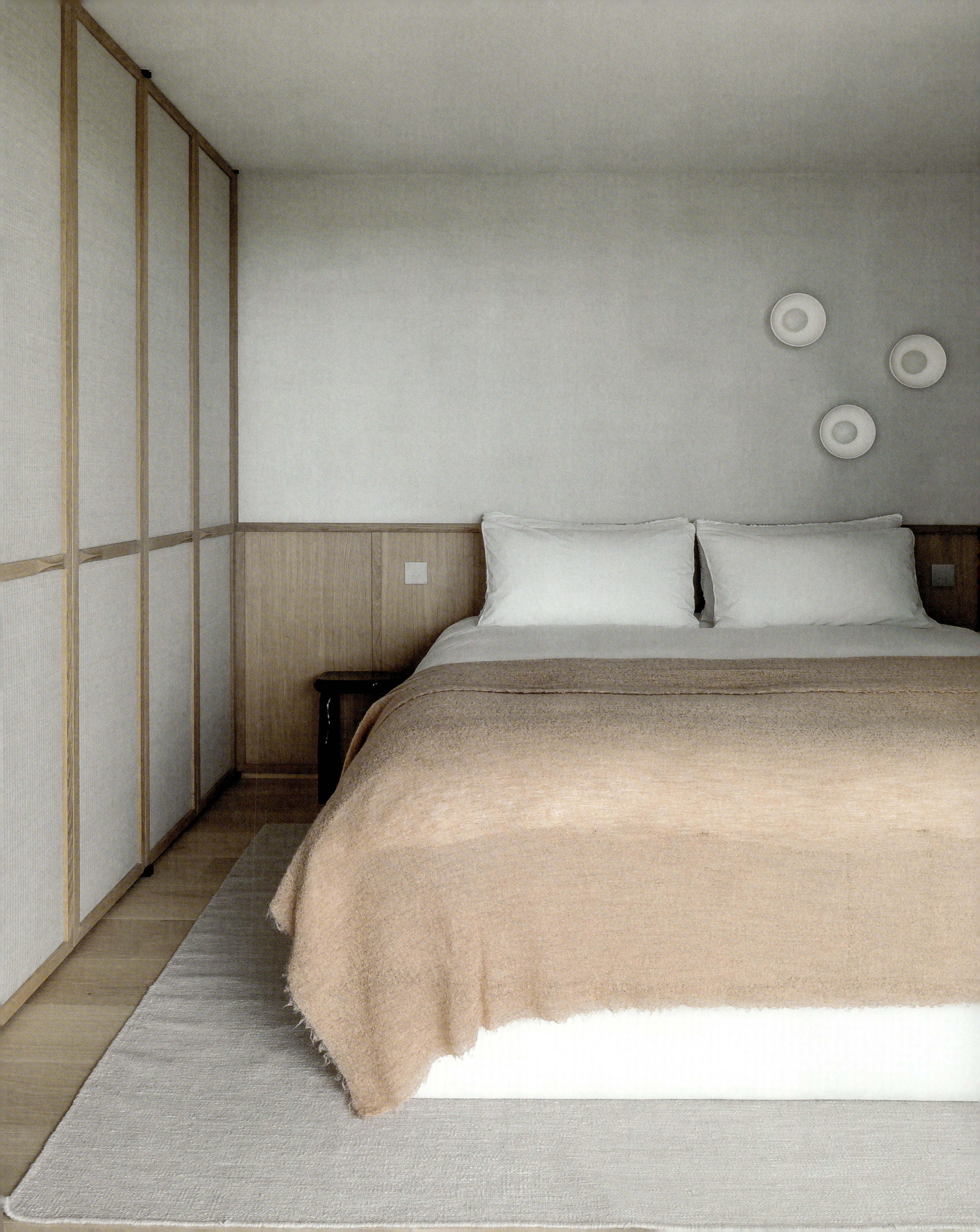

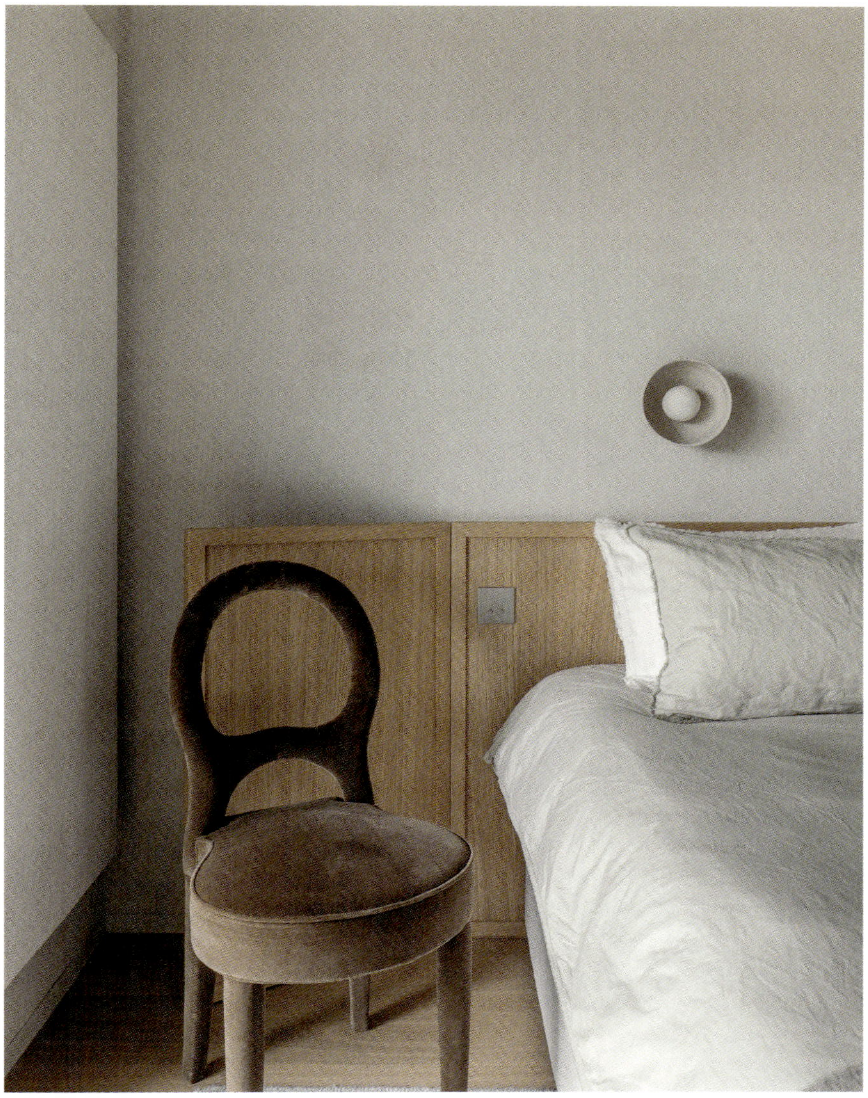

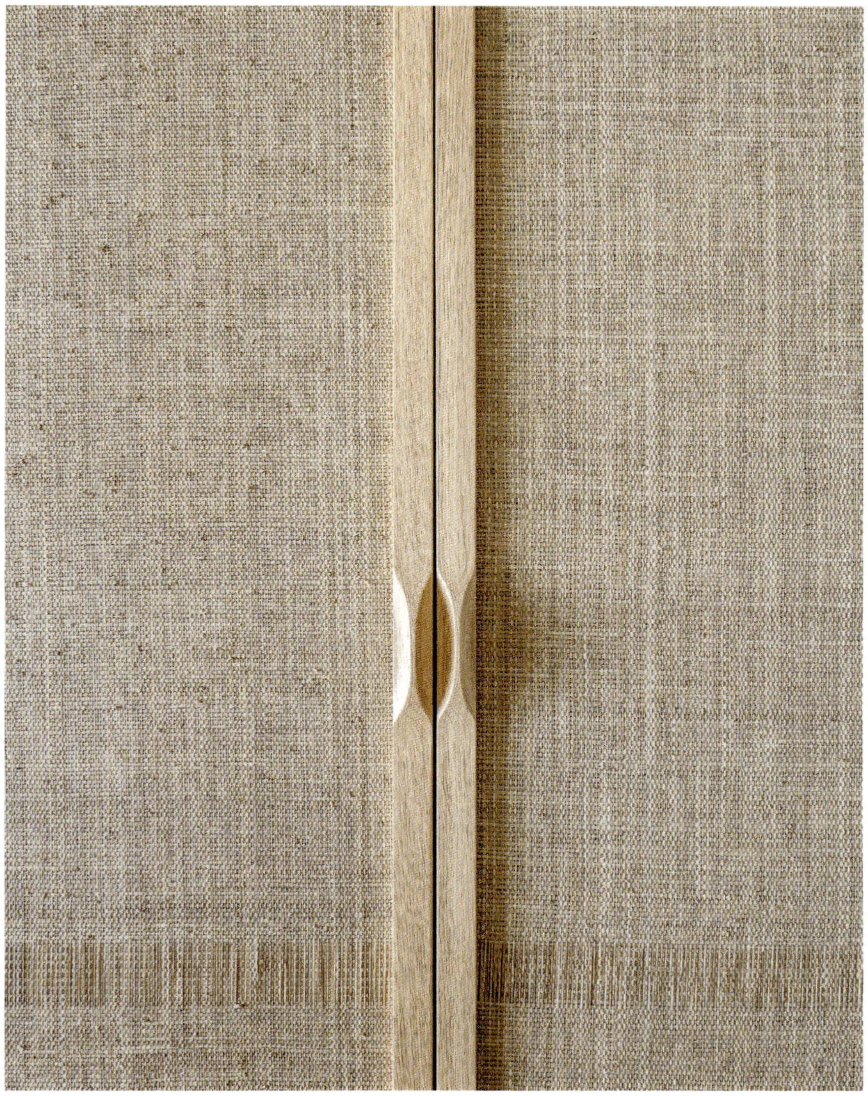

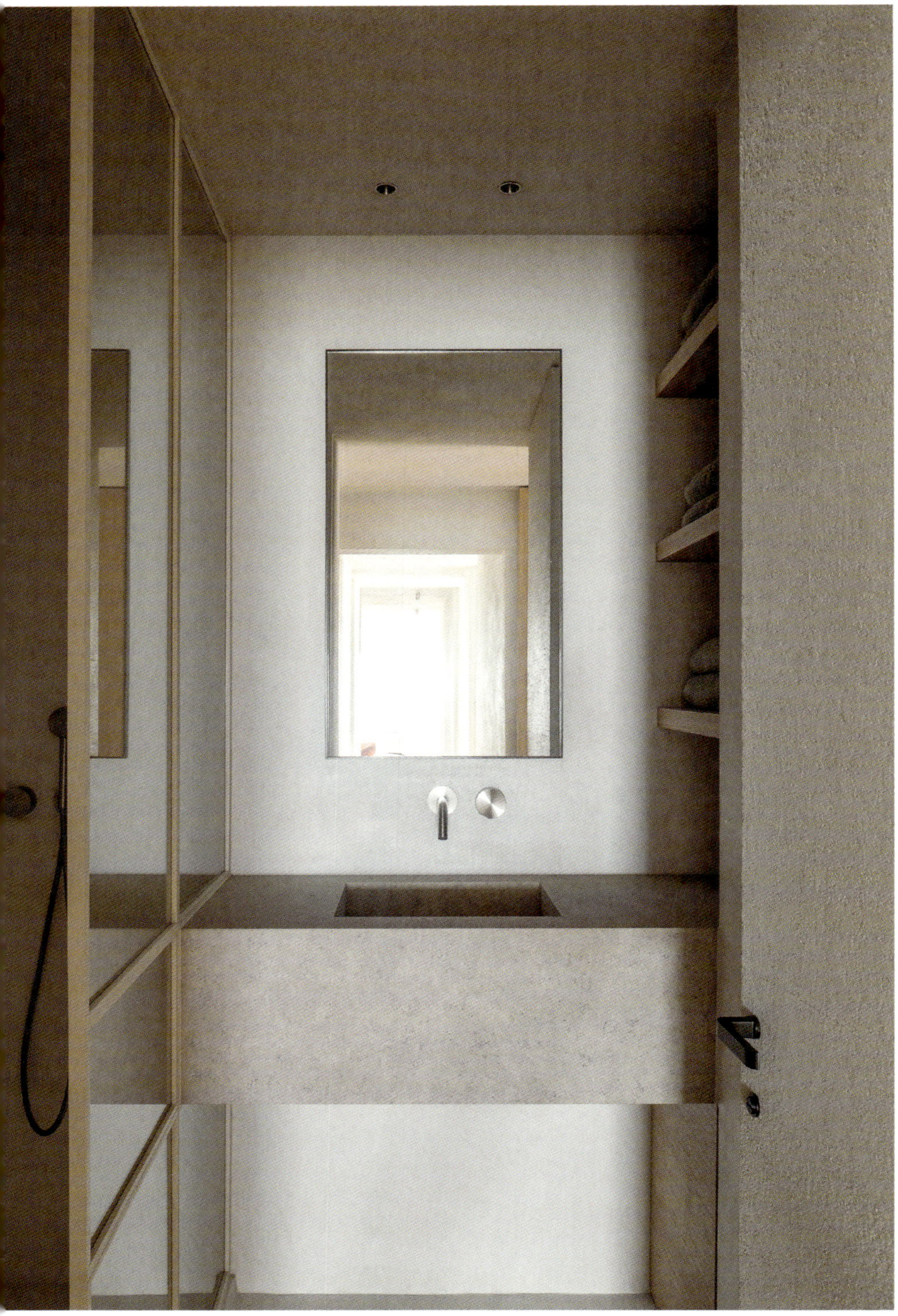

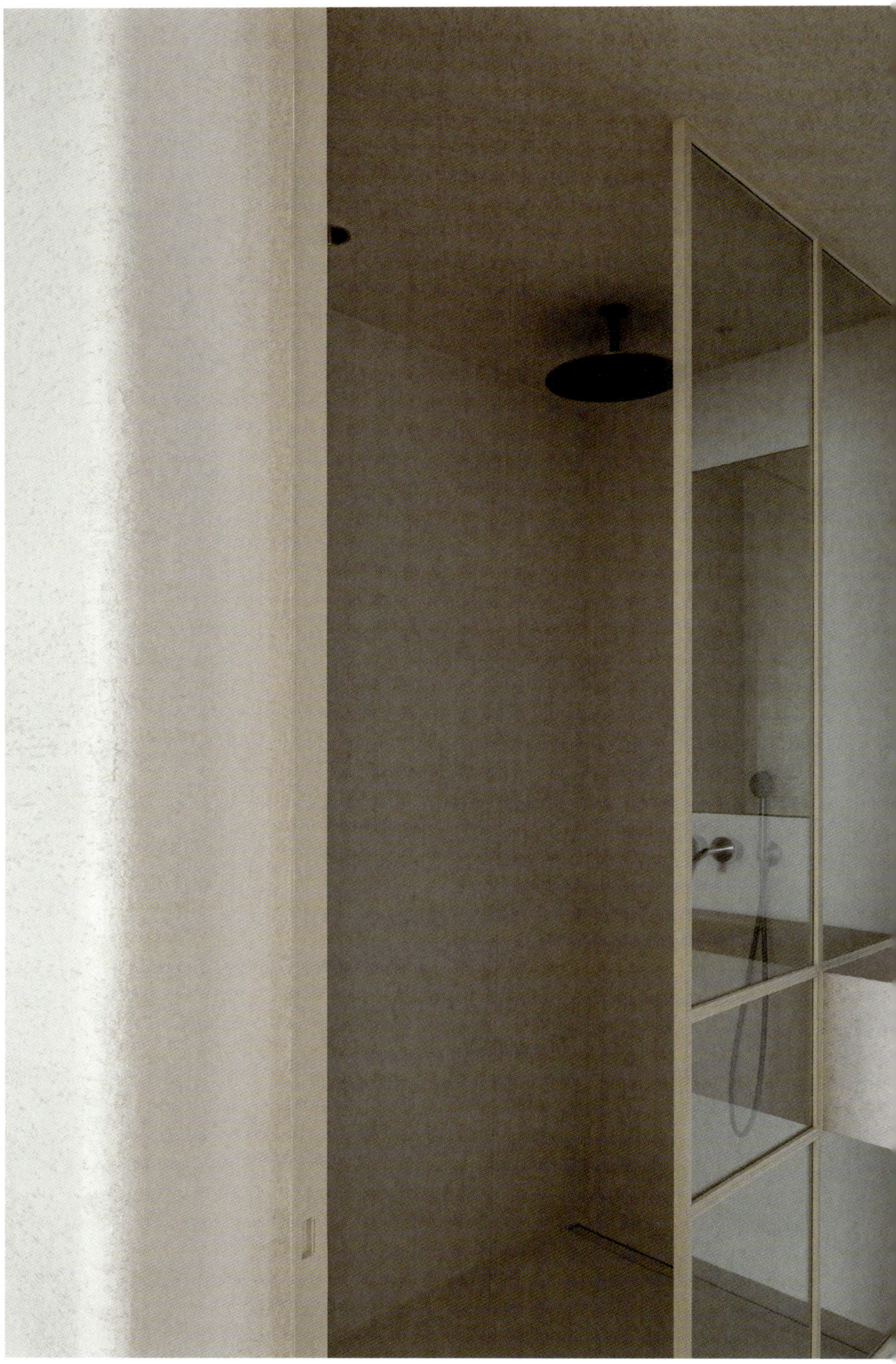

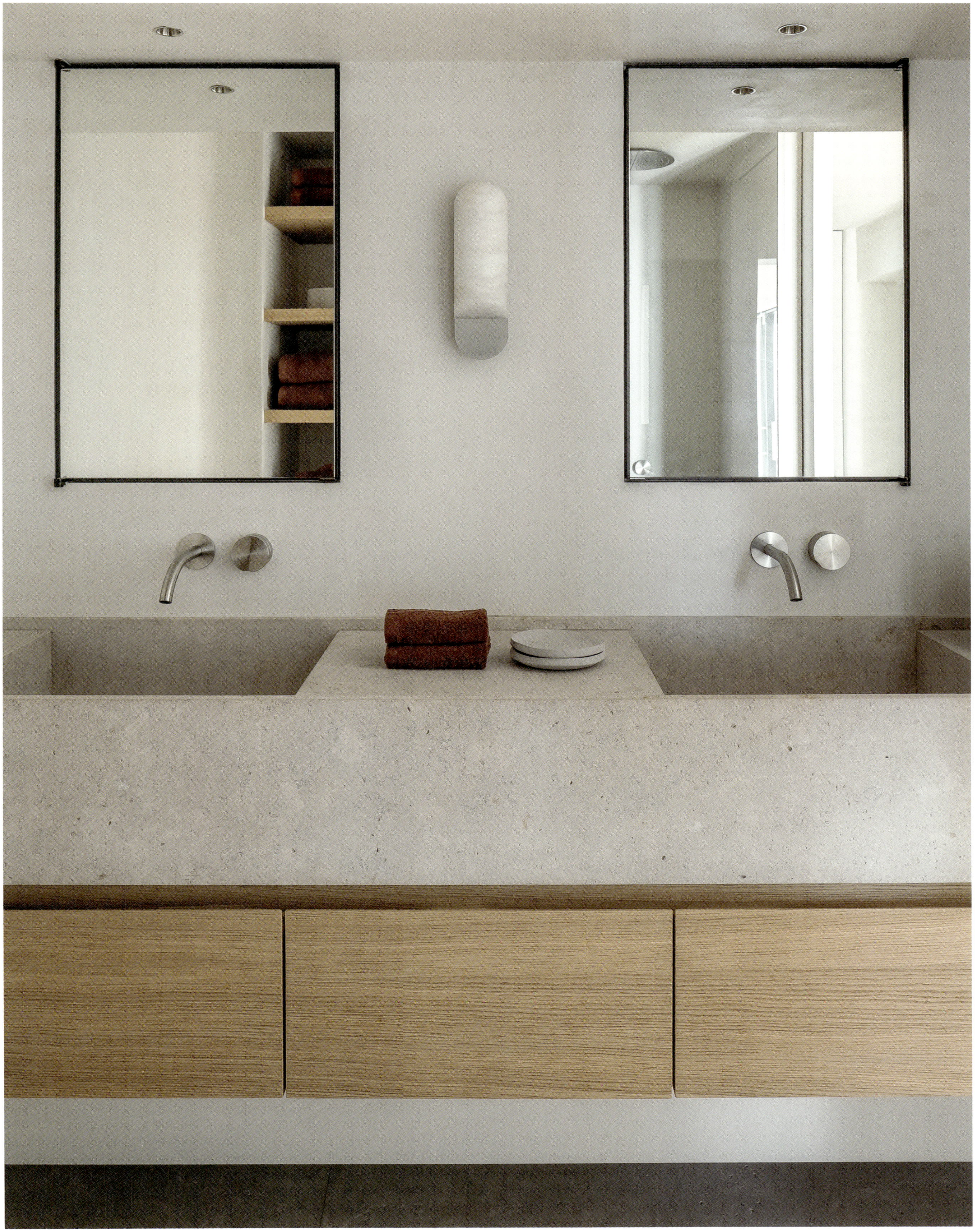

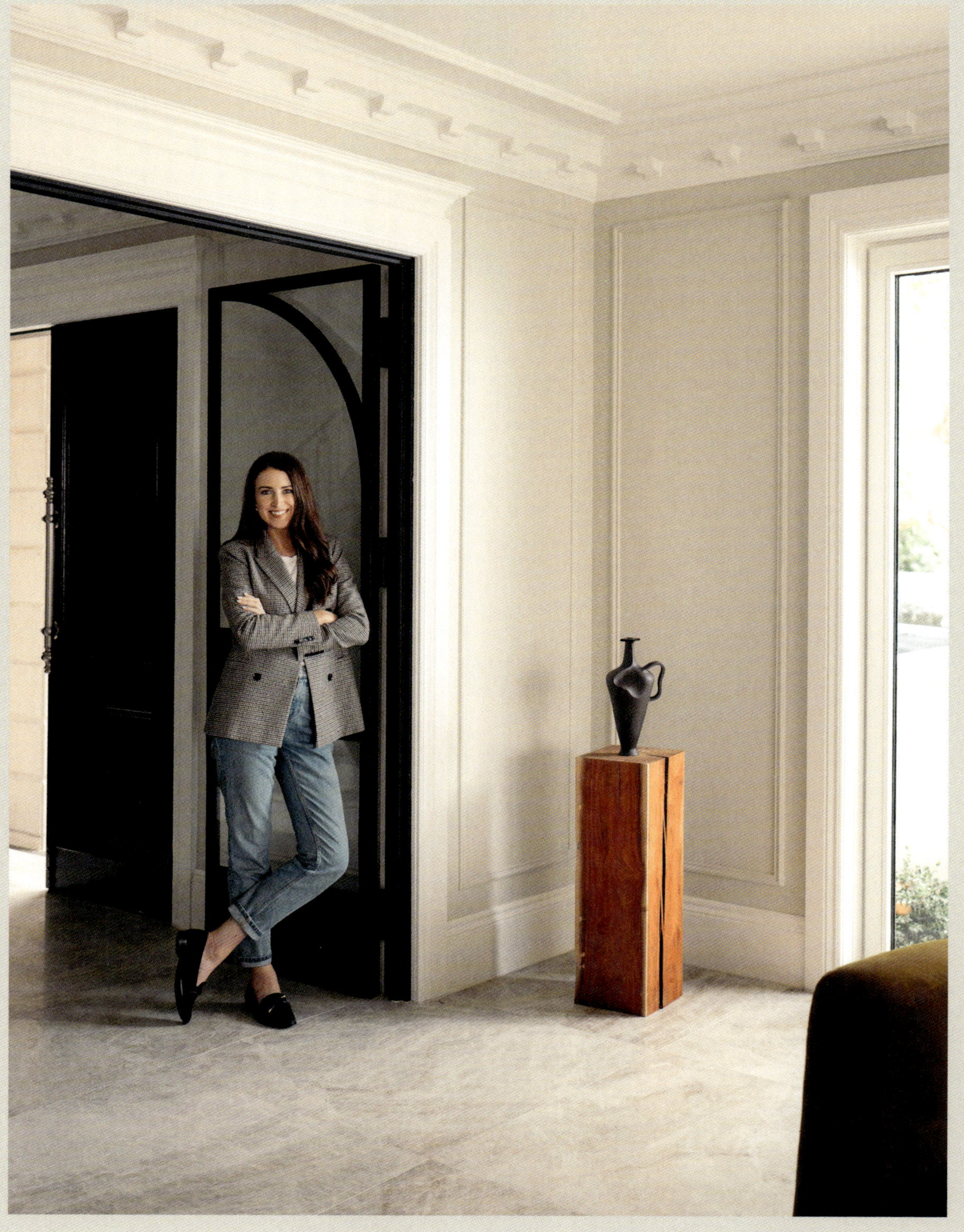

Carla Barton

Carla Barton grew up as the daughter of a Melbourne-born interior designer and furniture importer. From a young age, she was surrounded by beautiful objects and creative processes that shaped her artistic sensibilities.

Interior Design and Real Estate were Carla's parallel passions in her early years. After studying real estate, she gained valuable experience in real estate sales. Carla followed her true calling and earned a degree in interior design from the University of Canberra in 2009. During her five-year residency in Canberra, she had the valuable opportunity to work with architects and interior designers to expand her knowledge and skills.

In 2012, Carla returned to Sydney. As a Senior Interior Designer at Hamel & Associates for eight years, she worked on numerous high-end residential projects in Sydney, Melbourne and New York.

Carla launched her design firm in 2021 and quickly gained a reputation as one of Sydney's leading designers.

The basis of her work is attention to detail and the further development of the architectural language. Carla and her team have a long history of working with local and international leading artisans, whom they collaborate with to create unique pieces for their clients' homes. She has gained a reputation for her interior design expertise, with her projects featured in highly regarded publications and on prestigious platforms.

Exceptional talent and attention to detail earned her nominations at the prestigious Fanuli Belle Awards 2022 for Best Emerging Interior Designer and Best Bathroom Design and in 2023 for Best Residential Interior Design. Furthermore, Carla's work is often published in Belle magazine, showing her thoughtful designs and artistic vision.

www.carlabarton.com.au

Photography: Felix Forest

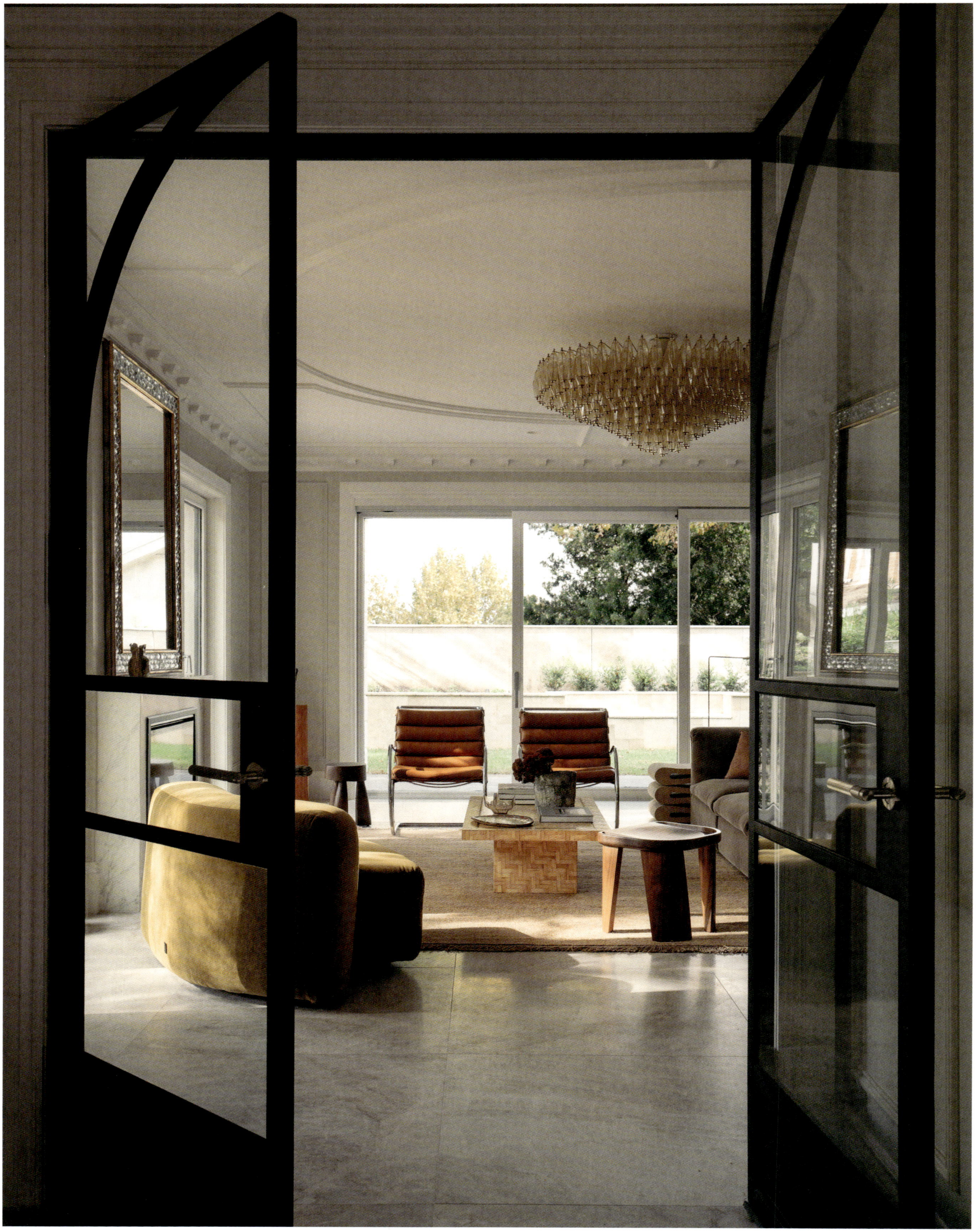

Carla Barton designed the interior of this newly built 2 storey home on a corner block in Double Bay (NSW, Australia).

The property was constructed in a distinctive New Georgian period style. The house features an entry foyer, a dining room and a kitchen, a laundry, a powder room, a study and a double garage on the ground floor. There are three bedrooms with en suites and walk-in robes on the upper floor. The stone and iron staircase is in the centre of the home.

This house is situated in a great location, only three blocks away from the main shopping district in Double Bay. This was an opportunity for the owner, who buys and renovates or rebuilds single dwelling properties in the eastern suburbs. The family has three adult children, with only one of the daughters still living at home. Now that the children are moving out, the owners thought this would be a good home to downsize.

This new construction downsizer of Grand proportions was meticulously designed and built to reflect the client and designers' appreciation alike for timeless and quality design. At the core of the interior brief was hard wearing materials and "easy to clean" finishes, which was achieved with flat panel joinery doors, minimal cabinetry hardware and quartzite natural stones. The home is soft and understated with a strong use of natural materials such as timber veneers, stones, metals, plaster, and Murano glass to layer, add warmth and glamorize.

Architectural layers formed the canvas for the interior brief, stone coining, architraves, ceiling patterns, wall panelling, Georgian tooth cornicing were all thoughtfully considered to feel purposefully placed and honest to the referenced style of the home.

Carla Barton describes the home's style as one that, taking a step inside, you immediately forget that you are in Double Bay. This could be anywhere in the world. It's an eclectic mix of Georgian architectural style with contemporary joinery and fittings, and mid-century lighting and furniture. It is really transitional.

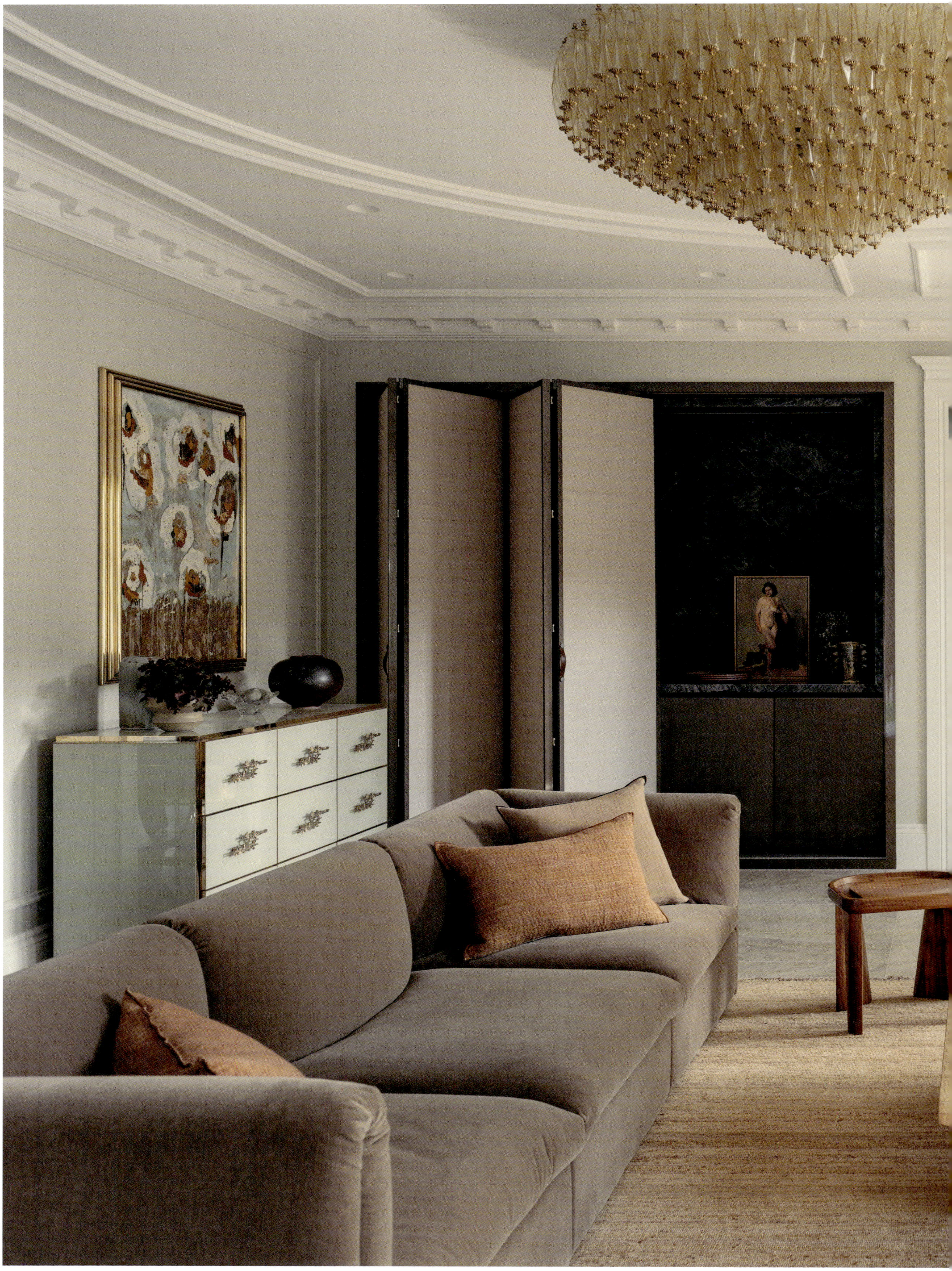

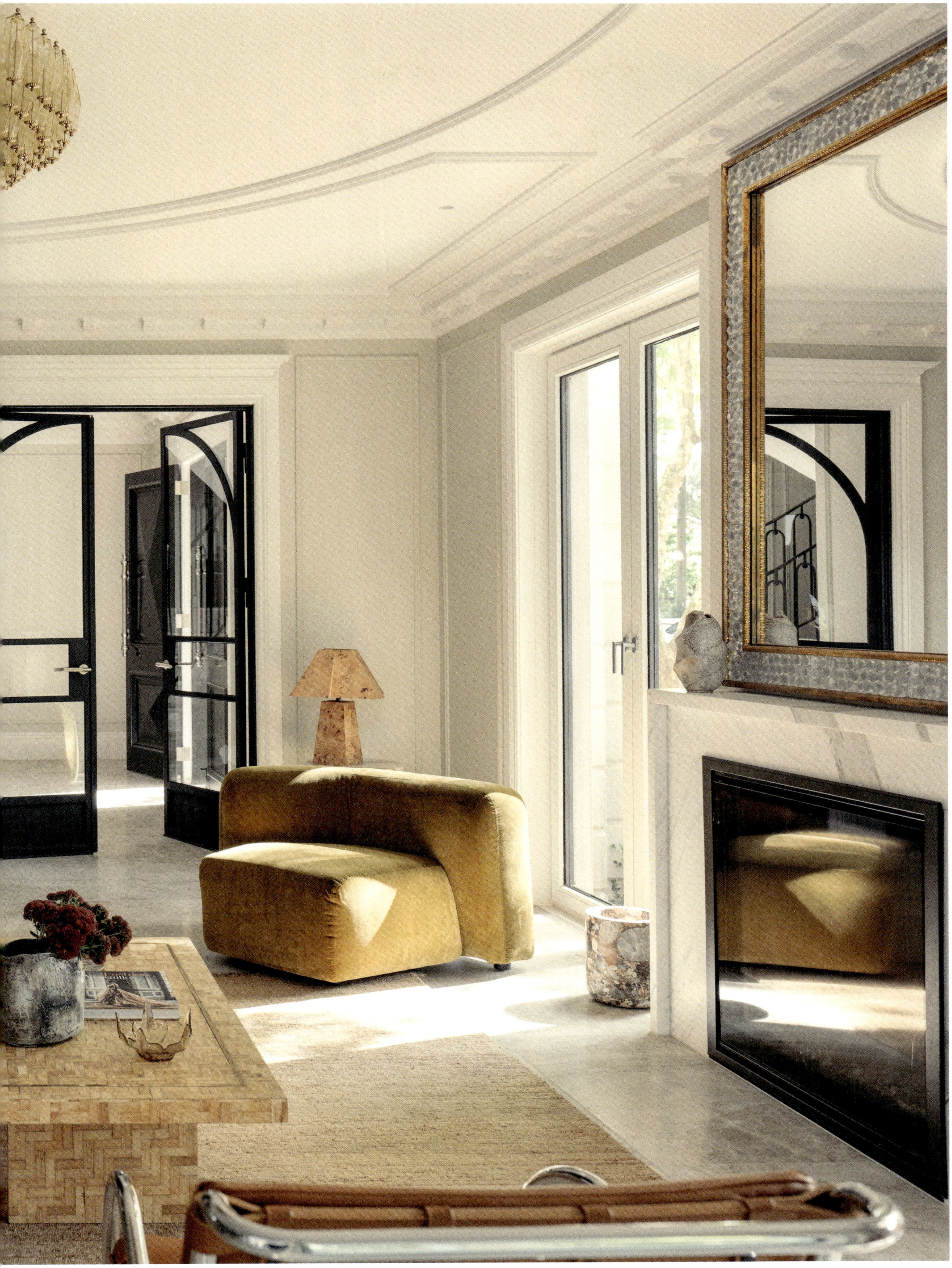

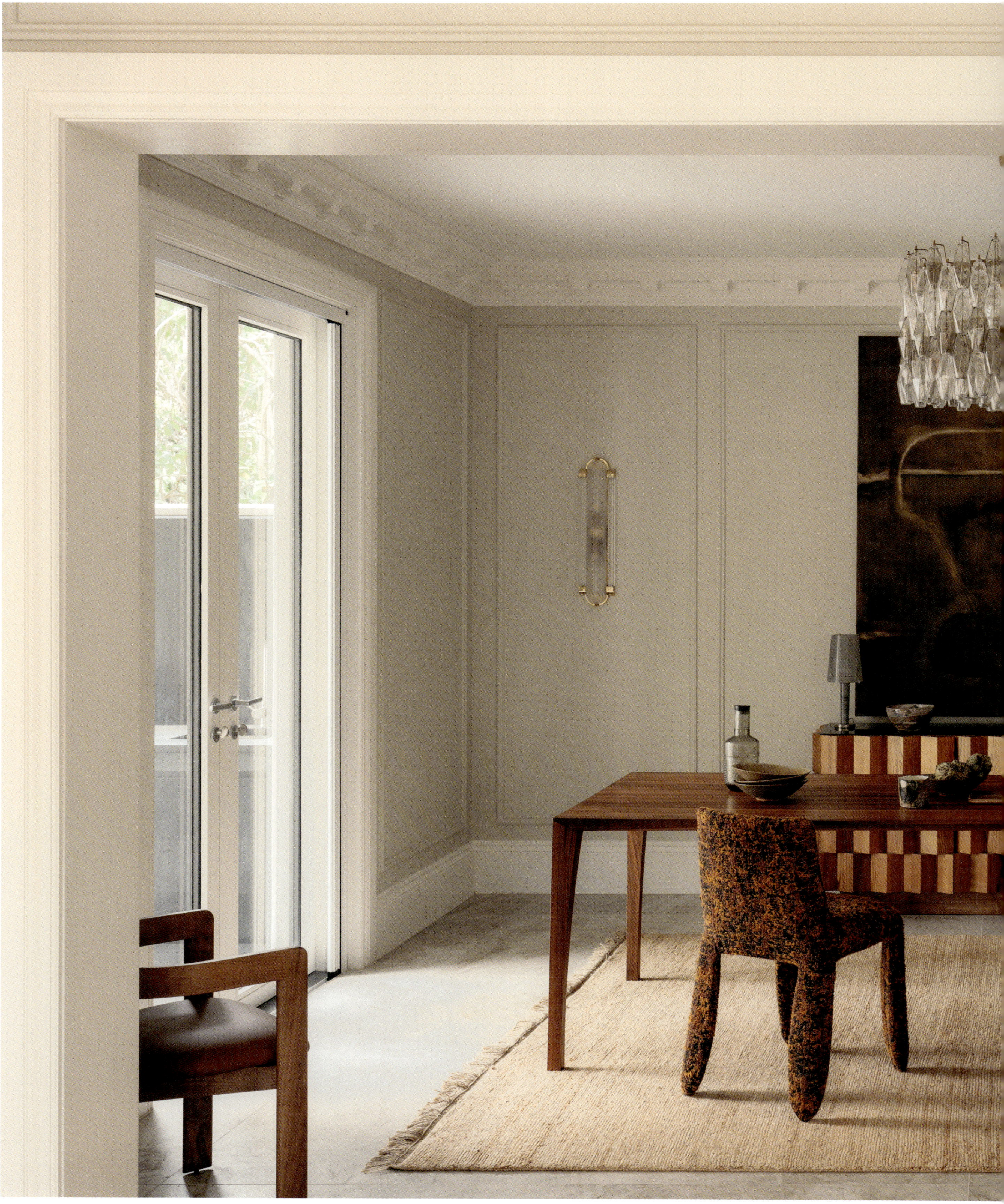

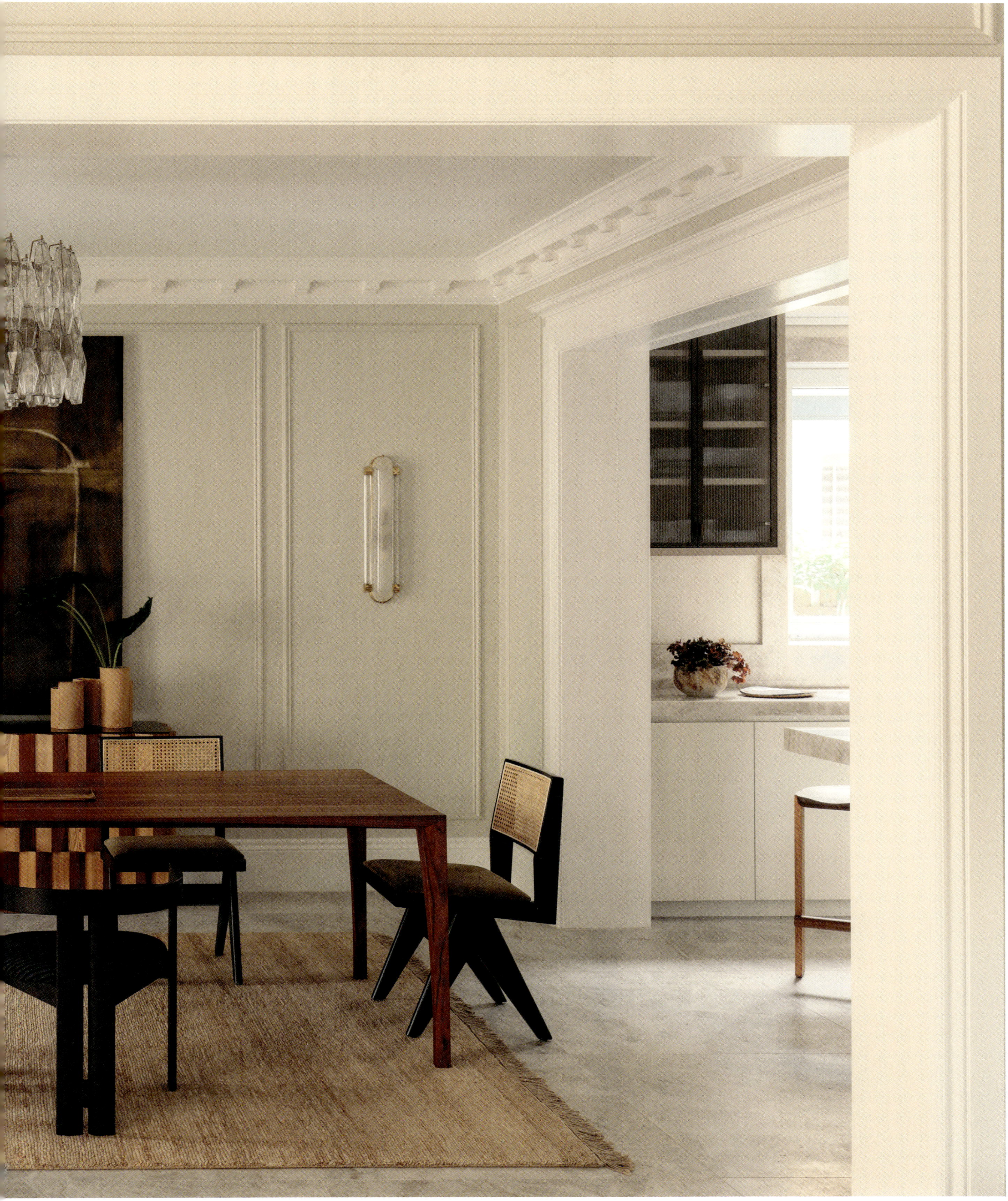

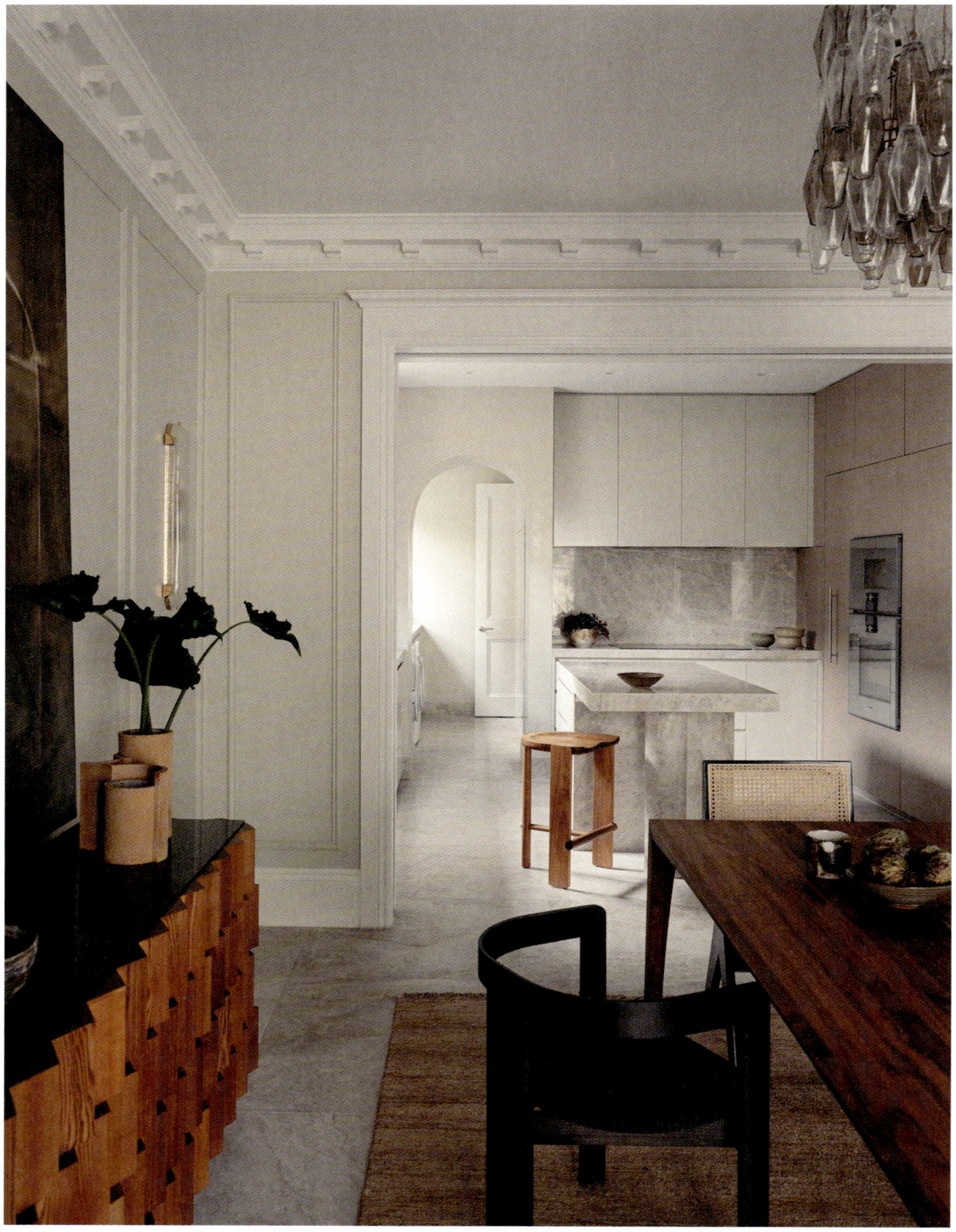

199

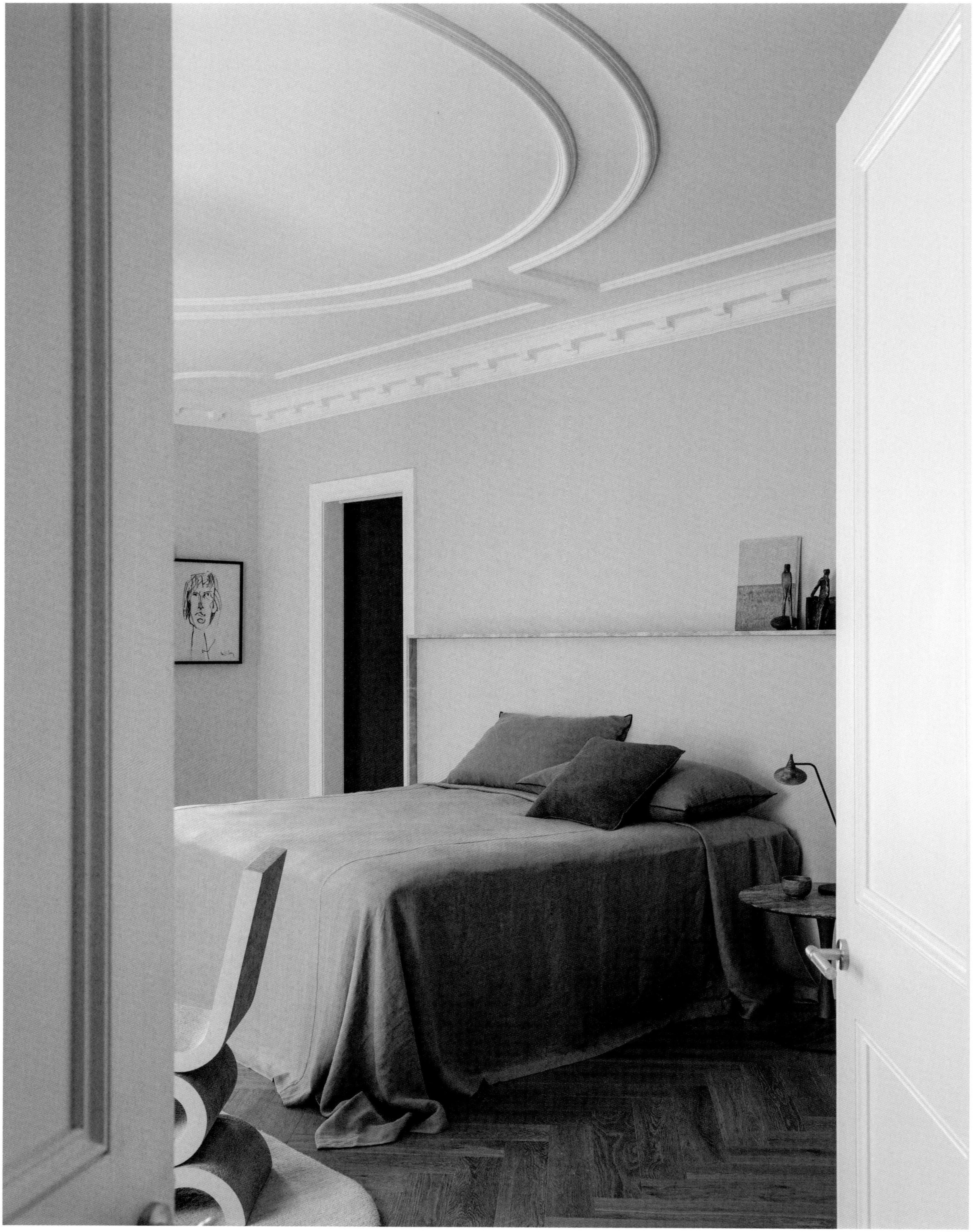

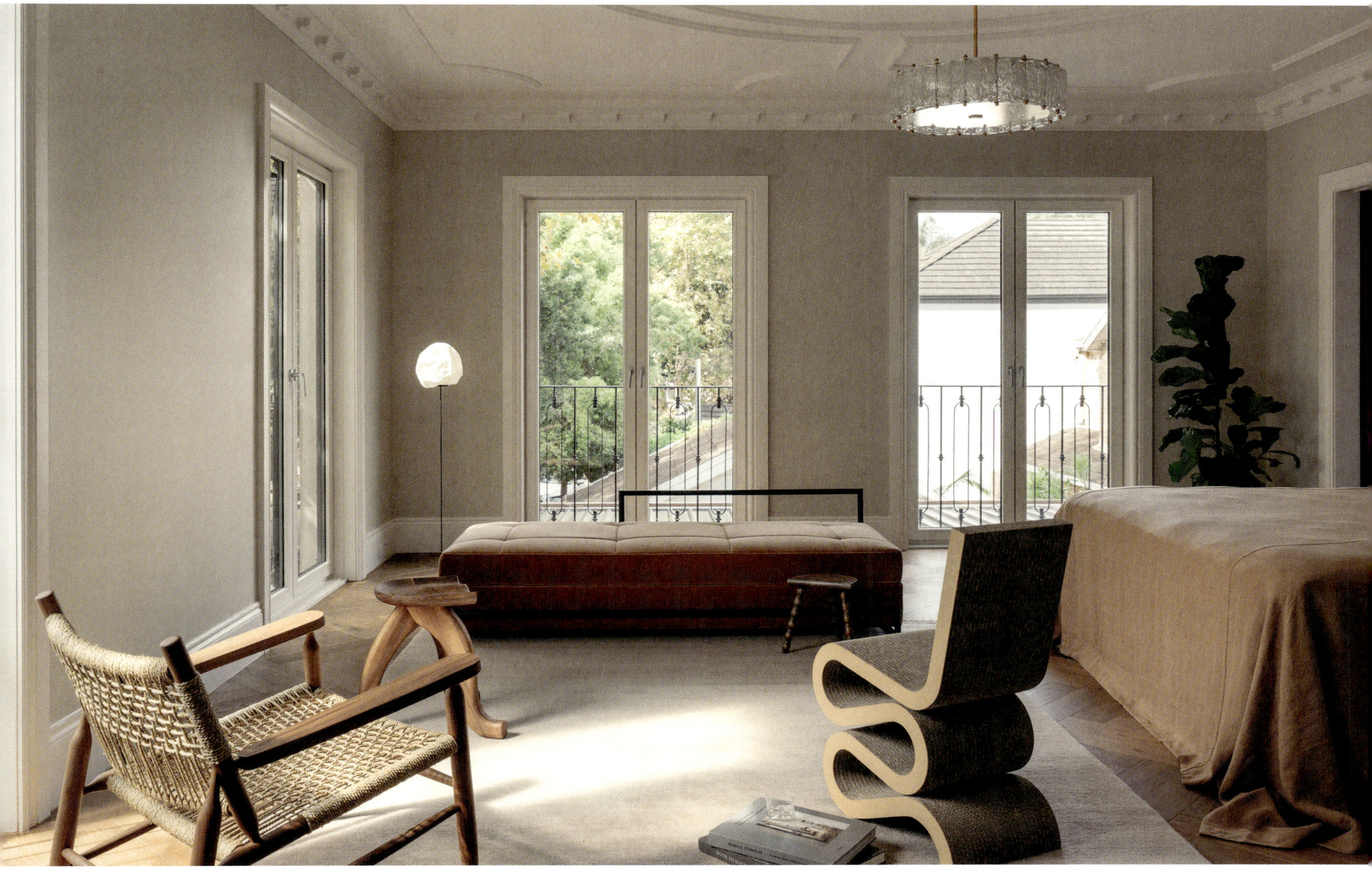

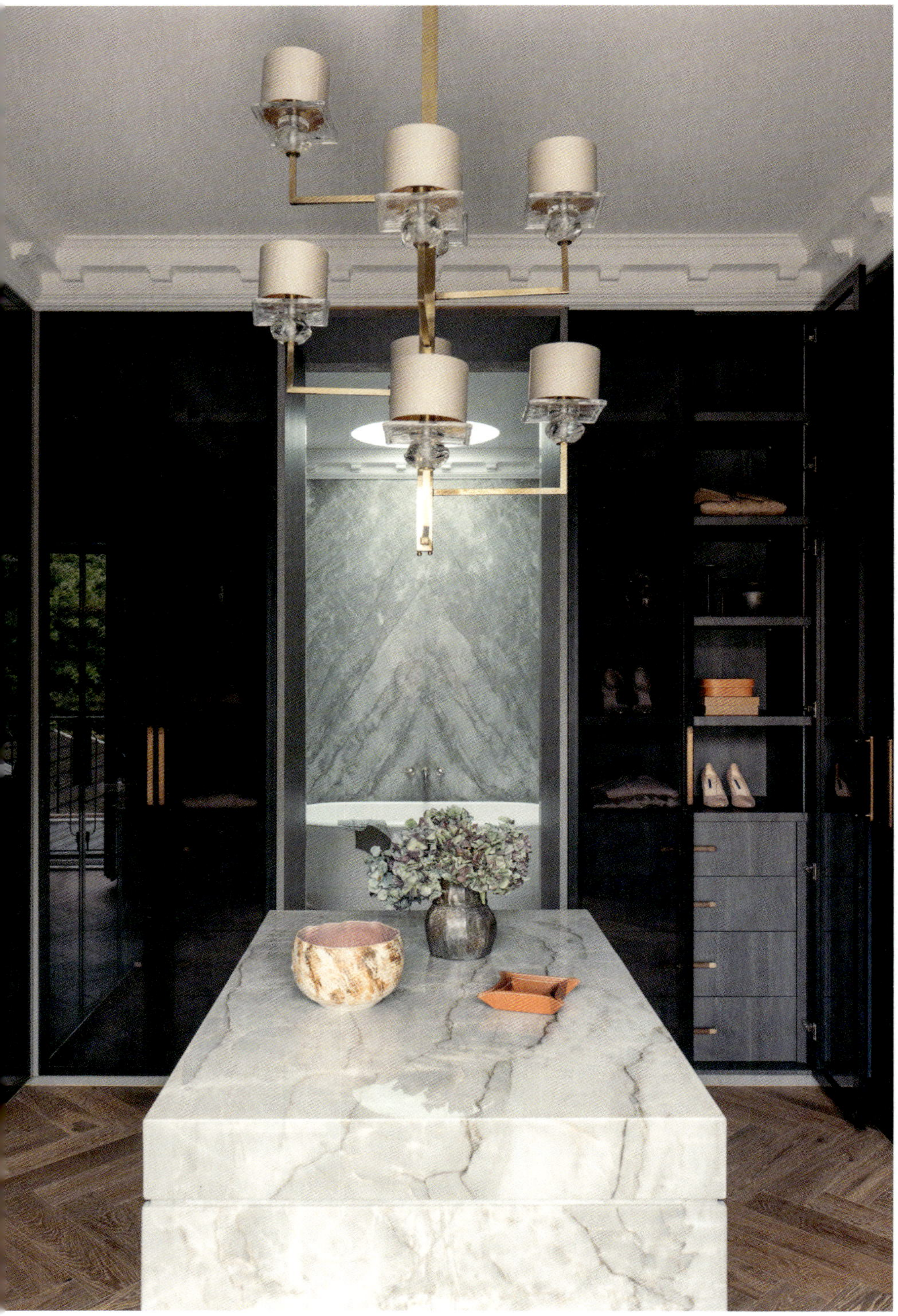

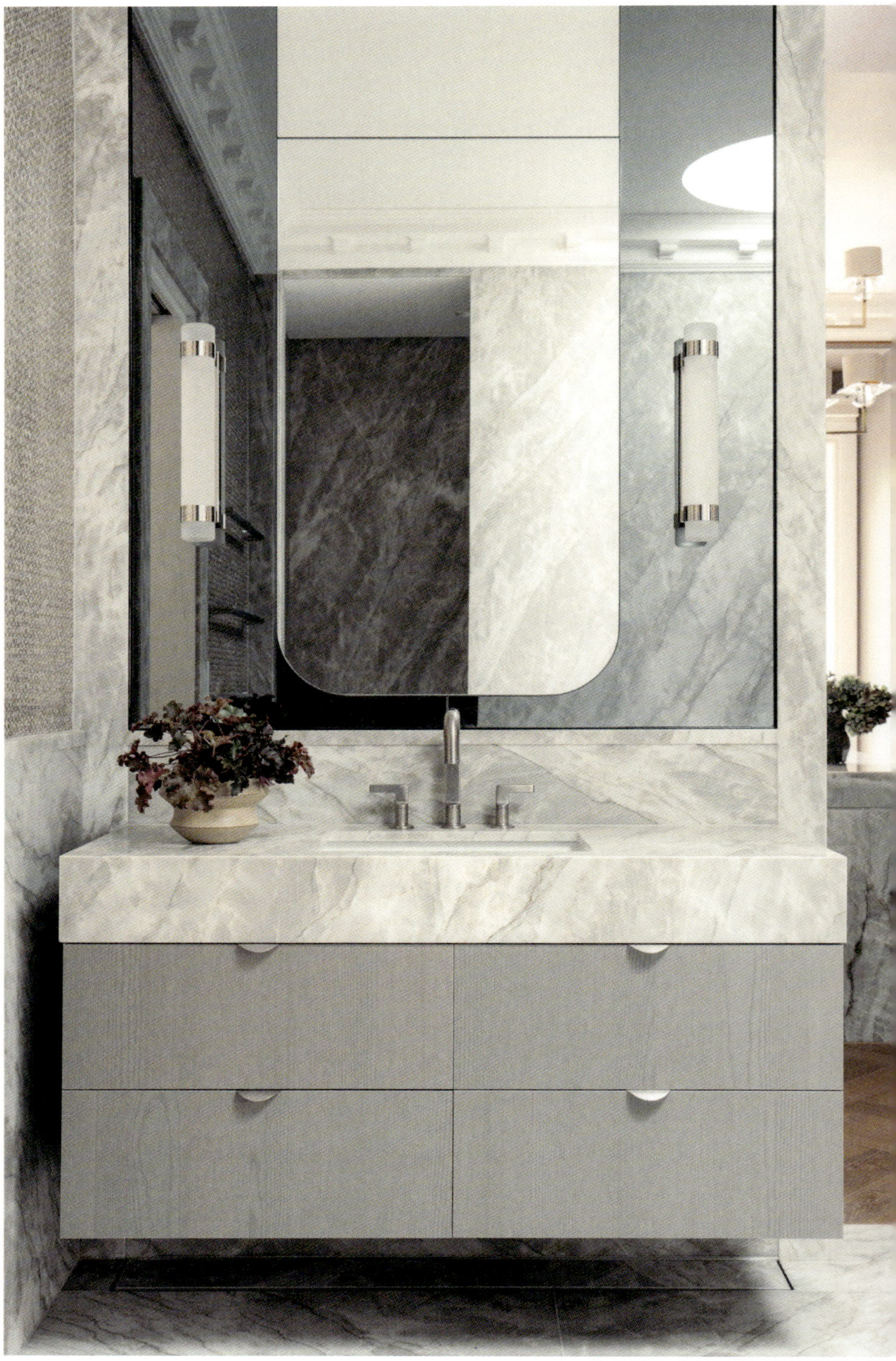

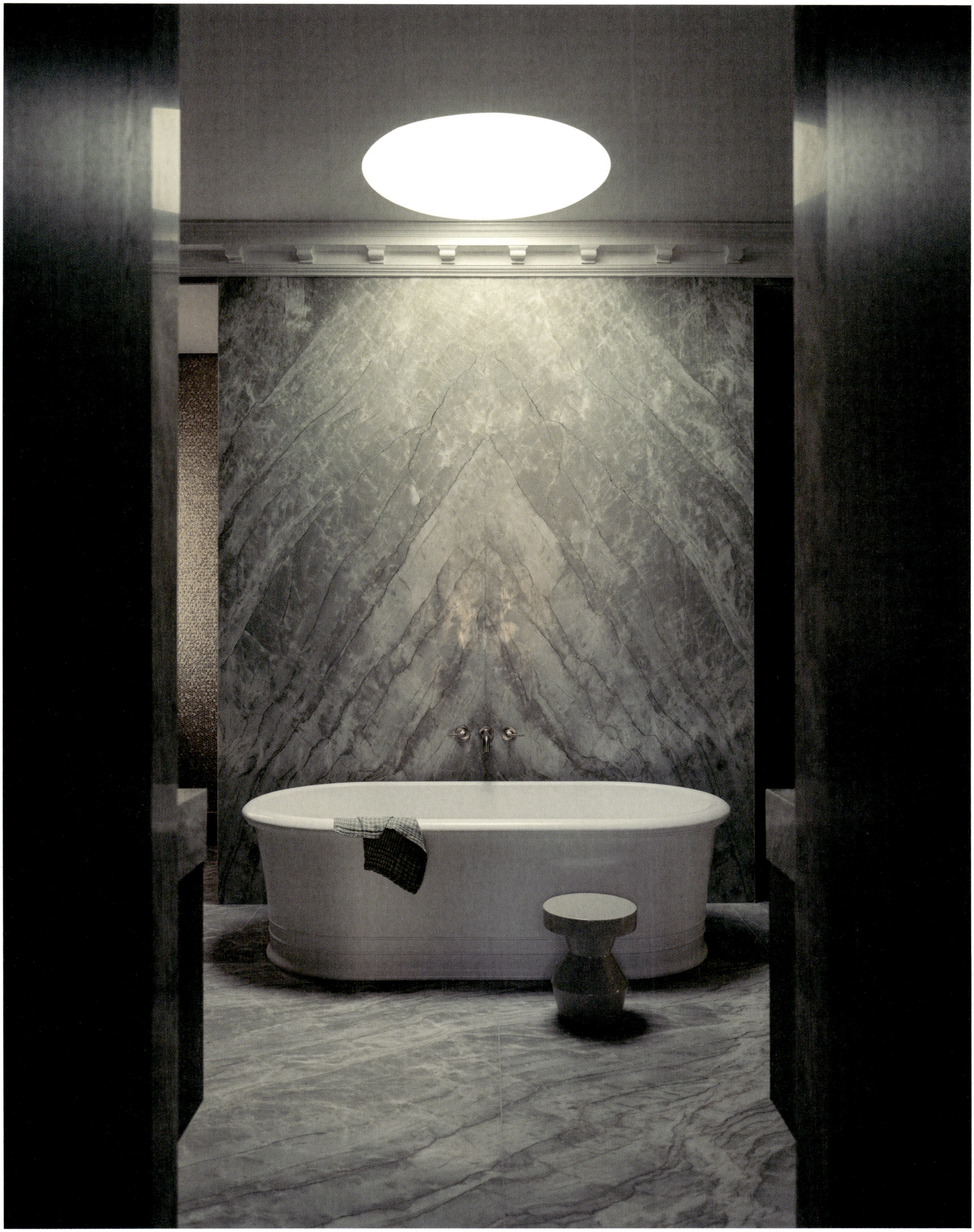

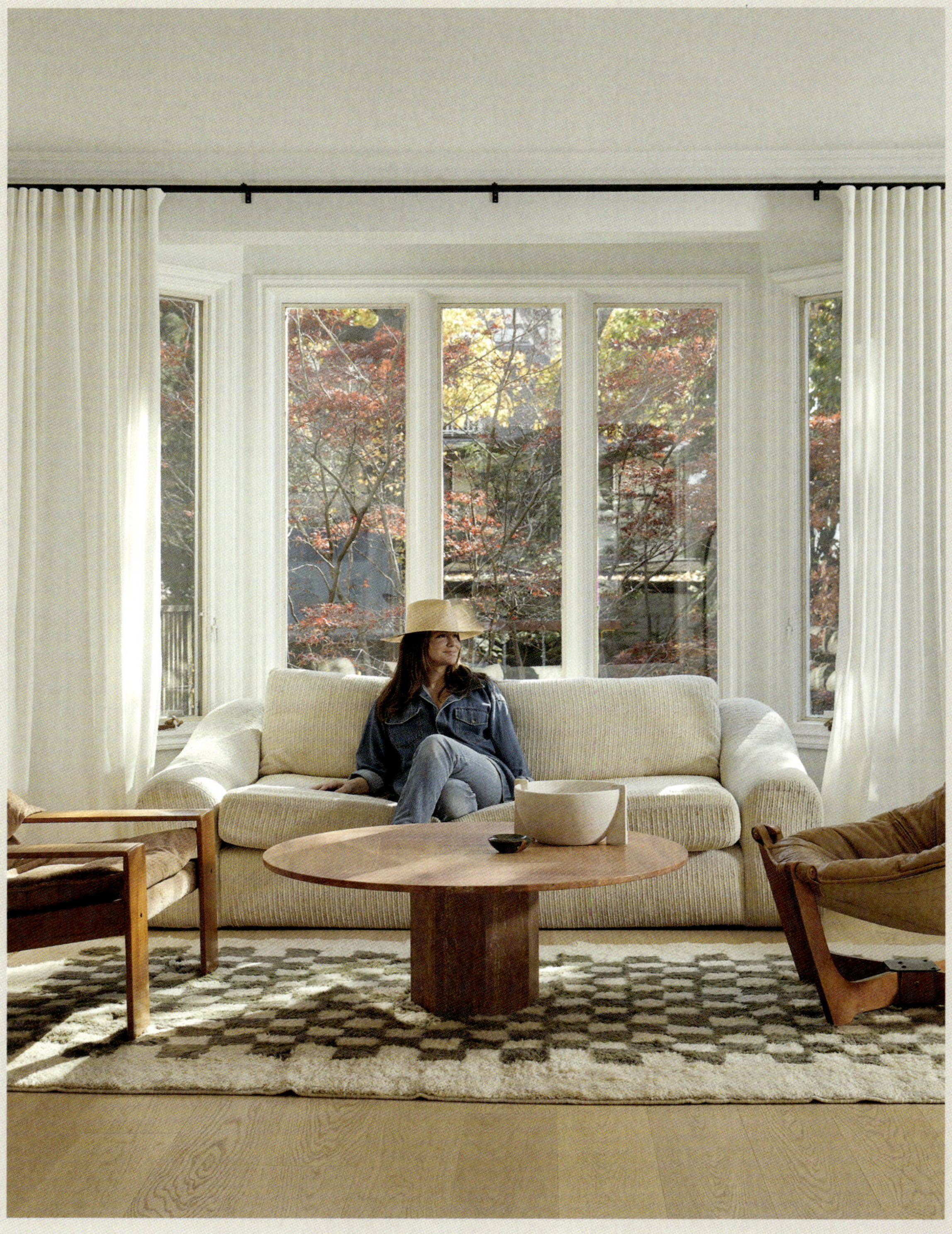

Montana Burnett

Montana Burnett Design is a full service residential and commercial design firm based in Toronto, Canada.

Known for her fresh and eclectic style, Montana brings her original perspective to every project.

Having begun her career as an editor for Canadian House and Home Magazine, Montana has a wide breadth of experience and exposure to all of the best in style.

Her regular travels inject a unique character to her style and the results are always beautifully curated spaces.

www.montanaburnettdesign.com

Photography: Lauren Miller

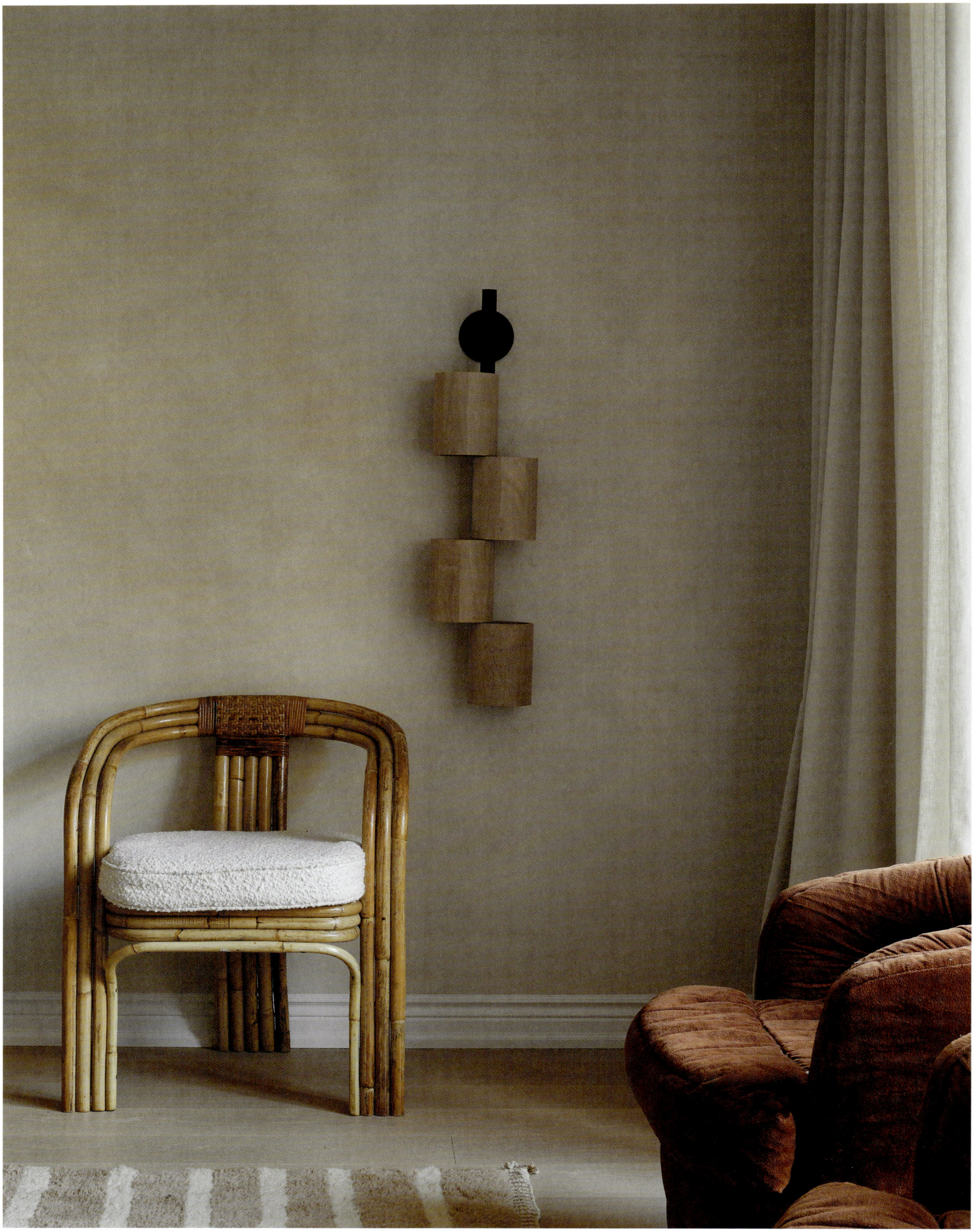

An amalgamation of Mediterranean earthiness and vintage 70's flare informed Montana Burnett Design in its approach to celebrity-chef Eden Grinshpan's renovation.

After leaving NYC and Brooklyn living, Eden and her family moved to a 90's built home in Toronto, Canada. The Eden's House project was born out of this home craving clean updates and an injection of Eden's distinct, eclectic style.

As a full-home renovation in progress, Burnett and Grinshpan work closely and in collaboration to bring to life this serenely clean yet whimsically unique home. So far, Eden's House has realized a clean palette with new flooring and an intentional one-tone paint job. Odes to the 70s dance through the home from its fully redesigned chef's kitchen with soft pink hues and warm woods, new powder room, as well as its inviting fireplace mantles.

Eden's House is perfect for entertaining, family life, and cooking up Eden's next new recipe.

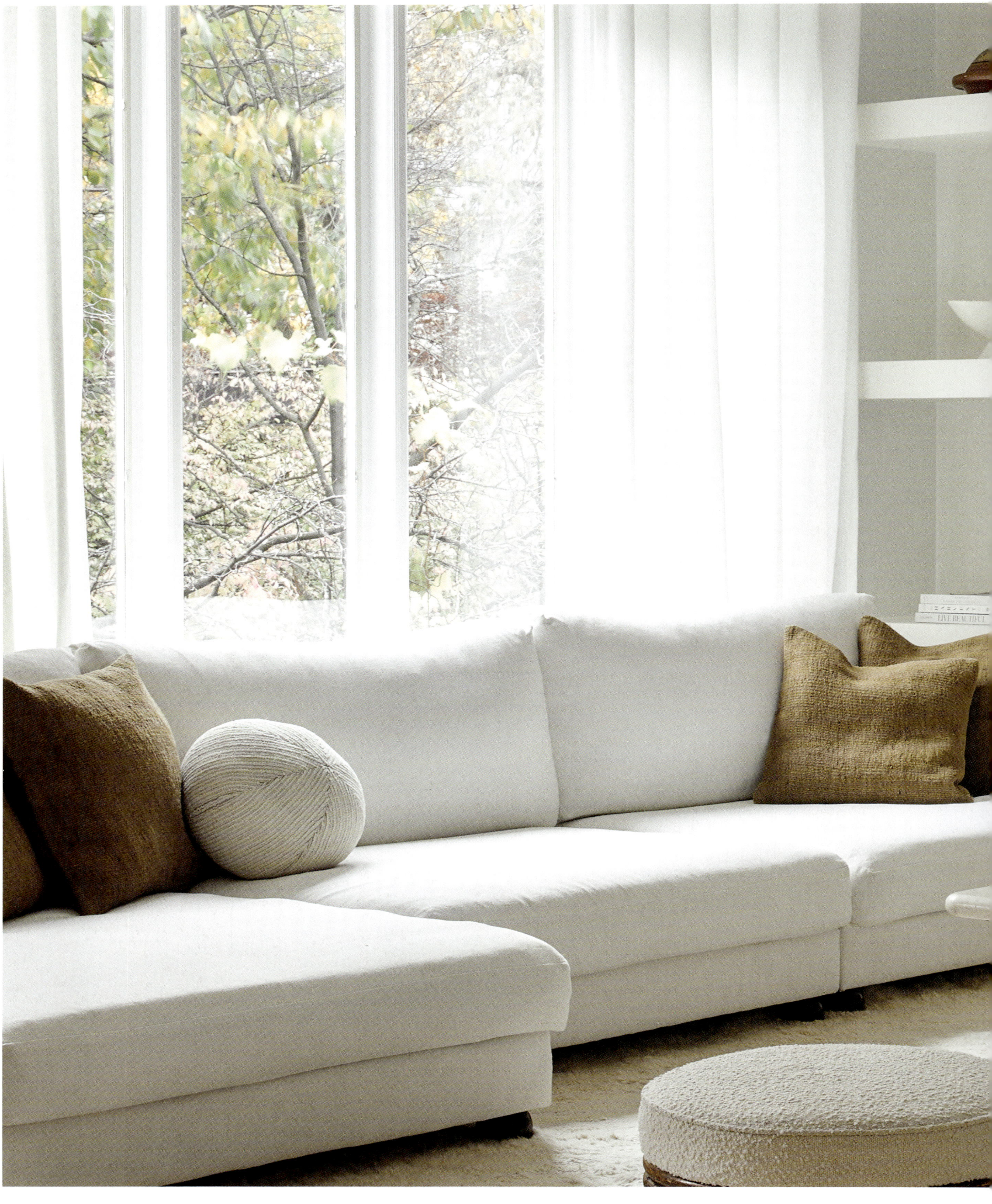
LIVE BEAUTIFUL

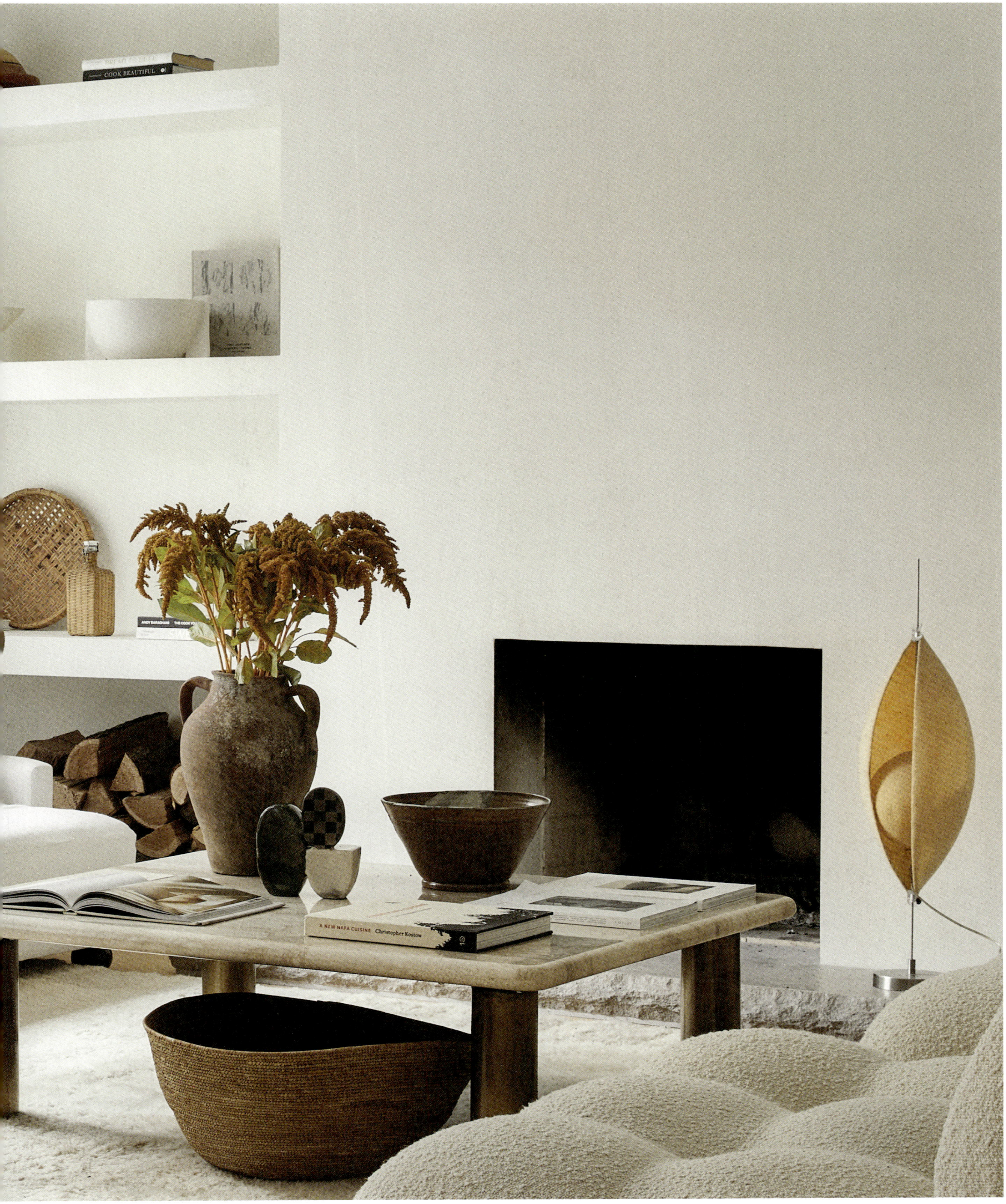
COOK BEAUTIFUL
A NEW NAPA CUISINE Christopher Kostow

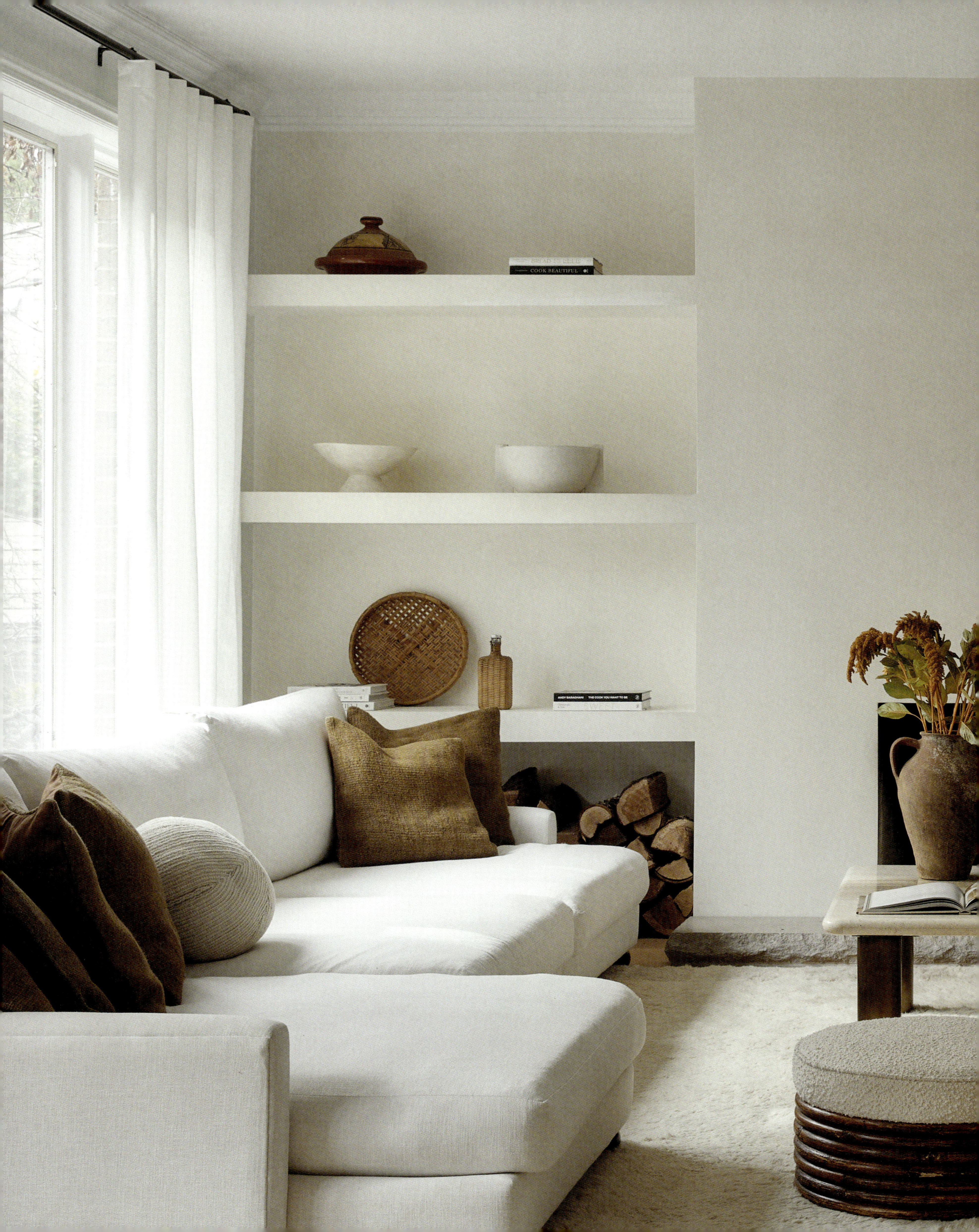
COOK BEAUTIFUL

FRENCH COUNTRY CUISINE
EATING OUT LOUD
A NEW NAPA CUISINE Christopher Kostow

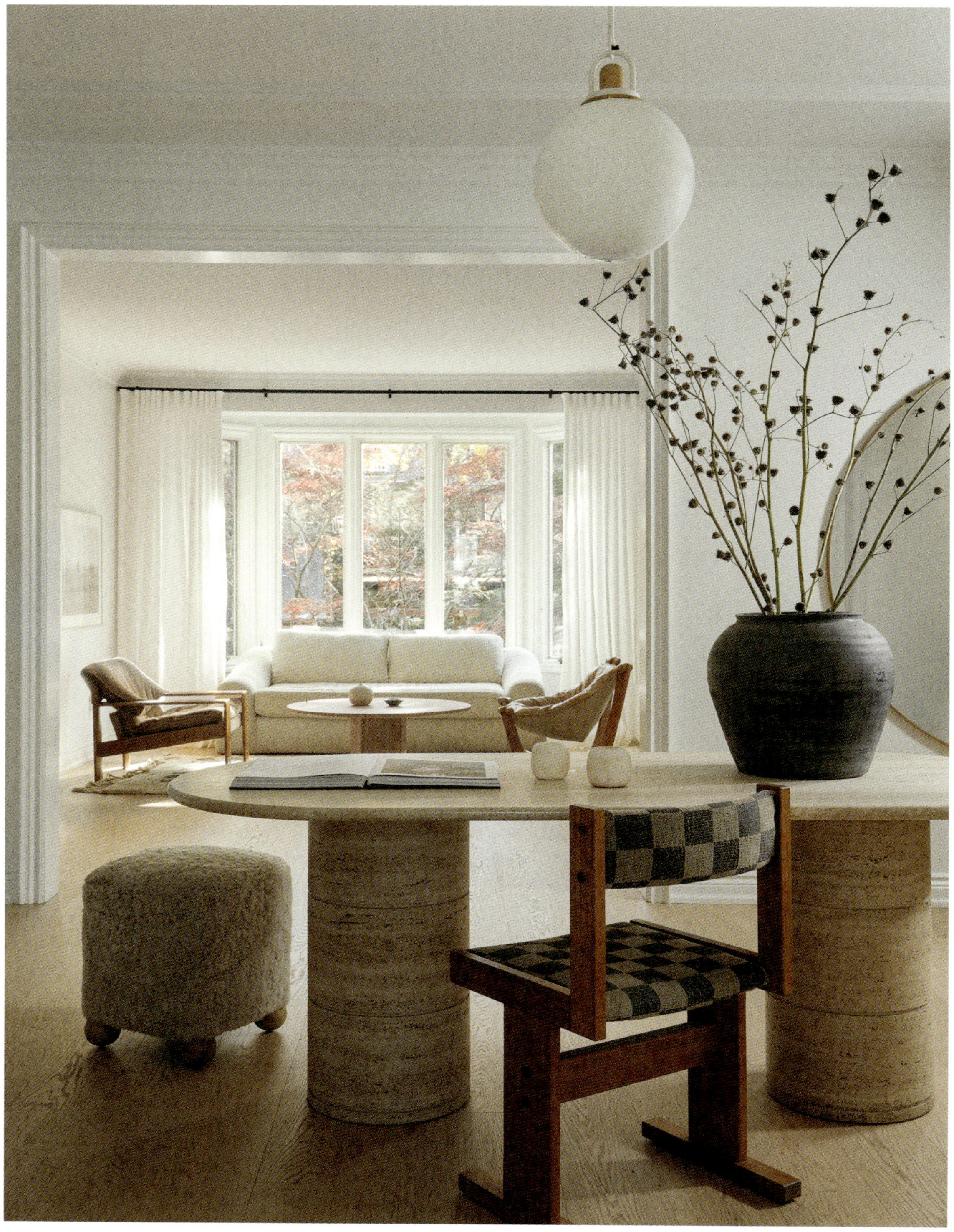

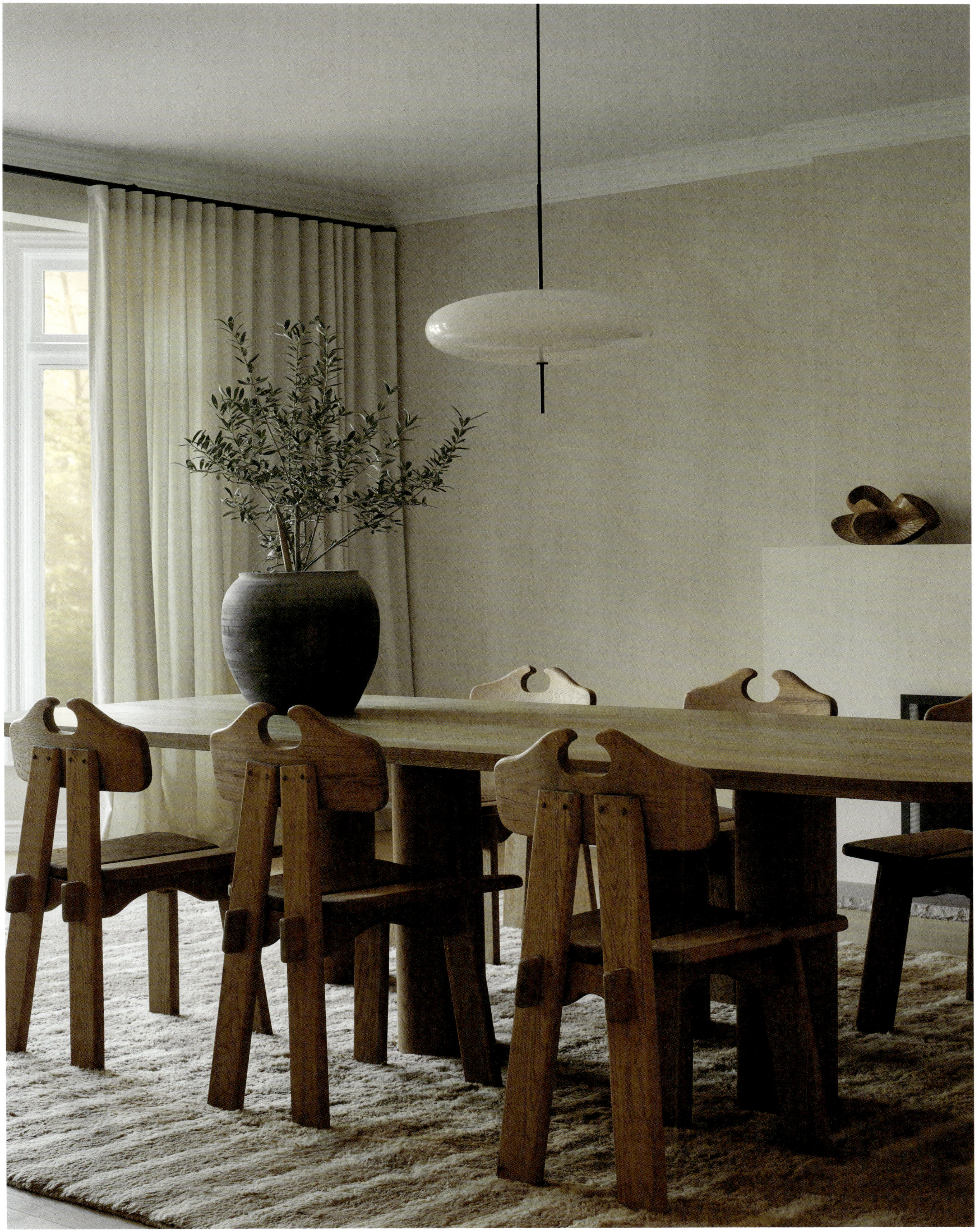

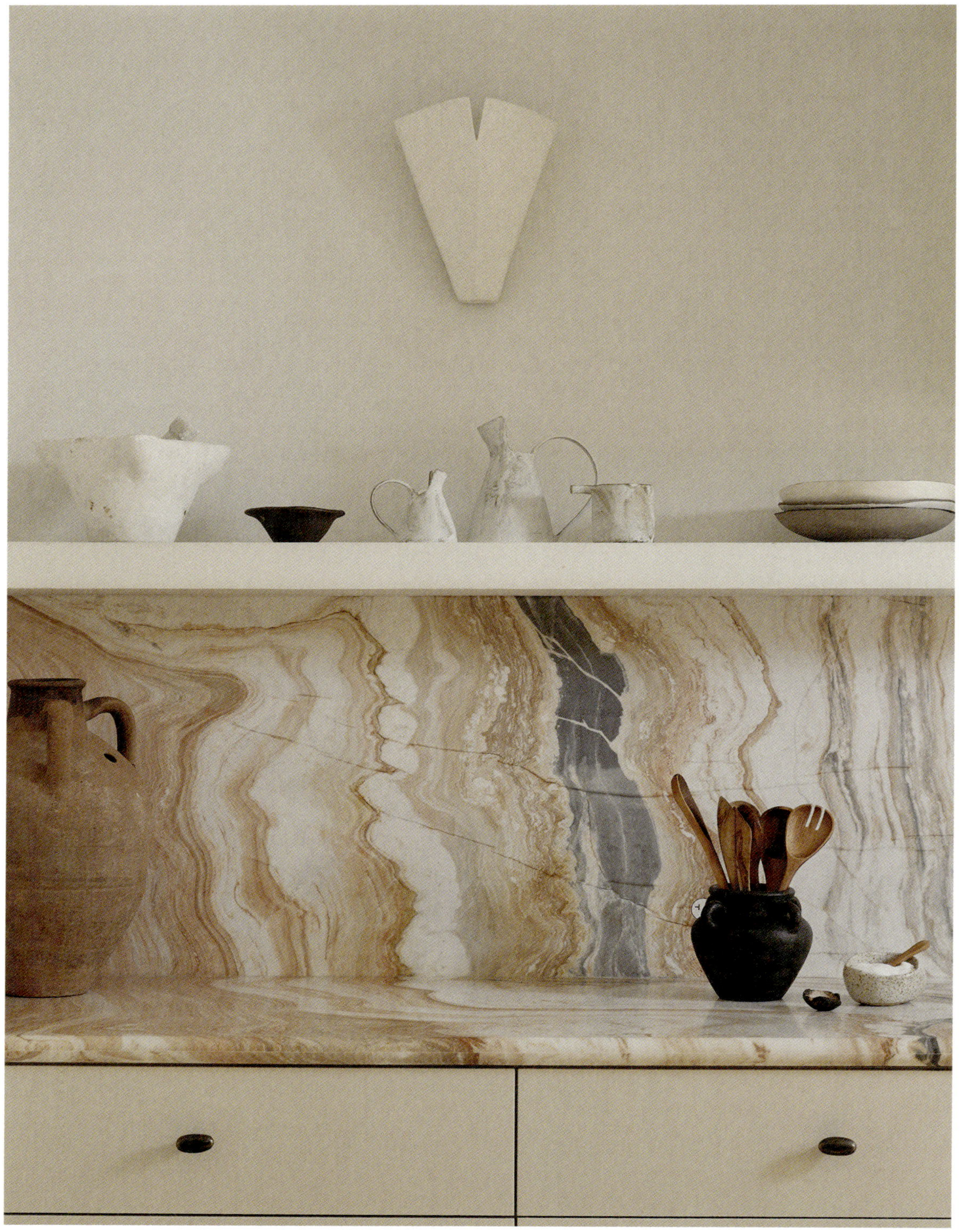

215

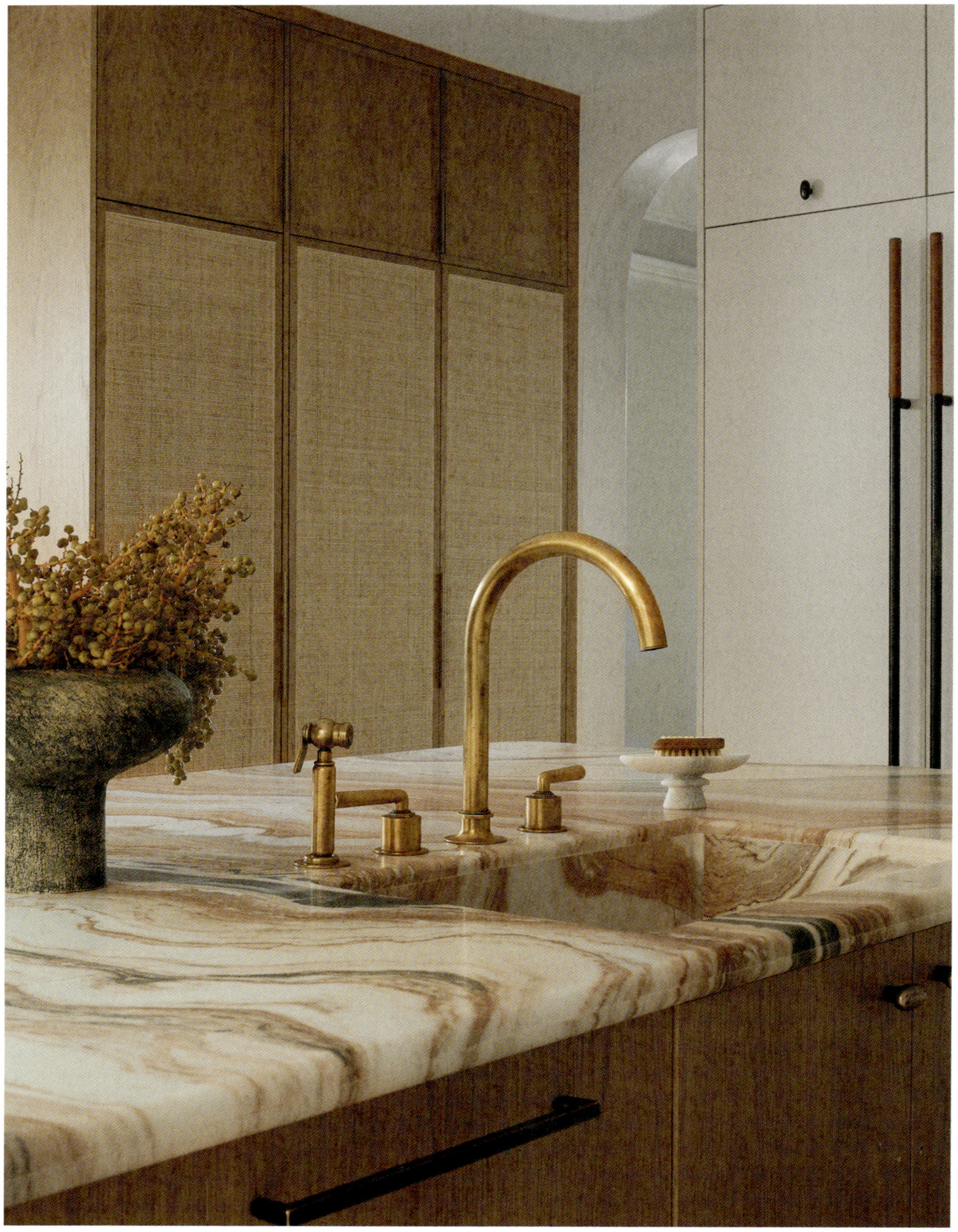

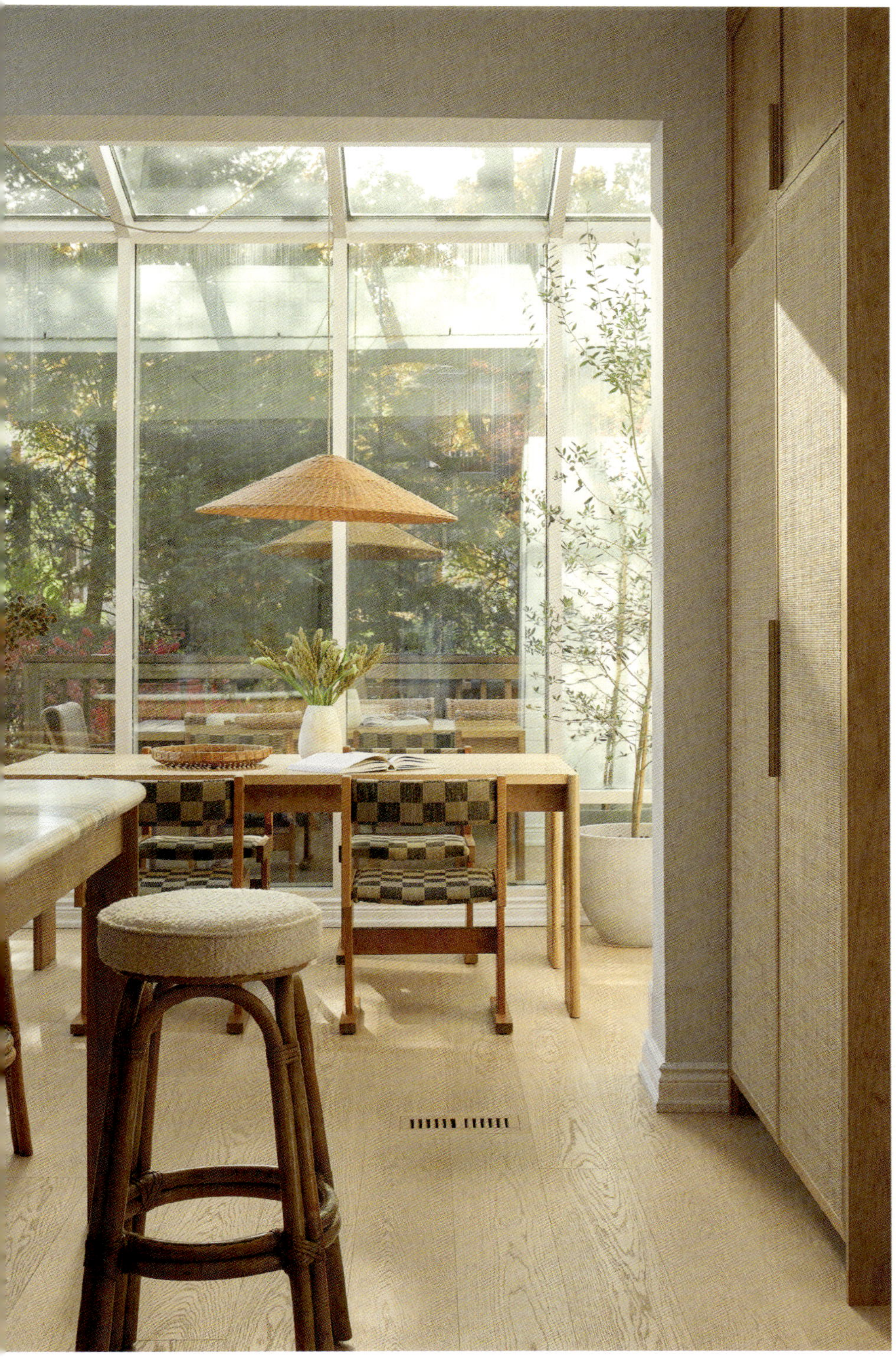

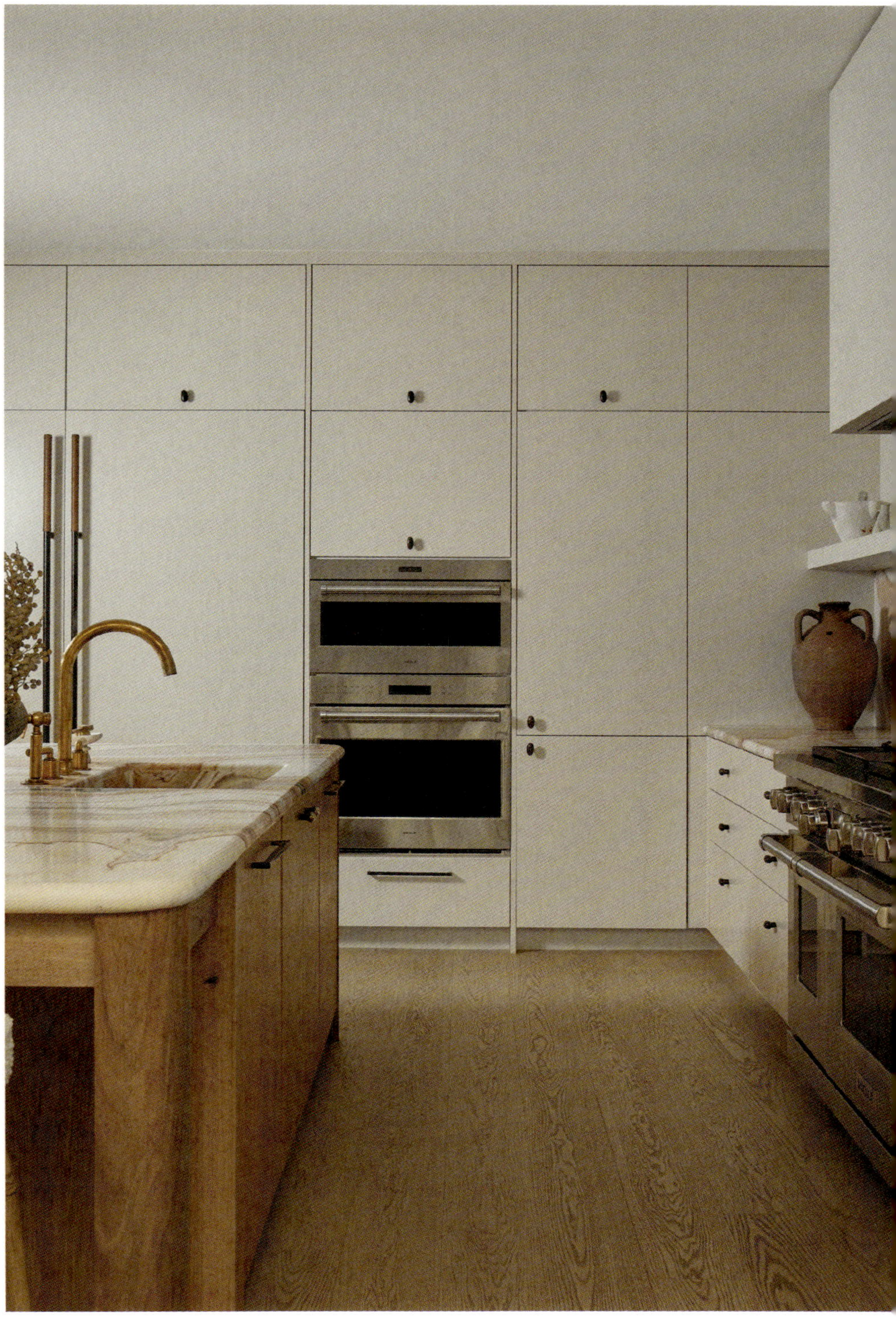

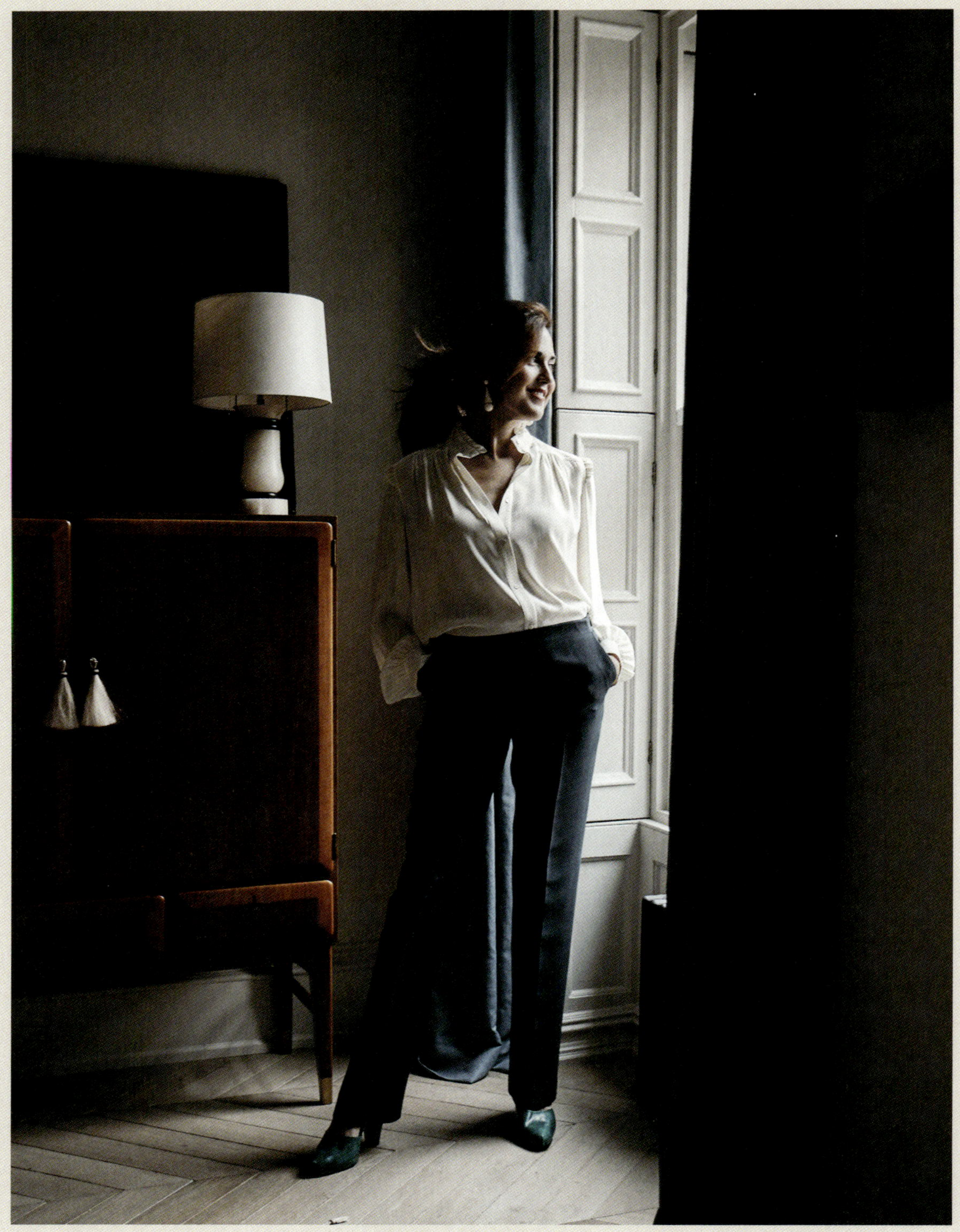

Chused & Co

After 20 years as an entrepreneur, designer, stylist, editor, and buyer, Jenna Chused followed her true passion and in 2015 established her Brooklyn-based interior design firm, Chused & Co. Chused's unique creative background conveys a distinct awareness of color, pattern, and texture. Layering selected modern elements and unexpected vintage pieces, her interiors are richly layered spaces that show an acquired eclecticism. She continues to receive global recognition for her interiors that feel unpretentious yet luxe, straddling both the modern and the traditional.

Starting a career in fashion at Donna Karan, she then moved to the editorial side as a fashion stylist for publications including Italian Vogue, Vanity Fair, and Elle. Eventually transitioning from fashion to home, Jenna spent the next 13 years building the highly successful lifestyle brand DwellStudio. She was involved in all aspects of the business, from product design and development to creating the brand's showrooms and the New York flagship store. Chused helped take the company from a small wholesale business to an internationally recognized brand. In 2013 the company was sold to Wayfair, presenting the opportunity for Chused to start her interior design studio - Chused & Co.

Originally hailing from the South, Jenna has resided in New York for over 25 years and lives in Brooklyn, New York with her husband and two sons.

www.chusedandco.com

Photography: Jeff Holt

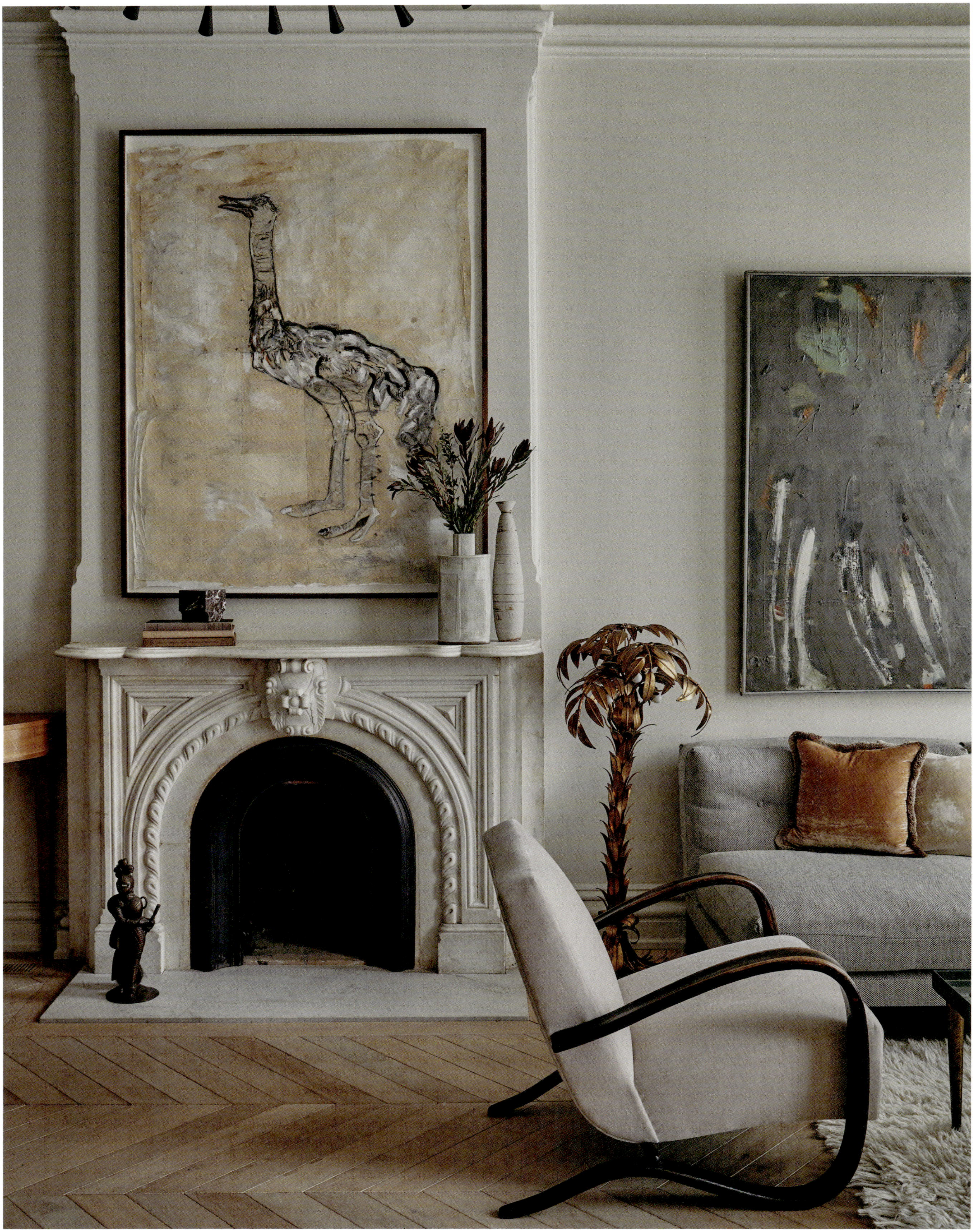

This is the own home, elegant yet family-friendly, of Jenna Chused and her family in the Fort Greene neighborhood in Brooklyn, New York. Light-filled yet at times moody, with a combination of vintage and custom pieces, this chic town house has soaring ceilings and several marble mantles. Jenna realized the home of her dreams, with a grand European feel, in keeping with the antiques, especially the decorative arts of the 1940s which she adores.

The house had already been renovated previously (in 2005), but Jenna designed all-new bathrooms and a brand new kitchen at the rear of the parlor floor with a new window and new doors. She did away with some upstairs closets and reconceived the imposing arched opening into the living room to gain more living space, moved doorways and redid all the floors with new planks laid in a herringbone pattern. What had been a separate garden-floor apartment was incorporated into the rest to make the building a single-family. The downstairs front room is now a sienna-colored music room with vintage slipper chairs, a polished brass Cubist-style Italian chandelier from the 1960s by Gaetano Sciolari and a grand piano played by everyone in the family (Jenna's husband is a composer).

Almost all the furnishings in the house are vintage, including the lighting, with a show-stopping ceiling fixture in almost every room. Jenna salvaged a wide archway that had once been in another house and replaced the doorway's existing pair of double doors with pocket doors to gain precious inches for furniture placement in the front parlor. Armless sofas from Ochre are among the only new furnishings in the house. A Brazilian mid-century coffee table, a pair of low-slung armchairs by Czech designer Jindrich Halabala and a Moroccan rug round out the room's decor. Most of the art and lighting in the home are pieces Chused purchased and squirreled away over the years. She found the Italian metal '60s chandelier at auction; it once hung in a hotel in Rome. The ostrich painting over the mantel was found rolled up at a Paris flea market in 2000. The dining area in the middle of the parlor floor is distinguished by an antique Belgian tapestry on the wall, chairs by Angelo Mangiarotti, and an oval table and bouclé-covered banquette Chused had custom made. In the kitchen, glossy burgundy cabinetry was achieved with a hand-done Old World lacquer technique. The white range with gold-toned knobs is from Lacanche. The clean-lined fireplace wall replaces the original ornate mantel, relocated upstairs to the primary bedroom. The elaborately carved mantel came from what is now the kitchen. A gleaming Swedish cabinet, French '40s ceiling fixture from Paris and vintage Moroccan rug echo themes found elsewhere in the house. Chused removed two closets to allow for a spacious sitting room adjacent to the primary bedroom. A panoramic wallpaper mural from Ananbo envelops the atmospheric space. She had the rolled-arm sofa custom made. The velvet armchair is a design by Guglielmo Ulrich for Cassina, the sculptural fiberglass chandelier a 20th century icon by Achille Castiglioni. Even the TV room at the rear of the garden level received an extra-special wallpaper treatment - a 1930s pattern of lush vegetation from the French wallpaper company Isidore Leroy.

The result of this major renovation is astonishing. As Architectural Digest describes it, "it's clear that Chused has masterfully forged latitude and a lively sense of family life into a seemingly narrow town house. The definition of luxury in a city."

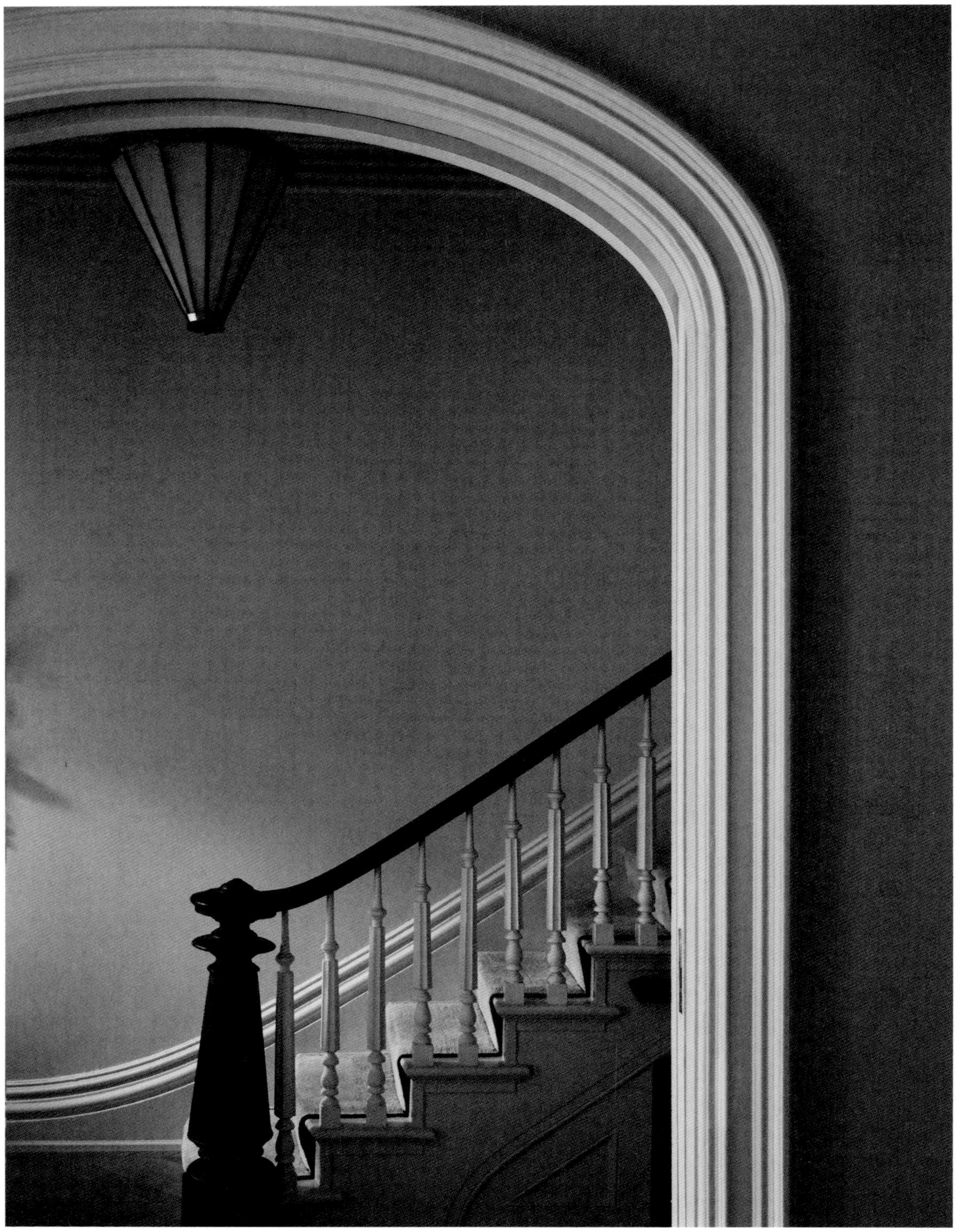

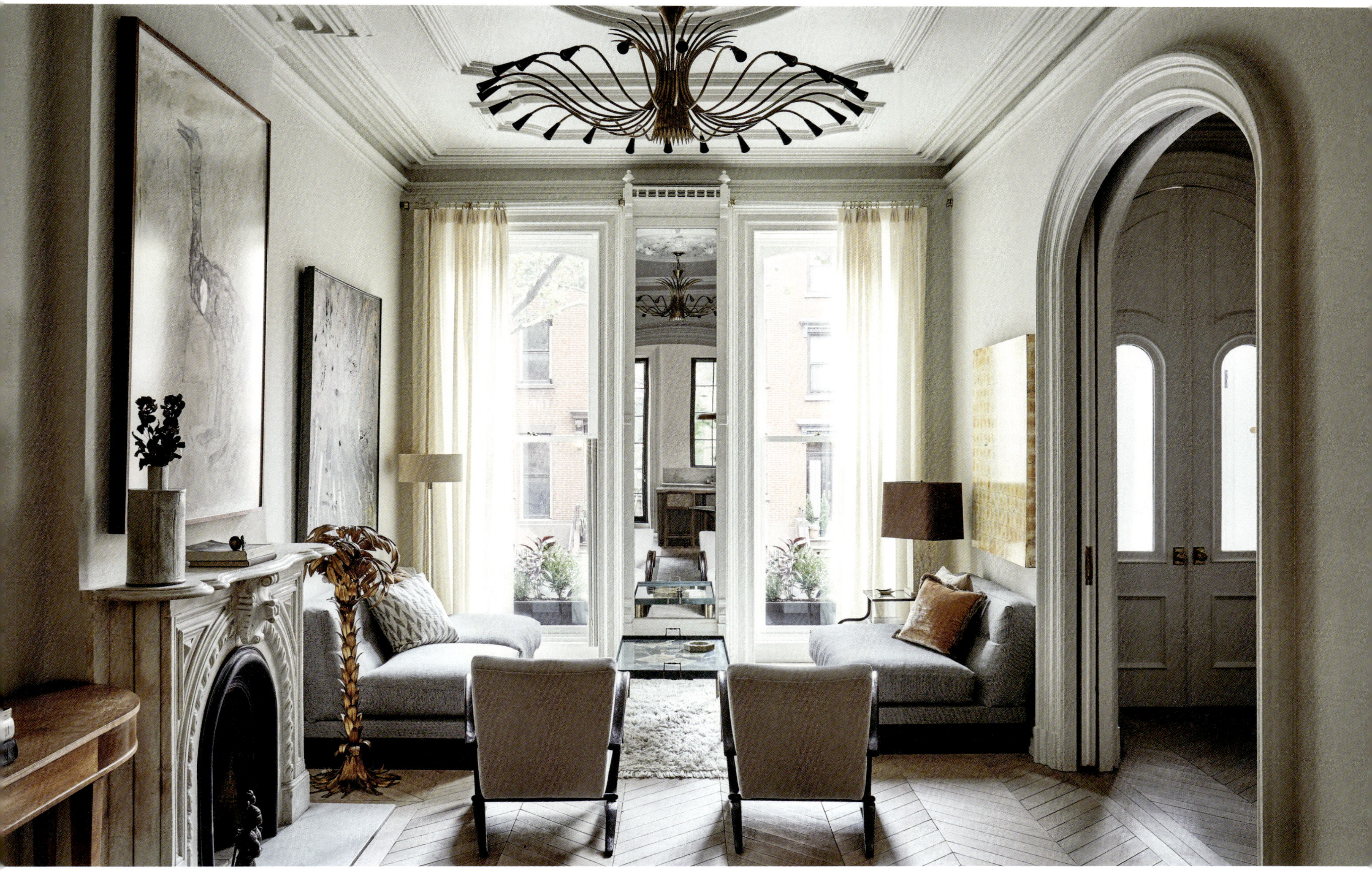

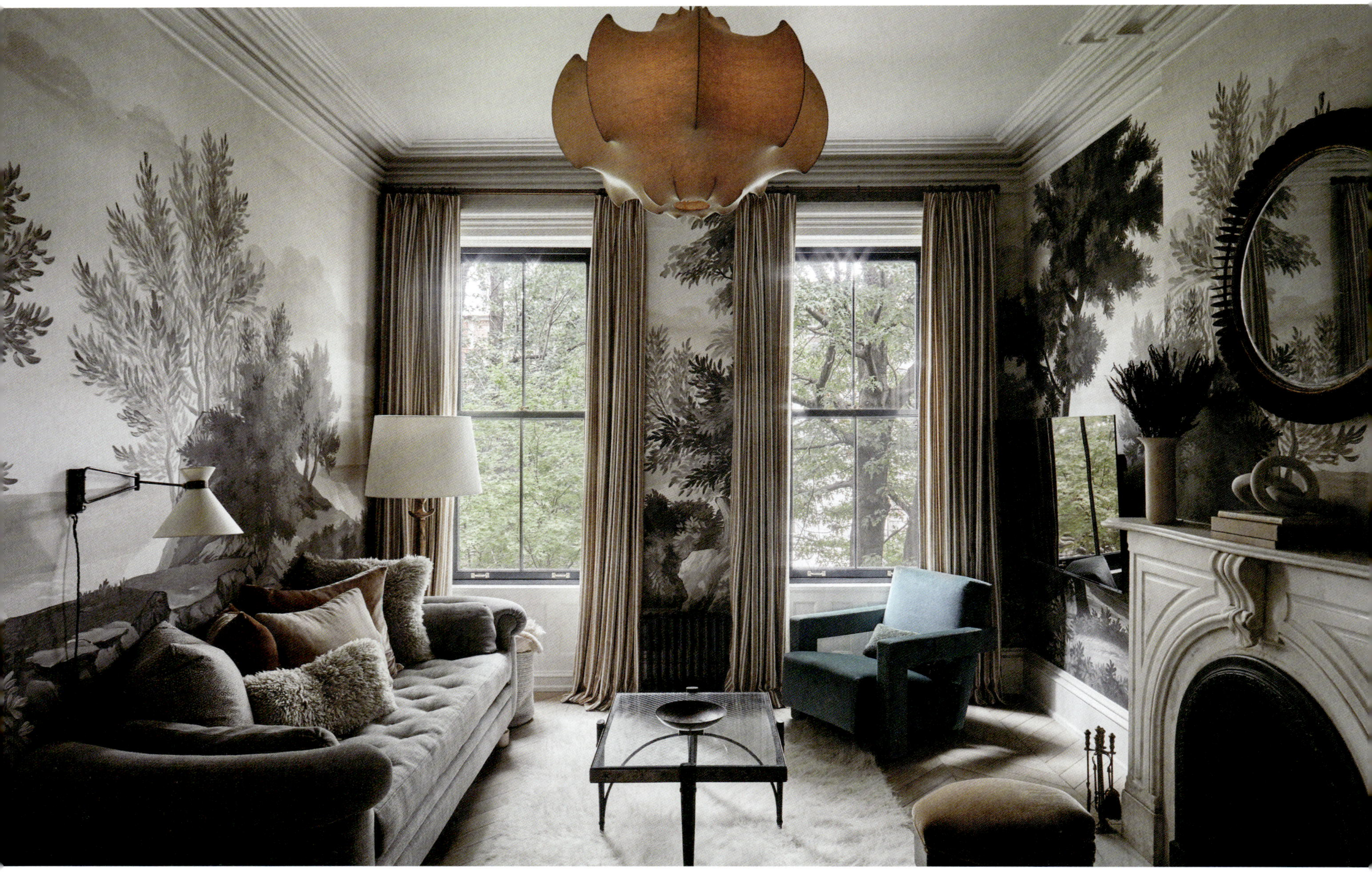

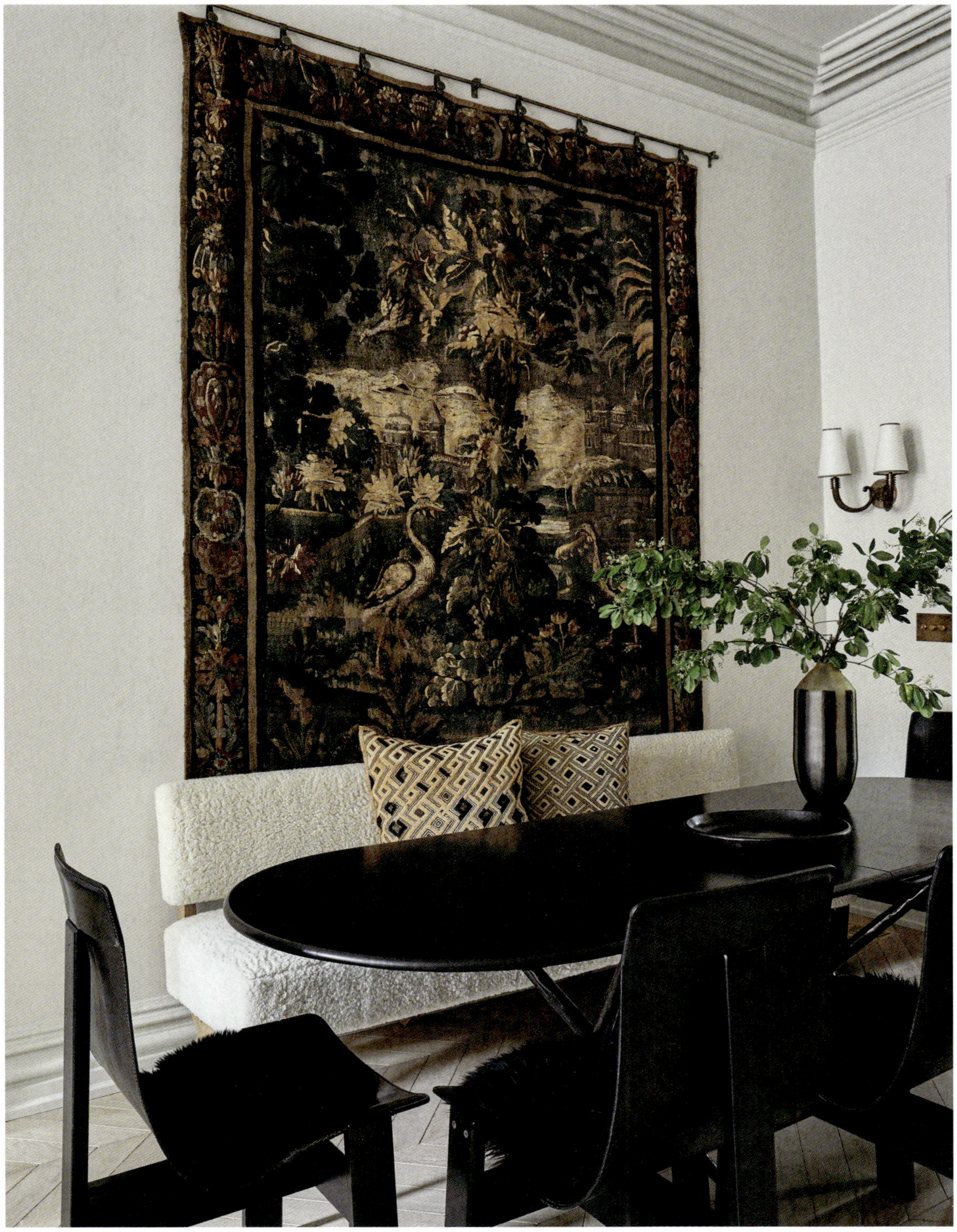

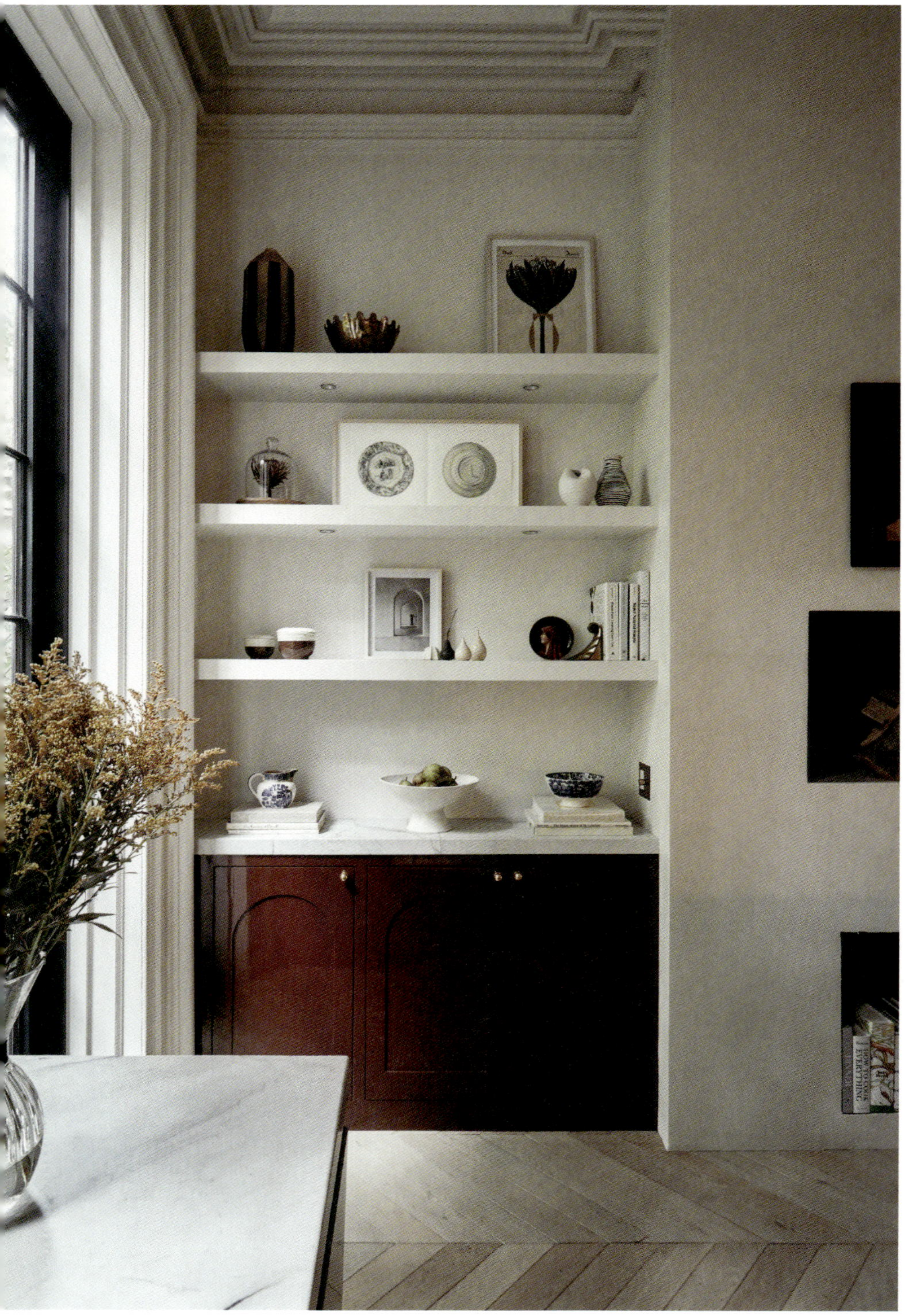
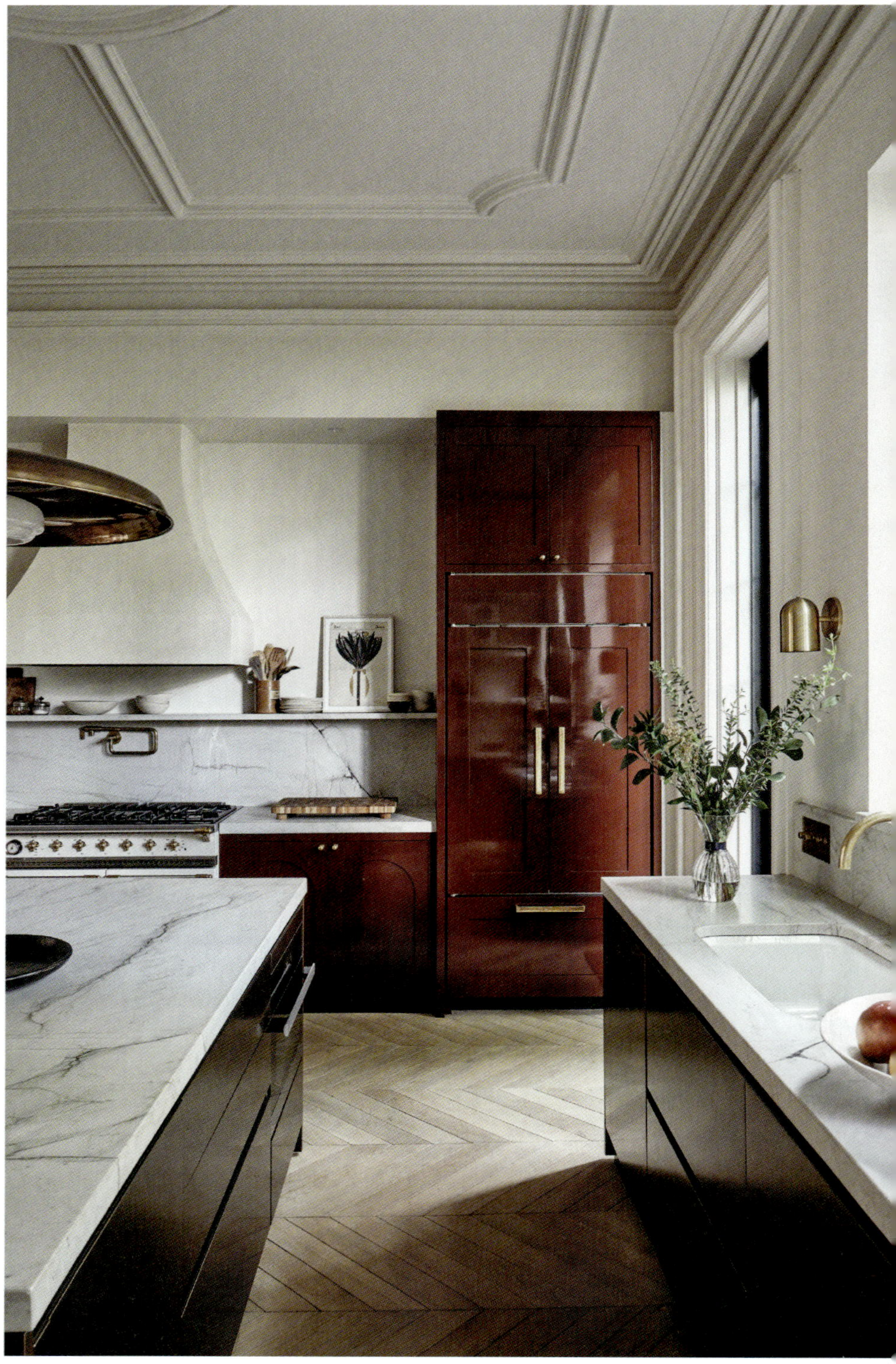

227

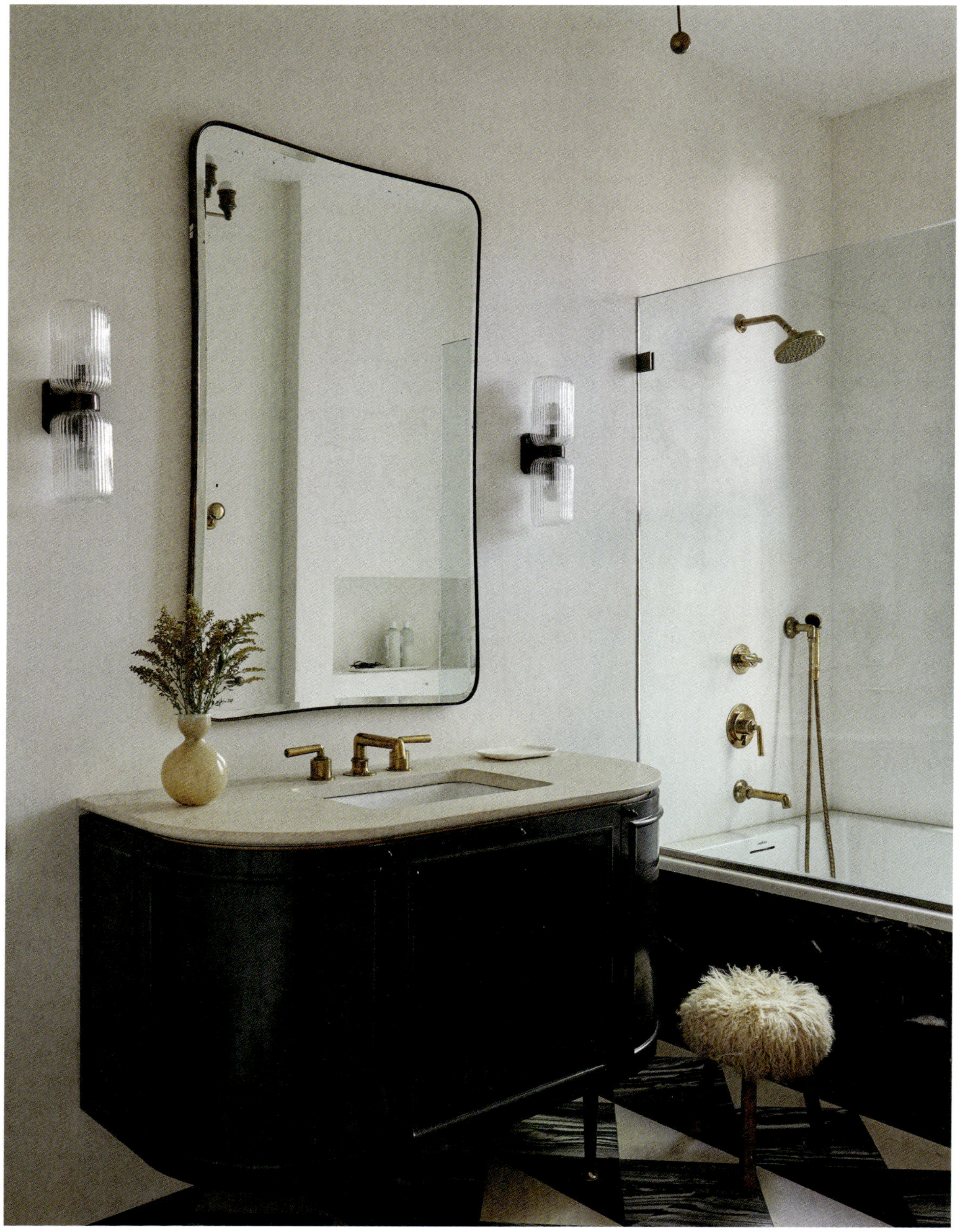

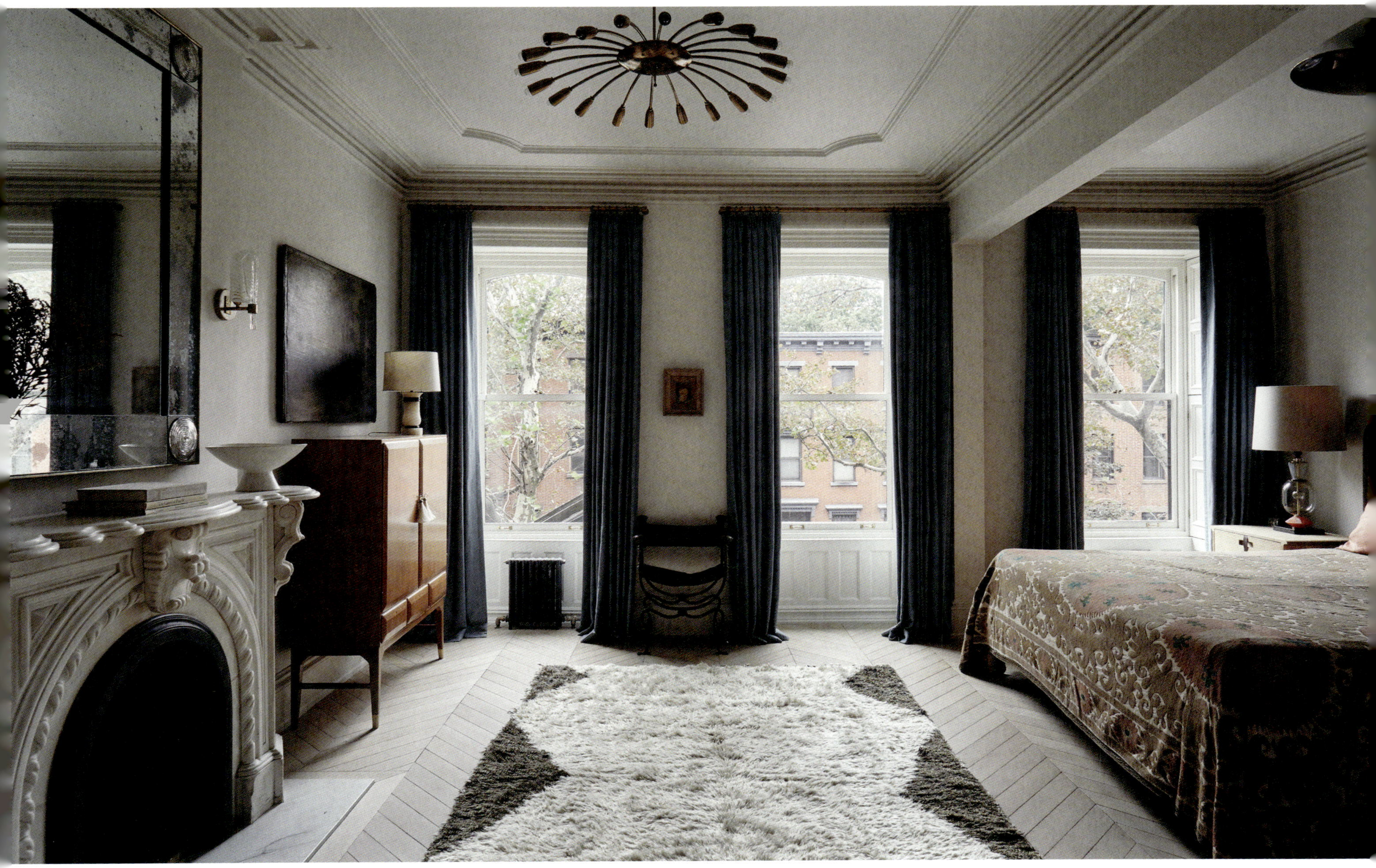

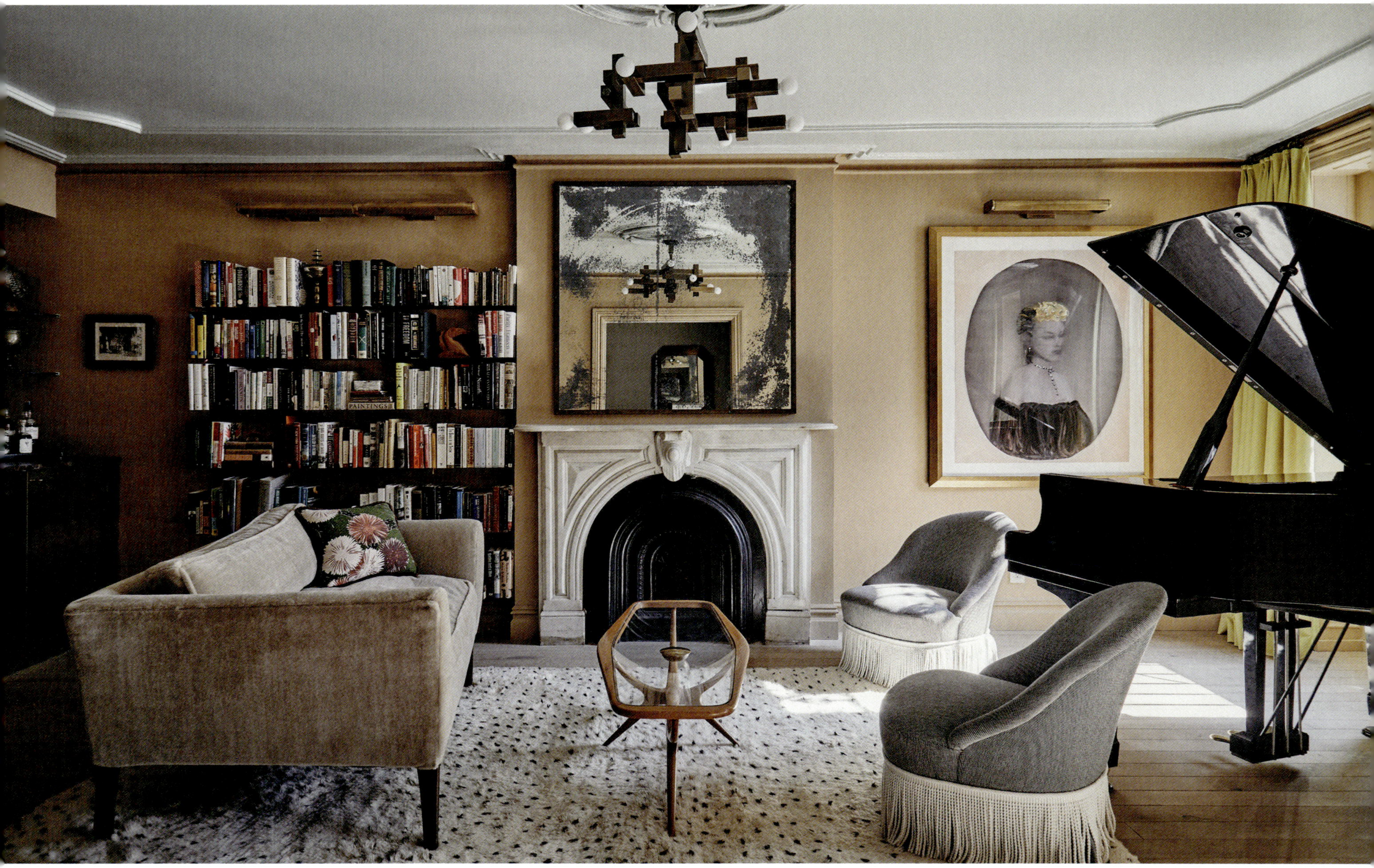

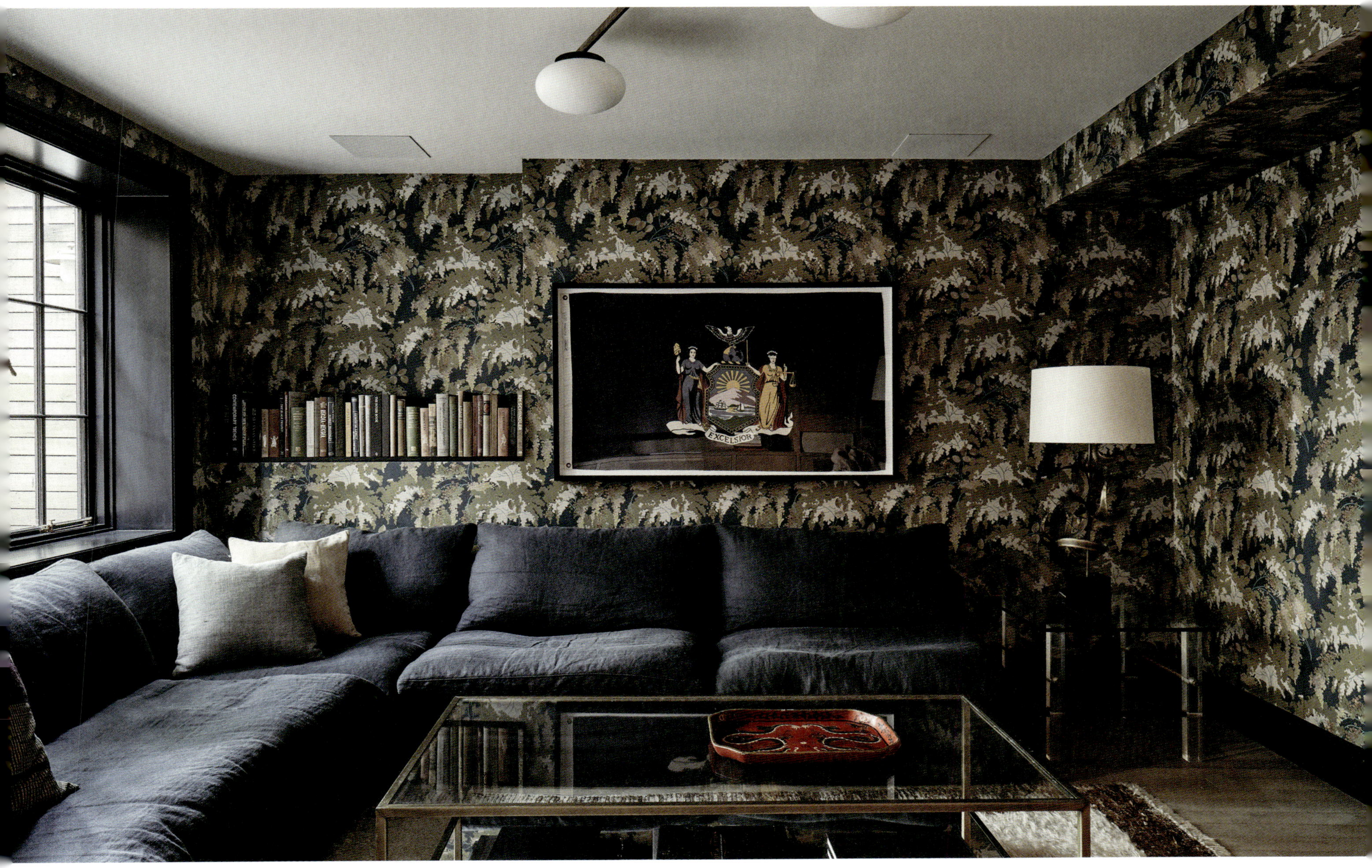

Portrait by Julie Ansiau

Véronique Cotrel

Véronique Cotrel is an interior design agency founded in Paris in 2010. She has developed expertise in the design and implementation of total renovation projects in Paris and throughout France and the rest of the world.

Véronique and her team work in all sectors of the building industry: homes, offices, hotels, restaurants and boutiques. Today, the agency has offices in Paris and New York and a staff of around 15.

Its work is based on one guiding principle: to strike the right balance between ergonomics and the soul of a place. Indeed, the first discussions with customers are always about lifestyle and needs, which form the specifications. Then, with her passion for art and architecture, Véronique Cotrel is keen to immerse herself in the place to better understand its history, style and codes. Once the project has been defined, she works with excellent craftsmen to bring these new settings to life, reflecting her vision of a new Parisian chic that blends tradition and modernity.

Left page: François Mille (director) and Véronique Cotrel (creative director).

www.verocotrel.fr

Photography: Amaury Laparra

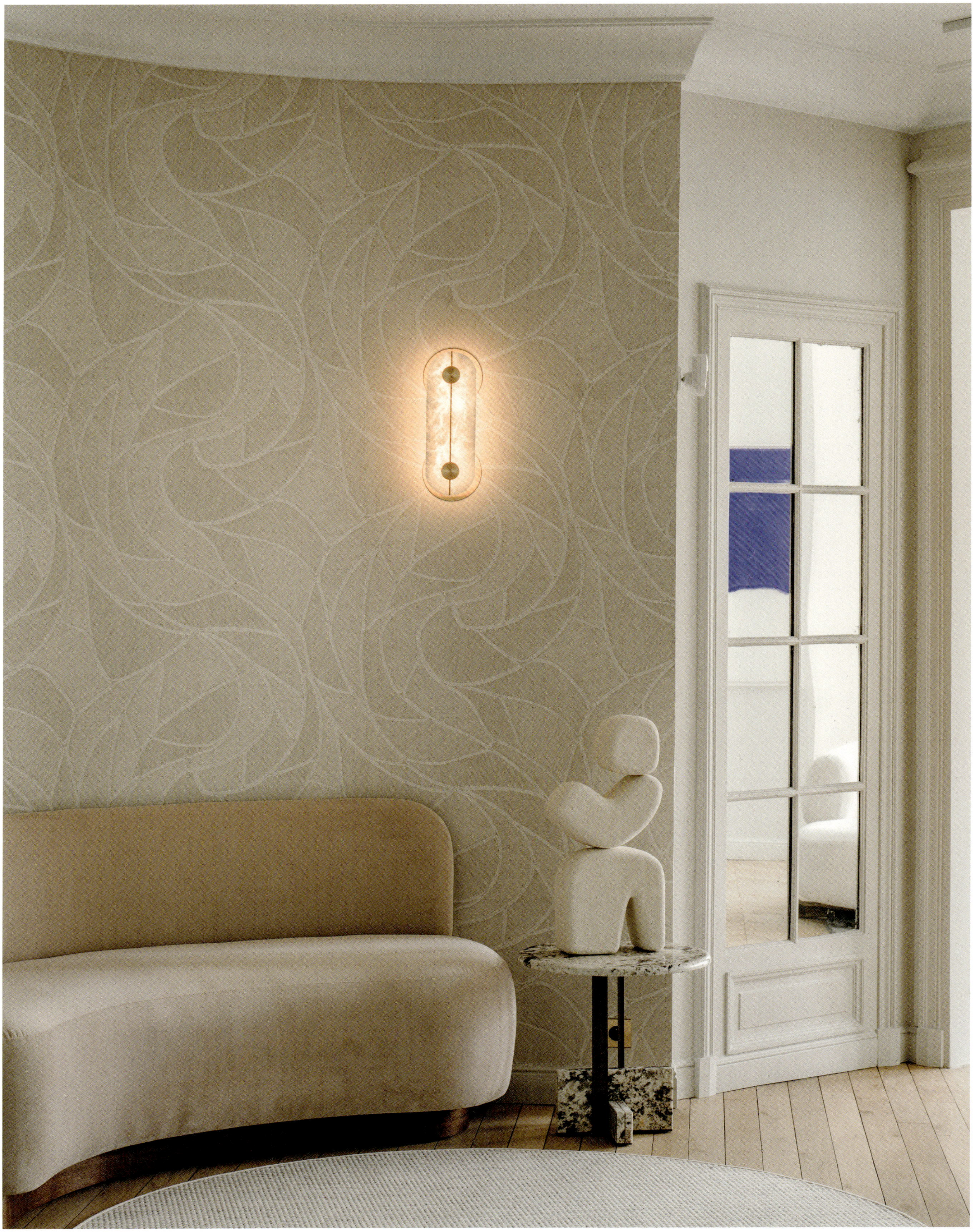

Located close to the Eiffel Tower, this apartment has the unique feature of being designed as a rotunda.

The living room is bathed in natural light throughout the day. The kitchen had to connect to this in a subtle and elegant way. The dining room acts as a link between the two spaces. The delineation is reinforced by the rounded wooden skylights designed by Véronique Cotrel. They are made of veneered and varnished walnut. This type of wood, often used in interior design, is also used for the fronts of the kitchen, which Véronique wanted to be made-to-measure. This option gives the designers the freedom to create a kitchen that isn't a kitchen at all! Totally integrated, its materials blend into the décor. The central island is lightened by this curved detail, and the airy walnut top.

This project underwent extensive restoration work, which had the advantage of rethinking the entire organization of the living spaces. As part of this reorganization, the moldings were either renovated or added to adapt to the new layout and form a common thread that harmonizes the spaces. The floors have been completely redesigned to meet both a comfort criterion by incorporating a heating system, and an aesthetic criterion by enlarging the outlook. Véronique Cotrel chose a layout, format and shade that respect the way parquet floors were laid in the Haussmann era.

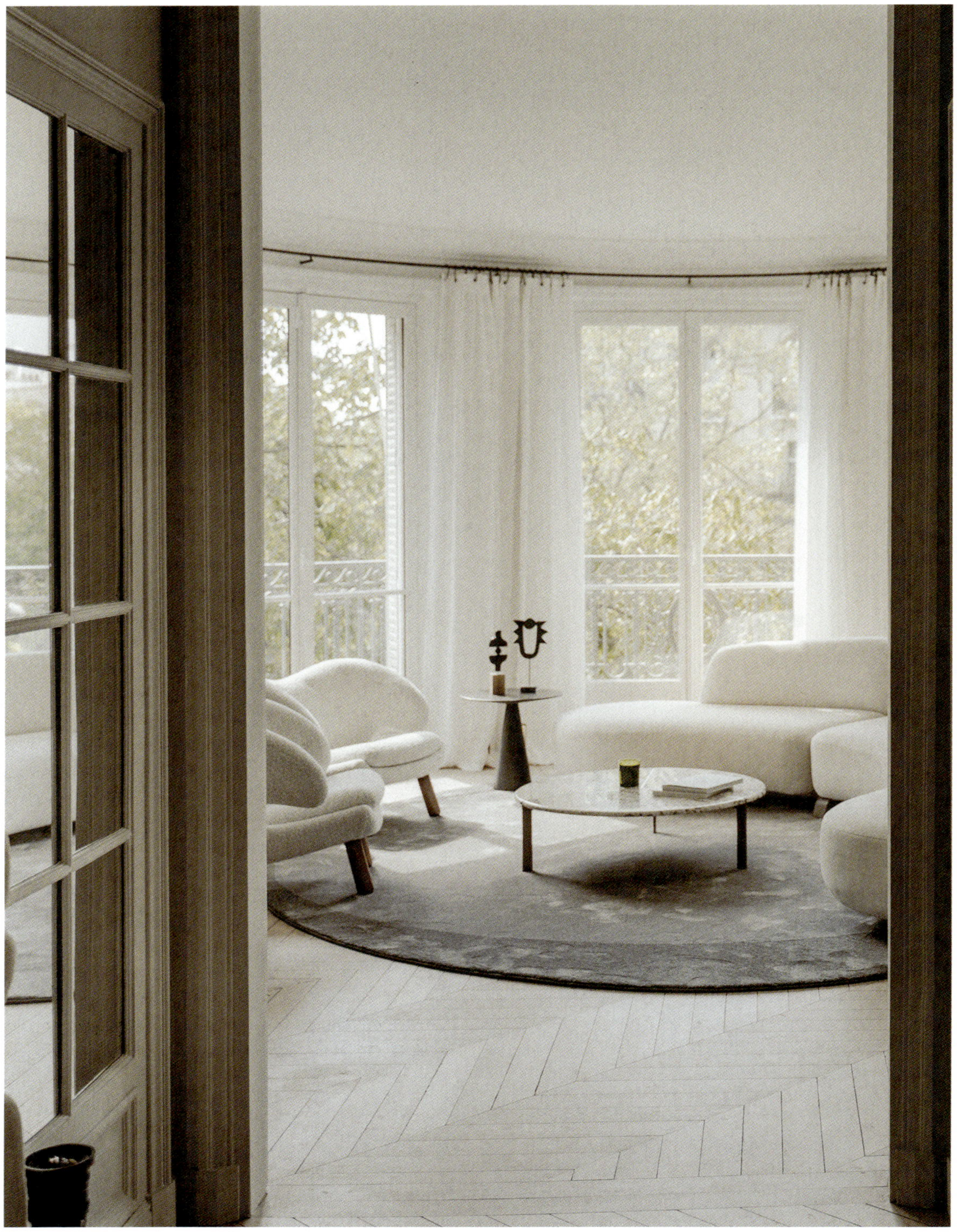

237

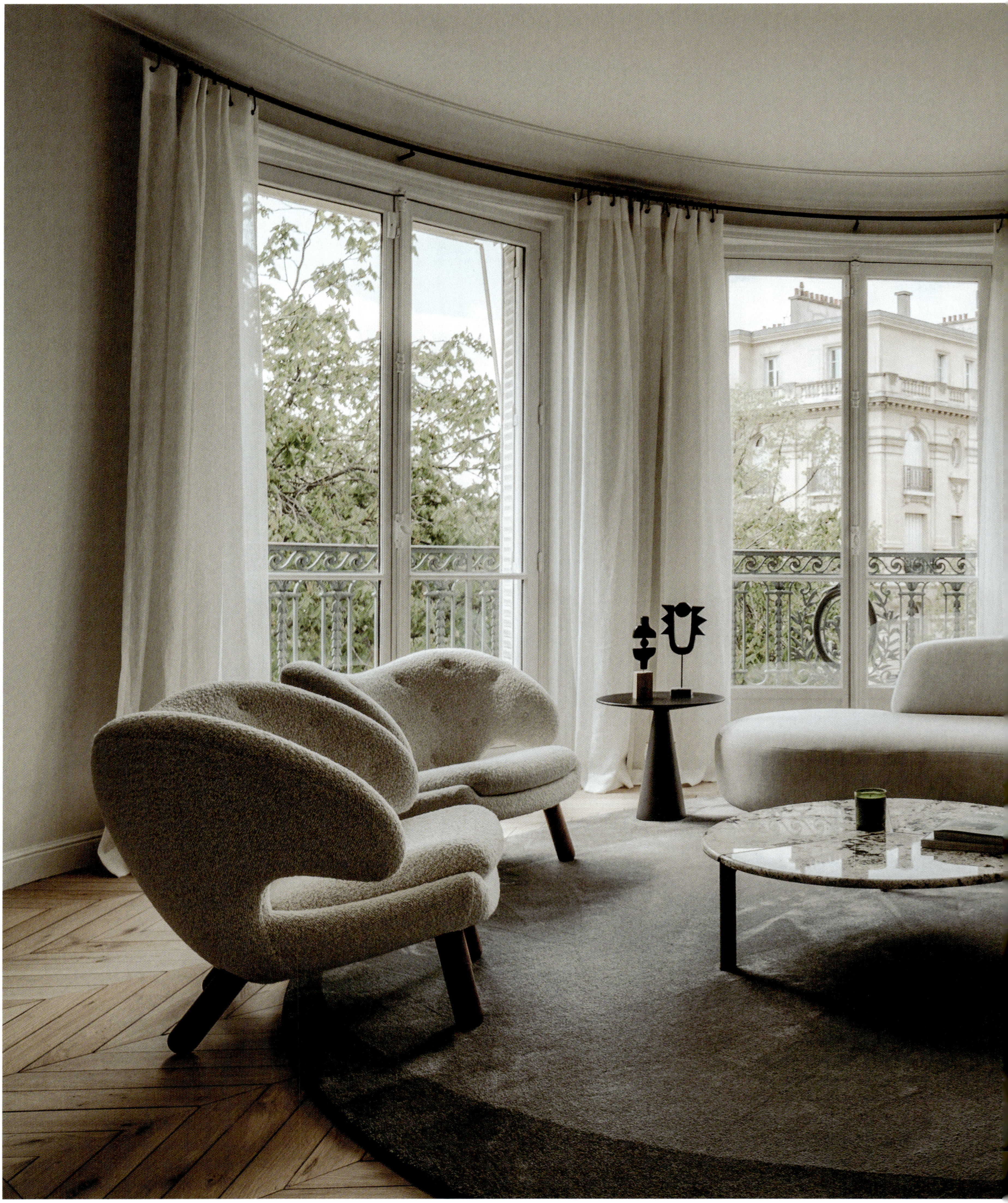

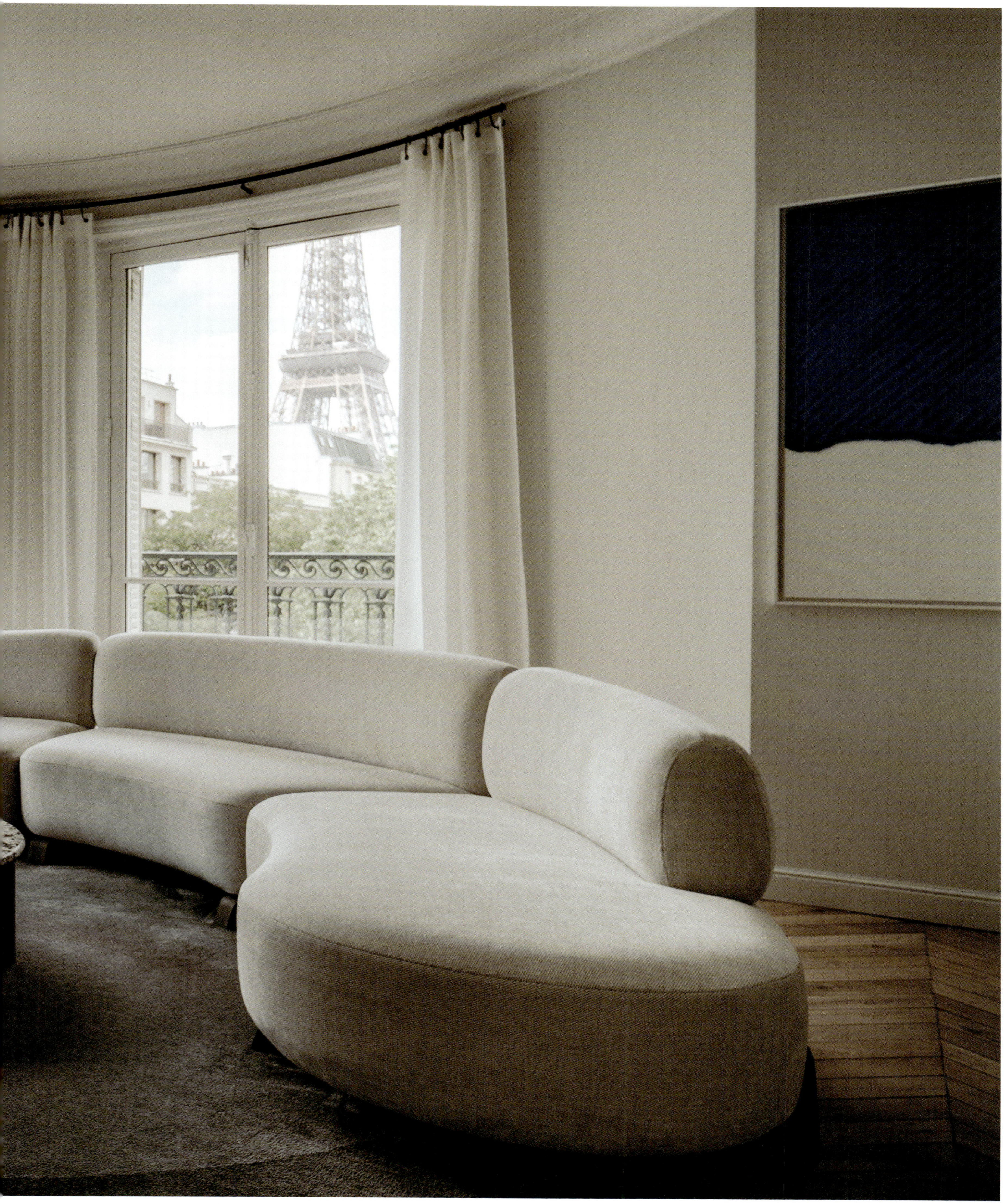

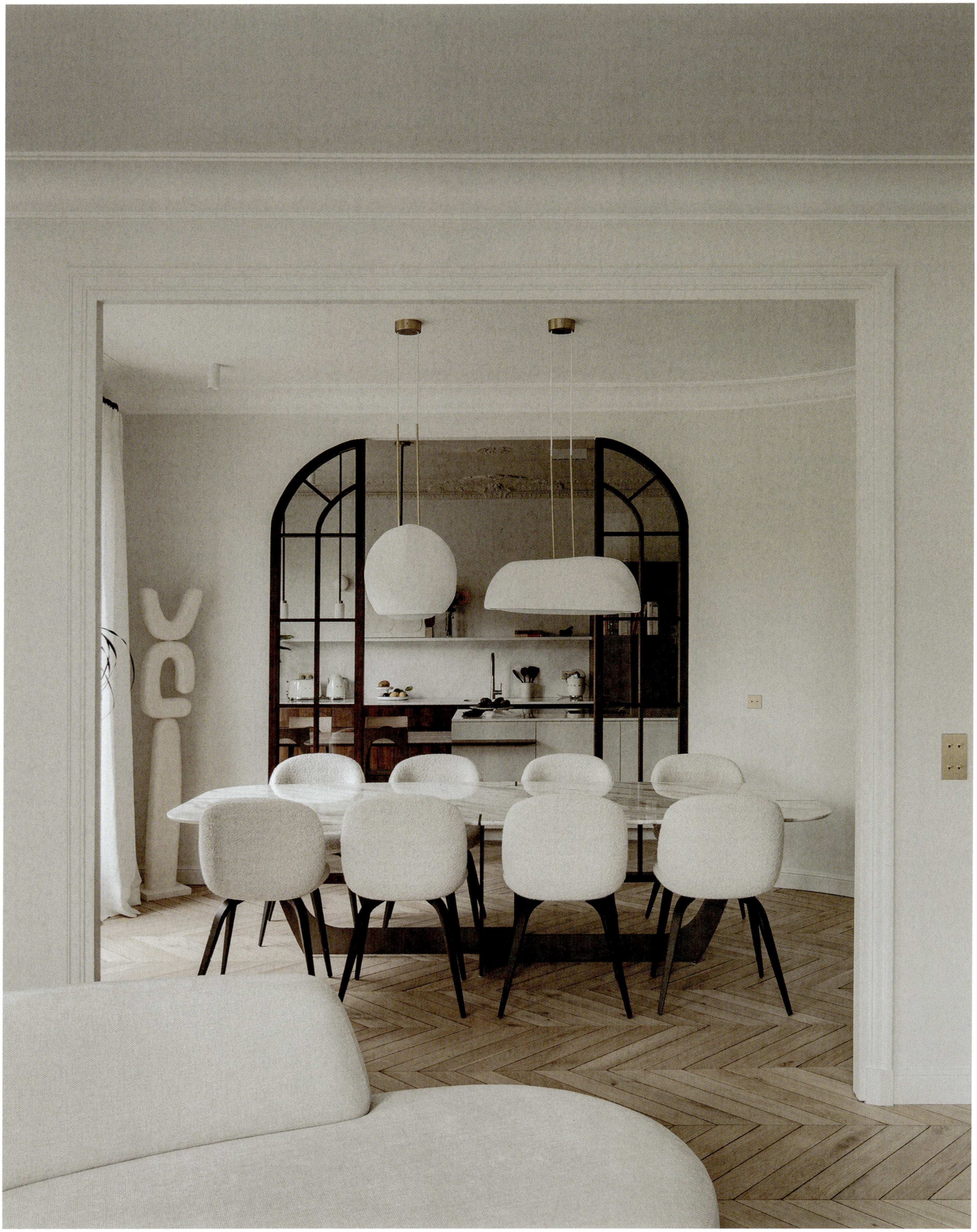

241

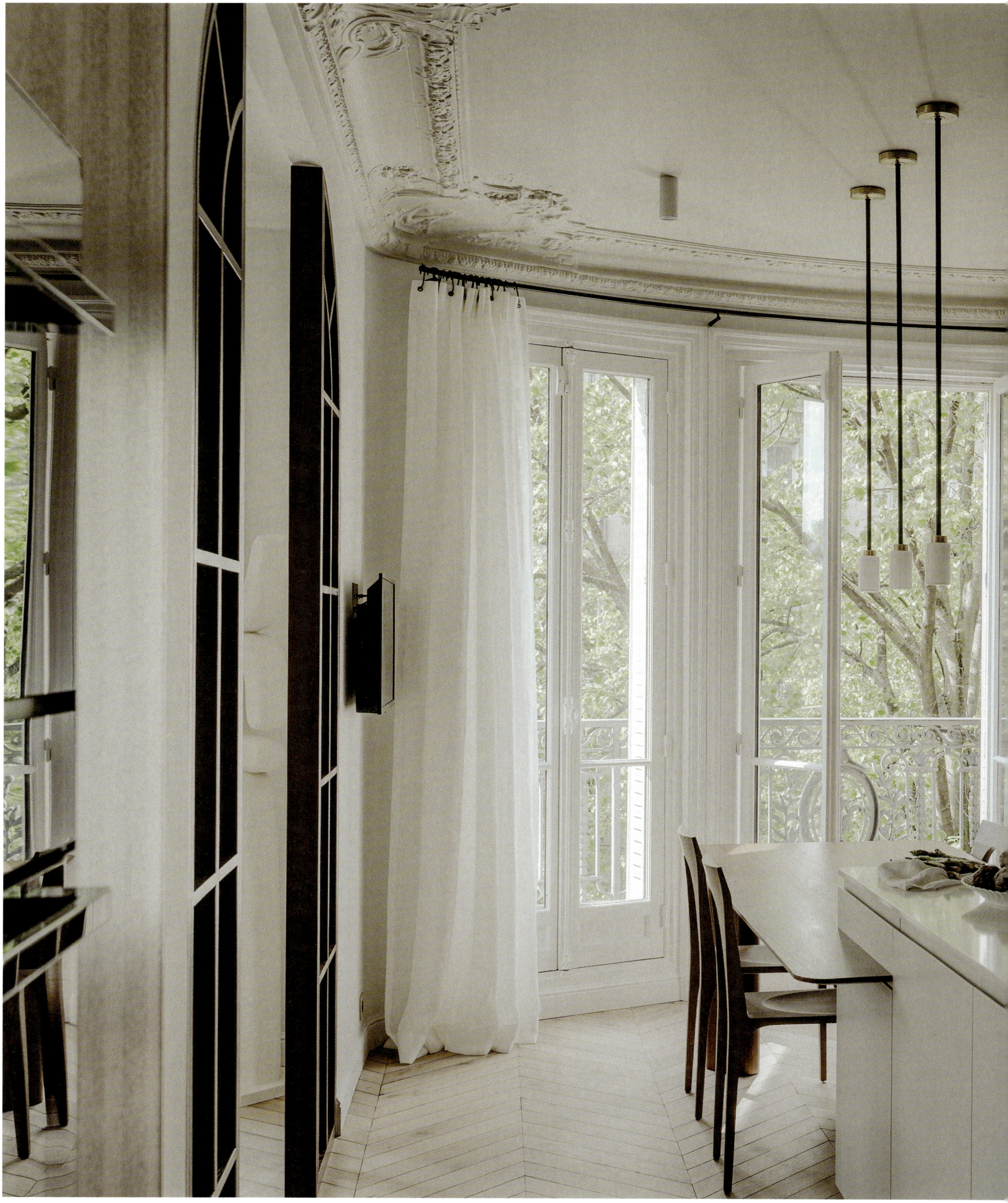

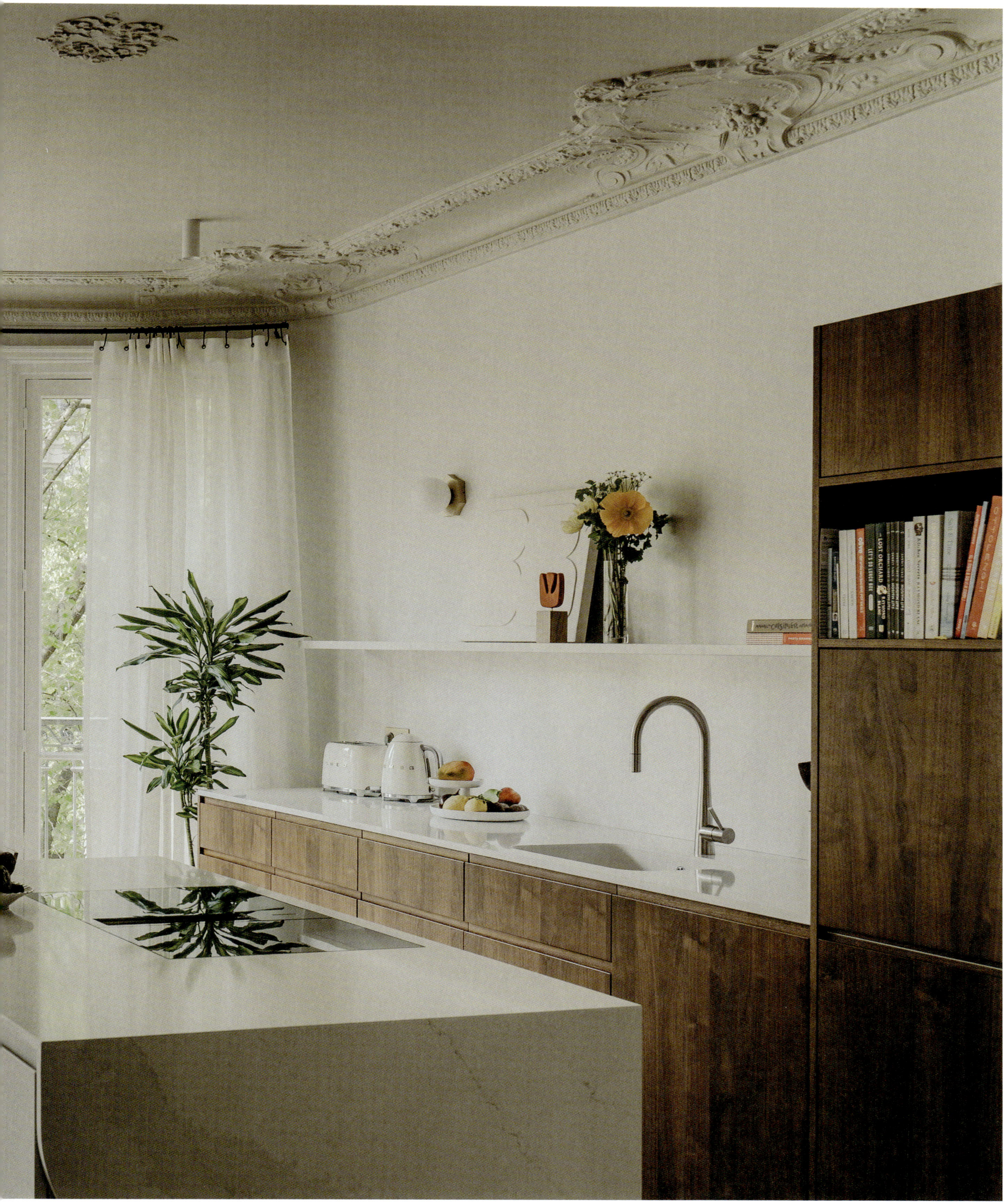

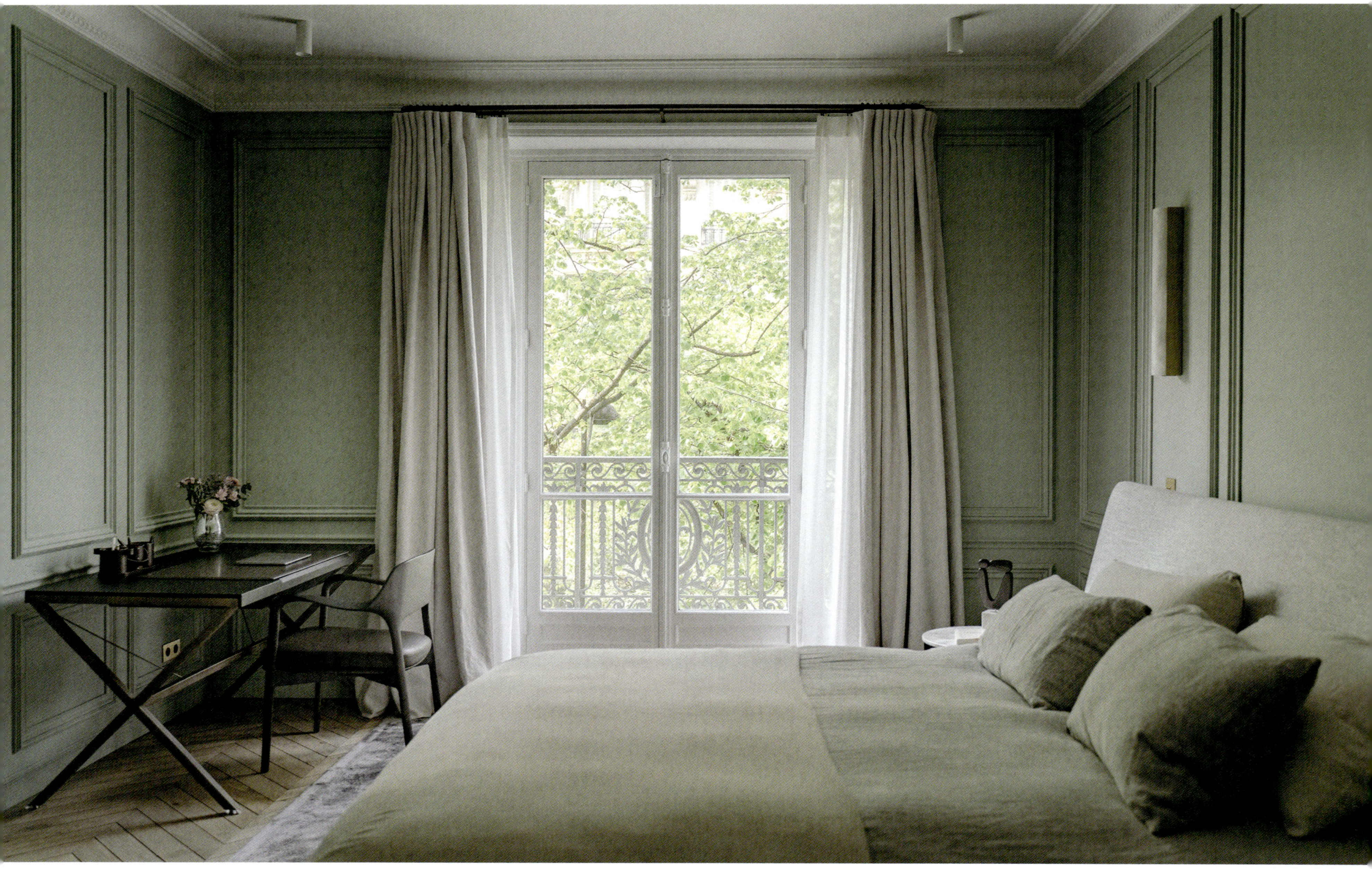

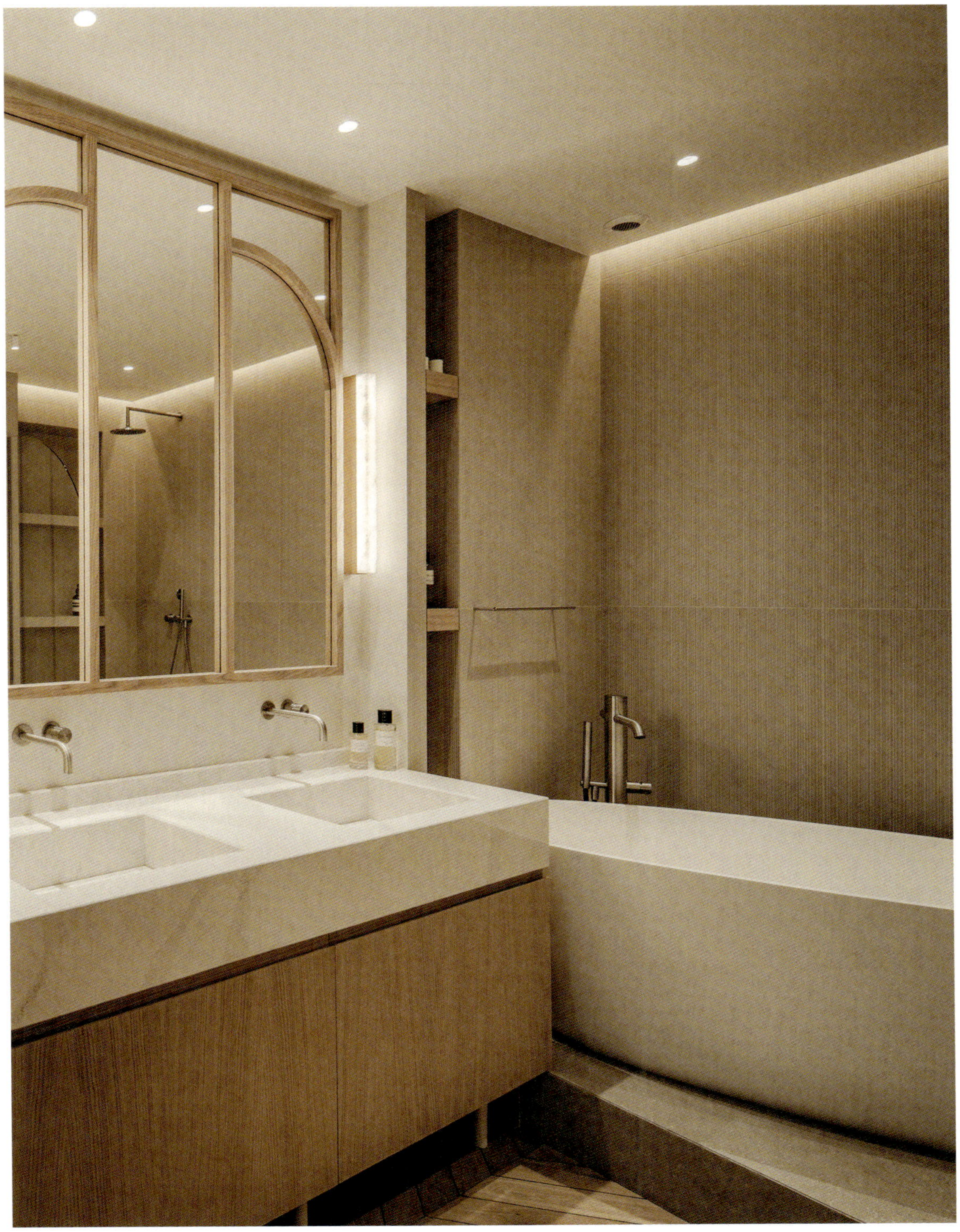

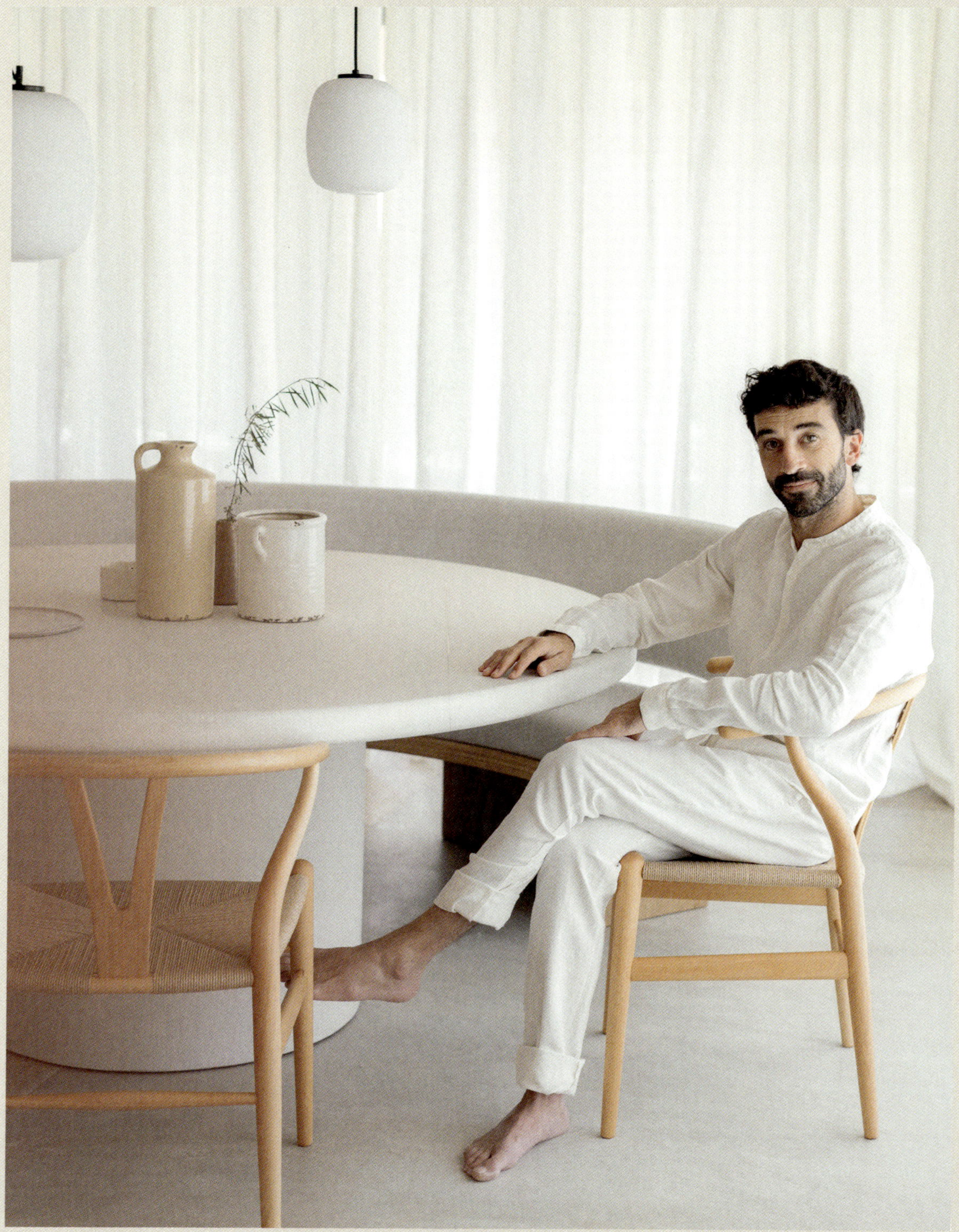

Angel Martin

Angel Martin and his team design with a contemporary language but without losing the essence of simplicity and austerity. At Angel Martin Studio they create spaces that enhance the lifestyle and value of companies.

From their studio in Palma de Mallorca, they are open to any international project.

They create architecture and design with passion and enthusiasm, reimagining the idea of the extraordinary. They advocate the natural and timeless, with an emphasis on local and sustainable production. Angel and his collaborators are attracted to simple and not so sophisticated elements while combining technology with craftsmanship. Martin's style is based on working with natural materials and unique objects, respecting their characteristics and applying light as an essential element of the spaces.

www.angelmartin.studio

Photography: Eugeni Pons & Silvia Foz. Styling Susana Ocaña.

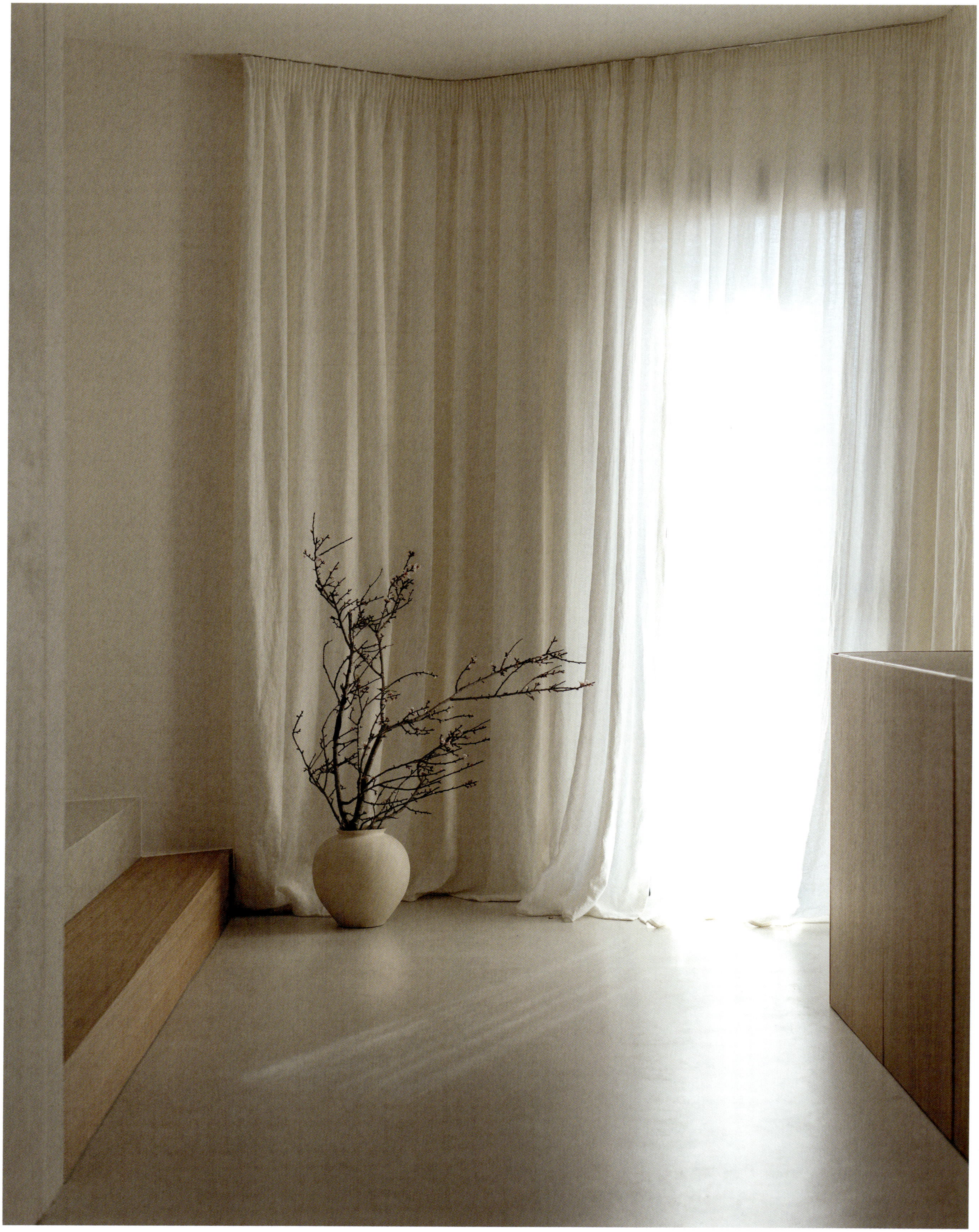

Located in Ses Salines, in the south of Mallorca, this old "village house" has been transformed in depth to multiply the sensation of spaciousness and homogenise the spaces through the materials and shapes.

The doors and walls are made of lime mortar and the floor, on the other hand, is made from a natural stucco that extends the length of the house and coexists with the oak of the bedrooms on the first floor. The curved shapes of the tables and washbasins designed by the studio give continuity and calm to a reduced dwelling that opens onto a small geometric courtyard with a swimming pool. Nuanced and restrained, this small residential refuge from which the island of Cabrera can be glimpsed, combines traditional and contemporary features.

An investment project treated by Angel Martin Studio with a lot of love and care. Collaboration architect: Maria Jose Duch.

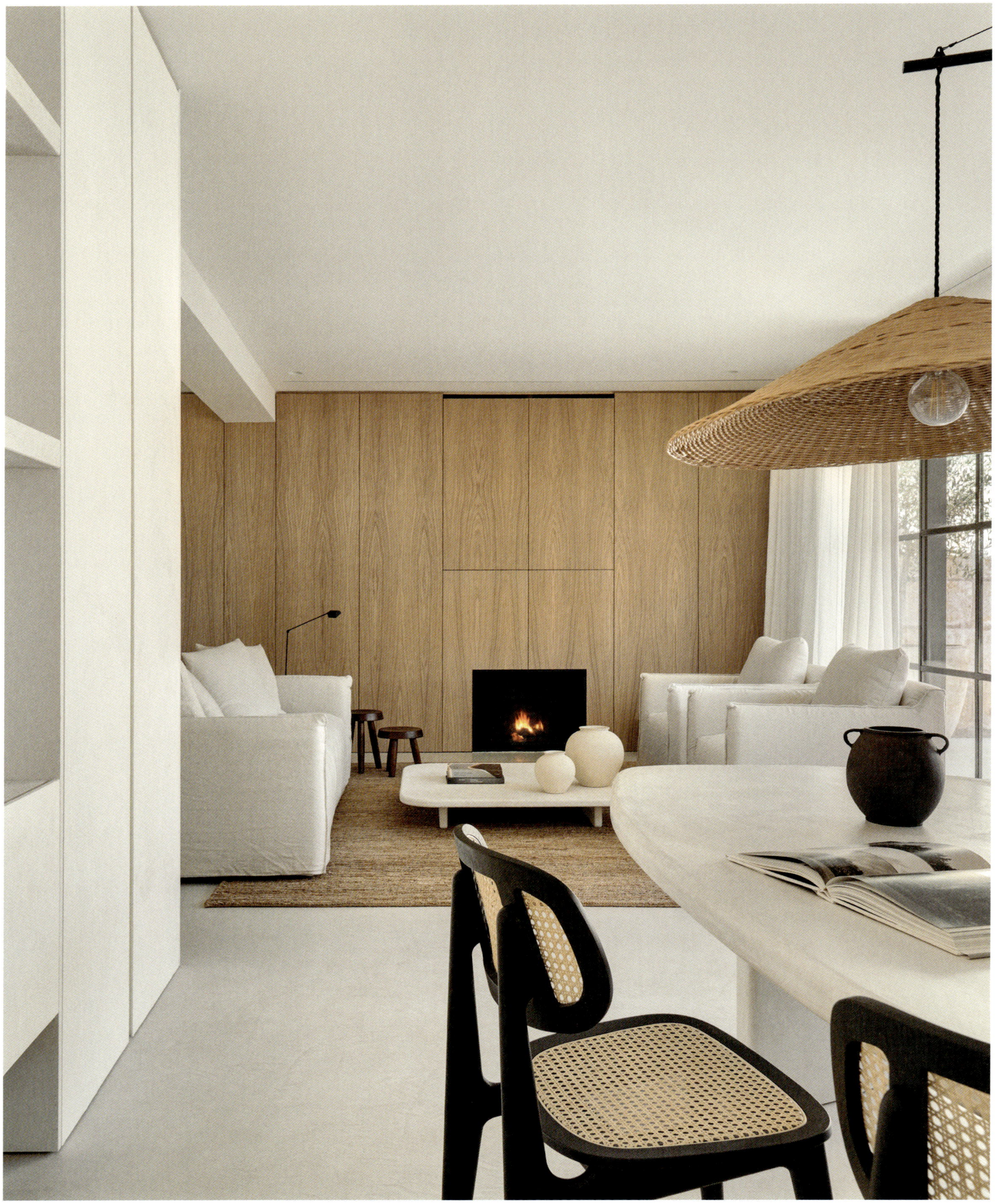

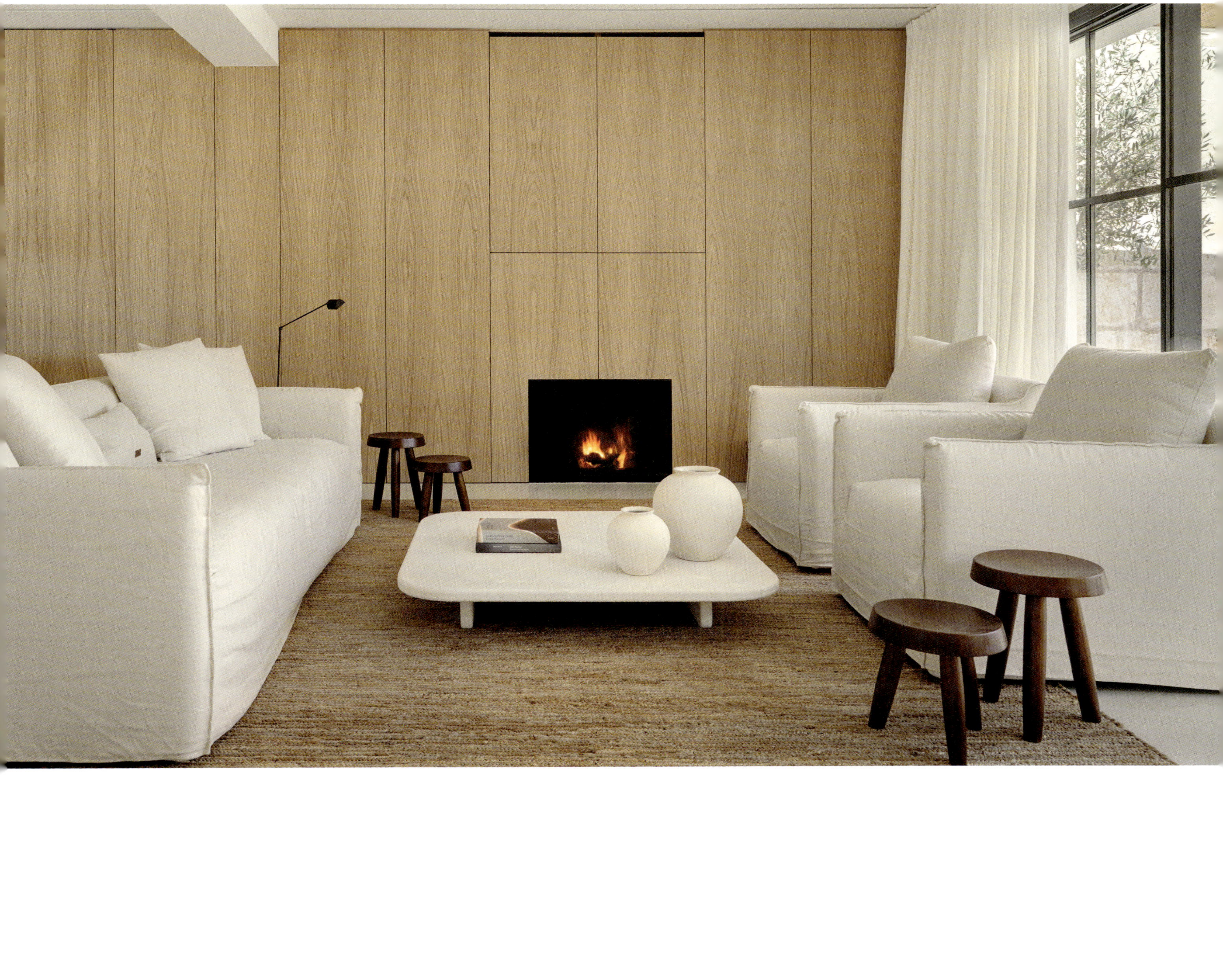

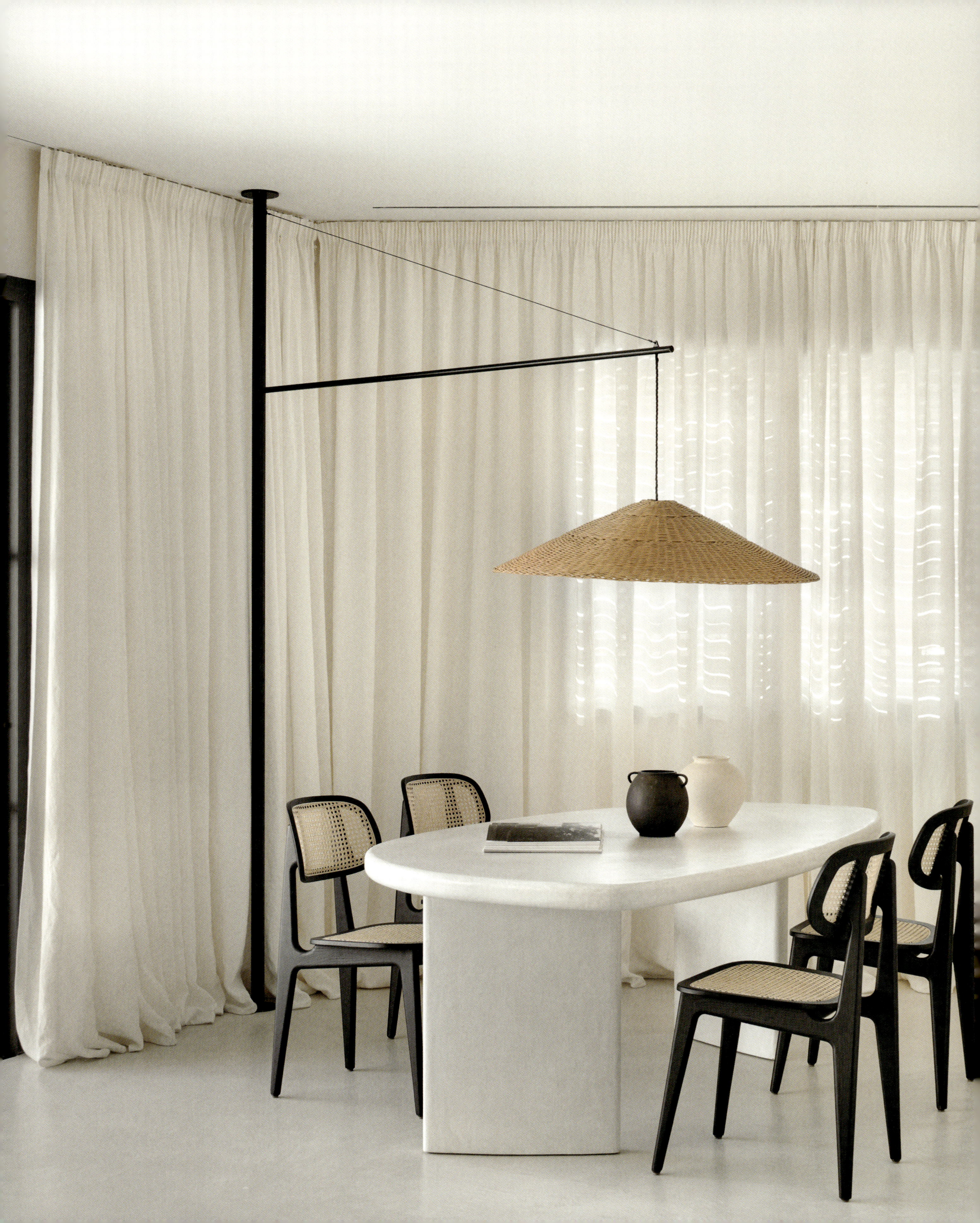

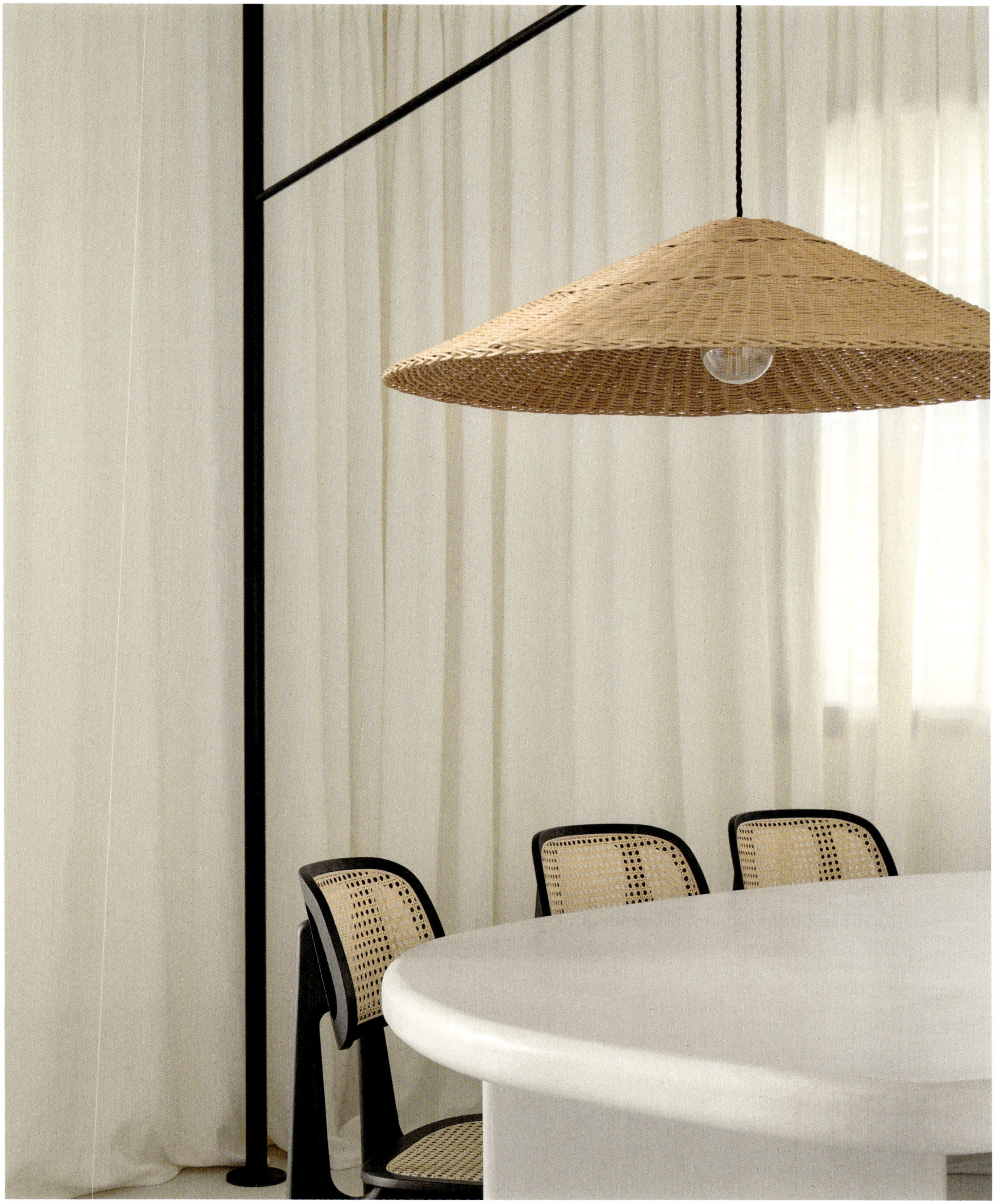

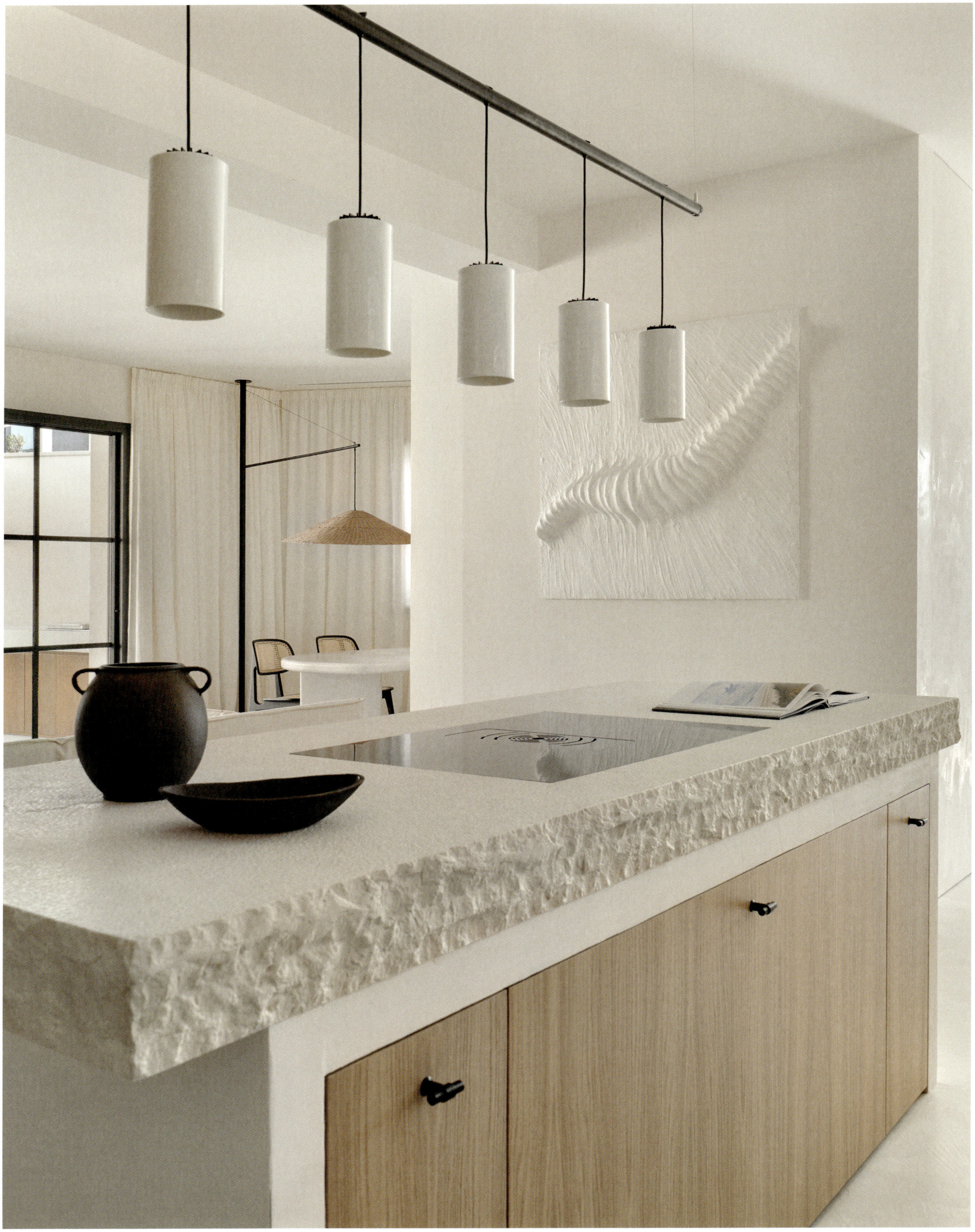

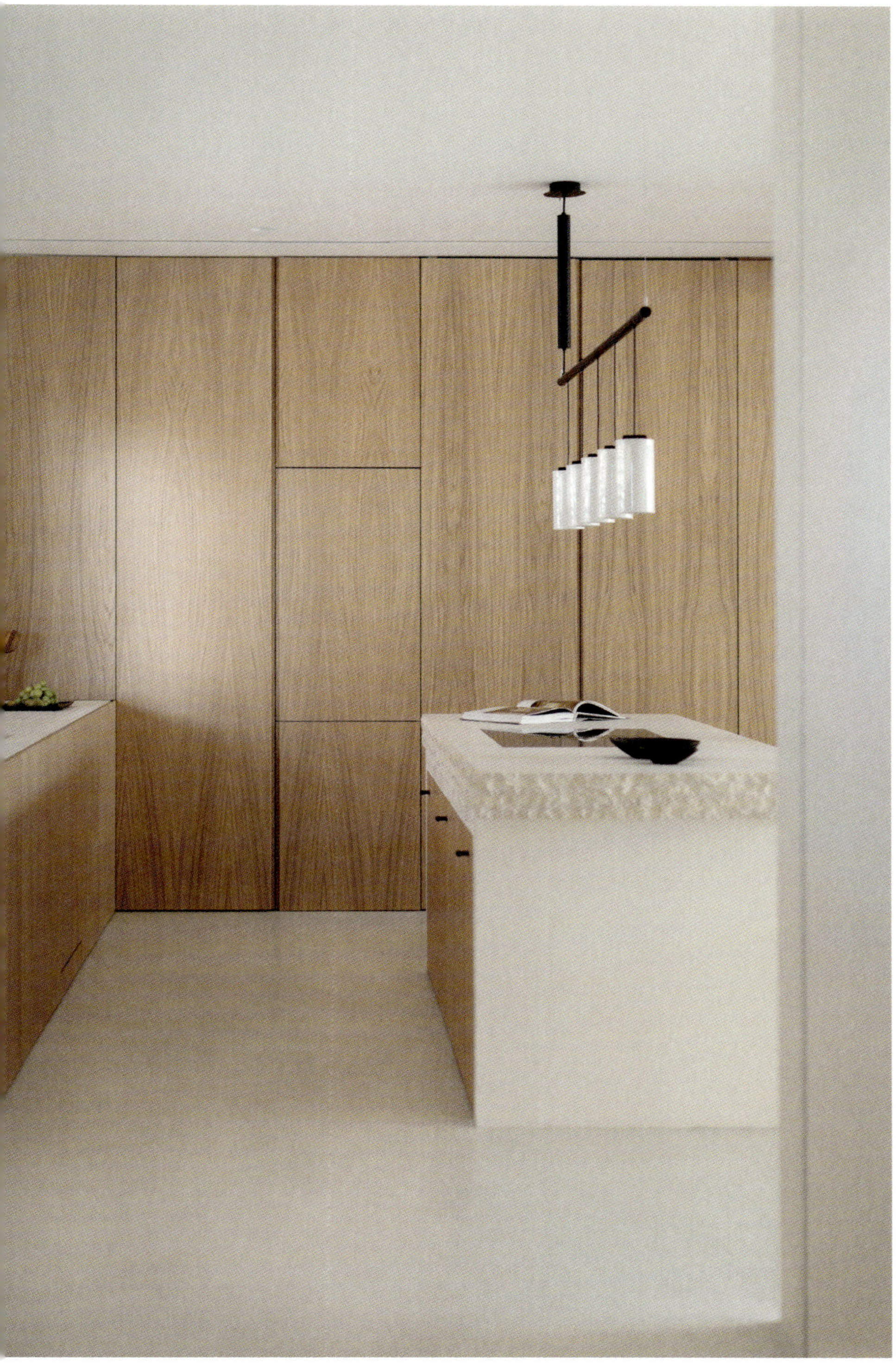
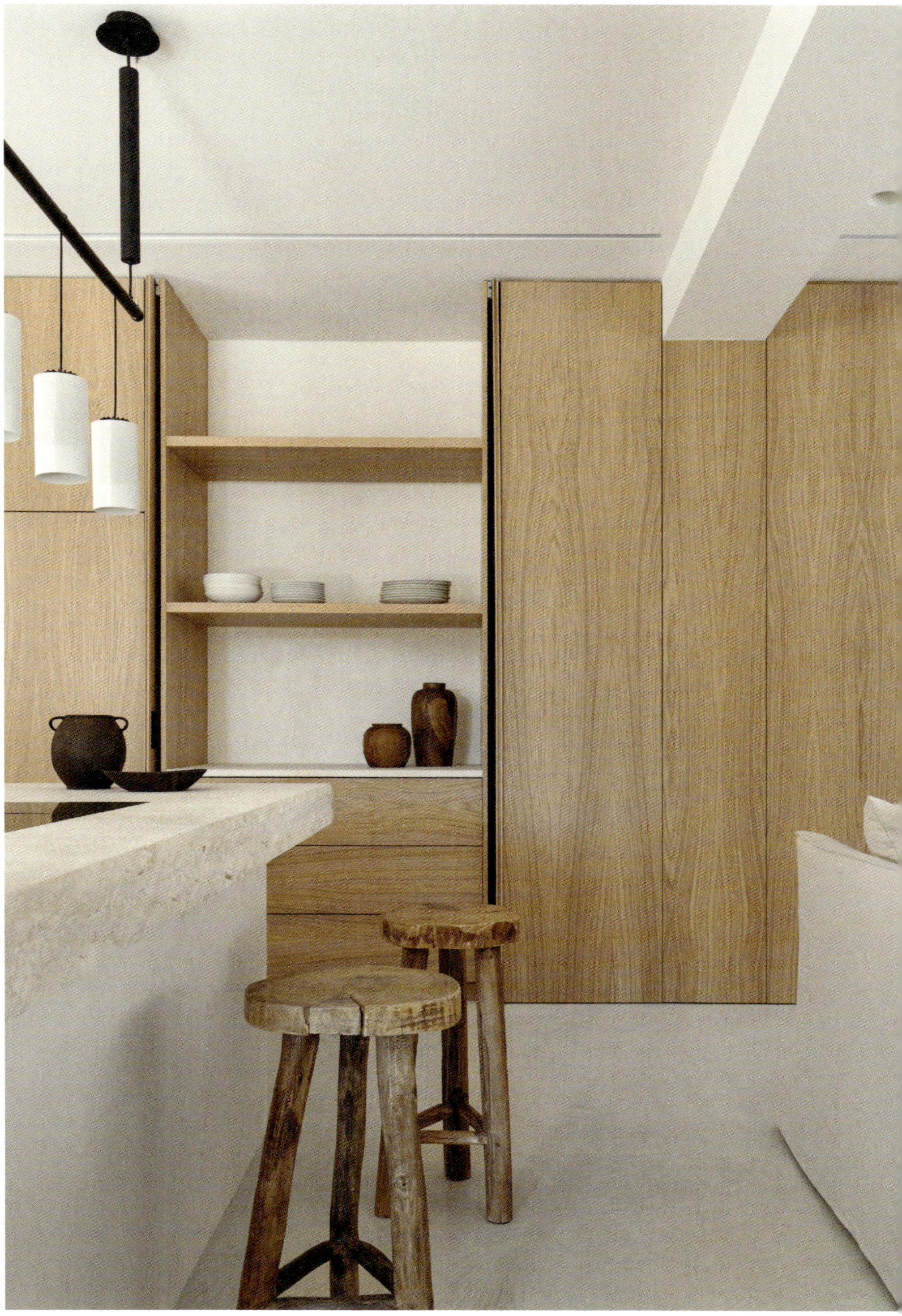

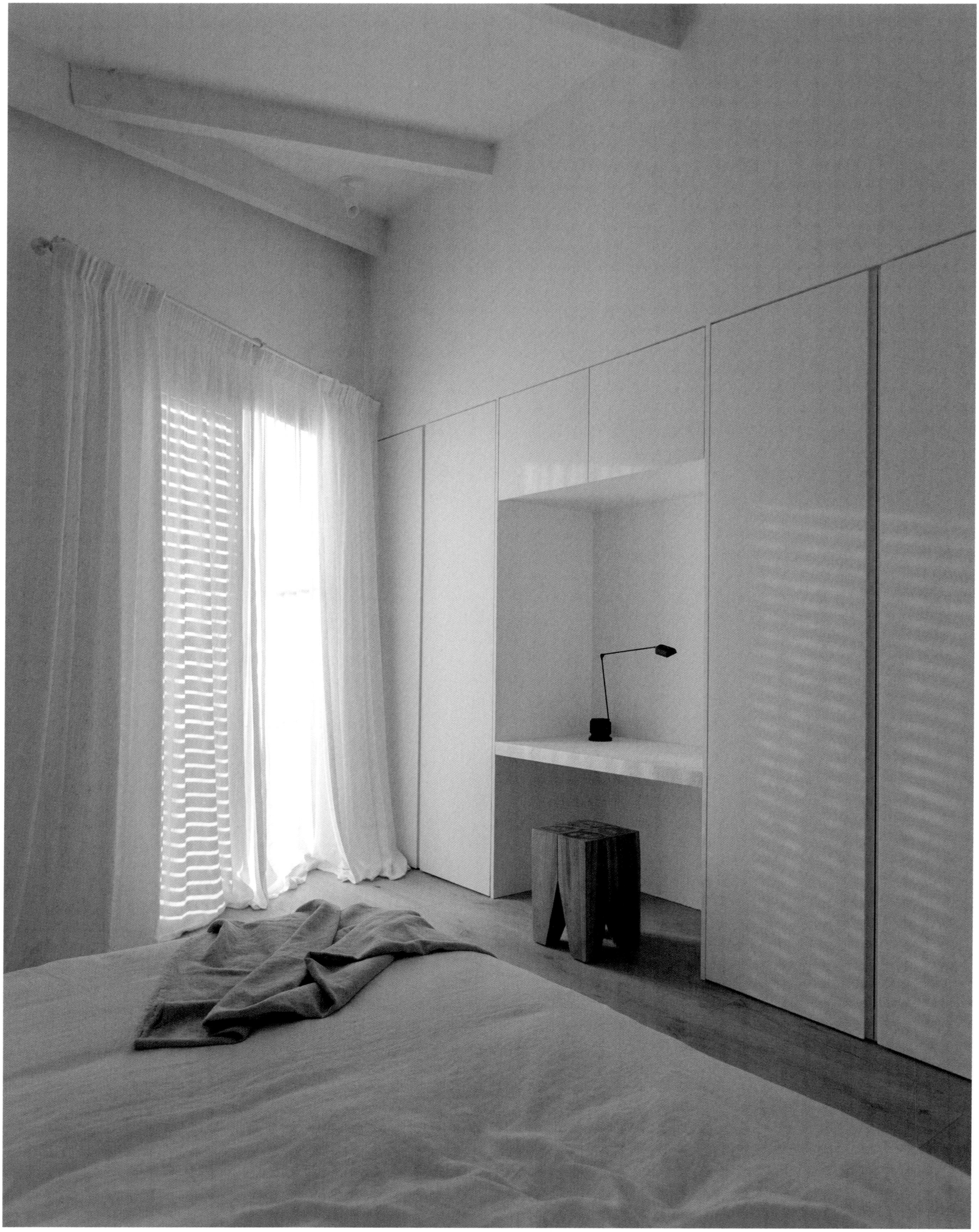

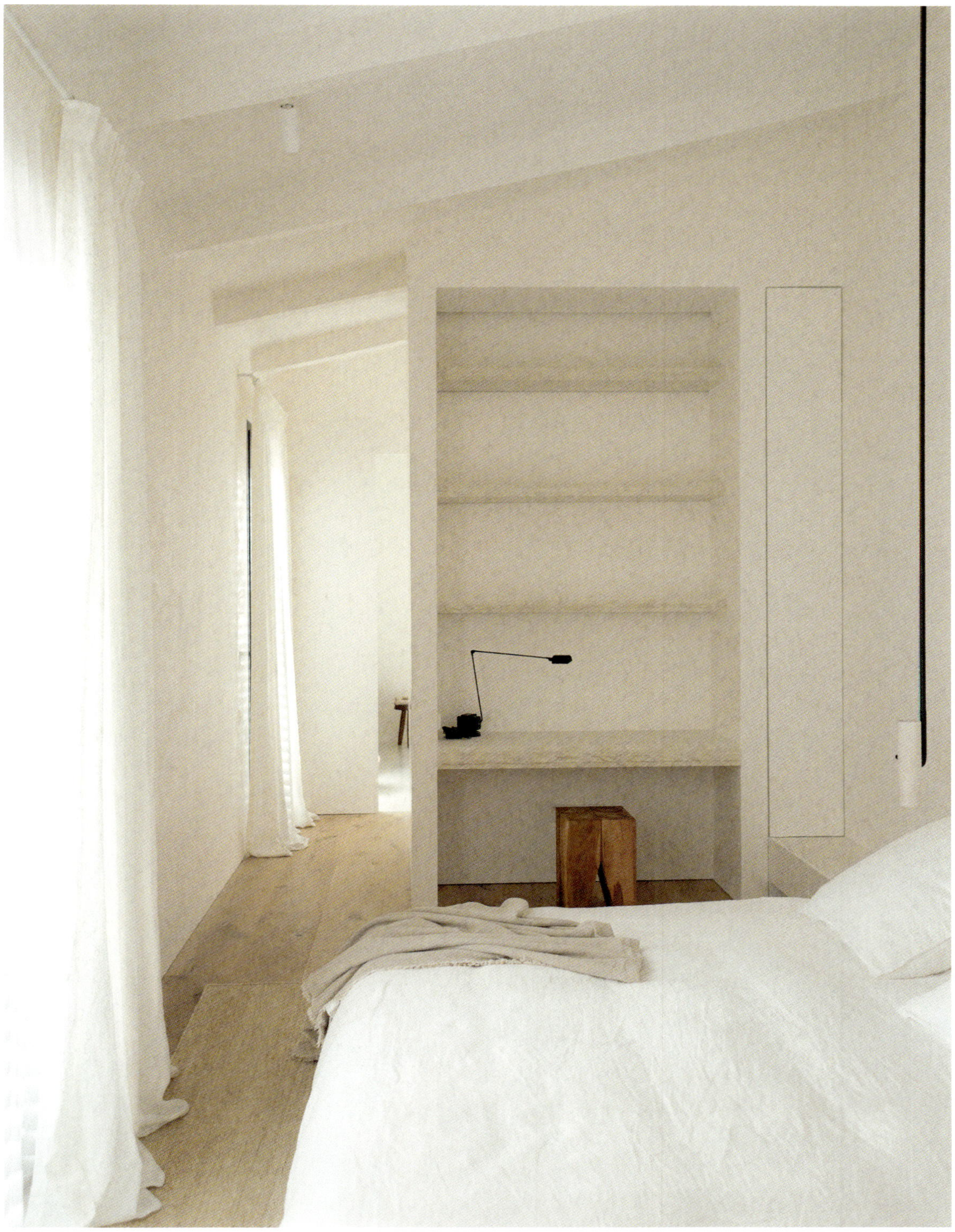

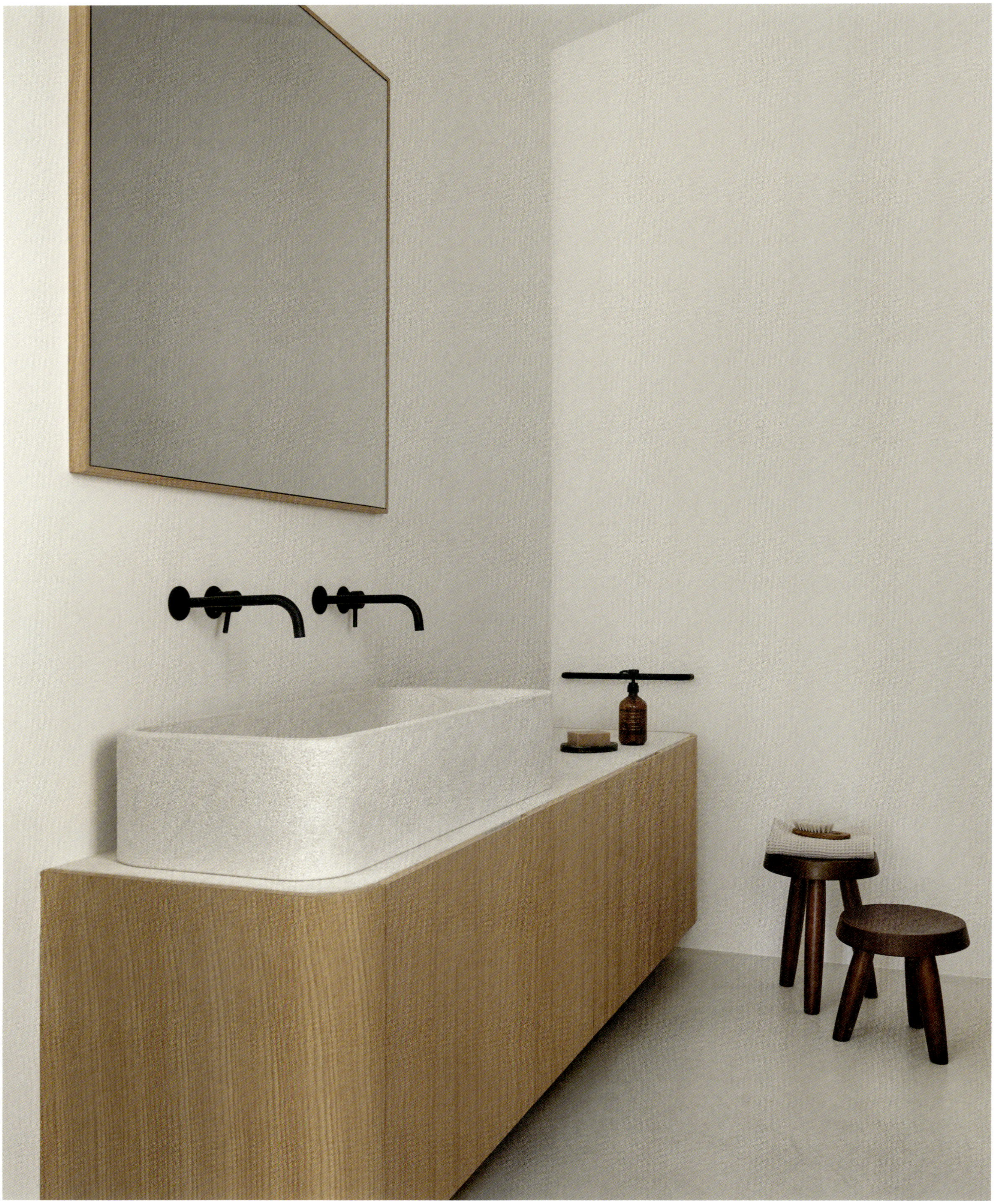

259

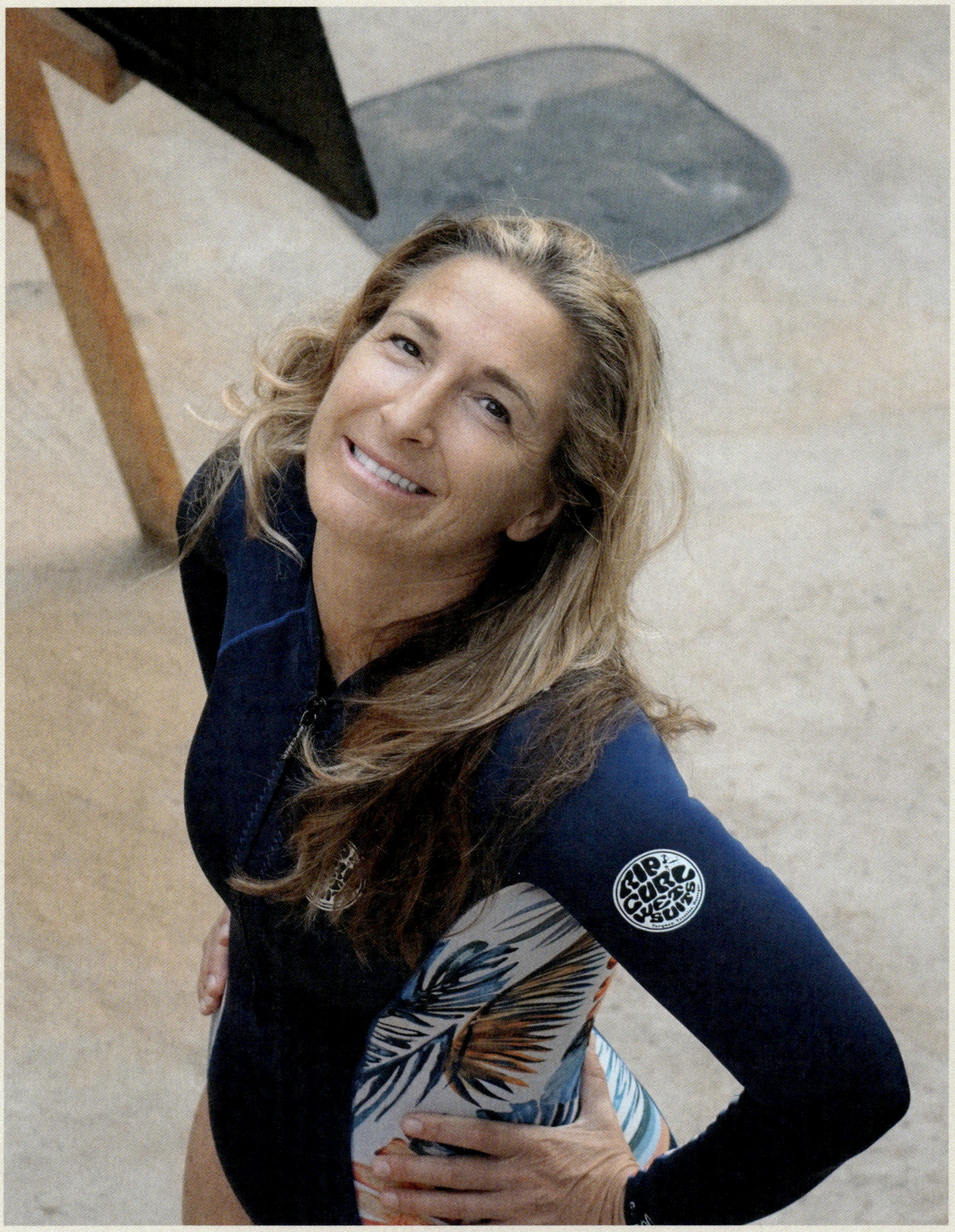

Marie-Emilie Geerinckx

Marie-Emilie graduated as an architect in 2003 before joining Art&Build in Brussels to start her internship where she ended in 2004 co-designing the interior of a new generation sail boat and first designs of the Wiels museum. She then joined the Robelco team to develop the Thurn und Taxis site in Brussels into offices and was responsible for the follow-up of clients wishing an «à la carte» interior. Being a young mother just after those internship years, she decided to raise her kids while working on smaller and close to home projects for her family.

In 2014 she gradually got back to her passion in a professional way restoring a classic Brussels townhouse for a good friend. That was the start of a new career into (interior) architecture from concept and design to complete follow-up. Her technical background, her no nonsense practical attitude and her love for beautiful things create an optimal and "out of the box" result. A few years later, some nice collegeas joined Marie-Emilie and MEG studio is now a cozy and laid-back, yet organized office where ideas get the time to evolve over time as they exchange with the clients.

Everything starts by listening to their dreams and aspirations and understanding their needs and way of life. The given canvas also sets a direction. The classic Brussels townhouse, the Comporta retro house, the classic Flemish villa and the Costa Rican surf hideaways all have a different spirit.

MEG Studio creates every time another look and feel, it is not about aesthetics only. A house should not be a showroom but a place to experience good moments and to create or store memories.

Before starting every project, MEG studio also partly compensate the carbon footprint of their project by planting five trees per square meter with Go Forest or grow coral or restore mangroves with Go Ocean as we often forget where all our beautiful materials come from.

www.marieemiliegeerinckx.be

Photography: Alohafred (Frédéric Swennen) / p. 270-275 Cafeine (Thomas De Bruyne)

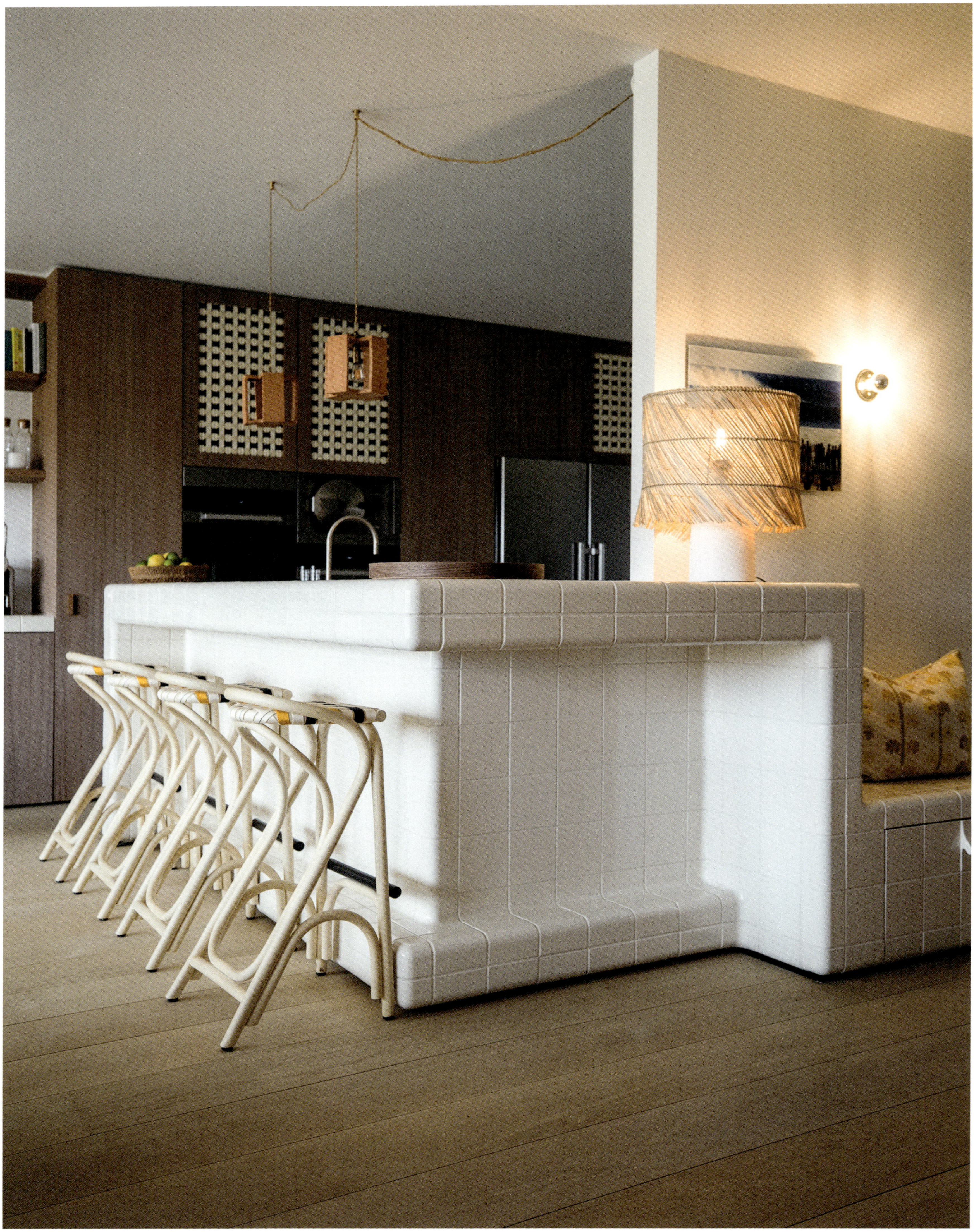

In this publication, Marie-Emilie presents four of her most recent - and favorite - projects.

On pages 262 to 265: a retro inspired seafront apartment for a young windsurfers' family in Oostduinkerke - the perfect weekend hideaway for these sea and nature lovers, laid-back parents with young children who need a practical yet cozy and bulletproof interior. The simple but qualitative materials and precise design and realization create a relaxed atmosphere.

On pages 264 to 267: the renovation of a pool, spa, TV room and bar in Sint-Martens-Latem. Deep surgery of a leaking 1990's pool and surrounding areas. Everything was stripped, the leaking pool got an invisible overflow and was brought back to life by the technical wisdom and realization of Frederic Hoste in XXL ceramic tiles that look like hammered natural stone. The whole ceiling was replaced by an acoustic mineral plaster and the walls were realized in thermowood to ease the acoustic problems you often get in a pool. The ventilation and humidity regulation are fully integrated to avoid any condensation. On the daybed and in the hammam you get a beautiful view of the pool into the garden. The family bar overlooking the garden is located between the TV room and the pool. A place to relax and gather.

On pages 268 and 269: a full renovation of a classic country house in Vinderhoute. The house had to be "refreshed"... but only the outside walls remained and it was rebuilt with the Art Deco elements but with the implementation of modern techniques. Classic elements were reintroduced with a modern twist. The construction meetings were a mix of know-how and real craftsmanship with a passion for good work.

On pages 270 to 275: this underground relaxation space with bar is the ultimate paradise for men. Every car lover, wine taster and sportive family man would love this man cave / addendum to his existing house. The garage fits six cars and family bikes but has an acoustic ceiling to create a good in-house discotheque when the teenagers need to get loose at night or rollerskate on rainy days. Once you pass the closets and security door you get to the gym, the fully climatized wine room and the spa with sauna and hammam. All ceilings are acoustic to create a very calm atmosphere even when kids are running around. The spa and wine cellar have two different ventilation systems integrated in the floors and ceilings to avoid condensation on the windows of the wine cellar. Every light, temperature, music is remote controlled through the fully integrated domestics system. The old upstairs garages were transformed into a bar and TV room for family and friends ...

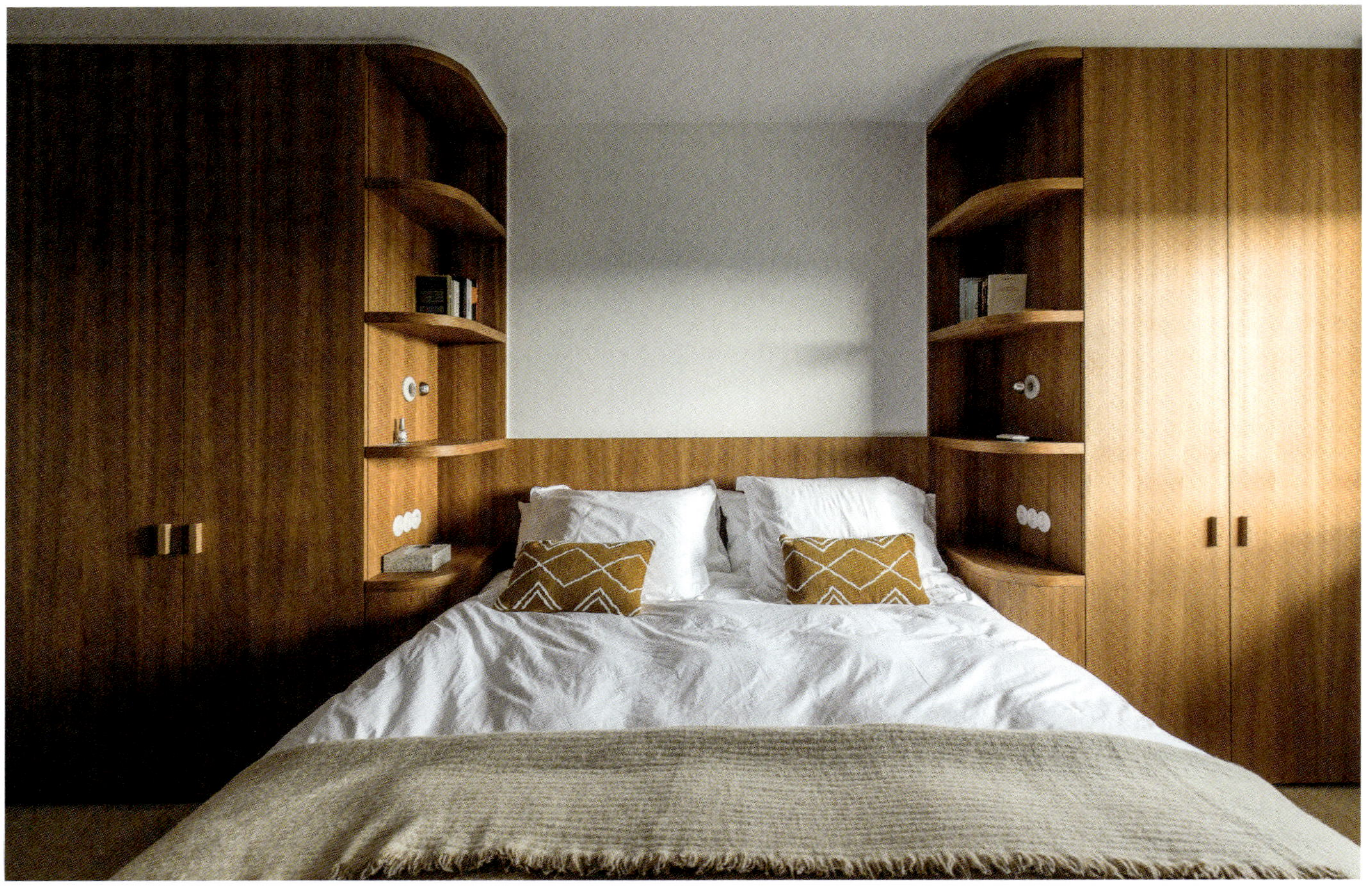

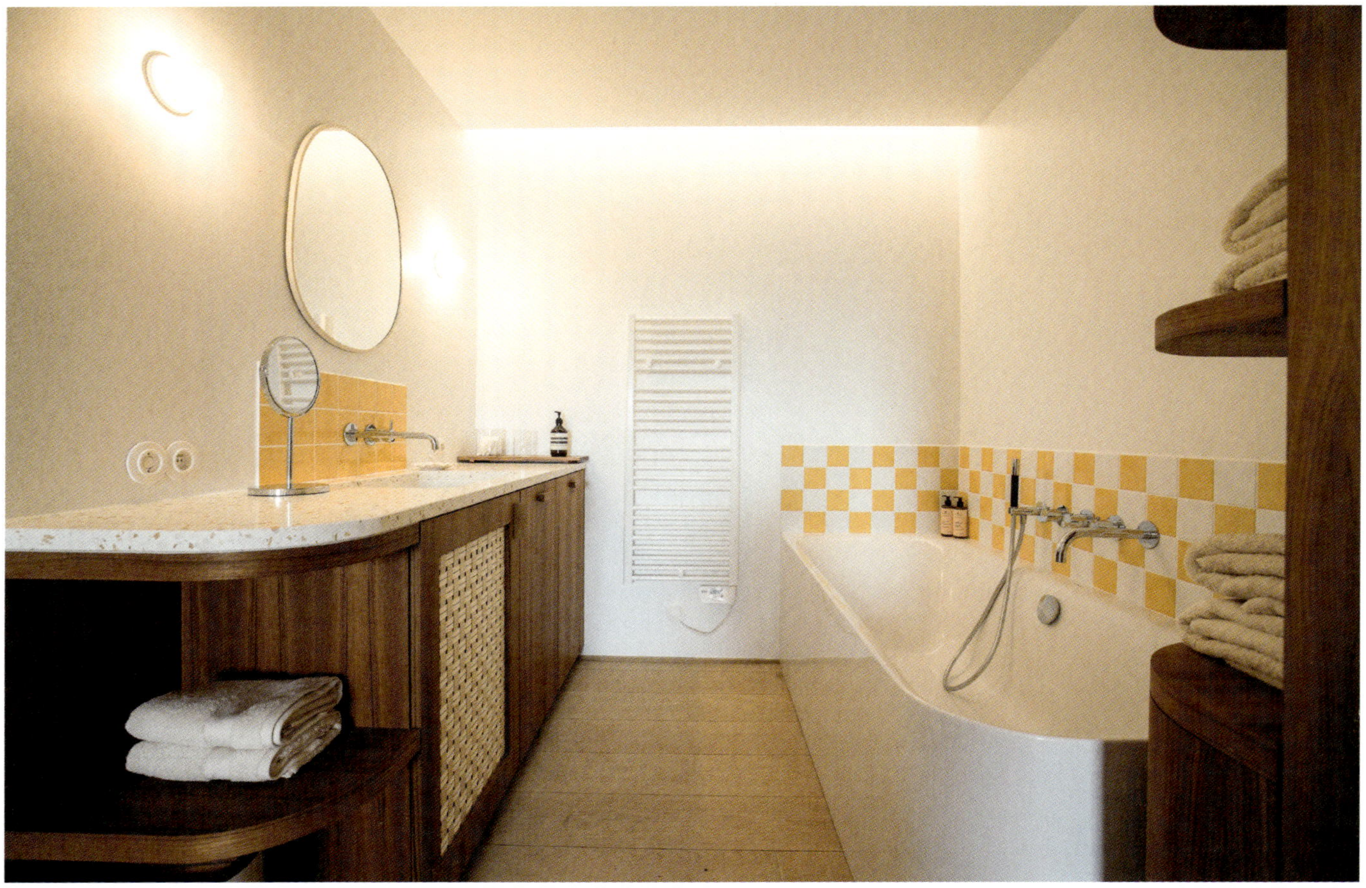

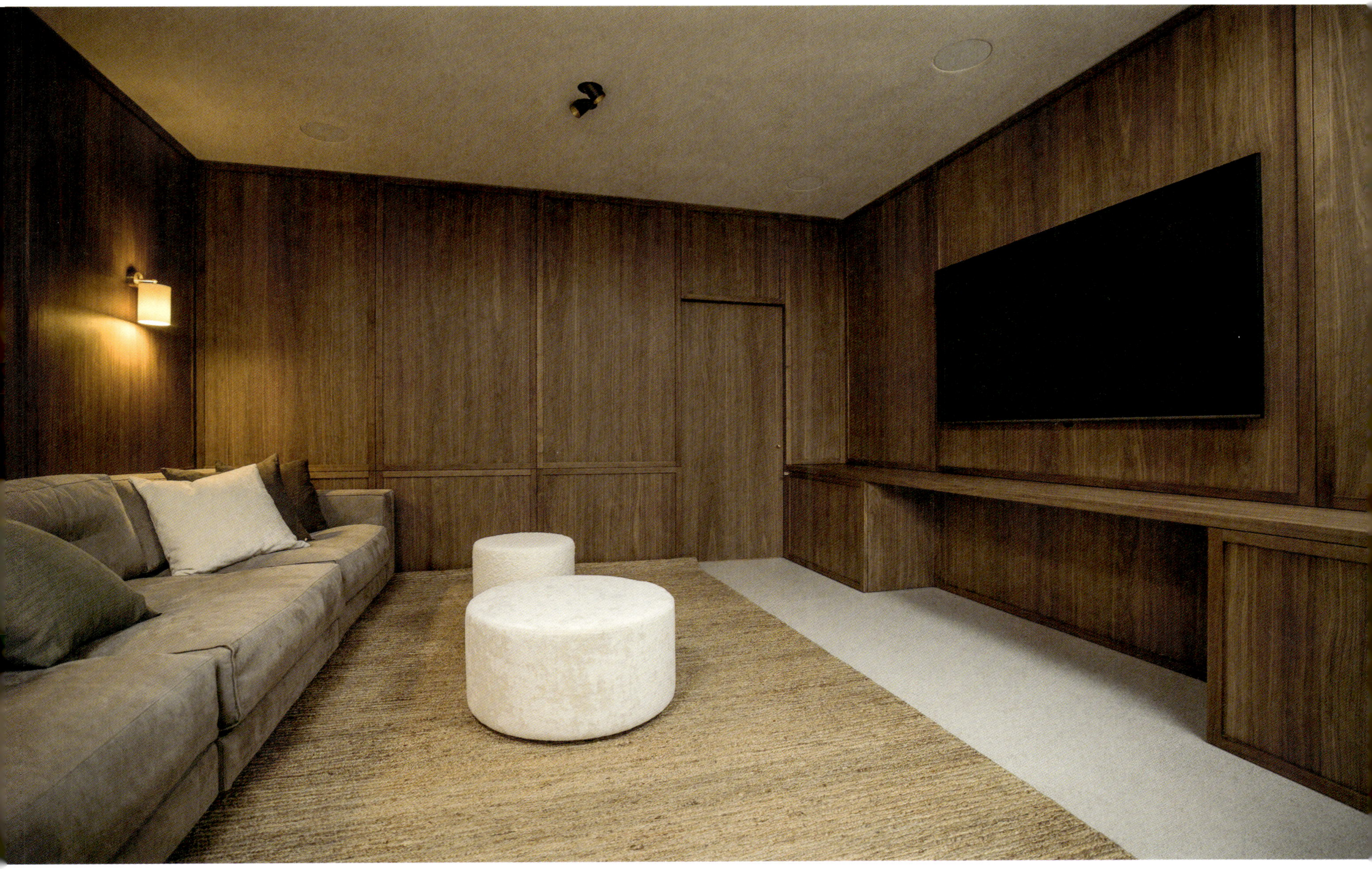

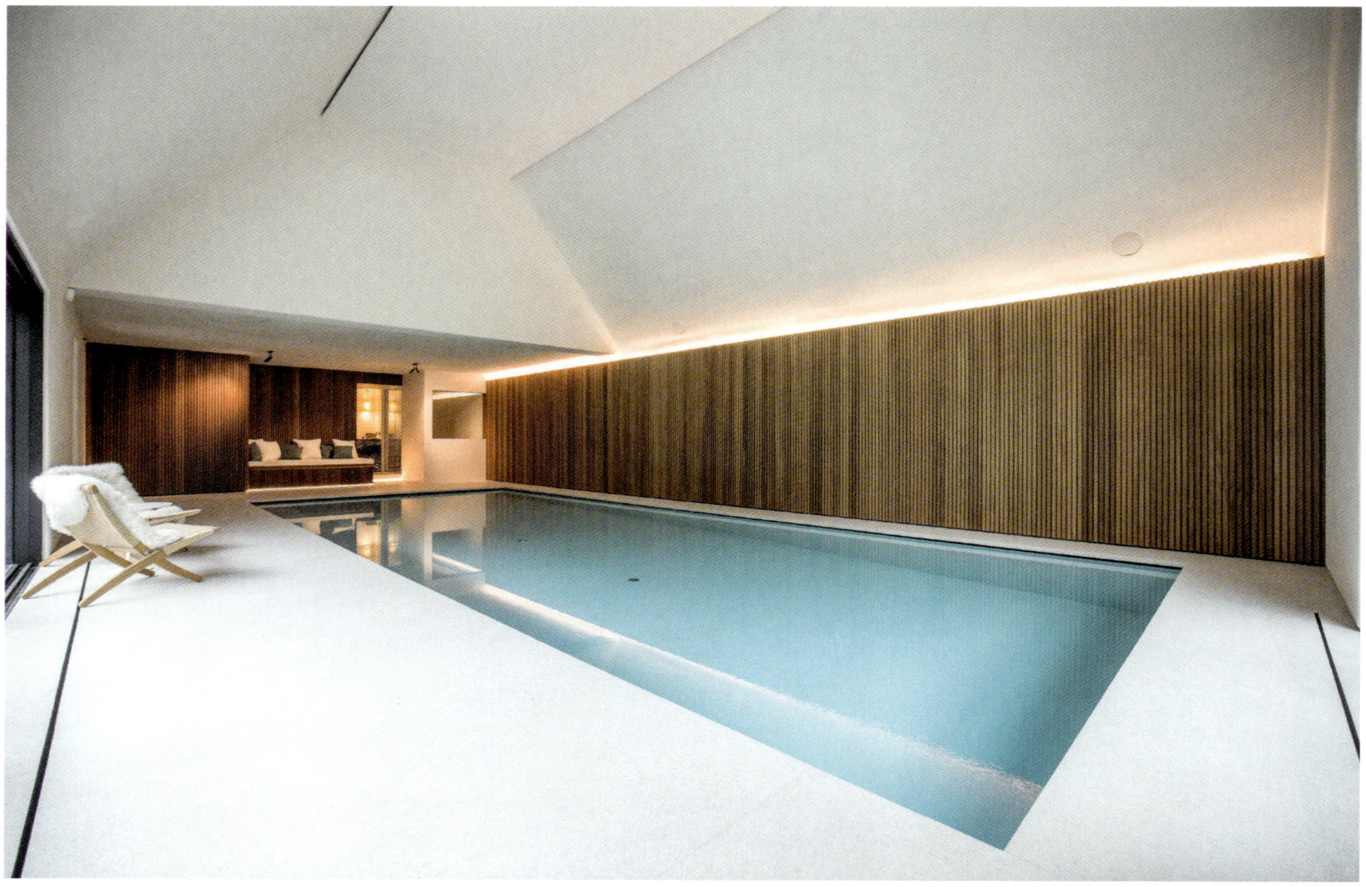

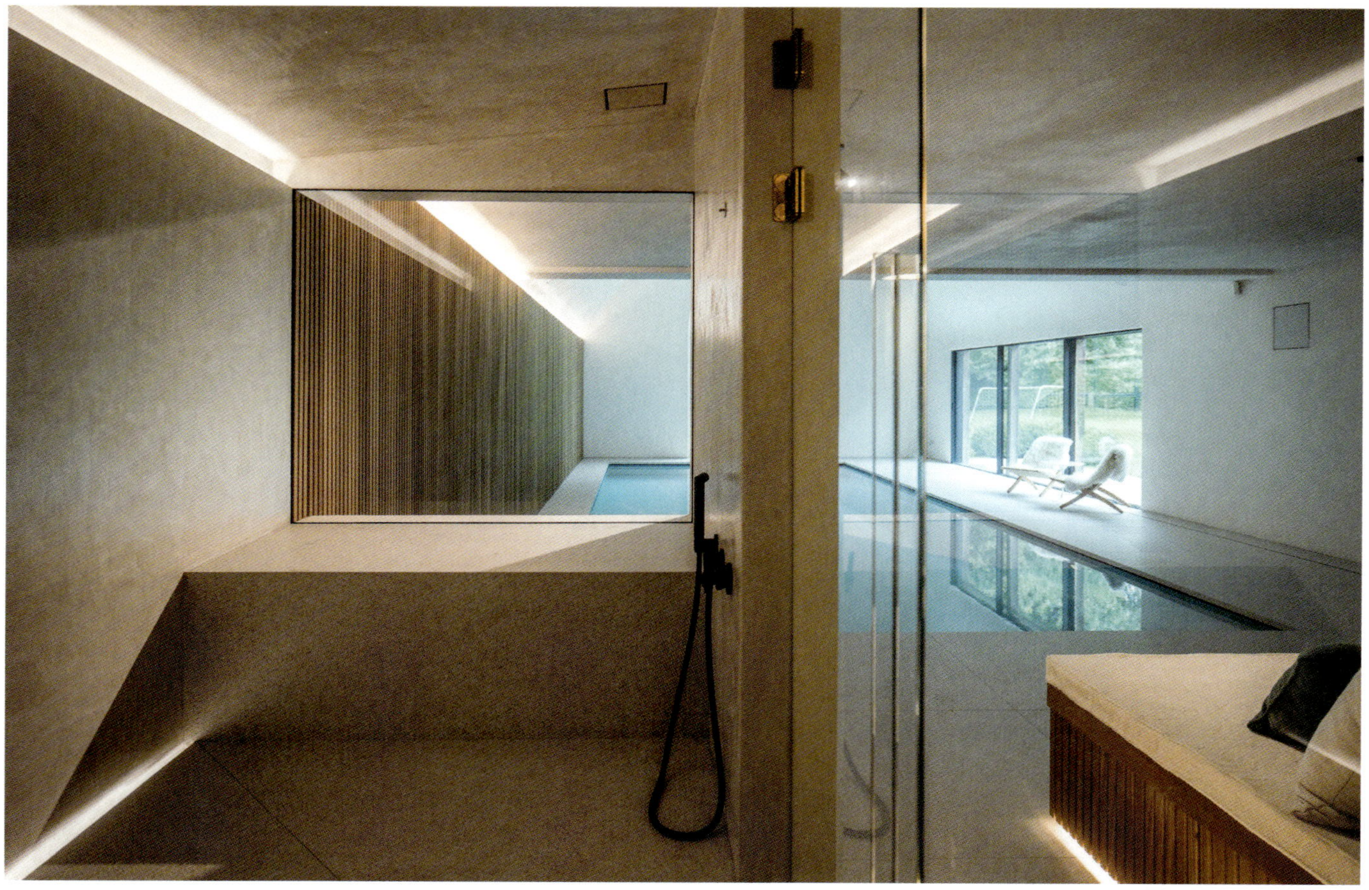

267

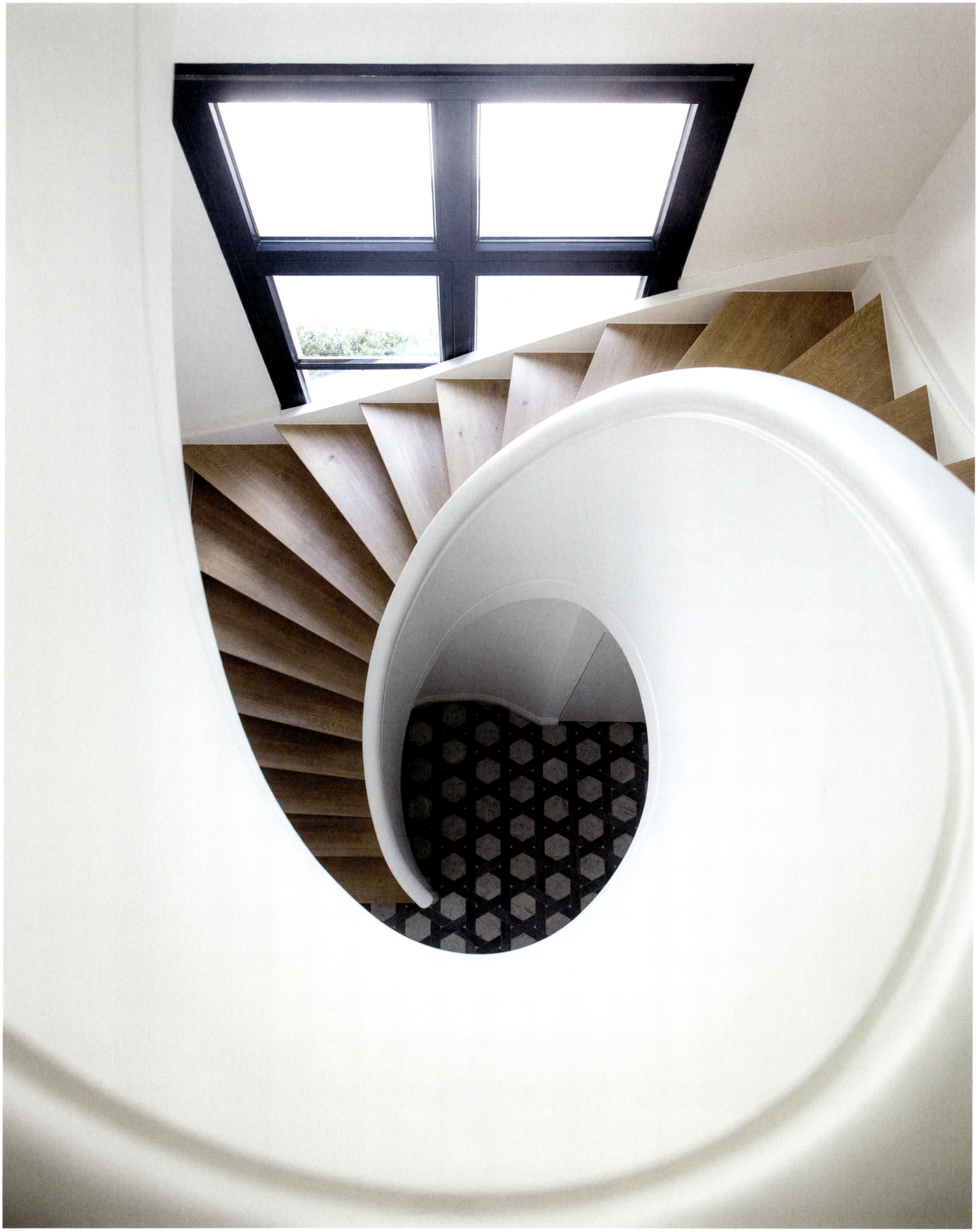

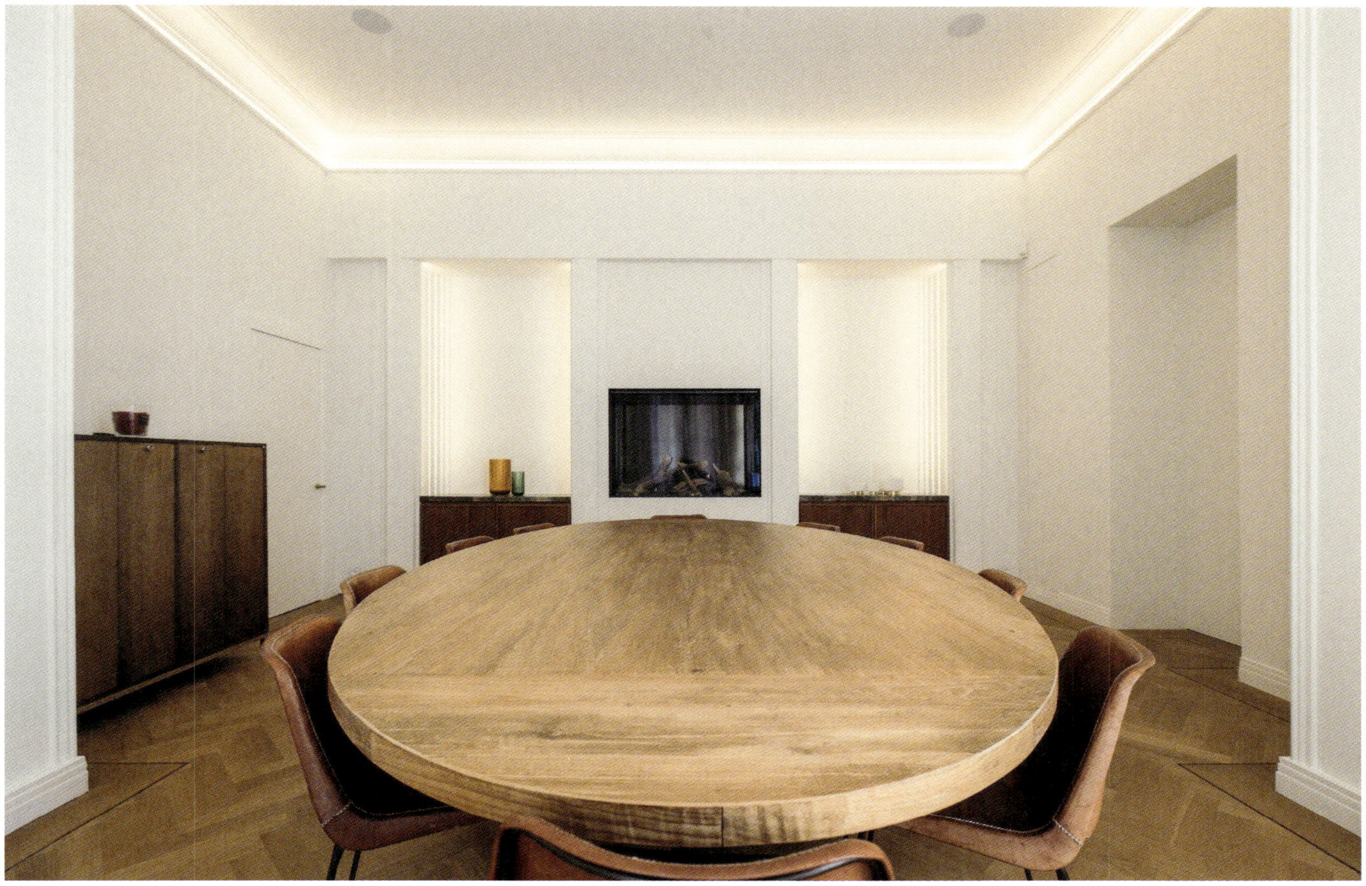

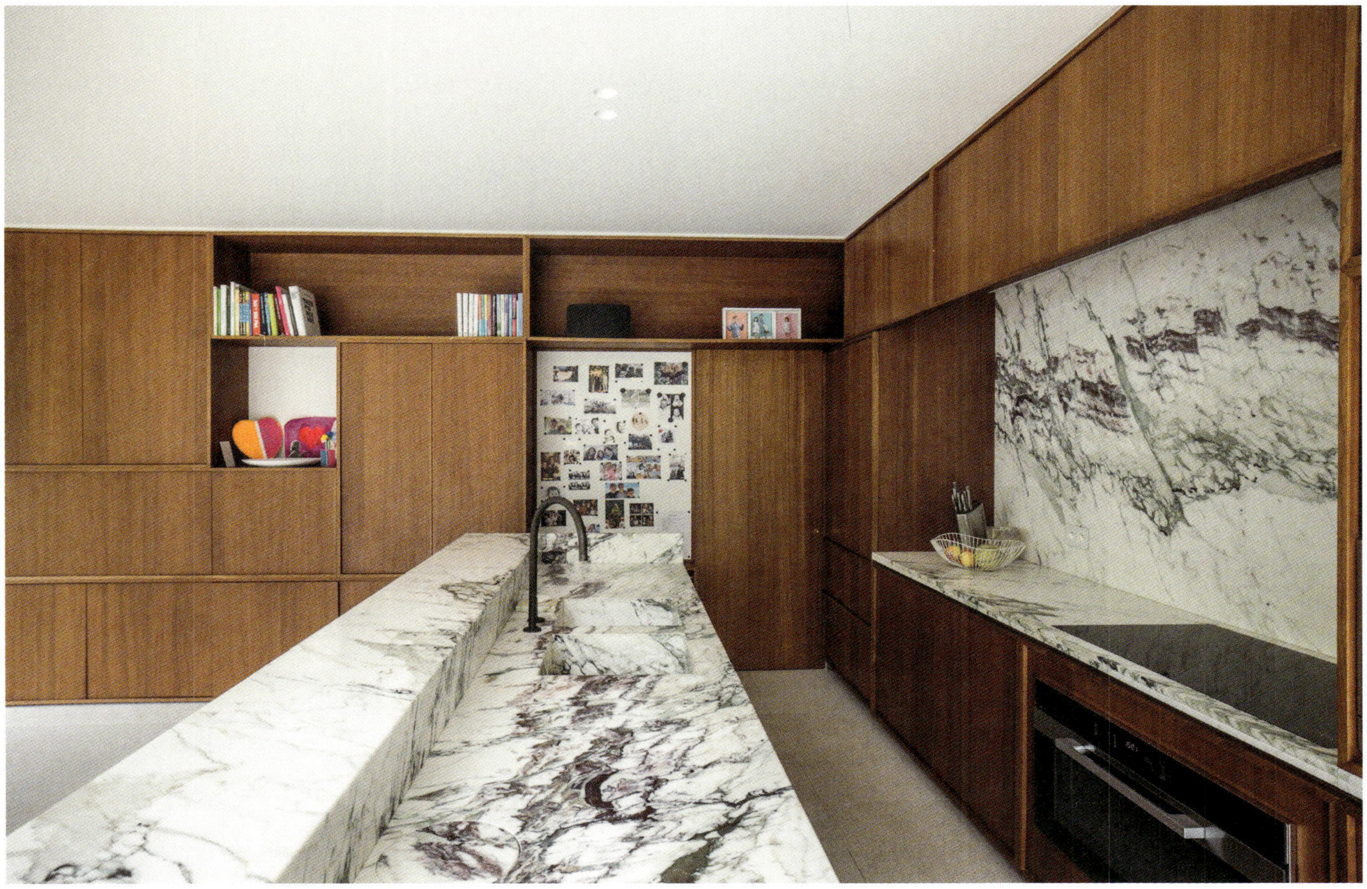

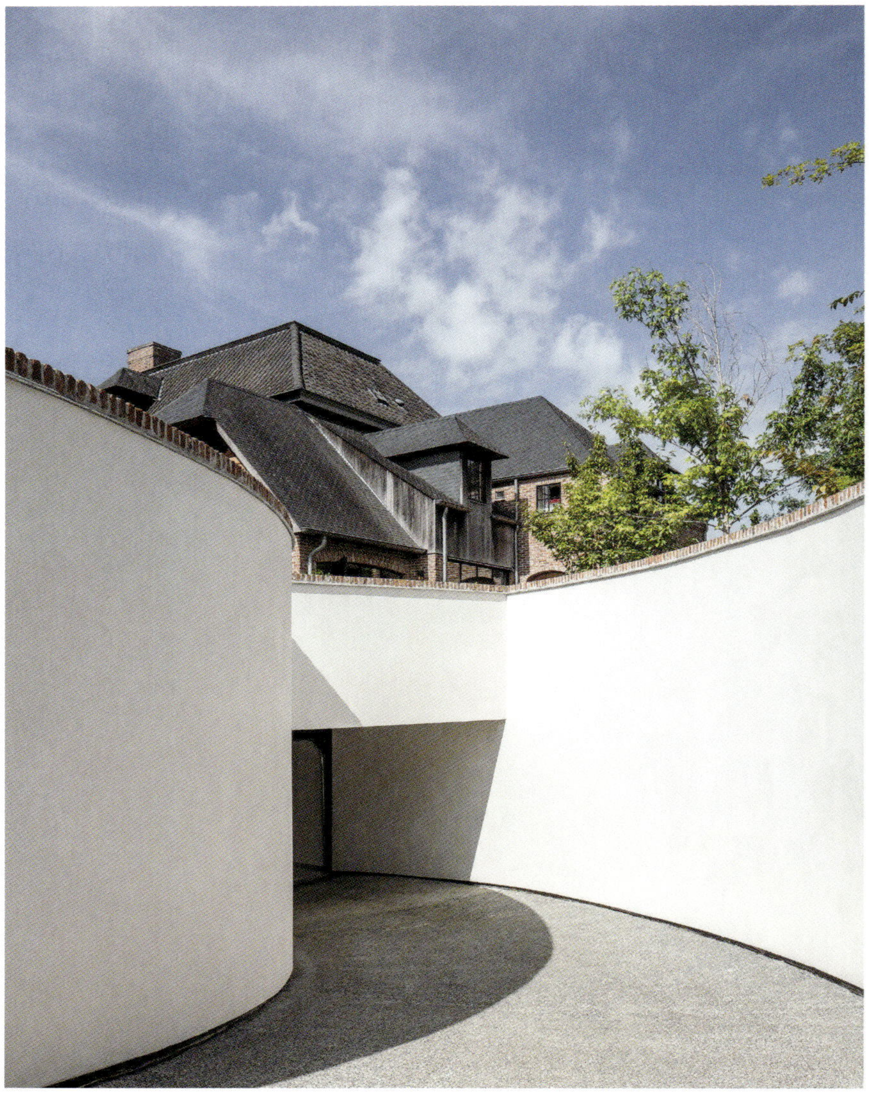

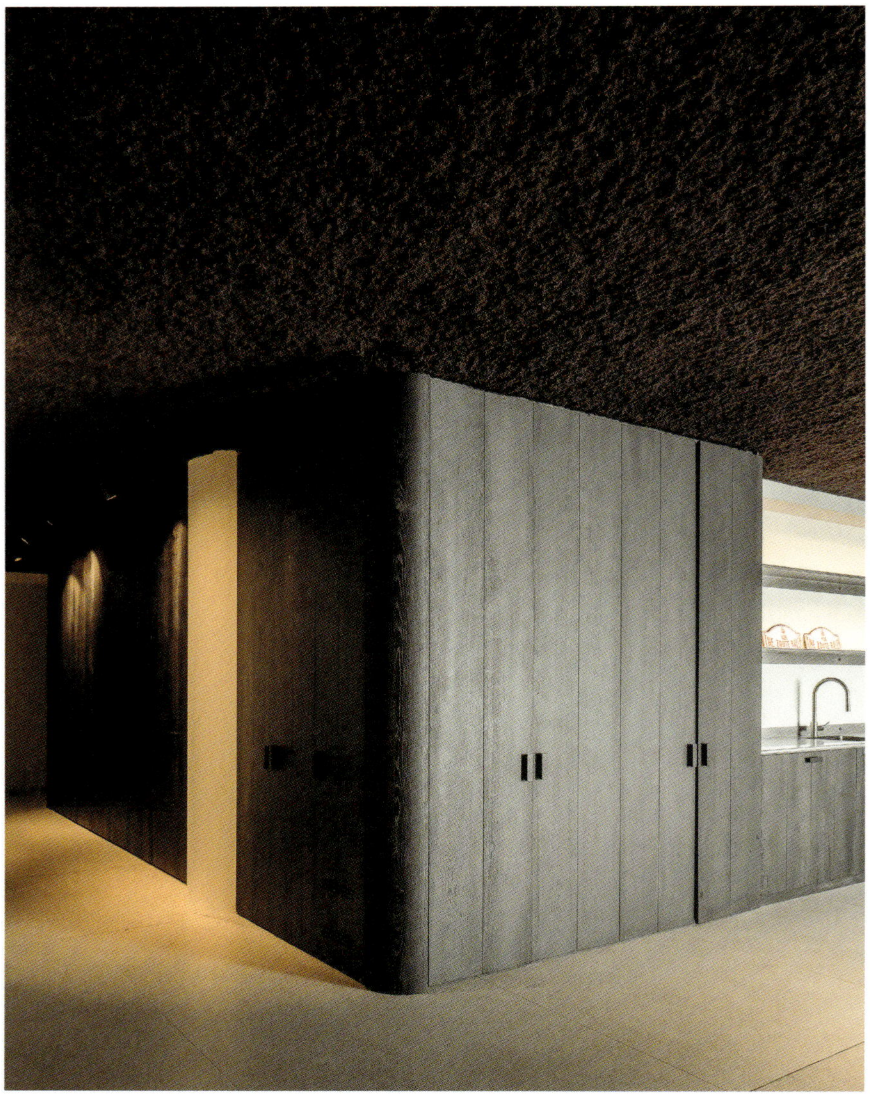

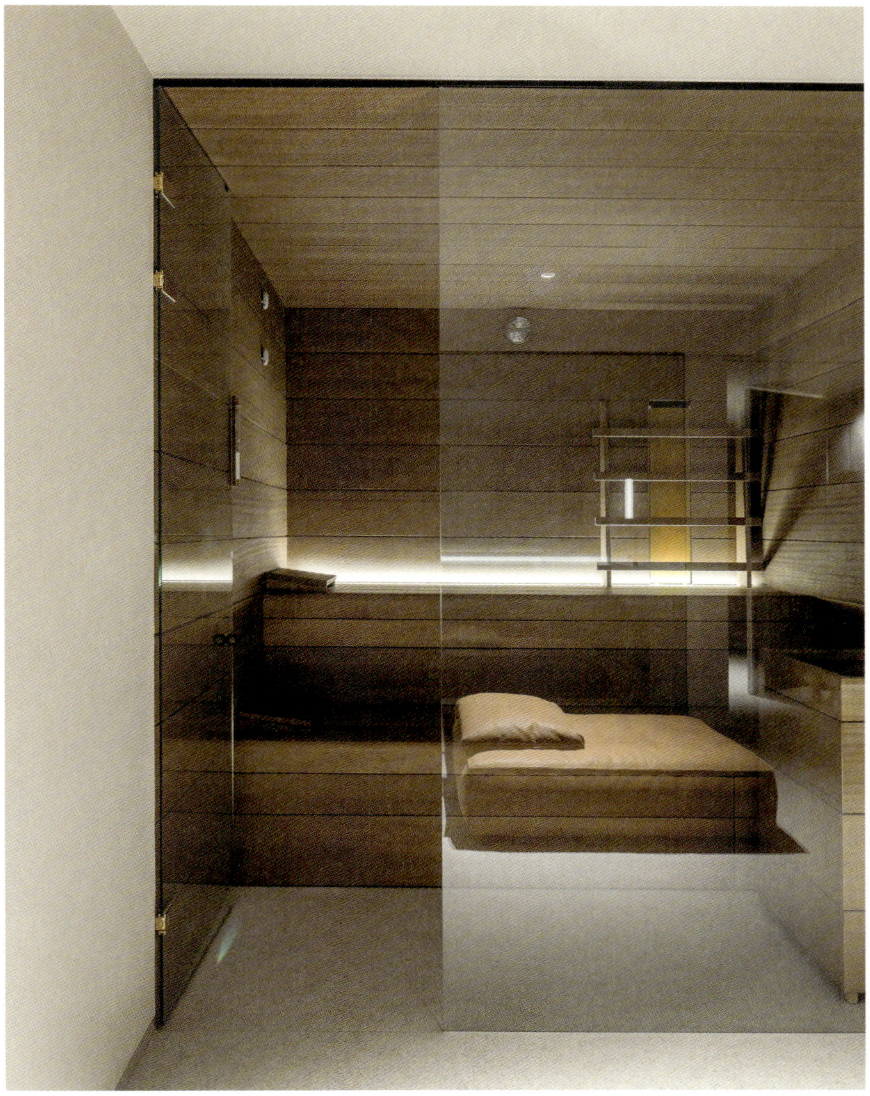

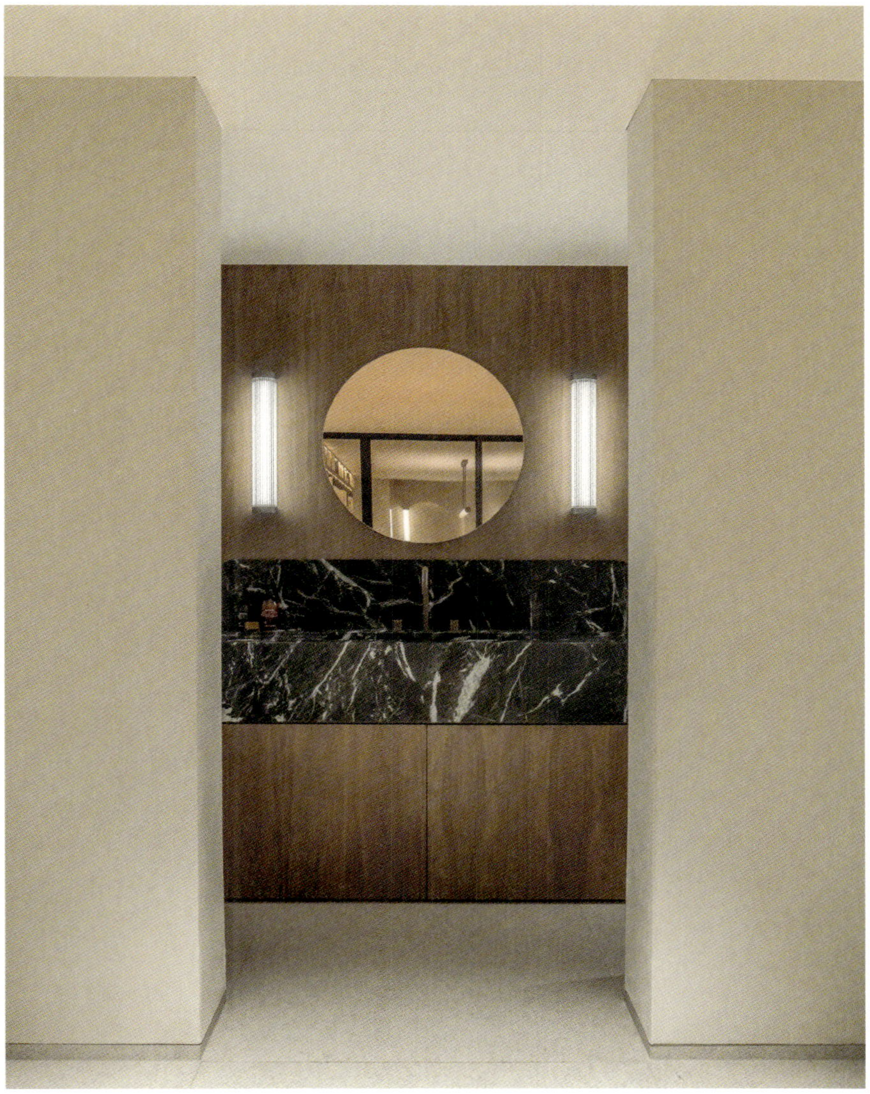

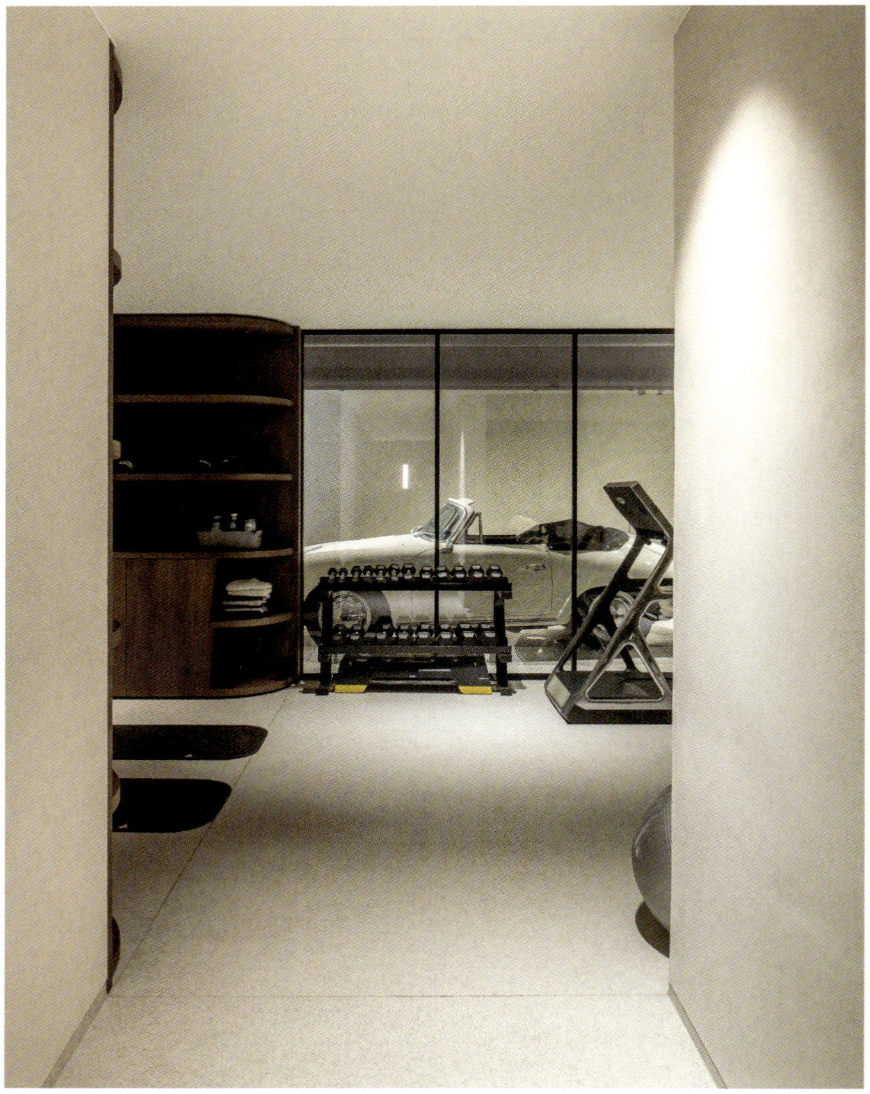

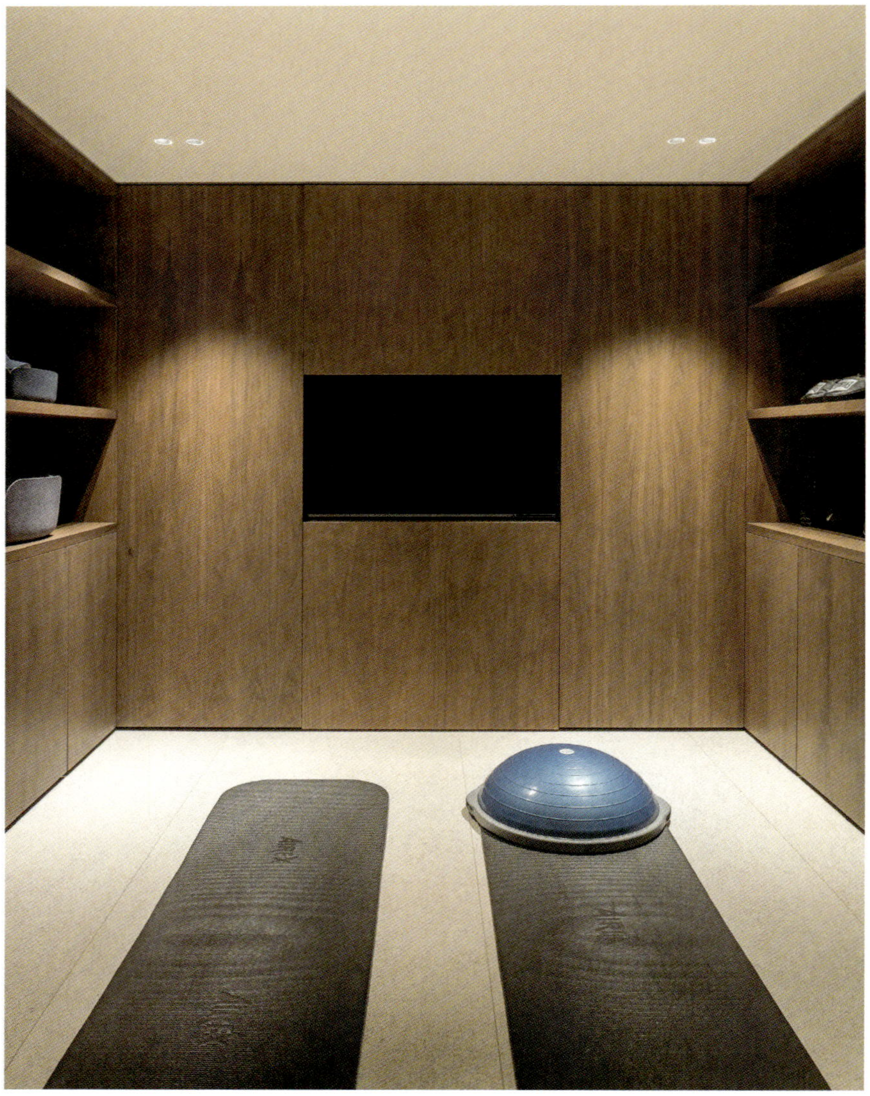

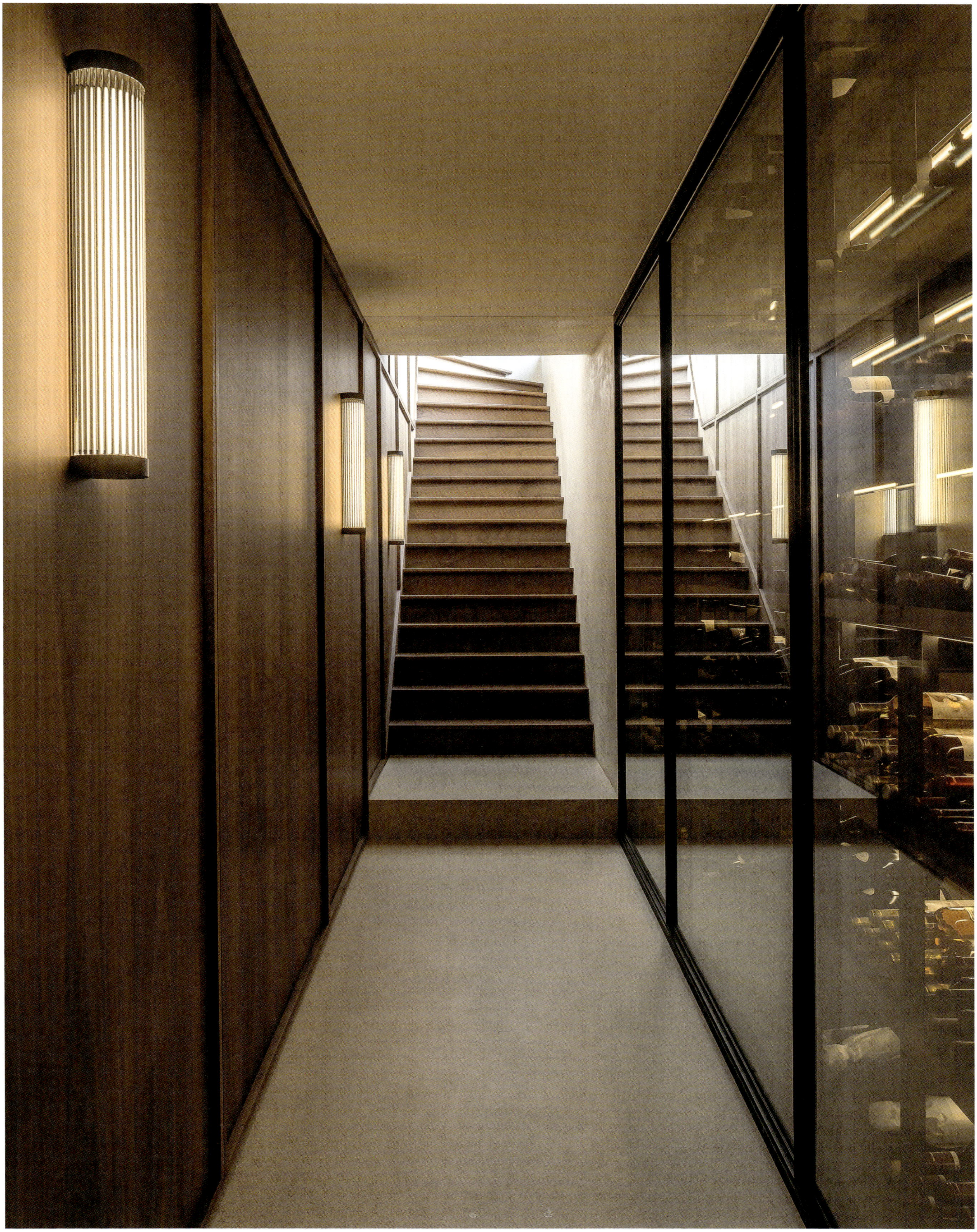

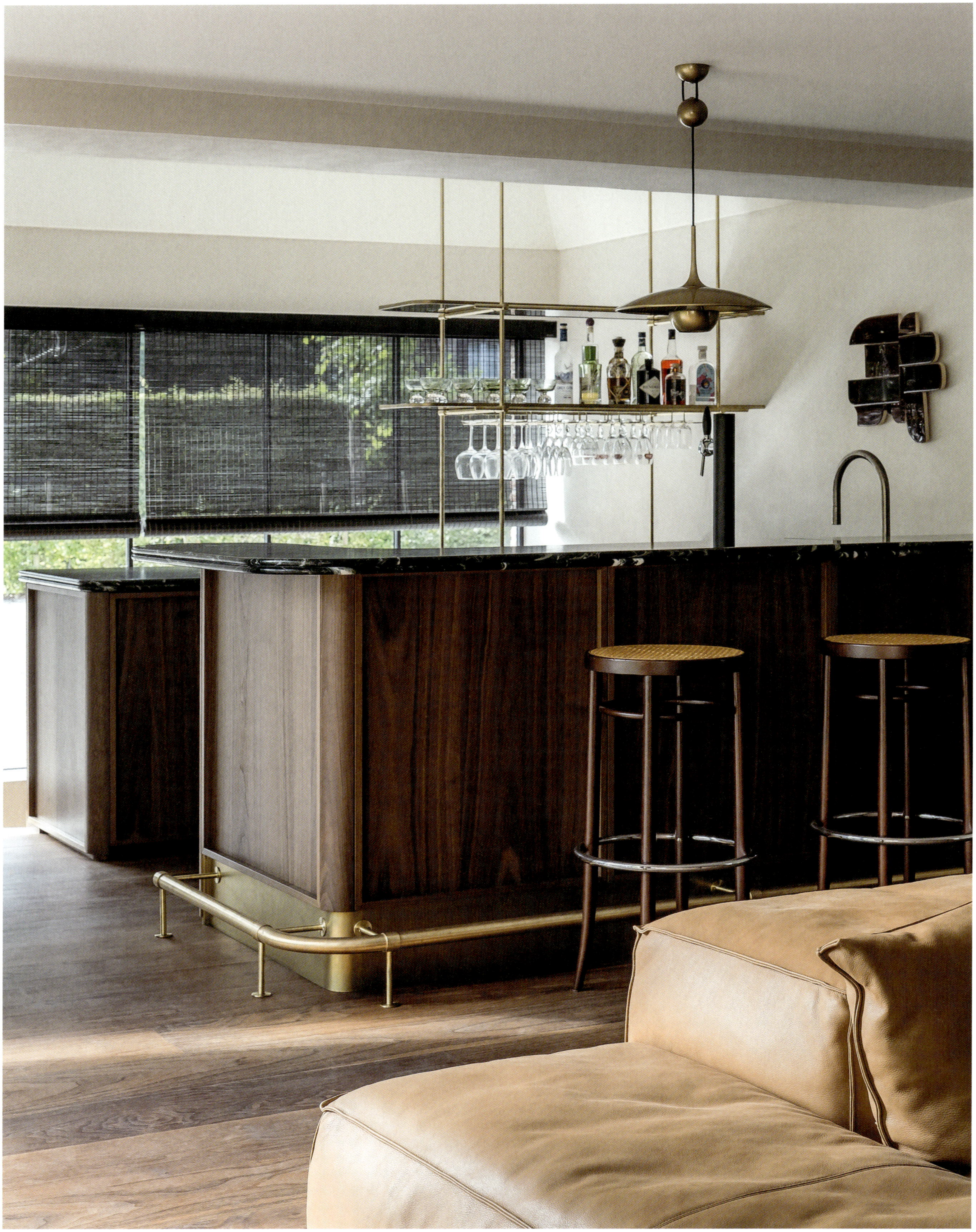

I drink to make other people
more interesting
Ernest Hemingway

Portrait by Jonathan Hökklo

Studio Zung

Studio Zung is a modern design studio integrating architecture, interiors and the artistry of living.

Founder and principal Tommy Zung has over 30 years of experience in the design world, starting in architecture, delving into fashion, and his most recent endeavor: an eponymous architecture and design studio, Tommy Zung has transformed what it means to be a designer in today's world. His unique and balanced perspective - a mix of professional experience countered with years spent surfing, negotiating the oceans unpredictable and formidable nature, gives rise to his commitment to a mindful, holistic lifestyle and modern, sensorial design.

Studio Zung is a team of architects, thinkers, designers and makers inspired by a holistic lifestyle and sensorial, mindful design. They develop concepts in architecture, interiors, and products as a team of multidisciplinary creatives; architects, interior designers, and visual marketeers who help clients realize the artistry of living. Tommy and his team have torn down walls between architecture, design, and built environments so their clients get the best creativity, in the most efficient way.

Studio Zung's approach is immersive; a fluid union of ideas and aesthetics that combines the physical and sensuous storytelling of architecture and design. They believe that every project starts with a smart, visionary idea, and ends with a beautiful, sustainable, and memorable human environment.

www.studiozung.com

Photography: Jonathan Hökklo (p. 278-283) / Adrian Gaut (p. 284-289)

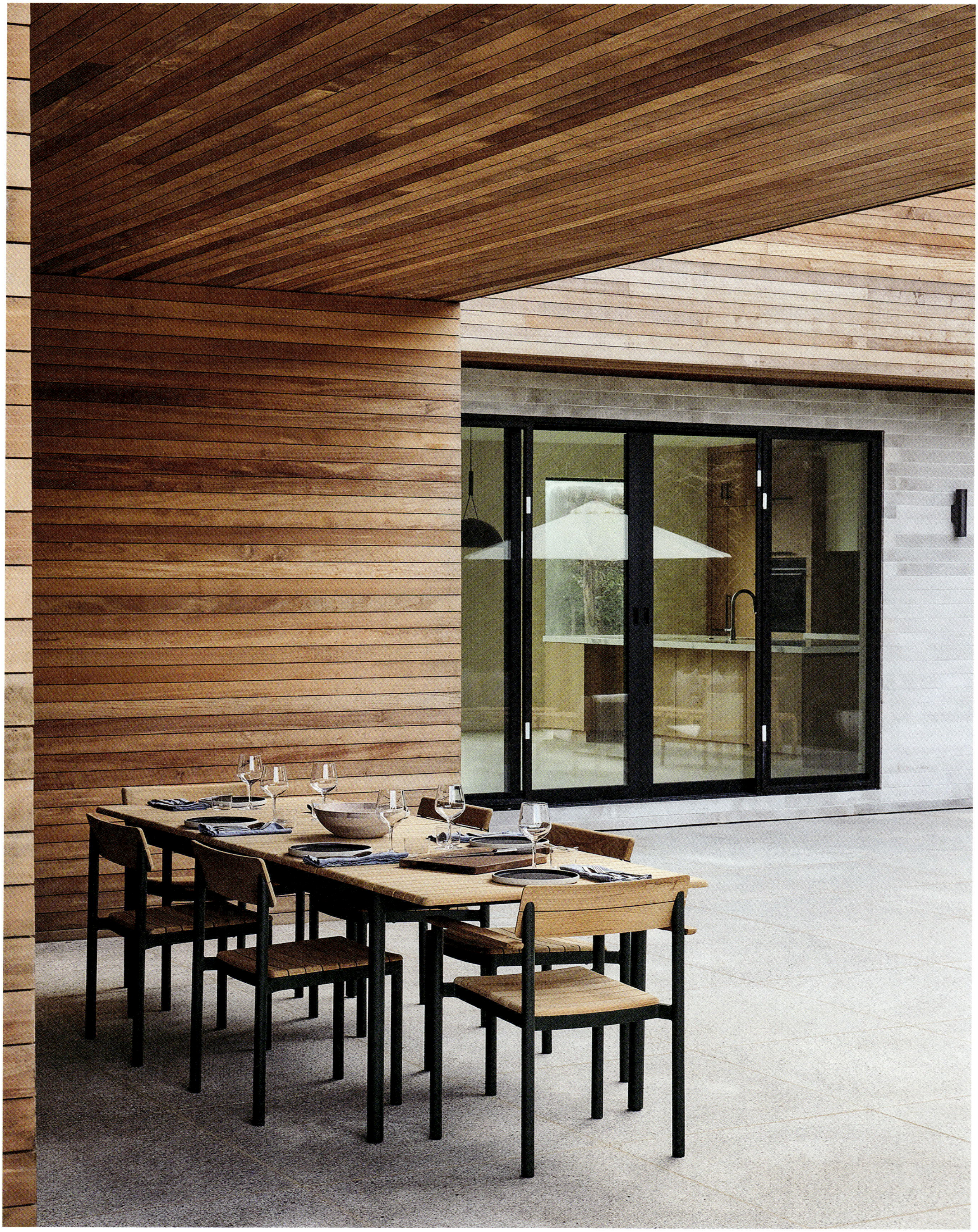

In this publication, we present two of Studio Zung's creations: Atelier 96 and Atelier 211.

Atelier 96 is a modern beach home with 190-degree ocean views accessible from every public living space, private bedroom, and nook. Nestled within Atlantic Beach and Amagansett Lanes, Atelier 96 fosters a connection to the natural luxuries that surround and envelope the home. The master bedroom opens to the master deck with views of the boundless Atlantic Ocean with the guest suite having private access to its own outdoor deck. Unobstructed ocean views continue through moments in the home and onto the rooftop deck with an open fire pit and outdoor seating. The residence represents the duality of our daily life, balancing luxury with a scent of simplicity.

With sweeping vistas of one of the best views Amagansett has to offer, Atelier 211 is designed around the breathtaking natural environment and continues the story into the home. Honoring the natural luxuries and fostering connections, Atelier 211 is an ocean-view, modern A-Frame beach residence within Atlantic Beach and Amagansett Lanes. The residence features a Scandinavian-inspired chef's kitchen and a serene wellness spa encompassing a separate cedar sauna and steam room inspired by the Swedish bath experience dedicated to wellness and tranquility.

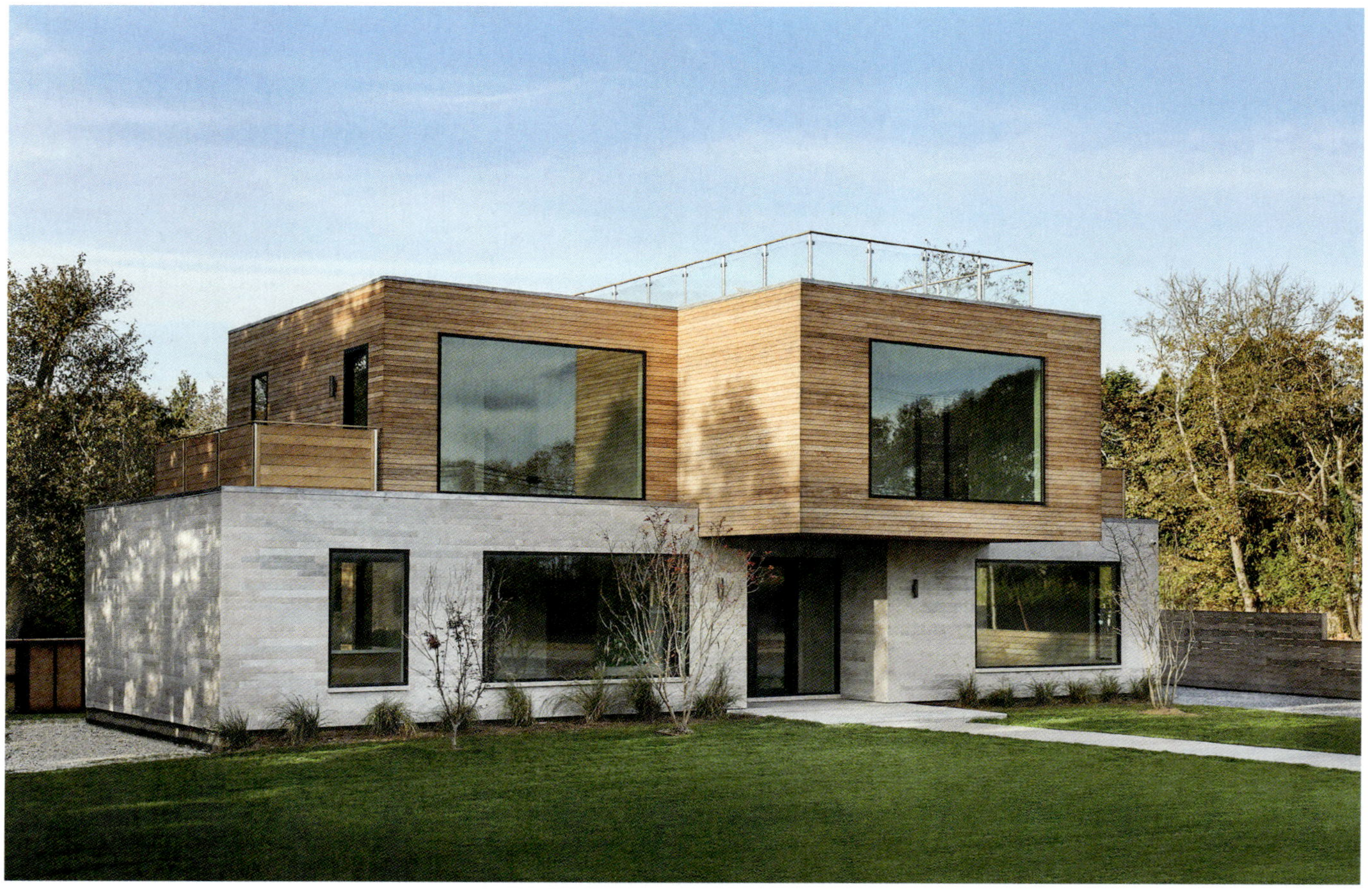

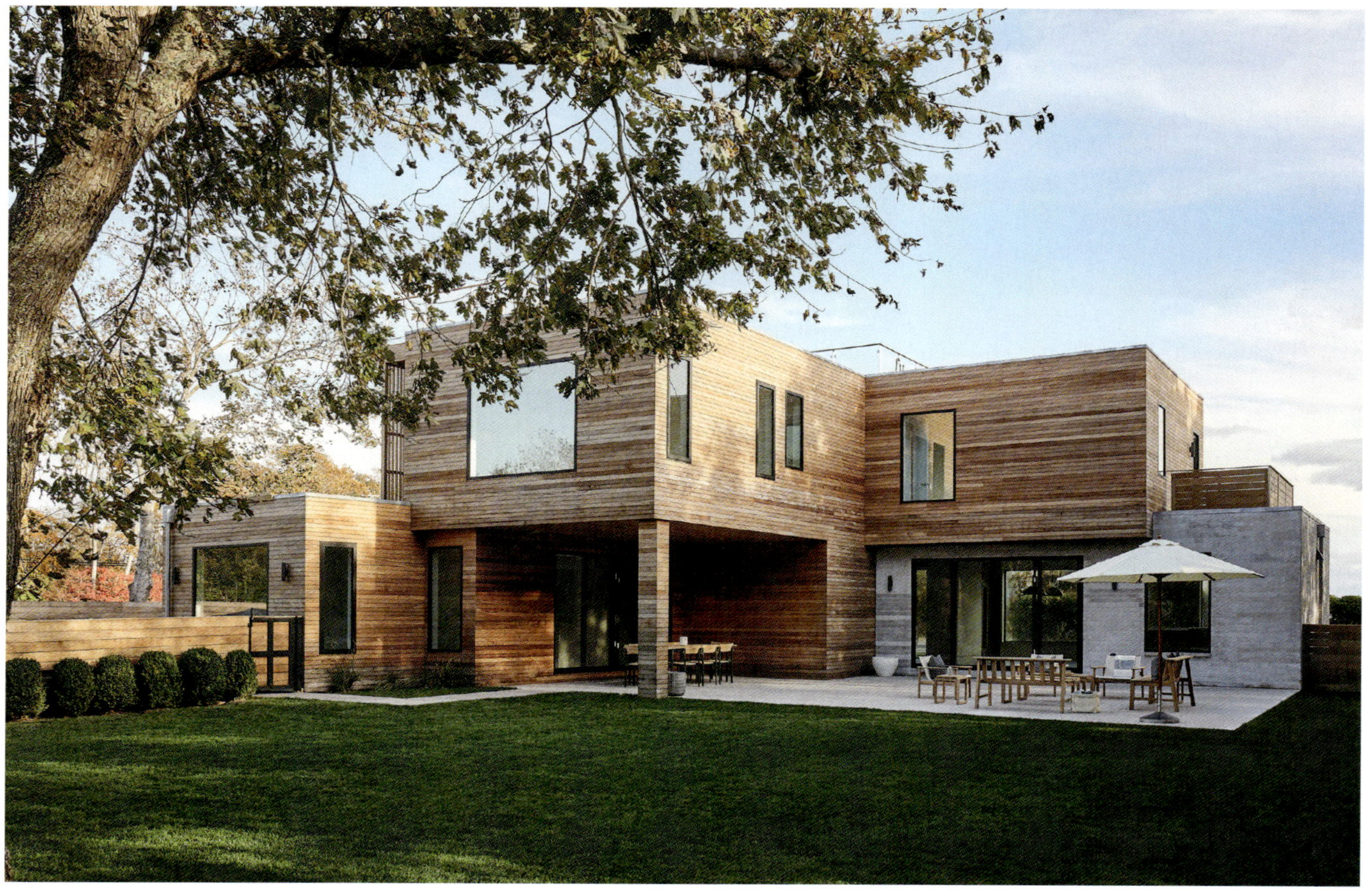

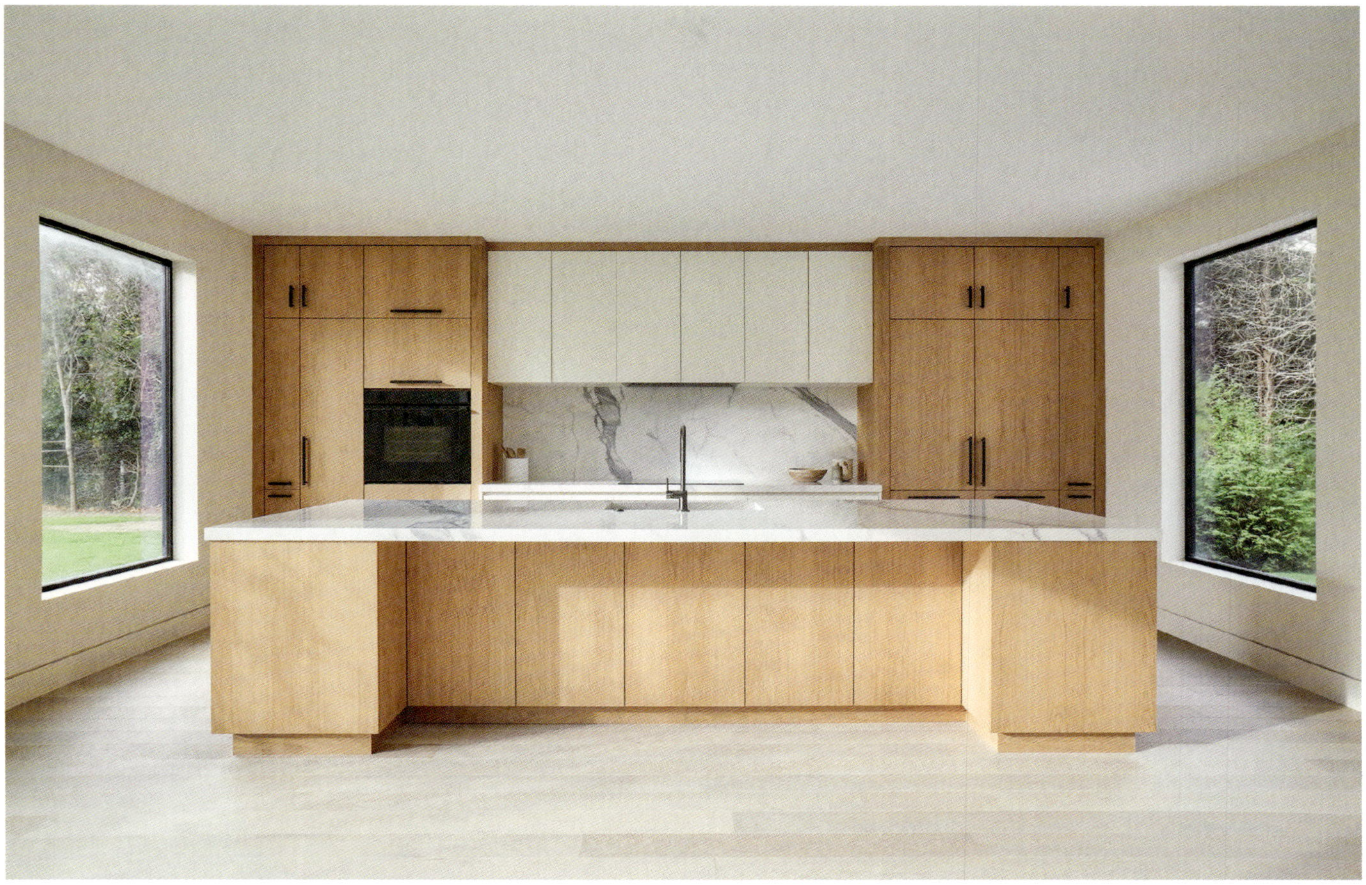

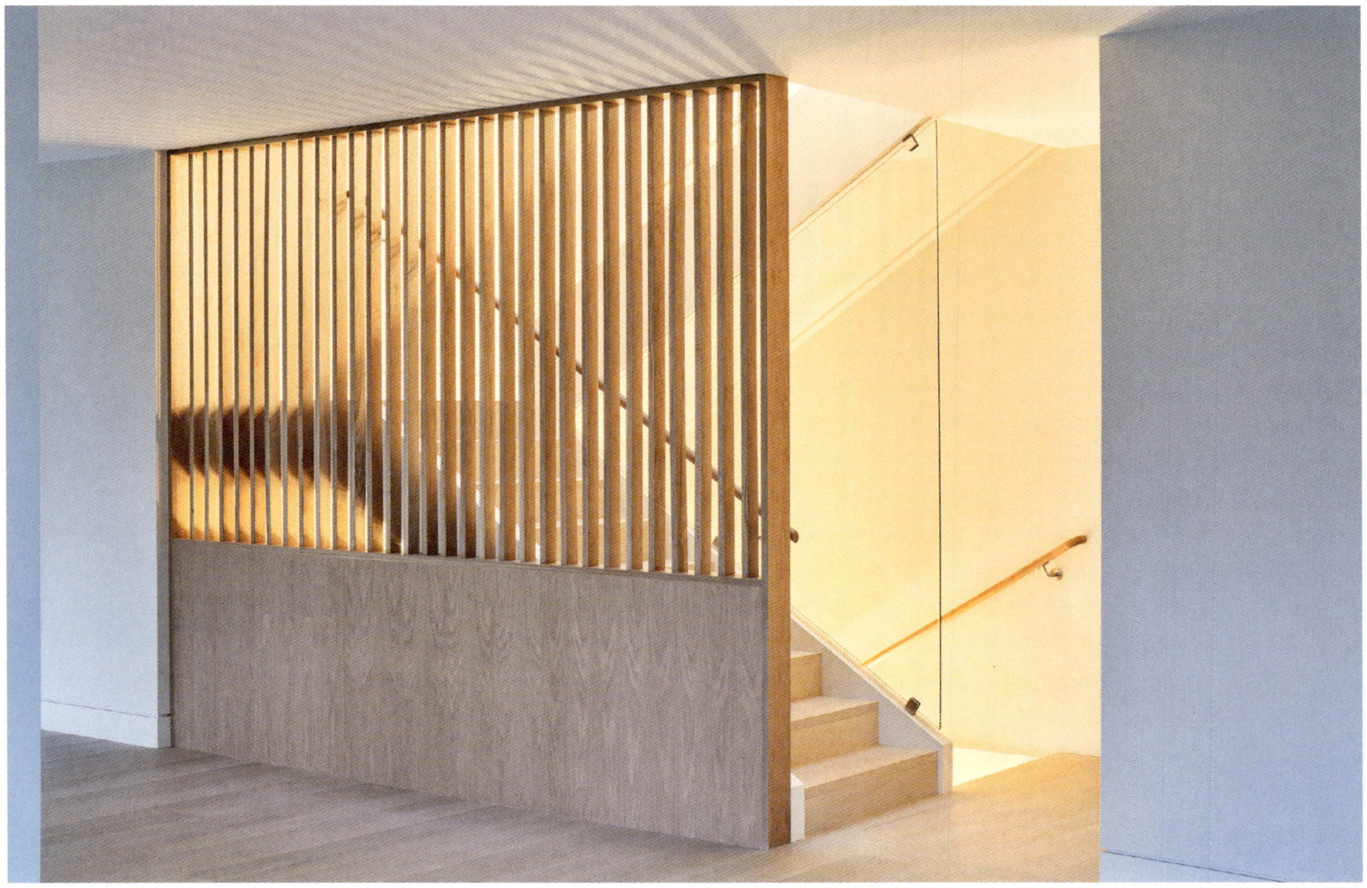

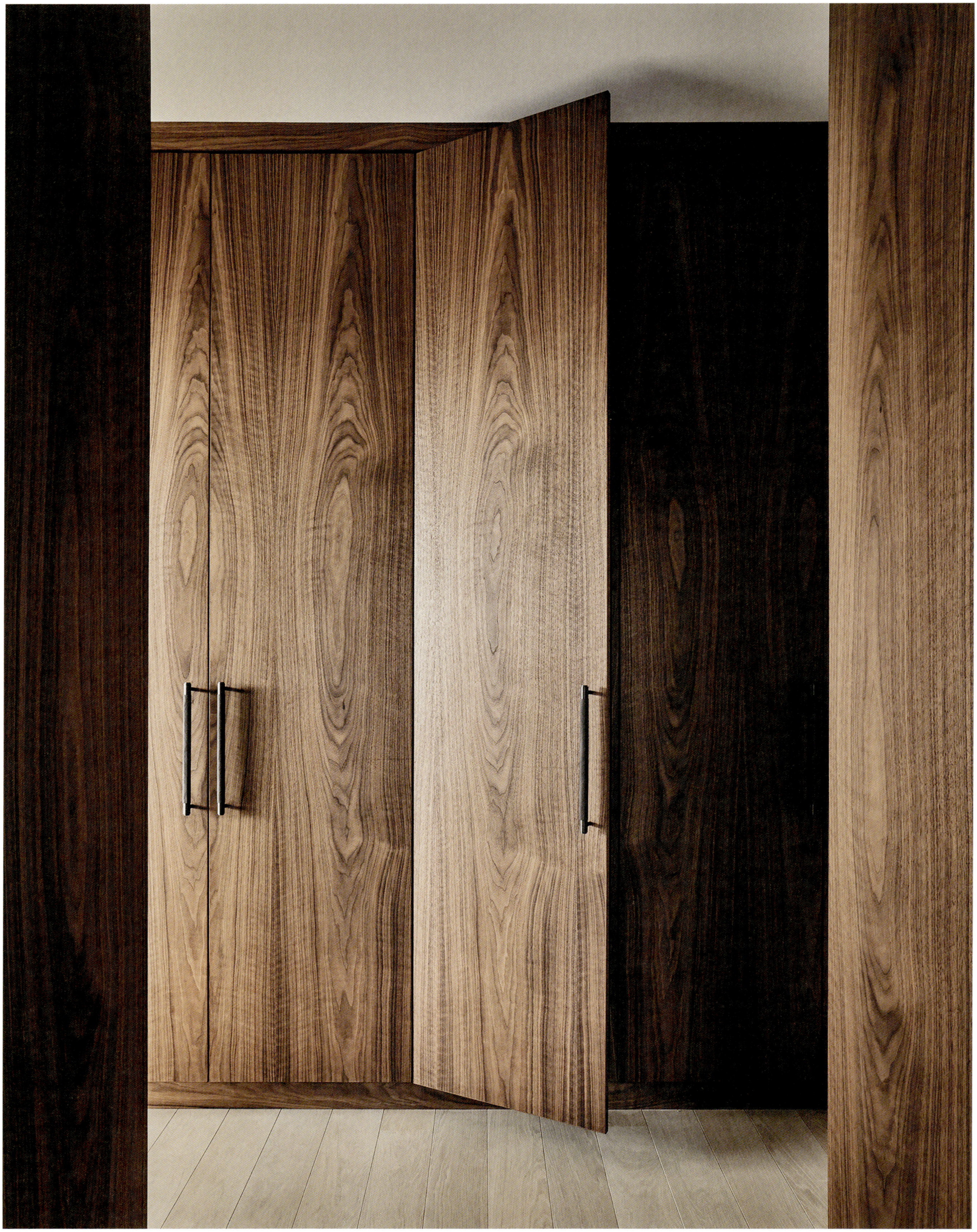

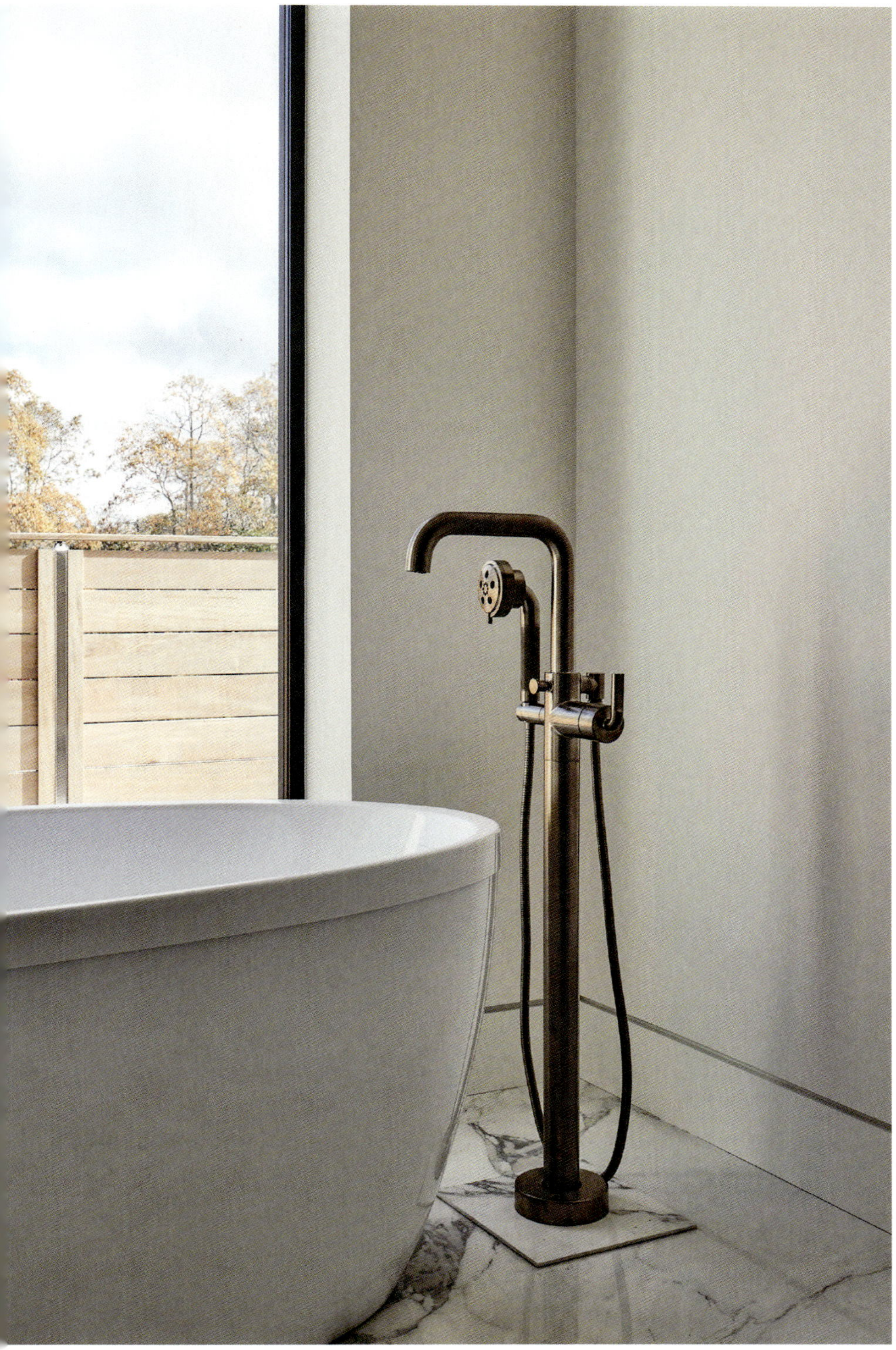

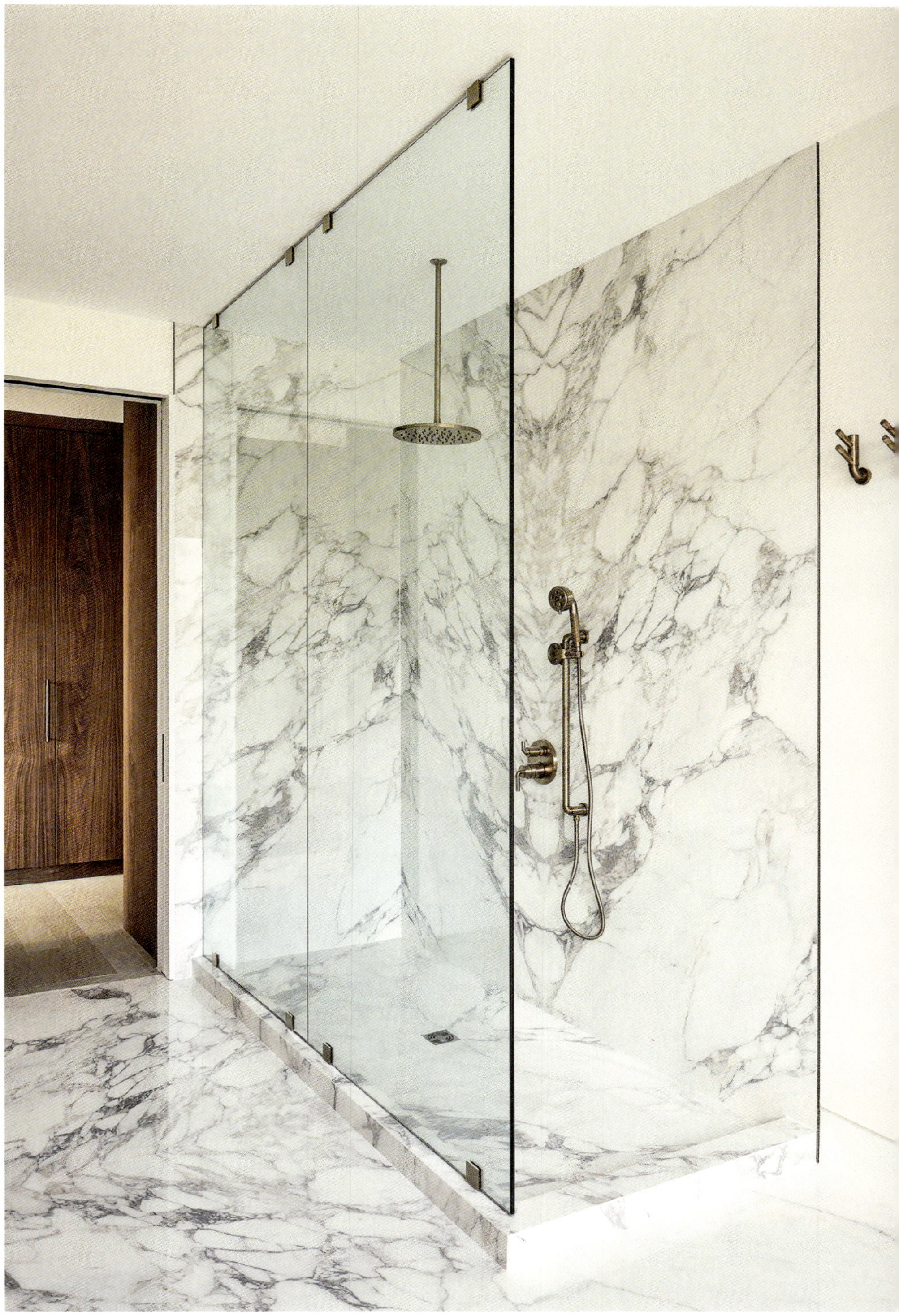

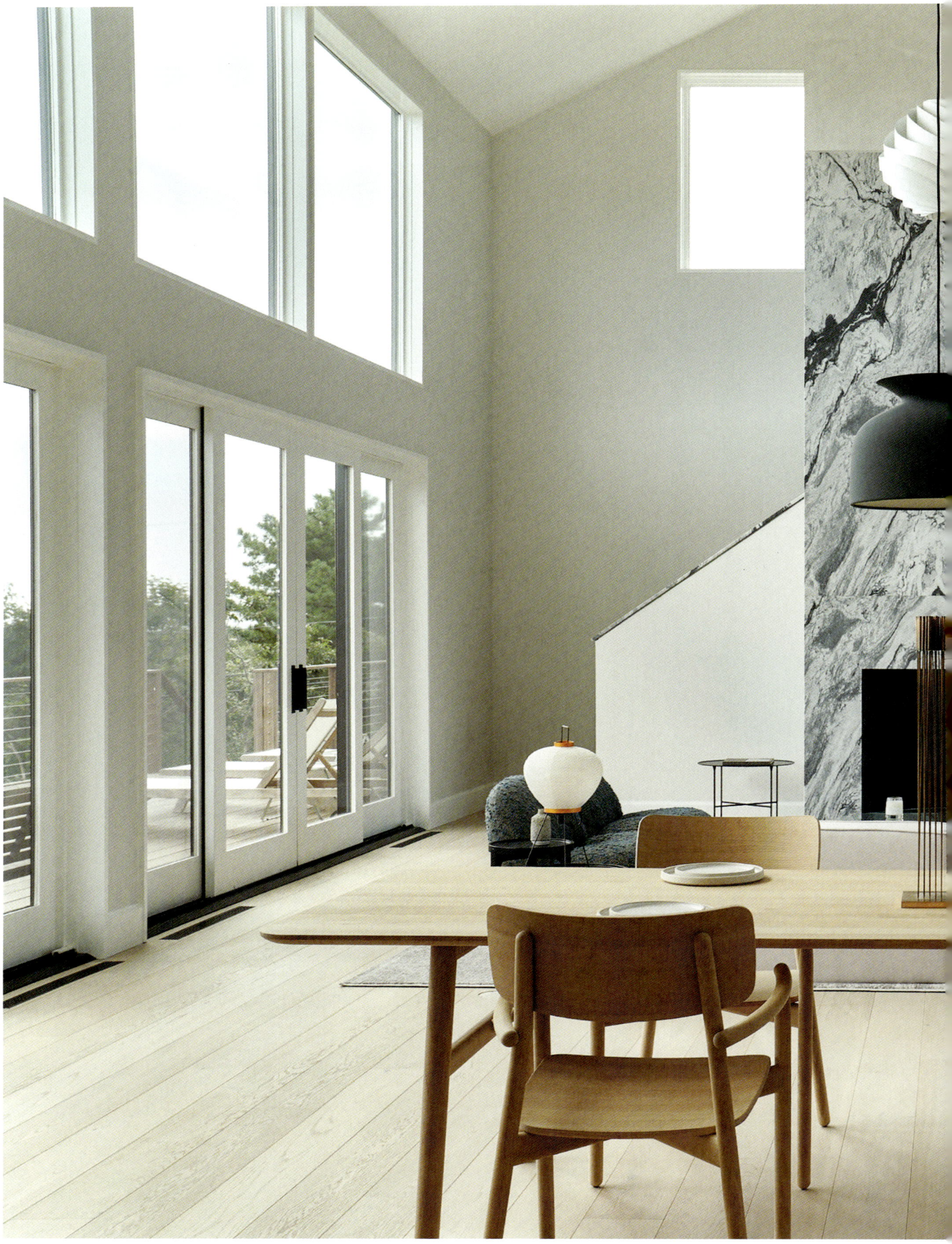

285

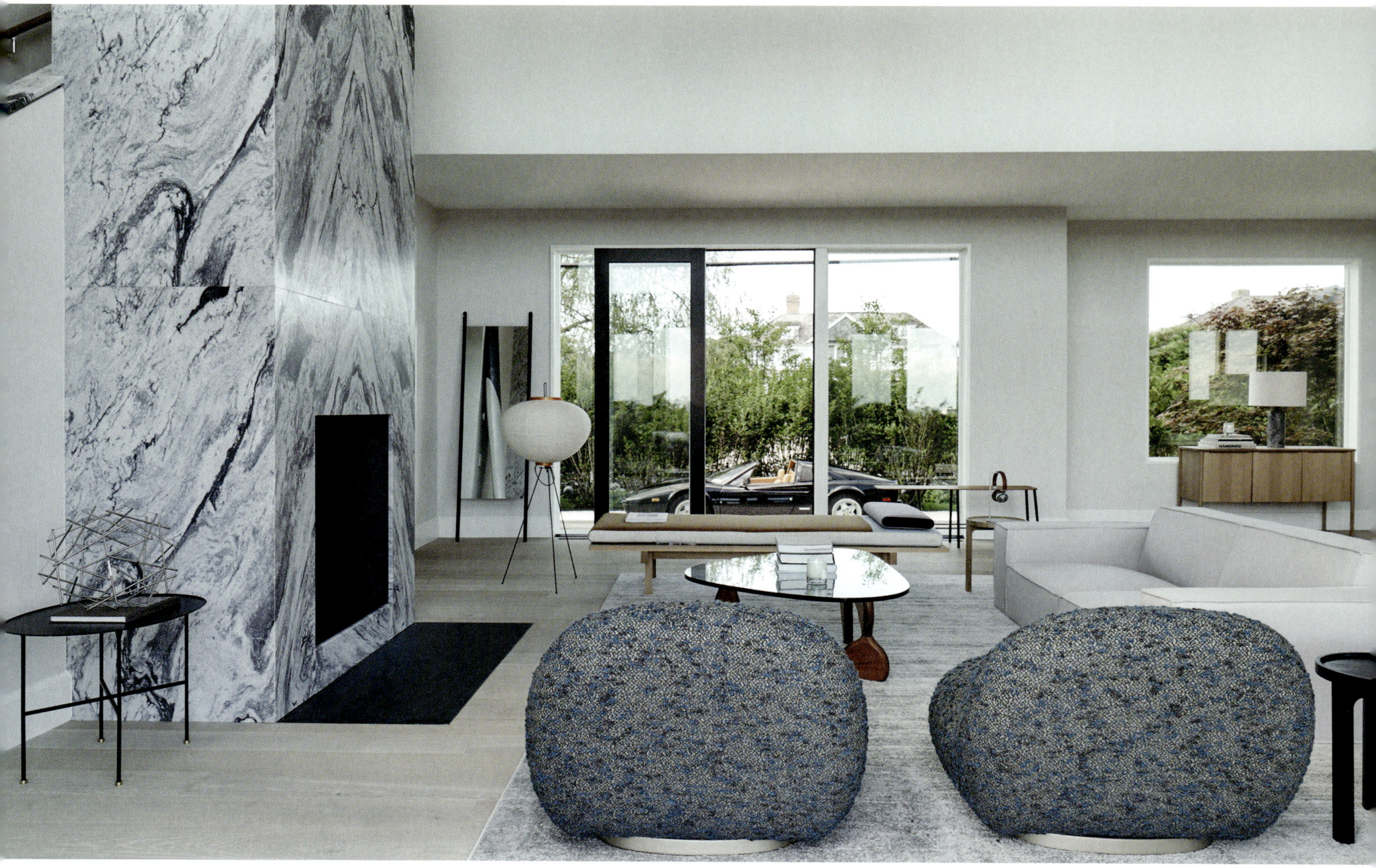

287

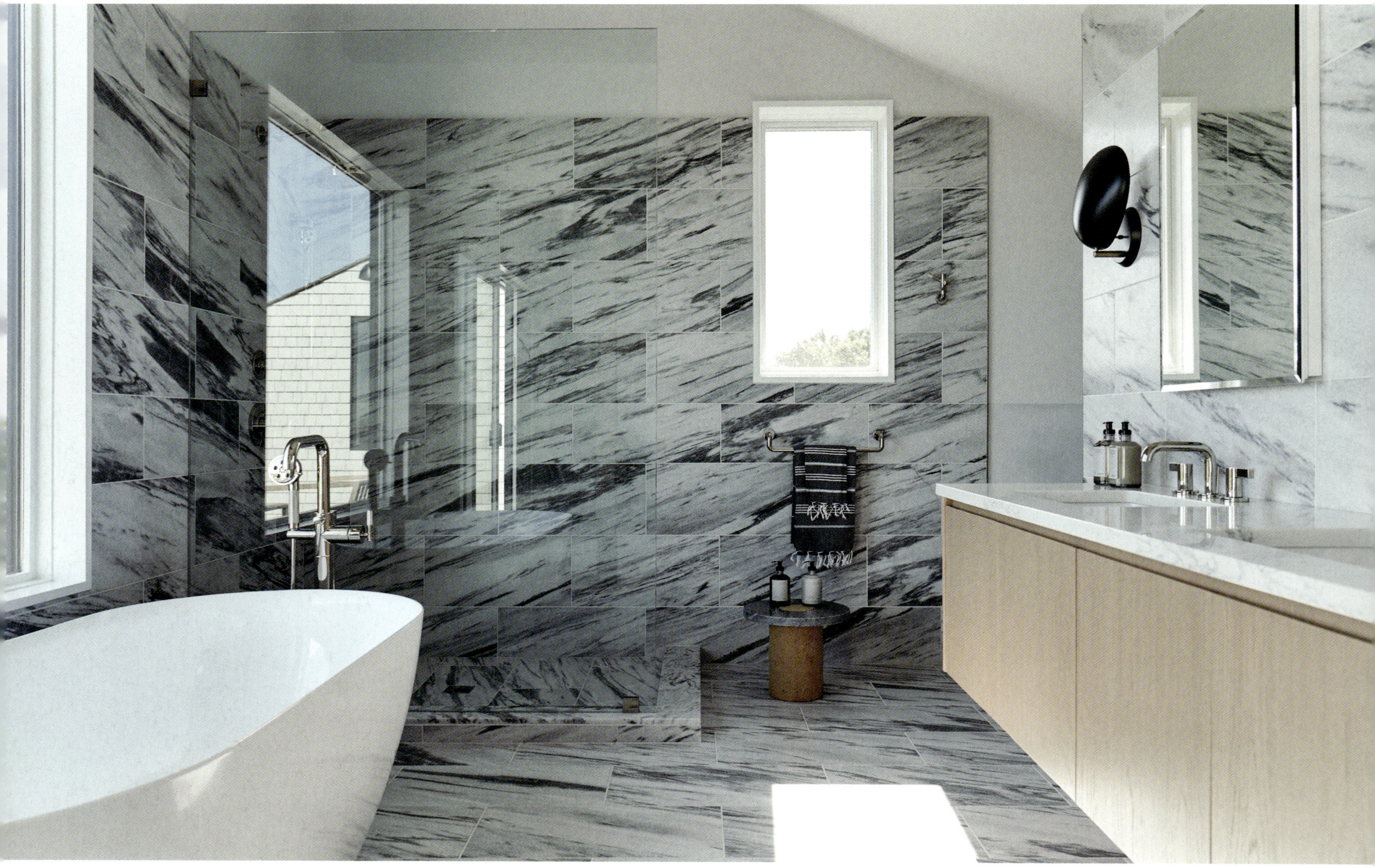

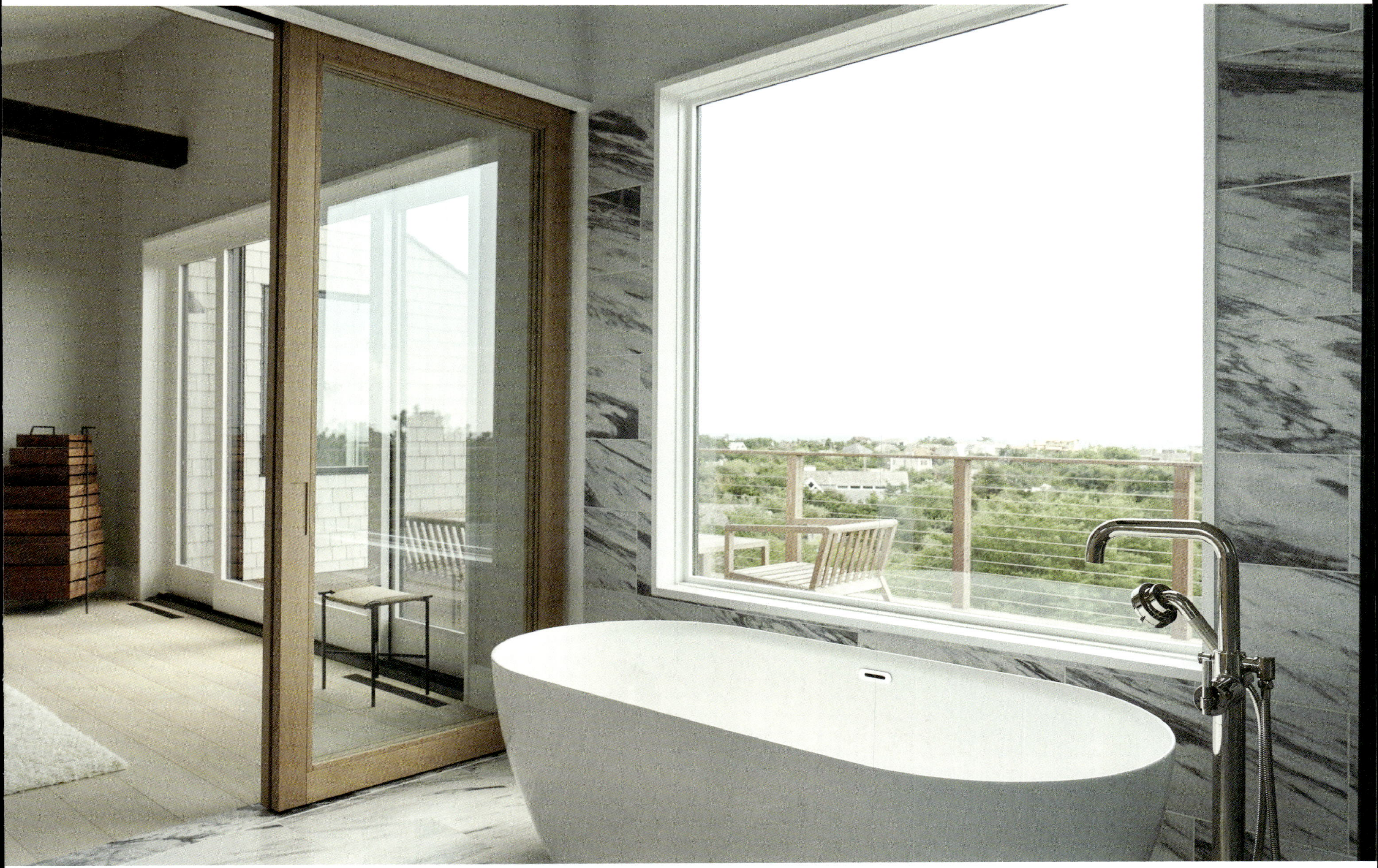

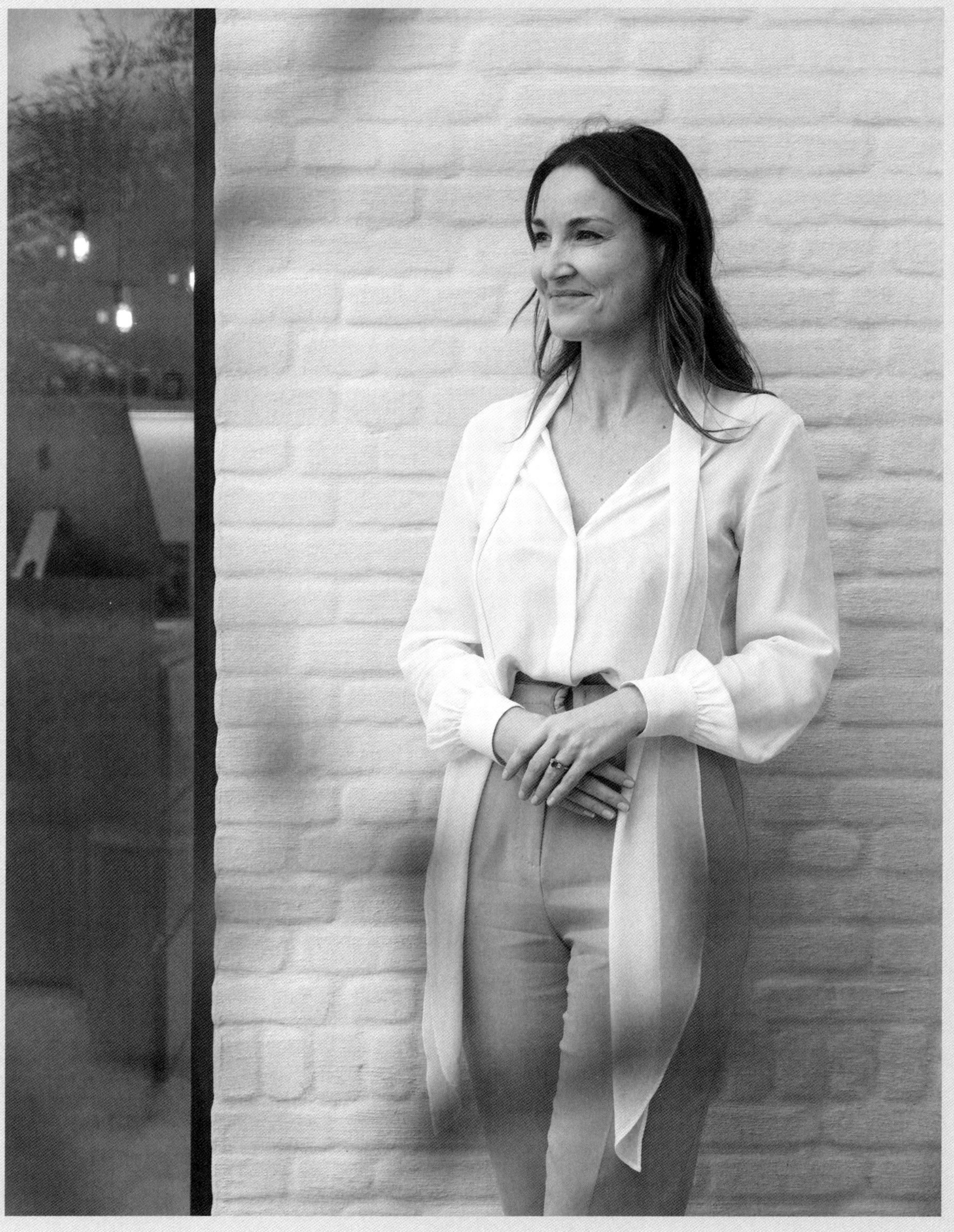

Ann-Sophie Princen

Princen Concepts is a young and dynamic company founded in 2020 by Ann-Sophie Princen. An architect with a strong sense for high-end total concepts that connect in a flowing way.

Ann-Sophie Princen started her 4-year studies in interior architecture at the University of Diepenbeek, after which, under the impetus of her mentor, she started an additional 4-year course in architecture at the University of Maastricht. She is very strong in surveyable work where not only interior and exterior seamlessly merge into one another, but also the different spaces. Softness and warmth that surround her like an invisible force can be found in everything she does. The sense of beauty and making beautiful nestled in her DNA make the projects she takes on not just a job but a real passion.

That sense of belonging works through not only in the projects she undertakes but also in the way she interacts with her clients. The cocoon, which represents her design, is brought to life with the soul of the clients placed in it with care. After all, it is for them that she creates and executes the designs. But Ann-Sophie does not do this alone, although her company is currently 1-woman-strong, she is surrounded by a whole trust team, partners she carefully chose to strengthen her. In this team you will find not only partners in construction, but also, for example, the photographer who knows how to capture the soul of the end result so precisely in images, is an indispensable link. Everything stands and falls with trust hence Ann-Sophie only works with the partners she evolved with in her process and entrepreneurship and who share the same values and standards. Boa Interior is hereby the ideal match as a general contractor, they know exactly what Ann-Sophie means and thus materialize her thoughts and instructions, down to the smallest details. This experienced and driven company, started 17 years ago as a joinery and thus keeps a finger on the pulse of pure craftsmanship and is an established value in the interior and construction world.

Ann-Sophie stands for minimalist timelessness, sustainability and understated luxury. The spaces come to life through a continuous line of materials and textures. Nothing is too much, but also nothing too little, designs connected by the right balance of details that support and even enhance the design.

www.princenconcepts.be - www.boa-interior.be

Photography: Stéphanie Mathias

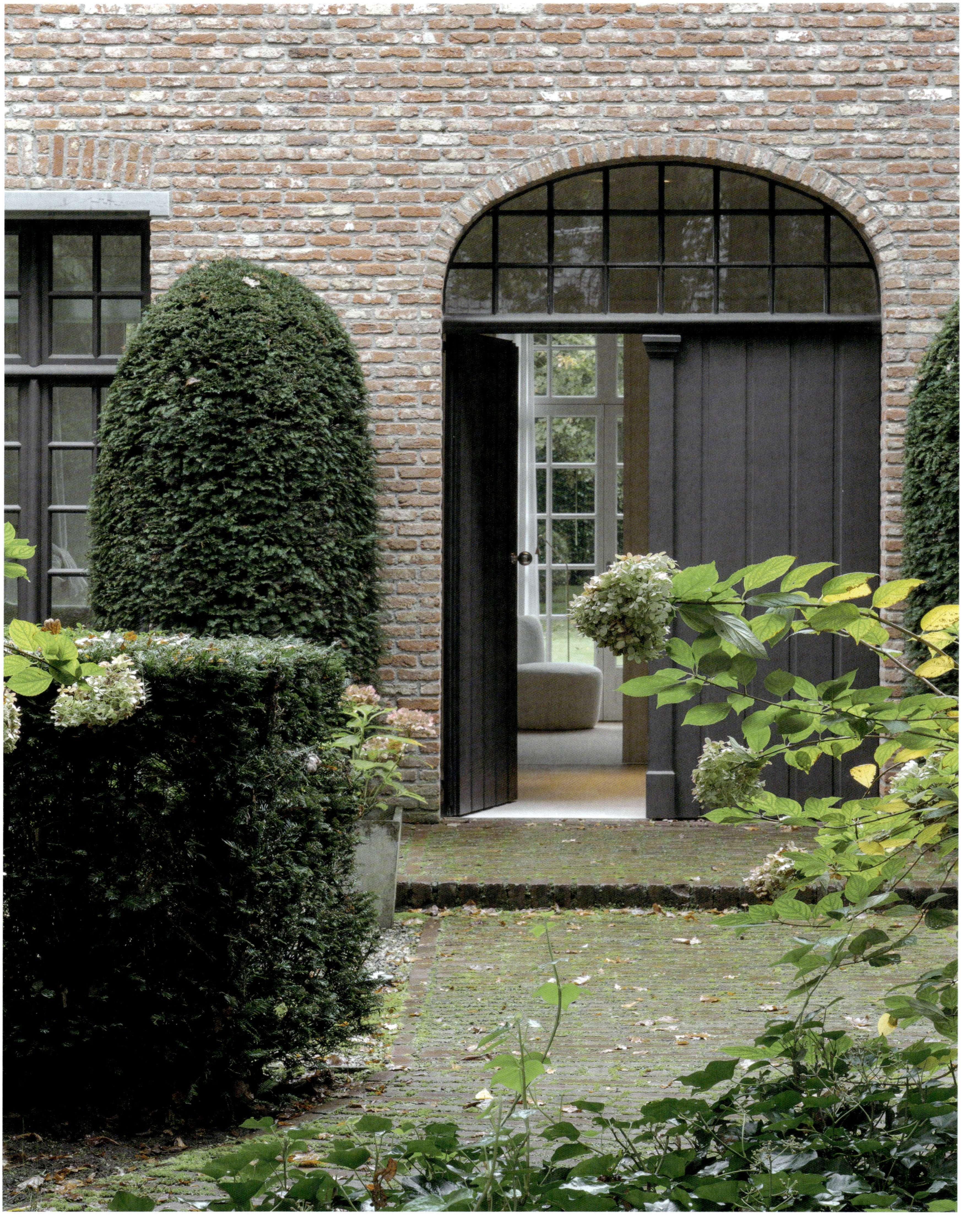

The renovation of this detached villa is an excellent example of how to draw a flowing yet powerful line from existing architecture to an updated interior. The classic architecture called for a soft, connecting approach so that there is no clash between inside and outside. At the same time, an innovative and timeless interpretation.

On the first floor of the villa, the design revolves around the heart of the home: the kitchen, the place where the residents spend most time together. The tranquility and warmth of the floors laid in Romanesque pattern with Pietra di Cortado limestone, bespoke furniture with touches of natural brushed light oak and the sheer stucco textures on cabinet fronts and walls, form a flowing unity resulting in silence, tranquility and harmony for the residents.

The luxury of lush nature is drawn inward in a yet understated way with the addition of a cold-placed window in the kitchen, completely in line with the showpiece of this space: the kitchen island. This architectural addition creates a warm abundance of light. The dining area is seamlessly threaded to this central space by infusing materials, colors and textures. This place becomes a valuable space because of the organically shaped dining table that occupies a modest but full place because of the hanging light elements above it. These light elements not only anchor the dining table but also connect the different horizontal layers, thus enhancing the multidimensional feel of the spaces.

The spaces are also given more breathing space with the addition of architectural details such as the room-high doorways, which make you flow silently from one space to another.

This whole infill of materials and colors that make you breathe freely are carried through to the rest of the home in the same harmonious way. The entire home exudes a warm and welcoming feeling, the definition of understated luxury. Princen Concepts' signature softness, fluidity and connection is felt throughout.

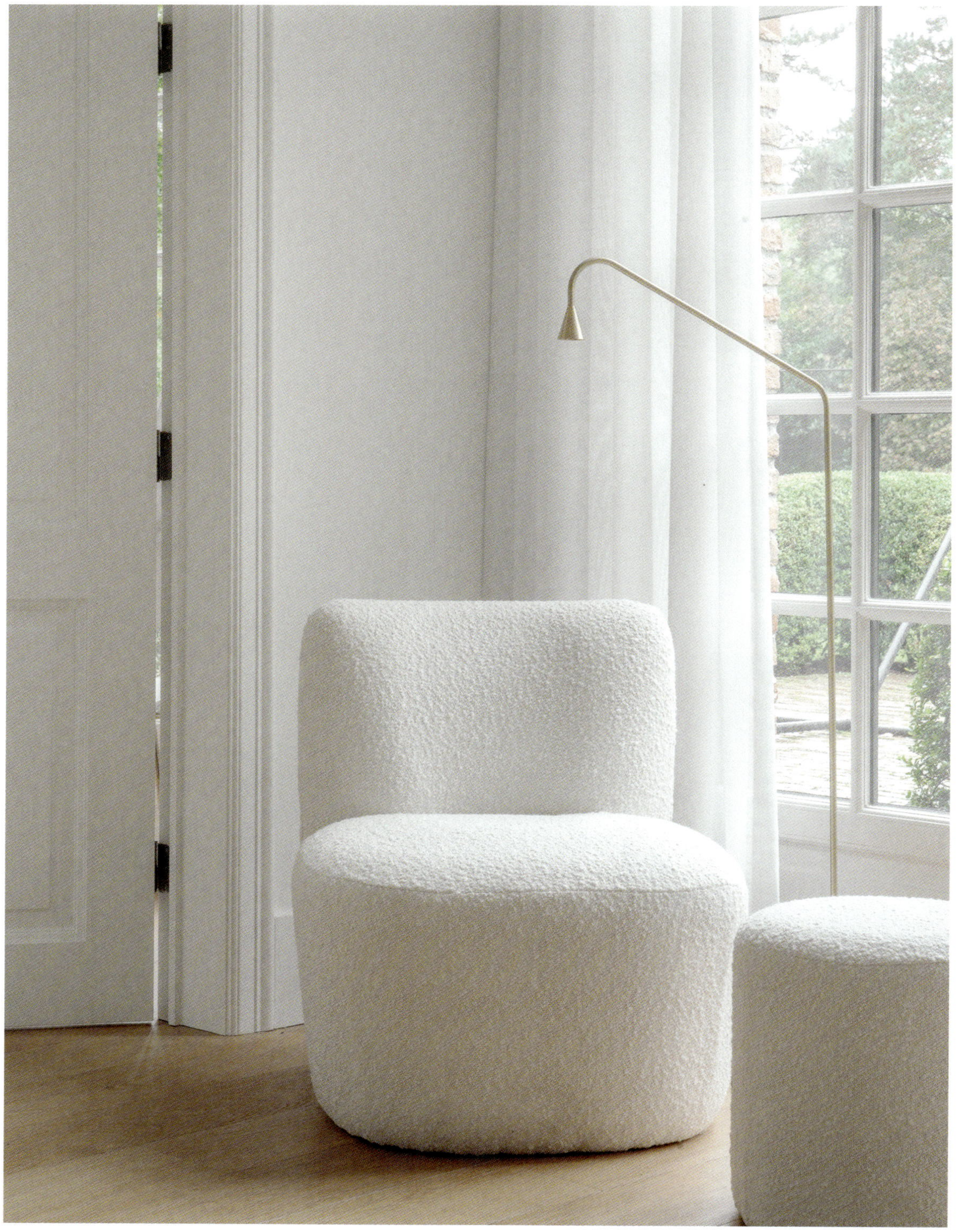

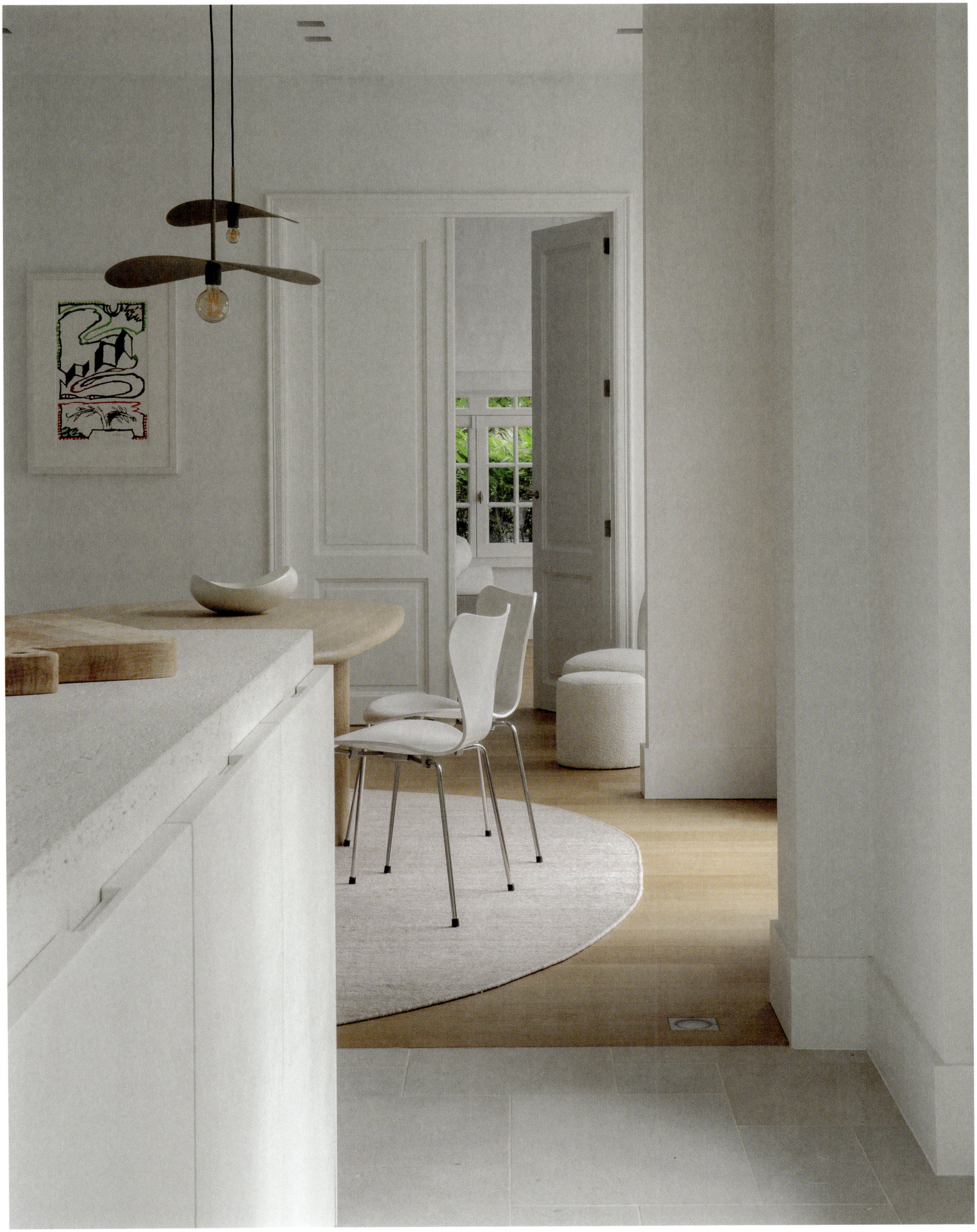

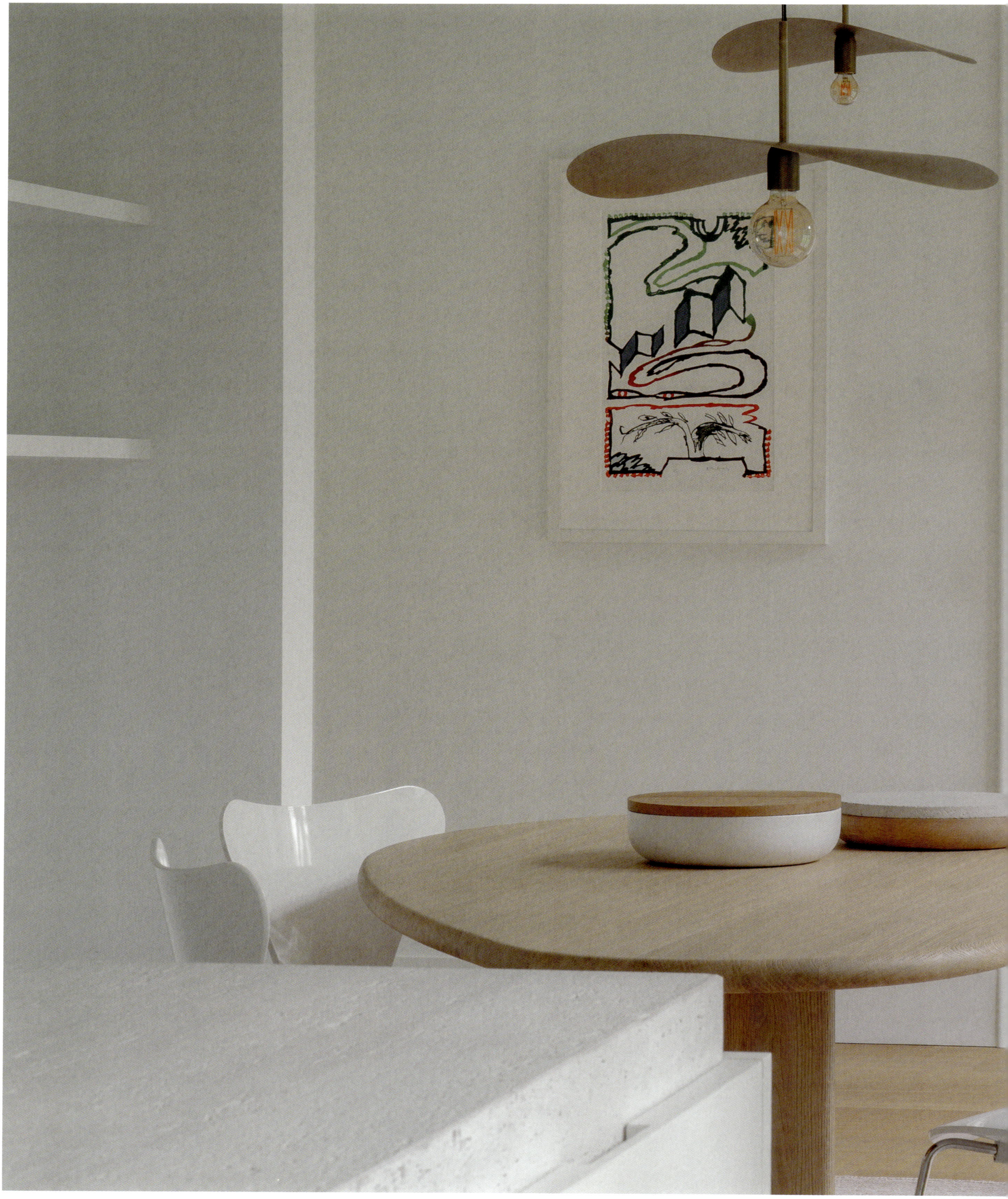

297

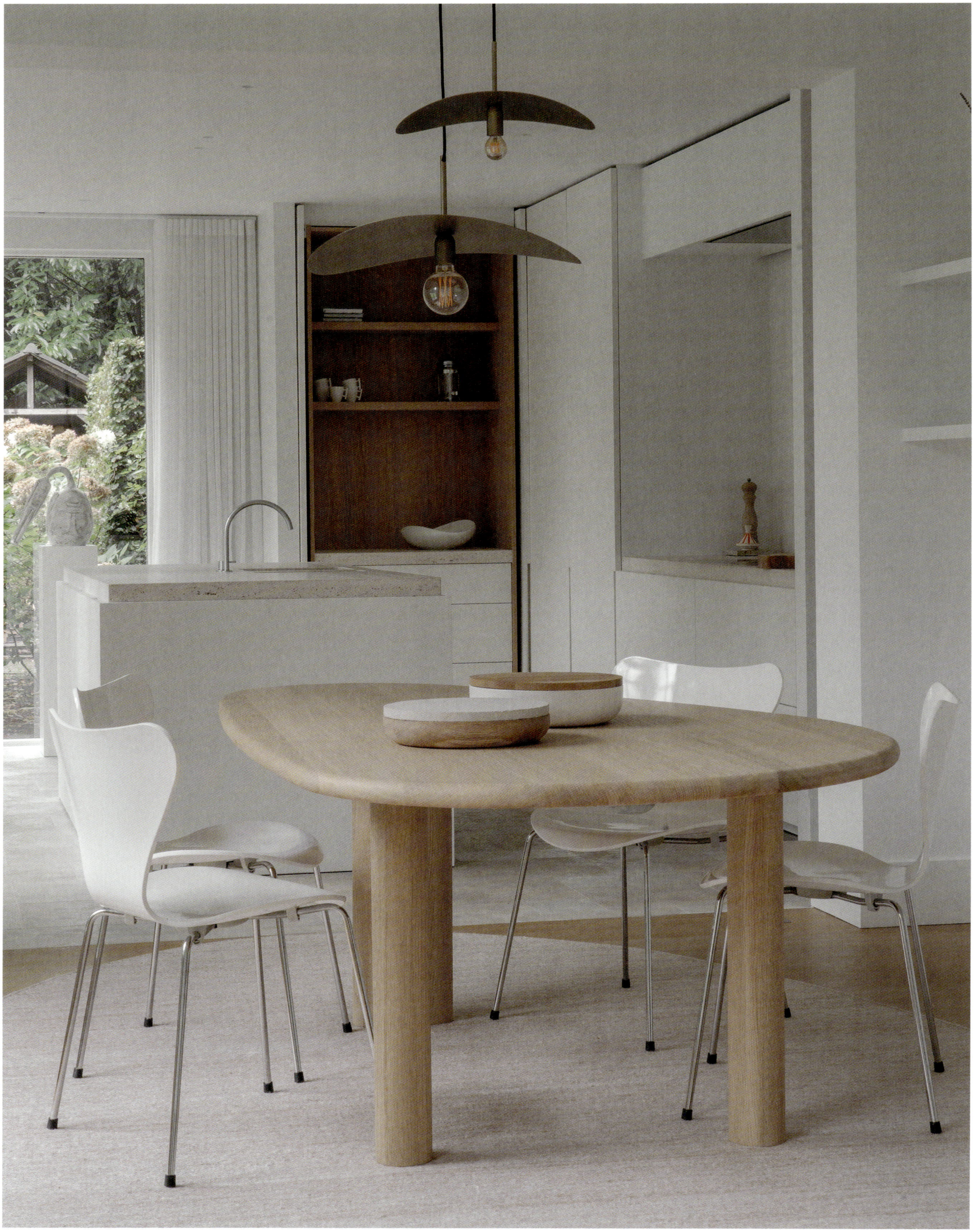

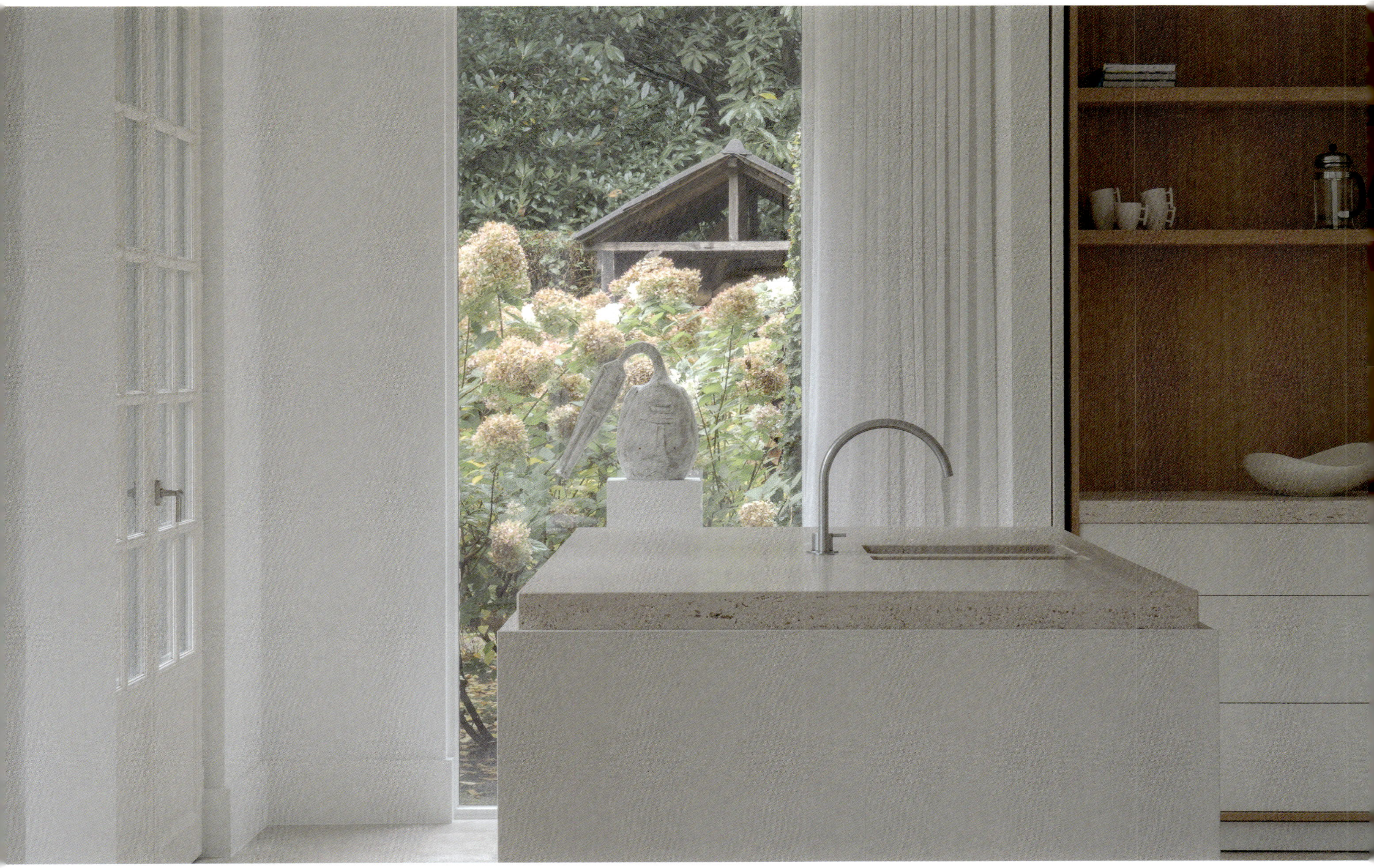

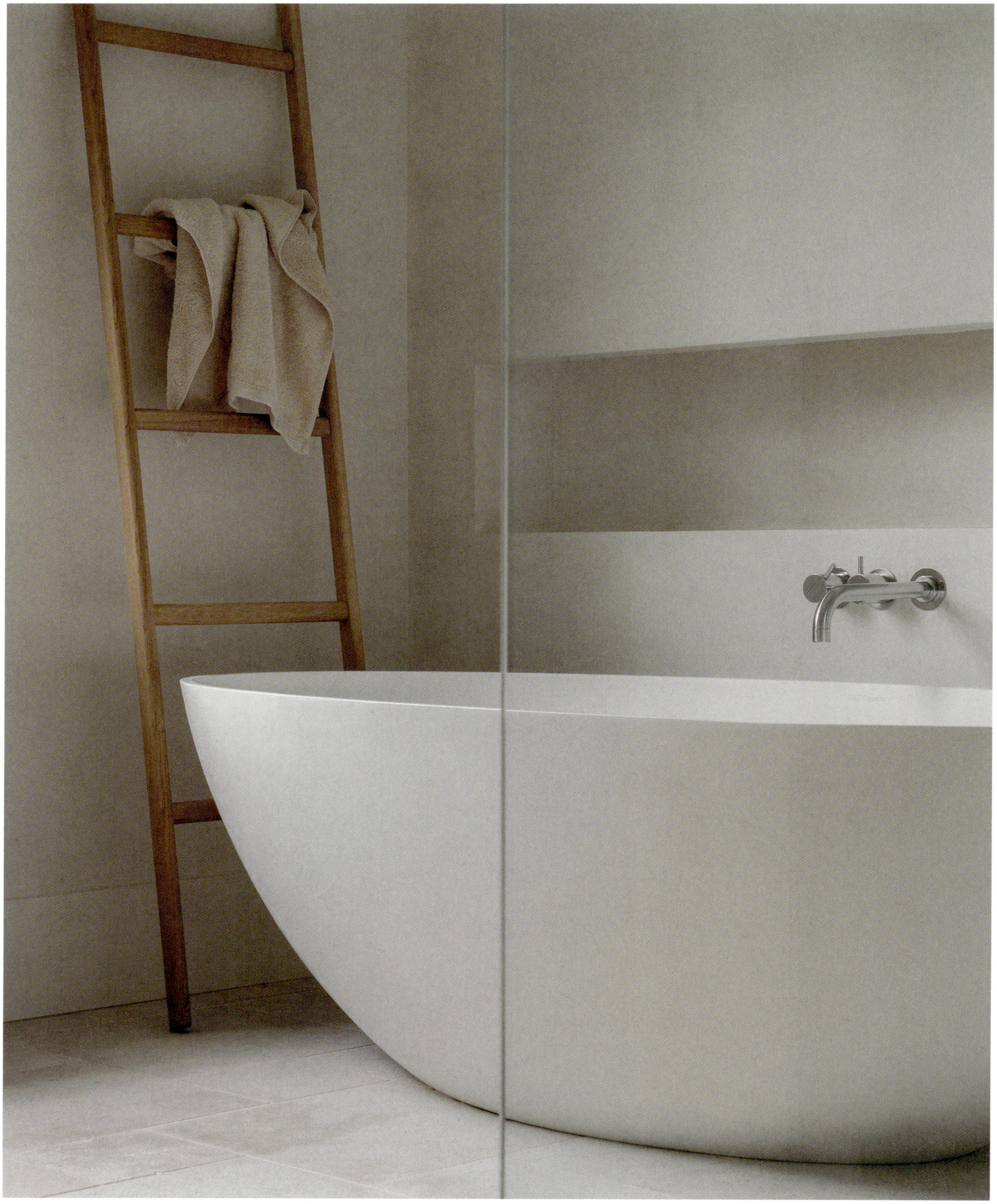

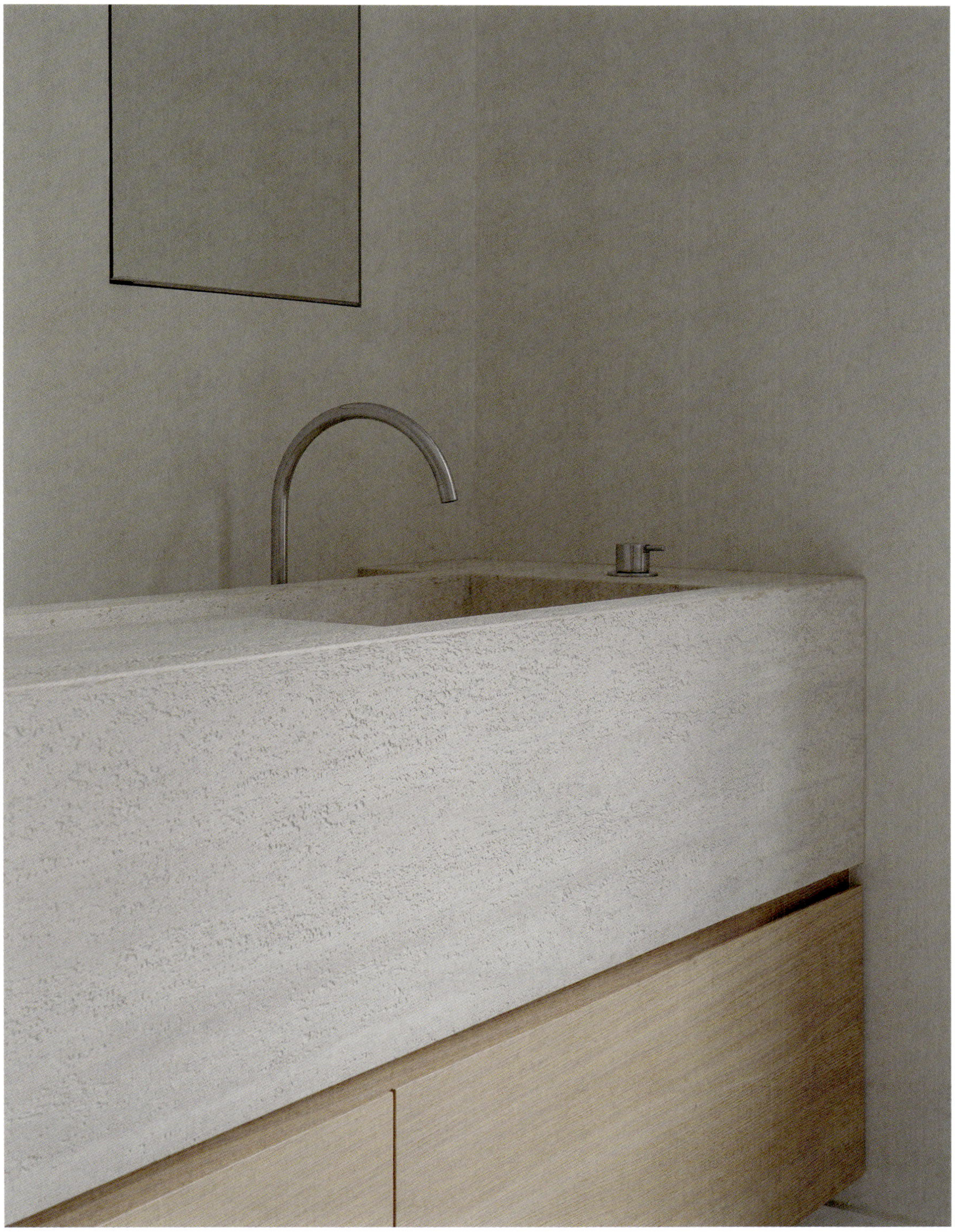

Portrait by Lieven Dirckx

Grain Designoffice

Grain Designoffice is a creative studio founded by Sander Bullynck and Nick De Moor in 2016. Grain creates residential interiors and what they call branded architecture - fully integrating brand strategy and architecture.

Sander and Nick forge close relationships with their clients; supporting them on a journey from good-to-great and helping them translate their ideas into engaging private, hospitality or development concepts. In other words — they know how to serve your early stage needs and simultaneously build the foundation for a great future. By observing what makes people listen carefully, sit close, keep a distance, get up and start dancing or fall in love, they know how to put people in the right mood.

Grain Designoffice has only one great ambition: creating things that are still relevant 20 years from now. A strong story is the foundation for everything. It's what makes their guest's experience so meaningful they'll share it often, come back for it time and again or what makes you feel at home. In creating that story, they would like to add some 'grain'. A twist to spice things up, add a texture, in order to create unique and immersive experiences.

Grain Designoffice's services include: interior design, branding, architecture, strategy, furniture selection, web design and playlist curation. They focus on what they do best, and for all other matters they have developed a high quality network of partners on anything from photography, to 3D modeling or even copywriting. They will make sure it all fits.

www.grain-office.be

Photography: Piet-Albert Goethals (pages 304-317) / Tijs Vervecken (pages 318-321)

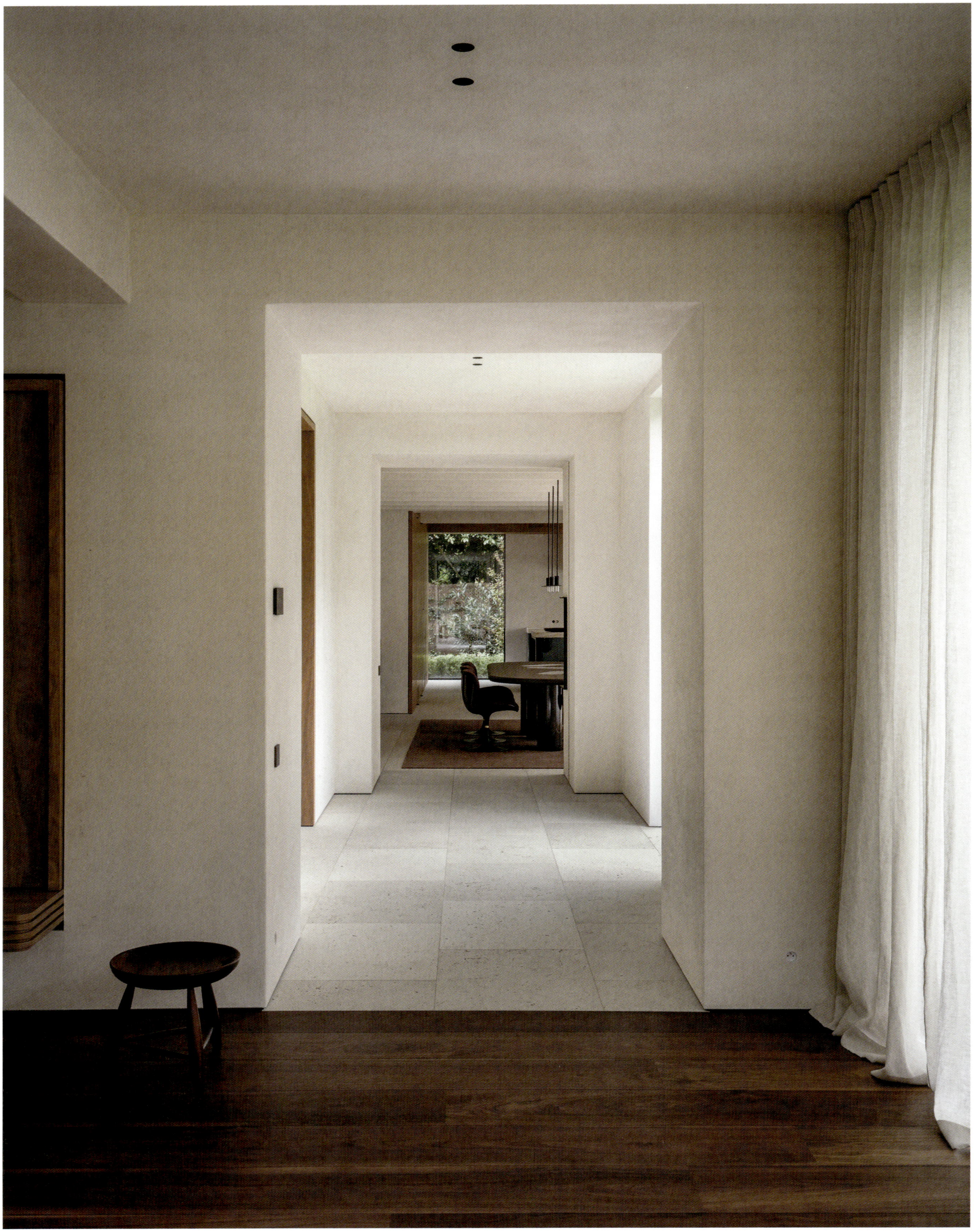

In this publication, Grain Designoffice presents two recent projects: a large villa in Schilde (on pages 306 to 317) and a small seaside apartment (on pages 318 to 321).

On pages 306-317: Nestled in Schilde, Antwerp, this home embraces practical luxury for a vibrant young family. Warmth and sophistication merge seamlessly as American walnut graces the spaces, creating a rich, inviting atmosphere. The floors on the ground floor are dressed in Pietra dei Medici natural stone, ensuring durability without compromising on aesthetics. The kitchen, a focal point, boasts an onyx natural stone island. A luxurious centerpiece that elevates both style and functionality. Together with the loam plastered walls these more classical materials set the stage for some more daring choices in details and furniture. The polished green elements in the custom joinery, or the Marilyn chairs by Baxter for example create an interesting contrast to elevate the living spaces. While the facade of the house kept its more traditional elements, extra attention went to strong perspectives and openness resulting in a very contemporary interior without forgetting its relation to the outside.

On pages 318-321: Grain Designoffice renovated this small 60 square meter apartment overlooking the Belgian North Sea as a compact holiday home for a family in Duinbergen. With one master bedroom, two bathrooms and a kids room with bunk beds, smart usage of space was essential. The kitchen is at the core of the retreat. The central marble island - which got its unique form by embracing the unusual shape of the apartment - is more than just a place for cooking; it also extends to a 'vide-poche', or a place to gather for drinks. Custom shelving creates openness in the space and opportunity for display. The material palette immediately sets the tone from entry, confronting visitors with the Royal Purple natural stone block. It dictates the color scheme throughout the whole of the apartment; translating into stained cherry paneling and deep blue hues. Where cherry wood isn't dressing the walls, the tactile lime finish creates a soft matte effect for extra intimacy. Terra floor was placed throughout the apartment for easy flow from one space to the next and as a hard-wearing material to accommodate its visitors on the beachside location.

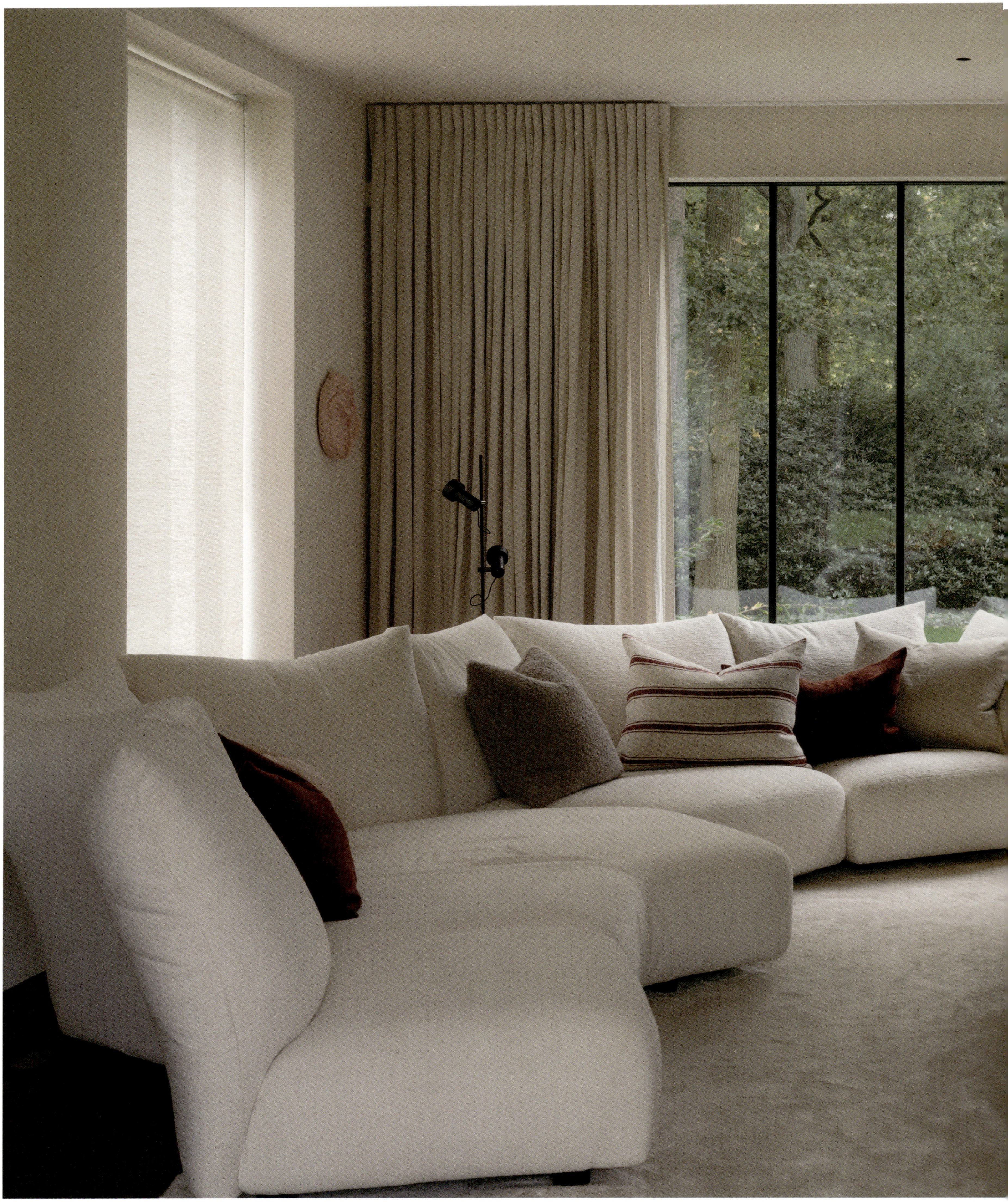

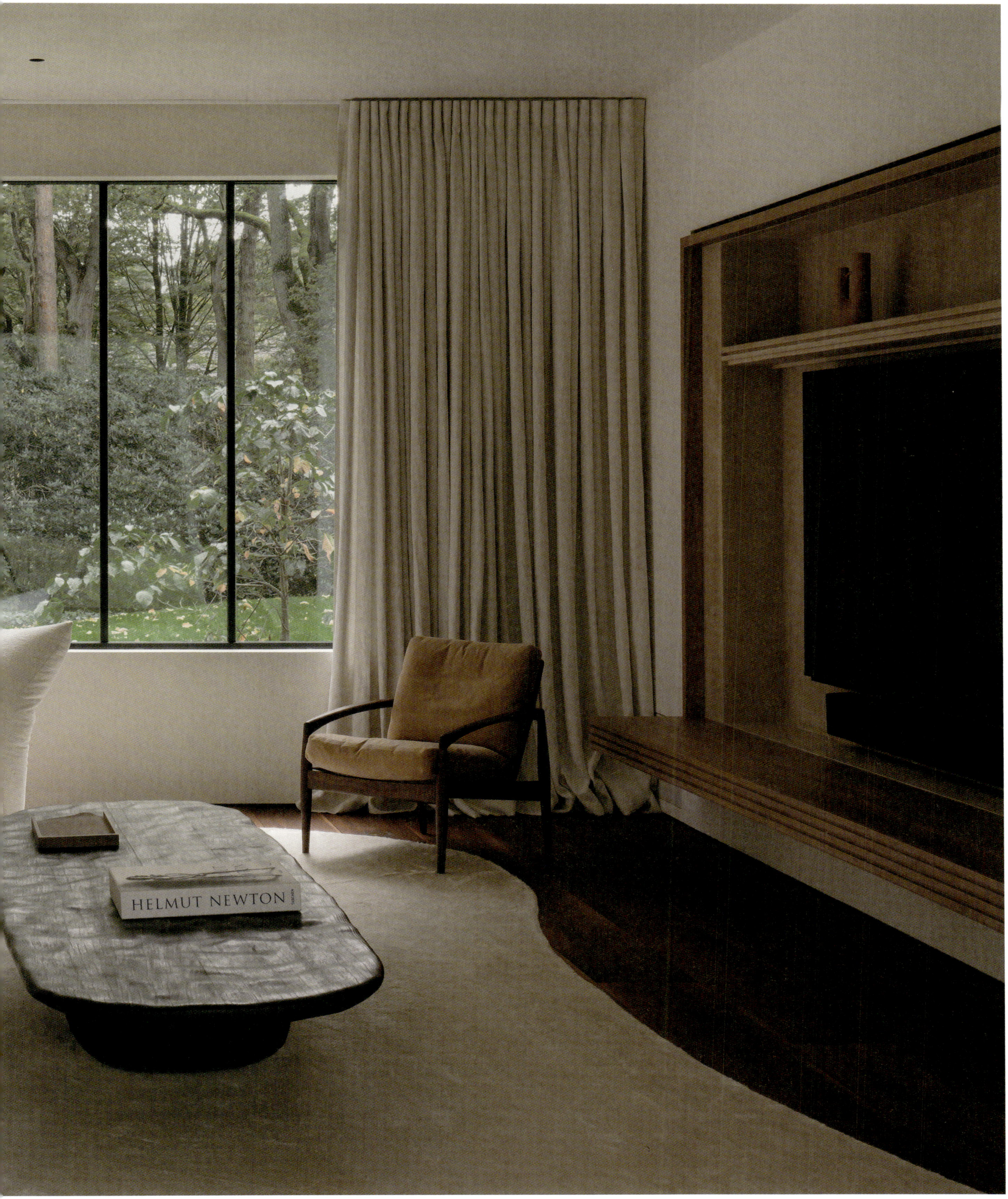
HELMUT NEWTON

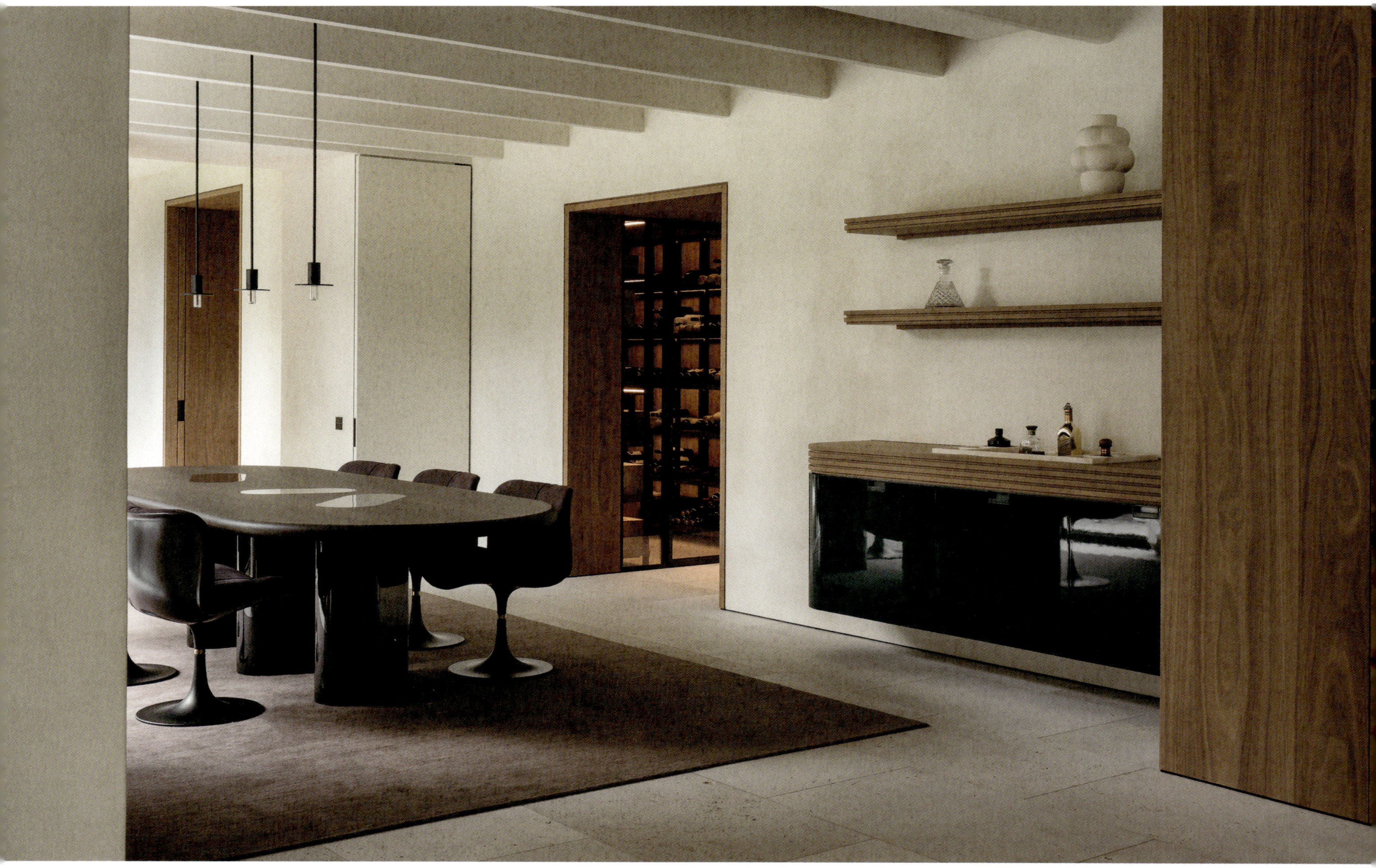

309

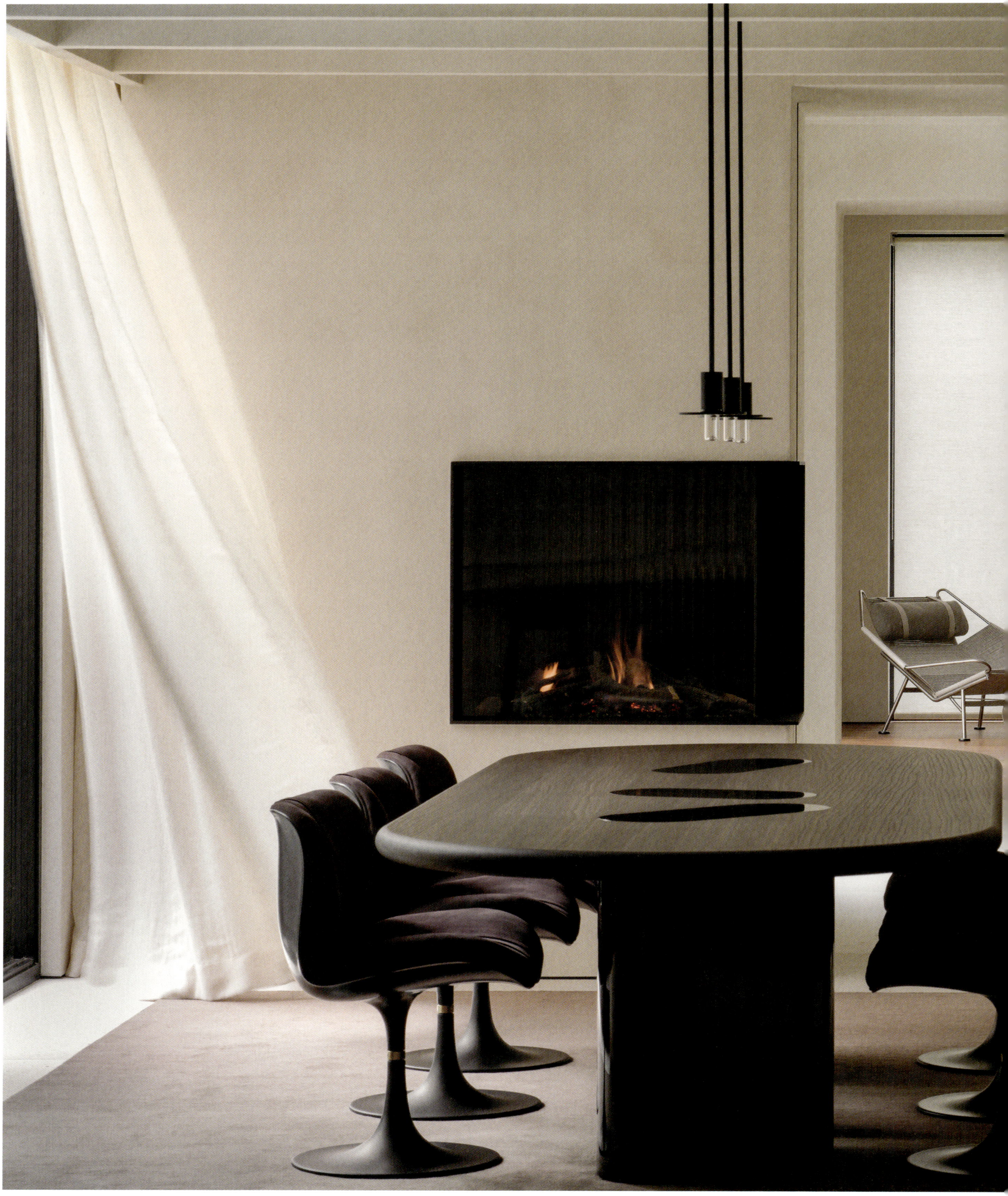

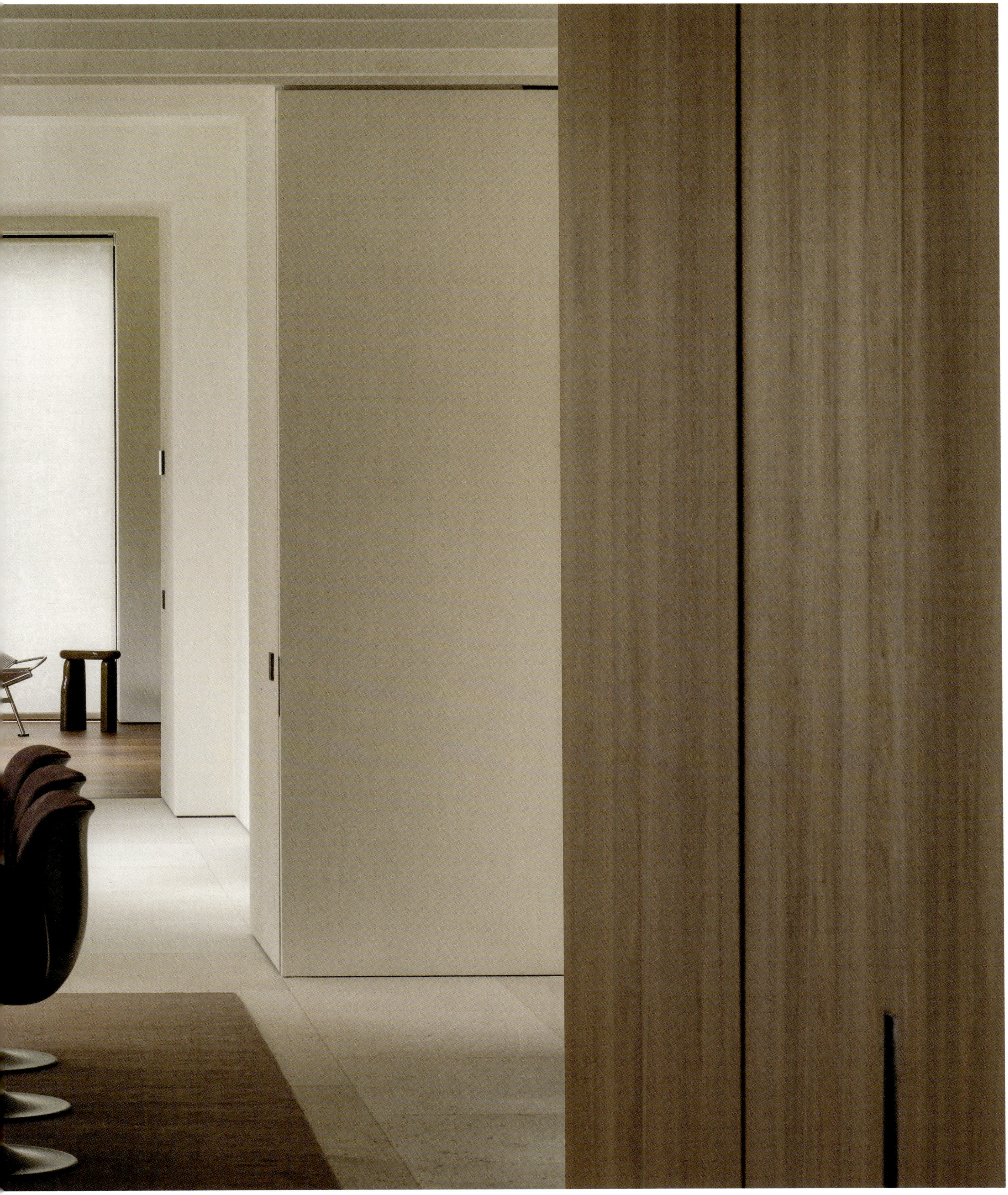

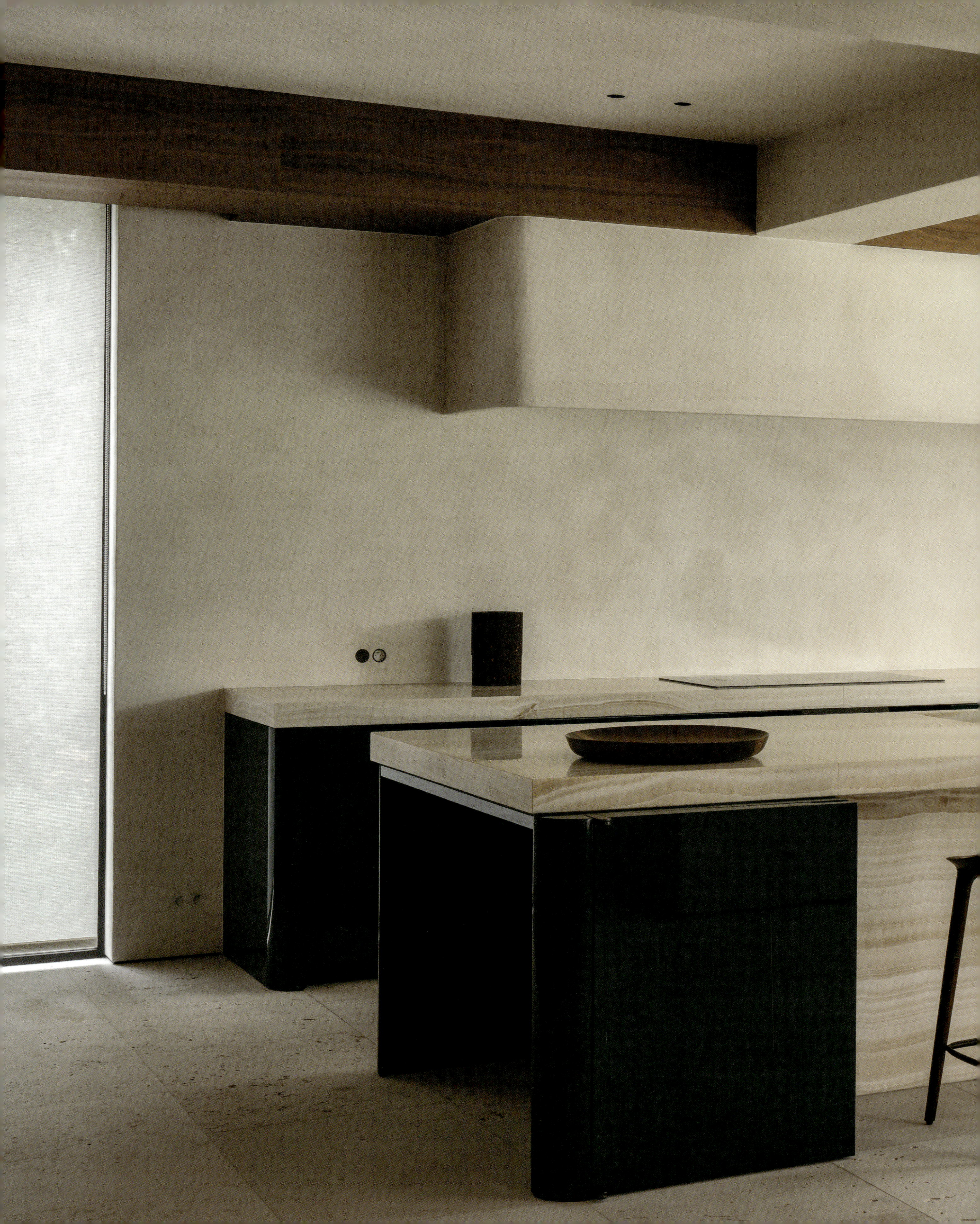

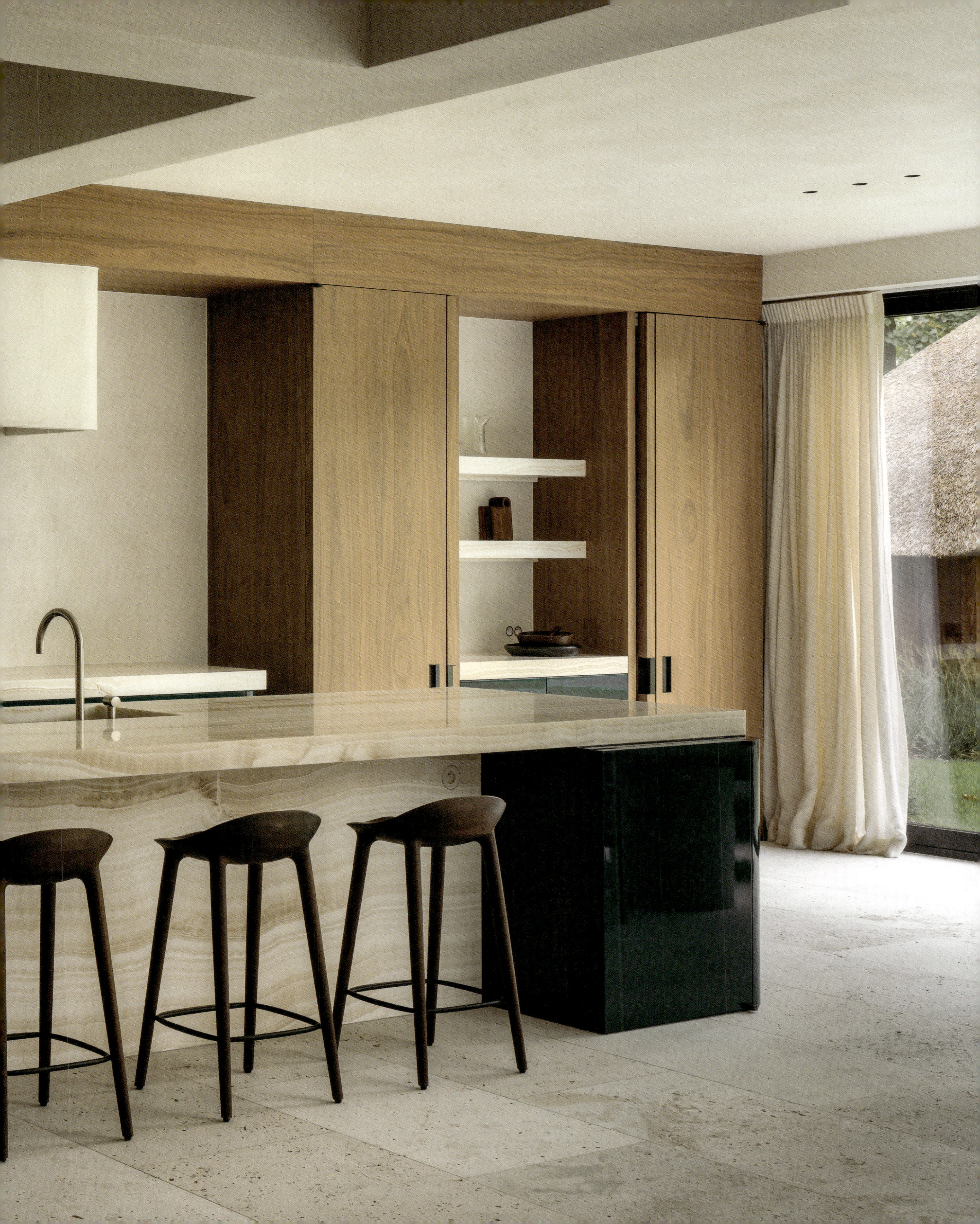

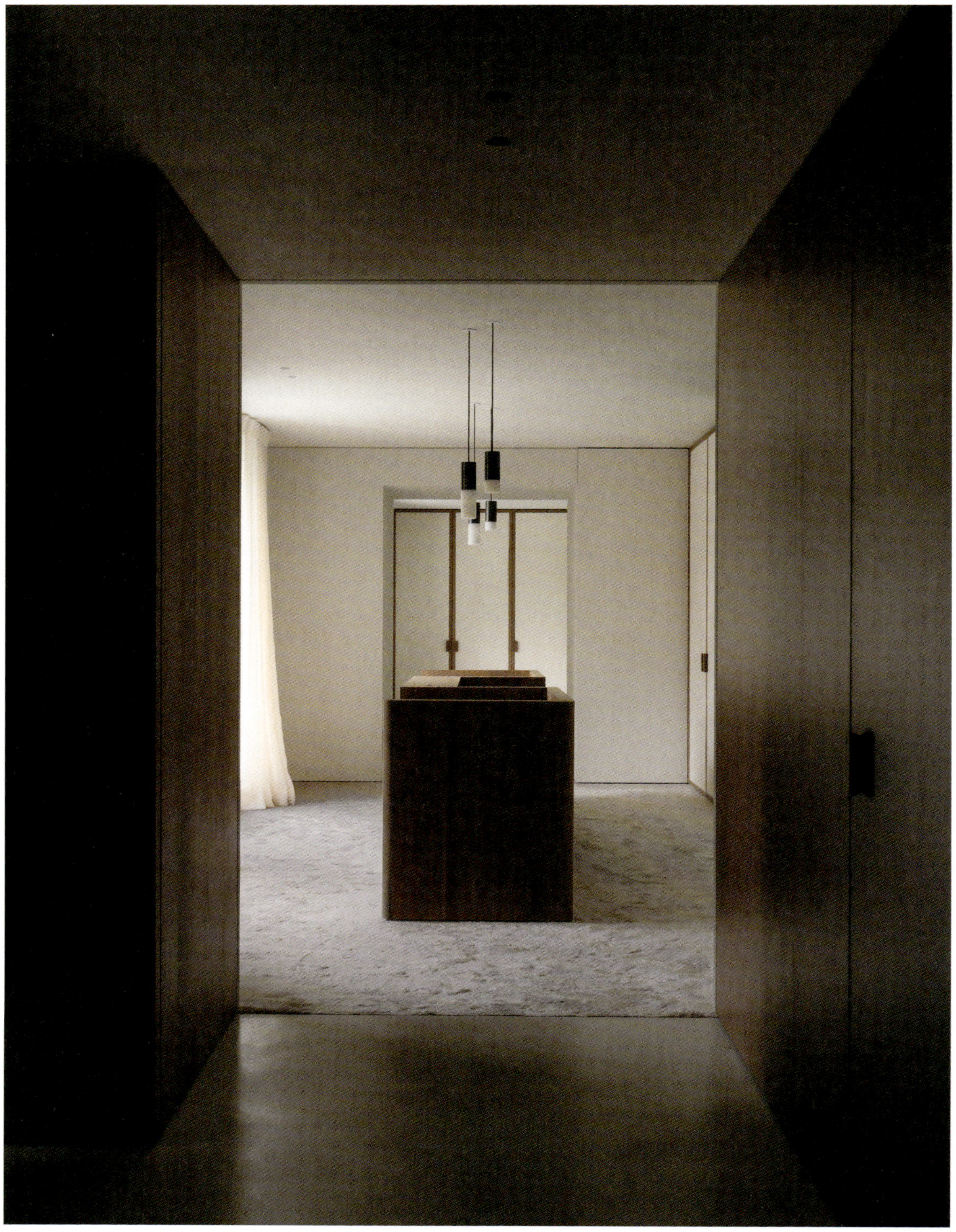

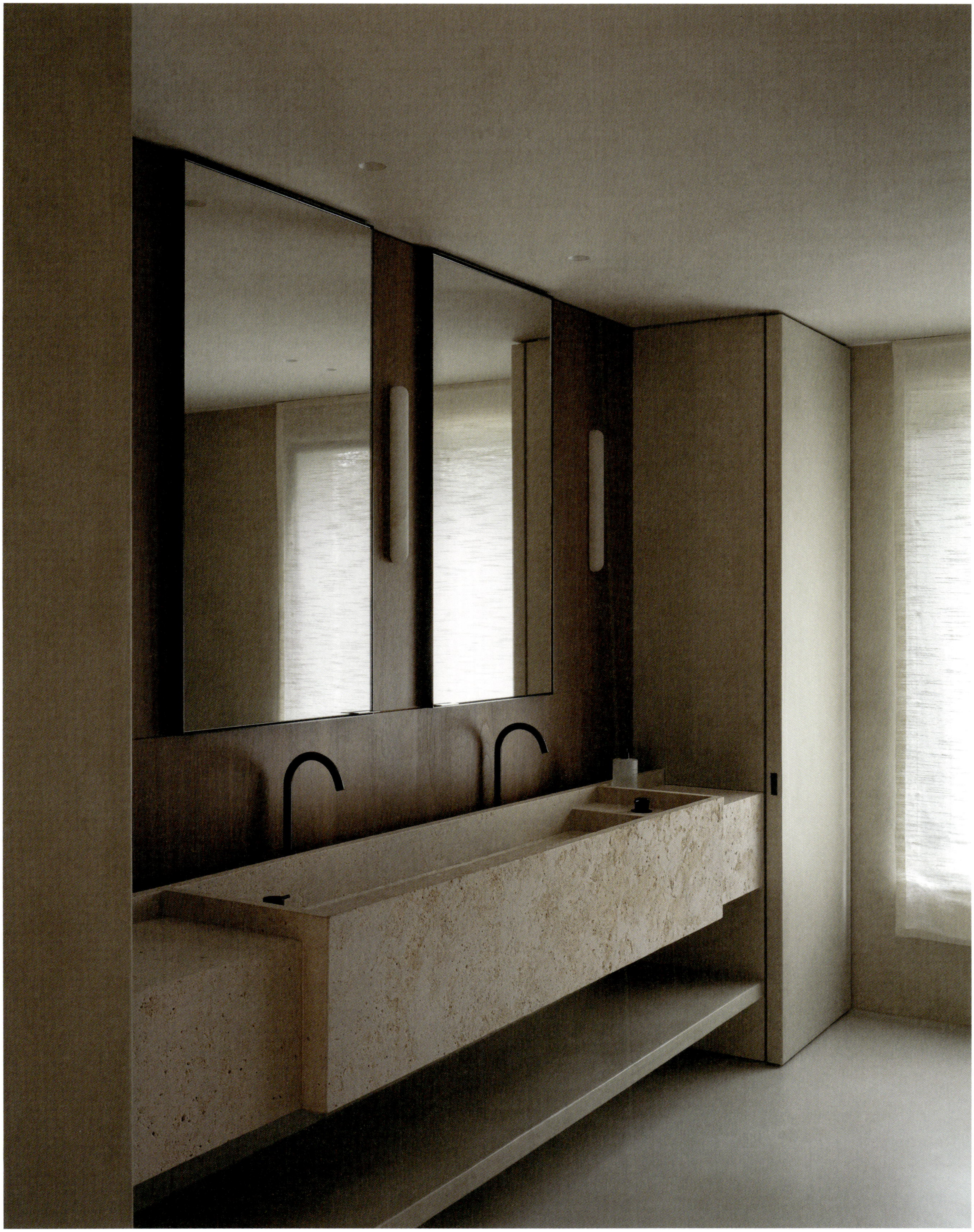

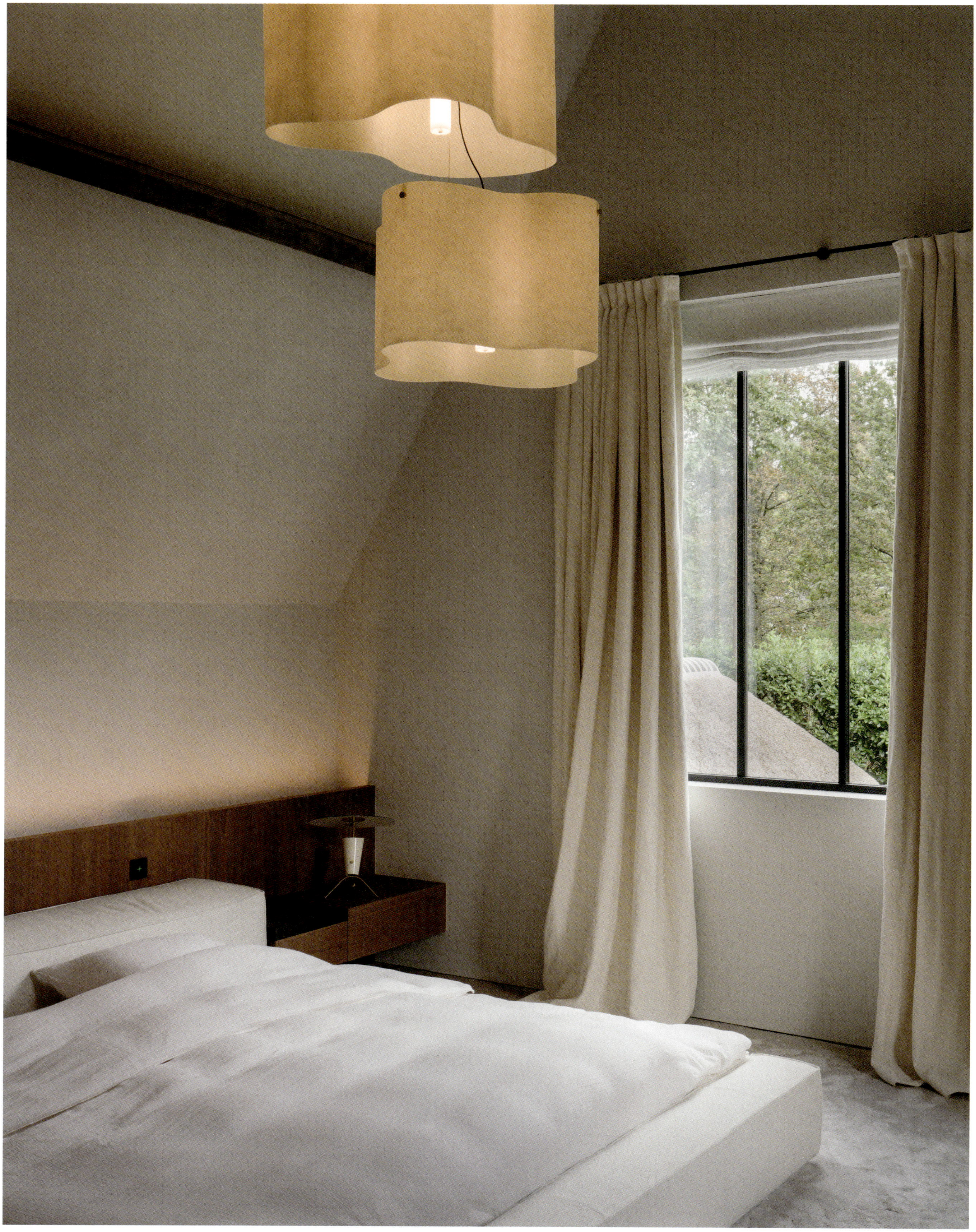

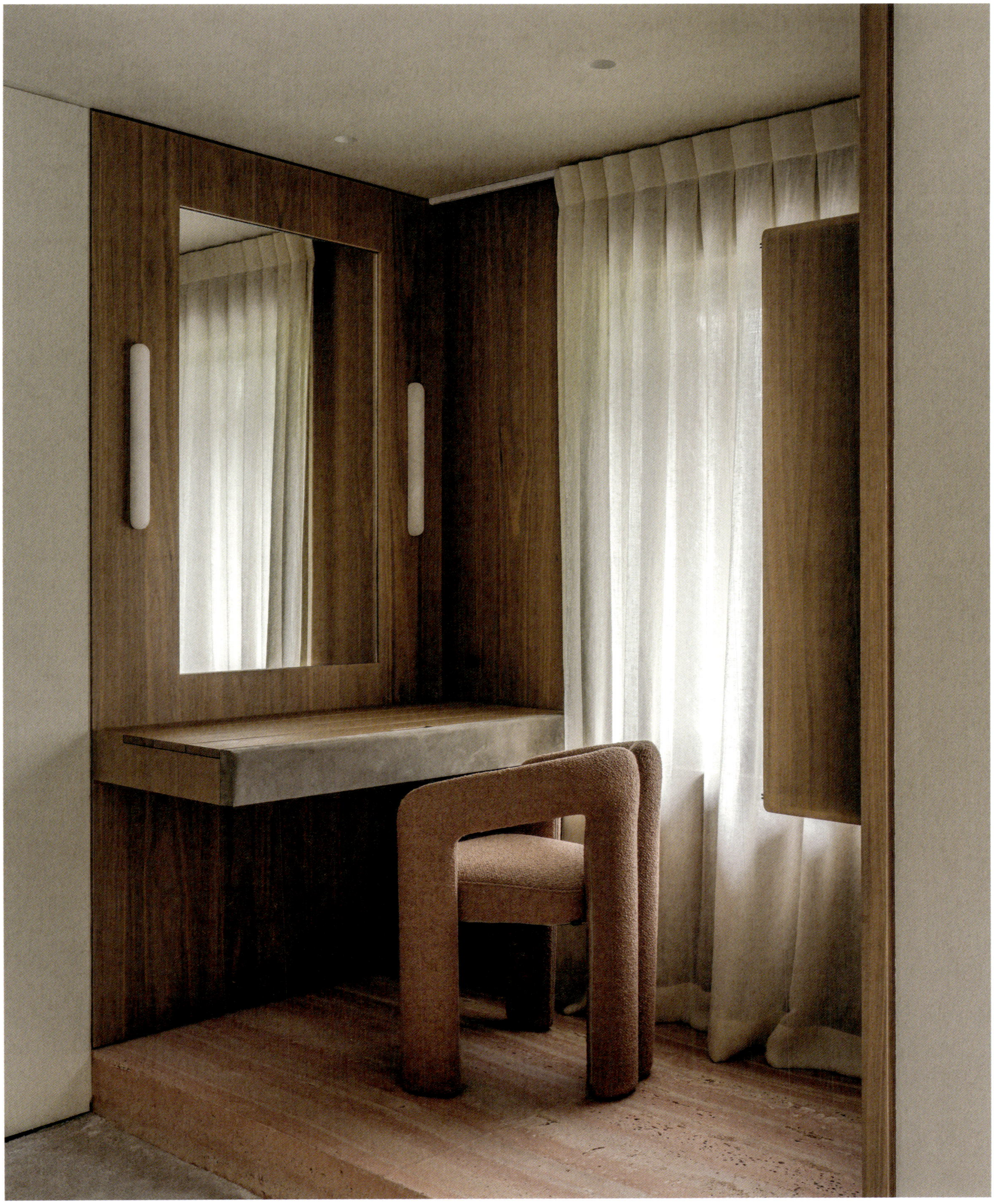

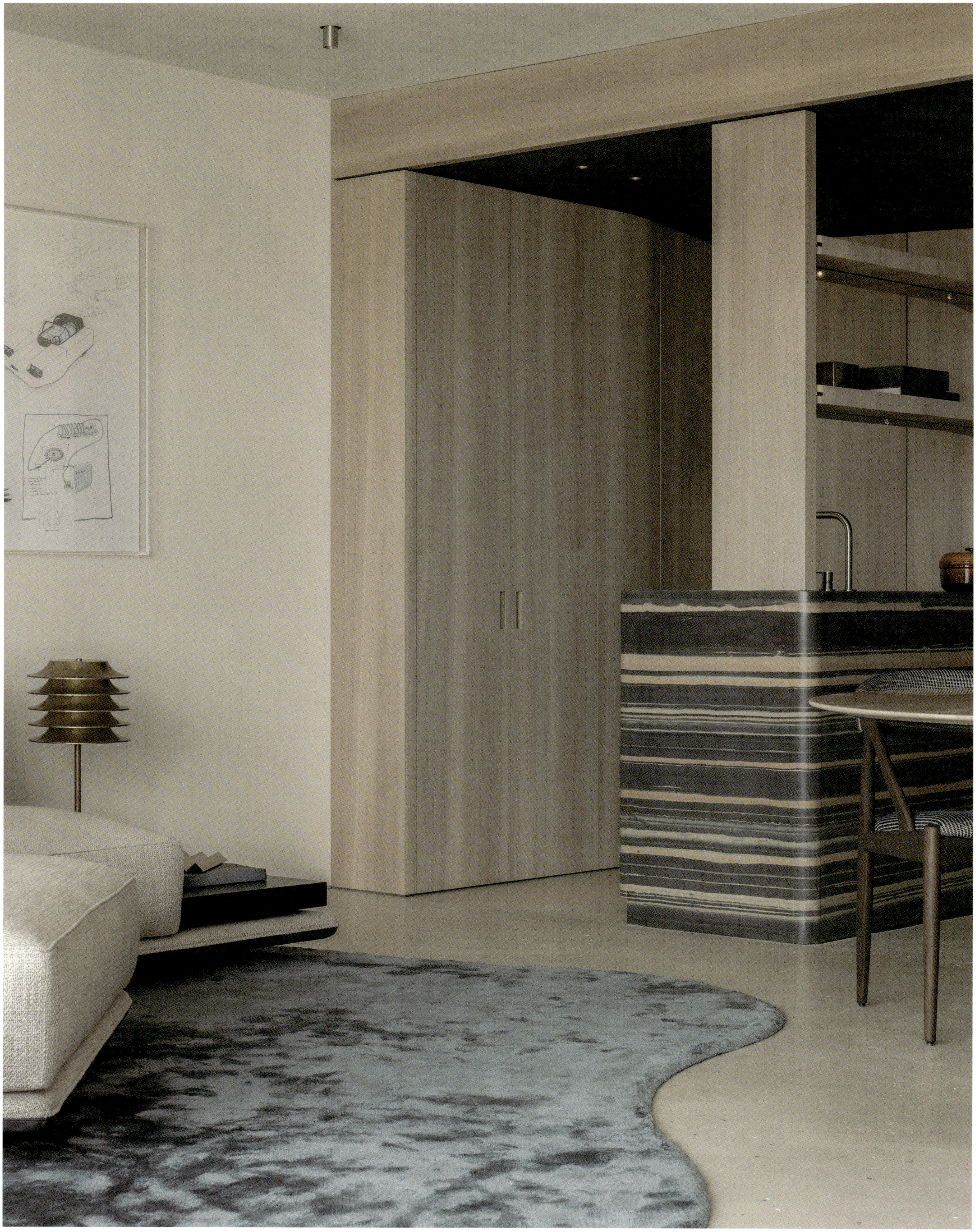

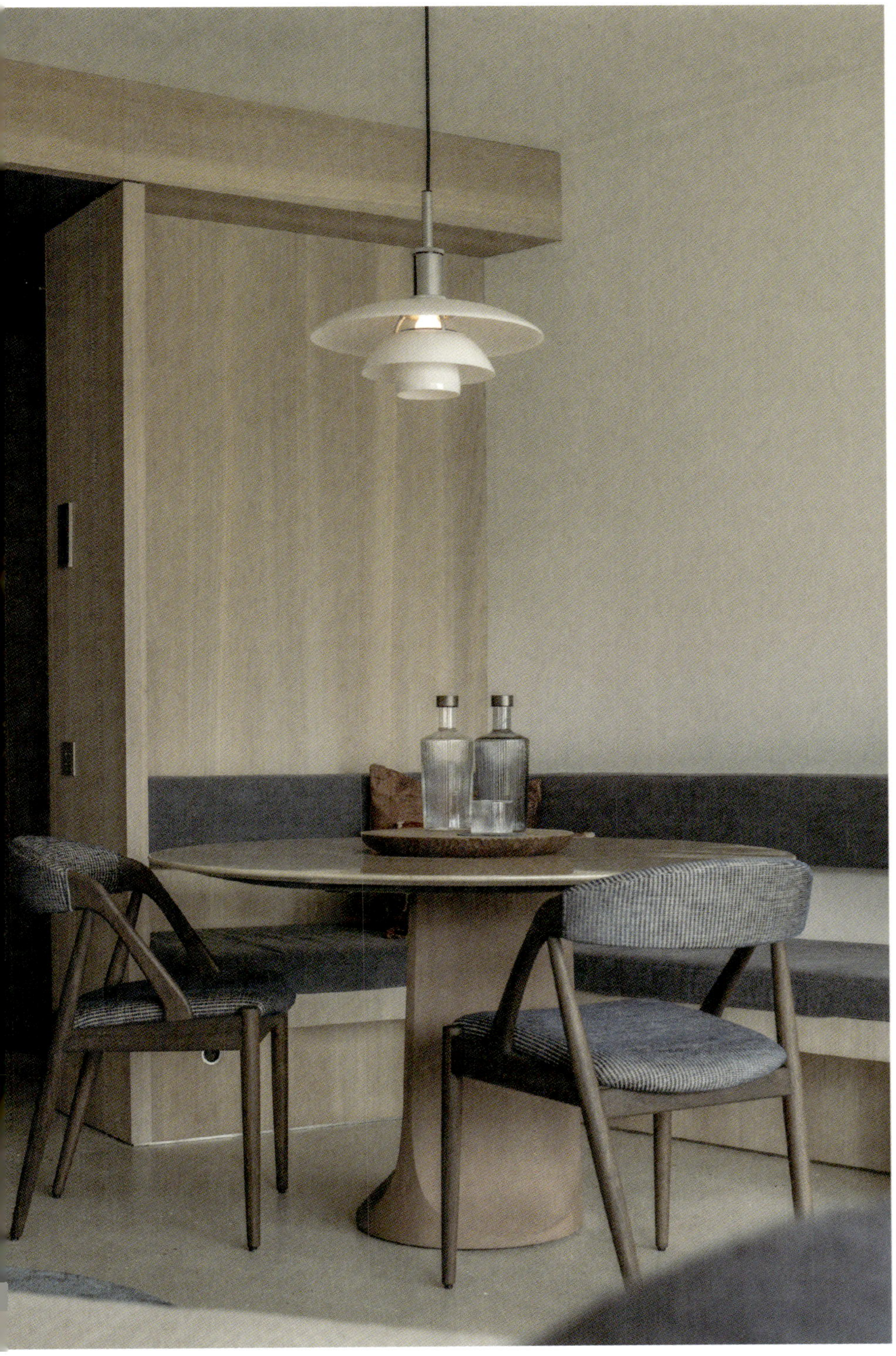
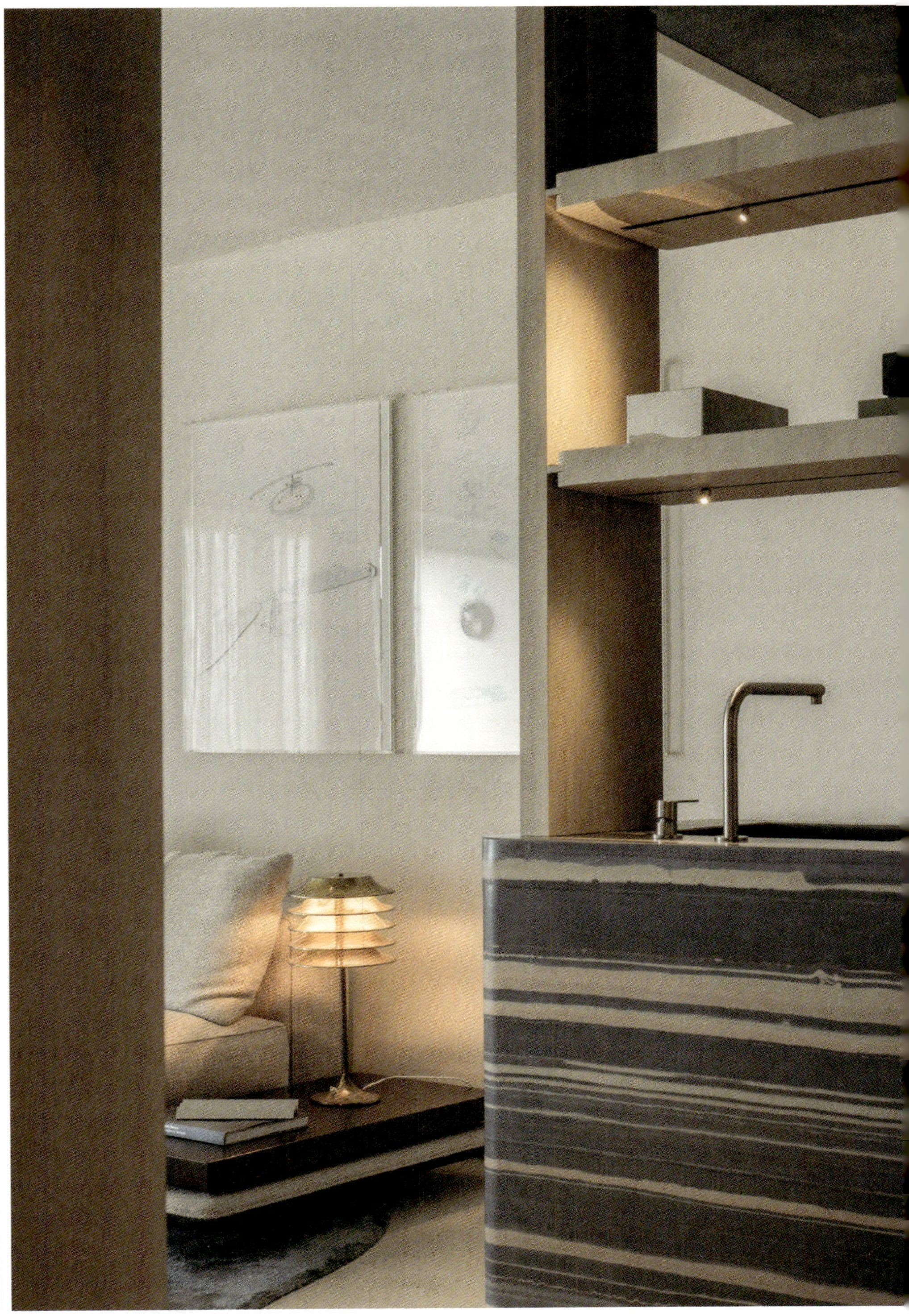

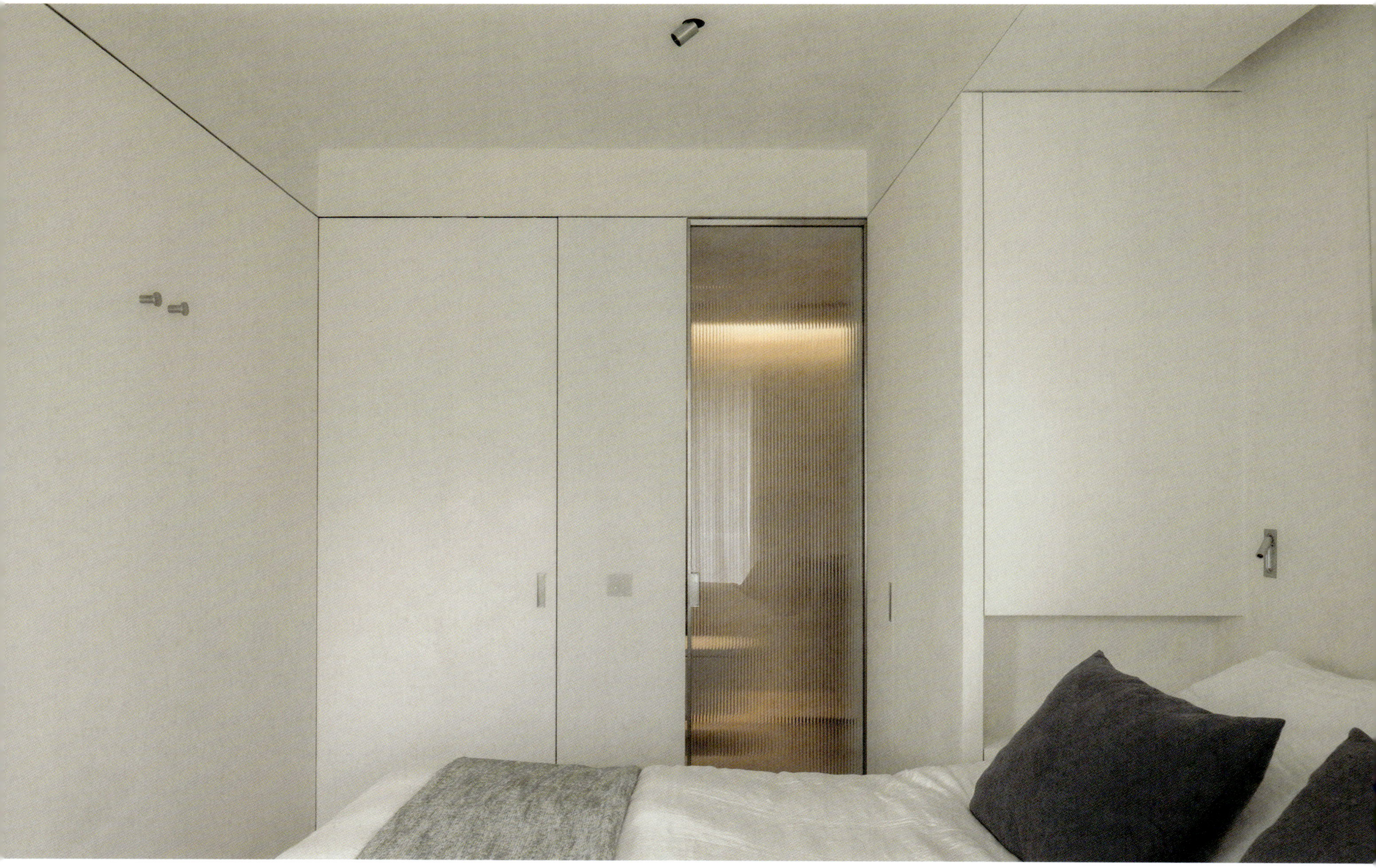

321

Portrait by Bella Francis

Meg Cassidy

Studio Meg Cassidy is a full service design firm dedicated to residential interiors.

The firm, headquartered in Toronto, has work spanning across North America and includes full scale builds and renovations. Meg Cassidy's approach is highly collaborative and includes working with professionals across all trades and disciplines for seamless execution and beautiful results.

She and her team are passionate story tellers looking to uncover the opportunities of each space in order to make them unique to each of their clients.

They are also creators of custom furniture pieces that truly embody the essence of the space and act as an extension of the sophisticated and paired back approach to their interior designs.

Meg initially began her career in event marketing only later to begin freelancing in the design space before she officially started her own firm in 2017. In 2019, Meg was named Top 40 Under 40 most promising designers by Beta-Plus Publishing.

www.megcassidy.com

Photography: Kirsten Francis

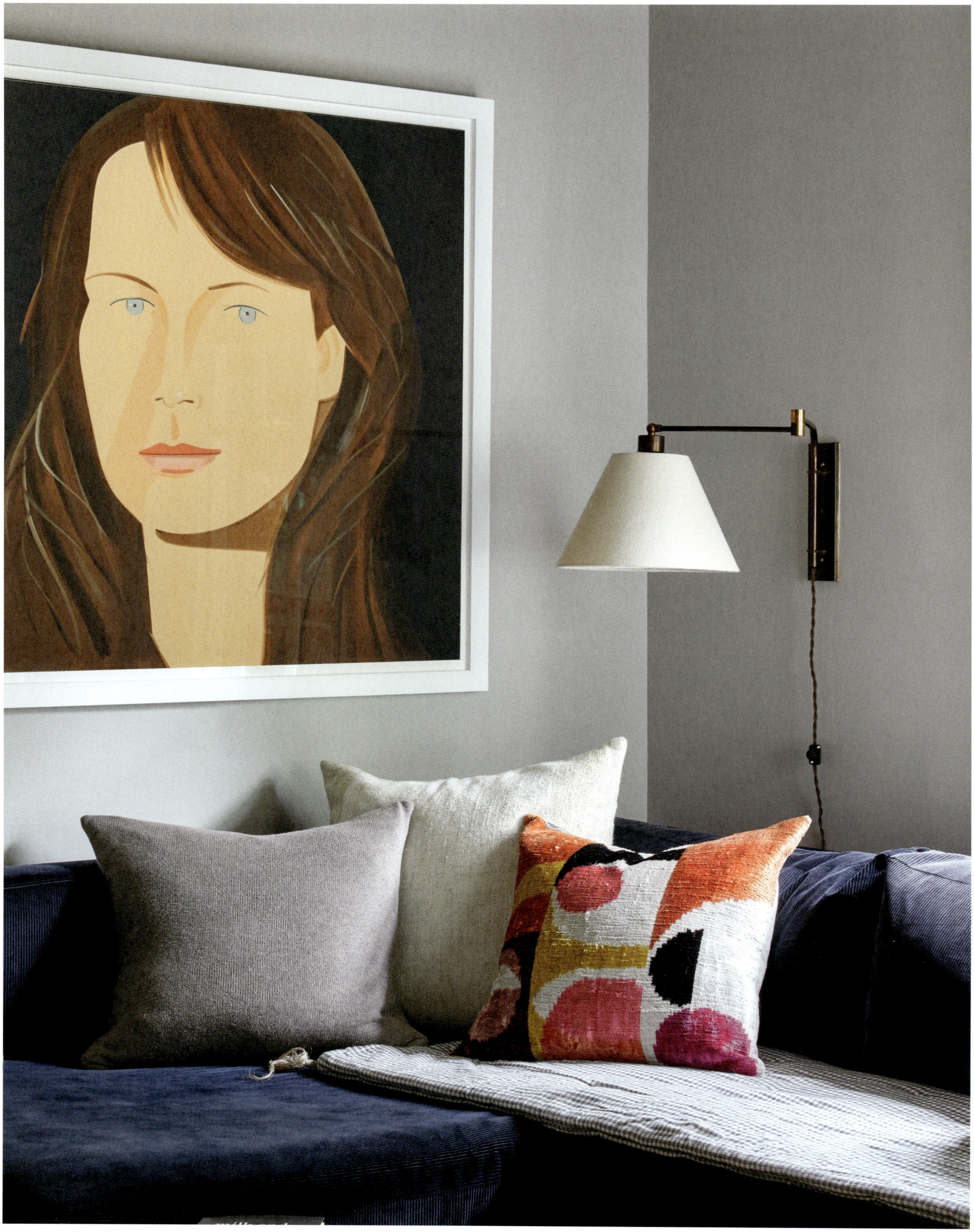

This midwest home in Chicago, was a truly collaborative design between Studio Meg Cassidy and the homeowners.

A beautiful architectural plan and clients with exceptional taste, the foundation for this project was well established for the Studio Meg Cassidy team to help layer and bring the project to completion.

A modern home with classic and traditional architectural details made for this seamless marriage of old and new.

The pallet was gentle yet had several moments of high contrast and visual interest. Most importantly, the little details became extremely important and evident throughout the home. There is a feeling in this space that truly is so inviting and pulls you in to linger just as long as you can.

Interior Design: Studio Meg Cassidy. Architect: Kipnis Architecture + Planning. Builder: Berliant Builders Inc.

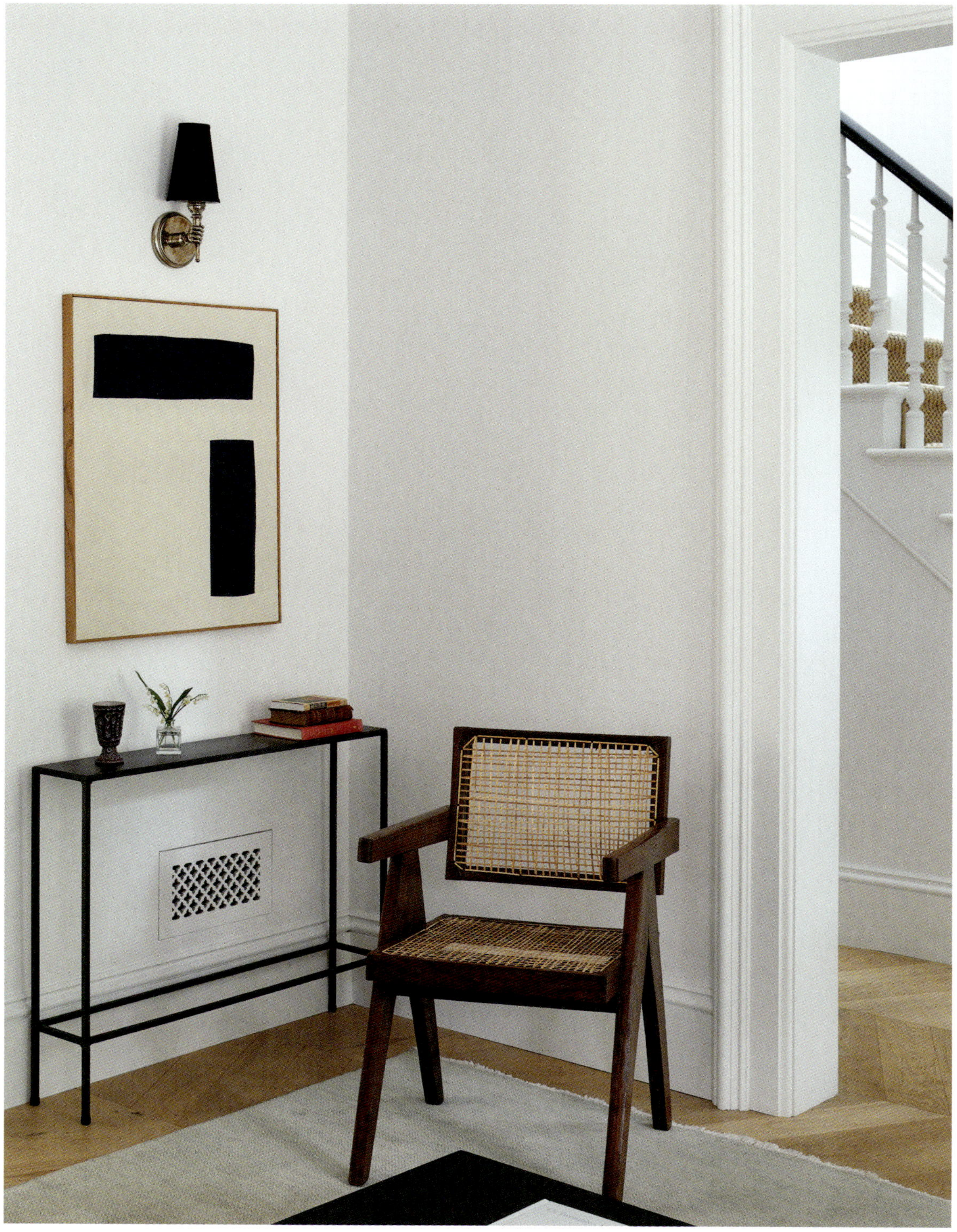

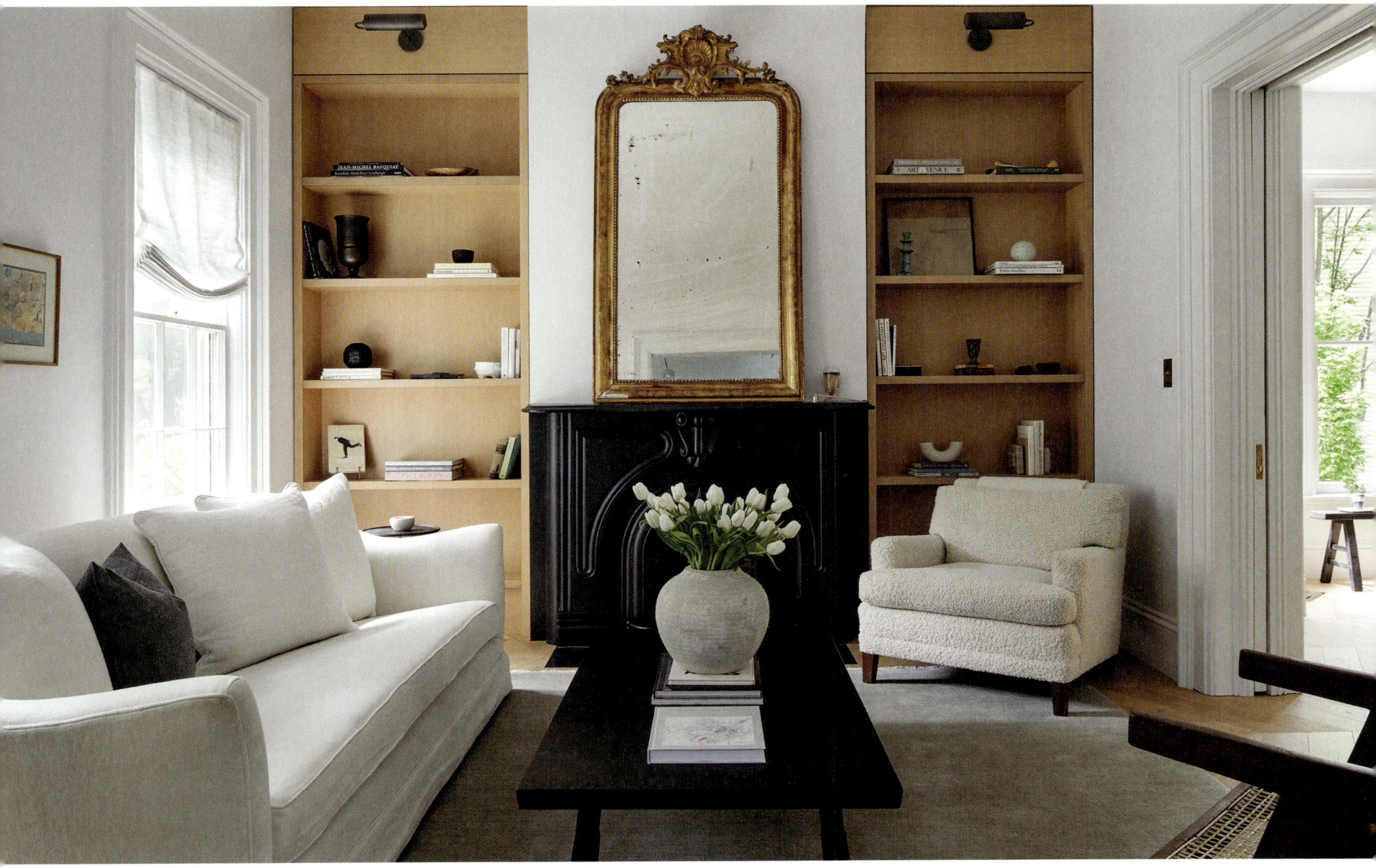

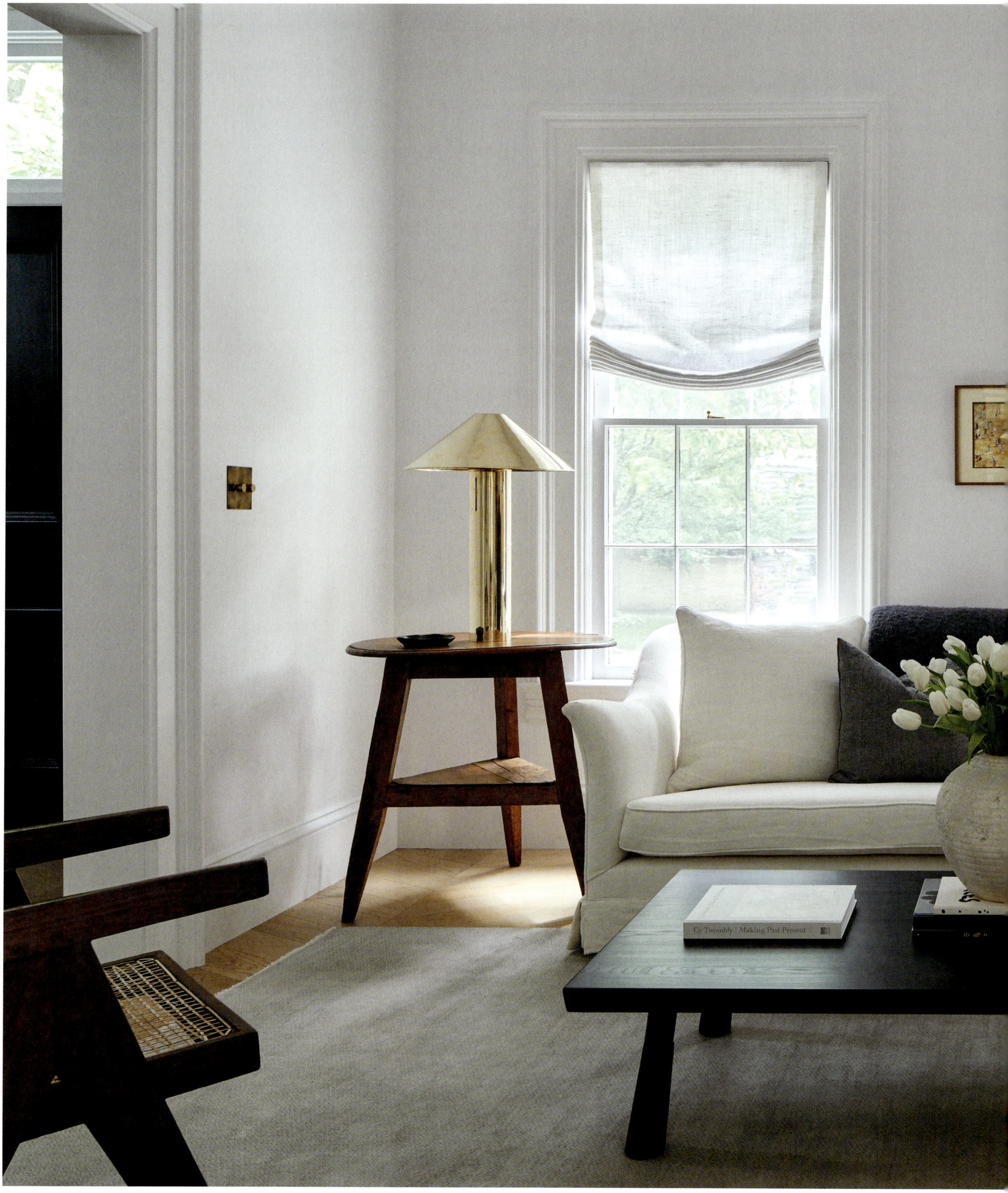
Cy Twombly | Making Past Present

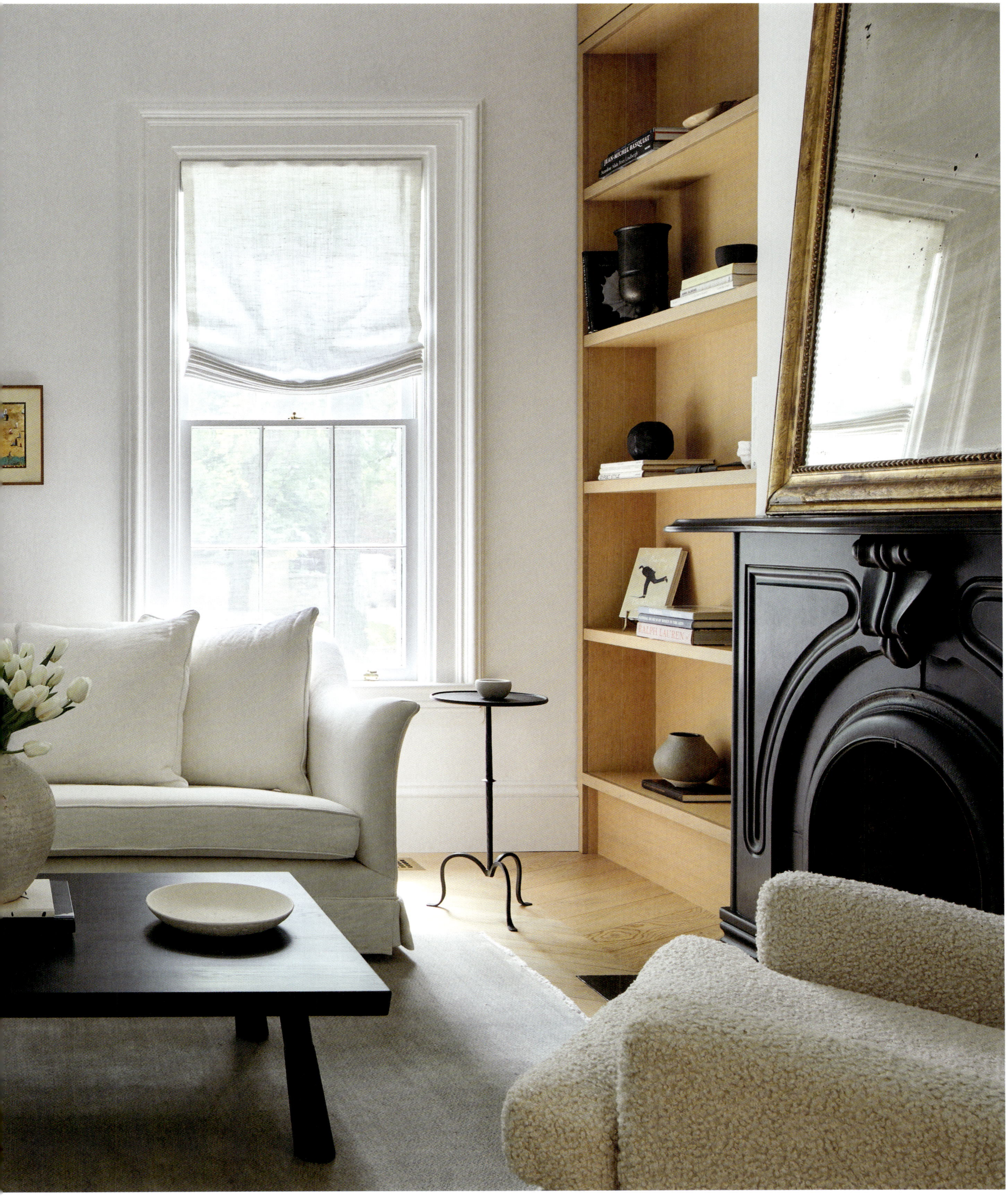
JEAN-MICHEL BASQUIAT
RALPH LAUREN

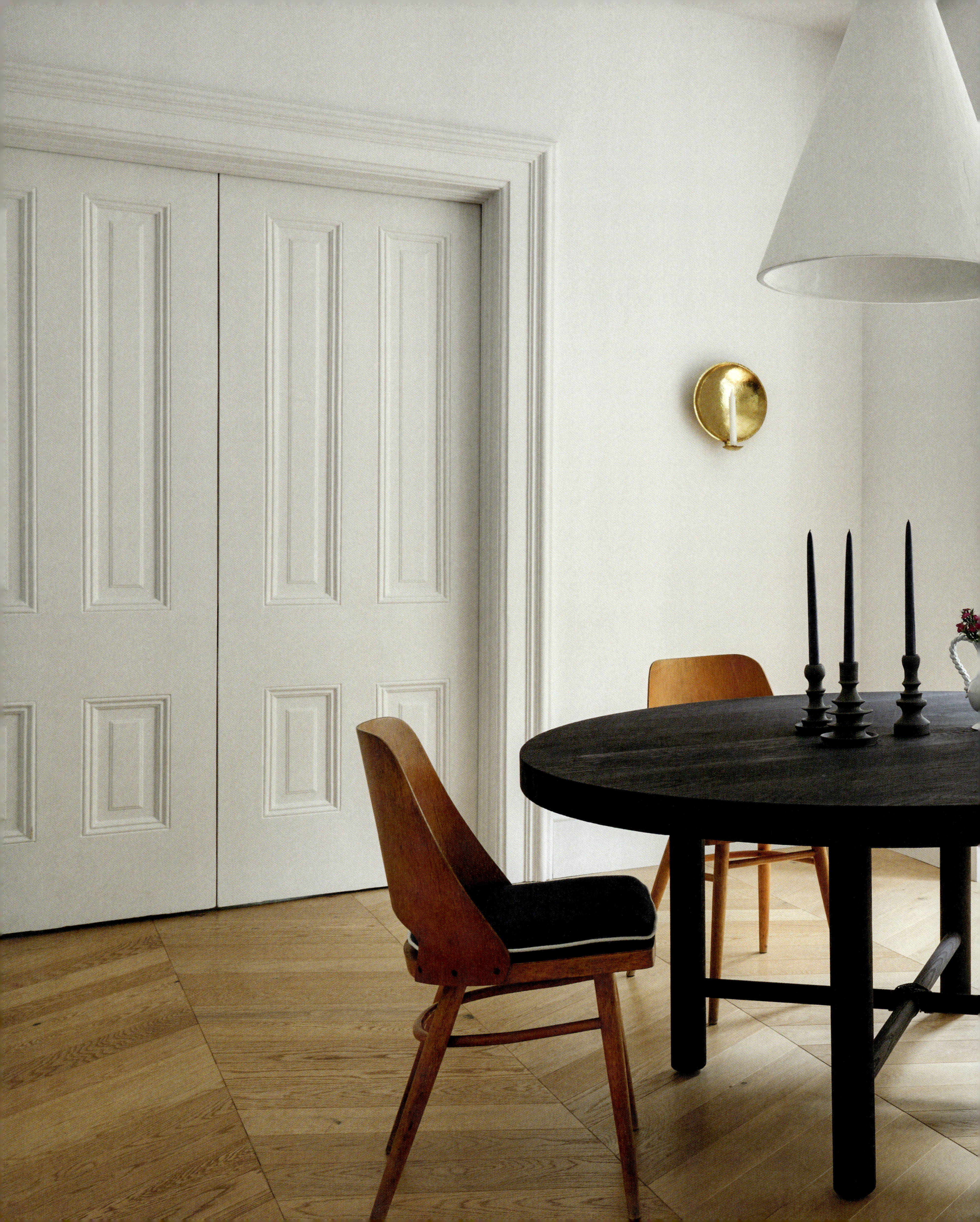

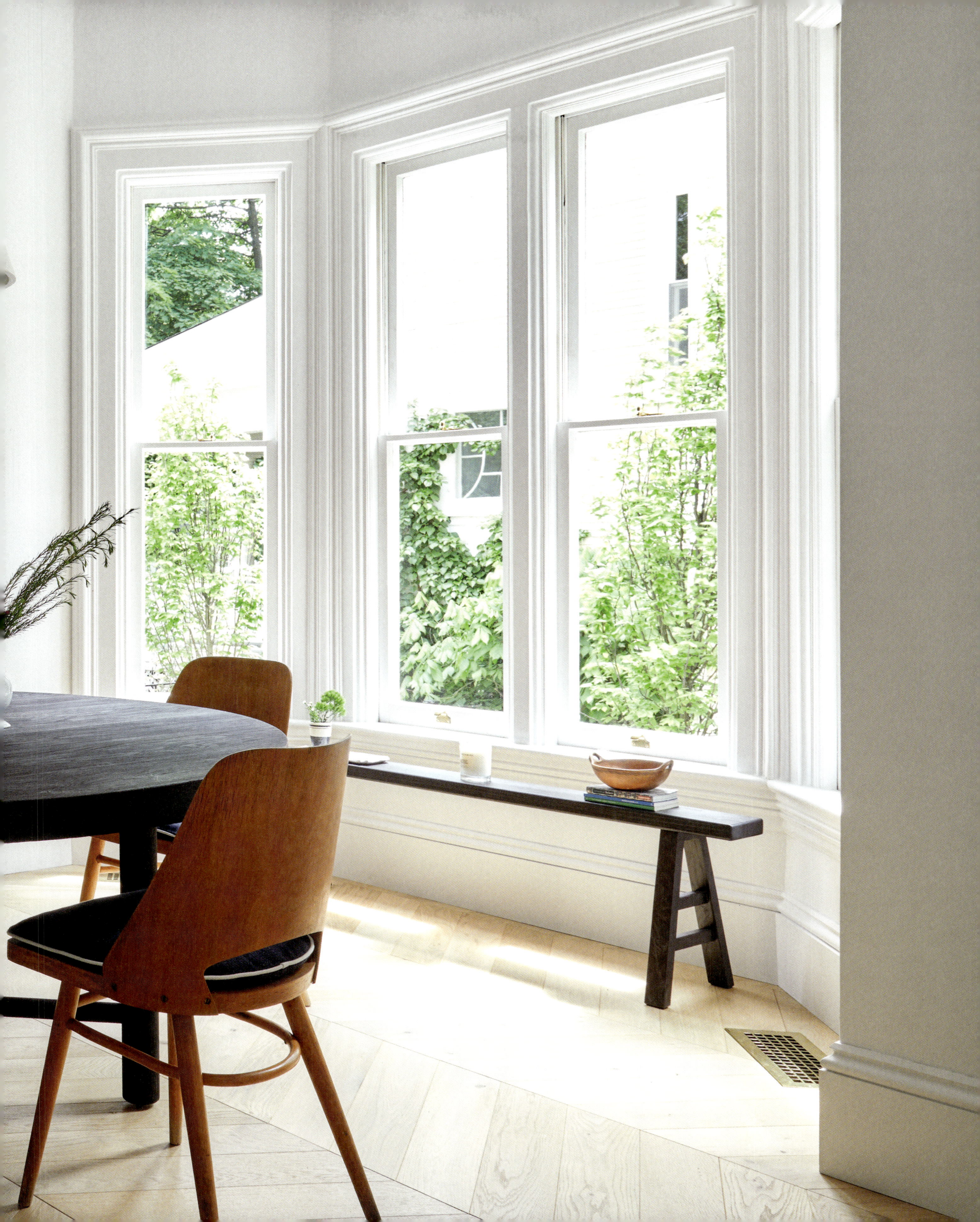

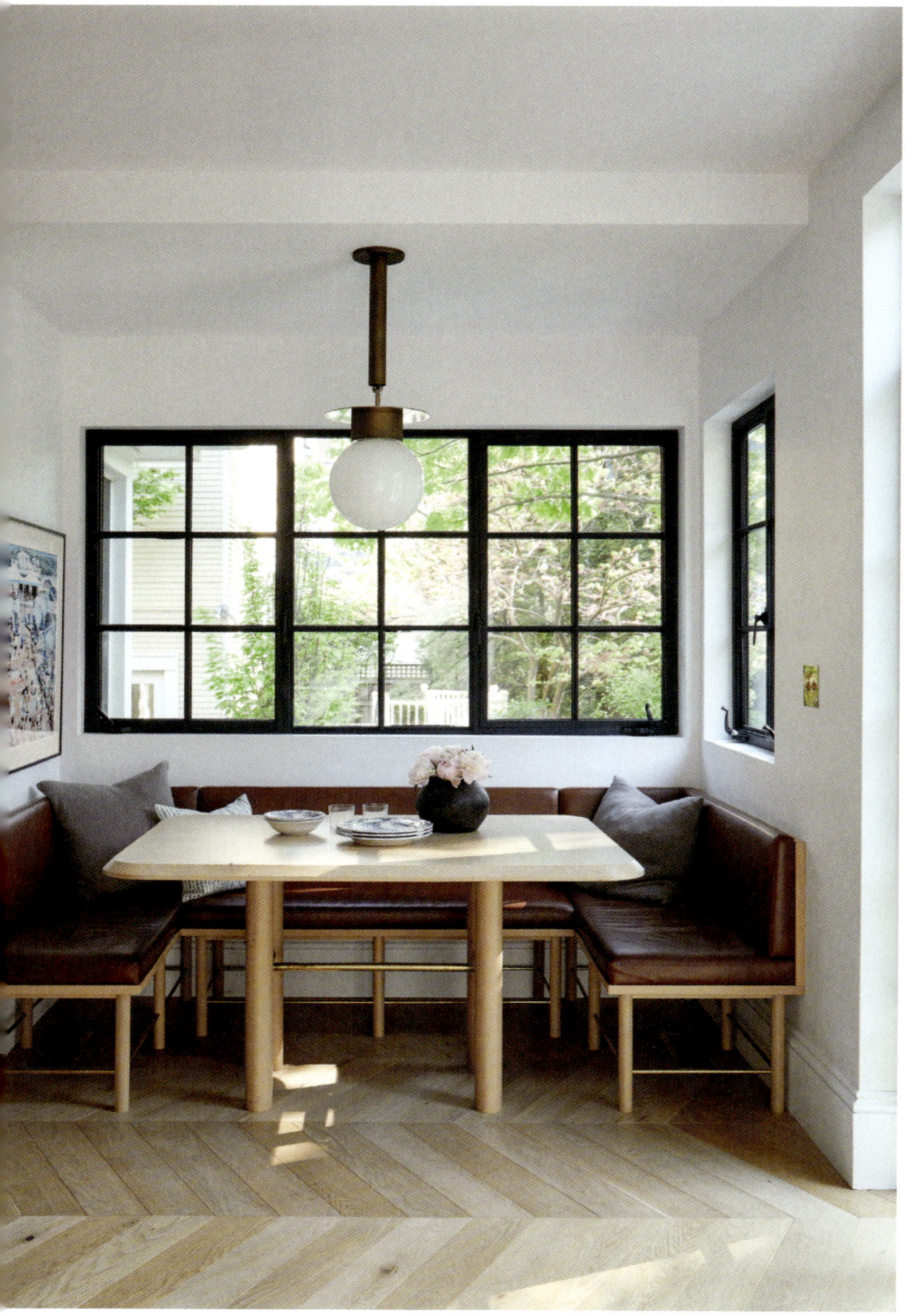

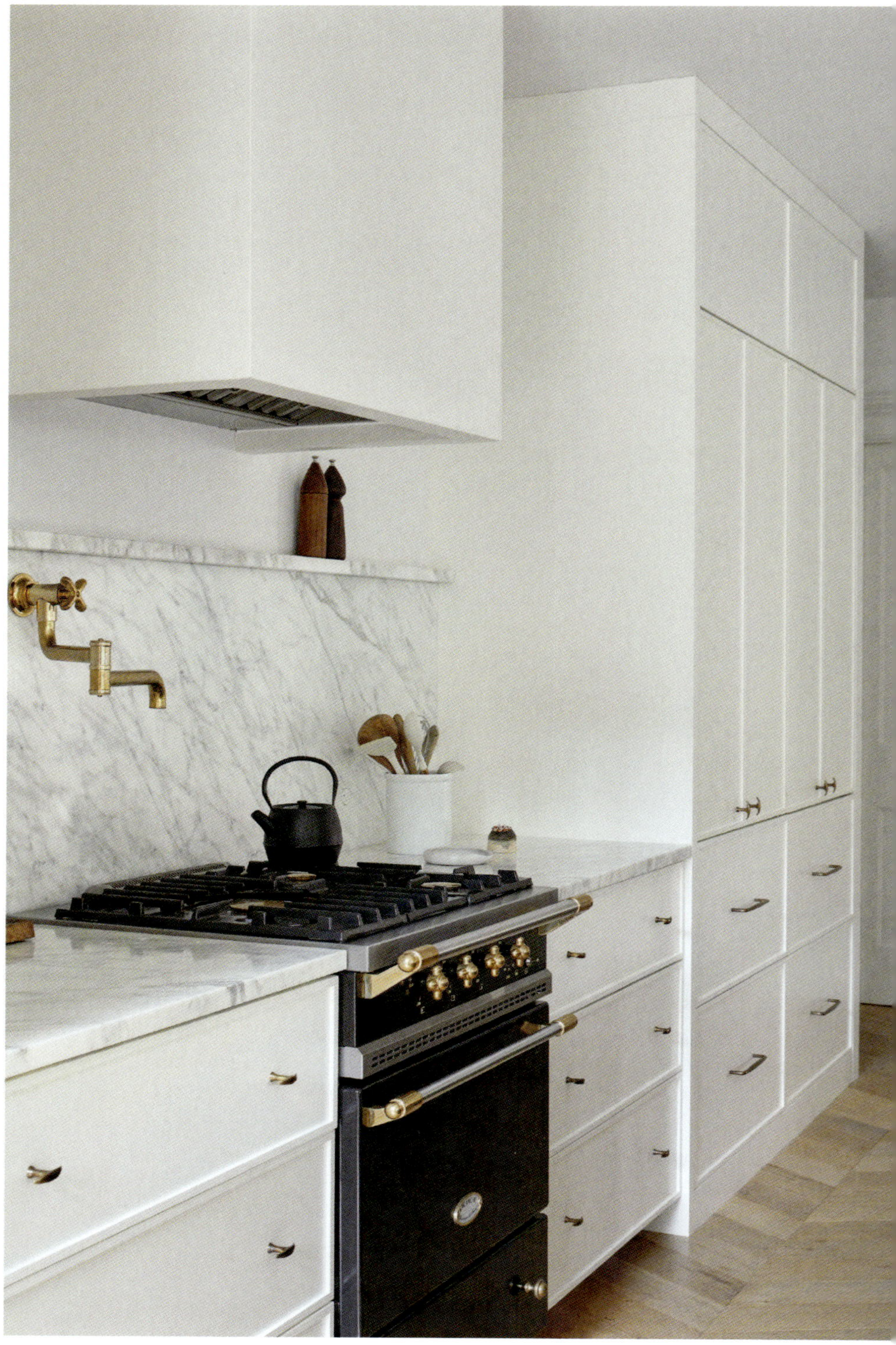

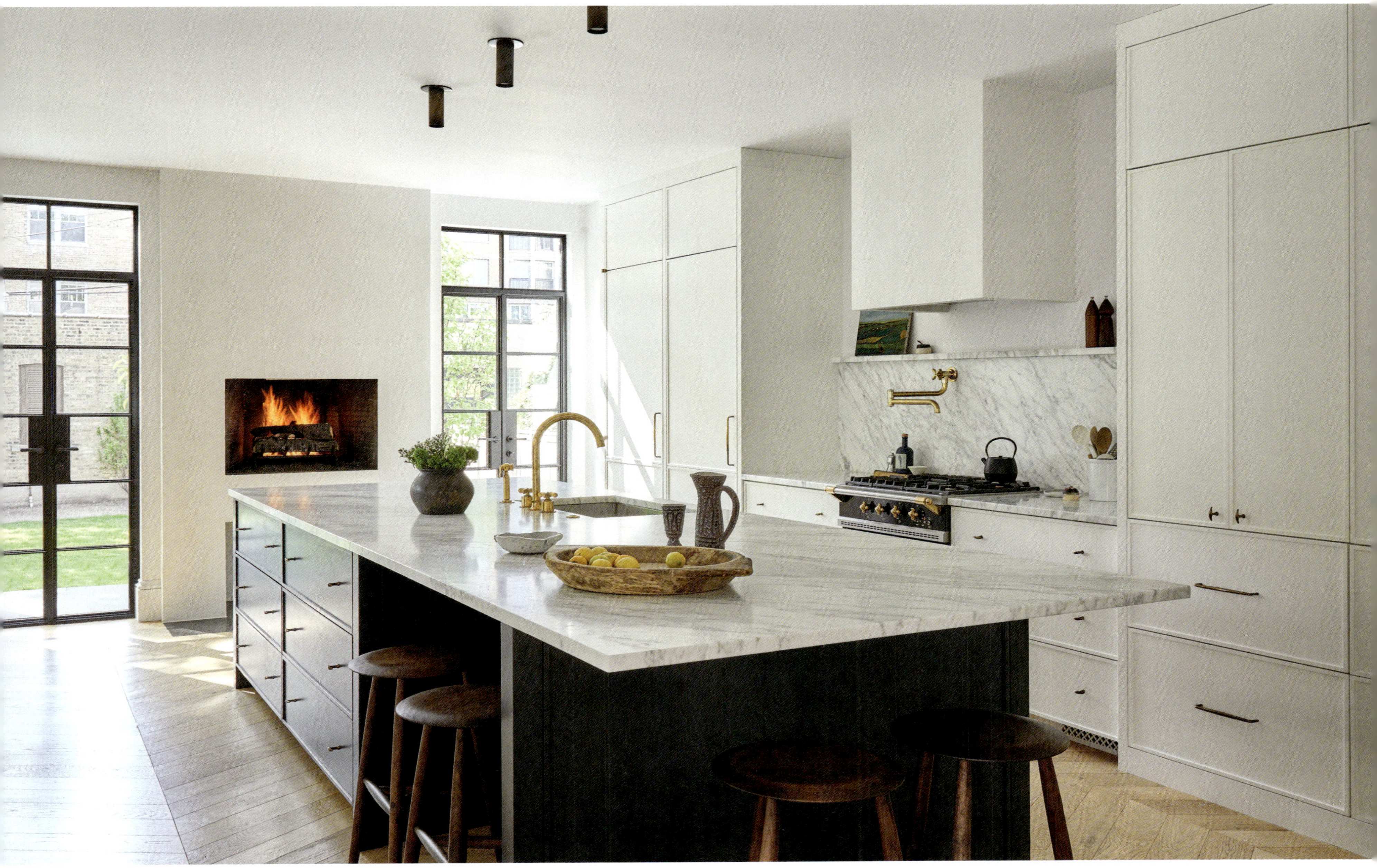

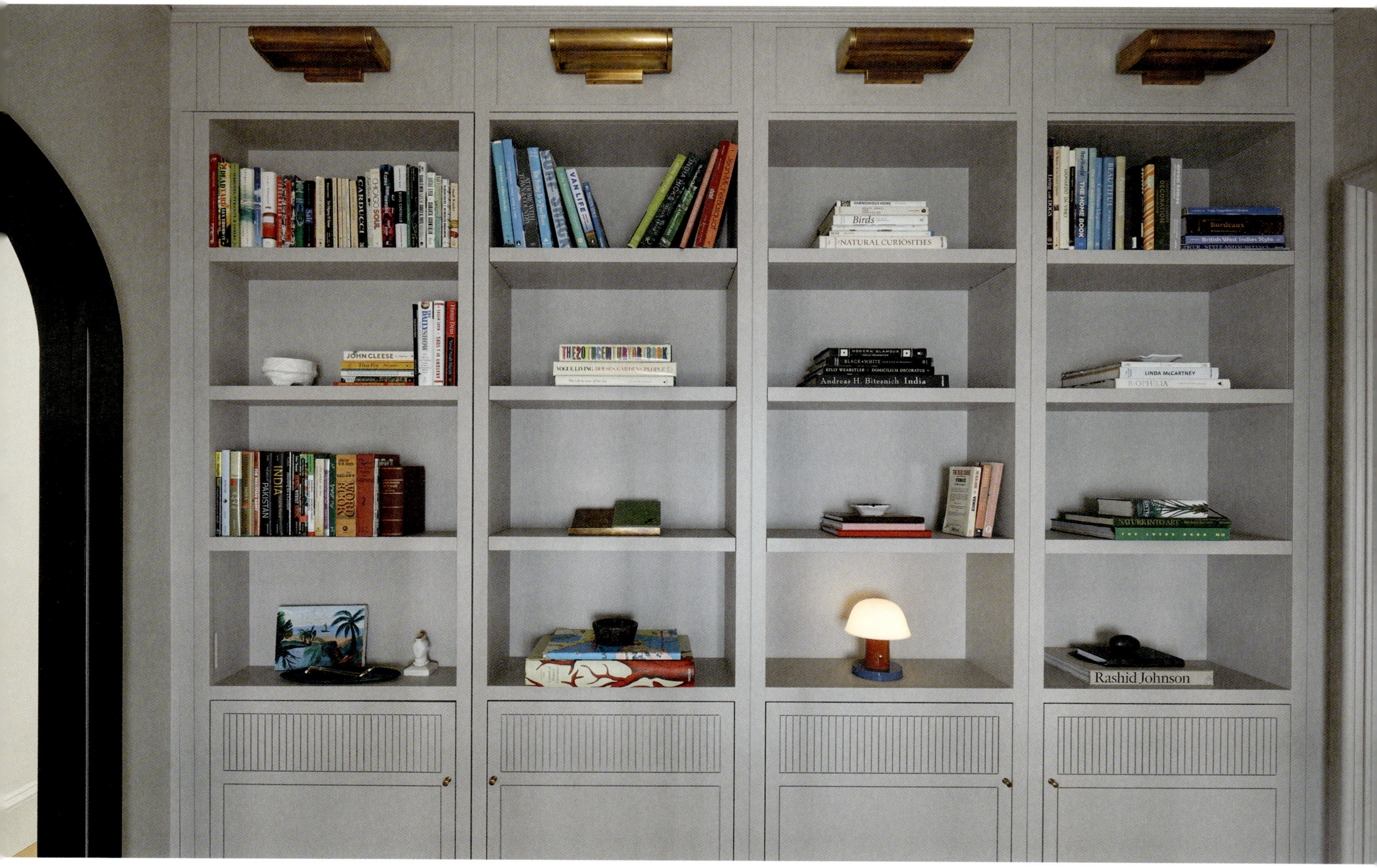

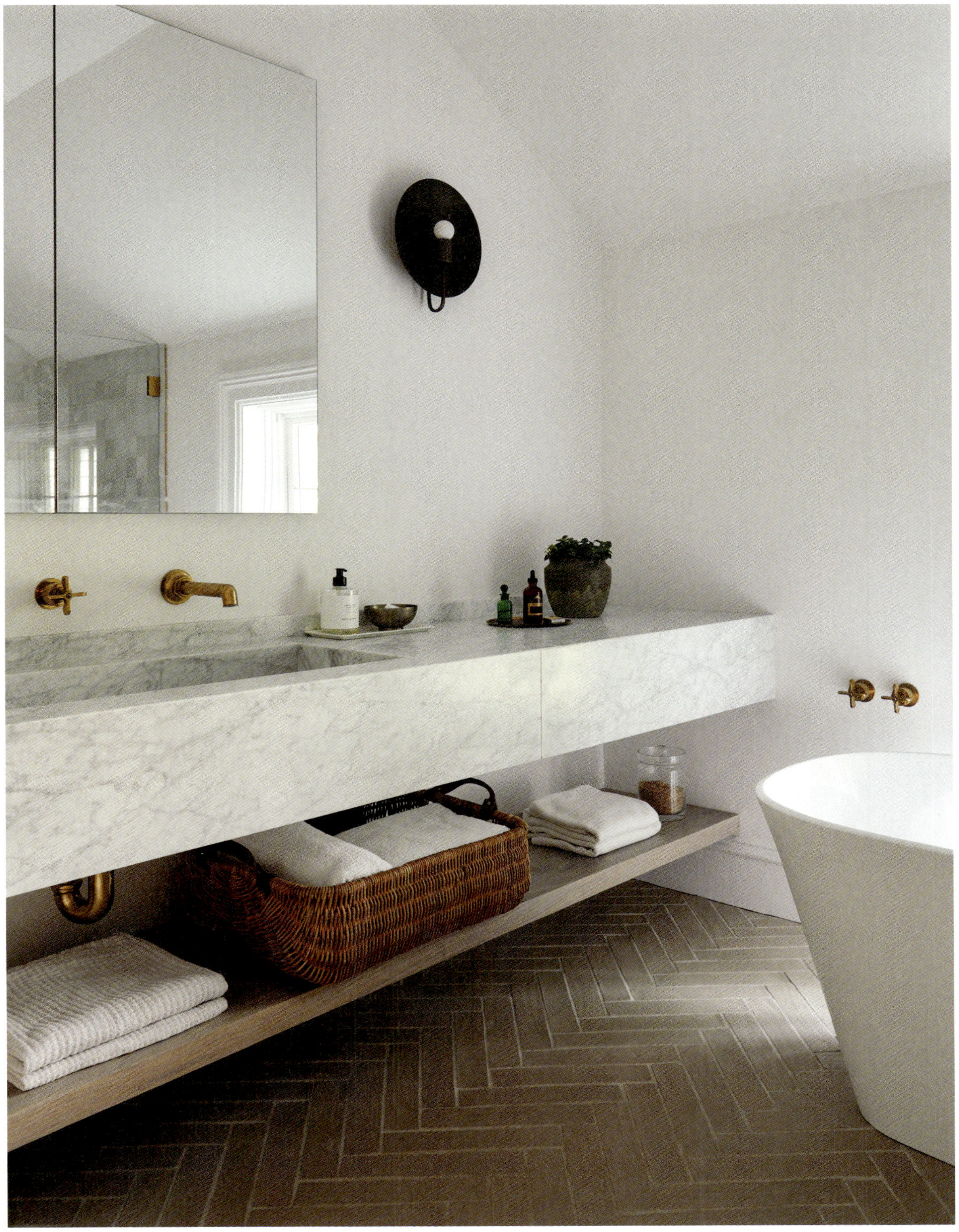

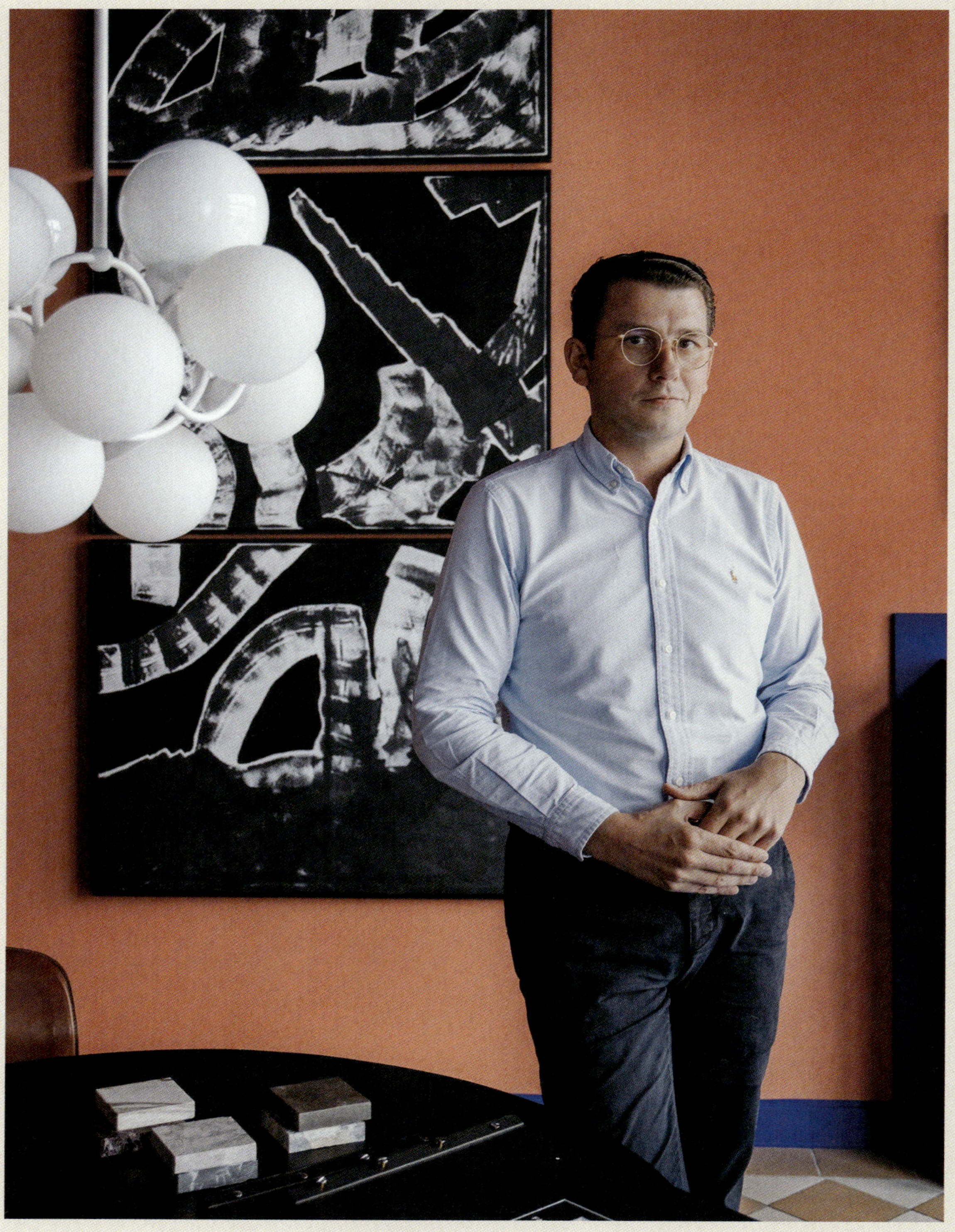

Fabian Freytag

Fabian Freytag was born in Hamburg in 1984 and moved to Berlin in 2004 to study architecture at the University of the Arts.

In the first few years, he already realized projects in the fields of set design, product design and interior design. The combination of these disciplines with art and architecture characterizes his work to this day and led to the founding of Fabian Freytag Studio in 2012.

The focus of the office is on living, which, in Fabian Freytag's opinion, unites all disciplines in a precise way. In 2020, the studio and its team moved into a coach house in Berlin's Mitte district. This is also home to the suite, as a showroom, and the gallery in the front building.

Fabian Freytag works with his team on publications, products and art objects that are presented at the furniture fairs in Milan and Copenhagen. The studio's gently radical approach is not just a motto, but a serious statement, because in Fabian Freytag's opinion, design should first and foremost be fun.

www.fabianfreytag.com

Photography: Kozy Studio Berlin

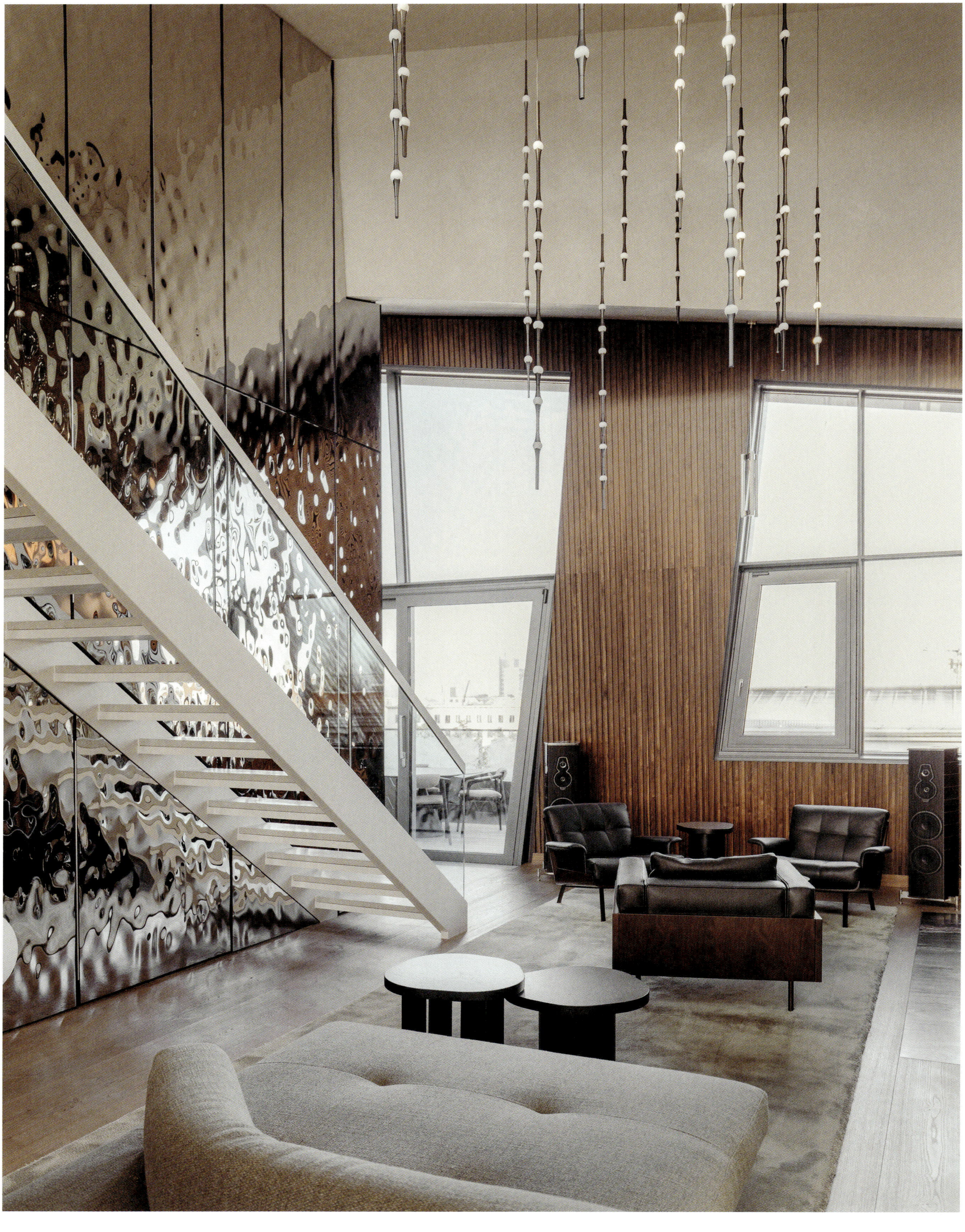

Penthouse 106 is a recent project by Fabian Freytag Studio located in Daniel Libeskind's Sapphire building in Berlin Mitte.

Slated windows, sloping surfaces and lines that only in the rarest of cases do they meet at a 90 degrees angle... A basis for interior planning that could hardly be more challenging. The Fabian Freytag Studio meets the sculptural design inside the penthouse with a concept that is individualized and sets a symphonic play of surfaces.

What at first glance sounds like an overwhelming abundance of materials is in reality a unique interplay of organic surfaces. The diagonal walnut picks up on the daylight streaming in from above. The reflections of the hammered steel lend lightness to the soaring spaces. Patterns enclosed in the natural stone act like frozen forces of nature and paradoxically give the rooms something soft and calming. The interior by Fabian Freytag Studio breathes something human into the abstract forms of Libeskind's architecture, creating a homely retreat in the sculptural building.

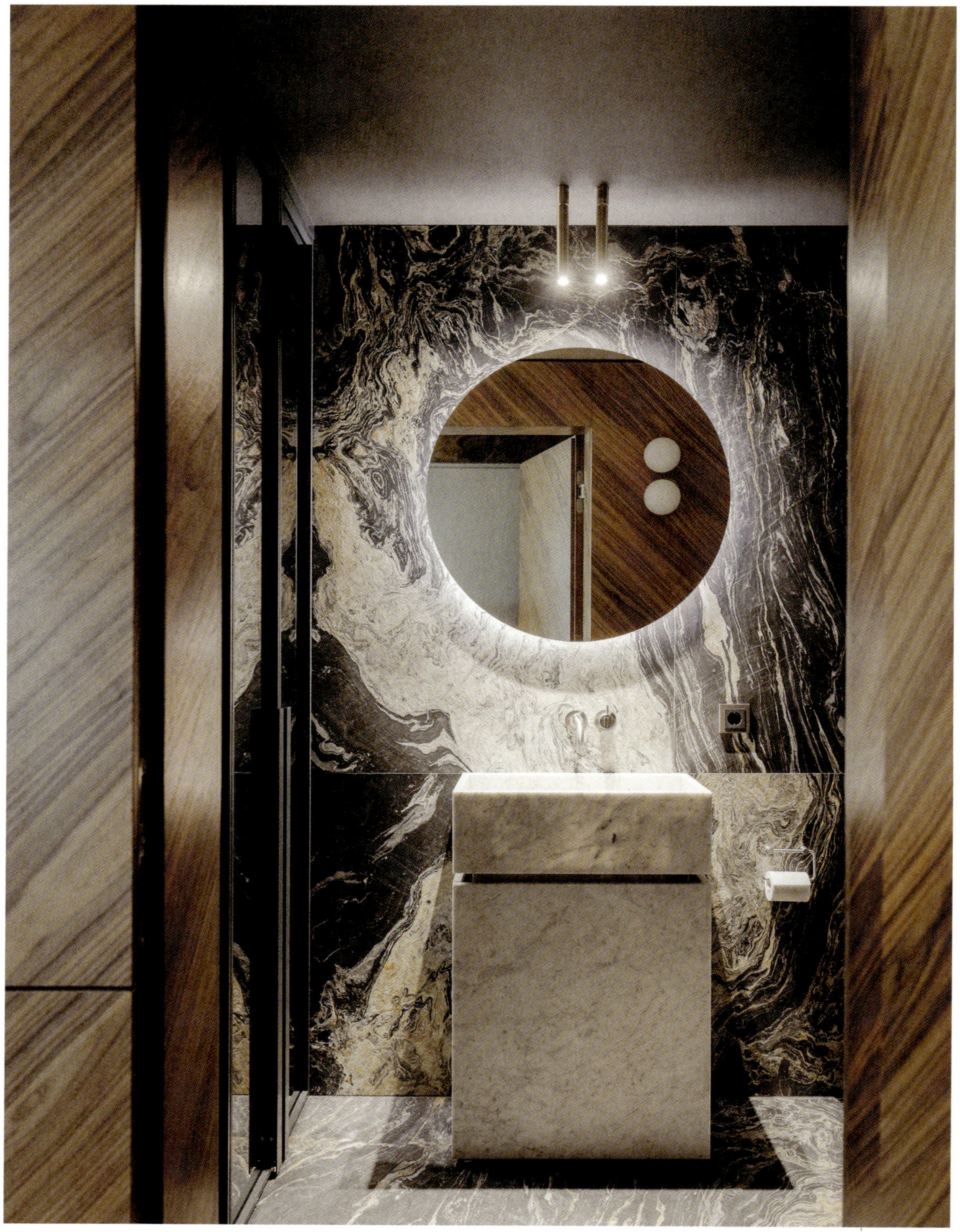

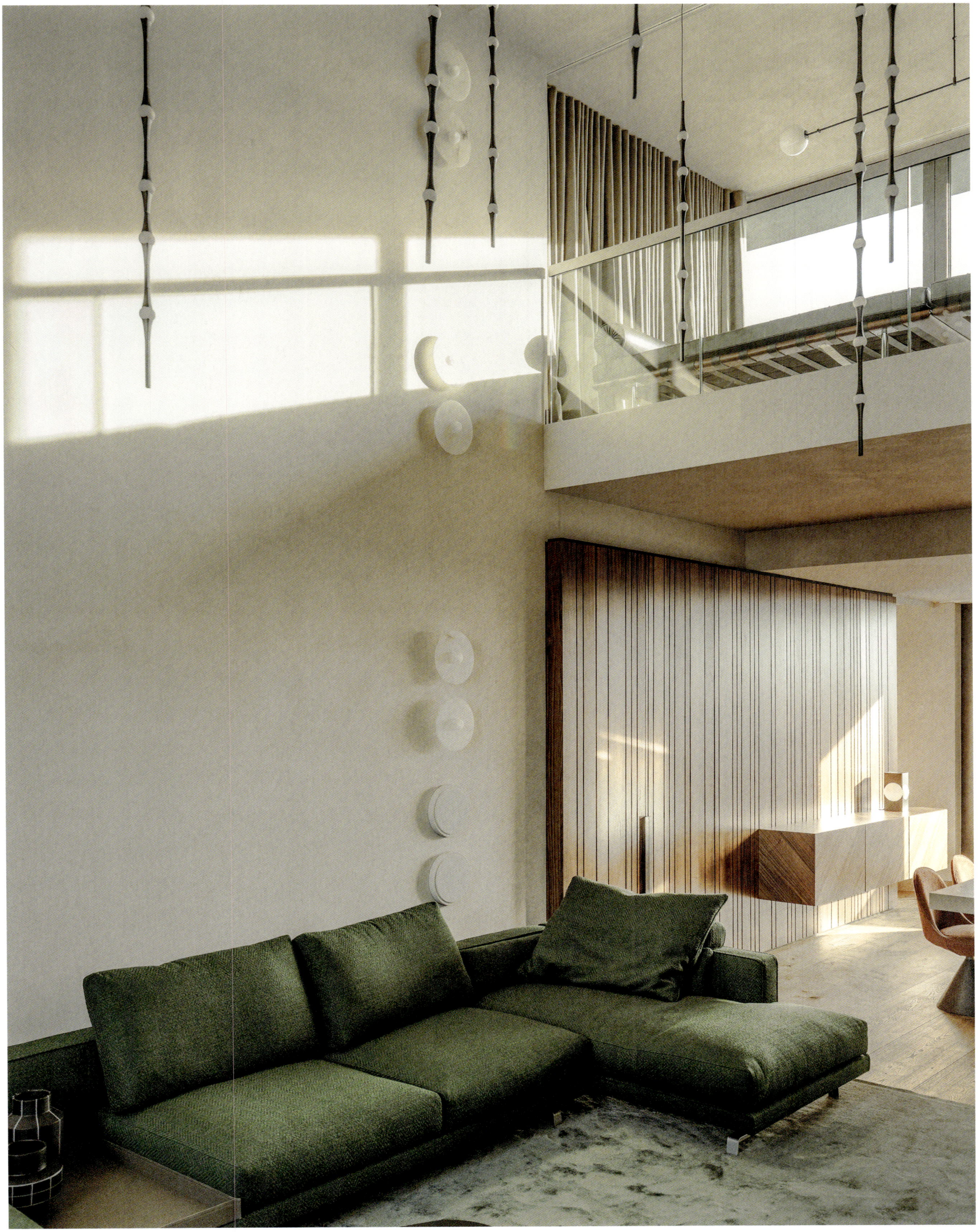

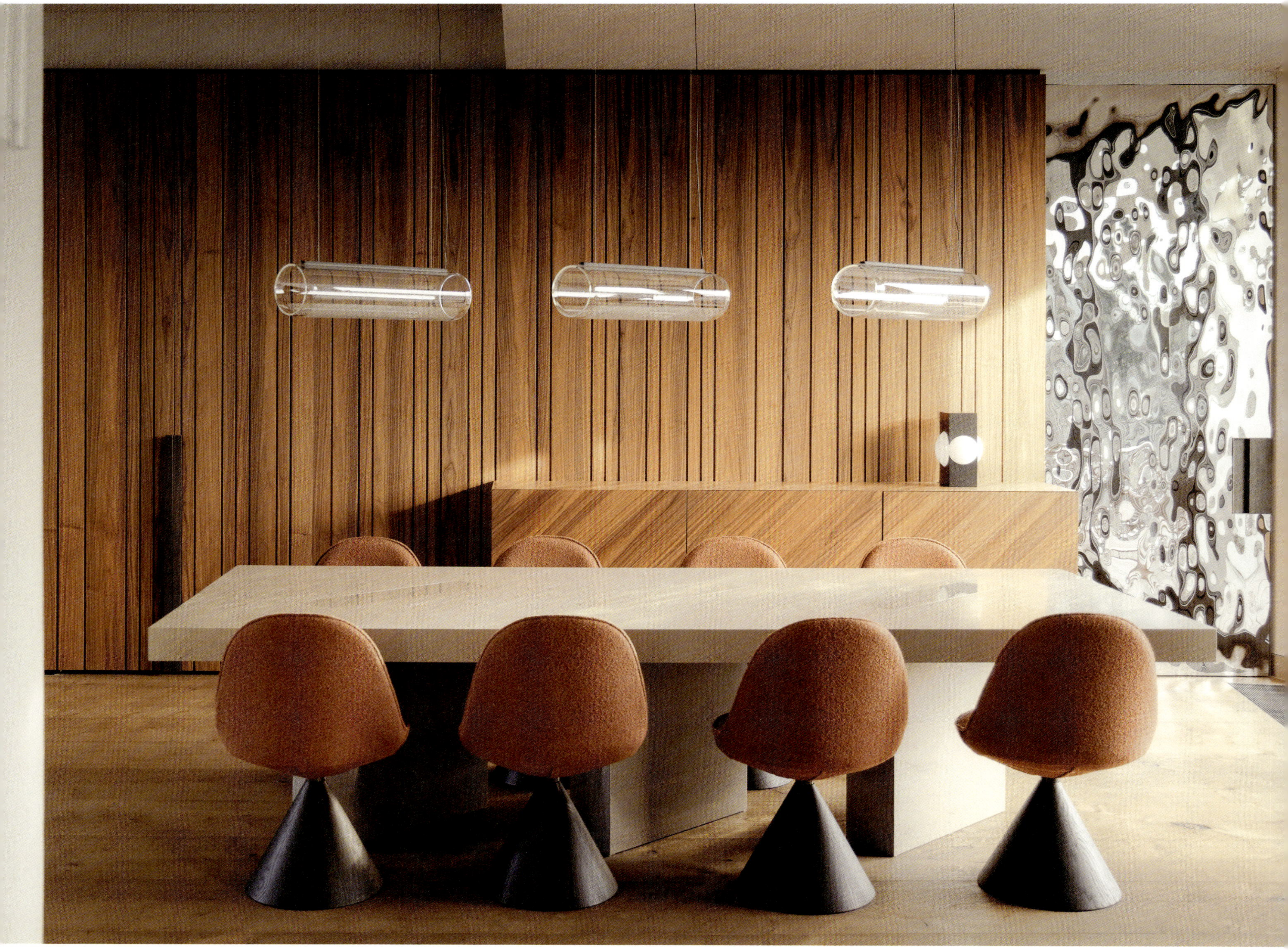

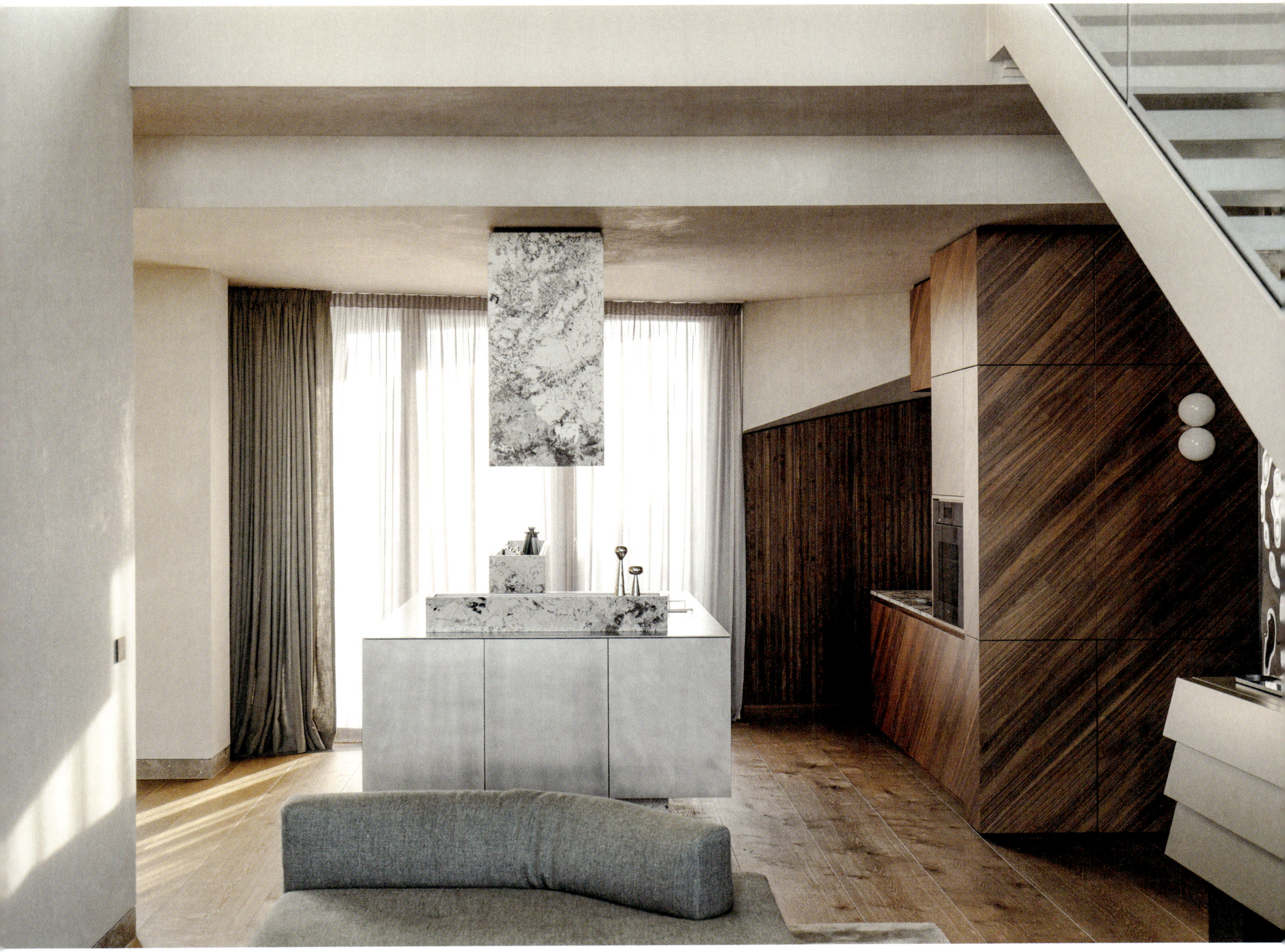

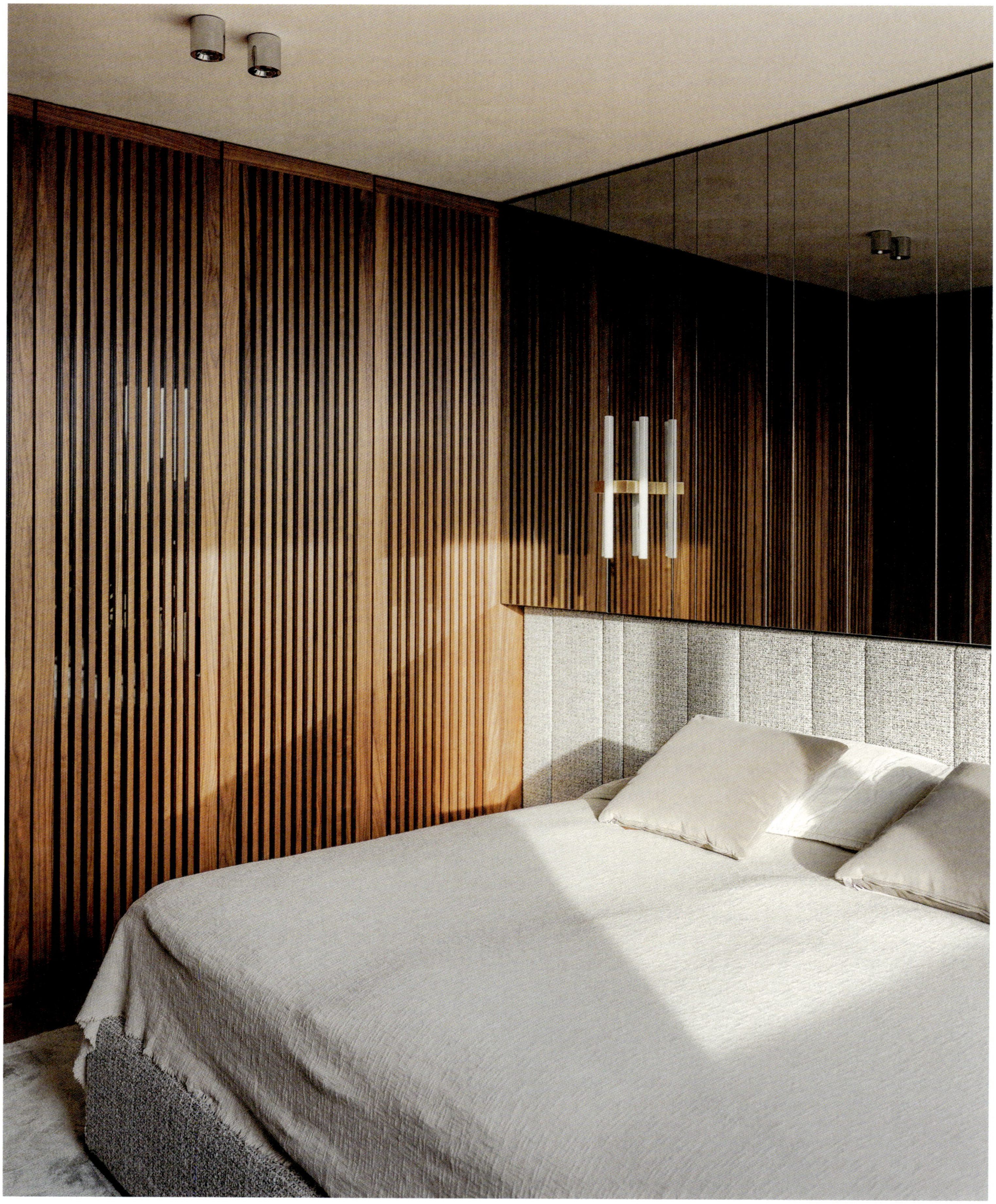

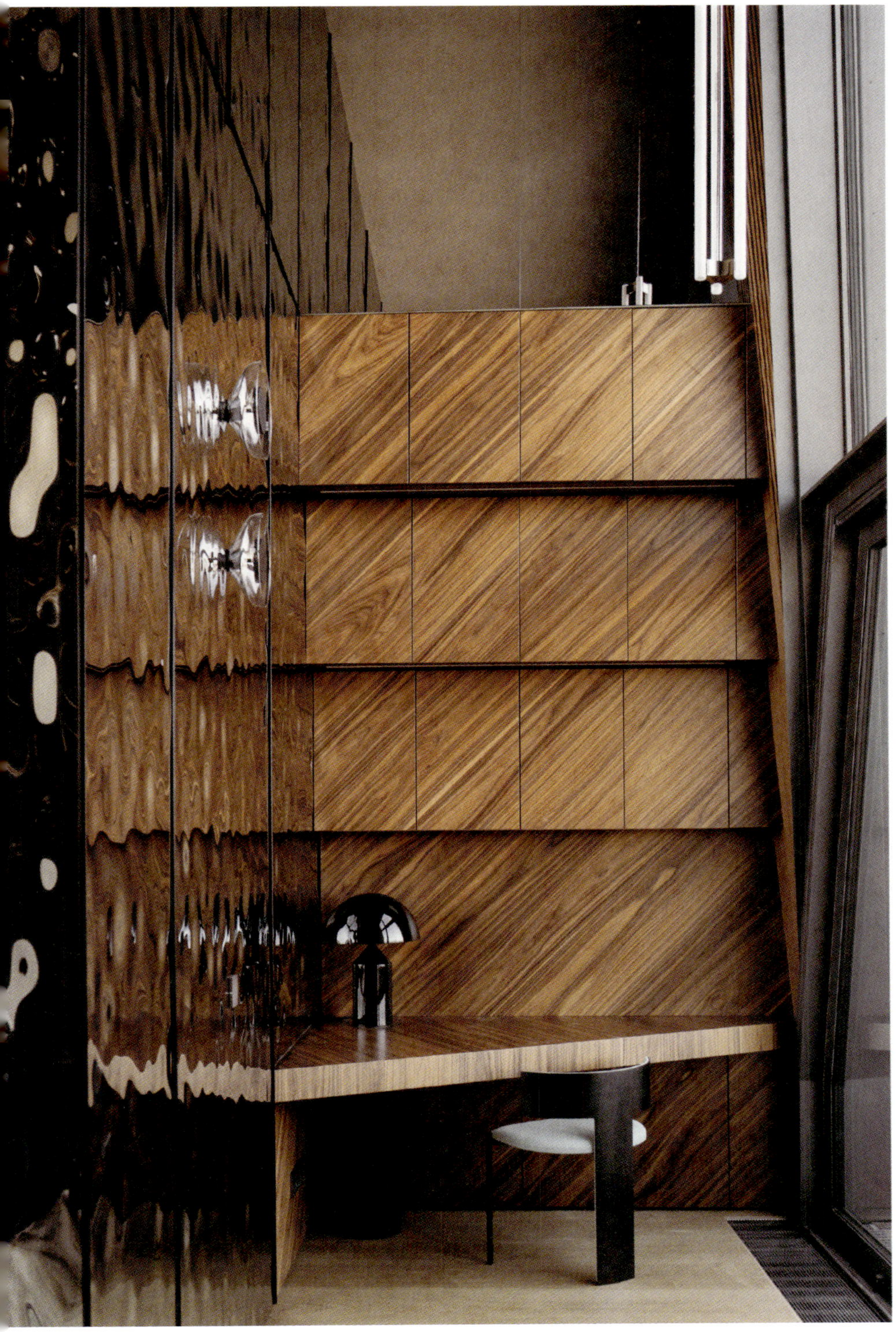
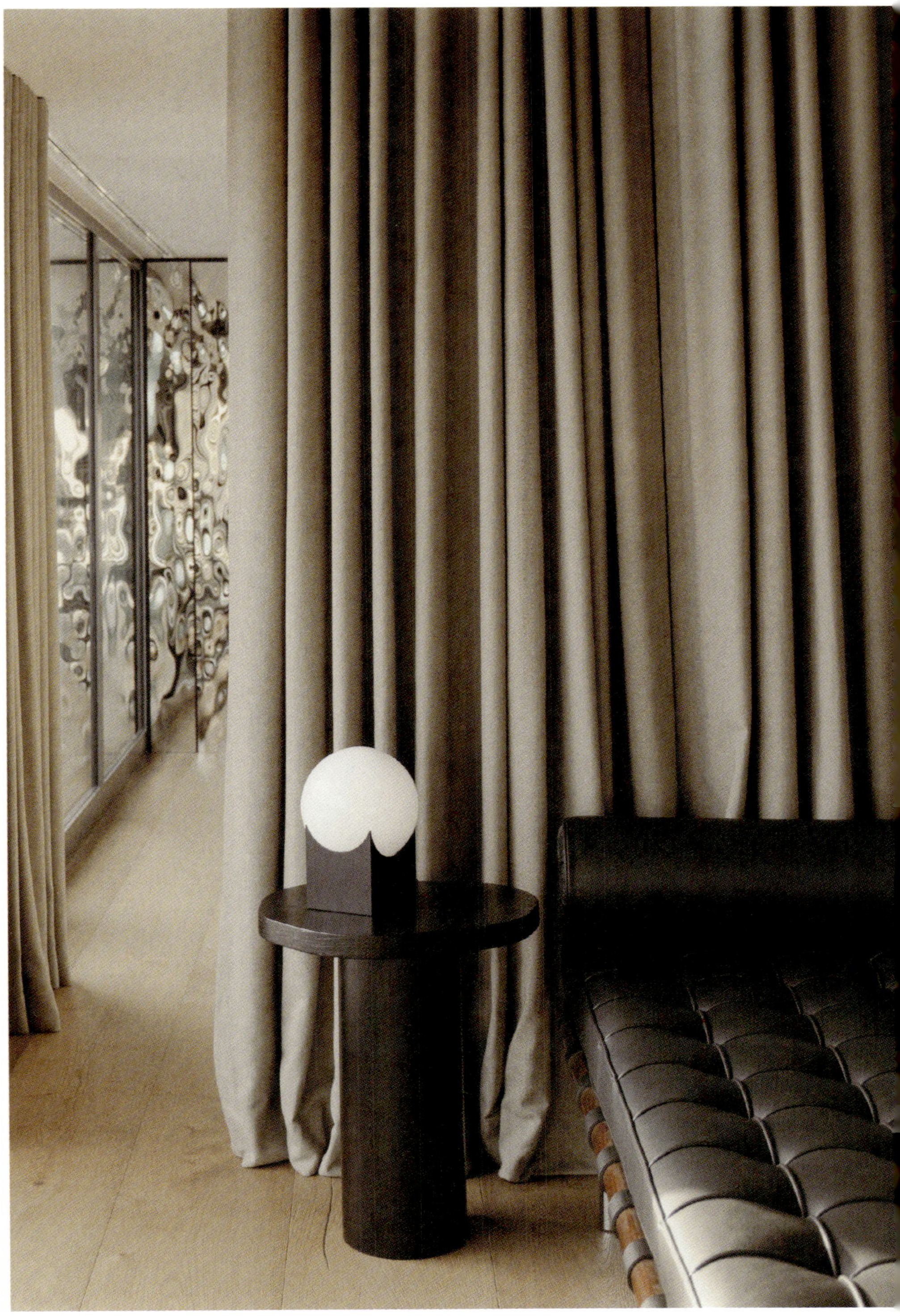

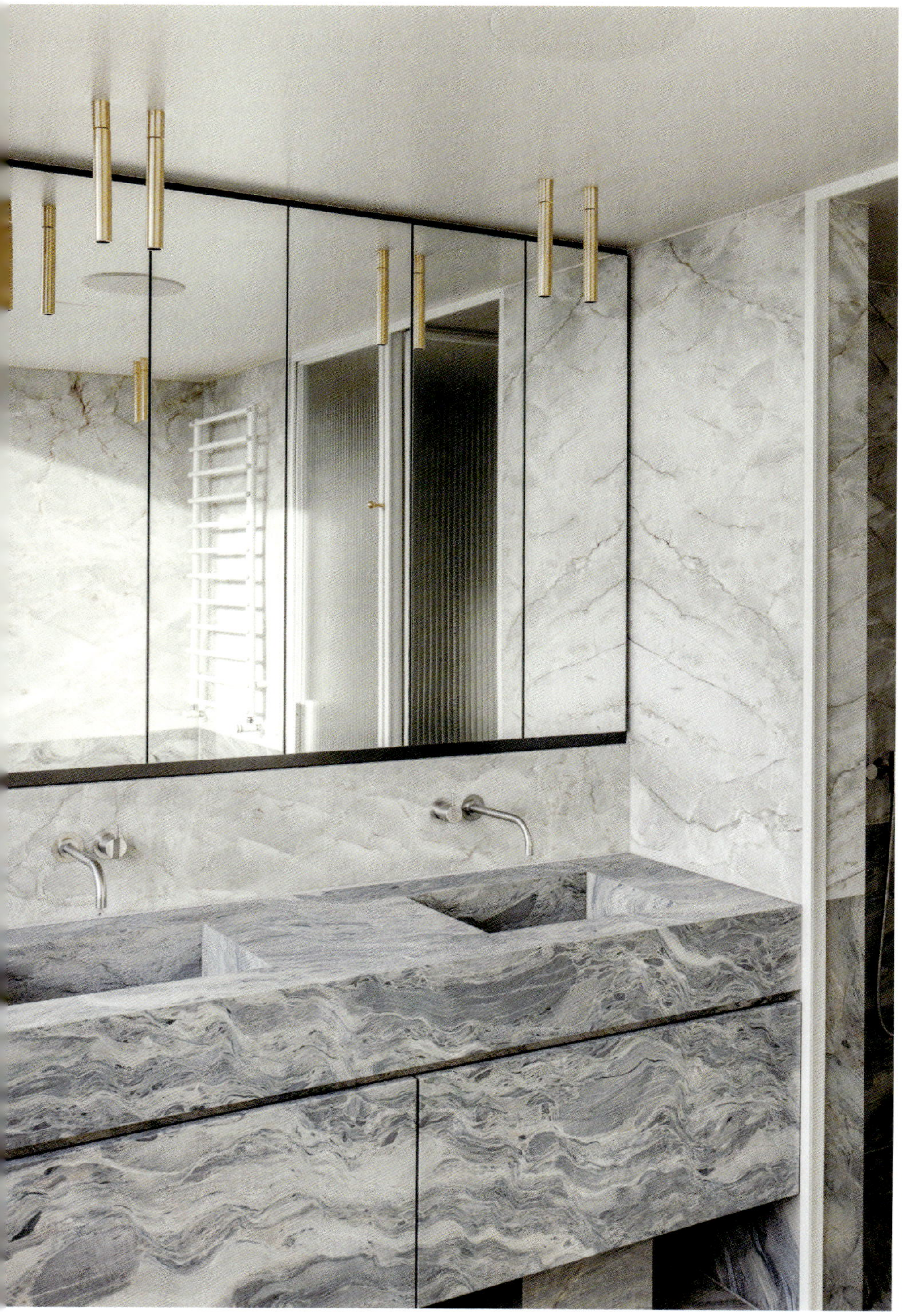
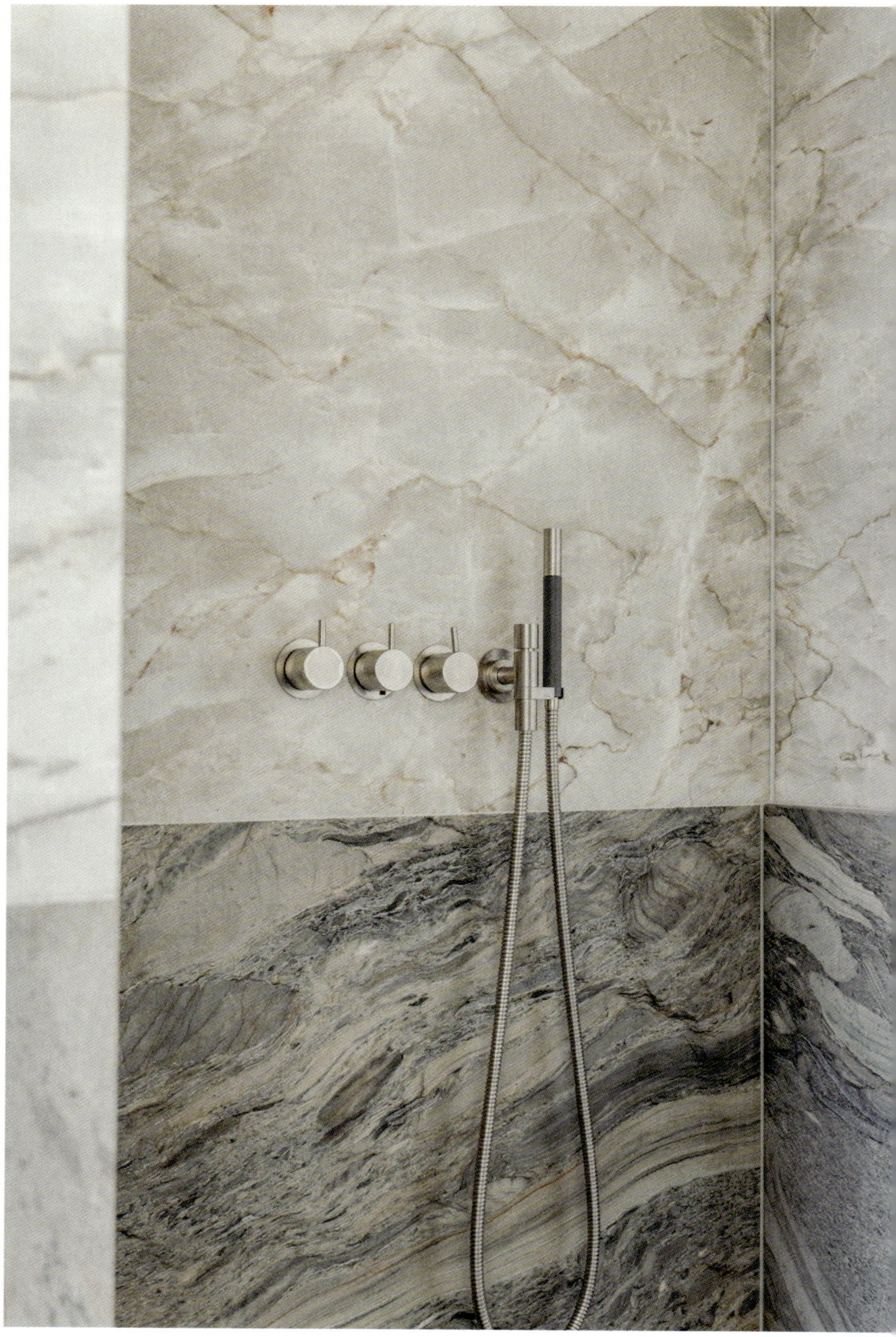

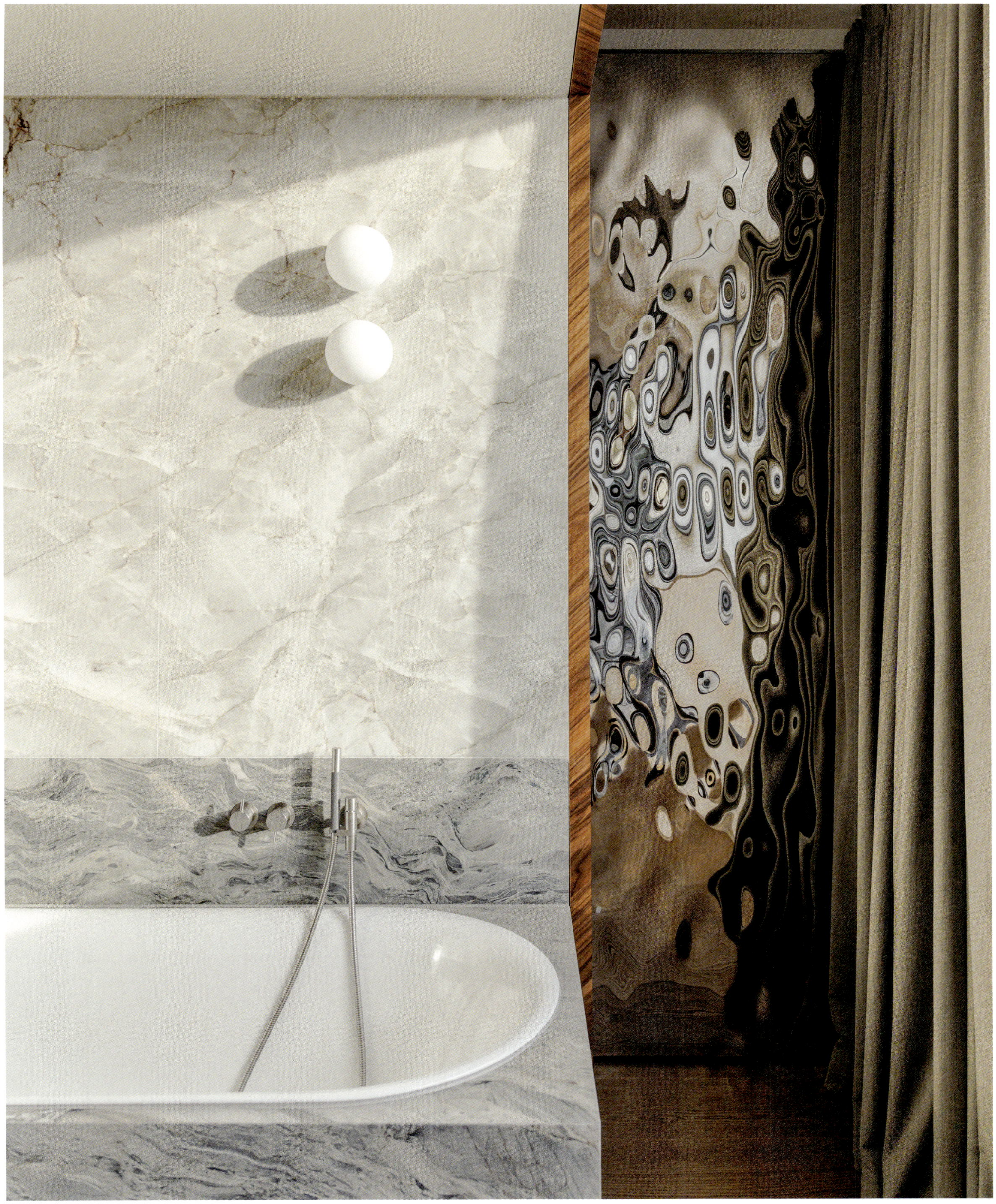

Portrait by Charlotte Lauwers

Paulien De Lange

As an interior designer, Paulien specializes in renovations and challenging restorations, carefully fusing the existing architecture with an aesthetic and functional interior.

With work experiences at a shipyard and subsequently as a yacht designer, the passion for designs and materials was formed, which proved to be the guiding principle through Paulien's trajectory.

The interior design studio Studio Pien led by Paulien, invariably believes that interior design, both for private and professional projects, is the ultimate 'tool' to not only shape a space that reflects the clients and the spirit of the place, but also makes them extremely happy.

Studio Pien takes a very personal approach, and puts the ultimate experience and 'feel-good' content of the project at the center.

www.studio-pien.com

Photography: Pilar Shoots (pages 350-361) / Charlotte Lauwers (pages 362-365)

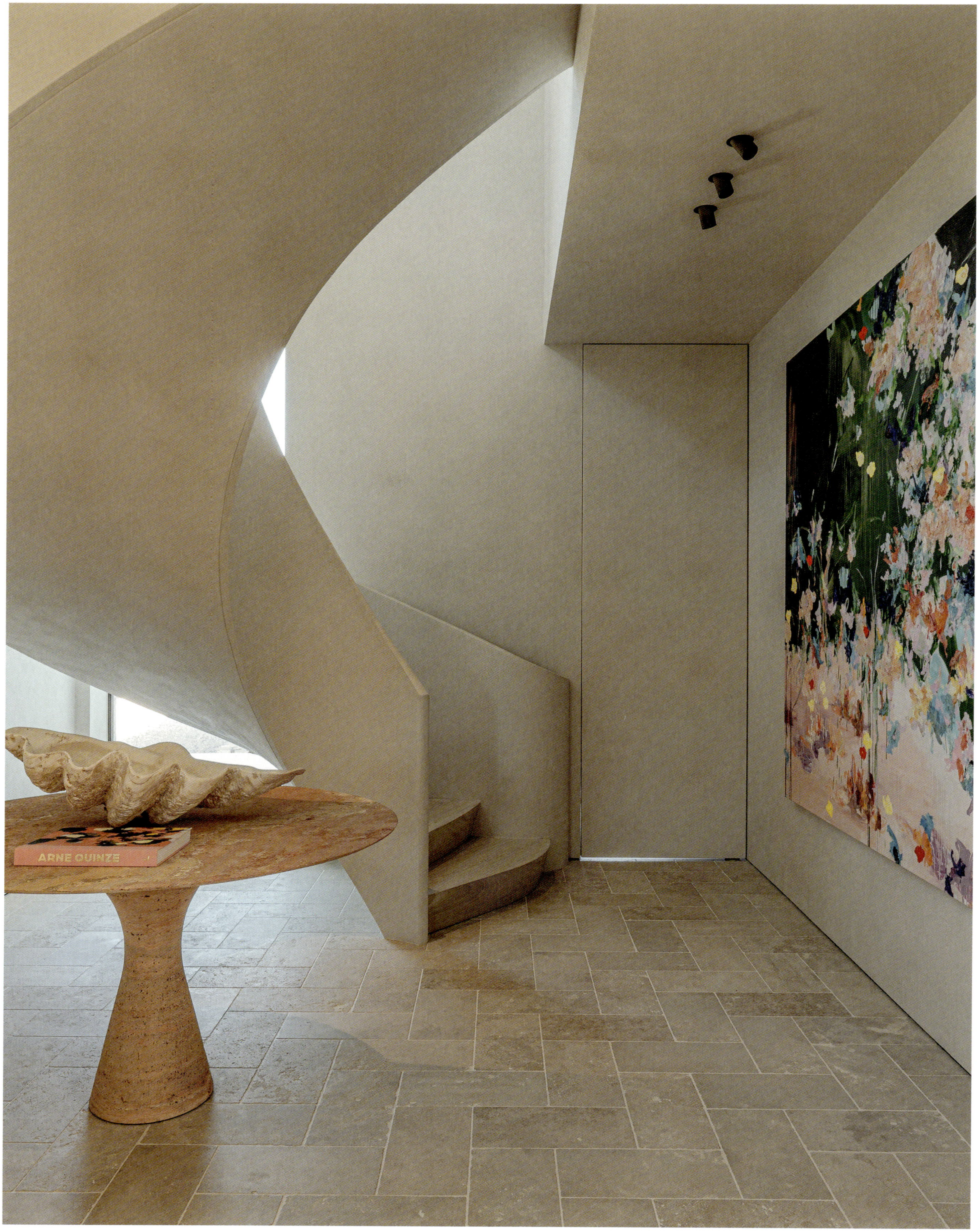
ARNE QUINZE

In this publication, Paulien De Lange (Studio Pien) shows two recent residential projects: a villa in De Haan and a seaside penthouse at the Belgian seaside.

Project Villa De Haan (pages 350-361): the initial brief for the design of this permanent home ranged from 'warm minimalism' to a "Spanish finca". The brief started with finding the right flow for a family of six, where functionality was paramount, followed by the separate specific experience of each space - from entrance hall to the heart of the home; the kitchen. The result is an extremely detailed project, where the choice of materials guided the final composition of the interior. Solid brass appears in spotlights, doors, handles and switchgear, interspersed with different types of marble, colored tiling, subtle wood tones, punchy color accents, finished with carefully selected art on a background of fine painting techniques.

Project Seaside Penthouse (pages 362-365): the lateral view to the sea on the one hand and the beautiful belle-epoque neighborhood in De Haan on the other, was the common thread the design of this penthouse. The living spaces are maximally oriented to vistas, with the 'get-together' feeling of the residents being central. The kitchen with attached bench and console, is central to the space. The materialization is "airy" with some design classics, where the "four seasons" marble provided impetus for the rest of the color use. In the end, the interior still feels warm with the addition of walnut throughout the penthouse. A place for the perfect summer evening, but also the cold winter days.

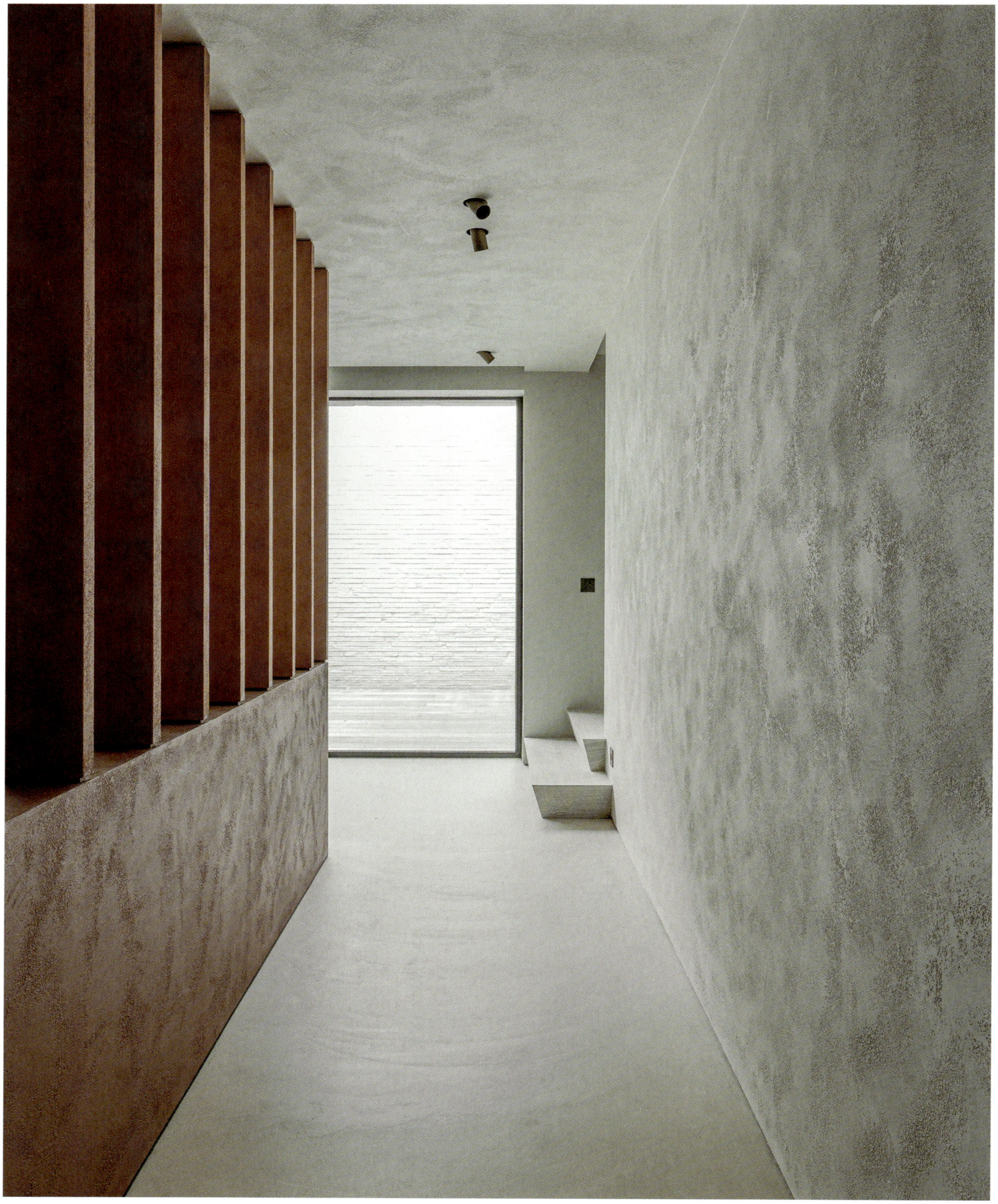

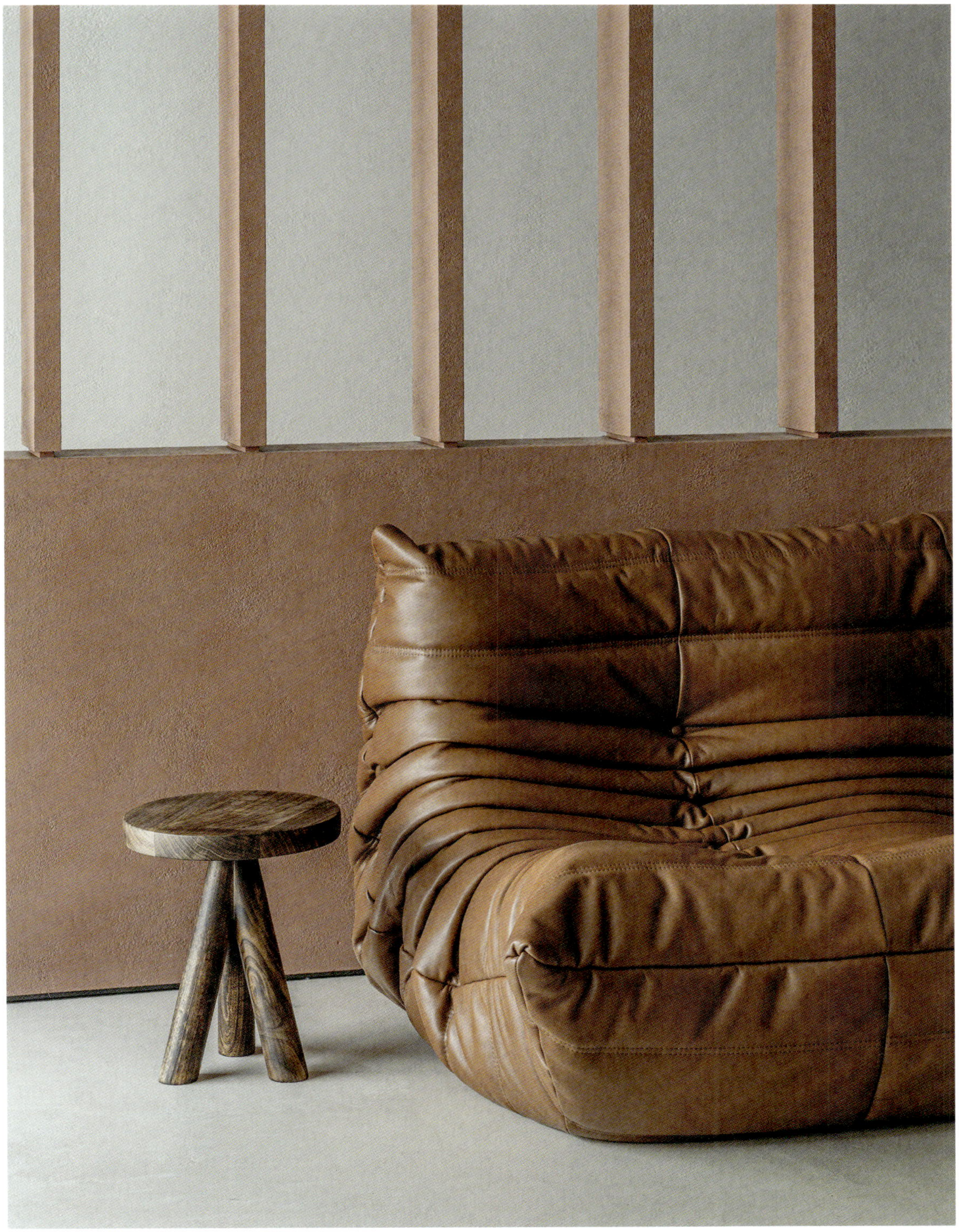

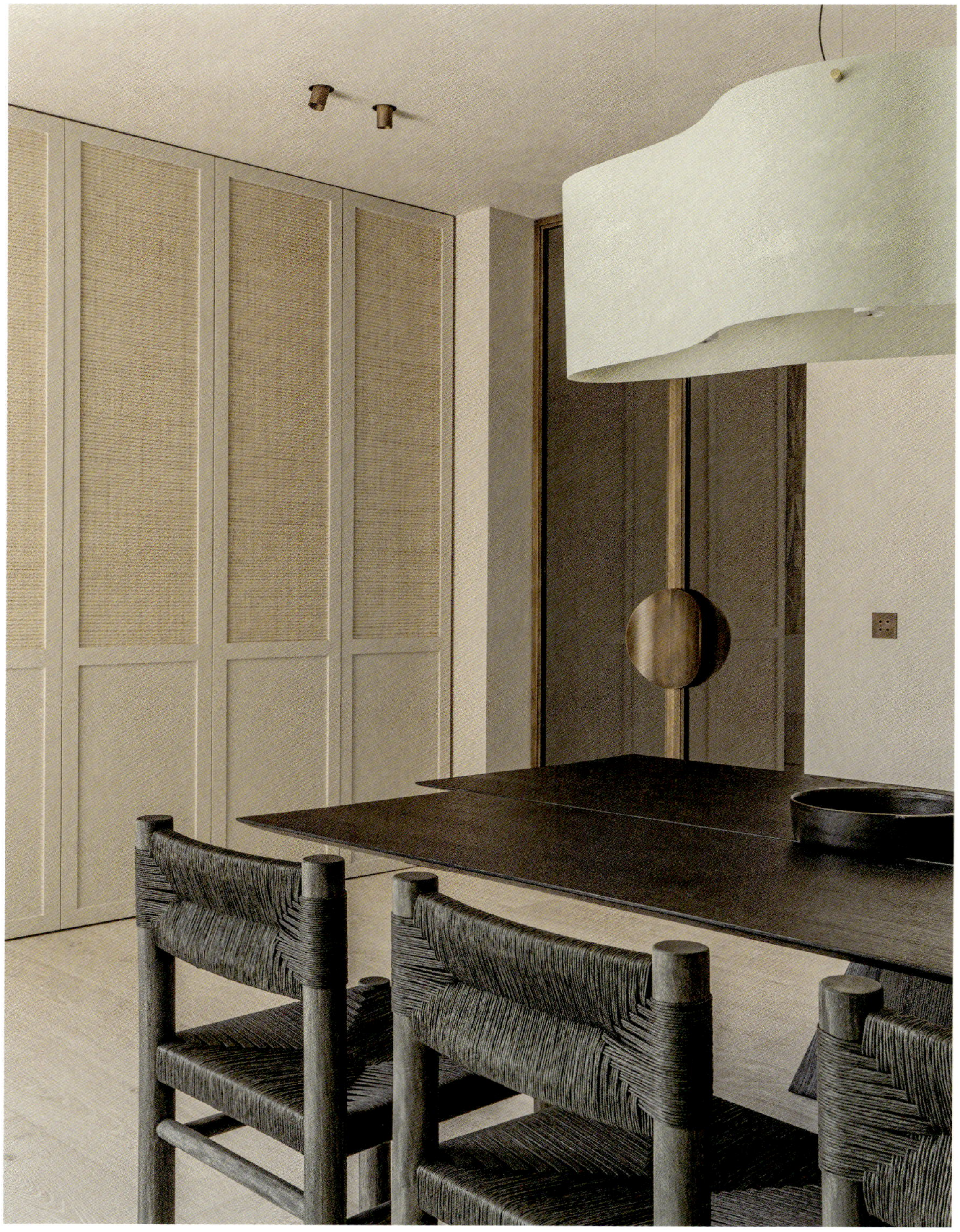

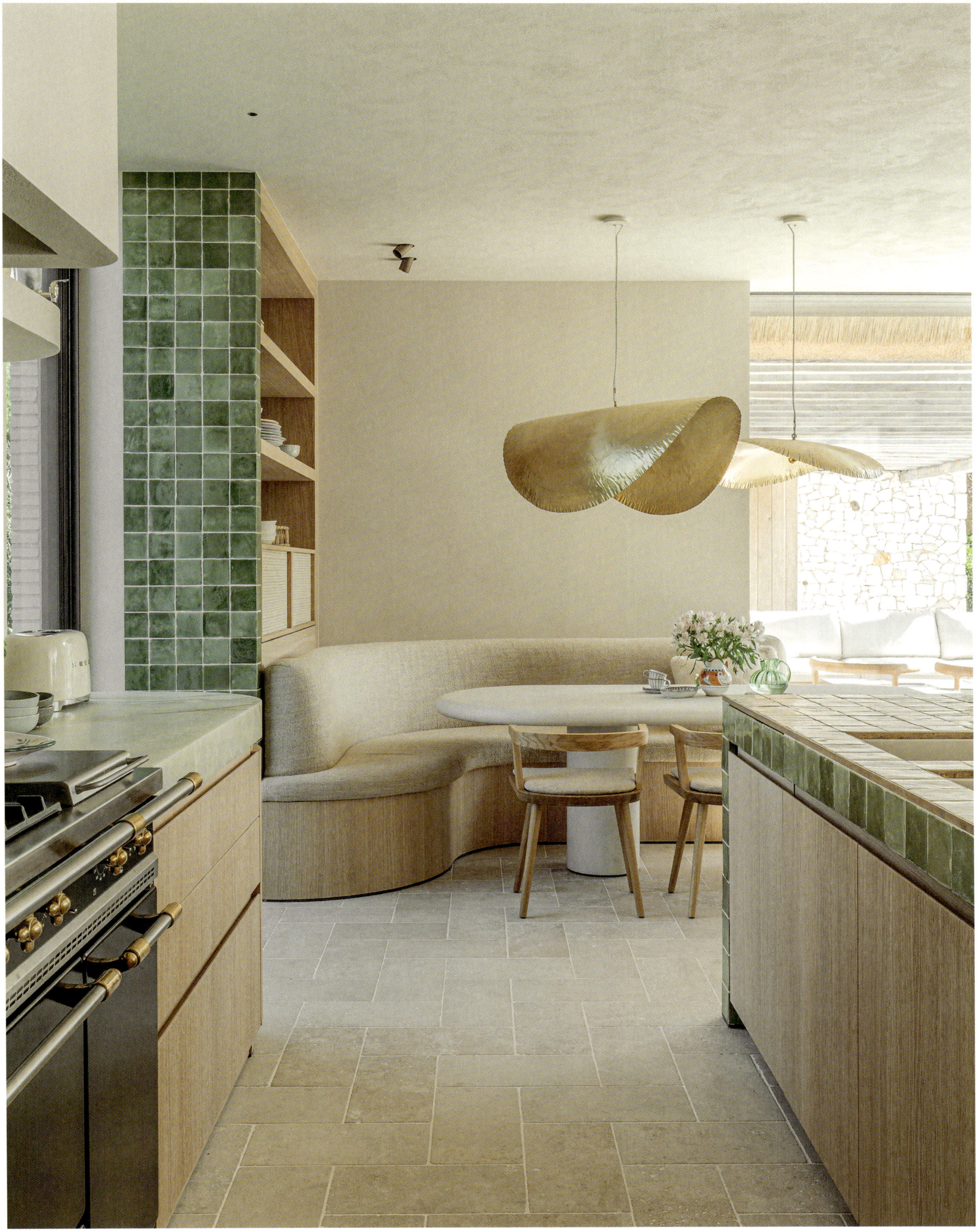

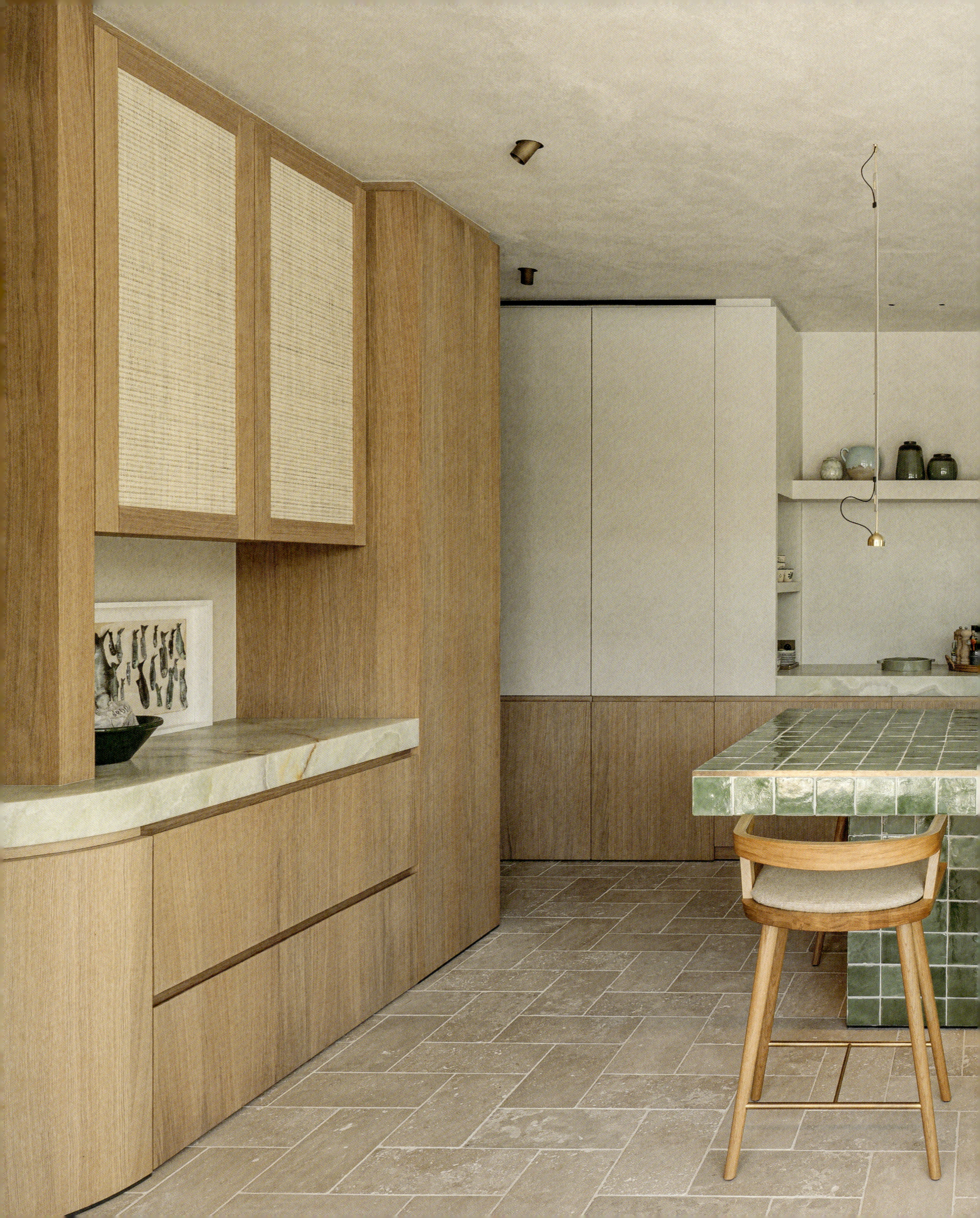

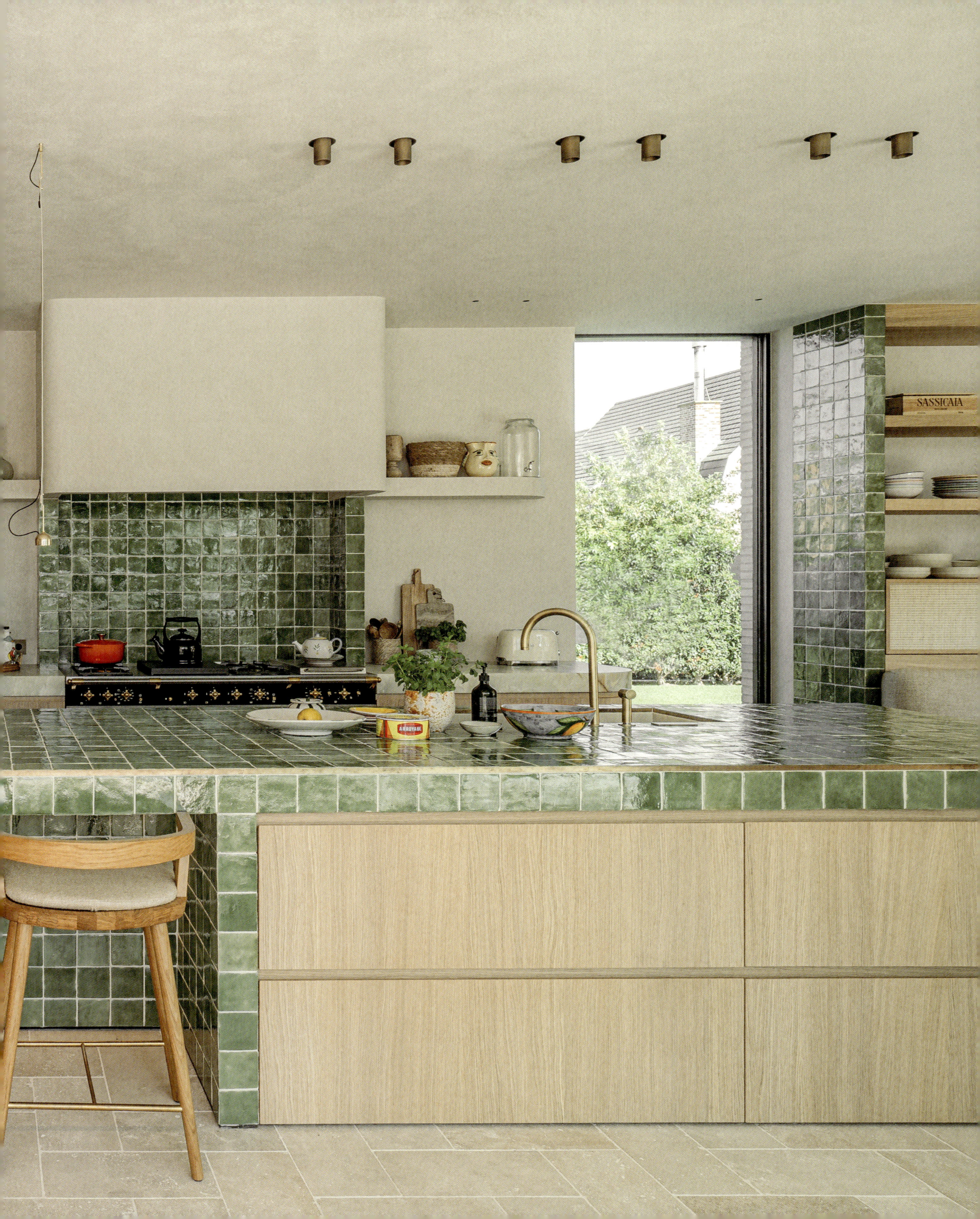
SASSICAIA

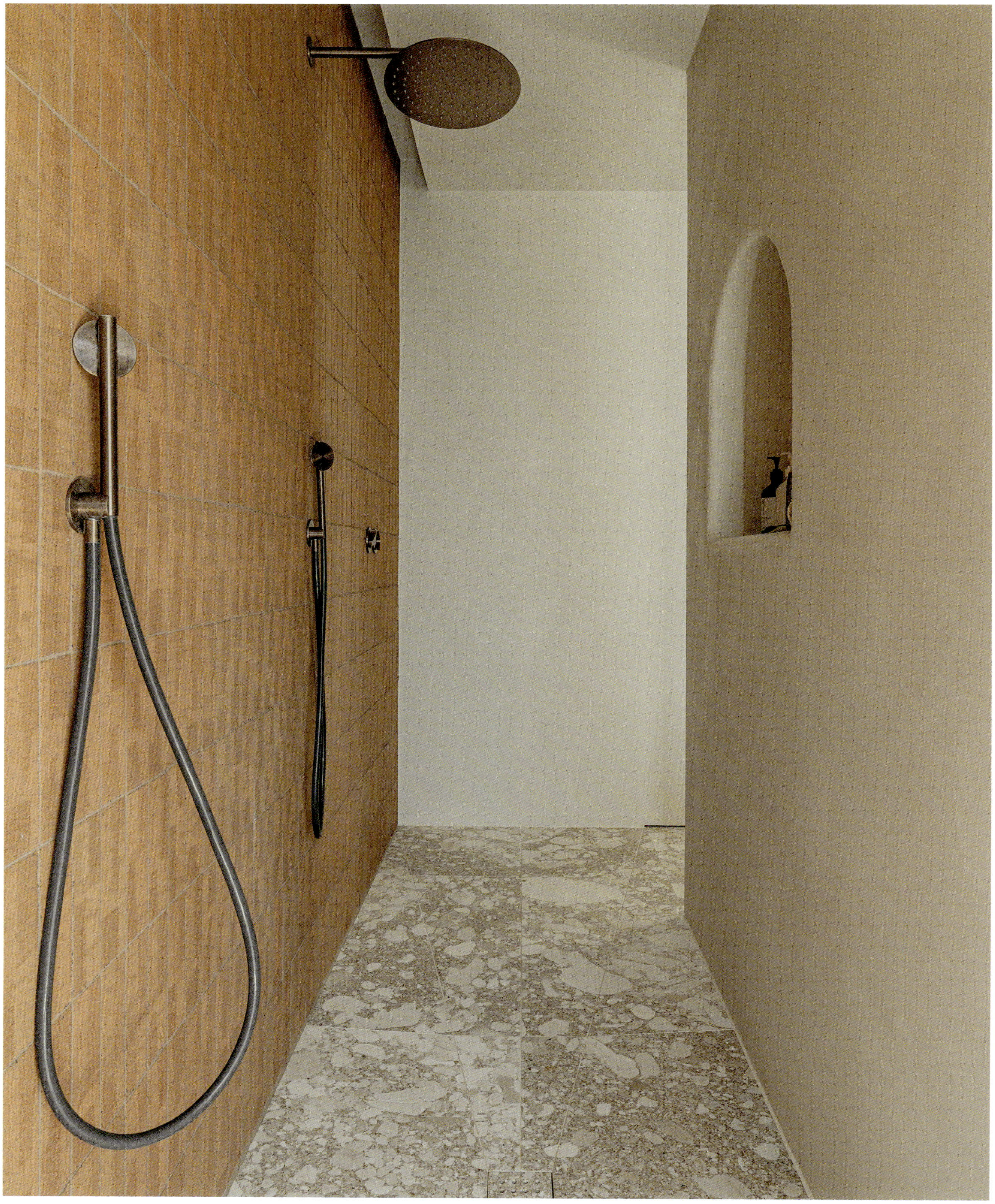

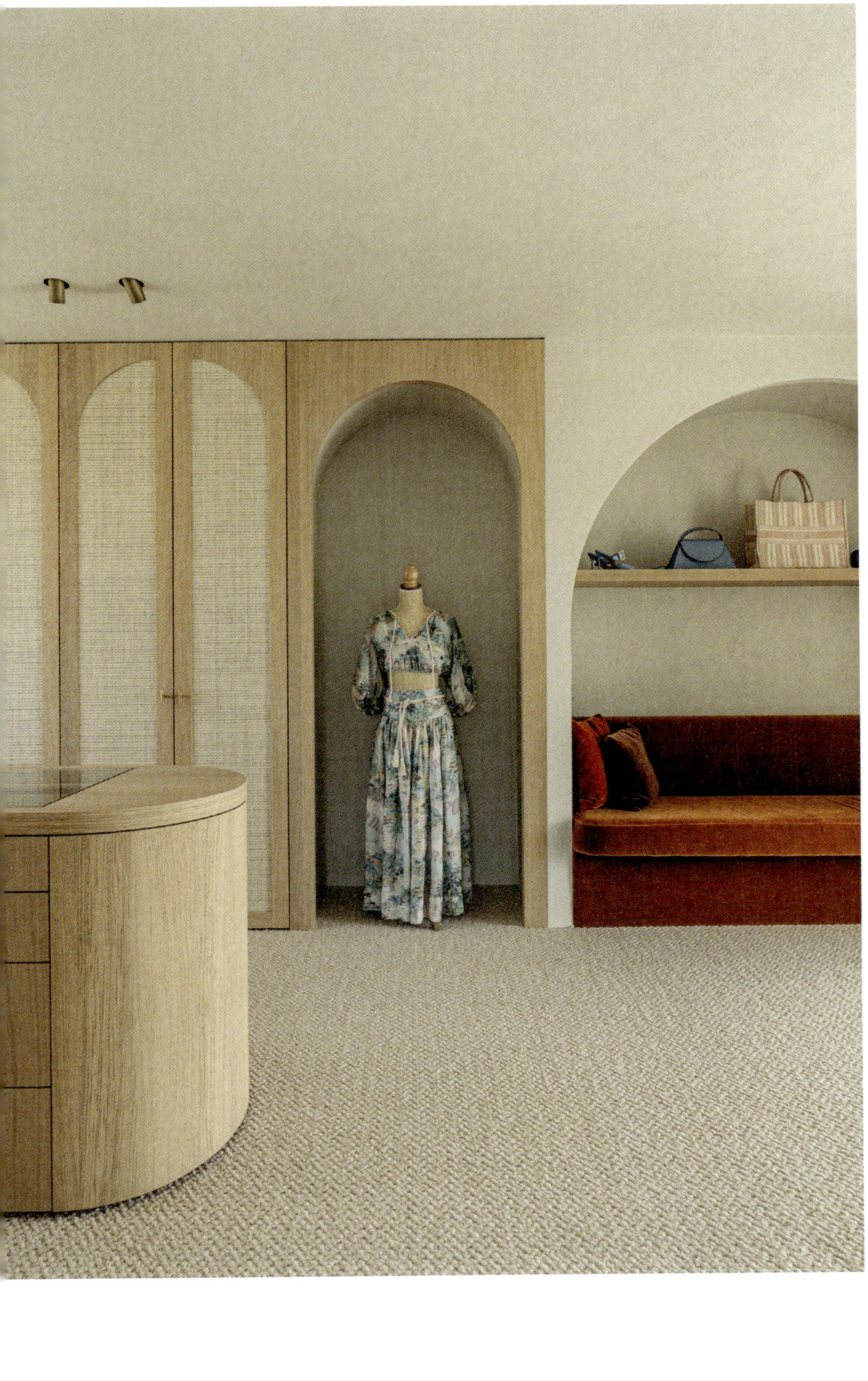

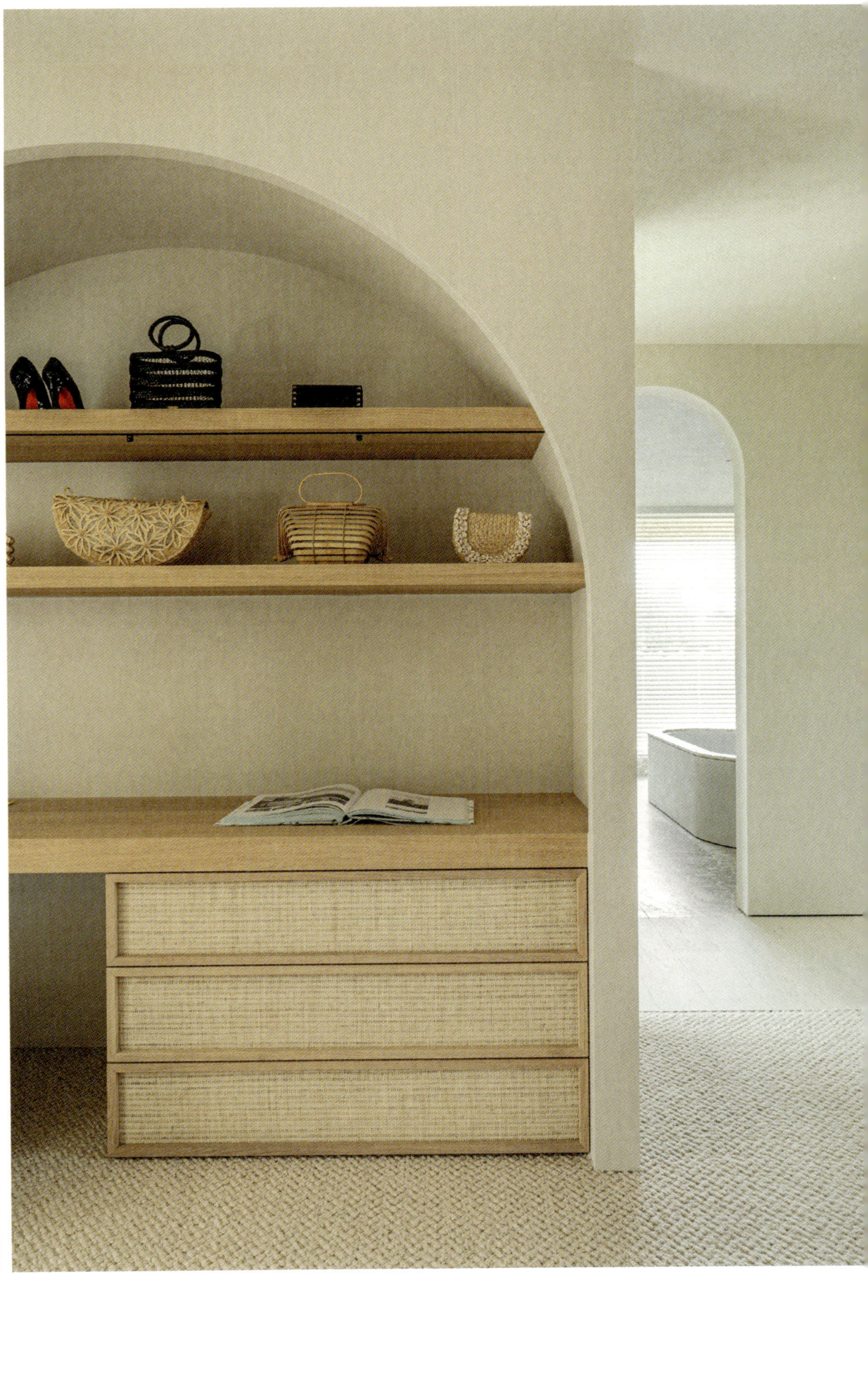

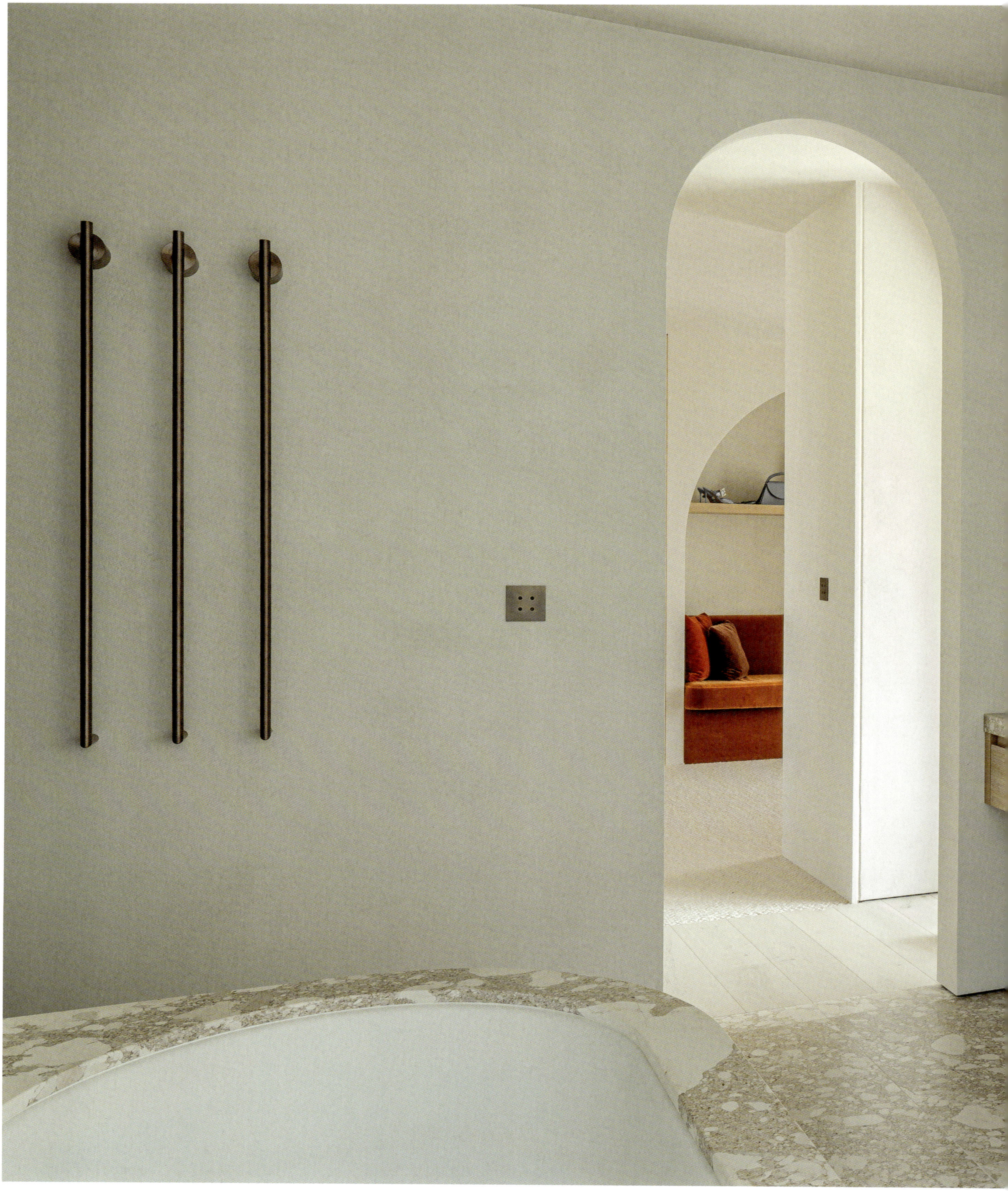

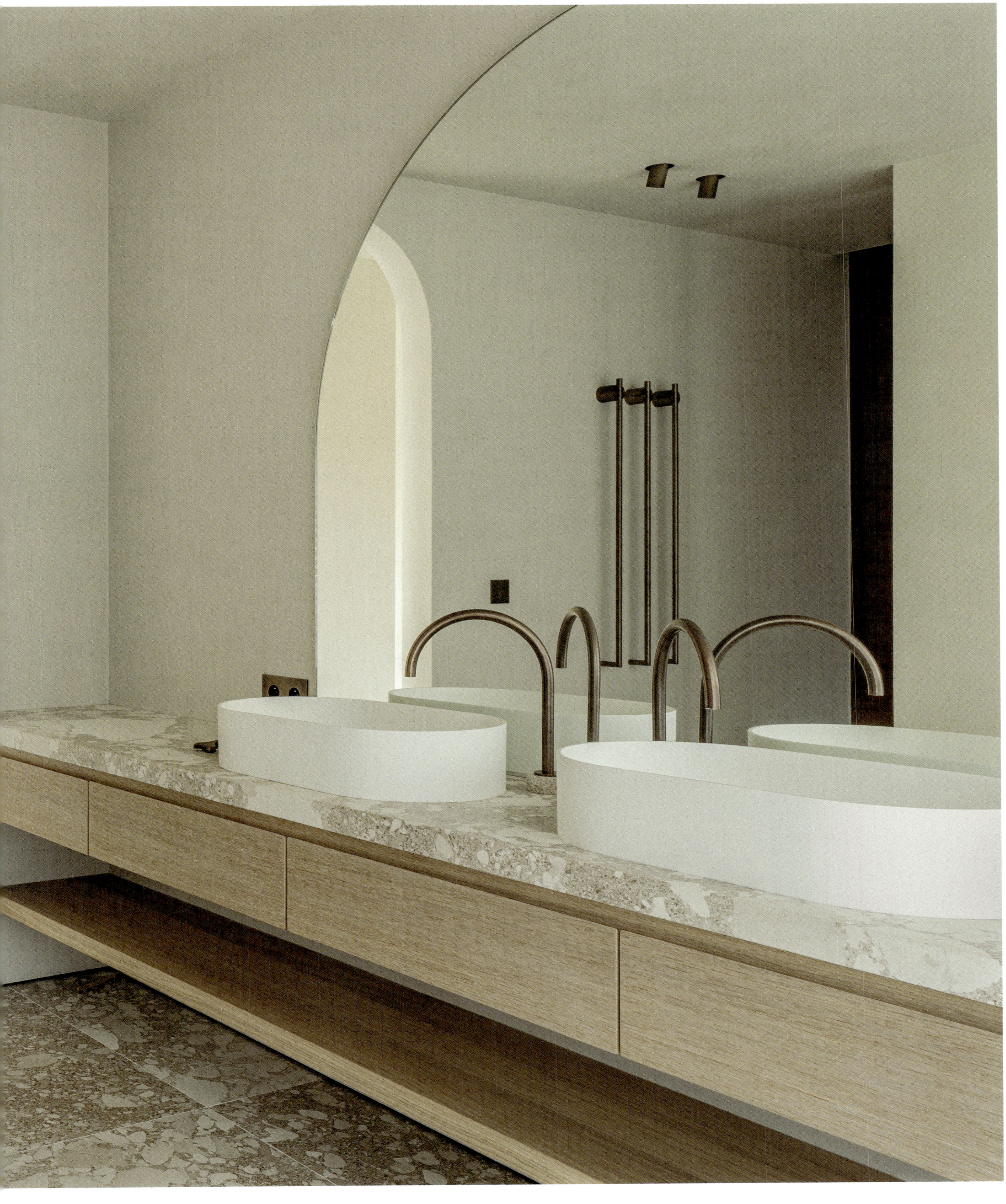

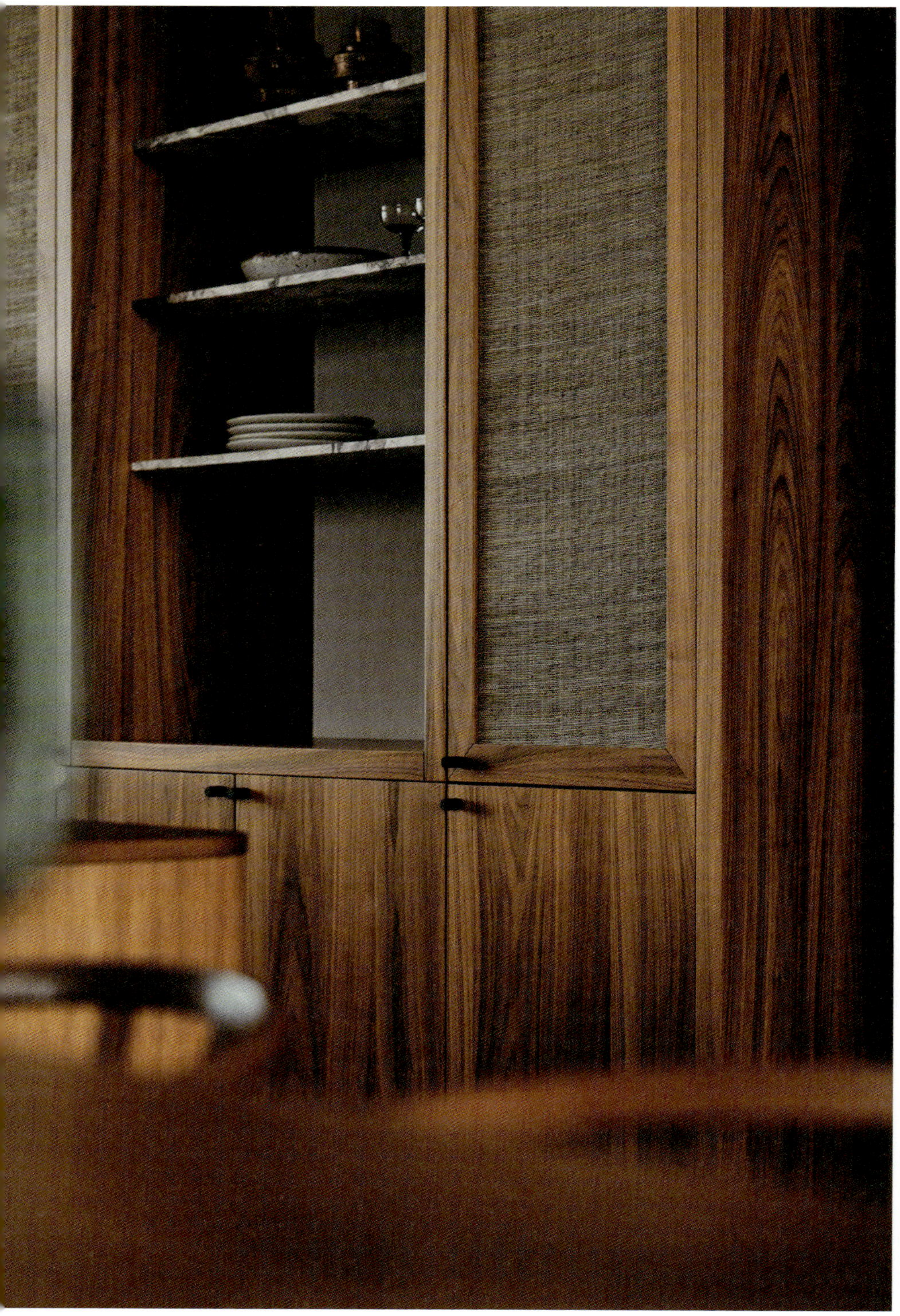

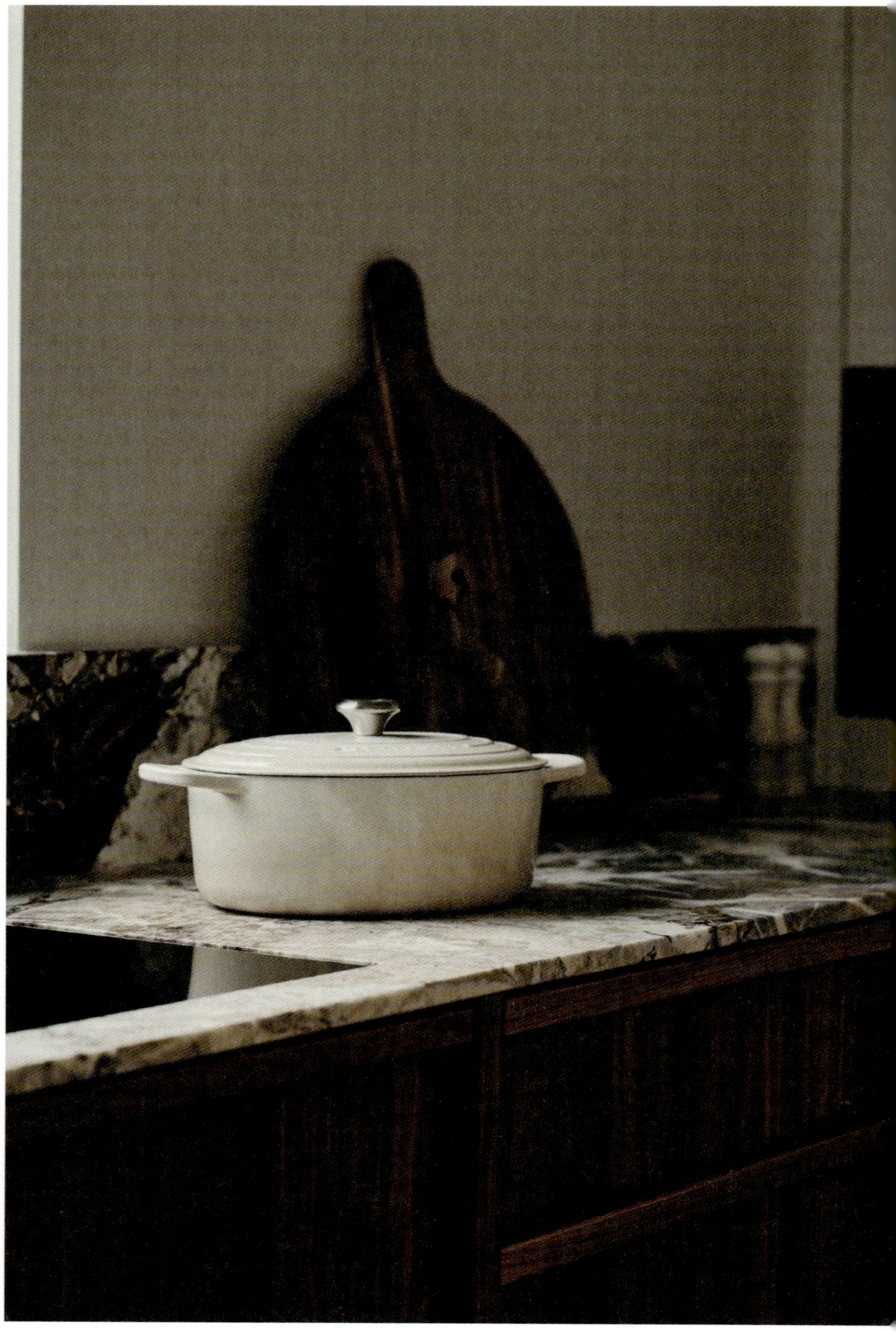

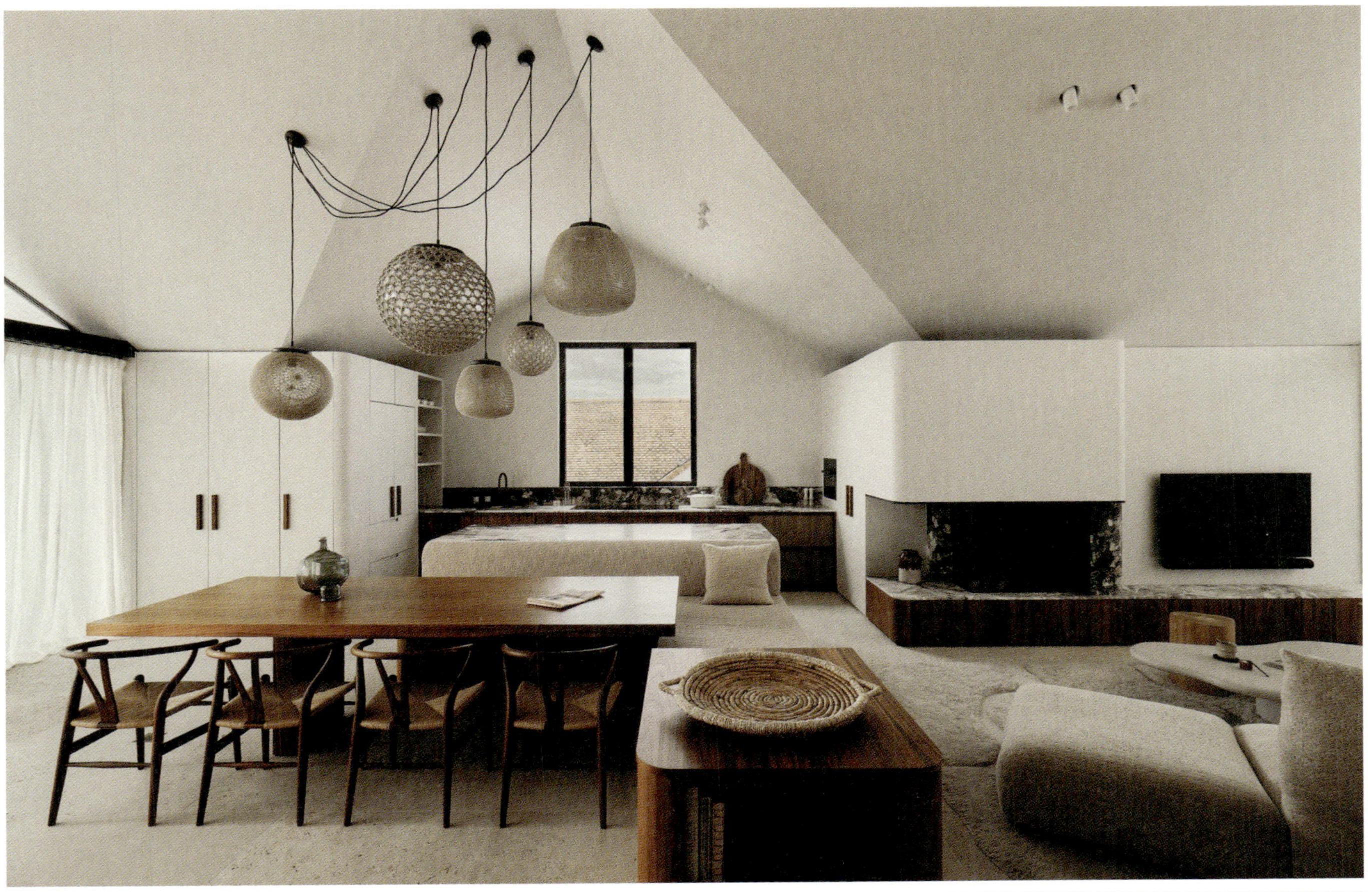

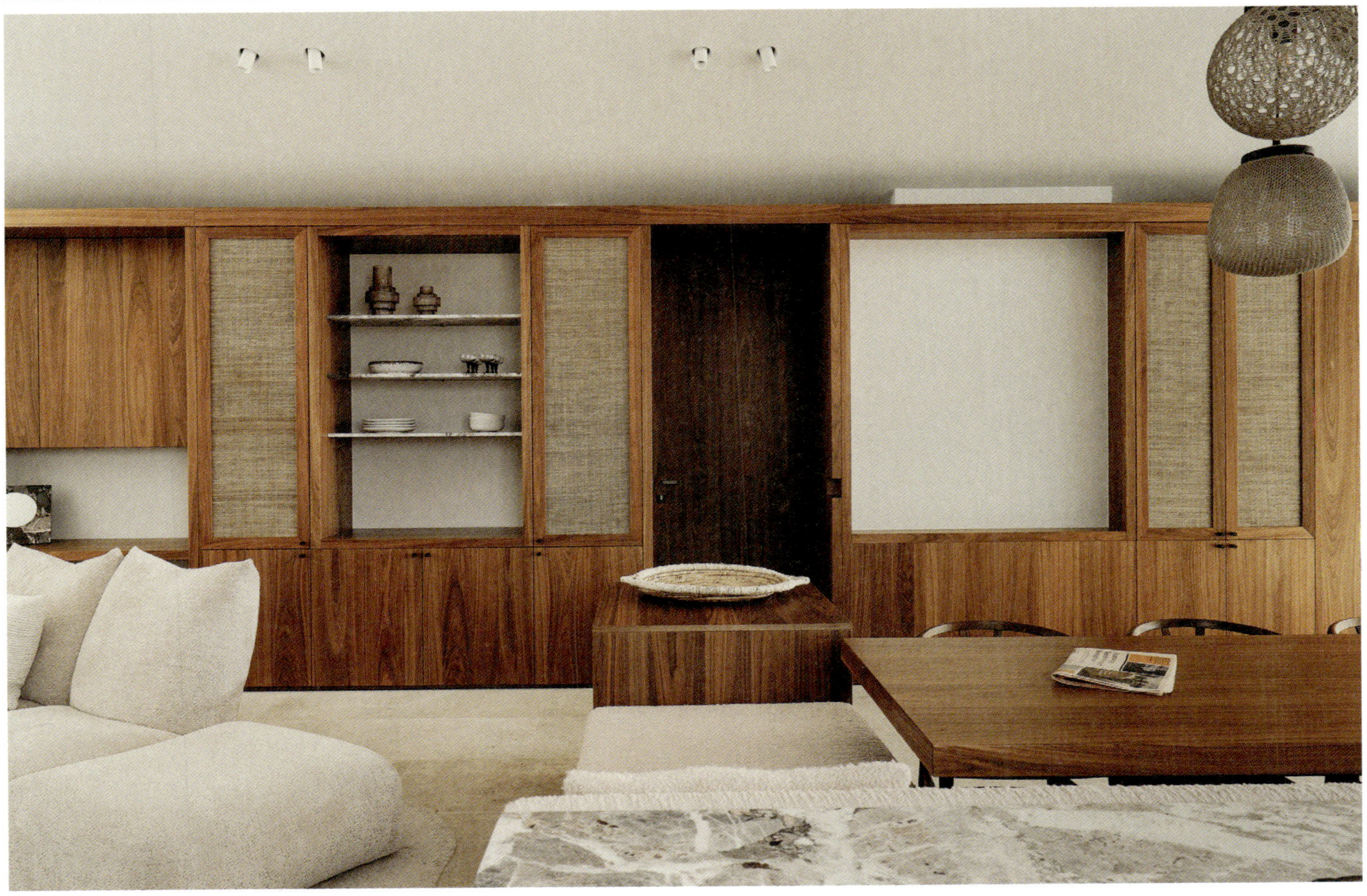

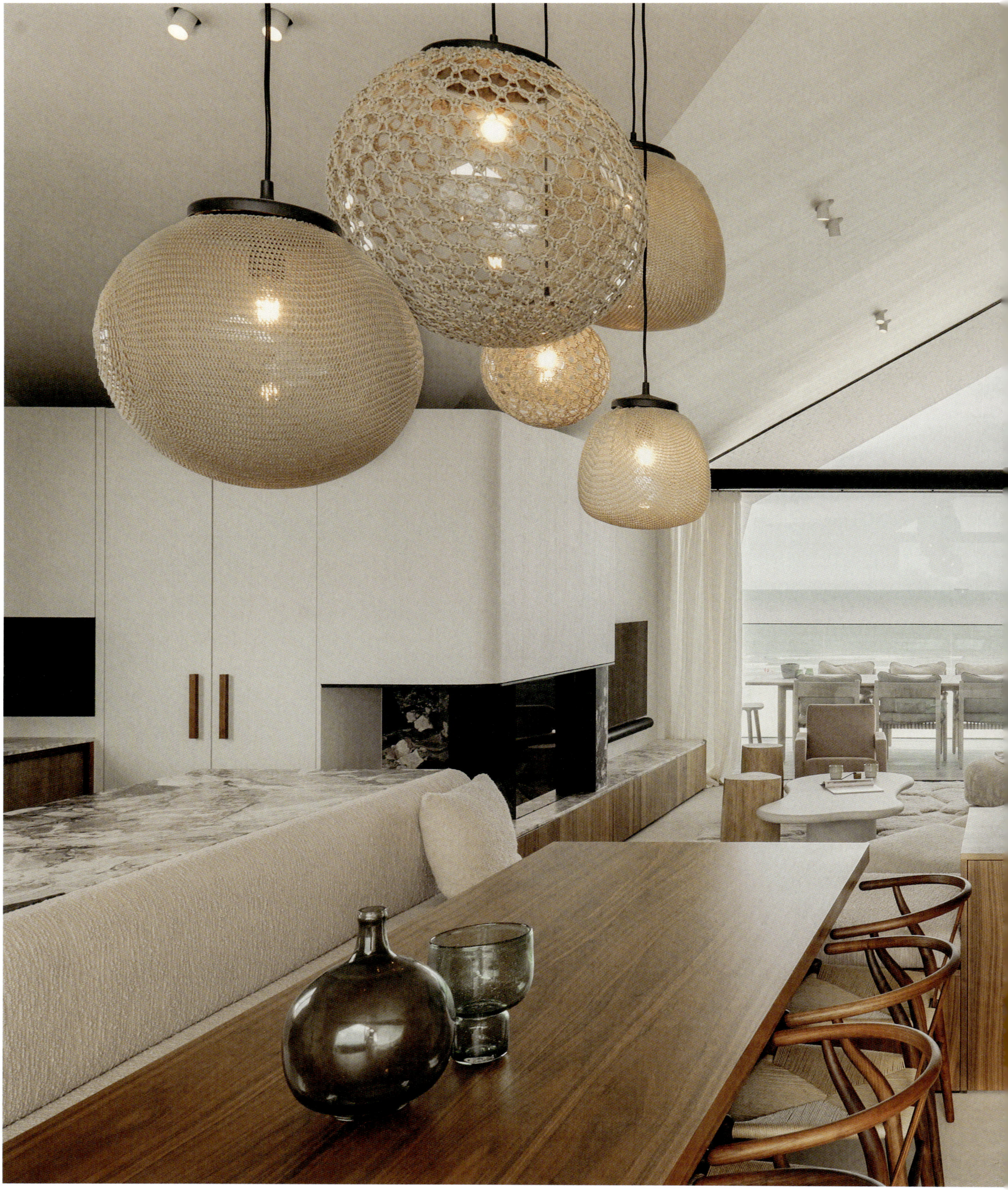

365

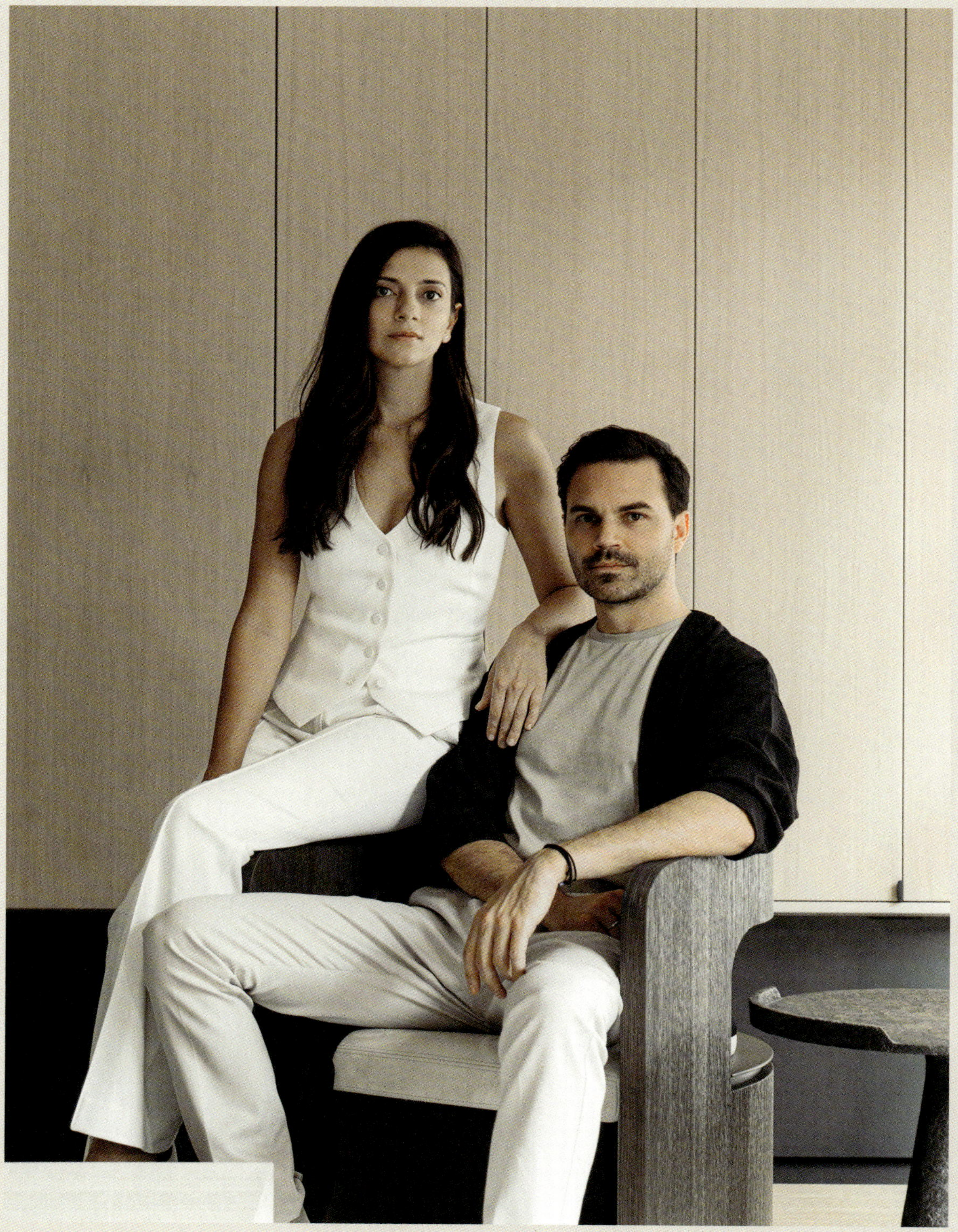

Özge Öztürk & Alexandre Simeray (OZA Design)

OZA Design is a London-based architecture and design studio founded in 2011 by architects Özge Öztürk and Alexandre Simeray.

Özge is from Türkiye and Alexandre from France, and they brought together their different backgrounds and traditions to create something new and unique.

OZA Design has also recently launched a first furniture and lighting collection, "Warrior".

OZA is more than a design agency; it is a complete creative vision of design that continues to expand into new projects. OZA can't be framed. It exists in every detail in its projects, from the woodgrain of its furniture to the glow of its lights; from the softness of the fabrics to the sharpness of the metal. OZA can't be defined by a style, it always reinvents itself and translates atmospheres into physical expressions.

They do not design simply to meet an expected aesthetic. OZA disrupts your preconceptions to produce a work that is as unique as the places they transform. OZA is born out of a desire to create unforgettable design experiences and to develop its own unique language away from inexpressive contemporary styles. With an ever-expanding scope of work including architecture, interior design, concept creation, FF&E design, and styling; OZA simultaneously disturbs and redefines an era of spatial experiences grounded by the desire to tell authentic stories. They thrive to meet the client's needs with unparalleled design solutions that yield emotive, human-conscious, and functional responses through the highest quality of design. They created OZA because they believe in the human need for emotion and connection in their environment. The duo approaches each project with desire to provide our clients with a bespoke and timeless creation, tailoring their experience from the very beginning through to completion.

www.ozadesign.com

Photography: Edvinas Bruzas

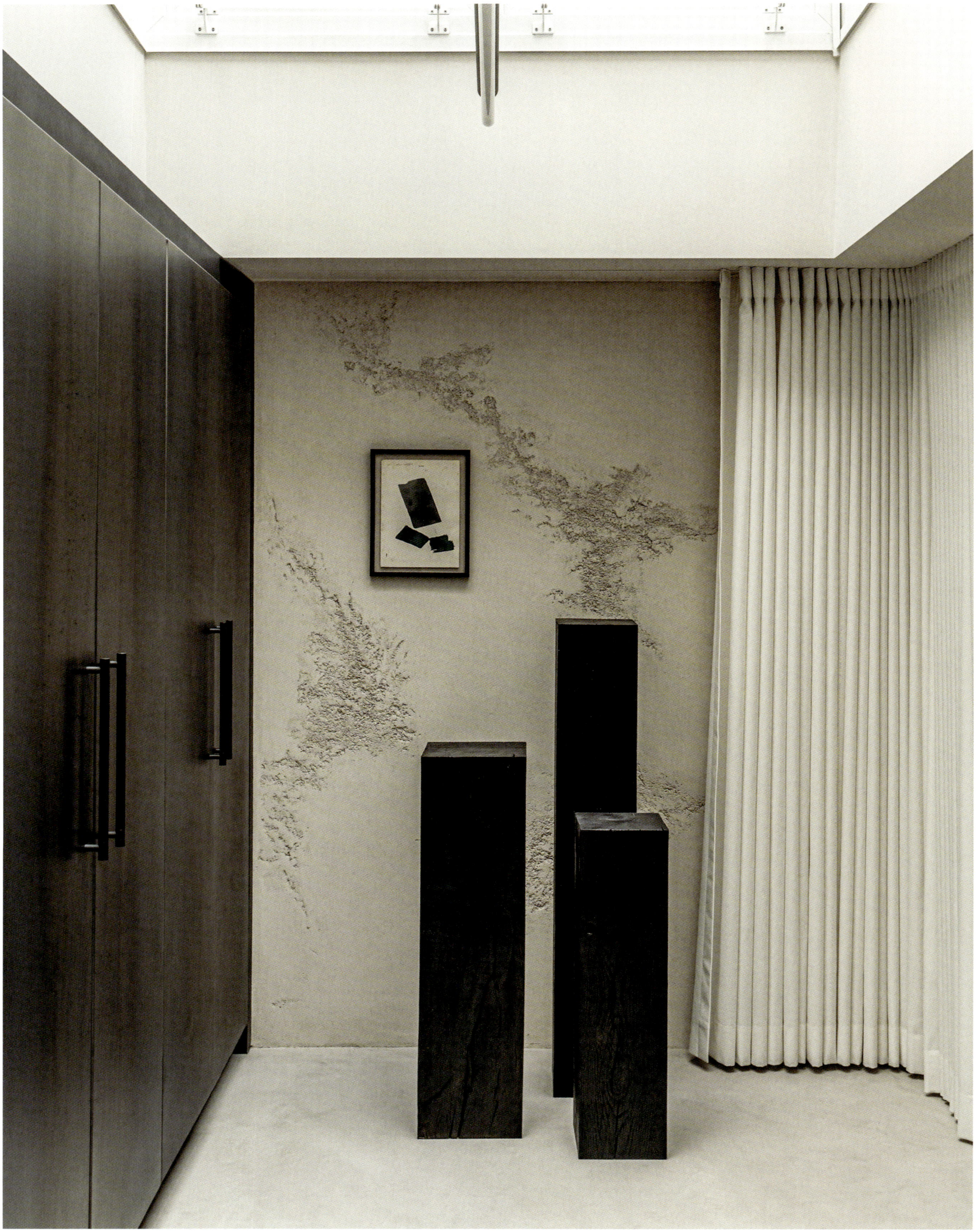

Tucked away in the heart of London, this Chelsea House by OZA Design explores balance and harmony through every design element to create an urban refuge. This home is a testament to their passion for creative distinctive design experiences by focusing on curation, craftsmanship, art, and culture. The designers travelled to different countries in search of the best craftsmen to create their first collection of furniture and lighting. The emphasis is on a minimalist approach, raw natural materials and a soft colour palette, accentuating the natural beauty of the space.

Chelsea House was originally built as a small outbuilding at the rear of the historic Cranley Gardens House, and they have retained its rich history through thoughtful design to modernize the interior. There is no pretentious architectural detailing, no fake patina to shine, and every material comes in its raw appearance to enhance its natural beauty.

The pied-à-terre harmoniously merges private and public spaces. The ground floor features communal living spaces, and the upper floor serves as both a private area and a secluded workspace; every space in the house seamlessly flows to create an inviting yet calm atmosphere. OZA Design deliberately removed all unnecessary doors and increased the size of the architraves to allow light to flood the space, creating a visible thread that connects each area.

The living area, as well as the other rooms, features carefully curated, custom-made furniture from their first design collection, "Warrior". The dining area features bespoke pieces, including an integrated wine cellar, sculptural charred oak plinths, and custom-patterned timber flooring-also designed by OZA Design.

A textural yet neutral palette plays to the soft and calm theme throughout. The light-filled living area features marble stone, travertine accents, and light oak timber flooring, as well as clay-clad walls in warm beige that initiate a considered interplay between form and texture.

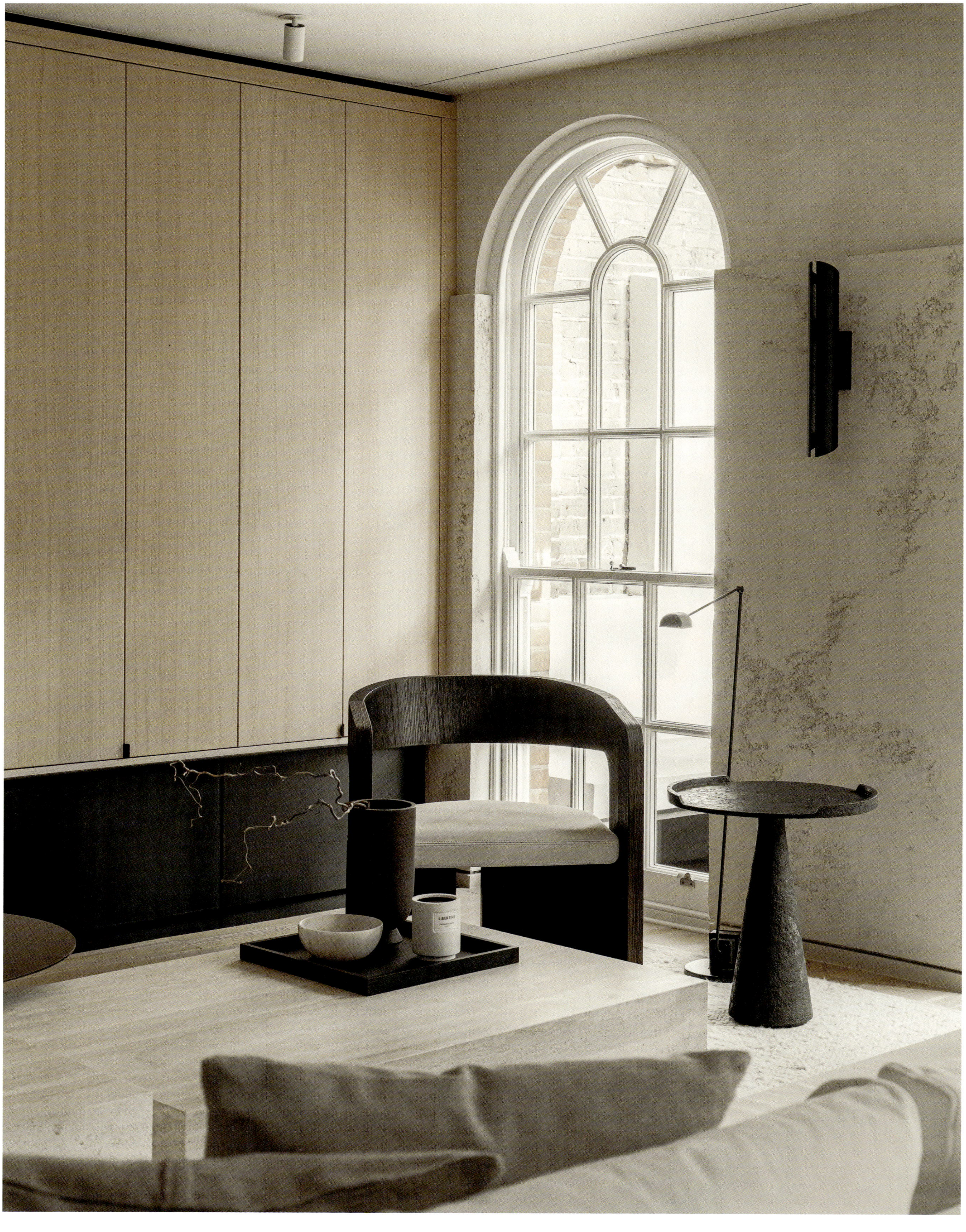

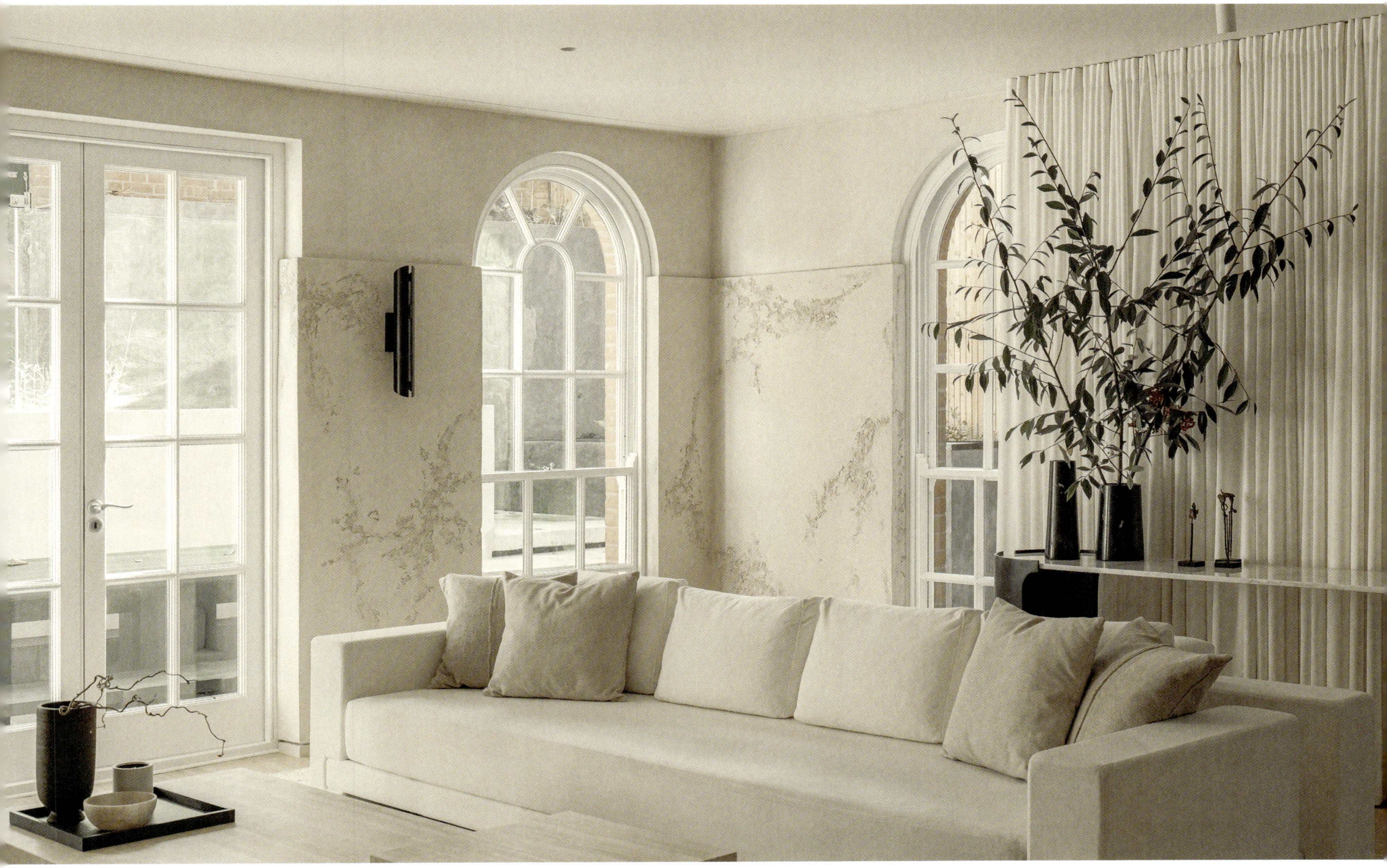

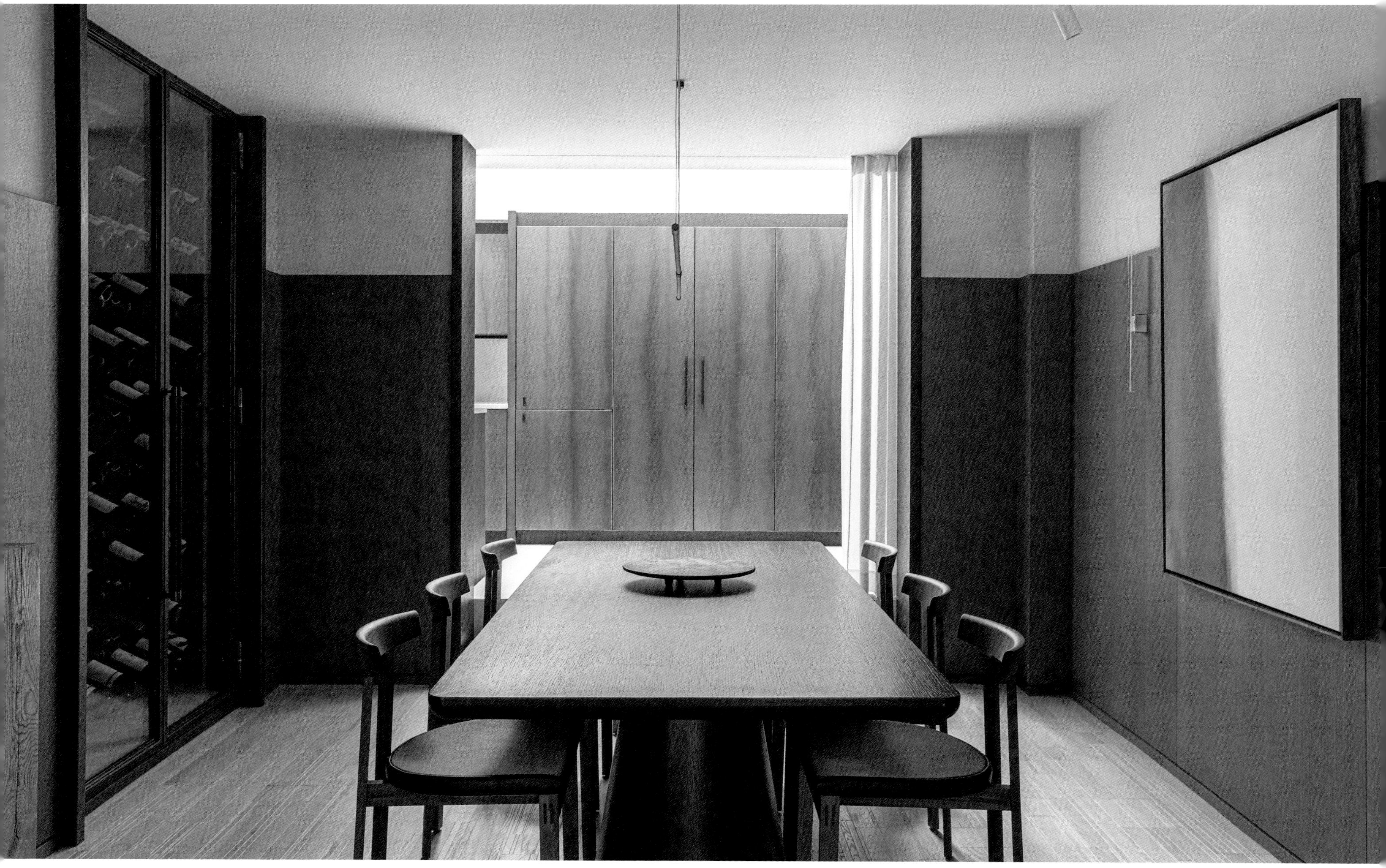

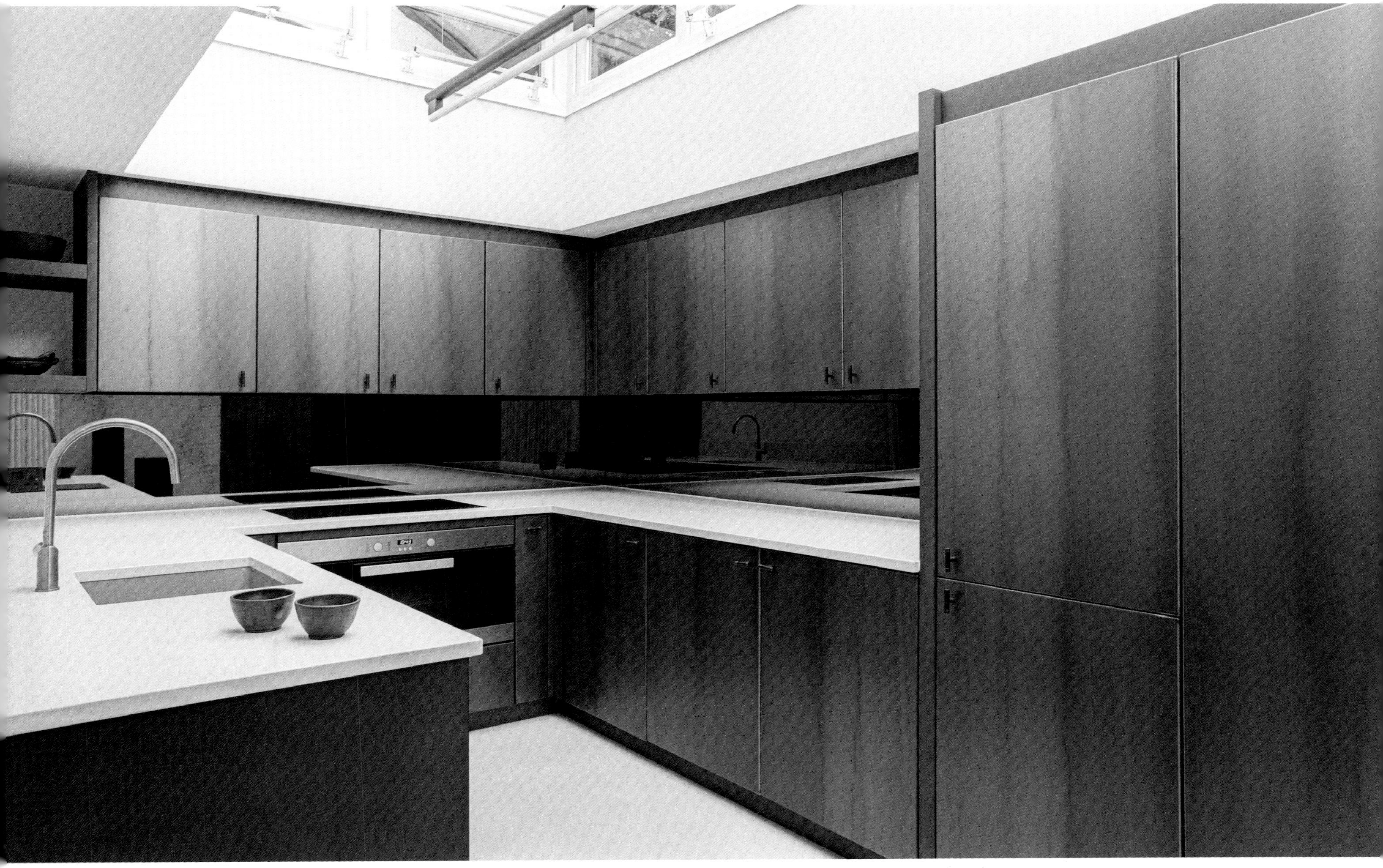

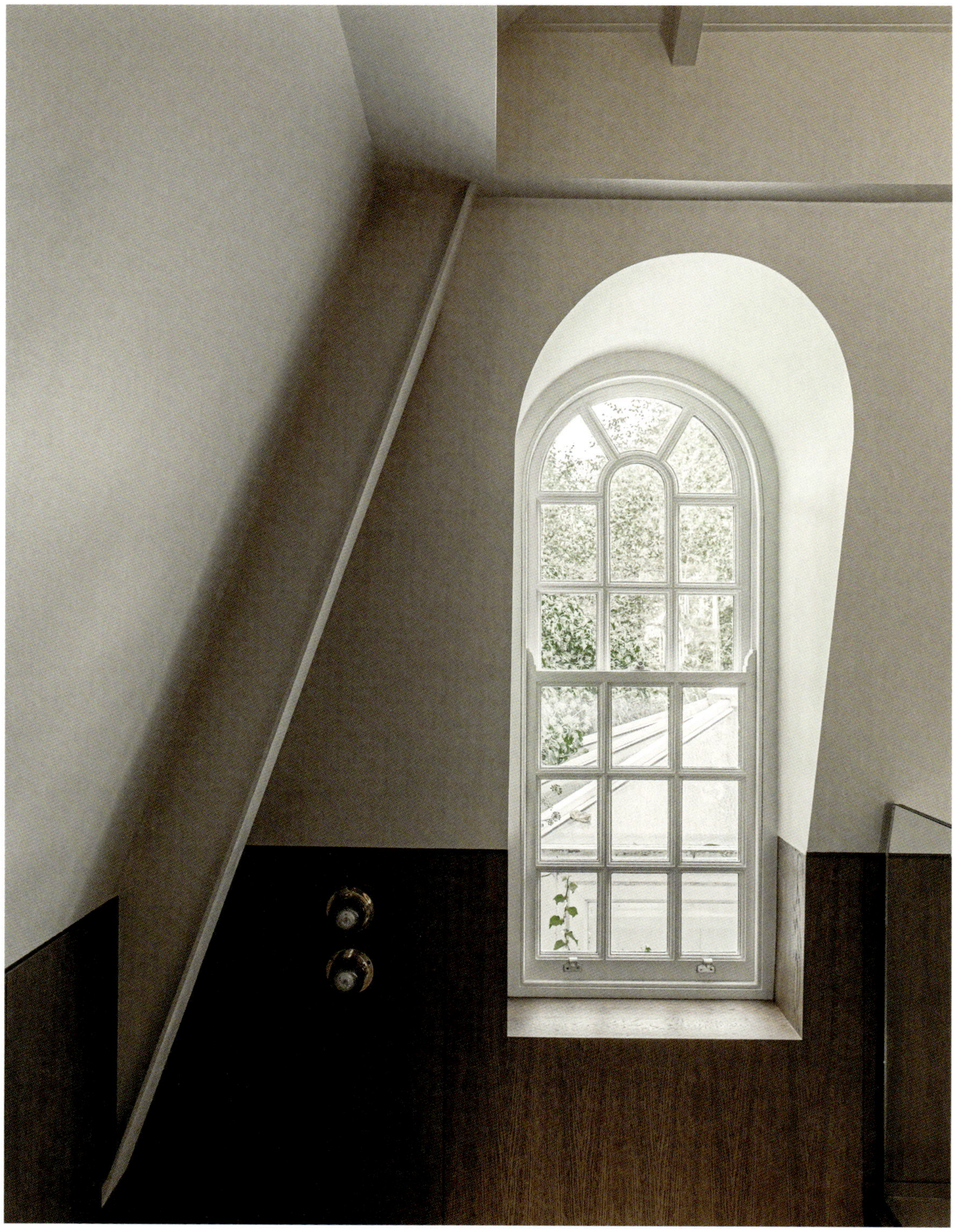

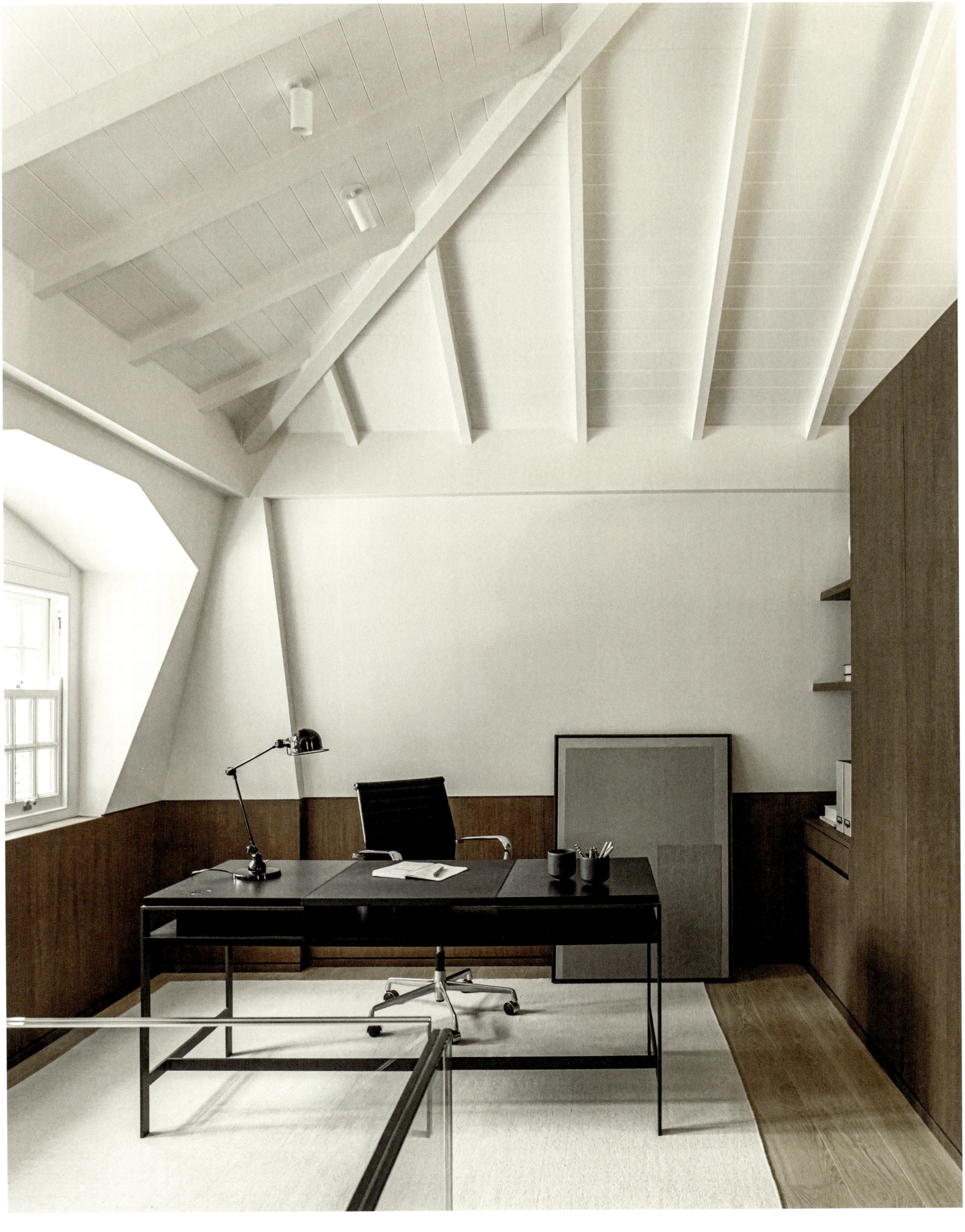

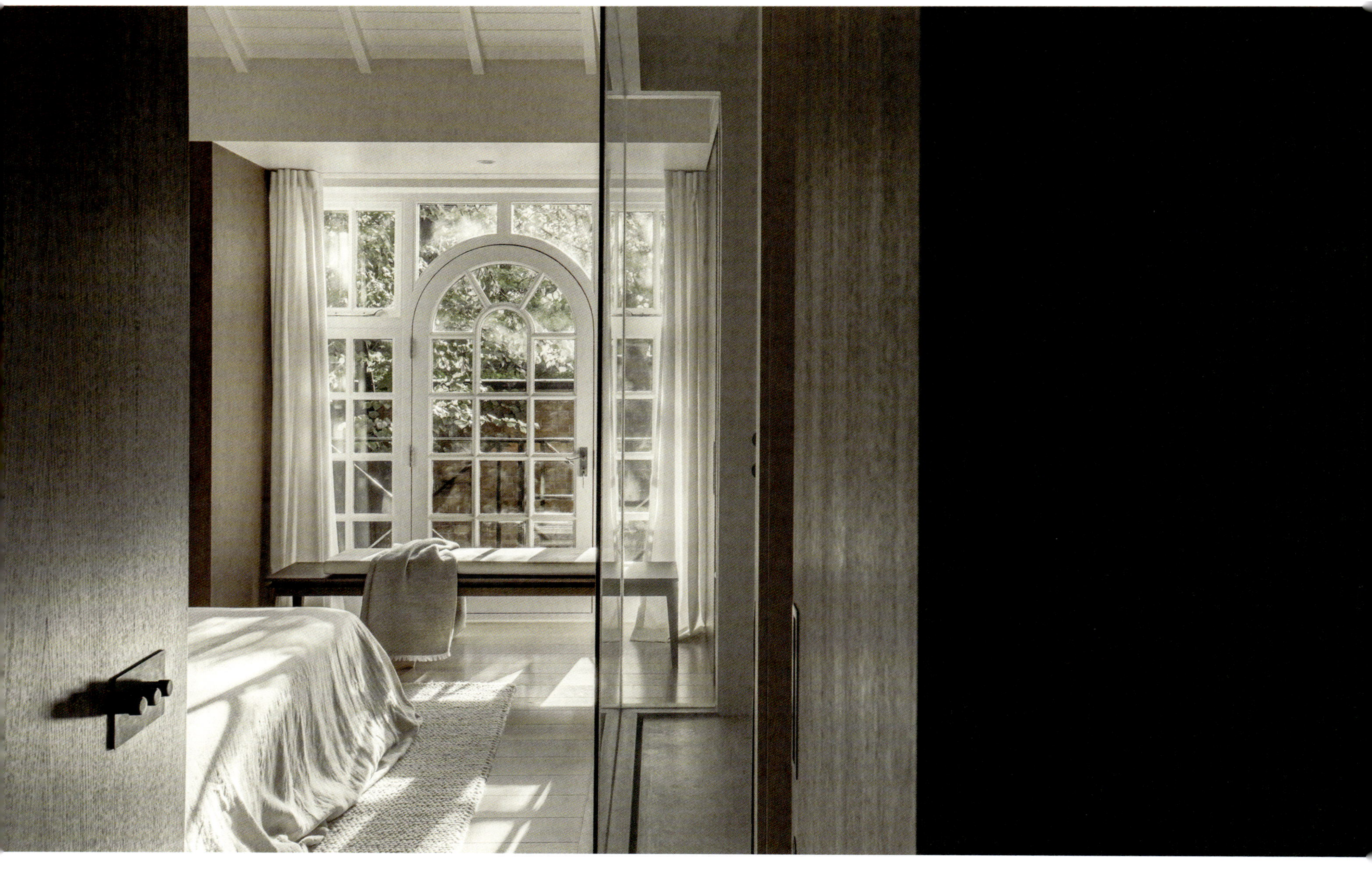

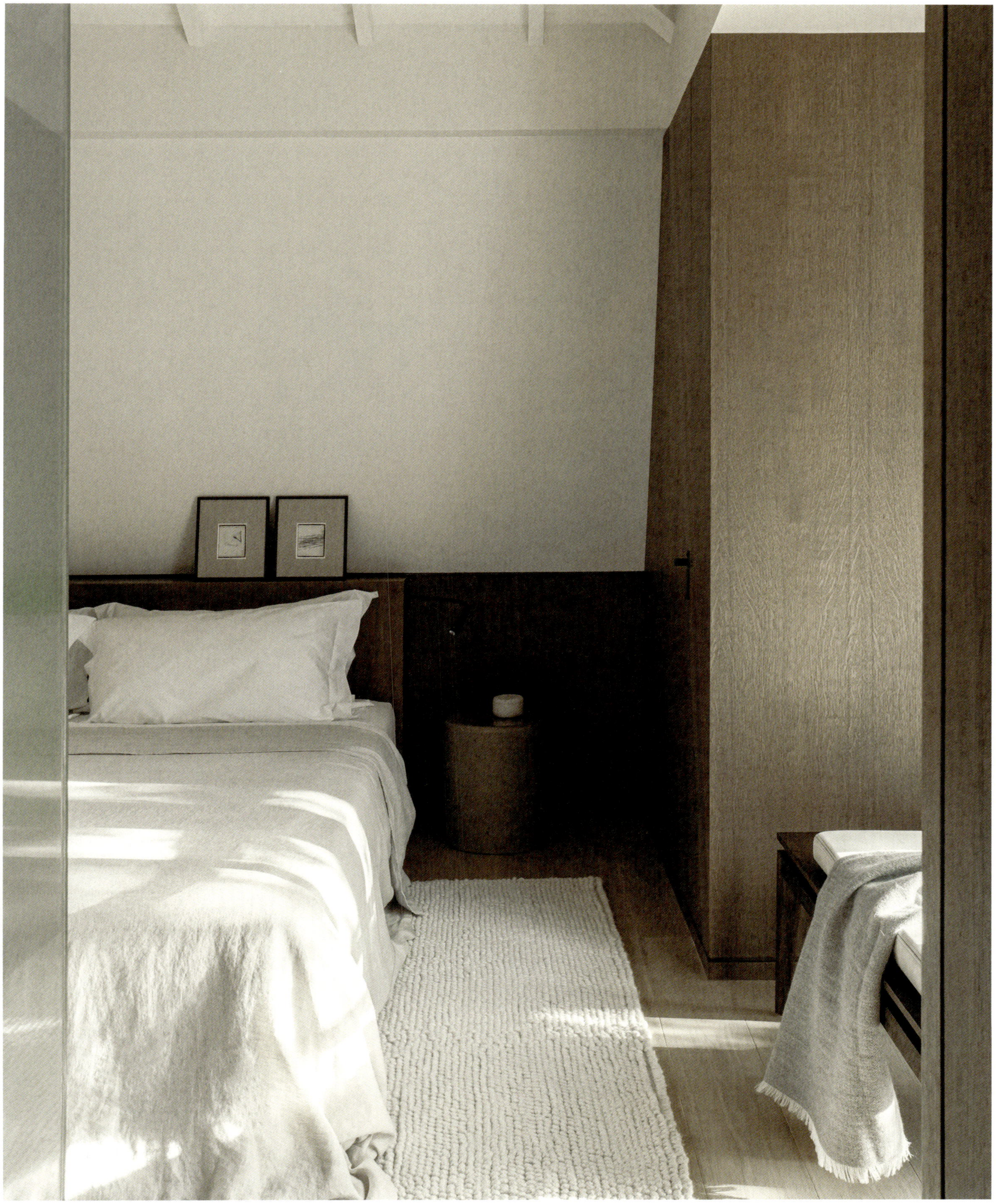

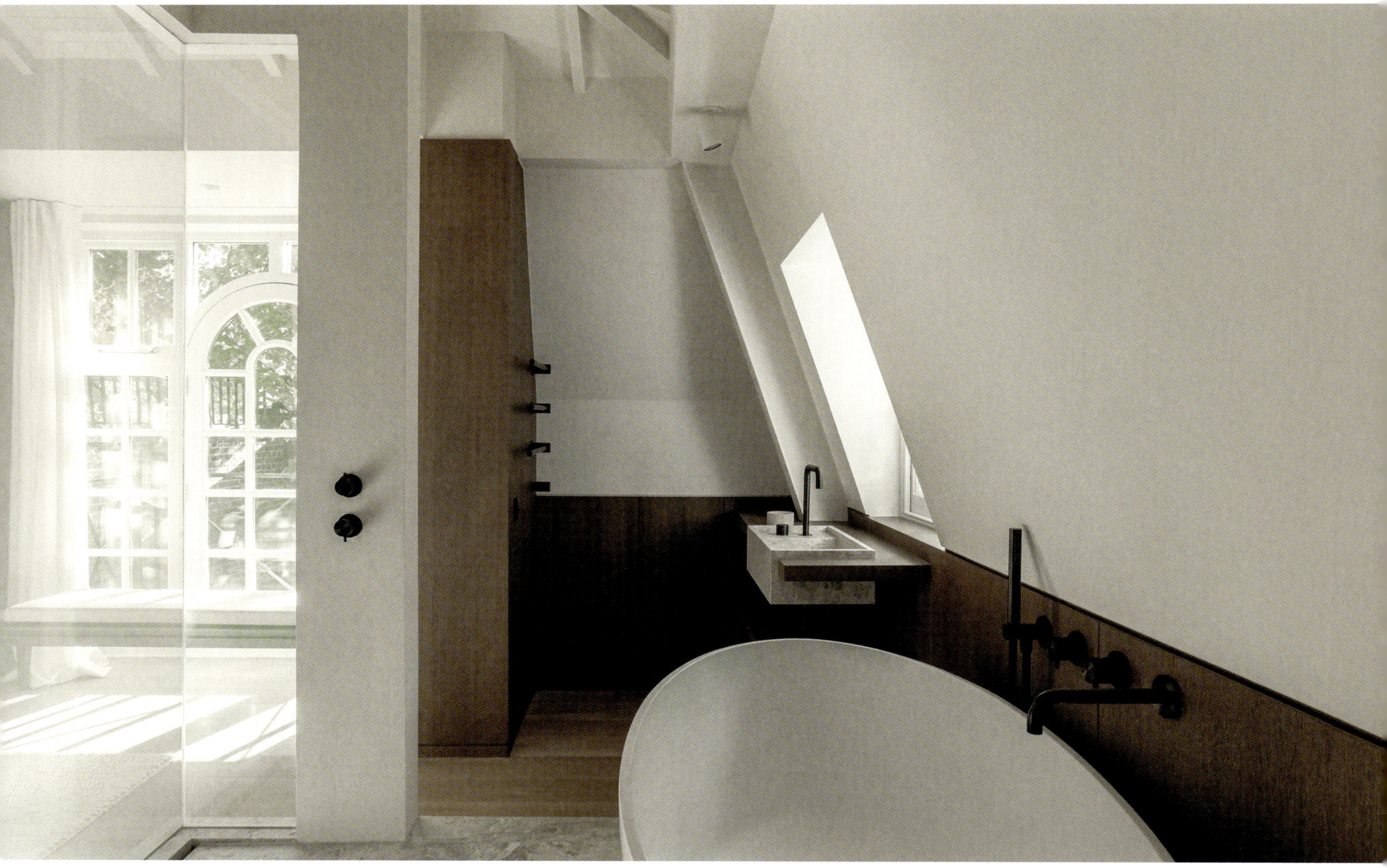

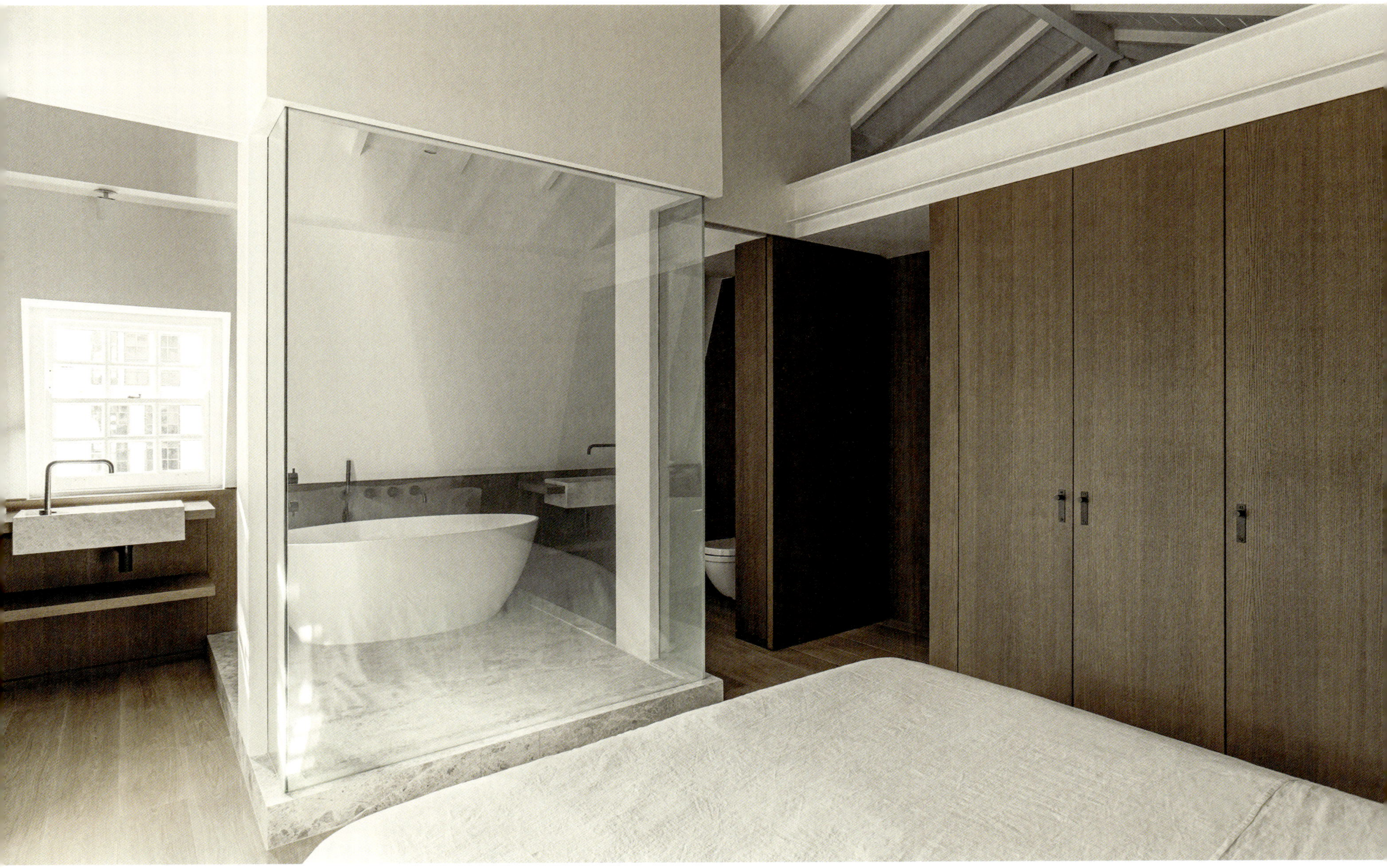

Portrait by Pilar Shoots (Thibault Debaene)

Laura Sainderichin

LO is the architectural office of Laura Sainderichin, where both architecture and interior are given a place, where total concepts are custom-tailored and where interior and exterior are in harmony with each other.

Laura and her team design spaces from the inside, through intimacy on the one hand, and through movement on the other hand.

Every project is based on specific conditions such as program, users, budget, surroundings... with these elements Laura tries to create a feeling more than a rational solution.

Without compromising functionality and comfort, she tries to clear all unnecessary things and to create an architecture with a soul.

Laura likes natural, honest and classical materials, which are used in a modern way resulting in a timeless architecture.

www.lo-ar.be

Photography: Thibault De Schepper

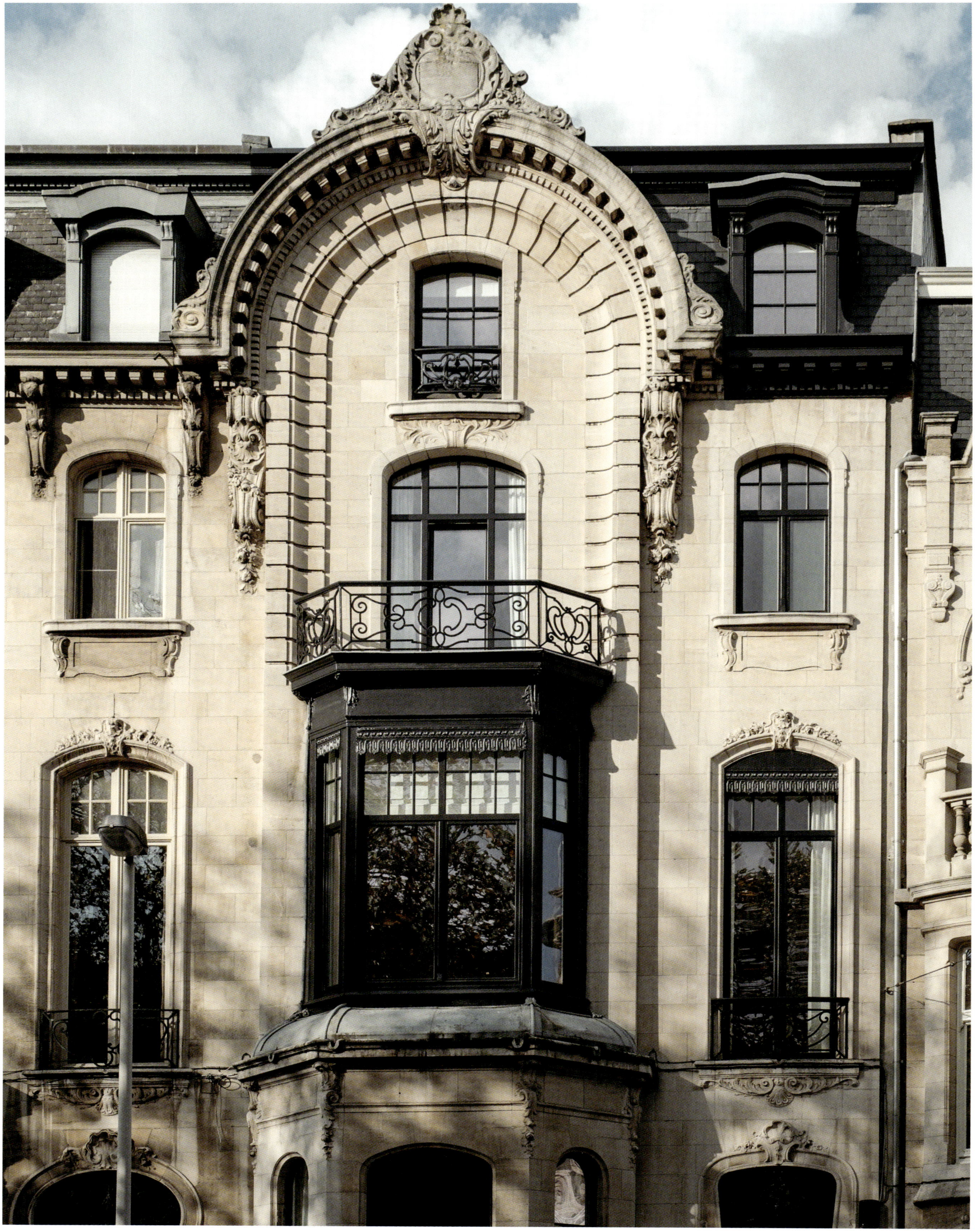

Laura Sainderichin was approached in 2019 by a family, who had just purchased a large neo-classical mansion in Antwerp. It is a beautiful house of about 700 square meters overlooking a tree-lined well-known avenue. The house also has a nice city garden.

The mansion had been previously renovated in the 1980s with little respect for the original architectural details that Laura loves to work with in her renovation projects. So Laura and her team had to figure out how to revive the original spirit of this home while restructuring it according to this family's desired program. They introduced a warm and minimal materials palette to create a blend of the past and present.

While they wanted to bring back the original charm of the home, they also had to find a way to create easy circulations that you don't normally experience in a typical townhouse. The current phenomenal vestibule with staircase and stained glass dome at the top were thoroughly restored. A new glass roof was placed above for protection. This intervention returned natural light to the heart of this home. A new compact staircase and elevator were designed to connect all other floors.

The converted back facade with small windows was completely redesigned to original model and facade with large molded authentic windows. By applying this to the rear façade and adding glass steel partitions in the interior, the home is flooded with light throughout the day, creating a seemingly contradictory sense of overwhelming tranquility.

The kitchen was positioned on the "bel étage" rear facing the renovated city garden and richly ornamented dining area. Tucked behind the kitchen, a new staircase that connects the basement to the main floor and allows for easy daily circulation. Laura introduced strong but understated material elements, a mix of dark wood, natural stone and glass that harmonized in color and texture and combined well with the beautiful historic character of this home.

Art was an important factor for this client. Therefore, timely consideration was given to the proper lighting, positioning and color of the interior in function of the artworks.

384

385

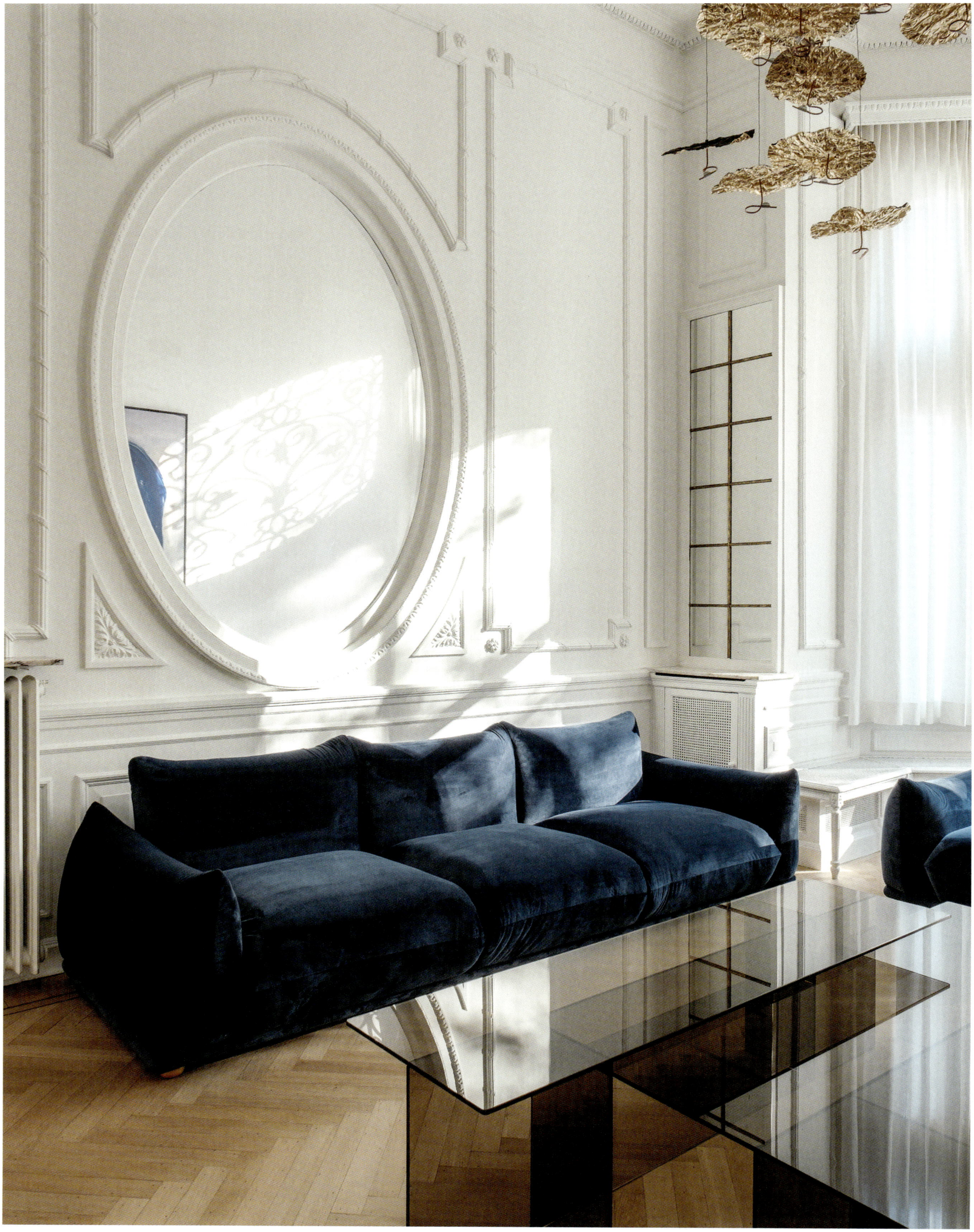

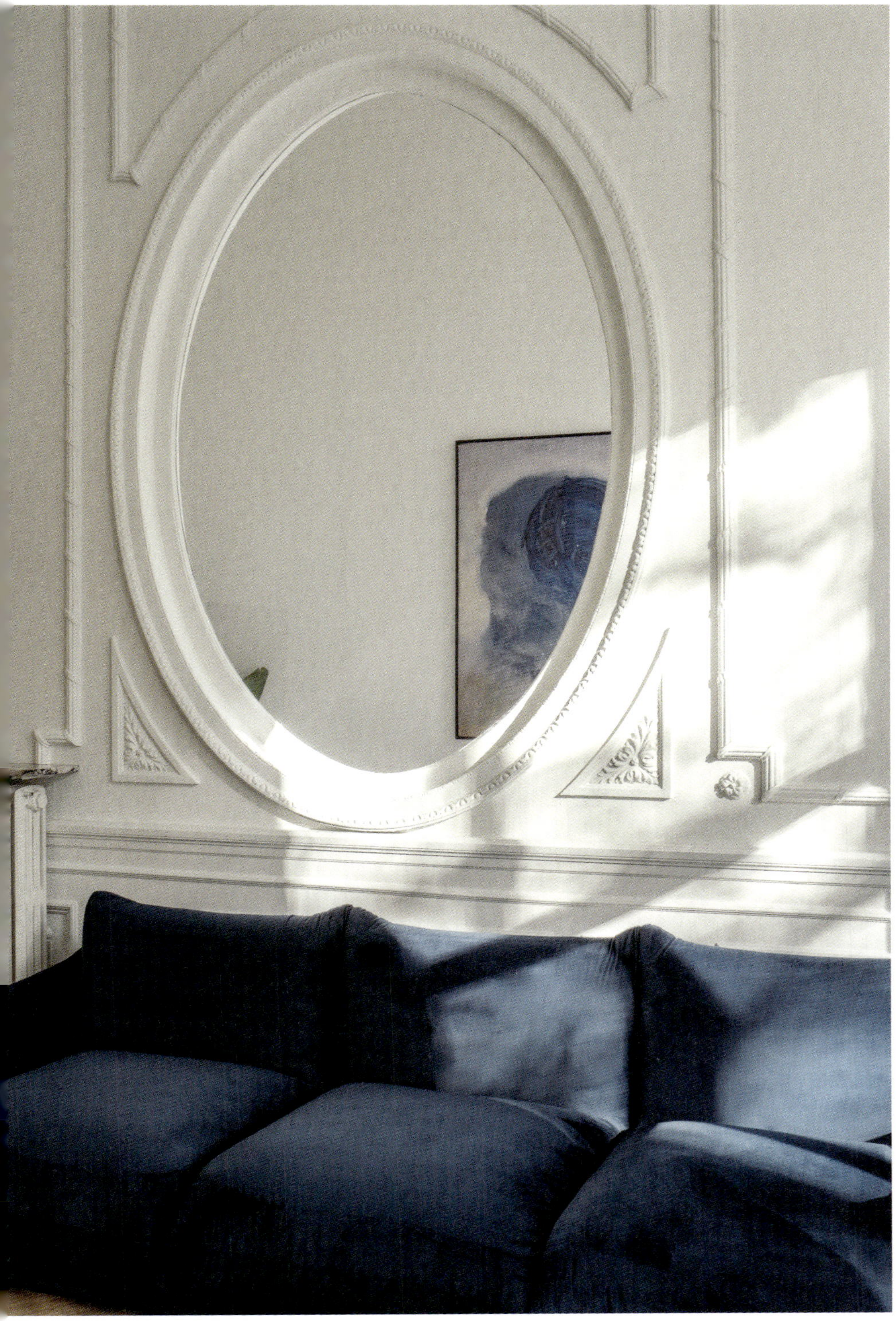
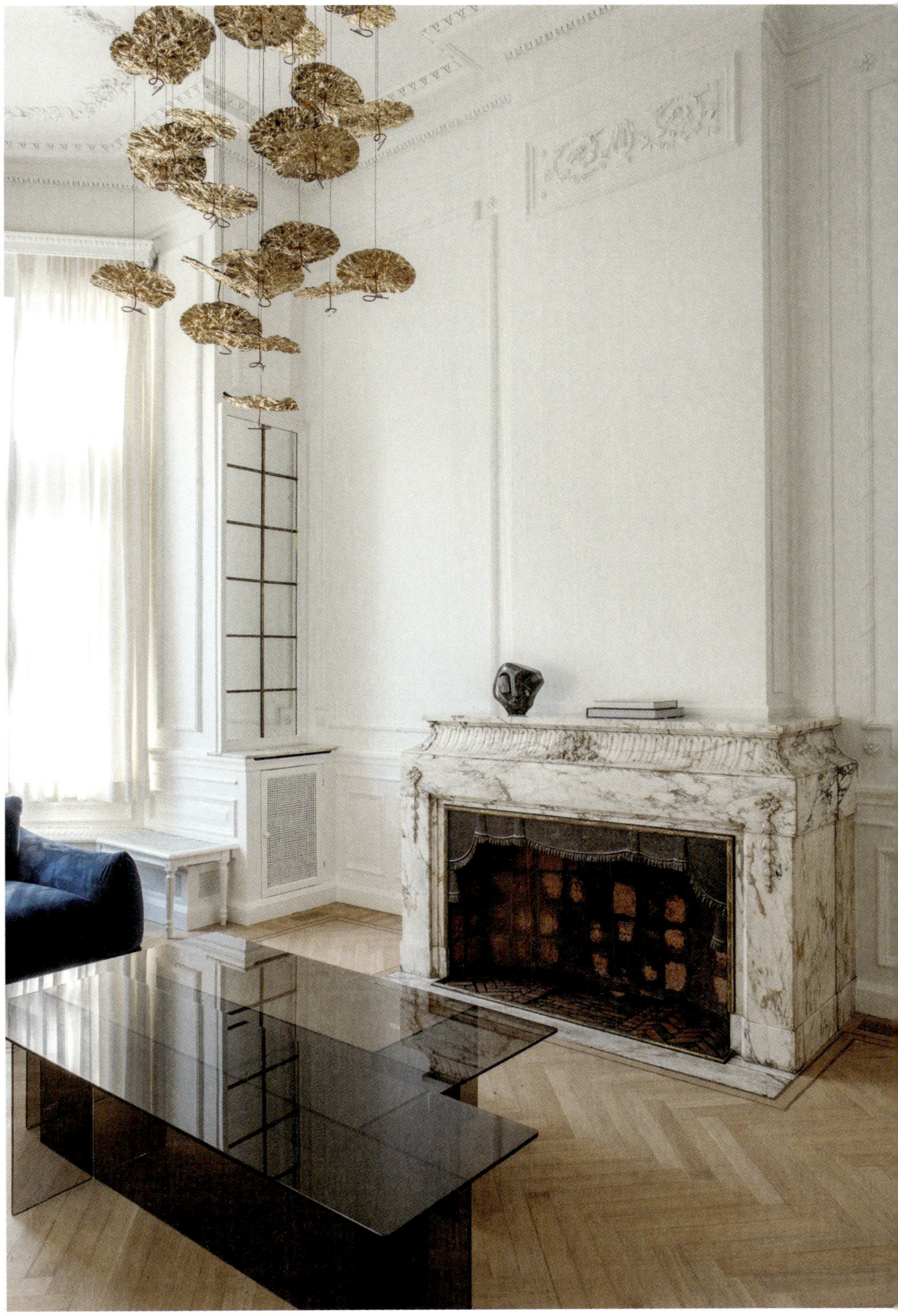

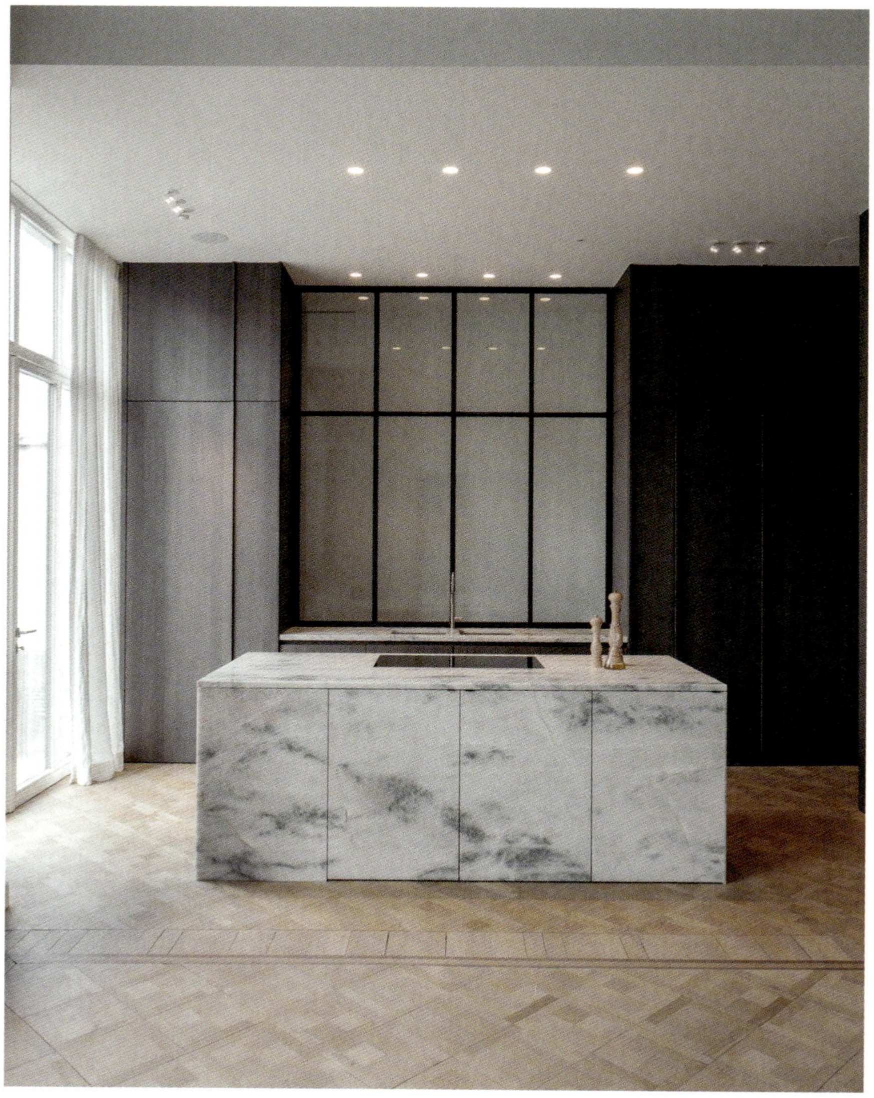

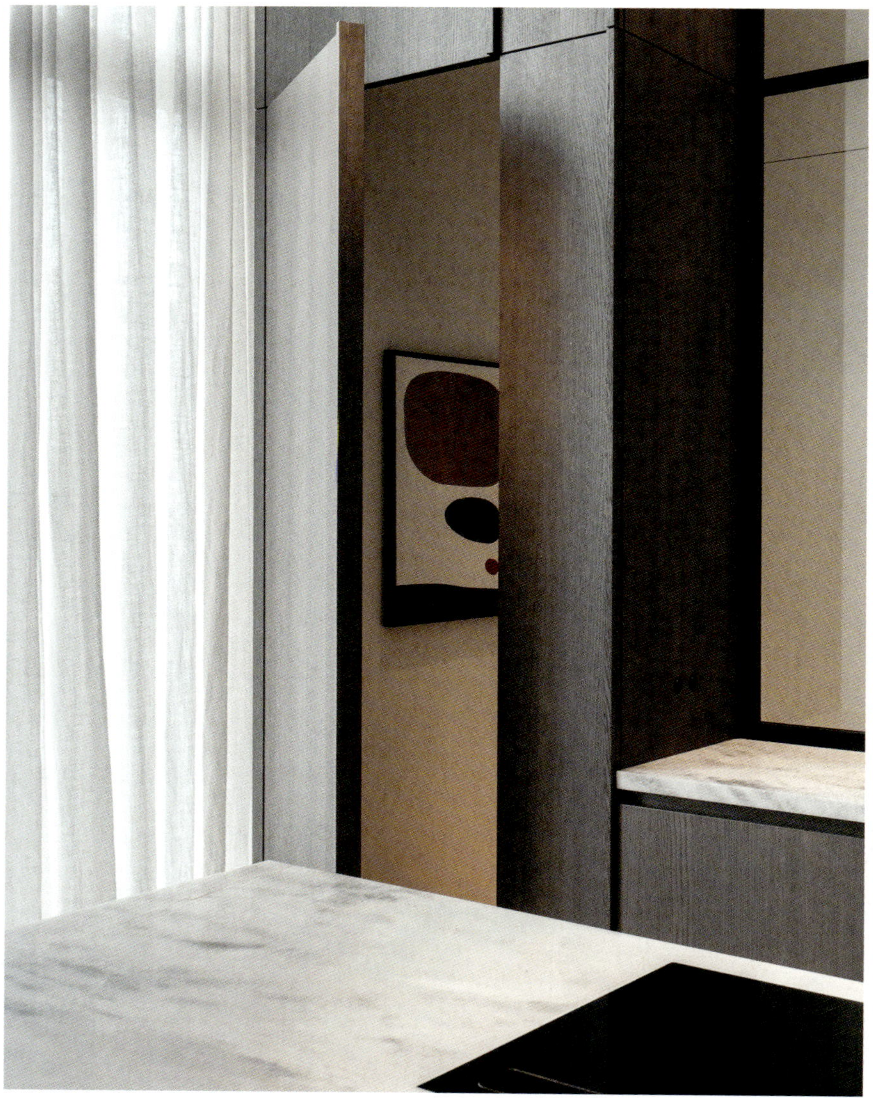

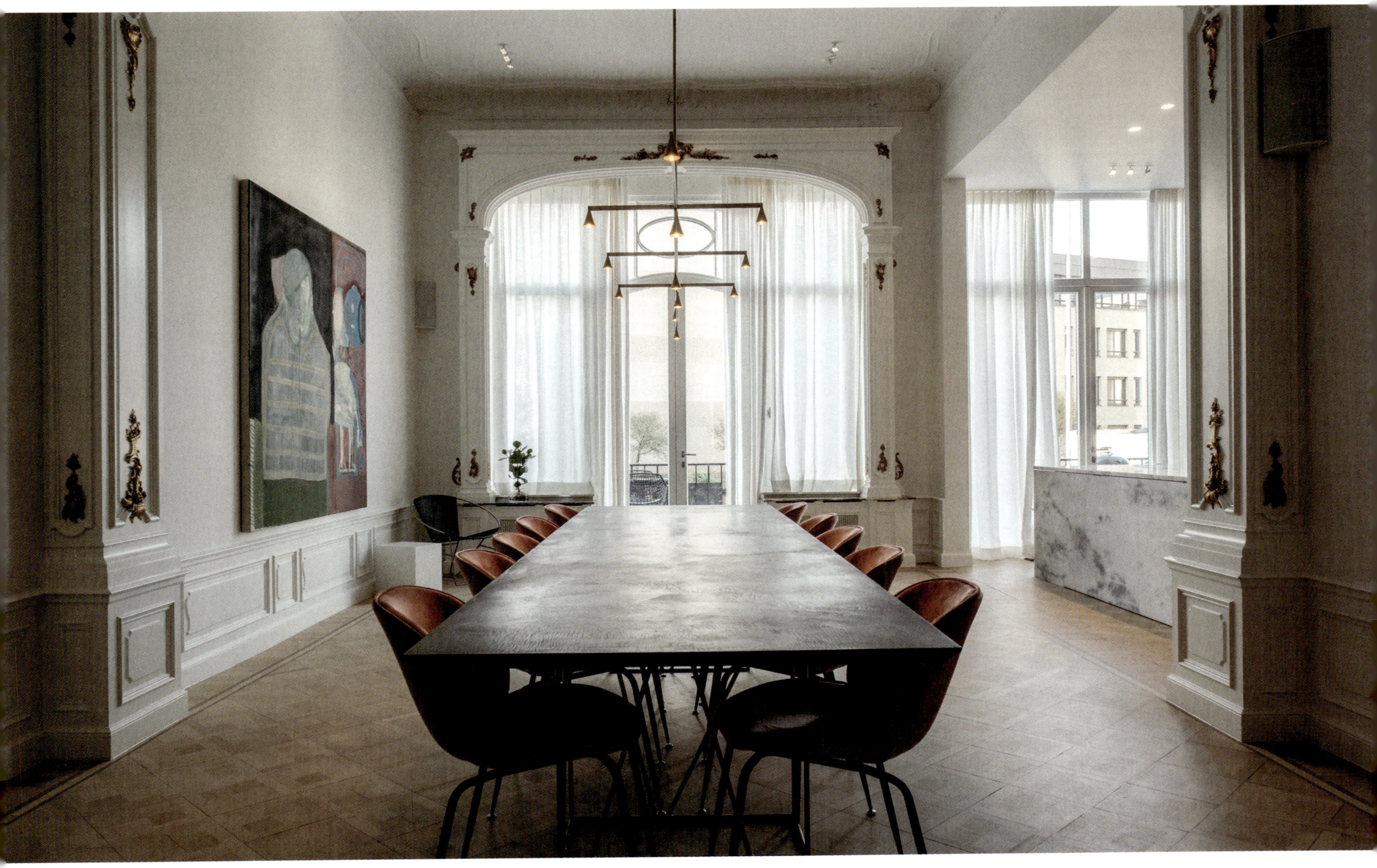

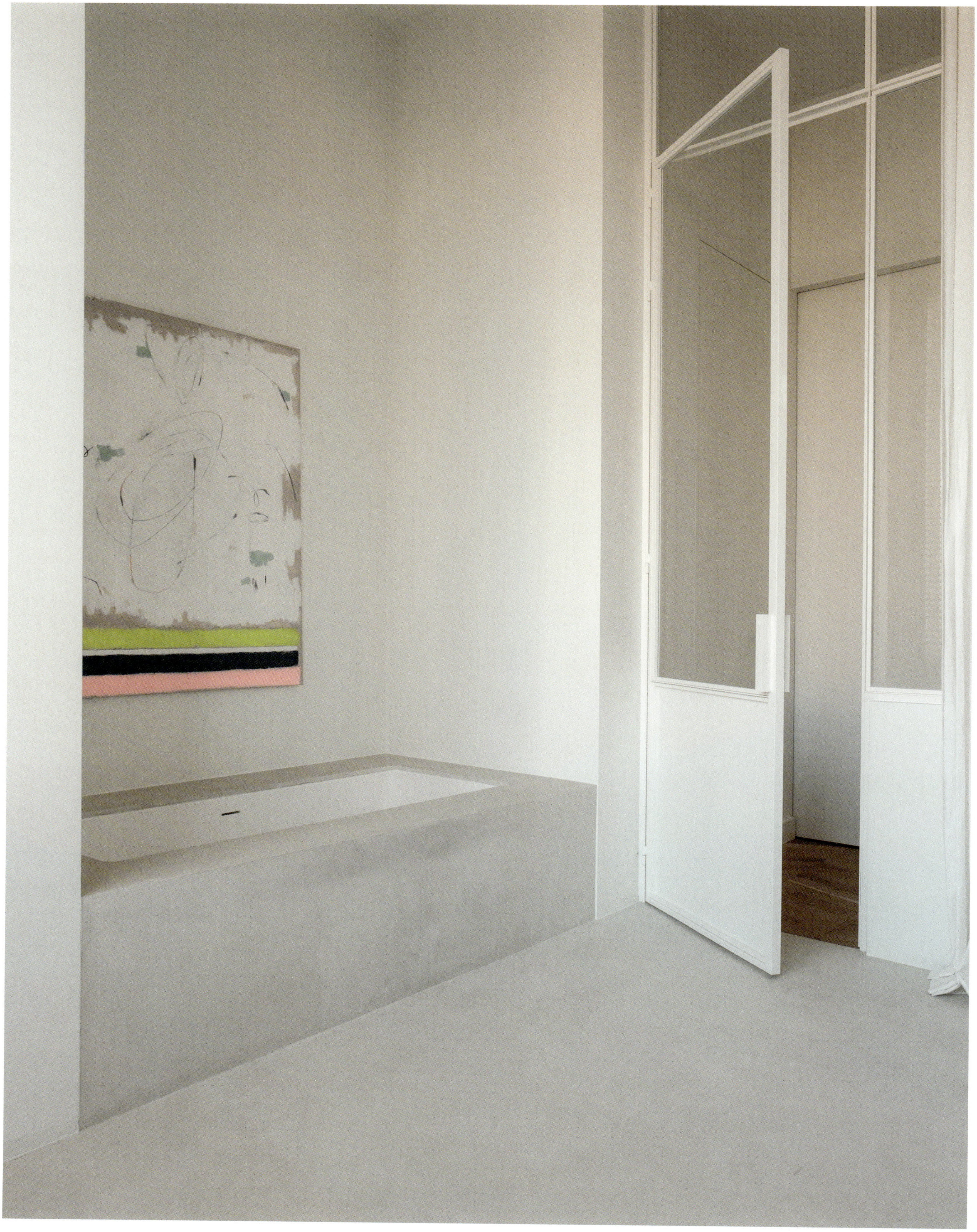

391

PUBLISHER
BETA-PLUS nv/sa
Avenue Louise 367
B-1050 Brussels
www.betaplus.com

DESIGN
Patrick Pierre

Cover & page 4: project by Arjaan De Feyter. Photography: Jan Liégeois
Double page 2-3: project by Chused & Co. Photography: Jeff Holt
Page 6: project by Studio Pien. Photography: Pilar Shoots (Thibault Debaene)

© 2024, BETA-PLUS

All rights reserved.
No part of this publication may be reproduced,
stored in a retrieval system, or transmitted
in any form or by any means.

Printed in Belgium.

FSC
www.fsc.org
MIX
Paper | Supporting responsible forestry
FSC® C014767